the Best RV and Tent Campgrounds in the Southwest & South Central Plains

Arkansas, Colorado, Kansas, Missouri, New Mexico, Oklahoma & Texas

Other Titles in the Unofficial Guide
<u>Best RV and Tent Campgrounds Series</u>

California & the West
Florida & the Southeast
Great Lakes States
The Northeast
Mid-Atlantic States
Northwest & Central Plains
U.S.A.

Other Unofficial Guides

Beyond Disney: The Unofficial Guide to Universal, SeaWorld, and the Best of Central Florida

Inside Disney: The Incredible Story of Walt Disney World and the Man Behind the Mouse

Mini Las Vegas: The Pocket-Sized Unofficial Guide to Las Vegas

Mini-Mickey: The Pocket-Sized Unofficial Guide to Walt Disney World

The Unofficial Guides to Bed & Breakfasts and Country Inns:
California Great Lakes New England
Northwest Rockies Southeast Southwest

The Unofficial Guides to the Best RV and Tent Campgrounds:
California & the West Florida & the Southeast Great Lakes
Mid-Atlantic States Northeast Northwest Southwest U.S.A.

The Unofficial Guide to Branson, Missouri

The Unofficial Guide to Chicago

The Unofficial Guide to Cruises

The Unofficial Guide to Disneyland

The Unofficial Guide to Disneyland Paris

The Unofficial Guide to Florence, Rome, and the Heart of Italy

The Unofficial Guide to the Great Smoky and Blue Ridge Region

The Unofficial Guide to Golf Vacations in the Eastern U.S.

The Unofficial Guide to Hawaii

The Unofficial Guide to Las Vegas

The Unofficial Guide to London

The Unofficial Guide to New Orleans

The Unofficial Guide to New York City

The Unofficial Guide to Paris

The Unofficial Guide to San Francisco

The Unofficial Guide to South Florida, including Miami and the Keys

The Unofficial Guides to Traveling with Kids:
California Florida Mid-Atlantic New England and New York
Walt Disney World

The Unofficial Guide to Walt Disney World

The Unofficial Guide to Walt Disney World for Grown-Ups

The Unofficial Guide to Washington, D.C.

The Unofficial Guide to the World's Best Diving Vacations

the Unofficial Guide® to the Best RV and Tent Campgrounds in the Southwest & South Central Plains

1st Edition

Arkansas, Colorado, Kansas, Missouri, New Mexico, Oklahoma & Texas

Stuart Hamby with Grace Walton

Hungry Minds™

Best-Selling Books • Digital Downloads • e-Books • Answer Networks • e-Newsletters
Branded Web Sites • e-Learning

New York, NY • Indianapolis, IN • Cleveland, OH

Your safety is important to us, so we encourage you to stay alert and be aware of your surroundings. Keep a close eye on cameras, purses, and wallets, all favorite targets of thieves and pickpockets.

Published by Hungry Minds, Inc.
909 Third Avenue
New York, NY 10022

Produced by Menasha Ridge Press
COVER DESIGN BY MICHAEL J. FREELAND
INTERIOR DESIGN BY MICHELE LASEAU

ISBN 0-7645-6423-4

ISSN 1536-9706

Manufactured in the United States of America

10 9 8 7 6 5 4 3 2

Contents

the Unofficial Guide® to

the Best RV and Tent Campgrounds in the Southwest & South Central Plains

Introduction

Why Unofficial?

The material in this guide has not been edited or in any way reviewed by the campgrounds profiled. In this "unofficial" guide we represent and serve you, the consumer. By way of contrast with other campground directories, no ads were sold to campgrounds, and no campground paid to be included. Through our independence, we're able to offer you the sort of objective information necessary to select a campground efficiently and with confidence.

Why Another Guide to Campgrounds?

We developed *The Unofficial Guide to the Best RV and Tent Campgrounds in the Southwest and South Central Plains* because we recognized that campers are as discriminating about their choice of campgrounds as most travelers are about their choice of hotels. As a camper, you don't want to stay in every campground along your route. Rather, you prefer to camp only in the best. A comprehensive directory with limited information on each campground listed does little to help you narrow your choices. What you need is a reference that tells you straight out which campgrounds are the best, and that supplies detailed information, collected by independent inspectors, that differentiates those campgrounds from all of the also-rans. This is exactly what *The Unofficial Guide to the Best RV and Tent Campgrounds* delivers.

The Choice Is All Yours

Life is short, and life is about choices. You can stay in a gravel lot, elbow to elbow with other campers, with tractor-trailers roaring by just beyond the fence, or with this guide, you can spend the night in a roomy, shaded site, overlooking a sparkling blue lake. The choice is yours.

The authors of this guide have combed the Southwestern and South Central states inspecting and comparing hundreds of campgrounds. Their objective was to create a hit parade of the very best, so that no matter where you travel, you'll never have to spend another night in a dumpy, gravel lot.

The best campgrounds in each state are described in detail in individual profiles so you'll know exactly what to expect. In addition to the fully profiled campgrounds, we provide a Supplemental Directory of Campgrounds that lists hundreds of additional properties that are quite adequate, but that didn't make the cut for the top 350 in the guide. Thus, no matter where you are, you'll have plenty of campgrounds to choose from. None of the campgrounds appearing in this guide, whether fully profiled or in the supplemental list, paid to be included. Rather, each earned its place by offering a superior product. Period.

Letters, Comments, and Questions from Readers

Many who use the Unofficial Guides write to us with questions, comments, and reports of their camping experiences. We appreciate all such input, both positive and critical. Readers' comments are frequently incorporated into revised editions of the Unofficial Guides and have contributed immeasurably to their improvement. Please write to:

The Unofficial Guide to the Best RV and Tent Campgrounds
P.O. Box 43673
Birmingham, AL 35243
UnofficialGuides@menasharidge.com

For letters sent through the mail, please put your return address on both your letter and envelope; the two sometimes become separated. Also include your phone number and email address if you are available for a possible interview.

How to Use This Guide

Using this guide is quick and easy. We begin with this introduction followed by "Campground Awards," a list of the best campgrounds for RVers, tenters, families, and more. Then we profile the best 350 campgrounds in the Southwestern and South Central Plains states. Next is a supplemental list of hundreds of additional campgrounds including details about prices, hookups, and more. Bringing up the rear is an alphabetical index of all campgrounds included in the guide.

Both the profiled section and the supplemental directory are ordered alphabetically, first by state and then by city. To see what campgrounds are available:

- Find the section covering the state in question.
- Within that section, look up the city alphabetically.
- Under the city, look up the campgrounds alphabetically.

You can choose and locate campgrounds in four different ways.

1. **Use the Map** If a city appears with a black, solid bullet on our map, at least one of our profiled or listed campgrounds will be located there. The converse is also the case: if the city has a hollow, outlined bullet, you can assume that we do not cover any campgrounds in that city.

2. **Check the Campground Profiles** In the section where we profile campgrounds, look up any city where you hope to find a campground. If the city isn't listed, it means we do not profile any campgrounds there.

3. **Check the Supplemental Directory of Campgrounds** Check for the same city in the supplemental listings.

4. **Use the Index** If you want to see if a specific campground is profiled or listed in the guide, look up the name of the campground in the alphabetical index at the back of the book.

When looking up campgrounds, remember that the best campgrounds are found in the profiled section; always check there first before turning to the Supplemental Directory of Campgrounds.

Understanding the Profiles

Each profile has seven important sections:

Campground Name, Address, and Contact Information In addition to the street address, we also provide phone and fax numbers as well as website and email addresses.

Ratings Using the familiar one- to five-star rating with five stars being best, we offer one overall rating for RV campers and a second overall rating for tent campers. The overall rating for each type of camper is based on a rough weighted average of the following eight individually rated categories:

Category	Weight
Beauty	15%
Site Privacy	10%
Site Spaciousness	10%
Quiet	15%
Security	13%
Cleanliness/upkeep	13%
Insect Control	10%
Facilities	14%

Beauty This rates the natural setting of the campground in terms of its visual appeal. The highest ratings are reserved for campgrounds where the beauty of the campground can be enjoyed and appreciated both at individual campsites and at the campground's public areas. Views, vistas, landscaping, and foliage are likewise taken into consideration.

Site Privacy This category rates the extent to which the campsites are set apart and/or in some way buffered (usually by trees and shrubs) from adjacent or nearby campsites. The farther campsites are from one another the better. This rating also reflects how busy the access road to the campsites is in terms of traffic. Campgrounds that arrange their sites on a number of cul-de-sacs, for example, will offer quieter sites than a campground where the sites are situated off of a busy loop or along a heavily traveled access road.

Site Spaciousness This rates the size of the campsite. Generally, the larger the better.

Quiet This rating indicates the relative quietness of the campground. There are three key considerations. The first is where the campground is located. Campgrounds situated along busy highways or in cities or towns are usually noisier, for example, than rural or wilderness campgrounds removed from major thoroughfares. The second consideration relates to how noise is managed at the campground. Does the campground forbid playing of radios or enforce a "quiet time" after a certain hour? Is there someone on site at night to respond to complaints about other campers being loud or unruly at a late hour? Finally, the rating considers the extent to which trees, shrubs, and the natural topography serve to muffle noise within the campground.

Security This rating reflects the extent (if any) to which management monitors the campground during the day and night. Physical security is also included in this rating: Is the campground fenced? Is the campground gated? If so, is the gate manned? Generally, a campground located in a city or along a busy road is more exposed to thieves or vandals than a more remote campground, and should more actively supervise access.

Cleanliness This rates the cleanliness, serviceability, and state of repair of the campground, including grounds, sites, and facilities.

Insect Control This rating addresses questions regarding insect and pest control. Does management spray or take other steps to control the presence of mosquitoes and other insect pests? Does the campground drain efficiently following a rain? Are garbage and sewage properly collected and disposed of?

Facilities This rates the overall variety and quality of facilities to include bath house/toilets, swimming pool, retail shops, docks, pavilions, playgrounds, etc. If the quality of respective facilities vary considerably within a given campground, inconsistencies are explained in the prose description of the campground.

Campground Description This is an informative, consumer-oriented description of the campground. It includes what makes the campground special or unique and what differentiates it from other area campgrounds. The description may additionally include the following:

- The general layout of the campground.
- Where the campground is located relative to an easily referenced city or highway.
- The general setting (wilderness, rural, or urban).
- Description of the campsites including most and least desirable sites.
- Prevailing weather considerations and best time to visit.
- Mention of any unusual, exceptional, or deficient facilities.
- Security considerations, if any (gates that are locked at night, accessibility of campground to non-campers, etc.).

Basics Key information about the campground including:

- *Operated By* Who owns and/or operates the campground.
- *Open* Dates or seasons the campground is open.
- *Site Assignment* How sites are most commonly obtained (first-come, first served; reservations accepted; reservations only; assigned on check-in, etc. Deposit and refund policy.
- *Registration* Where the camper registers on arrival. Information on how and where to register after normal business hours (late arrival).
- *Fee* Cost of a standard campsite for one night for RV sites and tent sites respectively. Forms of payment accepted. Uses the following abbreviations for credit cards: V = VISA, AE = American Express, MC = MasterCard, D = Discover, CB = Carte Blanche, and DC = Diner's Club International.
- *Parking* Usual entry will be "At campsite" or "On road," though some campgrounds have a central parking lot from which tent campers must carry their gear to their campsite.

Facilities This is a brief data presentation that provides information on the availability of specific facilities and services.

- *Number of RV Sites* Any site where RVs are permitted.
- *Number of Tent-Only Sites* Sites set aside specifically for tent camping, including pop-up tent trailers.
- *Hookups* Possible hookups include electric, water, sewer, cable TV, phone, and Internet connection. Electrical hookups vary from campground to campground. Where electrical hookups are available, the amperage available is stated parenthetically, for example: "Hookups: Electric (20 amps), water."
- *Each Site* List of equipment such as grill, picnic table, lantern pole, fire pit, water faucet, electrical outlet, etc., provided at each campsite.
- *Dump station, laundry, pay phone, restrooms and showers, fuel, propane, RV service, general store, vending, playground* Are these items or services available on site? Their respective fields indicate the answer.
- *Internal Roads* Indicates the road type (gravel, paved, dirt), and condition.
- *Market* Location and distance of closest supermarket or large grocery store.
- *Restaurant* Location and distance of closest restaurant.
- *Other* Boat ramp, dining pavilion, miniature golf, tennis court, lounge, etc.
- *Activities* Activities available at the campground or in the area.
- *Nearby Attractions* Can be natural or manmade.
- *Additional Information* The best sources to call for general information on area activities and attractions. Sources include local or area chambers of commerce, tourist bureaus, visitors and convention authorities, forest service, etc.

Restrictions Any restrictions that apply, including:

- *Pets* Conditions under which pets are allowed or not.
- *Fires* Campground rules for fires and fire safety.
- *Alcoholic Beverages* Campground rules regarding the consumption of alcoholic beverages.
- *Vehicle Maximum Length* Length in feet of the maximum size vehicle the campground can accommodate.
- *Other* Any other rules or restrictions, to include minimum and maximum stays; age or group size restrictions; areas off-limits to vehicular traffic; security constraints such as locking the main gate during the night; etc.

How to Get There Clear and specific directions, including mileage and landmarks, for finding the campground.

Supplemental Directory of Campgrounds

If you're looking for a campground within the territory covered in this guide and can't find a profiled campground that is close or convenient to your route, check the Supplemental Directory of Campgrounds. This directory of hundreds of additional campgrounds is organized alphabetically by state and city name. Each entry provides the campground's name, address, reservations phone, fax, website, number of sites, average fee per night, and hookups available.

To Alaska
BRITISH COLUMBIA
ALBERTA
SASKATCHEWAN
MANITOBA
Calgary
Saskatoon
Regina
Winnipeg
Vancouver
Victoria
Seattle
Olympia
Spokane
Yakima
Portland
Salem
Eugene
Medford
Lewiston
Missoula
Great Falls
Helena
Butte
Billings
Bismarck
Grand Forks
Fargo
Pierre
Rapid City
Sioux Falls
Sioux City
Lincoln
CANADA
UNITED STATES
Missouri
WASHINGTON
OREGON
IDAHO
MONTANA
NORTH DAKOTA
SOUTH DAKOTA
WYOMING
NEBRASKA
NEVADA
UTAH
COLORADO
KANSAS
OKLAHOMA
CALIFORNIA
ARIZONA
NEW MEXICO
TEXAS
ROCKY MOUNTAINS
Boise
Idaho Falls
Twin Falls
Pocatello
Sheridan
Casper
Great Salt Lake
Salt Lake City
Provo
Laramie
Cheyenne
Fort Collins
Boulder
Denver
Colorado Springs
Pueblo
Grand Junction
Salina
Wichita
Eureka
Redding
Chico
Reno
Carson City
Sacramento
San Francisco
San Jose
Monterey
Fresno
Bakersfield
Las Vegas
St. George
Colorado
Flagstaff
Santa Fe
Albuquerque
Oklahoma City
Amarillo
Lubbock
Roswell
Santa Barbara
Los Angeles
Palm Springs
Phoenix
San Diego
Mexicali
Tucson
Las Cruces
El Paso
Odessa
Abilene
Dallas
Waco
Austin
San Antonio
Del Rio
Rio Grande
Laredo
Corpus Christi
Monterrey
Saltillo
Hermosillo
Chihuahua
UNITED STATES
MEXICO
PACIFIC OCEAN
MEXICO
500 mi
500 km
Barrow
RUSSIA
Fort Yukon
Nome
Fairbanks
ALASKA
CANADA
Bering Sea
Anchorage
Cordova
Juneau
Unalaska
PACIFIC OCEAN

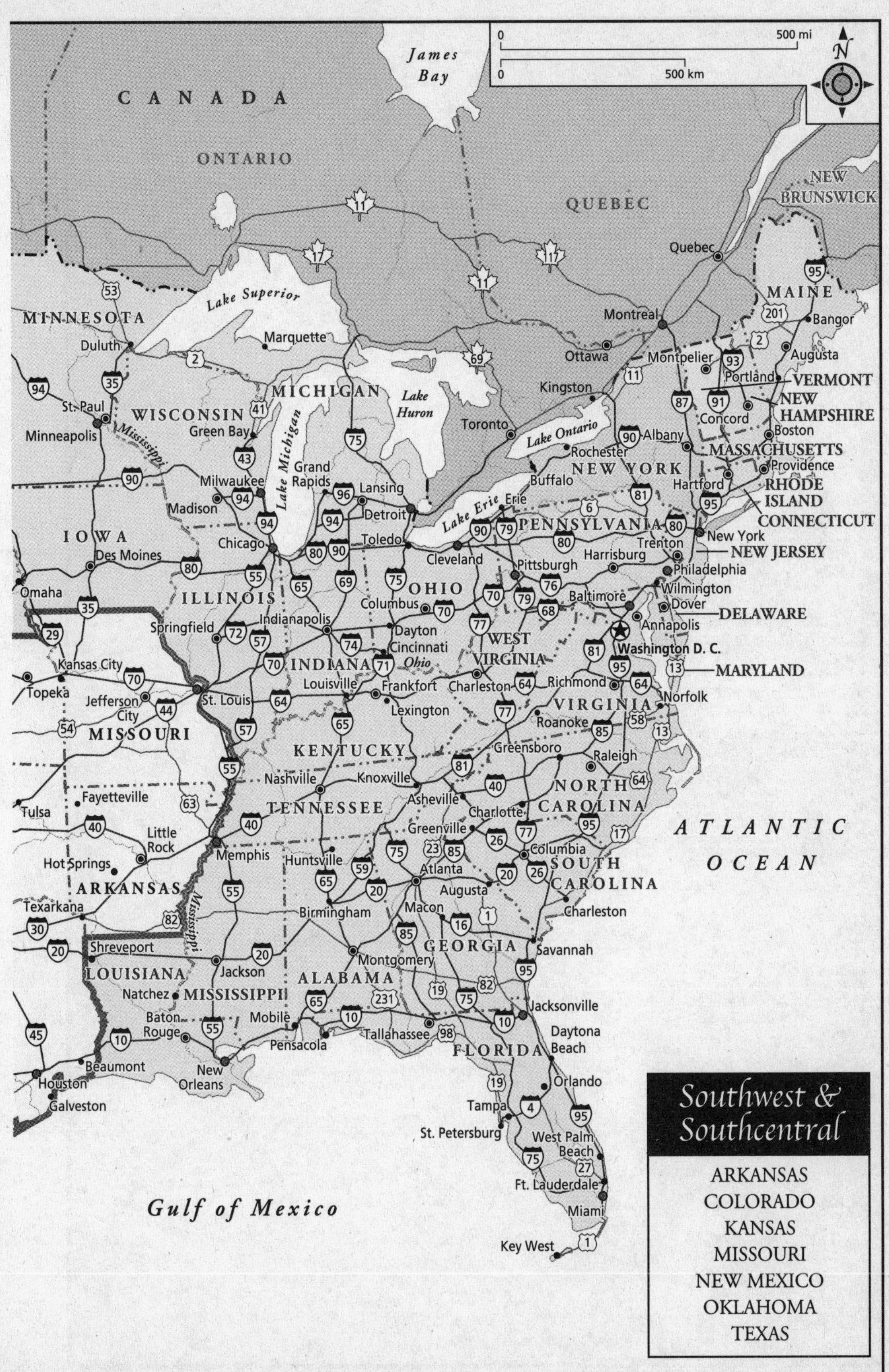
0
500 mi
0
500 km
N
James Bay
CANADA
ONTARIO
QUEBEC
NEW BRUNSWICK
Lake Superior
Lake Michigan
Lake Huron
Lake Ontario
Lake Erie
MINNESOTA
WISCONSIN
MICHIGAN
IOWA
ILLINOIS
INDIANA
OHIO
PENNSYLVANIA
NEW YORK
MAINE
VERMONT
NEW HAMPSHIRE
MASSACHUSETTS
RHODE ISLAND
CONNECTICUT
NEW JERSEY
DELAWARE
MARYLAND
WEST VIRGINIA
VIRGINIA
KENTUCKY
MISSOURI
TENNESSEE
NORTH CAROLINA
SOUTH CAROLINA
ARKANSAS
GEORGIA
ALABAMA
MISSISSIPPI
LOUISIANA
FLORIDA
Mississippi
Ohio
Duluth
Marquette
St. Paul
Minneapolis
Green Bay
Milwaukee
Madison
Grand Rapids
Lansing
Detroit
Chicago
Des Moines
Omaha
Toledo
Cleveland
Erie
Buffalo
Toronto
Kingston
Ottawa
Montreal
Quebec
Montpelier
Portland
Bangor
Augusta
Concord
Boston
Providence
Hartford
Albany
Rochester
New York
Trenton
Philadelphia
Wilmington
Dover
Annapolis
Baltimore
Washington D. C.
Harrisburg
Pittsburgh
Columbus
Dayton
Cincinnati
Indianapolis
Springfield
Kansas City
Topeka
Jefferson City
St. Louis
Louisville
Frankfort
Lexington
Charleston
Richmond
Norfolk
Roanoke
Greensboro
Raleigh
Nashville
Knoxville
Asheville
Charlotte
Greenville
Columbia
Charleston
Atlanta
Augusta
Macon
Savannah
Huntsville
Birmingham
Montgomery
Memphis
Little Rock
Hot Springs
Fayetteville
Tulsa
Texarkana
Shreveport
Jackson
Natchez
Baton Rouge
New Orleans
Mobile
Pensacola
Tallahassee
Jacksonville
Daytona Beach
Orlando
Tampa
St. Petersburg
West Palm Beach
Ft. Lauderdale
Miami
Key West
Beaumont
Houston
Galveston
ATLANTIC OCEAN
Gulf of Mexico
Southwest & Southcentral
ARKANSAS
COLORADO
KANSAS
MISSOURI
NEW MEXICO
OKLAHOMA
TEXAS

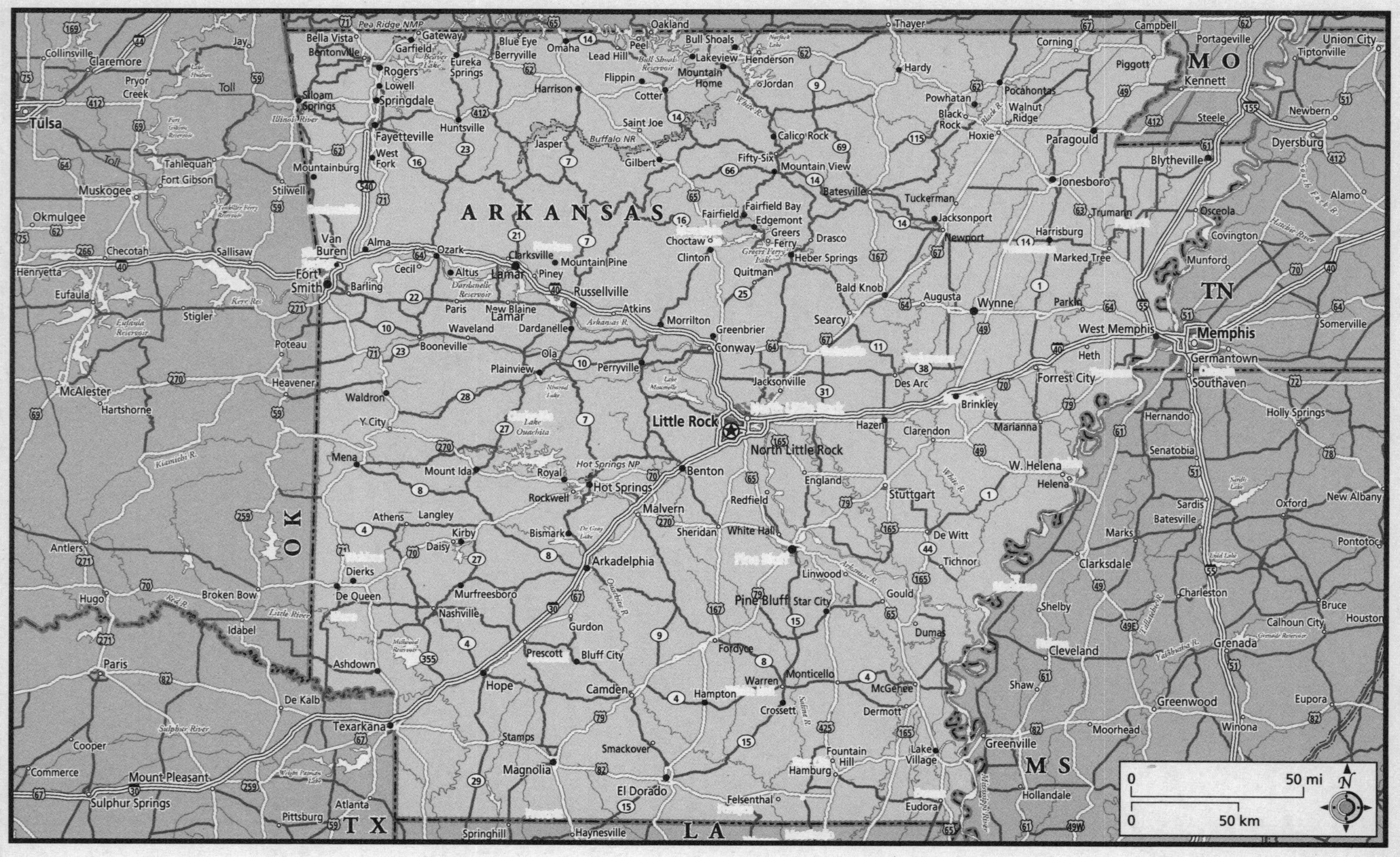
ARKANSAS
MO
TN
MS
LA
TX
OK
Little Rock
North Little Rock
Memphis
West Memphis
Fort Smith
Fayetteville
Hot Springs
Pine Bluff
Jonesboro
Texarkana
El Dorado
Tulsa
50 mi
50 km
N

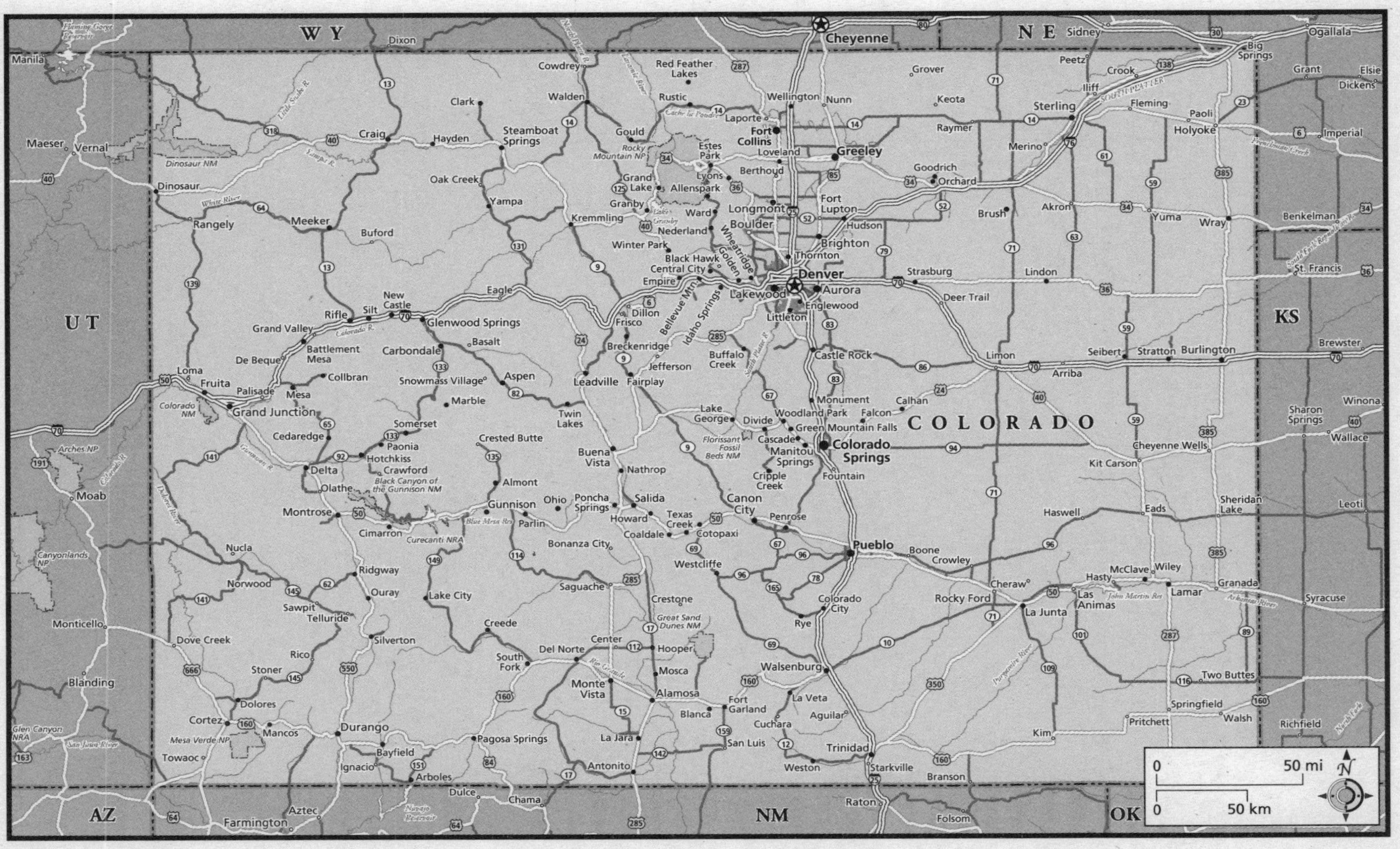

WY
NE
KS
OK
NM
AZ
UT
COLORADO
Cheyenne
Denver
Aurora
Lakewood
Englewood
Littleton
Thornton
Brighton
Boulder
Longmont
Loveland
Fort Collins
Greeley
Wellington
Laporte
Estes Park
Lyons
Golden
Wheatridge
Idaho Springs
Central City
Black Hawk
Nederland
Castle Rock
Monument
Colorado Springs
Manitou Springs
Cripple Creek
Pueblo
Canon City
Trinidad
Walsenburg
Alamosa
La Junta
Lamar
Las Animas
Rocky Ford
Sterling
Limon
Burlington
Leadville
Breckenridge
Frisco
Dillon
Fairplay
Buena Vista
Salida
Gunnison
Aspen
Glenwood Springs
Carbondale
Eagle
Rifle
Grand Junction
Fruita
Palisade
Delta
Montrose
Ouray
Telluride
Silverton
Durango
Cortez
Pagosa Springs
Craig
Meeker
Rangely
Steamboat Springs
Walden
Kremmling
Granby
Grand Lake
Winter Park
Rocky Mountain NP
Dinosaur NM
Colorado NM
Black Canyon of the Gunnison NM
Great Sand Dunes NM
Mesa Verde NP
Florissant Fossil Beds NM
Curecanti NRA
Arches NP
Canyonlands NP
Moab
Vernal
Farmington
Raton
Ogallala
50 mi
50 km

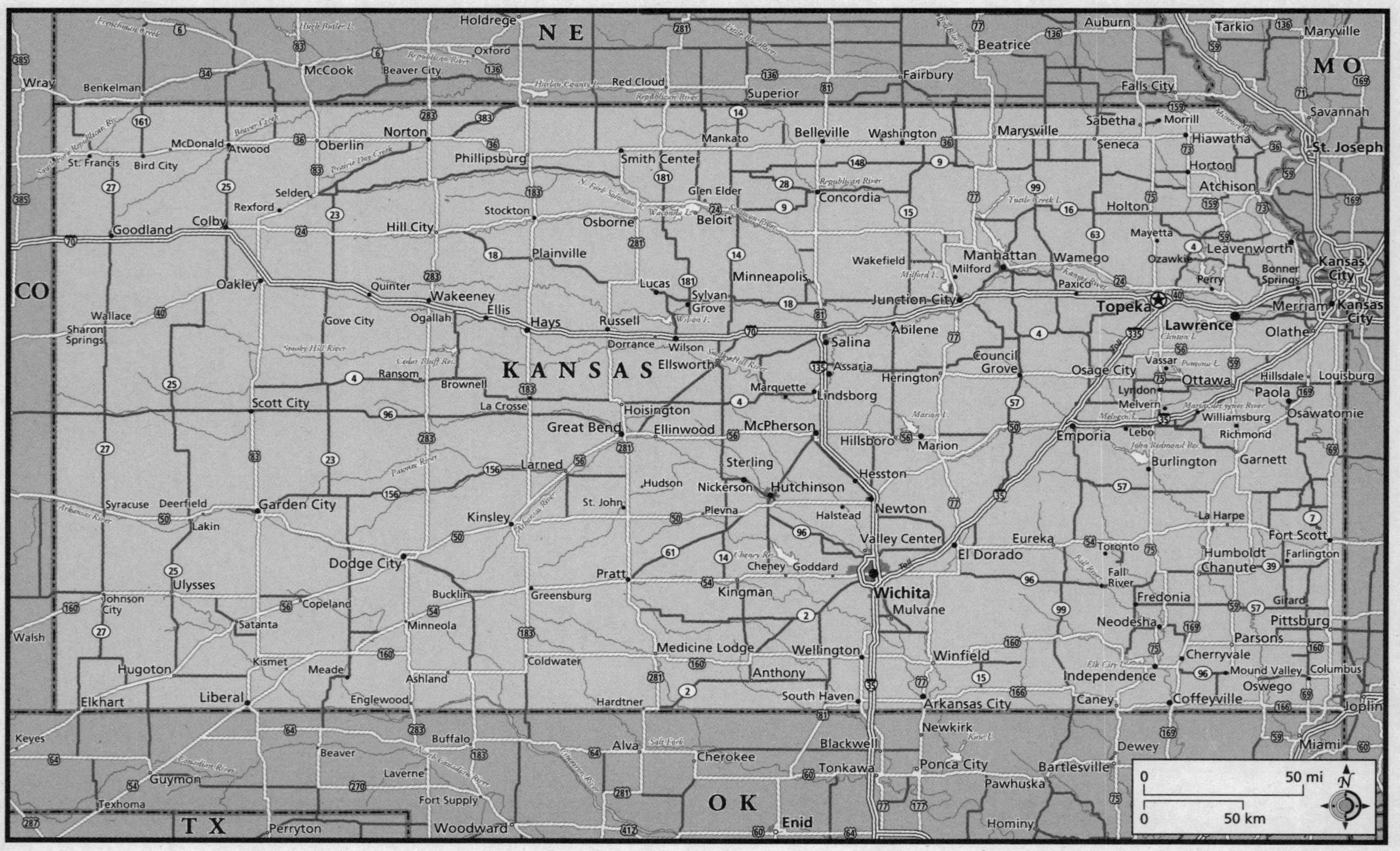
KANSAS
NE
MO
CO
OK
TX
0
50 mi
0
50 km
N
Topeka
Wichita
Kansas City
Lawrence
Olathe
Merriam
Leavenworth
Bonner Springs
St. Joseph
Atchison
Manhattan
Junction City
Salina
Abilene
Emporia
Hutchinson
Newton
McPherson
Great Bend
Hays
Dodge City
Garden City
Liberal
Goodland
Colby
Oakley
Scott City
Pratt
Ottawa
Paola
Osawatomie
Fort Scott
Pittsburg
Parsons
Chanute
Independence
Coffeyville
El Dorado
Winfield
Arkansas City
Wellington
Concordia
Belleville
Marysville
Beloit
Russell
Ellsworth
Lindsborg
Larned
Kingman
Medicine Lodge
Ulysses
Hugoton
Elkhart
Norton
Phillipsburg
Oberlin
Atwood
St. Francis
Joplin
Miami
Enid
Ponca City
Bartlesville
Guymon
Woodward
Beatrice
Fairbury
McCook
Holdrege
Wray

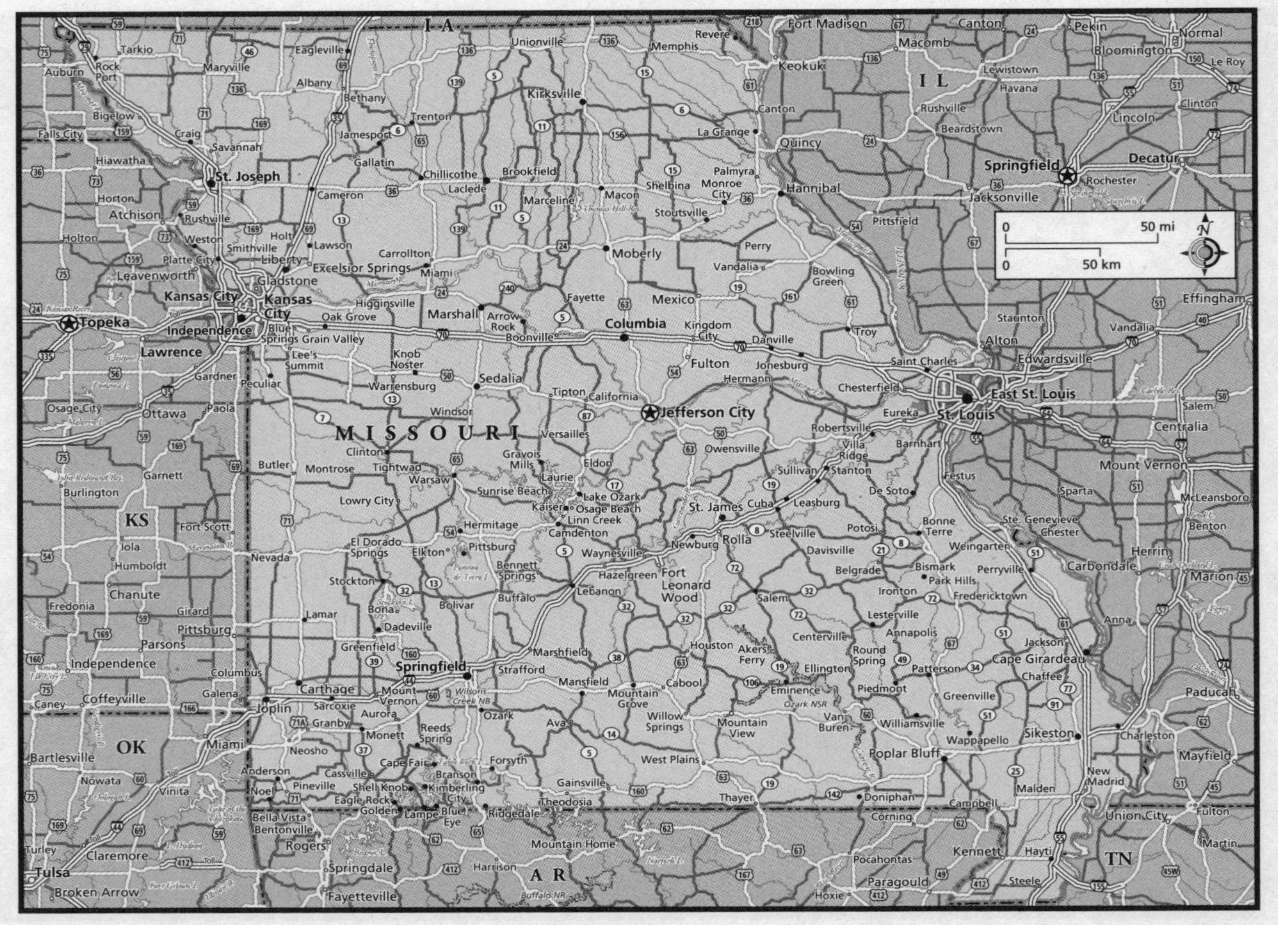
MISSOURI
IA
IL
KS
OK
AR
TN
0 50 mi
0 50 km
N
Kansas City
St. Joseph
Independence
Lawrence
Topeka
Columbia
Jefferson City
St. Louis
East St. Louis
Springfield
Joplin
Cape Girardeau
Hannibal
Quincy
Decatur
Sedalia
Rolla
Fort Leonard Wood
Poplar Bluff
Sikeston
Branson
Lake Ozark
Osage Beach
Carthage
Moberly
Mexico
Fulton
Kirksville
Chillicothe
Warrensburg
Lebanon
Carbondale
Paducah
Mount Vernon
Edwardsville
Alton
Tulsa

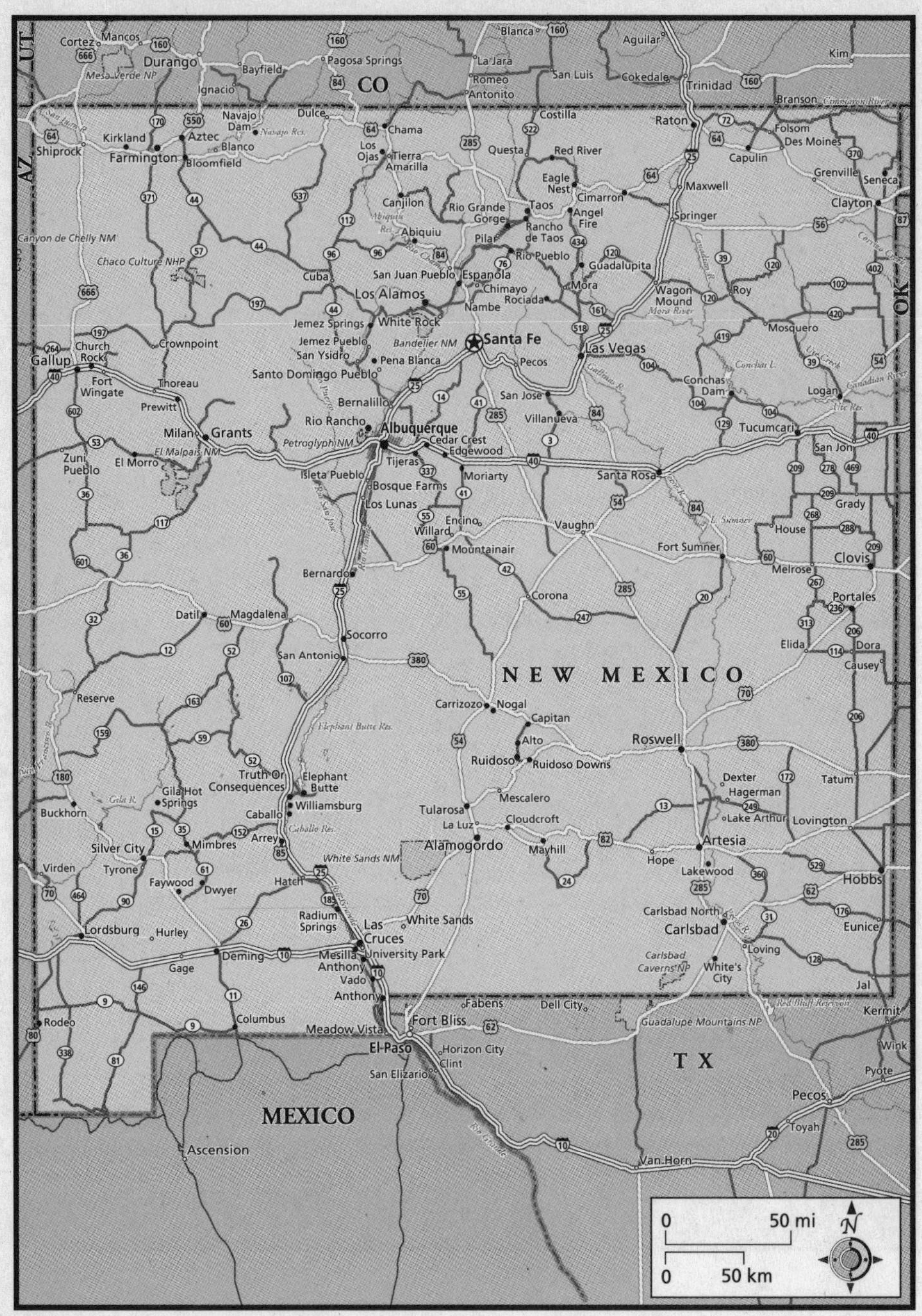

UT
CO
AZ
OK
TX
NEW MEXICO
MEXICO
Cortez
Mancos
Durango
Mesa Verde NP
Bayfield
Pagosa Springs
Ignacio
La Jara
Romeo
Antonito
Blanca
San Luis
Aguilar
Cokedale
Trinidad
Kim
Branson
Navajo Dam
Dulce
Chama
Kirkland
Aztec
Shiprock
Farmington
Blanco
Bloomfield
Los Ojas
Tierra Amarilla
Costilla
Questa
Red River
Eagle Nest
Raton
Folsom
Des Moines
Capulin
Grenville
Seneca
Maxwell
Cimarron
Clayton
Canjilon
Rio Grande Gorge
Taos
Angel Fire
Rancho de Taos
Springer
Canyon de Chelly NM
Abiquiu
Pilar
Rio Pueblo
Guadalupita
Chaco Culture NHP
Cuba
San Juan Pueblo
Española
Chimayo
Mora
Roy
Los Alamos
Nambe
Rociada
Wagon Mound
Jemez Springs
White Rock
Mosquero
Jemez Pueblo
Bandelier NM
Santa Fe
Las Vegas
Gallup
Church Rock
Crownpoint
San Ysidro
Pena Blanca
Pecos
Santo Domingo Pueblo
Fort Wingate
Thoreau
Conchas Dam
Logan
Prewitt
Bernalillo
San Jose
Rio Rancho
Villanueva
Milan
Grants
Albuquerque
Tucumcari
Petroglyph NM
Cedar Crest
Edgewood
San Jon
Zuni Pueblo
El Morro
El Malpais NM
Tijeras
Santa Rosa
Isleta Pueblo
Moriarty
Bosque Farms
Los Lunas
Grady
Encino
Vaughn
Willard
House
Mountainair
Fort Sumner
Clovis
Melrose
Bernardo
Corona
Portales
Datil
Magdalena
Socorro
Elida
Dora
San Antonio
Causey
Reserve
Carrizozo
Nogal
Capitan
Alto
Roswell
Ruidoso
Ruidoso Downs
Truth Or Consequences
Elephant Butte
Dexter
Hagerman
Tatum
Gila Hot Springs
Williamsburg
Mescalero
Buckhorn
Caballo
Tularosa
Lake Arthur
Lovington
La Luz
Cloudcroft
Silver City
Mimbres
Arrey
Alamogordo
Artesia
Virden
Tyrone
White Sands NM
Mayhill
Hope
Lakewood
Faywood
Dwyer
Hatch
Hobbs
Radium Springs
Carlsbad North
Lordsburg
Hurley
Las Cruces
White Sands
Carlsbad
Eunice
Deming
Mesilla
University Park
Loving
Gage
Anthony
Carlsbad Caverns NP
White's City
Vado
Jal
Fabens
Dell City
Kermit
Rodeo
Columbus
Meadow Vista
Fort Bliss
Guadalupe Mountains NP
Wink
El Paso
Horizon City
Clint
San Elizario
Pyote
Pecos
Toyah
Ascension
Van Horn
0 50 mi
0 50 km
N

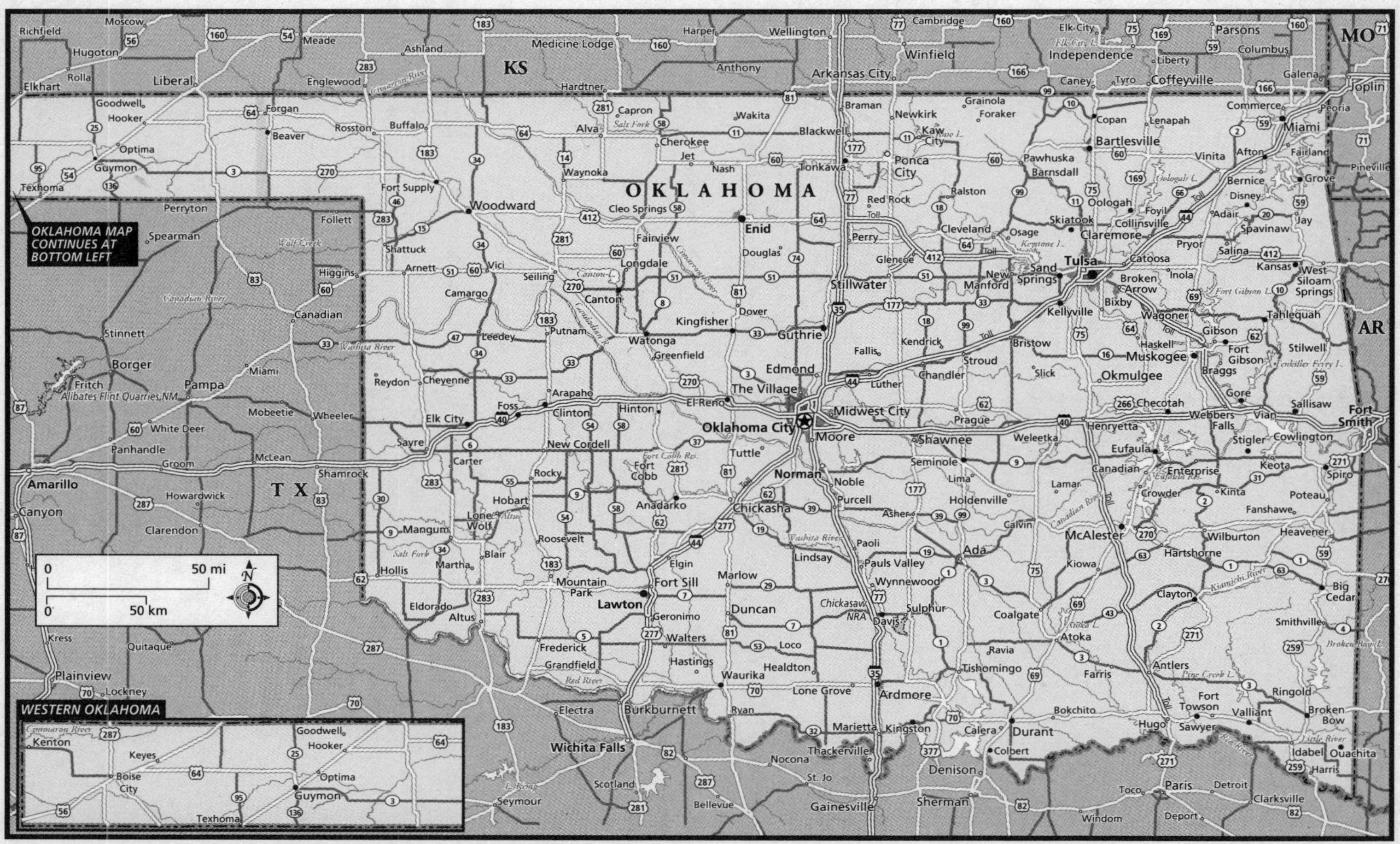
OKLAHOMA
KS
MO
AR
TX
OKLAHOMA MAP CONTINUES AT BOTTOM LEFT
WESTERN OKLAHOMA
0
50 mi
0
50 km
N
Oklahoma City
The Village
Edmond
Midwest City
Moore
Norman
Tulsa
Sand Springs
Broken Arrow
Lawton
Fort Sill
Enid
Stillwater
Guthrie
Muskogee
Okmulgee
Bartlesville
Ponca City
Shawnee
Chickasha
Ada
McAlester
Ardmore
Durant
Woodward
Guymon
Miami
Tahlequah
Fort Smith
Joplin
Amarillo
Wichita Falls
Liberal
Arkansas City
Independence
Coffeyville
Sherman
Denison
Gainesville
Paris
Chickasaw NRA

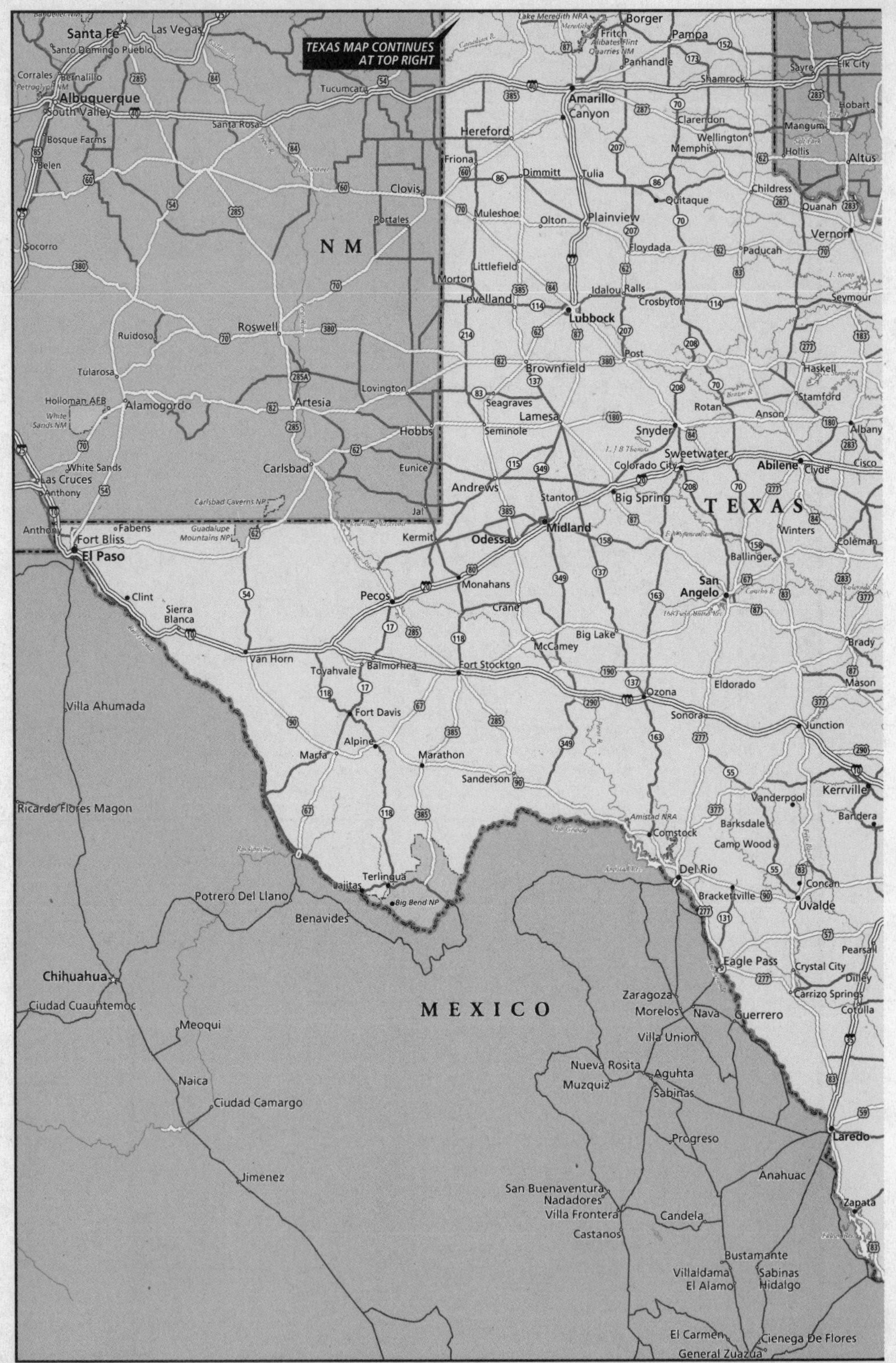
TEXAS MAP CONTINUES AT TOP RIGHT
NM
TEXAS
MEXICO
Santa Fe
Las Vegas
Santo Domingo Pueblo
Corrales
Bernalillo
Albuquerque
South Valley
Bosque Farms
Belen
Socorro
Tucumcari
Santa Rosa
Clovis
Portales
Roswell
Ruidoso
Tularosa
Holloman AFB
Alamogordo
White Sands NM
Artesia
Lovington
Hobbs
Carlsbad
Eunice
Jal
White Sands
Las Cruces
Anthony
Carlsbad Caverns NP
Fabens
Guadalupe Mountains NP
Fort Bliss
El Paso
Clint
Sierra Blanca
Van Horn
Kermit
Pecos
Monahans
Odessa
Midland
Andrews
Stanton
Big Spring
Crane
McCamey
Big Lake
Fort Stockton
Toyahvale
Balmorhea
Fort Davis
Alpine
Marfa
Marathon
Sanderson
Terlingua
Lajitas
Big Bend NP
Ozona
Sonora
Eldorado
Junction
Kerrville
Vanderpool
Bandera
Barksdale
Camp Wood
Concan
Uvalde
Brackettville
Del Rio
Comstock
Amistad NRA
Eagle Pass
Crystal City
Carrizo Springs
Pearsall
Dilley
Cotulla
Laredo
Zapata
Borger
Pampa
Fritch
Panhandle
Shamrock
Amarillo
Canyon
Hereford
Clarendon
Wellington
Memphis
Friona
Dimmitt
Tulia
Quitaque
Childress
Quanah
Muleshoe
Olton
Plainview
Floydada
Paducah
Vernon
Littlefield
Morton
Levelland
Idalou
Ralls
Crosbyton
Lubbock
Seymour
Post
Brownfield
Seagraves
Lamesa
Seminole
Snyder
Haskell
Stamford
Rotan
Anson
Albany
Sweetwater
Colorado City
Abilene
Clyde
Cisco
Winters
Ballinger
Coleman
San Angelo
Brady
Mason
Elk City
Sayre
Hobart
Mangum
Hollis
Altus
Villa Ahumada
Ricardo Flores Magon
Potrero Del Llano
Benavides
Chihuahua
Ciudad Cuauhtemoc
Meoqui
Naica
Ciudad Camargo
Jimenez
Zaragoza
Morelos
Nava
Guerrero
Villa Union
Nueva Rosita
Muzquiz
Aguhta
Sabinas
Progreso
Anahuac
San Buenaventura
Nadadores
Villa Frontera
Candela
Castanos
Bustamante
Villaldama
El Alamo
Sabinas Hidalgo
El Carmen
General Zuazua
Cienega De Flores

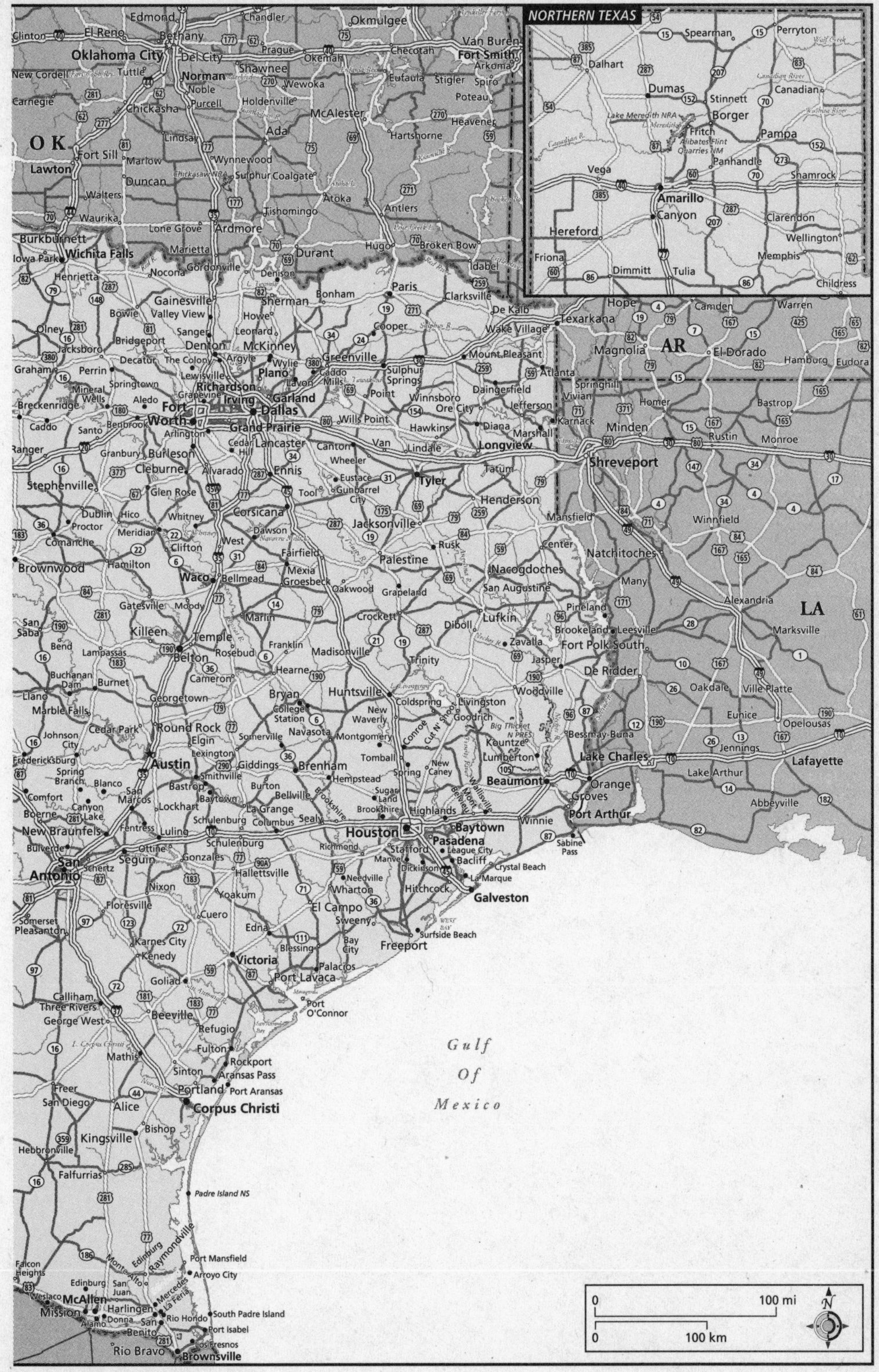
NORTHERN TEXAS
Spearman
Perryton
Dalhart
Dumas
Stinnett
Canadian
Borger
Lake Meredith NRA
Fritch
Alibates Flint Quarries NM
Pampa
Panhandle
Vega
Shamrock
Amarillo
Canyon
Clarendon
Hereford
Wellington
Friona
Memphis
Dimmitt
Tulia
Childress
OK
Edmond
Chandler
Okmulgee
Clinton
El Reno
Bethany
Van Buren
Oklahoma City
Del City
Prague
Checotah
Fort Smith
Arkoma
Okemah
New Cordell
Tuttle
Shawnee
Norman
Wewoka
Eufaula
Stigler
Spiro
Noble
Carnegie
Purcell
Holdenville
Poteau
Chickasha
McAlester
Heavener
Ada
Lindsay
Hartshorne
Fort Sill
Marlow
Wynnewood
Lawton
Duncan
Sulphur
Coalgate
Walters
Atoka
Antlers
Tishomingo
Waurika
Lone Grove
Ardmore
Burkburnett
Marietta
Durant
Hugo
Broken Bow
Wichita Falls
Iowa Park
Nocona
Gordonville
Denison
Idabel
Henrietta
Paris
Bonham
Clarksville
Sherman
Gainesville
Bowie
Valley View
Howe
De Kalb
Hope
Camden
Warren
Texarkana
Olney
Cooper
Sanger
Leonard
Wake Village
Jacksboro
Bridgeport
Denton
McKinney
Magnolia
AR
El Dorado
Decatur
The Colony
Argyle
Greenville
Mount Pleasant
Hamburg
Eudora
Graham
Perrin
Lewisville
Wylie
Sulphur Springs
Atlanta
Springtown
Richardson
Plano
Caddo Mills
Springhill
Mineral Wells
Grapevine
Irving
Garland
Lavon
Point
Winnsboro
Daingerfield
Vivian
Homer
Bastrop
Breckenridge
Aledo
Fort Worth
Dallas
Ore City
Jefferson
Caddo
Santo
Benbrook
Arlington
Grand Prairie
Wills Point
Hawkins
Diana
Karnack
Marshall
Minden
Ruston
Monroe
Ranger
Granbury
Burleson
Cedar Hill
Lancaster
Canton
Van
Lindale
Longview
Shreveport
Wheeler
Cleburne
Alvarado
Ennis
Tatum
Stephenville
Eustace
Tyler
Glen Rose
Tool
Gunbarrel City
Henderson
Dublin
Hico
Whitney
Corsicana
Proctor
Dawson
Jacksonville
Mansfield
Winnfield
Comanche
Meridian
Clifton
West
Rusk
Center
Natchitoches
Brownwood
Hamilton
Fairfield
Palestine
Mexia
Nacogdoches
Waco
Bellmead
Groesbeck
Many
Oakwood
Grapeland
San Augustine
Gatesville
Moody
Pineland
Alexandria
LA
Marlin
Crockett
Diboll
Lufkin
San Saba
Killeen
Temple
Brookeland
Leesville
Marksville
Bend
Franklin
Zavalla
Fort Polk South
Lampasas
Belton
Rosebud
Madisonville
Trinity
Jasper
Buchanan Dam
Burnet
Hearne
De Ridder
Cameron
Bryan
Huntsville
Woodville
Oakdale
Ville Platte
Llano
Georgetown
College Station
Coldspring
Livingston
Marble Falls
New Waverly
Goodrich
Eunice
Cedar Park
Round Rock
Navasota
Big Thicket N PRES
Bessmay-Buna
Opelousas
Johnson City
Elgin
Somerville
Montgomery
Conroe
Cut N' Shoot
Kountze
Jennings
Fredericksburg
Lexington
Tomball
Lumberton
Lake Charles
Lafayette
Spring Branch
Austin
Giddings
Brenham
New Caney
Spring
Blanco
Smithville
Hempstead
Beaumont
Lake Arthur
Comfort
San Marcos
Bastrop
Burton
Sugar Land
Orange
Canyon Lake
Lockhart
Bellville
Groves
Abbeyville
Boerne
Baytown
La Grange
Brookshire
Highlands
Schulenburg
Columbus
Sealy
Port Arthur
New Braunfels
Fentress
Luling
Winnie
Houston
Bulverde
Richmond
Pasadena
Sabine Pass
San Antonio
Seguin
Ottine
Gonzales
Stafford
League City
Schertz
Manvel
Bacliff
Crystal Beach
Hallettsville
Dickinson
La Marque
Needville
Nixon
Wharton
Hitchcock
Galveston
Yoakum
Floresville
El Campo
Cuero
Sweeny
Somerset
Pleasanton
Edna
Surfside Beach
Karnes City
Freeport
Blessing
Bay City
Kenedy
Victoria
Palacios
Goliad
Port Lavaca
Calliham
Three Rivers
Port O'Connor
George West
Beeville
Refugio
Gulf Of Mexico
Fulton
Mathis
Rockport
Sinton
Aransas Pass
Freer
Portland
Port Aransas
San Diego
Alice
Corpus Christi
Bishop
Kingsville
Hebbronville
Falfurrias
Padre Island NS
Port Mansfield
Falcon Heights
Edinburg
Raymondville
Arroyo City
San Juan
Weslaco
McAllen
Harlingen
Mercedes
La Feria
Mission
Donna
Alamo
San Benito
Rio Hondo
South Padre Island
Port Isabel
Los Fresnos
Rio Bravo
Brownsville
0
100 mi
0
100 km
N

Campground Awards

ARKANSAS

Best RV Camping

Shadow Mountain, Mena

Best Tent Camping

Crowley's Ridge State Park, Paragould
Petit Jean State Park, Morrilton
Shadow Mountain, Mena
Jacksonport State Park, Jacksonport
Eureka Springs KOA, Eureka Springs
Cedar Ridge, Calico Rock

Most Beautiful Campgrounds

Petit Jean State Park, Morrilton
Jacksonport State Park, Jacksonport
Eureka Springs KOA, Eureka Springs
Blue Clouds RV & Cabin Resort, Edgemont
Cedar Ridge, Calico Rock

Most Private Campsites

Cedar Ridge, Calico Rock
Whispering Pines RV Park, Clinton
Moro Bay State Park, El Dorado
Hardy Camper Park, Hardy
Jacksonport State Park, Jacksonport
Pecan Grove RV Park, Lake Village
Petit Jean State Park, Morrilton
Wilderness Hills RV Park & Campground, Siloam Springs

Most Spacious Campsites

Whispering Pines RV Park, Clinton
Moro Bay State Park, El Dorado
Hardy Camper Park, Hardy
Parkers RV Park, Harrison
Jacksonport State Park, Jacksonport
Pecan Grove RV Park, Lake Village
Petit Jean State Park, Morrilton
Crowley's Ridge State Park, Paragould
Old Davidsonville State Park, Pocahontas
Wilderness Hills RV Park & Campground, Siloam Springs

Quietest Campgrounds

Cedar Ridge, Calico Rock
Moro Bay State Park, El Dorado
Jacksonport State Park, Jacksonport
Craighead Forest Park, Jonesboro
Petit Jean State Park, Morrilton
Crowley's Ridge State Park, Paragould
Saracen Trace RV Park, Pine Bluff
Old Davidsonville State Park, Pocahontas
Rogers/Pea Ridge KOA, Rogers
Wilderness Hills RV Park & Campground, Siloam Springs
Village Creek State Park, Wynne

Most Secure Campgrounds

Petit Jean State Park, Morrilton
Shadow Mountain, Mena
Pecan Grove RV Park, Lake Village
Craighead Forest Park, Jonesboro
Jacksonport State Park, Jacksonport
Young's Lakeshore RV Resort, Hot Springs
Fair Park RV Park, Hope
Hardy Camper Park, Hardy
Cedar Ridge, Calico Rock

Cleanest Campgrounds

Eureka Springs KOA, Eureka Springs
Parkers RV Park, Harrison
Jacksonport State Park, Jacksonport
Shadow Mountain, Mena

ARKANSAS (continued)

Cleanest Campgrounds (continued)
Rogers/Pea Ridge KOA, Rogers
Trav-L-Park, West Memphis

Best Campground Facilities
Eureka Springs KOA, Eureka Springs
Fair Park RV Park, Hope
Little Rock North KOA, Little Rock
Trav-L-Park, West Memphis

Best Rural, Farm, or Ranch Settings
Pecan Grove RV Park, Lake Village

Best Urban and Suburban Settings
Hardy Camper Park, Hardy
Heritage Inn & RV Park, Brinkley

Best Waterfront Settings
Bull Shoals Recreationea, Bull Shoals
Moro Bay State Park, El Dorado

Most Romantic Campgrounds
Eureka Springs KOA, Eureka Springs

Best Family-Oriented Campgrounds
Petit Jean State Park, Morrliton

Best Swimming Pools
Arkadelphia KOA, Arkadelphia
Petit Jean State Park, Carrliton
Eureka Springs KOA, Eureka Springs
Trav-L-Park, West Memphis
Rogers KOA, Rogers

COLORADO

Best RV Camping
Grape Creek RV Park, Westcliffe
Four Seasons RV Park, Salida
RV Ranch at Grand Junction, Grand Junction
North Park/Gould KOA, Gould
Lost Burro, Cripple Creek
Mt Views at River's Edge RV Resort, Creede
Pueblo South/Colorado City KOA, Colorado City
Gambler's Edge RV Park, Central City
Aspen Trails Campground and Resort, Cedaredge
Tiger Run RV Resort, Breckenridge

Best Tent Camping
Idlewild Campground, Winter Park
Camp Dick, Ward
North Park/Gould KOA, Gould
Horsetooth Campground (Stout Campground), Fort Collins
Pueblo South/Colorado City KOA, Colorado City
Steamboat Lake State Park, Clark
Aspen Trails Campground and Resort, Cedaredge
Arkansas River Rim Campground & RV Park, Buena Vista

Most Beautiful Campgrounds
Stillwater Campground, Yampa
Camp Dick, Ward
Parry Peak Campground, Twin Lakes
Rifle Falls/Rifle Gap, Rifle
Dowdy Lake Campground, Red Feather
Paonia State Park, Paonia
North Park/Gould KOA, Gould
Horsetooth Campground (Stout Campground), Fort Collins
Estes Park KOA, Estes Park
Lost Burro, Cripple Creek
Gambler's Edge RV Park, Central City
Bonny Lake State Park Campground, Burlington
Kelsey Campground, Buffalo Creek
Arkansas River Rim Campground & RV Park, Buena Vista
Tiger Run RV Resort, Breckenridge
Olive Ridge Campground, Allenspark

Most Private Campsites
Tiger Run RV Resort, Breckenridge
Castle Rock KOA, Castle Rock
Mt Views at River's Edge RV Resort, Creede
Lost Burro, Cripple Creek
Horsetooth Campground (Stout Campground), Fort Collins
North Park/Gould KOA, Gould
Four Seasons RV Park, Salida
Stillwater Campground, Yampa

Most Spacious Campsites
Tiger Run RV Resort, Breckenridge
Castle Rock KOA, Castle Rock

COLORADO (continued)

Mt Views at River's Edge RV Resort, Creede
Lost Burro, Cripple Creek
Horsetooth Campground (Stout Campground), Fort Collins
Stagecoach Campground, Meeker
Four Seasons RV Park, Salida
Stillwater Campground, Yampa

Quietest Campgrounds

Battlement Mesa RV Park, Battlement Mesa
Tiger Run RV Resort, Breckenridge
Bonny Lake State Park Campground, Burlington
Aspen Trails Campground and Resort, Cedaredge
Gambler's Edge RV Park, Central City
Steamboat Lake State Park, Clark
Mt Views at River's Edge RV Resort, Creede
Lost Burro, Cripple Creek
North Park/Gould KOA, Gould
Meadowlark Cafe, Motel & RV Park, Lindon
Montrose RV Resort (formerly KOA), Montrose
Ridgway State Park, Ridgway
Rifle Falls/Rifle Gap, Rifle
Glen Echo Resort, Rustic
Silver Summit, Silverton
Camp Dick, Ward
Grape Creek RV Park, Westcliffe
Stillwater Campground, Yampa

Most Secure Campgrounds

Prospect RV Park, Wheat Ridge
Denver North Campground & RV Park, Thornton
Yogi Bear Jellystone Camp Resort, Sterling
Pueblo KOA, Pueblo
Blue Mountain Village, Dinosaur
Pueblo South/Colorado City KOA, Colorado City
Gambler's Edge RV Park, Central City
Castle Rock KOA, Castle Rock
Tiger Run RV Resort, Breckenridge

Cleanest Campgrounds

Josey's Mogote Meadow, Antonito
Pinon Park Campground and RV Resort, Arboles
Aspen-Basalt Campground, Aspen
Battlement Mesa RV Park, Battlement Mesa
Tiger Run RV Resort, Breckenridge
Bonny Lake State Park Campground, Burlington
Castle Rock KOA, Castle Rock
Gambler's Edge RV Park, Central City
Cortez/Mesa Verde KOA, Cortez
Craig KOA Kampground, Craig
Mt Views at River's Edge RV Resort, Creede
Lost Burro, Cripple Creek
Durango East KOA, Durango
Estes Park KOA, Estes Park
Ami's Acres, Glenwood Springs
North Park/Gould KOA, Gould
RV Ranch at Grand Junction, Grand Junction
Elk Creek Campground, Grand Lake
Gunnison KOA, Gunnison
Red Mountain RV Park, Kremmling
Carter Valley Campground, Loveland
Montrose RV Resort (formerly KOA), Montrose
Cool Pines RV Park, Pagosa Springs
Pueblo KOA, Pueblo
Rifle Falls/Rifle Gap, Rifle
Glen Echo Resort, Rustic
Four Seasons RV Park, Salida
Silver Summit, Silverton
Denver North Campground & RV Park, Thornton
Fort Collins/Wellington KOA, Wellington
Grape Creek RV Park, Westcliffe
Prospect RV Park, Wheat Ridge

Best Campground Facilities

Aspen-Basalt Campground, Aspen
Tiger Run RV Resort, Breckenridge
Aspen Trails Campground and Resort, Cedaredge
Cortez/Mesa Verde KOA, Cortez
Craig KOA Kampground, Craig
Mt Views at River's Edge RV Resort, Creede
Durango East KOA, Durango
Estes Park KOA, Estes Park
North Park/Gould KOA, Gould
RV Ranch at Grand Junction, Grand Junction
Elk Creek Campground, Grand Lake
Gunnison KOA, Gunnison
Montrose RV Resort (formerly KOA), Montrose
Four Seasons RV Park, Salida
Steamboat Campground (formerly KOA), Steamboat Springs
Denver North Campground & RV Park, Thornton
Fort Collins/Wellington KOA, Wellington

Best Rural, Farm, or Ranch Settings

Meadowlark Cafe, Motel & RV Park, Lindon
Hitchin' Post RV Park, Wray

Best Urban and Suburban Settings

Deluxe RV Park, Denver
La Junta KOA, La Junta

COLORADO (continued)

Best Urban and Suburban Settings (continued)

La Junta KOA, La Junta
Memorial Park, Brush
Riverwood Inn, Delta

Best Mountain Settings

Battlement Mesa RV Park, Battlement Mesa
Tiger Run RV Resort, Breckenridge
Lost Burro, Cripple Creek
Mt Views at River's Edge RV Resort, Creede
Steamboat Lake State Park, Clark
Horsetooth Reservoir (Stout Campground), Fort Collins
Chief Hosa Campground, Golden
Gould KOA, Gould
North Park/Gould KOA, Gould
Paonia State Park, Paonia
Silver Summit, Silverton
Camp Dick, Ward
Stillwater Campground, Yampa

Best Waterfront Settings

Bonny Lake State Park, Burlington
Pinon Park Campground & RV Resort, Boles
Tiger Run RV Resort, Breckenridge
BRB Crystal River Resort, Carbondale
Cotopaxi KOA, Cotopaxi
Steamboat Lake State Park, Clark
Riverwood Inn, Delta
Horsetooth Reservoir (Stout Campground), Fort Collins
Jackson Lake State Park, Goodrich
Dowdy Lake Campground, Red Feather
Ridgway State Park, Ridgway
Rifle Falls/Rifle Gap Campgrounds, Rifle
Parry Peak Campground, Twin Lakes
Stillwater Campground, Yampa

Most Romantic Campgrounds

Aspen Trails Campground & Resort, Cedaredge
BRB Crystal River Resort, Carbondale
Cedar Ridge, Calico Rock
Lost Burro, Cripple Creek
Mt Views at River's Edge RV Resort, Creede
Estes Park KOA, Estes Park KOA
Gould KOA, Gould
Battlement Mesa RV Park, Battlement Mesa
Grape Creek RV Park, Westcliffe
Stillwater Campground, Yampa

Best Family-Oriented Campgrounds

Alamosa KOA, Alamosa
Bonny Lake State Park, Burlington
Tiger Run RV Resort, Breckenridge
Colorado City KOA, Colorado City
Cotopaxi KOA, Cotopaxi
Craig KOA, Craig
Mt Views at River's Edge RV Resort, Creede
Durango KOA, Durango
Estes Park KOA, Estes Park
Gould KOA, Gould
Gunnison KOA, Gunnison
RV Ranch at Grand Junction, Grand Junction
La Junta KOA, La Junta
La Junta KOA, La Junta
Lamar KOA, Lamar
Montrose RV Resort (formerly KOA), Montrose
Pueblo KOA, Pueblo
Steamboat Campground (formerly KOA), Steamboat Springs
Yogi Bear Jellystone Campground Resort, Sterling

Best Swimming Pools

Memorial Park, Brush
Castle Rock KOA, Castle Rock
Cortez KOA, Cortez
Cotopaxi KOA, Cotopaxi
Craig KOA, Craig
Durango KOA, Durango
Hudson KOA, Hudson
La Junta KOA, La Junta
Lamar KOA, Lamar
Hud's Campground, McClave
Montrose RV Resort (formerly KOA), Montrose
Pike's Peak RV Park & Campground, Manitou Springs
Pueblo KOA, Pueblo
Steamboat Campground (formerly KOA), Steamboat Springs
Yogi Bear Jellystone Campground Resort, Sterling
Wellington KOA, Wellington

KANSAS

Best RV Camping

Topeka KOA, Topeka
Tuttle Creek State Park, Manhatten
Fort Scott Campground, Fort Scott
Crawford State Park, Farlington
Council Grove Lake, Council Grove
Brome Ridge RV Park, Concordia
Covered Wagon RV Resort, Abilene

Best Tent Camping

Camp Lakeside, Scott City
Prairie Dog State Park, Norton
Tuttle Creek State Park, Manhatten
Elk City State Park, Independence
Crawford State Park, Farlington
Council Grove Lake, Council Grove
Covered Wagon RV Resort, Abilene

Most Beautiful Campgrounds

Elk City State Park, Independence
Crawford State Park, Farlington
Council Grove Lake, Council Grove
Evergreen Acres RV Park, Belleville

Most Private Campsites

Crawford State Park, Farlington
Tuttle Creek State Park, Manhatten

Most Spacious Campsites

Council Grove Lake, Council Grove
Crawford State Park, Farlington
Tuttle Creek State Park, Manhatten
Prairie Dog State Park, Norton

Quietest Campgrounds

Evergreen Acres RV Park, Belleville
Council Grove Lake, Council Grove
Crawford State Park, Farlington
Elk City State Park, Independence
Tuttle Creek State Park, Manhatten
Prairie Dog State Park, Norton
Webster State Park, Stockton

Most Secure Campgrounds

Garden City KOA Kampground, Garden City

Cleanest Campgrounds

Evergreen Acres RV Park, Belleville
Emporia RV Park, Emporia
Crawford State Park, Farlington
Fort Scott Campground, Fort Scott
Garden City KOA Kampground, Garden City
Country Squire Motel & RV Park, Hiawatha
Elk City State Park, Independence
Tuttle Creek State Park, Manhatten
Camp Lakeside, Scott City
Topeka KOA, Topeka
Wakeeney KOA Kampground, Wakeeney
USI RV Park, Wichita

Best Campground Facilities

Garden City KOA Kampground, Garden City
Goodland KOA, Goodland
Lawrence/Kansas City KOA, Lawrence
Topeka KOA, Topeka
Wakeeney KOA Kampground, Wakeeney
Wheatland RV Park, Wellington

Best Rural, Farm, or Ranch Settings

Evergreen Acres & RV Park, Belleville
Homewood RV Park, Ottawa-Williamsburg
Topeka KOA, Topeka

Best Urban and Suburban Settings

USI RV Park, Wichita

Best Waterfront Settings

Lake Atwood, Atwood
Evergreen Acres & RV Park, Belleville
Watersports Campground, Dodge City
Council Grove Lake,uncil Grove
Crawford State Park, Girard
Elk City State Park, Independence
Tuttle Creek State Park, Manhattan
Prairie Dog State Park, Norton
Camp Lakeside, Scott City
Webster State Park, Stockton
Topeka KOA, Topeka
Homewood RV Park, Ottawa-Williamsburg
Brome Ridge RV Park, Concordia

Most Romantic Campgrounds

Ft Scott Campground, Ft Scott

Best Family-Oriented Campgrounds

Watersports Campground, Dodge City
Ft Scott Campground, Fort Scott
Garden City KOA, Garden City
Goodland KOA, Goodland
Camp Lakeside, Scott City
Wakeeney KOA, Wakeeney

KANSAS (continued)

Best Swimming Pools

Covered Wagon RV Resort, Abilene
Ft Scott Campground, Fort Scott
Goodland KOA, Goodland
Lawrence KOA, Lawrence
Camp Inn & RV Park, Oakley
Wakeeney KOA, Wakeeney
Wheatland RV Park, Wellington

MISSOURI

Best RV Camping

Basswood Country Inn & RV Resort, Platte City
Perryville/Cape Girardeau KOA, Perryville
Peculiar Park Place, Peculiar
Kan-Do Kampground RV Park, Danville
Cottonwoods RV Park, Columbia

Best Tent Camping

Lake Wappapello State Park, Williamsville
Native Experience Adventure Campground, Sullivan
Perryville/Cape Girardeau KOA, Perryville
Long Branch Lake State Park, Macon
Gravois Creek Campground, Gravois Mills
Jacks Fork Campground, Eminence
Kan-Do Kampground RV Park, Danville
Trail of Tears State Park, Cape Girardeau
Down Under Camp Resort, Cameron

Most Beautiful Campgrounds

Lake Wappapello State Park, Williamsville
Pheasant Acres, St. James
Travelers Park Campground, Springfield
Elk River Floats Wayside Campground, Noel
Long Branch Lake State Park, Macon
Gravois Creek Campground, Gravois Mills
McCullough Park Campground, Chillicothe
Heavenly Days Resort & Campground, Camdenton

Most Private Campsites

Lamar KOA, Lamar
Pine Trails RV Ranch, Monett
Pheasant Acres, St. James
Lake Wappapello State Park, Williamsville

Most Spacious Campsites

McCullough Park Campground, Chillicothe
Jacks Fork Campground, Eminence
Lamar KOA, Lamar
Travelers Park Campground, Springfield
Lake Wappapello State Park, Williamsville

Quietest Campgrounds

Down Under Camp Resort, Cameron
Trail of Tears State Park, Cape Girardeau
McCullough Park Campground, Chillicothe
Parks Bluff Campground, Lesterville
Long Branch Lake State Park, Macon
Thompson Campground, Moberly
Pheasant Acres, St. James
Lake Wappapello State Park, Williamsville

Most Secure Campgrounds

Lake Wappapello State Park, Williamsville
Native Experience Adventure Campground, Sullivan
St. Louis RV Park, St. Louis
Pheasant Acres, St. James
Hinton Park, Sikeston
Basswood Country Inn & RV Resort, Platte City
Peculiar Park Place, Peculiar
Elk River Floats Wayside Campground, Noel
Pine Trails RV Ranch, Monett
Thompson Campground, Moberly
Long Branch Lake State Park, Macon
Parks Bluff Campground, Lesterville
Injun Joe Campground, Hannibal
Gravois Creek Campground, Gravois Mills
Rocky River Resort, Doniphan
Cottonwoods RV Park, Columbia
McCullough Park Campground, Chillicothe
Ballard's Campground, Carthage
Trail of Tears State Park, Cape Girardeau
Down Under Camp Resort, Cameron

Cleanest Campgrounds

Cottonwoods RV Park, Columbia
Kan-Do Kampground RV Park, Danville
Hayti-Portageville KOA, Hayti
Lamar KOA, Lamar
Lebanon KOA, Lebanon
Pine Trails RV Ranch, Monett
Peculiar Park Place, Peculiar

MISSOURI (continued)

Perryville/Cape Girardeau KOA, Perryville
Basswood Country Inn & RV Resort, Platte City
Pheasant Acres, St. James
St. Louis RV Park, St. Louis
Native Experience Adventure Campground, Sullivan

Best Campground Facilities

Cottonwoods RV Park, Columbia
Hayti-Portageville KOA, Hayti
Lamar KOA, Lamar
Lebanon KOA, Lebanon
Perryville/Cape Girardeau KOA, Perryville
Basswood Country Inn & RV Resort, Platte City
Native Experience Adventure Campground, Sullivan

Best Rural, Farm, or Ranch Settings

McCullough Park Campground, Chillicothe
Kan-Do Kampground & RV Park, Danville
Pheasant Acres Campground, St James

Best Urban and Suburban Settings

Ozark RV Park, Ozark
St Louis RV Park, St Louis

Best Waterfront Settings

Heavenly Days Resort & Campground, Camdenton
Trail of Tears State Park, Cape Girardeau
Truman Lake State Park (Sparrofoot Campground), Clinton
Gravois Creek Campground, Gravois Mills
Thousand Hills State Park, Kirksville
Parks Bluff Campground, Lesterville
Long Branch State Park, Macon
Elk River Floats Wayside Campground, Noel
Lake Wappapello State Park, Williamsville

Most Romantic Campgrounds

Heavenly Days Resort & Campground, Camdenton
Basswooduntry Inn & RV Resort, Platte City

Best Family-Oriented Campgrounds

Down Under Camp Resort, Cameron
Heavenly Days Resort & Campground, Camdenton
McCullough Park Campground, Chillicothe
Trail of Tears State Park, Cape Girardeau
Truman Lake State Park (Sparrofoot Campground), Clinton
Injun Joe Campground, Hannibal
Injun Joe Campground, Hannibal
KOA Hayti-Portageville, Hayti
Lamar KOA, Lamar
Lebanon KOA, Lebanon
Elk River Floats Wayside Campground, Noel
Oak Grove KOA, Oak Grove
Basswooduntry Inn & RV Resort, Platte City
Perryville KOA, Perryville
Native Experience Adventure Campground, Sullivan

Best Swimming Pools

Down Under Camp Resort, Cameron
Kan-Do Kampground & RV Park, Danville
Injun Joe Campground, Hannibal
KOA Hayti-Portageville, Hayti
Lamar KOA, Lamar
Lebanon KOA, Lebanon
Miller's Kampark, Liberty
Lazy Days Campground, Marshall
Missouri Park Campground, Mountain Grove
Thompson Campground, Moberly
Oak Grove KOA, Oak Grove
Basswooduntry Inn & RV Resort, Platte City
Perryville KOA, Perryville
AOK Overnite Kampground, St Joseph
Native Experience Adventure Campground, Sullivan
Pheasant Acres Campground, St James
St Louis RV Park, St Louis
Traveler's Park Campground, Springfield

NEW MEXICO

Best RV Camping

Manzano's RV Park, Silver City
Santa Fe Skies RV Park, Santa Fe
Rio Penasco RV Camp, Mayhill
Best View RV Park, Las Cruces
Trail's End RV Park, Jemez Springs
Lakeside RV Park, Elephant Butte
Pancho Villa State Park, Columbus
Rio Chama RV Park, Chama
Alamogordo KOA, Alamogordo

NEW MEXICO (continued)

Best Tent Camping
Pecos River Campground, San Jose
Bluewater Lake State Park, Prewitt
Trail's End RV Park, Jemez Springs
Faywood Hot Springs, Dwyer
Rio Chama RV Park, Chama
Riana Campground, Abiquiu

Most Beautiful Campgrounds
Monte Bello RV Park, Taos
Manzano's RV Park, Silver City
Santa Fe Skies RV Park, Santa Fe
Bluewater Lake State Park, Prewitt
Manzano Mountains State Park, Mountainair
Trail's End RV Park, Jemez Springs
Faywood Hot Springs, Dwyer
Pancho Villa State Park, Columbus
Rio Chama RV Park, Chama
Sierra Bonita Cabins & RV Park, Angel Fire
Riana Campground, Abiquiu

Most Private Campsites
Alamogordo KOA, Alamogordo
Artesia RV Park, Artesia
Kiva RV Park & Horse Motel, Bernardo
Rio Chama RV Park, Chama
Pancho Villa State Park, Columbus
Faywood Hot Springs, Dwyer
Lakeside RV Park, Elephant Butte
Trail's End RV Park, Jemez Springs
Ute Lake State Park, Logan
Lordsburg KOA, Lordsburg
Manzano Mountains State Park, Mountainair
Manzano's RV Park, Silver City

Most Spacious Campsites
Artesia RV Park, Artesia
Kiva RV Park & Horse Motel, Bernardo
Pancho Villa State Park, Columbus
Faywood Hot Springs, Dwyer
Lakeside RV Park, Elephant Butte
Trail's End RV Park, Jemez Springs
Ute Lake State Park, Logan
Lordsburg KOA, Lordsburg
Bluewater Lake State Park, Prewitt
Manzano's RV Park, Silver City
Monte Bello RV Park, Taos

Quietest Campgrounds
Riana Campground, Abiquiu
Faywood Hot Springs, Dwyer
Trail's End RV Park, Jemez Springs
Rio Penasco RV Camp, Mayhill
Manzano Mountains State Park, Mountainair
Bluewater Lake State Park, Prewitt
Bosque Birdwatcher's RV Park, San Antonio
Pecos River Campground, San Jose
Santa Fe Skies RV Park, Santa Fe
Manzano's RV Park, Silver City

Most Secure Campgrounds
Manzano's RV Park, Silver City
Pecos River Campground, San Jose
Bosque Birdwatcher's RV Park, San Antonio
Rodeo RV Park & Country Store, Rodeo
Best View RV Park, Las Cruces
Paramount RV Park, Kirtland
Trail's End RV Park, Jemez Springs
Gallup KOA, Gallup
Dad's RV Park, Farmington
Cottonwood RV Park, Espanola
Lakeside RV Park, Elephant Butte
Faywood Hot Springs, Dwyer
Ponil Campground, Cimarron
Rio Chama RV Park, Chama
Artesia RV Park, Artesia

Cleanest Campgrounds
Albuquerque Central KOA, Albuquerque
Sierra Bonita Cabins & RV Park, Angel Fire
Artesia RV Park, Artesia
Carlsbad RV Park & Campground, Carlsbad
Ponil Campground, Cimarron
Meadowlark KOA, Clayton
Faywood Hot Springs, Dwyer
West Lake RV Park, Eagle Nest
Lakeside RV Park, Elephant Butte
Gallup KOA, Gallup
Trail's End RV Park, Jemez Springs
Lordsburg KOA, Lordsburg
Rio Penasco RV Camp, Mayhill
Manzano Mountains State Park, Mountainair
Santa Fe Skies RV Park, Santa Fe
Manzano's RV Park, Silver City
Monte Bello RV Park, Taos

Best Campground Facilities
Alamogordo KOA, Alamogordo
Albuquerque Central KOA, Albuquerque
Carlsbad RV Park & Campground, Carlsbad
Gallup KOA, Gallup

NEW MEXICO (continued)

Best View RV Park, Las Cruces
Lordsburg KOA, Lordsburg

Best Rural, Farm, or Ranch Settings

Kiva RV Park, Bernardo
Faywood Hot Springs, Dwyer
Cottonwood RV Park, Espanola
Bosque Birdwatcher's RV Park, San Antonio

Best Urban and Suburban Settings

Artesia RV Park, Artesia
Dad's RV Park, Farmington
Sands RV Park & Motel, Carrizozo
Vegas RV Overnite Park, Las Vegas

Best Mountain Settings

Coyote Creek State Park, Angelfire
Riana Campground, Abiquiu
Trail's End RV Park, Jemez Springs
Manzano Mountains State Park, Mountainair

Best Waterfront Settings

Riana Campground, Abiquiu
Ute Lake State Park, Logan
Bluewater Lake State Park, Prewitt

Most Romantic Campgrounds

Coyote Creek State Park, Angelfire
Riana Campground, Abiquiu
Lakeside RV Park, Elephant Butte
Pancho Villa State Park, Columbus
Rio Chama RV Park, Chama
Faywood Hot Springs, Dwyer
Trail's End RV Park, Jemez Springs
Bosque Birdwatcher's RV Park, San Antonio
Manzano's RV Park, Silver City
Pecos River Campground, San Jose
Santa Fe Skies RV Park, Santa Fe

Best Family-Oriented Campgrounds

Alamogordo KOA, Alamogordo
Albuquerque KOA, Albuquerque
Riana Campground, Abiquiu
Carlsbad RV Park & Campground, Carlsbad
Clayton KOA, Clayton
Gallup KOA, Gallup
Lordsburg KOA, Lordsburg
Ute Lake State Park, Logan

Best Swimming Pools

Alamogordo KOA, Alamogordo
Albuquerque KOA, Albuquerque
Carlsbad RV Park & Campground, Carlsbad
Faywood Hot Springs, Dwyer
Redrow Campground, Edgewood
Gallup KOA, Gallup
Best View RV Park, Las Cruces
Lordsburg KOA, Lordsburg
Vado RV Park, Vado
AAA White's City RV Park, White's City

OKLAHOMA

Best RV Camping

Sawyer RV Park, Sawyer
Cedar Oaks RV Resort, Grove
High Point RV Park, Enid

Best Tent Camping

Red Rock Canyon State Park, Hinton
MarVal Family Resort, Gore
Cherokee State Park (Riverside Campground), Disney
Clayton Lake State Park, Clayton

Most Beautiful Campgrounds

Sawyer RV Park, Sawyer
Red Rock Canyon State Park, Hinton
Cedar Oaks RV Resort, Grove
Cherokee State Park (Riverside Campground), Disney

Most Private Campsites

High Point RV Park, Enid
Lakeside RV Park, Sallisaw

Most Spacious Campsites

Cherokee State Park (Riverside Campground), Disney
High Point RV Park, Enid
Lakeside RV Park, Sallisaw

Quietest Campgrounds

Indian City USA, Anadarko
Big Cedar RV Park, Big Cedar
Cherokee State Park (Riverside Campground), Disney
High Point RV Park, Enid
Cedar Oaks RV Resort, Grove
Red Rock Canyon State Park, Hinton

OKLAHOMA (continued)

Quietest Campgrounds (continued)

Sawyer RV Park, Sawyer
Diamondhead Resort, Talequah
Moneka Park, Waurika

Most Secure Campgrounds

Diamondhead Resort, Talequah
Sawyer RV Park, Sawyer
Cedar Oaks RV Resort, Grove
MarVal Family Resort, Gore
Bridgeport RV Park, Eufaula
High Point RV Park, Enid
Cherokee State Park (Riverside Campground), Disney
Big Cedar RV Park, Big Cedar

Cleanest Campgrounds

Ardmore/Marietta KOA, Ardmore
Big Cedar RV Park, Big Cedar
Wink's RV Park, Clinton
Best Western, El Reno
Bridgeport RV Park, Eufaula
Cedar Oaks RV Resort, Grove
Lakeside RV Park, Sallisaw
Sawyer RV Park, Sawyer
Tulsa NE KOA, Tulsa

Best Campground Facilities

Cedar Oaks RV Resort, Grove

Best Rural, Farm, or Ranch Settings

Ardmore/Marietta KOA, Ardmore
KOA Ardmore-Marietta, Ardmore
Oak Hill RV Park, Davis
Simmons RV Park, Durant
Southwind RV Park, Guymon
Sleepee Hollo, Kingfisher
Rockin' Horse RV Park, Spiro
Sawyer RV Park, Sawyer
Sawyer RV Park, Sawyer

Best Urban and Suburban Settings

Corky's Get & Go, Woodward

Best Waterfront Settings

Cherokee Riverside Campground, Disney
Cedar Oaks RV Park, Grove
MarVal Family Resort, Gore
Diamondhead Resort, Talequah

Best Family-Oriented Campgrounds

KOA Ardmore-Marietta, Ardmore
MarVal Family Resort, Gore
Diamondhead Resort, Talequah
Tulsa KOA, Tulsa

Best Swimming Pools

Indian City USA, Anadarko
Riverside RV Resort, Bartlesville
Sherrard RV KOA, Colbert
MarVal Family Resort, Gore
Red Rock Canyon State Park, Hinton
Sandstel, Oklahoma City
Lakeside RV Park, Sallisaw
Tulsa KOA, Tulsa

TEXAS

Best RV Camping

Angelina National Forest, Boykin Springs and Sandy Creek Recreation Areas, Zavalla
Guadalupe River State Park, Spring Branch
Lake Somerville State Park & Trailway, Somerville, Ledbetter
Buescher State Park, Smithville
Caprock Canyons State Park and Trailway, Quitaque
Lake Mineral Wells State Park and Trailway, Mineral Wells
Caddo Lake State Park, Karnack
Pedernales Falls State Park, Johnson City
Daingerfield State Park, Daingerfield
Seminole Canyon State Historical Park, Comstock
Cedar Hill State Park, Cedar Hill
Big Bend National Park Chisos Basin and Cottonwood Campgrounds, Big Bend National Park

Best Tent Camping

Cooper Lake State Park (South Sulpher Unit), Sulpher Springs
Guadalupe River State Park, Spring Branch
Lake Somerville State Park & Trailway, Somerville, Ledbetter
Buescher State Park, Smithville
Caprock Canyons State Park and Trailway, Quitaque

TEXAS (continued)

Mustang Island State Park, Port Aransas
Lake Mineral Wells State Park and Trailway, Mineral Wells
Meridian State Park, Meridian
Caddo Lake State Park, Karnack
Pedernales Falls State Park, Johnson City
Daingerfield State Park, Daingerfield
Cooper Lake State Park (Doctor's Creek Unit), Cooper
Garner State Park, Concan
Seminole Canyon State Historical Park, Comstock
Cedar Hill State Park, Cedar Hill
Big Bend National Park Chisos Basin and Cottonwood Campgrounds, Big Bend National Park
Atlanta State Park, Atlanta
Angelina National Forest, Boykin Springs and Sandy Creek Recreation Areas,

Most Beautiful Campgrounds

Angelina National Forest, Boykin Springs and Sandy Creek Recreation Areas, Zavalla
Lost Maples State Natural Area, Vanderpool
Guadalupe River State Park, Spring Branch
Lake Somerville State Park & Trailway, Somerville, Ledbetter
Buescher State Park, Smithville
Caprock Canyons State Park and Trailway, Quitaque
Bentson-Rio Grande Valley State Park, Mission
Lake Mineral Wells State Park and Trailway, Mineral Wells
Fort Parker State Park, Mexia
Meridian State Park, Meridian
Caddo Lake State Park, Karnack
Pedernales Falls State Park, Johnson City
Daingerfield State Park, Daingerfield
Garner State Park, Concan
Seminole Canyon State Historical Park, Comstock
Cedar Hill State Park, Cedar Hill
River Bend Resort, Brownsville
Big Bend National Park Chisos Basin and Cottonwood Campgrounds, Big Bend National Park
Bastrop State Park, Bastrop

Most Private Campsites

Daingerfield State Park, Daingerfield
Pedernales Falls State Park, Johnson City
Lake Mineral Wells State Park and Trailway, Mineral Wells
Buescher State Park, Smithville
Lake Somerville State Park & Trailway, Somerville, Ledbetter
Angelina National Forest, Boykin Springs and Sandy Creek Recreation Areas, Zavalla

Most Spacious Campsites

Daingerfield State Park, Daingerfield
Pedernales Falls State Park, Johnson City
Lake Mineral Wells State Park and Trailway, Mineral Wells
Caprock Canyons State Park and Trailway, Quitaque
Buescher State Park, Smithville
Lake Somerville State Park & Trailway, Somerville, Ledbetter
Guadalupe River State Park, Spring Branch
Angelina National Forest, Boykin Springs and Sandy Creek Recreation Areas, Zavalla

Quietest Campgrounds

Atlanta State Park, Atlanta
Big Bend National Park Chisos Basin and Cottonwood Campgrounds, Big Bend National Park
Cedar Hill State Park, Cedar Hill
Seminole Canyon State Historical Park, Comstock
Cooper Lake State Park (Doctor's Creek Unit), Cooper
Daingerfield State Park, Daingerfield
Eisenhower State Park, Denison
Pedernales Falls State Park, Johnson City
Caddo Lake State Park, Karnack
Village Creek State Park, Lumberton
Meridian State Park, Meridian
Fort Parker State Park, Mexia
Lake Mineral Wells State Park and Trailway, Mineral Wells
Caprock Canyons State Park and Trailway, Quitaque
Buescher State Park, Smithville
Lake Somerville State Park & Trailway, Somerville, Ledbetter
Guadalupe River State Park, Spring Branch
Cooper Lake State Park (South Sulpher Unit), Sulpher Springs
Ray Roberts State Park (Johnson Branch Unit), Valley View
Angelina National Forest, Boykin Springs and Sandy Creek Recreation Areas, Zavalla

Most Secure Campgrounds

Lost Maples State Natural Area, Vanderpool
Guadalupe River State Park, Spring Branch
Long Island Village, Port Isabel
Village Creek State Park, Lumberton
Mission RV Park, El Paso

TEXAS (continued)

Most Secure Campgrounds (continued)

Seminole Canyon State Historical Park, Comstock
Cedar Hill State Park, Cedar Hill
Palo Duro Canyon State Park, Canyon
Choke Canyon State Park, Calliham, Three Rivers
Possum Kingdom State Park, Caddo
Big Bend National Park Chisos Basin and Cottonwood Campgrounds, Big Bend National Park

Cleanest Campgrounds

Big Bend National Park Chisos Basin and Cottonwood Campgrounds, Big Bend National Park
River Bend Resort, Brownsville
Seminole Canyon State Historical Park, Comstock
Mission RV Park, El Paso
Pedernales Falls State Park, Johnson City
Long Island Village, Port Isabel
Caprock Canyons State Park and Trailway, Quitaque
Admiralty RV Resort, San Antonio
Lake Somerville State Park & Trailway, Somerville, Ledbetter
Ray Roberts State Park (Johnson Branch Unit), Valley View
Lost Maples State Natural Area, Vanderpool

Best Campground Facilities

Bastrop State Park, Bastrop
River Bend Resort, Brownsville
Choke Canyon State Park, Calliham, Three Rivers
Cedar Hill State Park, Cedar Hill
Garner State Park, Concan
Mission RV Park, El Paso
Long Island Village, Port Isabel
Buescher State Park, Smithville
Wagon Wheel Dude Ranch, Snyder

Best Rural, Farm, or Ranch Settings

Cedar Hill State Park, Cedar Hill
Wagon Wheel Dude Ranch, Snyder

Best Urban and Suburban Settings

Admiralty RV Resort, San Antonio
Austin Lone Star Resort, Austin
Bentson-Rio Grande Valley State Park, Mission
Chimney RV Park, Mission
Colonia del Rey RV Park, Corpus Christi
Fun 'n' Sun, San Benito
Galveston Island State Park, Galveston
Houston Leisure RV Resort, Houston
Long Island Village, Port Isabel
Pioneer RV Resort, Port Aransas
River Bend Resort, Brownsville
Trader's Village RV Park & Campground, Dallas/Fort Worth
Treetops RV Village, Arlington
United RV Resort, San Marcos
Victoria Palms, Donna

Best Mountain Settings

Big Bend National Park, Big Bend

Best Waterfront Settings

River Bend Resort, Brownsville
Cedar Hill State Park, Cedar Hill
Huntsville State Park, Huntsville
Guadalupe River RV Resort, Kerrville
Lake Corpus Christi State Park, Mathis
Fort Parker State Park, Mexia
Lake Mineral Wells State Park, Mineral Wells
Bentson-Rio Grande Valley State Park, Mission
Padre Island National Seashore, Padre Island
Pioneer RV Resort, Port Aransas
Long Island Village, Port Isabel
Buescher State Park, Smithville
Lake Somerville State Park, Somerville
Angelina National Forest, Zavalla

Most Romantic Campgrounds

Big Bend National Park, Big Bend
Seminole Canyon State Historical Park, Comstock
Pedernales Falls State Park, Johnson City
Lake Miner al Wells State Park, Mineral Wells
Buescher State Park, Smithville
Lake Somerville State Park, Somerville
Angelina National Forest, Zavalla

Best Family-Oriented Campgrounds

Cedar Hill State Park, Cedar Hill
Guadalupe River RV Resort, Kerrville
Rusk/Palestine State Park, Rusk
Wagon Wheel Dude Ranch, Snyder

Best Swimming Pools

Alamo Palms, Alamo
Austin Lone Star RV Resort, Austin
Cowtown RV Park, Aledo
Treetops RV Village, Arlington
Alamo Fiesta RV Resort, Boerne
Bastrop State Park, Bastrop
River Bend Resort, Brownsville
Choke Canyon State Park, Calliham
Colonia del Rey RV Park, Corpus Christi

TEXAS (continued)

Trader's Village RV Park & Campground, Dallas-Fort Worth
Victoria Palms, Donna
Houston Leisure RV Resort, Houston
Guadalupe River RV Resort, Kerrville
Chimney RV Park, Mission
Las Aves RV Resort, Medina
Long Island Village, Port Isabel
Pioneer RV Resort, Port Aransas
Admiralty RV Resort, San Antonio
Fun 'n' Sun, San Benito
United RV Resort, San Marcos
Wagon Wheel Dude Ranch, Snyder

Arkansas

Rice paddies. Catfish filets. Only country-and-western radio stations. A polite "Sir" or "Madam" in every sentence. Life in Arkansas draws on the Deep South in ways outsiders may consider out of sync with modern America. With county bans on alcohol sales reminiscent of Prohibition, one native went so far as to call the state "backwards," but that depends on your perception. Residents possess an intimate knowledge and palpable love of the land they inhabit, and visitors are welcomed warmly in the best tradition of Southern hospitality.

Arkansas calls itself "The Natural State," and this moniker is reinforced by its inhabitants—even businessmen don safety orange for a weekend hunting trip. Nearly everyone you meet has a fishing pole, knows where to catch a trophy bass (or maybe just dinner), or has photos in his pocket from his last fishing trip. Perhaps the best way to get to know this state is to camp at some of the many state parks—they give you a feel for the breadth of the state's natural diversity and the depth of its history.

Aside from the hunting, the fishing, the boating, and the hot springs, even just driving Arkansas is a pleasure. Lush vegetation wraps around small roads like snug clothing. Wildlife abounds, including armadillos and even alligators. Go for a drive through the **Ozark National Forest** or along the **Mississippi River,** and you'll never think of Arkansas the same way again. Arkansas is such a verdent state you can't help but revel in its greenery. **Bull Shoals** and the **Ouachita Mountains** are as representative of Arkansas as **Little Rock** and **Texarkana.**

The question to ask yourself isn't "Why should I go to *Arkansas*?" but "Why haven't I gone there before?"

The following facilities accept payment in checks or cash only:

- Craighead Forest Park, Jonesboro
- Crossett Harbor RV Park, Crossett
- Fair Park RV Park, Hope
- Freppon's RV Park, Bald Knob
- Hardy Camper Park, Hardy
- Pecan Grove RV Park, Lake Village
- Whispering Pines RV Park, Clinton
- Wilderness Hills RV Park & Campground, Siloam Springs
- Young's Lakeshore RV Resort, Hot Springs

The following facilities feature 20 sites or fewer:

- Bull Shoals Recreation Area, Bull Shoals
- Cedar Ridge, Calico Rock
- Jacksonport State Park, Jacksonport
- Wiederkehr Wine Cellars RV Park, Altus

ALTUS
Wiederkehr Wine Cellars RV Park

3324 Swiss Family Dr., Altus 72821. T: (800) 622-WINE or (501) 468-WINE; F: (501) 468-4791; winear62@ar-digit.net.

RV ★★★ Tent ★★★

Beauty: ★★★★ Site Privacy: ★★★
Spaciousness: ★★★ Quiet: ★★★★
Security: ★★★★ Cleanliness: ★★★★
Insect Control: ★★★★ Facilities: ★★

This campground is west of a restaurant, gift shop, and office complex, and north of Arkansas River Valley vineyards. The park itself is little more than a large open parking lot of a gravel, grass, and dirt. Sites 1–10 back up to woods, while 11–20 back up to a pretty agricultural setting. Site 1 is partly in long prairie-type grass, but is close to a shade tree. Sites 7 and 8 are shaded, as is 20. This latter site is probably in the nicest location, as it is furthest from the restaurant complex and next to a large tree. Sites 9–12 are closest to the visitor parking lot. While there is no real maximum length to the vehicles this park can accommodate during off-season, it is unrealistic to haul more than 50 feet during the wine fest—the best time to come to this park (at least, if you don't mind crowds). Tents can cover the entire field to the west during the September wine fest, making it difficult to find a spot. There are few trees anyway, so most tenters will be in the same boat—camping on a hill with no shower facility. Of course, the atmosphere of the festival can override other concerns, but tenters (and RVers without indoor showers) must remember that they will have to spend a day or so without showering. There is one modern unisex rest room that must surely be packed during the festival. This campground is a somewhat dull park without many facilities, although the atmosphere of the restaurant and the wine fest help make up for these shortcomings.

Basics

Operated By: Don Neumeier. **Open:** All year. **Site Assignment:** First come, first served (reservations only for wine fest) **Registration:** In office, shop, or restaurant. (Late arrivals select an available site & pay in the morning.) **Fee:** RV $10 (water, electric), tent $10 (checks, MC, AE, D, CB, DC). **Parking:** At site.

Facilities

Number of RV Sites: 20. **Number of Tent-Only Sites:** Undesignated sites. **Hookups:** Water, electric (30 amps). **Dump Station:** No. **Laundry:** No. **Pay Phone:** Yes. **Rest Rooms and Showers:** Rest rooms; no shower. **Fuel:** No. **Propane:** No. **Internal Roads:** Gravel. **RV Service:** No. **Market:** 2 mi. to Altus. **Restaurant:** On site. **General Store:** No. **Vending:** No. **Swimming:** No. **Playground:** No. **Other:** Gift shop, vineyards **Activities:** Picnics in vineyards, shopping, wine tasting. **Nearby Attractions:** Wineries, antique shops. **Additional Information:** Altus Chamber of Commerce, (501) 468-4684.

Restrictions

Pets: On leash, cleaned up after. **Fires:** In grills only; subject to seasonal bans. **Alcoholic Beverages:** At sites. **Vehicle Maximum Length:** None.

To Get There

From I-40 (Exit 41), turn south onto Hwy. 186 and go 4.6 mi. Turn right at the sign into the entrance.

ARKADELPHIA
Arkadelphia KOA

221 Frost Rd., Arkadelphia 71923. T: (800) KOA-4207 or (870) 246-4922; F: (870) 246-4922; www.koa.com.

RV ★★★★ Tent ★★★

Beauty: ★★★★ Site Privacy: ★★★
Spaciousness: ★★★ Quiet: ★★★
Security: ★★★★ Cleanliness: ★★★★
Insect Control: ★★★★ Facilities: ★★★★

Most of the sites in this campground are well-shaded, which is good news to summer campers in this part of the state. Laid out in an arc with internal sites, the main camping area has 12 sites around the perimeter that can be used for tents or for small RVs. Site 1 is very close to the road that leads to the northern camping area, and all other sites (except 7 and 8) require either pitching a tent on a serious slope or right on the internal road. RVers may find this normal, but tenters will not like the space. Sites 7 and 8 are the exceptions, with larger spaces and nice trees. Site 24 is an enormous (100-feet-long) pull-through, while the sites next to it (20–23) are half the size and only pull-throughs if the adjacent site is unoccupied. These sites are all next to the forest, under a canopy of trees. Nice 50-foot back-ins that are likewise shaded include 50, 52, 59, and 62. These sites are in the north area of the campground, off the main camping area. Pull-throughs include 51, 55, 58, 60, and 62, which can accommodate a rig of any size. Less pleasant are sites 30 and 31, which are very open, and site 27, which is close to the entrance, Frost Rd., and the propane vending area. The laundry room is clean and spacious, and has a television to help while away the time while your clothes are being cleaned. The rest room is very clean but looks a little outdated. The campground is undergoing remodeling, and hopefully the rest rooms are slated for modernization. Overall, this is a nice campground, although RVers will enjoy it a little more than tenters.

Basics

Operated By: The Cristoffersons. **Open:** All year. **Site Assignment:** Assigned upon registration (Credit card required for reservations, recommended during holidays. Cancellation by 4 p.m. the day before arrival) **Registration:** In office. (Late arrivals use drop box.) **Fee:** RV $20 (full), $18 (water, electric), tent $14. **Parking:** At site.

Facilities

Number of RV Sites: 44. **Number of Tent-Only Sites:** 12. **Hookups:** Water, sewer, electric (30, 50 amps), cable. **Each Site:** Picnic table. **Dump Station:** Yes. **Laundry:** Yes. **Pay Phone:** Yes. **Rest Rooms and Showers:** Yes. **Fuel:** No. **Propane:** Yes. **Internal Roads:** Gravel. **RV Service:** No. **Market:** 7 mi. (Exit 73). **Restaurant:** 1 mi. **General Store:** Yes. **Vending:** No. **Swimming:** Pool. **Playground:** Yes. **Other:** Pet walk area, cabins, fishing pond, cottage (w/kitchen). **Activities:** Fishing, horseshoes, tetherball, hopscotch, hiking, biking. **Nearby Attractions:** Lake DeGray, Lake Hamilton, Lake Catherine, Lake Ouachita, Hot Springs, Crater of Diamonds. **Additional Information:** Arkadelphia Area Chamber of Commerce (870) 246-5542.

Restrictions

Pets: On leash, cleaned up after. **Fires:** In grills; subject to seasonal bans. **Alcoholic Beverages:** At sites, not by pool, subject to dry county regulations. **Vehicle Maximum Length:** None.

To Get There

From I-30, take Exit 78 and turn north onto Hwy. 7. Go 0.25 mi. and turn right onto Frost Rd. Go 1.5 mi. and turn left at the sign into the entrance.

BALD KNOB

Freppon's RV Park

Hwy. 167 North, Bald Knob 72010. T: (501) 724-6476.

RV ★★★ | Tent n/a

Beauty: ★★	Site Privacy: ★★★
Spaciousness: ★★★	Quiet: ★★★
Security: ★★★★	Cleanliness: ★★★
Insect Control: ★★★	Facilities: ★★

This campground has RV sites and mobile homes. RV sites are situated on the outside of a looped internal road around a large open grassy area. Sites 1–7 are 70-foot back-ins set in a row along the east side, close to the manager's house and the entrance. Sites 10–16, 45-foot back-ins along the north edge, back up to a forested area. Of these, sites 15 and 16 are less desirable, as they are so close to a storage unit that navigating a large rig into one of these sites may be problematic (especially 16). Back-ins 17–26 are located along the southern edge of the park. Of these 17 is the nicest, as it has a tree and more space than the others. There are five pull-throughs (also numbered 1–5) to the west of the manager's house. These are 75-foot sites, with grassy patches. The campground unfortunately does not offer rest rooms or showers, so self-contained units are the only RVs that should stop here. Campers who require outside rest room facilities may wish to press on.

Basics

Operated By: David Freppon. **Open:** All year. **Site Assignment:** Flexible when sites are available; verbal reservations OK. **Registration:** In mgr.'s house. (Late arrivals use drop box or settle in morning.) **Fee:** $15. **Parking:** At site.

Facilities

Number of RV Sites: 27. **Number of Tent-Only Sites:** 0. **Hookups:** Water, sewer, electric (30, 50 amps). **Dump Station:** Yes. **Laundry:** No. **Pay Phone:** No. **Rest Rooms and Showers:** No. **Fuel:** No. **Propane:** No. **Internal Roads:** Gravel. **RV Service:** No. **Market:** 3 mi. south. **Restaurant:** Less than 1 mi. south. **General Store:** No. **Vending:** No. **Swimming:** No. **Playground:** No. **Other:** Fishing pond. **Activities:** Fishing. **Nearby Attractions:** Bald Knob National Wildlife Reserve, Big Creek Natural Area. **Additional Information:** Bald Knob Chamber of Commerce, (501) 724-3140.

RESTRICTIONS

Pets: On leash, cleaned up after. **Fires:** In grills. **Alcoholic Beverages:** At sites subject to dry county regulations. **Vehicle Maximum Length:** None.

TO GET THERE

From the junction of Hwy. 64, 67, and 167, go 0.5 mi. north on Hwy. 167. Turn right at the sign into the campground.

BRINKLEY

Heritage Inn and RV Park

1507 North Hwy. 17, Brinkley 72021. T: (870) 734-2121; F: (870) 734-3538.

RV ★★★ Tent n/a

Beauty: ★★	Site Privacy: ★★★
Spaciousness: ★★★	Quiet: ★★★
Security: ★★★★	Cleanliness: ★★★
Insect Control: ★★★	Facilities: ★★★

Run in conjunction with a motel, this RV park is located in a commercial complex next to a gas station with convenience store, and it is within a block of Wal-Mart and several fast-food restaurants. Sites face either the motel or Wal-Mart. Sites are 75-foot pull-throughs with mostly gravel and some grass. Shade trees grow in even numbers 2–10 and odd numbers 11–21. End sites 1 and 22 seem shortchanged for space, and 9 is encroached upon by a storage shed. The campground offers the convenience of a commercial location, and the recreation possibilities of a pool.

BASICS

Operated By: Pam & Sam. **Open:** All year. **Site Assignment:** First come, first served Credit card required for reservations. 24 hour cancellation policy. **Registration:** In motel office. **Fee:** $17.22. **Parking:** At site.

FACILITIES

Number of RV Sites: 24. **Number of Tent Sites:** 0. **Hookups:** Water, sewer, electric (30, 50 amps). **Dump Station:** No (sewer at all sites). **Laundry:** No. **Pay Phone:** No. **Rest Rooms and Showers:** Yes. **Fuel:** No. **Propane:** No. **Internal Roads:** Gravel. **RV Service:** No. **Market:** Less than 0.25 mi. south. **Restaurant:** Less than 0.25 mi. south. **General Store:** No. **Vending:** Yes. **Swimming:** Pool. **Playground:** No. **Activities:** Swimming, hiking, wildlife watching. **Nearby Attractions:** White River Natural Wildlife Reserve. **Additional Information:** Chamber of Commerce, (870) 734-2262.

RESTRICTIONS

Pets: On leash, cleaned up after. **Fires:** In grills. **Alcoholic Beverages:** At sites. **Vehicle Maximum Length:** None.

TO GET THERE

From I-40, take Exit 216. Turn south onto Hwy. 49 and take the first right into the motel complex. Register in the motel office.

BULL SHOALS

Bull Shoals Recreation Area

P.O. Box 748, Bull Shoals 72619. T: (870) 445-4424 or (870) 445-4166; F: (870) 445-8354; www.bullshoals.com/boatdock; boatdock@bullshoals.net.

RV ★★★ Tent ★★★

Beauty: ★★★★	Site Privacy: ★★
Spaciousness: ★★★	Quiet: ★★★
Security: ★★★★	Cleanliness: ★★★
Insect Control: ★★★	Facilities: ★★★

Sites in this park are situated on a hill that overlooks the marina and the lake. All sites are 30-foot long and 40-foot wide paved back-ins, with the exception of 10, which is 40 feet Sites 1 and 2 have a partial view of the marina—for what it's worth. Sites 3 and 4, set further back into the woods, are combined, making them best for groups who arrive together—and a possible nuisance if incompatible groups are forced to share these sites. Sites 6–8 are forested sites located along the entrance in the northeast corner, but have the least impressive views. The remaining sites (9–12) are situated just above the marina parking lot, and are closest to the action. This can, however, be both good and bad: they have a great view, but are subjected to the most amount of traffic and noise from a loudspeaker. The pit toilet can get quite messy, and those who depend on it will likely not enjoy their stay as much as fully self-contained units. (Likewise, there are no showers.) This is definitely a place to come to enjoy your boat, and not a place to stay otherwise.

BASICS

Operated By: US Army Corps of Engineers. **Open:** All year. **Site Assignment:** First come, first served no reservations. **Registration:** Pick a site, then register in the office. **Fee:** $7.50 (water, electric), $15 (includes boat stall). **Parking:** At site.

Facilities

Number of RV Sites: 12. **Number of Tent-Only Sites:** 0. **Hookups:** Water, electric (30 amps). **Each Site:** Picnic table, grill, cement prep table. **Dump Station:** No. **Laundry:** No. **Pay Phone:** Yes. **Rest Rooms and Showers:** Rest rooms; no shower. **Fuel:** No. **Propane:** Yes. **Internal Roads:** Paved. **RV Service:** No. **Market:** 0.25 mi. north. **Restaurant:** 0.25 mi. north. **General Store:** Yes. **Vending:** No. **Swimming:** No. **Playground:** No. **Other:** Boat stall. **Activities:** Fishing, boating. **Nearby Attractions:** Mountain Village, Bull Shoals Caverns, Top O' The Ozarks. **Additional Information:** Bull Shoals Lake–White River Chamber of Commerce, (800) 447-1290, (870) 445-4443.

Restrictions

Pets: On leash, cleaned up after. **Fires:** In grills. **Alcoholic Beverages:** At sites; subject to dry county regulations. **Vehicle Maximum Length:** 30 ft.

To Get There

From the town's westernmost name sign, go 2.1 mi. west on Hwy. 178. Turn left onto Shorecrest Dr., then take the first left onto Boat Dock Rd., which leads to the marina.

CALICO ROCK
Cedar Ridge

P.O. Box 236, Calico Rock 72519. T: (870) 297-4282.

RV ★★★★★ Tent ★★★★★

Beauty: ★★★★★ Site Privacy: ★★★★★
Spaciousness: ★★★★ Quiet: ★★★★★
Security: ★★★★★ Cleanliness: ★★★★
Insect Control: ★★★★ Facilities: ★★

This campground is wild, undeveloped, natural, and quiet. It is subtlely but attractively landscaped with rock, cacti, and juniper. Sites 1–3 are 42-foot back-ins that back up to the (rather quiet) road. Site 4 is an unshaded site that also abuts the road, but backs to thick vegetation. Sites 5–7 are pull-throughs that average 55 feet in length; 5 and 7 are shaded, 6 is not. Two unnumbered sites in the northeast corner are in an open field, and can accommodate a rig of any size, as can a third site slightly below these two. (This third site, being sheltered somewhat by a juniper, is more welcoming than the two open sites next to it.) The largest sites are 9–11, which average 70 feet in length. The rest room and shower are contained in a single unit, which is modern and decently clean. There is an absolutely wonderful scenic view of the river down a gravel road at the southernmost edge of the campground, which campers should make a point of seeing. In fact, the campground itself is an extremely attractive natural setting that will please campers of all kinds—definitely a destination campground to return to.

Basics

Operated By: Gene & Reva Lockie. **Open:** Mar 1–Oct. 30. **Site Assignment:** First come, first served; verbal reservations OK. **Registration:** In office. (Late arrivals sign register; "Gene will see you later".) **Fee:** RV $12 (full), $10 (water, electric), tent $7. **Parking:** At site.

Facilities

Number of RV Sites: 17. **Number of Tent-Only Sites:** 3. **Hookups:** Water, sewer, electric (20, 30 amps). **Each Site:** Picnic table, grill. **Dump Station:** Yes. **Laundry:** No. **Pay Phone:** No. **Rest Rooms and Showers:** Yes. **Fuel:** No. **Propane:** No. **Internal Roads:** Gravel. **RV Service:** No. **Market:** 3 mi. into town. **Restaurant:** 1 mi. into town. **General Store:** No. **Vending:** No. **Swimming:** No. **Playground:** Yes. **Other:** Firewood. **Activities:** Fishing, hunting. **Nearby Attractions:** Blanchard Springs Caverns, White River. **Additional Information:** Mountain Home, Chamber of Commerce, (870) 425-5111.

Restrictions

Pets: On leash, cleaned up after. **Fires:** In grills. **Alcoholic Beverages:** At sites. **Vehicle Maximum Length:** None.

To Get There

From the junction of Hwy. 56 and Hwy. 5, go 1 block south on Hwy. 5 (Main St.) to Calico St. Turn right and go 0.7 mi. Turn left at the sign into the campground.

CLINTON

Whispering Pines RV Park

8575 Hwy. 65 North, Clinton 72031. T: (888) 745-4291 or (501) 745-4291.

RV ★★★★ Tent ★★★★

Beauty: ★★★★ Site Privacy: ★★★★★
Spaciousness: ★★★★★ Quiet: ★★★★
Security: ★★★★ Cleanliness: ★★★★
Insect Control: ★★★★ Facilities: ★★★

Located in a residential area, this property is a quiet, campground, with a large forested area at the back. Sites are extremely large (85 × 50 feet), with a mixture of pull-throughs and back-ins. Sites 1–14 are divided up into three rows, with 1–5 off to the west of the others. Site 11 is a particularly nice pull-through located next to the pavilion. Sites 15–24 are back-ins along the eastern edge of the property. These sites back up to a strip of trees, beyond which lies the highway. (This proximity to the road and the requirement that drivers back in make these sites a little less desirable.) Tenting is possible in a huge open field to the west, beyond which lie acres of forest. (The owner tells of a bear that has been seen in these woods, so hiding food and toiletries in your vehicle couldn't hurt.) Two other sites are located in front of the office, right off the highway, but you'd have to be crazy to camp there: they are literally a dozen steps from the road. The laundry facility is exceptionally clean and cozy, as are the rest rooms. The showers, while clean, are beginning to show their age and could use an overhaul. This is a cute campground with fruit trees, pines, and country kitsch decorating the grounds. RVers and tenters alike will be comfortable staying here.

BASICS

Operated By: Vilene Borgman & Donna Adkins. **Open:** Mar.–Nov. **Site Assignment:** Flexible, according to availbility; verbal reservations OK. **Registration:** In office. (Late arrivals pay in morning). **Fee:** RV $17 (full), tent $10. (checks, but no credit cards). **Parking:** At site.

FACILITIES

Number of RV Sites: 23. **Number of Tent-Only Sites:** Undesignated sites. **Hookups:** Water, sewer, electric (20, 30, 50 amps). **Each Site:** Picnic table, grill. **Dump Station:** No (sewer hookup at all sites). **Laundry:** Yes. **Pay Phone:** Yes. **Rest Rooms and Showers:** Yes. **Fuel:** No. **Propane:** No. **Internal Roads:** Gravel. **RV Service:** No. **Market:** 7.5 mi. south. **Restaurant:** 0.5 mi. north. **General Store:** Yes. **Vending:** No. **Swimming:** No. **Playground:** No. **Other:** Pavilion, dog run, rec room. **Activities:** Boating, swimming, fishing, darts, horseshoes. **Nearby Attractions:** Branson, Greers Ferry Lake. **Additional Information:** Clinton Chamber of Commerce, (501) 745-6500.

RESTRICTIONS

Pets: On leash, cleaned up after. **Fires:** In grills. **Alcoholic Beverages:** At sites. **Vehicle Maximum Length:** None.

TO GET THERE

From the junction of Hwy. 16 and Hwy. 65, turn north onto Hwy. 65 (towards Marshall), and go 7.3 mi. Turn left into the campground at the sign.

CROSSETT

Crossett Harbor RV Park

P.O. Box 338, Crossett 71635. T: (501) 364-6136.

RV ★★★★ Tent ★★★★

Beauty: ★★★★ Site Privacy: ★★★★
Spaciousness: ★★★★ Quiet: ★★★★
Security: ★★★★ Cleanliness: ★★
Insect Control: ★★★ Facilities: ★★★

This campground is divided into a south loop and an east loop. The south loop is further divided into an inner and outer loop. The most desirable sites are in general on the outer loop 9 especially even 102–106, 109, and odd 113–117), as they have more space and back up to forest, not other campsites. Site 85 is set back away from the other sites, and therefore has more privacy. Site 67 (and 69, to a lesser extent) is adjacent to a pond. Sites 86–91 are doubles. Some sites (especially 86, 87, 95, 97, and 98) seem prone to flooding after a rain. Sites on the outside of the east loop back to seemingly endless forest, and the loop feels more "lost" (in a good way) because of this. However, there is also a lot of stuff strewn about this part of the campground: an old bed frame, wood, and even the charred remains of a burnt vehicle! Sites 1–3 are smack dab on the intersection of two roads, and certainly must receive more passing traffic due to their location. Sites 31, 33, 35, 48, and 50 seem prone to flooding. The rest rooms in both areas look well used, and the floors are in a desperate need of a paint job. Despite the bizarre junk found in a few sites, the east loop seems the nicer of the two areas, and campers will certainly enjoy a stay here.

Basics

Operated By: US Army Corps of Engineers. **Open:** All year. **Site Assignment:** First come, first served; no reservations. **Registration:** In office (late arrivals check manager's trailer to left of registration kiosk) **Fee:** $12, $9 for seniors (no credit cards.) **Parking:** At site.

Facilities

Number of RV Sites: 119. **Number of Tent-Only Sites:** 0. **Hookups:** Water, electric (30, 50 amps). **Each Site:** Picnic table, grill, fire ring, 50-ft. camping pad, 18x12 tent pad, lantern pole. **Dump Station:** Yes. **Laundry:** No. **Pay Phone:** Yes. **Rest Rooms and Showers:** Yes. **Fuel:** No. **Propane:** No. **Internal Roads:** Paved. **RV Service:** No. **Market:** 9 mi. east. **Restaurant:** 8.5 mi. east. **General Store:** Yes. **Vending:** Yes. **Swimming:** No. **Playground:** Yes. **Other:** Boat ramp, picnic shelter. **Activities:** Hiking, boating, fishing. **Nearby Attractions:** Felsenthal Wildlife Refuge. **Additional Information:** Crossett Area Chamber of Commerce, (870) 364-6591, (870) 364-8648.

Restrictions

Pets: On leash, cleaned up after. **Fires:** In grills; subject to bans. **Alcoholic Beverages:** None. **Vehicle Maximum Length:** None.

To Get There

From the junction of Hwy. 133 and Hwy. 82 in town, turn west onto Hwy. 82 and go 8.1 mi. Turn left at the sign into the entrance.

EDGEMONT

Blue Clouds RV and Cabin Resort

10645 Edgemont Rd., Edgemont 72044. T: (501) 723-4999; www.greersferry.com/blueclouds.htm; bcrvcabins@aol.com.

RV: ★★★★ Tent: ★★★★

Beauty: ★★★★★ Site Privacy: ★★★★
Spaciousness: ★★★★ Quiet: ★★★★
Security: ★★★★ Cleanliness: ★★★★
Insect Control: ★★★★ Facilities: ★★★

This campground is built at the bottom of a hill, upon which are the office and the cafe. As a result there is a very nice forested view from many of the sites, which are all naturally landscaped. (While this has some appeal, the dirt road may be tricky for some rigs. Sites 1 and 9 are 90-foot pull-throughs, and 14 is a 120-foot pull-through, making it the longest site in the campground. Sites 2–6 are 40-foot back-ins, and 17–25 are 60-foot back-ins. Sites 40–48 back to woods on the south side, making them very attractive sites. All of the sites in this campground, however, are forested and therefore well-shaded. This is a very nice, natural campground for those who enjoy a woodsy feel without being 25 miles from the nearest conveniences. RVers and tenters alike will enjoy a stay here, although the forested setting and dirt road may make for challenging driving for long rigs—especially those with tows.

Basics

Operated By: Janice. **Open:** All year. **Site Assignment:** Assigned upon registration (Credit card required or telephone number for reservation. 24 hours cancellation policy.) **Registration:** In office. (Late arrivals select an available site & pay in the morning.) **Fee:** RV $15 (checks, V, MC, D). **Parking:** At site.

Facilities

Number of RV Sites: 25. **Number of Tent-Only Sites:** 0. **Hookups:** Water, sewer, electric (30, 50 amps). **Dump Station:** No. **Laundry:** Yes. **Pay Phone:** No. **Rest Rooms and Showers:** Yes. **Fuel:** No. **Propane:** Yes. **Internal Roads:** Dirt. **RV Service:** No. **Market:** 3 mi. east. **Restaurant:** 3 mi. east. **General Store:** No. **Vending:** Yes. **Swimming:** No. **Playground:** No. **Other:** Cabins. **Activities:** Fishing, boating, swimming, golfing, folk music. **Nearby Attractions:** Greers Ferry Lake. **Additional Information:** Heber Springs Chamber of Commerce, (501) 362-2444.

Restrictions

Pets: On leash, cleaned up after. **Fires:** In grills. **Alcoholic Beverages:** At sites. **Vehicle Maximum Length:** None.

To Get There

From the westernmost town name sign on Hwy. 16, go west on Hwy. 16 for 0.4 mi. Turn left at the sign into the entrance.

EL DORADO
Moro Bay State Park

6071 Hwy. 15 South, Jersey 71651. T: (870) 463-8555; www.arkansasstateparks.com.

RV ★★★★ Tent ★★★

Beauty: ★★★★	Site Privacy: ★★★★★
Spaciousness: ★★★★★	Quiet: ★★★★★
Security: ★★★★	Cleanliness: ★★★
Insect Control: ★★★	Facilities: ★★★

Sites 1–9 are built along the edge of a hill, and some of the space is unusable due to an extreme slope. However, there is a large fenced-in area that contains the picnic table and a large concrete slab for camping. Sites are 42-feet-long back-ins, with two pull-throughs (4 and 9), of 42 feet and 75 feet in length, respectively. Site 1 backs to a large open field, and can allow for recreation right off the site. The rest room is across from site 8, and noise from a large fan in the men's room may be bothersome at this site. The rest rooms are relatively clean and modern, but up on our visit the shower needed a good cleaning. Site 10 is located at the crossroads of two internal roads, and may receive more traffice because of this fact. The rest of the sites are along this other road, and are all 42-foot back-ins. Of the sites on this strip, 16 and 17 have a more secluded location at the end of the roundabout. The other sites are pretty much indistinguishable. Tenters will enjoy the wooded sites, but may wish for grassy ground cover instead of a more developed site. Campers of any stripe will enjoy this campground—however, especially those with boats.

Basics

Operated By: Arkansas State Parks. **Open:** All year. **Site Assignment:** First come, first served. Reservations require cash, credit card, or postal money order deposit; in case of cancellation, one night's fee is not refunded. **Registration:** In office. (Late arrivals occupy an available site & register at 8 the next morning.) **Fee:** $14. **Parking:** At site.

Facilities

Number of RV Sites: 20. **Number of Tent-Only Sites:** 0. **Hookups:** Water, electric (20, 30 amps). **Each Site:** Picnic table, grill, fire pit. **Dump Station:** Yes. **Laundry:** No. **Pay Phone:** Yes. **Rest Rooms and Showers:** Yes. **Fuel:** No. **Propane:** No. **Internal Roads:** Paved. **RV Service:** No. **Market:** 15 mi. to Strong or Hermitage. **Restaurant:** 15 mi. to Strong, Hermitage, or Union. **General Store:** Yes. **Vending:** Yes. **Swimming:** No. **Playground:** Yes. **Other:** Picnic area, hunting & fishing licenses. **Activities:** Boating, fishing, basketball, soccer, volleyball. **Nearby Attractions:** Ouachita River, South Arkansas Arbortoreum. **Additional Information:** El Dorado Chamber of Commerce, (870) 863-6113.

Restrictions

Pets: On leash, cleaned up after. **Fires:** In grills. **Alcoholic Beverages:** At sites. **Vehicle Maximum Length:** None.

To Get There

From the junction of Hwy. 167 and Hwy. 15, go 20 mi. northeast on Hwy. 15. Turn left at the sign and continue on to the park entrance.

EUREKA SPRINGS
Eureka Springs KOA

15020 Hwy. 187 South, Eureka Springs 72632. T: (501) 253-8036; F: (501) 253-2249; www.eureka-net.com/koa; koa4fun@ipa.net.

RV ★★★★ Tent ★★★★★

Beauty: ★★★★★	Site Privacy: ★★★
Spaciousness: ★★★	Quiet: ★★★
Security: ★★★★	Cleanliness: ★★★★★
Insect Control: ★★★★	Facilities: ★★★★★

There are loads of neat ornaments, plants, logs, rocks, and garden spots in this campground, giving it a somewhat artsy wilderness feel. All of the sites in this campground are forested, undeveloped gravel sites. Sites 1–19 ranging from 30 to 45-feet long on either side of an internal road. Of these, 1–12 back to a hedge, beyond which lies the highway. Sites 11 and 12 are fenced off, giving them added privacy. Site 32 is an exceptionally large (120 feet) pull-through, and 58–69 are only slightly shorter at 115 feet. Sites 41–44 are 60-foot back-ins by the Garden of Meditation, but are slightly sloped. Better sites by the garden are 49–51, which are also 60-foot back-ins, but more level. Tents sites are to the north, away from the RV sites. An exceptional feature of these tent pads is that they contain sawdust instead of crushed gravel, giving tenters a much more comfy bed to sleep on. These dirt sites are located under a canopy of trees, ensuring that all sites are shaded. Many of these sites are along the highway, which is normally quite quiet, but does, of course, carry the occasional vehicle. Sites M and N are the most remote, and R and S are also quite secluded. The rest rooms and showers are all very clean and spacious. Showers are all tile, which makes them seem as comfy as home. One really neat detail is the wooden number plates at each site, which each have a unique hand-carved cartoon. The Garden of Meditation, also a unique detail, comprises stone, twisted wood, plants, and sculptures, and is an extremely peaceful place to rest for a moment.

Basics

Operated By: Jane Shonka. **Open:** All year. **Site Assignment:** Assigned upon registration. Credit card required for reservation; 48 hours cancellation policy. **Registration:** In office. (Late arrivals select an available site & pay in the morning.) **Fee:** RV $24.00 (full), $22.00 (water, electric), tent $15.50. **Parking:** At site.

Facilities

Number of RV Sites: 65. **Number of Tent-Only Sites:** 24. **Hookups:** Water, sewer, electric (30, 50 amps). **Each Site:** Picnic table, fire pit. **Dump Station:** Yes. **Laundry:** Yes. **Pay Phone:** Yes. **Rest Rooms and Showers:** Yes. **Fuel:** No. **Propane:** Yes. **Internal Roads:** Paved. **RV Service:** No. **Market:** 5 mi. to Eureka Springs. **Restaurant:** 0.75 mi. towards Eureka. **General Store:** Yes. **Vending:** Yes. **Swimming:** Pool. **Playground:** Yes. **Other:** Mini golf, game room, dataport, picnic pavilion, Garden of Meditation. **Activities:** Fishing, boating, swimming. **Nearby Attractions:** White River, Beaver Lake, passion play, hoedowns, downtown (on National Registry of Historic Places), Onyx Cave Park. **Additional Information:** Eureka Springs Chamber of Commerce, (800) 638-7352 or (501) 253-8737.

Restrictions

Pets: On leash, cleaned up after. **Fires:** In grills. **Alcoholic Beverages:** At sites. **Vehicle Maximum Length:** None. **Other:** Consult handout when registering.

To Get There

From the junction of Hwy. 62 and Hwy. 187, turn south onto Hwy. 187 and go 1.1 mi. Turn left at the sign into the entrance.

FAYETTEVILLE

Fayetteville RV Park

2310 South School Ave., Fayetteville 72701. T: (501) 443-5864.

RV ★★★ Tent n/a

Beauty: ★★★	Site Privacy: ★★★
Spaciousness: ★★★	Quiet: ★★★
Security: ★★★★	Cleanliness: ★★★
Insect Control: ★★★★	Facilities: ★★

This park has gravel sites that average 45 × 27 feet Sites 1–7 are back-ins on the south side of the park, and 8–10 are open-ended back-ins on the north end. These latter sites may be able to accommodate slightly longer rigs. Sites 11–14 are 45-foot pull-throughs in the middle of the park. The best sites in the park, and the only ones with shade, are 3, 4, and 14. Much less desirable is site 1, which is crammed up against the house. This is a small park that is fine as a short stay for RVers. Tenters will have to move on, however.

Basics

Operated By: Private Operator. **Open:** All year. **Site Assignment:** First come, first served; verbal reservations OK. **Registration:** Park & pay when someone is around. (Late arrivals select an available site & pay in the morning.) **Fee:** RV $18 (checks, V, MC). **Parking:** At site, plus guest parking.

Facilities

Number of RV Sites: 13. **Number of Tent-Only Sites:** 0. **Hookups:** Water, sewer, electric (30, 50 amps), cable. **Dump Station:** No. **Laundry:** Yes. **Pay Phone:** No. **Rest Rooms and Showers:** Yes. **Fuel:** No. **Propane:** No. **Internal Roads:** Gravel. **RV Service:** No. **Market:** 5 mi. west. **Restaurant:** 3 mi. west. **General Store:** No. **Vending:** No. **Swimming:** No. **Playground:** No. **Activities:** Visiting museums. **Nearby Attractions:** Arkansas Air Museum, Fine Arts Center, University Museum. **Additional Information:** Fayetteville Chamber of Commerce, (800) 766-4626 or (501) 521-1710.

Restrictions

Pets: On leash, cleaned up after. **Fires:** In grills. **Alcoholic Beverages:** At sites. **Vehicle Maximum Length:** 45 ft.

To Get There

From I-540 (Exit 61), exit onto Hwy. 71 and go 1.3 mi. east. Get into the left-hand lane and turn left onto Hwy. 71B (School Ave.). Go 0.8 mi., then turn right at the sign into the entrance.

HARDY
Hardy Camper Park

P.O. Box 150 South Springs St., Hardy 72542. T: (870) 856-2356.

RV ★★★★ Tent ★★★

Beauty: ★★★ Site Privacy: ★★★★★
Spaciousness: ★★★★★ Quiet: ★★★★
Security: ★★★★★ Cleanliness: ★★★
Insect Control: ★★★★ Facilities: ★★

While the north and east sides of this campground face an industrial complex, the south has gorgeous rock cliffs over the river, and the west faces lush vegetation. Just 2 blocks from Main Street, this campground is convenient for visiting Old Hardy Town on foot, and has a comfortable, city park–like feel. RV sites are mostly open-ended, and can take a vehicle of any size. River sites (42-foot back-ins) have truly wonderful views, and are worth the slightly higher price. While you can't go wrong with any of these sites, 20–23 are definitely the best of the bunch: they are well-shaded and furthest from the entrance. Sites 10 and 11 are also well-shaded, and close to the bath house, while shaded sites 1–5 are closest to the entrance/exit. For a cheaper site (not on the river) or a pull-through, 58–63 are better than average. They are well-shaded, full-length (120-feet) pull-throughs. (The other pull-throughs have two sites in an area the same size.) The tenting area is a nice, unmarked grassy area behind the office. There is some shade, but no protection in the event of rain. The bathhouse is a disappointment. The inside is old cement with untreated cement floors. In stark contract with the attractiveness of the rest of the park, this is an obviously old facility in desperate need of renovation. (It might spur the city to action if enough campers contact the town of Hardy to let them know of this situation.) One further surprise arrives with every train—loud whistles and rumblings. While infrequent, this may be enough to put off some campers, which is a shame given the camp's enjoyable environment.

BASICS

Operated By: City of Hardy. **Open:** All year. **Site Assignment:** Flexible, depending on availability. Reservations require deposit if made more than 3 weeks in advance; cancellation requires 24-hours notice. **Registration:** In office. (Late arrivals either use drop box or pay in the morning.) **Fee:** Riverside, 17.50, other, $15.30, tent, $13.10. **Parking:** At site.

FACILITIES

Number of RV Sites: 76. **Number of Tent-Only Sites:** Undesignated sites. **Hookups:** Water, electric (15, 30, 50 amps). **Each Site:** Picnic table. **Dump Station:** Yes. **Laundry:** Yes. **Pay Phone:** Yes. **Rest Rooms and Showers:** Yes. **Fuel:** No. **Propane:** No. **Internal Roads:** Gravel/dirt. **RV Service:** No. **Market:** 2 blocks (on Main). **Restaurant:** 2 blocks (on Main). **General Store:** No. **Vending:** Yes. **Swimming:** River. **Playground:** No. **Activities:** Swimming, canoeing, fishing. **Nearby Attractions:** Veterans Military Museum, Old Hardy Town, antique stores. **Additional Information:** Spring River Area Chamber of Commerce, (870) 856-3210.

RESTRICTIONS

Pets: On leash, cleaned up after. **Fires:** In grills; subject to bans. **Alcoholic Beverages:** At sites, subject to dry county regulations. **Vehicle Maximum Length:** None. **Other:** Key for rest rooms in office.

TO GET THERE

From the junction of Hwy. 62/412 and Hwy. 63, go 0.25 mi. on Hwy. 62/412 (Main St.) to Spring St. Turn south onto Spring St. (at a building with a large mural). Go 0.2 mi. (just south of the train depot) and turn right at the sign into the campground.

HARRISON
Parkers RV Park

3629 Hwy. 65 North, Harrison 72601. T: (888) 590-2267 or (870) 743-2267; F: (870) 743-0011; www.parkersrvinc.com; parkersrv@critter.net.

RV ★★★★ Tent ★★★

Beauty: ★★★★ Site Privacy: ★★★★
Spaciousness: ★★★★★ Quiet: ★★★
Security: ★★★★ Cleanliness: ★★★★★
Insect Control: ★★★★ Facilities: ★★★

This campground has very cute landscaping (including shrubs and a bridge), and very tidy gravel and grass sites. sites 1–3 are 75 × 44-foot pull-throughs on the north side of the park, near the highway. These are some of the largest sites. (Site 4, for example, is only 52 feet long.) The only sites that are larger are 10 (a 90-foot pull-through) and 24, which can be a 105-foot pull-through if site 23 is unoccupied. A strip in the middle of the park contains sites 12–17, which are 66 × 44-foot back-ins. On the north side of the "island" in the middle, sites 18–22 are slightly smaller (60-feet) back-ins. For more shade, try sites 25–39, which back to woods on the south side of the campground. There is a covered pavilion between sites 29 and 30, which increases traffic near these two sites. Tenting is restricted to small parties of responsible adults. Tenting groups are discouraged. The rest room facility is one of the nicest you'll find. It is modern, very clean, and extremely comfortable. This park is a very nice stop for RVers, but tenters with children or groups of more than two or three should look elsewhere.

BASICS

Operated By: Gregg Parker. **Open:** All year. **Site Assignment:** Assigned upon registration. Credit card required for reservation; 24 hours cancellation policy. **Registration:** In office. (Late arrivals park, "someone will be out to see you".) **Fee:** RV $16.95, tent $. (checks, V, MC, AE, D). **Parking:** At site.

FACILITIES

Number of RV Sites: 42. **Number of Tent-Only Sites:** 0. **Hookups:** Water, sewer, electric (50 amps), cable. **Each Site:** Picnic table. **Dump Station:** Yes. **Laundry:** Yes. **Pay Phone:** Yes. **Rest Rooms and Showers:** Yes. **Fuel:** No. **Propane:** Yes. **Internal Roads:** Gravel. **RV Service:** No. **Market:** 1 mi. south. **Restaurant:** 1 mi. south. **General Store:** Yes. **Vending:** Yes. **Swimming:** No. **Playground:** No. **Other:** RV supplies, rec room, pool table, fooseball, dataport. **Activities:** Fishing, boating, swimming. **Nearby Attractions:** Buffalo River National Park, Hot Springs National Park. **Additional Information:** Harrison Chamber of Commerce, (870) 741-2659.

RESTRICTIONS

Pets: On leash, cleaned up after. **Fires:** In grills. **Alcoholic Beverages:** At sites. **Vehicle Maximum Length:** None. **Other:** No fireworks.

TO GET THERE

From the junction of Hwy. 62 and Hwy. 165/412, turn east onto Hwy. 62/65/412 and go 1.3 mi. Turn right at the sign into the entrance.

HAZEN

T. Ricks RV Park

3001 North Hwy. 11, Hazen 72064. T: (870) 255-4914.

RV ★★★ Tent ★★

Beauty: ★★★ Site Privacy: ★★★★
Spaciousness: ★★★★ Quiet: ★★
Security: ★★★★ Cleanliness: ★★★★
Insect Control: ★★★★ Facilities: ★★★

This campground is run by the convenience store adjacent to it. Sites are laid out in two strips of 65-foot pull-throughs (1–14 and 20–26) running from east (closest to the highway) to west (towards the forest). There is agricultural land to the south, which enhances the aesthetics of the campground. A strip of unfinished sites lies at the northwest end. The best sites are towards the western edge (9–14 and 20–22), as these sites have shade trees and are located furtehst from the convenience store and the highway. Less desirable sites are closer to the traffic: 1–3 and 26. There are swing chairs located between sites 10 and 11, 21 and 22, and 23 and 24. They say that tenting is possible on the RV sites, but a much better bet is a grassy area under one of the many trees around the perimter—especially towards the north side. This park provides visitors decent overnight stay. It does offer the convenience of a store and gas station, but the drawbacks include no showers, plenty of traffic noise, and not much to do or to look at.

BASICS

Operated By: Rick Adams & Rick Kent. **Open:** All year. **Site Assignment:** First come, first served; verbal reservations OK. **Registration:** In convenience store (Open 24 hrs.) **Fee:** RV $18 (30 amps), $20 (50 amps), tent $5. **Parking:** At site.

FACILITIES

Number of RV Sites: 21. **Number of Tent-Only Sites:** 0. **Hookups:** Water, sewer, electric (30, 50 amps). **Each Site:** Picnic table. **Dump Station:** Yes. **Laundry:** No. **Pay Phone:** Yes (in store). **Rest Rooms and Showers:** Yes; no shower. **Fuel:** Yes. **Propane:** Yes. **Internal Roads:** Gravel. **RV Service:** No. **Market:** 3 mi. south. **Restaurant:** Across street. **General Store:** Yes. **Vending:** No. **Swimming:** No. **Playground:** No. **Activities:** Fishing, boating, swimming, hiking. **Nearby Attractions:** Peckerwood Lake. **Additional Information:** Stuttgart Chamber of Commerce, (870) 673-1602.

Restrictions

Pets: On leash, cleaned up after. **Fires:** In grills. **Alcoholic Beverages:** At sites. **Vehicle Maximum Length:** None.

To Get There

From I-40, take Exit 193. Turn south onto Hwy. 63 and take first the right. Go straight into the entrance and register in the convenience store.

HOPE

Fair Park RV Park

P.O. Box 596, Hope 71802. T: (870) 777-7500.

RV: ★★★ Tent: ★★★

Beauty: ★★★	Site Privacy: ★★★★
Spaciousness: ★★★★	Quiet: ★★★★
Security: ★★★★★	Cleanliness: ★★★
Insect Control: ★★★	Facilities: ★★★★★

This campground is in a large city park, and there are hundreds of RV sites available, divided up into sections. Section A is open and grassy, to the north of the ballfield and the collesium, with open-ended pull-through sites. There are a few trees, but most sites are not shaded. A2 is between the barns and the collesium, and consists of open, grassy sites. Section B is to the south of A, and is likewise an open grassy field with no real shade. C is similar, but consists of open-ended back-ins around the baseball field. Section D backs to the woods on the perimeter of the park. Sites to the southeast are better shaded, and are some of the better sites in the park for this reason. Sections E and F are on either side of the office, closest to the rest rooms. This is where tenters are encouraged to stay. There is a decent grass covering, and a tree at the far end of the fence to the north of the office complex. The most outstanding area of the park, however, is Section G. This area is shaded, has full hookups, and backs to the woods. sites are open-ended pull-throughs, which means that any rig could fit in pretty much any site. RVers are advised to check out Section G, and tenters can pitch their tents in a number of pleasant spots at no cost.

Basics

Operated By: Paul G. Henley. **Open:** All year. **Site Assignment:** First come, first served; no reservations. **Registration:** In office. (Late arrivals use drop box.) **Fee:** RV $10, tent free (checks, no credit cards). **Parking:** At site.

Facilities

Number of RV Sites: 400. **Number of Tent-Only Sites:** Undesignated sites. **Hookups:** Water, sewer, electric (30 amps). **Dump Station:** Yes. **Laundry:** Yes. **Pay Phone:** Yes. **Rest Rooms and Showers:** Yes. **Fuel:** No. **Propane:** No (6 blocks away). **Internal Roads:** Paved. **RV Service:** No. **Market:** 6 blocks west. **Restaurant:** less than 1 mi. west. **General Store:** No. **Vending:** Yes. **Swimming:** Pool. **Playground:** Yes. **Other:** Arena, colliseum, wrestling matches, rodeo. **Activities:** Basketball, swimming, baseball/softball, tennis. **Nearby Attractions:** Watermelon festival. **Additional Information:** Hope Hempstead County Chamber of Commerce, (800) 777-3640.

Restrictions

Pets: On leash, cleaned up after. **Fires:** In grills. **Alcoholic Beverages:** At sites. **Vehicle Maximum Length:** None.

To Get There

From I-30, take Exit 30 and go 1.35 mi. south on Hwy. 4. Turn right onto Hwy. 67 and go 0.25 mi. west. Turn left onto Hwy. 174 and go 0.3 mi. south. Turn right onto Park Dr. and go 0.5 mi. through the park to the T intersection. Turn right and go 0.5 block to the office (green building) on the left.

HOT SPRINGS

Young's Lakeshore RV Resort

1601 Lakeshore Dr., Hot Springs 71913. T: (501) 767-7946; F: (501) 767-0084; www.hsnp.com/yougsrv; rvresort@hsnp.com.

RV: ★★★★ Tent: n/a

Beauty: ★★★★	Site Privacy: ★★★
Spaciousness: ★★★	Quiet: ★★★
Security: ★★★★★	Cleanliness: ★★★★
Insect Control: ★★★★	Facilities: ★★★

A campground whose motto is "in the city, on the lake", this RV park has nearly lakeside sites towards the back (37 is the closest). Most back-ins around the perimter are open-ended, with no maximum vehicle size. These sites back to a row of trees that provide some shade, but sites elsewhere in the park are open to the sun. Sites 1–6 are 42-feet back-ins in a strip on the north side of the park. Of these, 6 is the nicest, as it is closest to the trees and furthest from the entrance. Sites 7–20 are in two rows along the entrance road. These are 60-foot pull-throughs with grassy strips. Site 24 is next to both the propane and the entrance, making it less desirable. The lower numbered sites (1; 12, 13) are closer to the entrance, while the higher numbers (6; 7, 20) are further away. The laundry is slightly unkempt but clean and well-lit. The rest rooms are small with an open toilet, so guests may only want to use them one at a time (which is slightly inconvenient). Children must be accompanied and kept under supervision at all times, so families may want to reconsider this as a destination. Other campers who do not wish to camp with children will be happiest here.

Basics

Operated By: Jimmy & Ev Young. **Open:** All year. **Site Assignment:** Assigned upon registration; verbal reservations OK. **Registration:** In office. (Late arrivals use mailbox next to the door.) **Fee:** $21 (50 amps), $19 (30 amps). **Parking:** At site.

Facilities

Number of RV Sites: 40. **Number of Tent-Only Sites:** 0. **Hookups:** Water, sewer, electric (30, 50 amps), cable. **Each Site:** Picnic table. **Dump Station:** Yes. **Laundry:** Yes. **Pay Phone:** Yes. **Rest Rooms and Showers:** Yes. **Fuel:** No. **Propane:** Yes. **Internal Roads:** Gravel. **RV Service:** No. **Market:** 1.5 mi. east on Hwy. 7. **Restaurant:** 1.5 mi. west or east. **General Store:** No. **Vending:** Yes. **Swimming:** No. **Swimming:** No. **Playground:** No. **Other:** Dataport, boat ramp, lake beach, rec room, picnic area by lake. **Activities:** Fishing, boating, hot spring baths, canoeing, hiking. **Nearby Attractions:** Hot Springs National Park, Josephine Tussaud Wax Museum, Arkansas Alligator Farm & Petting Zoo. **Additional Information:** Hot Springs CVB: (800) 772-2489, (501) 321-2277.

Restrictions

Pets: On leash, cleaned up after. **Fires:** None. **Alcoholic Beverages:** At sites. **Vehicle Maximum Length:** None. **Other:** Adults preferred (children must be accompanied at all times).

To Get There

From Hwy. 270 (south of town), take Exit 3 and go west onto McLeod St. Go 0.25 mi. straight into the entrance of the park.

JACKSONPORT

Jacksonport State Park

Jacksonport State Park P.O. Box 8, Jacksonport 72075. T: (870) 523-2143; www.arkansas.com; jacksonport@arkansas.com.

RV ★★★★ Tent ★★★★★

Beauty: ★★★★★ Site Privacy: ★★★★★
Spaciousness: ★★★★★ Quiet: ★★★★★
Security: ★★★★★ Cleanliness: ★★★★★
Insect Control: ★★★★ Facilities: ★★★

This park is located in a wilderness setting about 5 miles out of town. There is a boat ramp, swimming beach, picnic area, and museum that explains the history of the area. All of the sites in this park are grassy 50-foot back-ins on either side of a looped road. Sites are extremely spacious, and most contain several shade trees. (All sites but 1, 10, and 11 are well-shaded.) Site 1 has a parking pad for an extra vehicle. Even numbered sites 4–10 and 9, 13, and 16 back to the river, while 2, 5, 7, 11, 12, 15, and 19 back to a large, open recreation field on the interior of the looped drive. Site 7 and 9 are closest to the rest rooms. The rest rooms and showers are very clean and modern, and quite comfortable.

Basics

Operated By: Arkansas Dept. of Parks & Tourism. **Open:** All year. **Site Assignment:** First come, first served; first night's reservation must be paid 5 days in advance of arrival date; no refunds. **Registration:** In Visitor Center or self-pay station. (Late arrivals use self-pay station.) **Fee:** $14.28 (checks, V, MC, AE, D) **Parking:** At site.

Facilities

Number of RV Sites: 20. **Number of Tent-Only Sites:** 0. **Hookups:** Water, electric (30 amps). **Each Site:** Picnic table, grill, fire pit, lantern pole. **Dump Station:** Yes. **Laundry:** No. **Pay Phone:** Yes. **Rest Rooms and Showers:** Yes. **Fuel:** No. **Propane:** No. **Internal Roads:** Paved. **RV Service:** No. **Market:** 3 mi. to Newport. **Restaurant:** 3 mi. to Newport. **General Store:** Yes. **Vending:** Yes. **Swimming:** River. **Playground:**

Yes. **Other:** Hunting & fishing licenses, picnic area, gift shop, boat ramp, nature trail. **Activities:** Fishing, swimming, boating, interpretative programs. **Nearby Attractions:** White River, Old Jacksonport Courthouse Museum. **Additional Information:** Newport Area Chamber of Commerce, (870) 523-3618.

RESTRICTIONS

Pets: On leash, cleaned up after. **Fires:** In grills or pits. **Alcoholic Beverages:** None. **Vehicle Maximum Length:** None. **Other:** No metal detectors, no glass near river.

TO GET THERE

From the junction of Hwy. 367 and Hwy. 69, go 2.9 mi. north. Turn left onto Hwy. 69 Spur (South), and go 0.8 mi. Take a tricky left turn at the sign into the campground entrance.

JONESBORO

Craighead Forest Park

P.O. Box 1845, Jonesboro 72403. T: (870) 933-4604.

RV ★★★★ Tent ★★★★

Beauty: ★★★★ Site Privacy: ★★★★
Spaciousness: ★★★★ Quiet: ★★★★★
Security: ★★★★★ Cleanliness: ★★★
Insect Control: ★★★ Facilities: ★★★

Situated in the easternmost edge of the park, this small campground has forested sites on either side of a single road. All sites back to the forest. Sites on the northwest side slope down towards the lake, while those on the southeast side back to flat land, making these sites a little longer than the 50-foot paved parking spaces. All campsites are extremely well-spaced: there is loads of room between you and your neighbor and plenty of space for extra vehicles. Sites 12–15 are closest to the fishing dock (but there is no swimming access). Sites 14 and 15 are the nicest, as they are adjacent to a grassy field that can be used for recreation and has picnic tables. The rest rooms are a little unkempt, but not any more than those who often camp in public forests might come to expect. This is a small and comfortable campground, well away from even the recreation areas within the park, offering a night of tranquility.

BASICS

Operated By: City of Jonesboro. **Open:** All year. **Site Assignment:** First come, first served; no reservations, no refunds. **Registration:** Campsite attendant (across from site 8). **Fee:** $15 (water, electric), tent $7 (checks, but no credits cards.) **Parking:** At site.

FACILITIES

Number of RV Sites: 26. **Number of Tent-Only Sites:** 0. **Hookups:** Water, electric (30 amps). **Each Site:** Picnic table, grill, trash. **Dump Station:** Yes. **Laundry:** No. **Pay Phone:** Yes. **Rest Rooms and Showers:** Yes. **Fuel:** No. **Propane:** No. **Internal Roads:** Paved. **RV Service:** No. **Market:** 4 mi. to Hwy. 63. **Restaurant:** 4 mi. to Hwy. 63. **General Store:** No. **Vending:** Yes. **Swimming:** Lake. **Playground:** Yes. **Other:** Picnic pavilions, ballfields, basketball court, paddle boat rentals, ATV trails. **Activities:** Boating, swimming, fishing, hiking, outdoor sports. **Nearby Attractions:** Craighead Forest Lake, Arkansas State University Museum. **Additional Information:** Chamber of Commerce, (870) 932-6691.

RESTRICTIONS

Pets: On leash, cleaned up after. **Fires:** In grills. **Alcoholic Beverages:** None. **Vehicle Maximum Length:** 50 ft. **Other:** No ATVs in campground, no fireworks.

TO GET THERE

From the junction of Hwy. 63 and Hwy. 1B, turn south onto Hwy. 1B and take the first right onto the service road (Parker Rd.). Follow this road 0.9 mi., then turn left onto Hwy. 141 (Culberhouse St.), and go 1.9 mi. Turn left onto Forest Park Dr. and go 1.25 mi. to the east end of Forest Park Loop, past pavilion 1, to the campground.

LAKE VILLAGE

Pecan Grove RV Park

3768 Hwy. 82 & 65 South, Lake Village 71653. T: (877) RV-4-FUNN or (870) 265-3005; F: (870) 265-2200; deebill@cei.net.

RV ★★★★ Tent ★★★★

Beauty: ★★★★ Site Privacy: ★★★★★
Spaciousness: ★★★★★ Quiet: ★★★
Security: ★★★★★ Cleanliness: ★★★
Insect Control: ★★★★ Facilities: ★★★★

An old pecan orchard, this campground has a small-farm feel to it. There is very cute landscaping around the grounds (flowers around trees and lightpoles), and remnants of the farm it once was (barn, farmhouse). Towering pecan trees grow at almost every site. There is also, however, an air of oldness that could be swept away: cobwebs in the corners, dirt from many hands opening doors, etc. The laundry is small, and while the rest rooms are clean, the building itself looks old. Further more, the cement walls are speckled with reddish paint. But don't let that scare you. The campground is very nice, and nearly every site is an excellent choice. Numbered sites in the first five rows are reserved for overnighters—the rest are for monthly renters. All sites are 80-foot pull-throughs on grassy patches. Sites at the far end of the highway (10, 27, and 35 especially) are the best, as they receive less traffic noise and not much passing traffic. (18, also an end site, is directly across from the bathhouse.) Those at the highway end are a little noisier (9, 17, 26, 34, 42). The tent area is to the northwest of the bathhouse. There is an excellent grass cover. Several large trees lend shade, but may be too high to provide much protection from rain. While the campground needs a nice spring cleaning and a little less traffic noise to earn a full rating, it is very nice, and a destination that many campers will be sure to return to.

Basics

Operated By: Bill & Dee Bunker. **Open:** All year. **Site Assignment:** Flexible, according to availability; verbal reservations OK. **Registration:** In office. (Late arrivals use drop box.) **Fee:** RV $16.67 (full), tent $12.50 (add $1 for cable or 50 amps.) **Parking:** At site.

Facilities

Number of RV Sites: 116. **Number of Tent-Only Sites:** 4. **Hookups:** Water, sewer, electric (30, 50 amps), cable. **Each Site:** Picnic table. **Dump Station:** No (sewer at all sites). **Laundry:** Yes. **Pay Phone:** Yes. **Rest Rooms and Showers:** Yes. **Fuel:** Next door. **Propane:** 1 mi. **Internal Roads:** Gravel. **RV Service:** On-call. **Market:** 1.5 mi. north. **Restaurant:** 1 mile north. **General Store:** Yes. **Vending:** Yes. **Swimming:** Lake. **Playground:** Yes. **Other:** Cabins, recreation hall, Lake Chicot, boat ramp, pavilion, dataport, dock, fish cleaning area. **Activities:** fishing, swimming, boating, volleyball, horseshoes. **Nearby Attractions:** Lake Chicot, Mississippi River. **Additional Information:** Chamber of Commerce, (870) 265-5997.

Restrictions

Pets: On leash, cleaned up after. **Fires:** In fire ring. **Alcoholic Beverages:** At sites. **Vehicle Maximum Length:** None.

To Get There

From the junction of Hwy. 65 South, 82 East, and 278 East, go 2.8 mi. on Hwy. 65/82. Turn right at the sign into the entrance. The office is the white house on the left.

LITTLE ROCK

Little Rock North KOA

7820 Crystal Hill Rd., North Little Rock 72118.T: (800) KOA-4598 or (501) 758-4598; www.koa.com; nlrkoa@aol.com.

RV ★★★★ Tent ★★★★

Beauty: ★★★★	Site Privacy: ★★★
Spaciousness: ★★★	Quiet: ★★
Security: ★★★★	Cleanliness: ★★★★
Insect Control: ★★★★	Facilities: ★★★★★

Campers in large rigs will be happy with the numerous pull-throughs in this campground, which include all sites except those around the perimter. Rows G19–24 and R8–14 are closest to the road, and include 40-foot back-ins. (G sites 15–24 are all in a forested corner of the campground, with gravel sites.) Sites R1–7 are well-shaded 56-foot pull-throughs, while G11– 14 are even longer (75 feet). Row B has 75-foot pull-throughs, of which 1–3 face a residence. B15–20 is along the northwest side of the grounds, and has 40-foot grassy back-ins. (19 is located directly next to the dog walk area.) Row Y, along the northern perimeter, has the least developed sites, but the many pine trees in this area give it a nice, natural feel. Sites Y1–13 are 75 pull-throughs amidst the trees, while Y14–28 back into the forest. Tent site T1 is off in the woods above RV site G24, and T2–3 are even more remote, in the northeast corner. All sites have a finely crushed gravel bed for a tent and plenty of trees. The rest room is very clean, and campers will be delighted to know that it has airconditioning. The toilet stalls are a little narrow, but everything is clean as a whistle. This is a fine campground to make your home base while exploring the Little Rock area. It has a nice woodsy feel and is close enough to the attractions to allow for plenty of day trips.

Basics

Operated By: The Clay Family. **Open:** All year. **Site Assignment:** Assigned upon registration. Reservations require credit card; cancellation requires 24 hours notice. **Registration:** In office. (Late arrivals use drop box.) **Fee:** RV $23–31, tent $20–23 (checks V, MC, AE, & D). **Parking:** At site.

Facilities

Number of RV Sites: 100. **Number of Tent-Only Sites:** 10. **Hookups:** Water, sewer, electric (20, 30, 50 amps), cable. **Each Site:** Picnic table, grill. **Dump Station:** Yes. **Laundry:** Yes. **Pay Phone:** Yes. **Rest Rooms and Showers:** Yes. **Fuel:** No. **Propane:** Yes. **Internal Roads:** Paved. **RV Service:** No. **Market:** 4 mi. west. **Restaurant:** Across street. **General Store:** Yes. **Vending:** Yes. **Swimming:** Pool. **Playground:** Yes. **Other:** Dataport, sauna, hot tub, exercise equipment, snack bar, pool table, dog walk. **Activities:** Basketball, volleyball, horseshoes, swimming, golf, shopping. **Nearby Attractions:** Burns Park, Wild River Country, Little Rock, Aerospace Education Center, State Capitol, Museum of Dy. **Additional Information:** North Little Rock Advertising & Promotion Commission, (800) 643-4690, (501) 758-1424.

Restrictions

Pets: On leash, cleaned up after; do not leave unattended. **Fires:** In grills only. **Alcoholic Beverages:** At sites. **Vehicle Maximum Length:** None.

To Get There

(If coming north from Little Rock on I-30, take I-40 West to I-40.) From I-40, take Exit 148. Turn west onto Crystal Hill Rd. and go 1.2 mi. Turn right at the sign into the entrance.

MENA

Shadow Mountain

3708 Hwy. 71 South, Mena 71953. T: (501) 394-6299; F: (501) 394-7378.

RV: ★★★★★ Tent: ★★★★★

Beauty: ★★★★	Site Privacy: ★★★★
Spaciousness: ★★★★	Quiet: ★★★★
Security: ★★★★★	Cleanliness: ★★★★★
Insect Control: ★★★★	Facilities: ★★★★

Touted by the proprietor as the "only full-service campground within 50 miles", this campground has full hookups, a pool, and modern facilities in a forested, rural setting. Sites in this campground are not overly developed, adding to the natural charm of the grounds. All RV sites are 65-foot pull-throughs. Sites at the ends of the rows on the east side (2, 7, 13, 14, 28) are generally the best, as they face the forest and are slightly away from the other sites in the rows. Sites 41–51 are right off the highway, making them less desirable than other sites. Unnumbered tent sites are situated down the slope of the RV park and to the south, towards the highway. Sites are grassy, with ample tree coverage, but due to some amount of passing traffic noise is inevitable. The rest rooms are very clean and fairly modern. Showers are very spacious. The laundry room is spacious and contains enough machines for a campground of this size. This is a nice little getaway with an off-the-beaten-path feel but the convenience of a highway location.

Basics

Operated By: Bonnie & Aaron Trawiek. **Open:** All year. **Site Assignment:** Assigned upon registration; reservations require credit card. **Registration:** In office. (Late arrivals use drop box.) **Fee:** RV $18 (full), $17 (water, electric), $13 (electric), tent $10. **Parking:** At site.

Facilities

Number of RV Sites: 51. **Number of Tent-Only Sites:** Undesignated sites. **Hookups:** Water, sewer, electric (30 amps). **Each Site:** Picnic table. **Dump Station:** Yes. **Laundry:** Yes. **Pay Phone:** Yes. **Rest Rooms and Showers:** Yes. **Fuel:** No. **Propane:** No. **Internal Roads:** Paved. **RV Service:** No. **Market:** 5 mi. to Mena. **Restaurant:** 5 mi. to Mena. **General Store:** Yes. **Vending:** Yes. **Swimming:** Pool. **Playground:** Yes. **Other:** Lake, antique soda fountain, firewood. **Activities:** Basketball, swimming. **Nearby Attractions:** Talimena scenic Drive, Ouachita National Forest, Janssen Park, Queen Wilhelmina State Park. **Additional Information:** Mean/Polk County Chamber of Commerce, (501) 394-2912.

Restrictions

Pets: On leash, cleaned up after. **Fires:** In rings. **Alcoholic Beverages:** At sites; subject to dry county regulations. **Vehicle Maximum Length:** None.

To Get There

From the junction of Hwy. 8 and Hwy. 59/71, in Mena, go 4.5 mi. south on Hwy. 59/71. Turn right at the sign into the entrance. The office is on the left; park to the right.

MORRILTON

Petit Jean State Park

1285 Petit Jean Mountain Rd., Morrilton 72110. T: (501) 727-5441; www.arkansasstateparks.com; petitjean@arkansas.com.

 ★★★★ ▲ ★★★★★

Beauty: ★★★★★ Site Privacy: ★★★★★
Spaciousness: ★★★★★ Quiet: ★★★★★
Security: ★★★★★ Cleanliness: ★★★★
Insect Control: ★★★★ Facilities: ★★★★

Sites in this state park, Arkansas' first, are divided into 4 areas, A–D. Area A is east of the Visitors Center, and contains sites 1–35, all 80-foot pull-throughs (except 32, which is 105 feet). Many of these sites are along (or near) the lake, and therefore are preferred or premium sites, costing more than the others. Premium sites closest to the lake are 19, 26, and 27. Preferred sites near the lake are 8, 9, 29, and 30. The end sites 1 and 35 are closest to the entrance, and may not be as desirable. Area B contains the reservable sites. Of these, 44–48 are the nicest, as they back to thick woods and are quieter than other sites. Sites 36–42 back to a road, and suffer from more noise as a result. Area C contains 45–50-foot back-ins. Sites 74–76, 89, and 91 back to thick woods, making them quite nice. Site 71 is across from the bathhouse, making access quite convenient. Site 77 is right by the entrance. Area D is for overflow camping. The rest rooms and showers in all of these areas are clean and spacious. This is a wonderful park with loads to do. It makes a great destination for families and anyone in a tent. RVers will enjoy their stay, but do not have the benefit of full hookups.

BASICS

Operated By: Arkansas State Parks. **Open:** All year. **Site Assignment:** Assigned upon registration during the day; first come, first served at night. Reservations require deposit of one's night's stay, made 5 days in advance; cancellation requires 5-days notice; first night's deposit non-refundable. **Registration:** In visitor's center. (Late arrivals select an available site & pay in the morning.) **Fee:** $17.50 (premium site), $16 (preferred site), $14.50 (water, electric). **Parking:** At site.

FACILITIES

Number of RV Sites: 127. **Number of Tent-Only Sites:** 0. **Hookups:** Water, electric (20, 30 amps). **Each Site:** Picnic table, grill, lantern pole. **Dump Station:** Yes. **Laundry:** No. **Pay Phone:** Yes. **Rest Rooms and Showers:** Yes. **Fuel:** No. **Propane:** No. **Internal Roads:** Paved. **RV Service:** No. **Market:** 20 mi. to Morrilton. **Restaurant:** On site; 20 mi. to Morrilton. **General Store:** Yes. **Vending:** Yes. **Swimming:** Pool. **Playground:** Yes. **Other:** Tennis courts, picnic pavilion, snack bar, boat rentals, amphitheater, Mather Lodge Restaurant, horse facilities. **Activities:** Fishing, boating, swimming, horseback riding, hiking, tennis. **Nearby Attractions:** Waterfall, Museum of Automobiles. **Additional Information:** Morrilton Chamber of Commerce, (501) 354-2393.

RESTRICTIONS

Pets: On leash, cleaned up after. **Fires:** In grills. **Alcoholic Beverages:** At sites. **Vehicle Maximum Length:** None.

TO GET THERE

From the junction of Hwy. 9 and Hwy. 154, turn west onto Hwy. 154 and go 11.3 mi. into the park.

MURFREESBORO

Miner's Camping and Rock Shop

2235 Hwy. 301 South, Murfreesboro 71958. T: (870) 285-2722; jgoodin776@aol.com.

★★★★ ▲ ★★★★

Beauty: ★★★★ Site Privacy: ★★★
Spaciousness: ★★★ Quiet: ★★★
Security: ★★★★ Cleanliness: ★★★
Insect Control: ★★★ Facilities: ★★★

This campground is divided into two sections on either side of the highway, the north and south sections. In the north section, sites are arranged on the outside of an internal loop. All sites are back-ins: 5–11 back to the forest, 12–17 to a dirt road. Sites are open-ended, meaning that a rig of any size can fit in most sites. Site 17 is somewhat less desirable due to its proximity to the highway. The main rest rooms are in this section, and are small, modern, and cozy. The shower is extremely spacious, but shares one drawback with the rest room—a cement floor. Sites on the south side of the park all back to the woods. Sites H–K are the best sites, as they are furthest from the highway. Site A is closest to the highway, and therefore less desirable. There are two non-flush toilets here, which are as clean as can be expected. (Take the time to cross the highway and use the full rest room!) Tenting is allowed in an open field on the south side, to the east of the RV sites. There is a good grass cover, but no trees for shade or protection from the elements. Rockhounds—and others—will enjoy this campground just south of Murfreesboro and a couple hundred feet from the Crater of Diamonds State Park. The services are decent, and the campground is cute and woodsy.

Basics

Operated By: J. Goodin. **Open:** All year. **Site Assignment:** Assigned upon registration. Verbal reservations OK; call to cancel.) **Registration:** In gift shop. (Late arrivals select an available site & settle in the morning.) **Fee:** RV $15 (full), $12 (water, electric), tent $10. **Parking:** At site.

Facilities

Number of RV Sites: 33. **Number of Tent-Only Sites:** 10. **Hookups:** Water, sewer, electric (30, 50 amps). **Each Site:** Picnic table, trash can. **Dump Station:** Yes. **Laundry:** No. **Pay Phone:** Yes. **Rest Rooms and Showers:** Yes. **Fuel:** No. **Propane:** No. **Internal Roads:** Dirt. **RV Service:** No. **Market:** 2 mi. north. **Restaurant:** 2 mi. north. **General Store:** No. **Vending:** Yes. **Swimming:** No. **Playground:** Yes. **Other:** Gift shop, 3 cabins, firewood, fishing pond, pavilion. **Activities:** Hiking, rock collecting. **Nearby Attractions:** Crater of Diamonds State Park, Ka-Do-Ha Indian Village, Hot Springs, Quartz Mines, Washington State Park. **Additional Information:** Murfreesboro Chamber of Commerce, (870) 425-5111.

Restrictions

Pets: On leash, cleaned up after. **Fires:** In pits. **Alcoholic Beverages:** Subject to dry county regulations. **Vehicle Maximum Length:** None. **Other:** No washing of vehicles.

To Get There

From the junction of Hwy. 26/27 and Hwy. 301, go 2.3 mi. east on Hwy. 301. Turn left at the sign into the entrance.

PARAGOULD

Crowley's Ridge State Park

2092 Hwy. 168 North, Paragould 72450. T: (800) 264-2405 or (870) 573-6751; F: (870) 573-6758; www.arkansasstateparks.com; crowleys@arkansas.com.

RV: ★★★★ Tent: ★★★★★

Beauty: ★★★★ Site Privacy: ★★★★
Spaciousness: ★★★★★ Quiet: ★★★★★
Security: ★★★★ Cleanliness: ★★★
Insect Control: ★★★ Facilities: ★★★

Campsites in the park are situated along a single internal road. Sites on the north side have a sudden slope at the rear, while those on the south side have a more gradual slope. (All parking strips are level.) Tent sites (19–26) are mostly 30 feet off the main road, although sites 22–24 are set back further. These are extremely spacious (45-feet-wide) dirt campsites set, as all campsites in the park are, back in the forest. Of the RV sites (so designated solely by their electric hookups), 1 is a gigantic (120-feet) pull-through, while the others are mostly 45–50-foot back-ins. (Site 7 is an exception, being only 30 feet long and set very close to the road.) Site 9 offers the most privacy, being set well back from the road; while 8 has much less privacy due to its proximity to a hiking trail head. The rest rooms and showers are astonishingly clean, modern, and spacious (but do lack air conditioning). This is an intimate state park with extraordinarily clean facilities that both tenters and RVers will definitely enjoy.

Basics

Operated By: Arkansas Dept. of Parks & Tourism. **Open:** All year. **Site Assignment:** First come, first served. Reservations require deposit of one's night's stay, made 5 days in advance; cancellation requires 5-days notice; first night's deposit non-refundable. **Registration:** In Visitors Center. (Late arrivals select available site & register next morning after 8.) **Fee:** $14 (water, electric), tent $8 (checks, V, MC, AE, & D). **Parking:** At site.

Facilities

Number of RV Sites: 18. **Number of Tent-Only Sites:** 8. **Hookups:** Water, electric (30 amps). **Each Site:** Picnic table, grill, lantern pole. **Dump Station:** Yes. **Laundry:** No. **Pay Phone:**

Yes. **Rest Rooms and Showers:** Yes. **Fuel:** No. **Propane:** No. **Internal Roads:** Paved. **RV Service:** No. **Market:** 9 mi. to Paragould. **Restaurant:** 9 mi. to Paragould. **General Store:** No. **Vending:** Yes. **Swimming:** Lake. **Playground:** Yes. **Other:** Gift shop. **Activities:** Boating, canoeing, hiking, swimming, paddleboating. **Nearby Attractions:** Lake Ponder, Walcott Lake. **Additional Information:** Paragould-Greene County Chamber of Commerce, (870) 236-7684.

Restrictions

Pets: On leash, cleaned up after. **Fires:** In pits. **Alcoholic Beverages:** At sites (preferably in nondescript containers). **Vehicle Maximum Length:** None.

To Get There

From the junction of Hwy. 49 and Hwy. 412, go 9 mi. west on Hwy. 412. Turn left onto Hwy. 168 and go 2 mi. Turn left at the sign into the campground.

PINE BLUFF

Saracen Trace RV Park

P.O. Box 7676, Pine Bluff 71611. T: (870) 536-0920; parks@seark.net.

RV: ★★★★ Tent: n/a

Beauty: ★★★★ Site Privacy: ★★★★
Spaciousness: ★★★★ Quiet: ★★★★★
Security: ★★★★ Cleanliness: ★★★★
Insect Control: ★★ Facilities: ★★★

Located within a large city park, this campground has open, grassy sites situated along a looped internal road. All sites are 60-foot back-ins, and most (if not all) are very well shaded. Sites on the eastern side of the campground (7–17) back to the lake, and seem to be sought after for this reason. Sites 21–24 back to a golf course adjacent to the campground. Site 43 is desirable for the large amount of open space (large enough for another RV site) adjacent to it. Sites 29 and 30, on the other hand, are less desirable, as they are very close to the entrance and receive more passing traffic than other sites. There is a disabled-access fishing pier between sites 12 and 13, which may also account for increased traffic past these two sites. This campground is on the whole a very pleasant, extremely quiet campground. Sites are grassy and shaded, and campers seeking a relaxing atmosphere should find them extremely comfortable.

Basics

Operated By: Pine Bluff Parks Commission. **Open:** All year. **Site Assignment:** First come, first served; no reservations. **Registration:** Registration kiosk. **Fee:** $10. **Parking:** At site.

Facilities

Number of RV Sites: 54. **Number of Tent-Only Sites:** 0. **Hookups:** Water, sewer, electric (20, 30 amps). **Each Site:** Picnic table, grill, trees. **Dump Station:** Yes. **Laundry:** Yes. **Pay Phone:** Yes. **Rest Rooms and Showers:** No. **Fuel:** No. **Propane:** No. **Internal Roads:** Paved. **RV Service:** No. **Market:** 6 mi. to town. **Restaurant:** 6 mi. to town. **General Store:** No. **Vending:** Yes. **Swimming:** Lake. **Playground:** Yes. **Activities:** Swimming, fishing, baseball, soccer, horseshoes, hiking, golf. **Nearby Attractions:** Lake Langhofer, The Band Museum, Southeast Arkansas Arts & Science Center. **Additional Information:** Greater Pine Bluff Area Chamber of Commerce, (870) 535-0110.

Restrictions

Pets: On leash, cleaned up after. **Fires:** In grills. **Alcoholic Beverages:** At sites. **Vehicle Maximum Length:** None.

To Get There

From the junction of Hwy. 79B and Hwy. 65B, go 1.2 mi. east on Hwy. 65B. Turn left at the light onto Convention Center Drive and follow this road into the park. The campground is at the extreme north end of the park.

POCAHONTAS

Old Davidsonville State Park

7953 Hwy. 166 South, Pocahontas 72455. T: (870) 892-4708 or (870) 892-7650; www.arkansasstateparks.com; olddavidson@arkansas.com.

RV: ★★★★ Tent: ★★★★

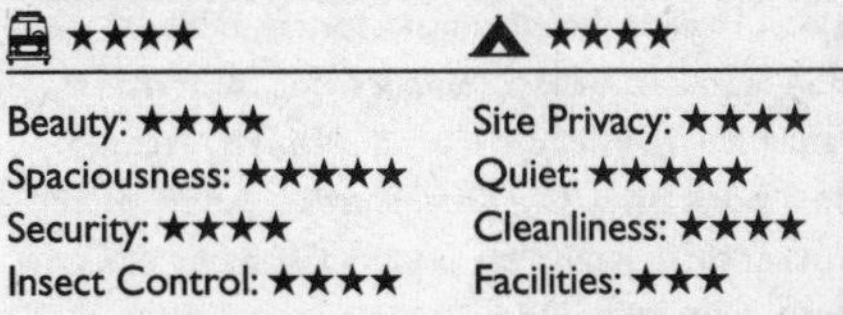

Beauty: ★★★★ Site Privacy: ★★★★
Spaciousness: ★★★★★ Quiet: ★★★★★
Security: ★★★★ Cleanliness: ★★★★
Insect Control: ★★★★ Facilities: ★★★

RV sites in this park are located on either side of a single internal looped road. Tent sites are walk-ins from a common parking area in the southeast corner. All campsites are spacious, forested spaces with a (mostly) dirt floor. Of the RV sites, 4, 8, 16, and 20 are 120-foot pull-throughs, while the rest of the sites run from 45 feet (1) or 75 feet (3) in length. Sites 10 and 11 are a double, suitable for a group camping. Sites 18, 19, and 24 are slightly less desirable sites: 18 is set right on the road, with little privacy; 19 is extremely close to several tent sites; and 24 is located right on the path that leads to the bath house, ensuring loads of passing foot traffic. All other sites are very nice, and even these three are only slightly worse-off. The tenting area consists of a very spacious walk-in area behind site 19. One (unnumbered) site in the northeast corner of this area is situated well away from the others, and therefore offers more privacy. The rest rooms and showers are extremely clean, modern, and spacious. The campground is very comfortable for both tenters and RVers, and offers a glimpse into frontier life in Arkansas from the early 1800s.

Basics

Operated By: Arkansas Dept. of Parks & Tourism. **Open:** All year (limited services Dec.–Feb.). **Site Assignment:** First come, first served; reservations require deposit of one's night's stay, made 5 days in advance; cancellation requires 5-days notice; first night's deposit non-refundable. **Registration:** In Visitor Center. (Late arrivals select available site & register next morning after 8.) **Fee:** $14.28 (water, electric), tent $8.16 (checks, V, MC, AE, & D). **Parking:** At site.

Facilities

Number of RV Sites: 24. **Number of Tent-Only Sites:** 15. **Hookups:** Water, electric (20 amps). **Each Site:** Picnic table, grill, fire pit, trees. **Dump Station:** Yes. **Laundry:** No. **Pay Phone:** Yes. **Rest Rooms and Showers:** Yes. **Fuel:** No. **Propane:** No. **Internal Roads:** Paved. **RV Service:** No. **Market:** 10 mi. to Pocahontas. **Restaurant:** 9 mi. to Pocahontas. **General Store:** No. **Vending:** Yes. **Swimming:** No. **Playground:** Yes. **Other:** Pavilion, boat ramp, historical exhibits, canoe rentals, gift shop, campfire ring. **Activities:** Boating, hiking, fishing, volleyball. **Nearby Attractions:** Black River, Old Davidsonville. **Additional Information:** Randolph County Chamber of Commerce, (870) 892-3956.

Restrictions

Pets: On leash, cleaned up after. **Fires:** In grills. **Alcoholic Beverages:** At sites (preferably in non-descript containers). **Vehicle Maximum Length:** None. **Other:** No fireworks, no firearms, no metal detectors, no excavating.

To Get There

From the junction of Hwy. 62 and Hwy. 166, turn south onto Hwy. 166 and go 8.5 mi. (Be sure to follow Hwy. 166 as it turns to the left after 8 mi.) Follow the road straight into the park.

ROGERS

Rogers/Pea Ridge KOA

P.O. Box 456, Rogers 72757. T: (800) 562-6572 or (501) 451-8566; www.koa.com.

RV ★★★★ Tent ★★★★

Beauty: ★★★★ Site Privacy: ★★★
Spaciousness: ★★★ Quiet: ★★★★★
Security: ★★★★ Cleanliness: ★★★★★
Insect Control: ★★★★ Facilities: ★★★★

Sites in this campground are mostly undeveloped, being grassy or, at most, gravel. However, this lends a natural feel to the entire campground that many campers will enjoy. Sites 1–15 are 75-foot pull-throughs, of which 1–8 are mostly without shade. (Sites 10–15 are forested.) Sites 22–26 are smaller (42–54-feet) back-ins, and a little crunched for space. 23 is a 60-foot pull-through at the tip of the island inside the looped road. Sites 44 and 45 are 75-foot back-ins that back to the forest, and are the most secluded sites in the park. The tent spaces, 32–40, are in fact one large open space fit for tents. This area has lots of trees but a rather thin grass cover. Tent sites 48 and 50, by the entrance, have crushed gravel pads and loads of shade. The laundry facility is small but very clean. The rest rooms are likewise clean and very bright. This campground is a very comfortable stay for both RVers and tenters.

Basics

Operated By: Leslie Thomas & Jack Maertens. **Open:** All year. **Site Assignment:** Assigned upon registration; V or MC required for reservation, 24-hours cancellation policy. **Registration:** In office. (Late arrivals use drop box.) **Fee:** RV $22 (full), $20 (water, electric), tent $13.50 (checks, V, MC). **Parking:** At site.

Facilities

Number of RV Sites: 41. **Number of Tent-Only Sites:** Undesignated sites. **Hookups:** Water, sewer, electric (20, 30, 50 amps). **Each Site:** Picnic table, grill. **Dump Station:** Yes. **Laundry:** Yes. **Pay**

Phone: Yes. **Rest Rooms and Showers:** Yes. **Fuel:** No. **Propane:** No. **Internal Roads:** Gravel. **RV Service:** No. **Market:** 2 mi. on Hwy. 62. **Restaurant:** 6 mi. west. **General Store:** Yes. **Vending:** No. **Swimming:** Pool. **Playground:** Yes. **Other:** Game room, within 15 minutes of fishing areas, cabins, pet walk. **Activities:** Fishing, boating, swimming. **Nearby Attractions:** Pea Ridge Military Park, War Eagle Cavern. **Additional Information:** Rogers Chamber of Commerce, (501) 636-1240.

Restrictions

Pets: On leash, cleaned up after. **Fires:** In grills. **Alcoholic Beverages:** At sites. **Vehicle Maximum Length:** None. **Other:** Extended-stay campers have a 3 dog limit.

To Get There

From I-340 (Exit 82), exit onto Hwy. 62 and go 10.6 mi. Turn left at the sign into the entrance.

RUSSELLVILLE

Outdoor Living Center RV Park

10 Outdoor Ct., Russellville 72802. T: (501) 968-7705; olcrv@mail.cswnet.com.

RV ★★★ | Tent n/a

Beauty: ★★ | Site Privacy: ★★★
Spaciousness: ★★★ | Quiet: ★★★
Security: ★★★★ | Cleanliness: ★★★★
Insect Control: ★★★★ | Facilities: ★★★

Although this campground is bordered to the northwest by woods, unsightly storage units to the south detract significantly from the beauty of this park. Sites are laid out in two central rows of 65-foot pull-throughs, with 60-foot back-ins around the perimiter. The nicest of the back-ins (17–25) are along the northern edge, just in front of the woods. Sites 1–16 also back to trees, but the trees don't shade the sites. The pull-throughs are grassy and level, but open to the sun. Site 25 is next to the rec room, and may receive more than the normal amount of passing foot traffic. Likewise, 46, closest to the rest rooms, may be a high-traffic site. The rest rooms are clean and comfortable, and kept locked for added security. This park is a decent overnight stay, but not a destination for most travelers. One word of note: during our visit, the managers were involved in multi-level marketing, and tended to push their product on visitors—to the extent of including a product brochure with each site map!

Basics

Operated By: Richard Shilling. **Open:** All year. **Site Assignment:** Flexible, depending on availability; reservations require credit card if arriving after 4 p.m.; cancellation requires 24-hours' notice. **Registration:** In office. (Late arrivals pay in morning.) **Fee:** RV $ 16.32 (50 amps), $ 15.30 (30 amps) (check, V, MC, & D). **Parking:** At site.

Facilities

Number of RV Sites: 50. **Number of Tent-Only Sites:** 0. **Hookups:** Water, sewer, electric (30, 50 amps), cable. **Dump Station:** Yes. **Laundry:** Yes. **Pay Phone:** Yes. **Rest Rooms and Showers:** Yes. **Fuel:** No. **Propane:** No. **Internal Roads:** Gravel/paved. **RV Service:** No. **Market:** 2 mi. south. **Restaurant:** 0.25 mi. south. **General Store:** Yes. **Vending:** Yes. **Swimming:** No. **Playground:** No. **Other:** Dataport, rec hall, RV supplies. **Activities:** Hot springs bathing, tours, hiking. **Nearby Attractions:** Lake Dardanelle State Park, Hot Springs National Park. **Additional Information:** Chamber of Commerce, (501) 968-2530.

Restrictions

Pets: On leash, cleaned up after; long-term residents may only have a "few" dogs. **Fires:** In grills; subject to bans. **Alcoholic Beverages:** At sites; subject to dry county regulations. **Vehicle Maximum Length:** 65 ft.

To Get There

From I-40 Exit 81, turn west onto Hwy. 7 and go 0.3 mi. north to campground entrance.

SILOAM SPRINGS

Wilderness Hills RV Park and Campground

13776 Taylor Orchard Rd., Gentry 72734. T: (501) 524-4955; F: (501) 524-4414; whcg@coxinternet. com.

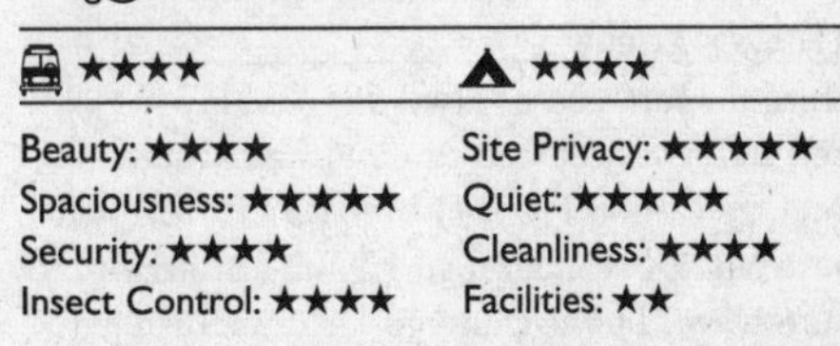

Located in a wilderness setting and surrounded by forest, this campground is shady and quiet. RV sites are huge pull-throughs (75–95-feet) laid out in two strips, and all are well-shaded. Sites 1–10 are furthest from the office, but closest to the entrance. (Sites 1–5 are the furthest from everything—but not by much.) Sites 3 and 4,as well as 5 and 6, are angled into each other, which makes them slightly less private. The longest sites in the campground are 11–15, which are an impressive 95 feet in length. Tenting space is located in the southeast corner. Like the RV sites, this area is well-shaded, and it is closest to the undeveloped forest. While there is but thin grass cover, the dirt is soft and will easily take tent spikes. Tenters will especially enjoy the "lost" atmosphere of this park, although anyone in search of a quiet night in the woods will appreciate it.

BASICS

Operated By: Robert Hammersla. **Open:** All year. **Site Assignment:** Assigned upon registration; verbal reservations OK. **Registration:** In office. (Late arrivals use drop box.) **Fee:** RV $15 (full), $12 (water, electric), tent $10 (checks, no credit cards.) **Parking:** At site.

FACILITIES

Number of RV Sites: 25. **Number of Tent-Only Sites:** Undesignated sites. **Hookups:** Water, sewer, electric (30, 50 amps). **Each Site:** Picnic table, grill. **Dump Station:** No (sewer at all sites). **Laundry:** No. **Pay Phone:** Yes. **Rest Rooms and Showers:** Yes. **Fuel:** No. **Propane:** No. **Internal Roads:** Gravel. **RV Service:** No. **Market:** 3 mi. southwest. **Restaurant:** 3 mi. southwest. **General Store:** No. **Vending:** Yes. **Swimming:** No. **Playground:** No. **Other:** Dataport, lake, stream, golf course, cabins. **Activities:** Fishing, golf, antique, flea markets. **Nearby Attractions:** Ozark National Forest, Beaver Lake. **Additional Information:** Chamber of Commerce, (501) 524-6466.

RESTRICTIONS

Pets: On leash, cleaned up after, quiet. **Fires:** In grills. **Alcoholic Beverages:** At sites. **Vehicle Maximum Length:** None.

TO GET THERE

From the junction of Hwy. 595 and Hwy. 412 East in town (just west of the Arkansas state line), go east on Hwy. 412 for 1.5 mi. Turn left onto Mt. Olive St. and go 1.9 mi. Turn right onto Dawn Hill Rd. and go 1.85 mi. Turn left onto Taylor Orchard Rd. and go 1.3 mi. Turn right at the sign into the campground.

TEXARKANA

Texarkana RV Park

8225 Camper Ln., Texarkana 71854. T: (870) 772-0751; rbparksr@msn.com.

RV: ★★★ Tent: n/a

Beauty: ★★★	Site Privacy: ★★★
Spaciousness: ★★★★	Quiet: ★★
Security: ★★★★	Cleanliness: ★★★★
Insect Control: ★★★★	Facilities: ★★★

Divided into three sections (A, B, and C), this campground has only RV sites, and does not accommodate tenting. Sites are all level, grassy pull-throughs. Row A has 65-foot sites that are all very open. Site 8 has the largest tree (across the internal road, by the grill), making it the best of this row. Site 12 is closest to the highway, making it the least desirbale. Row B has 45-foot sites that are mostly open—sites 8, 11, 12, and 14 have shade trees. Row C has 60-foot sites, with the best sites in the higher numbers. Sites 11–14 face a nice field to the north, and have trees across the internal road that provide some shade, but 14 is close to the highway. The campground in general is not highly developed, which lends a natural feel to the sites but also provides for a sometimes choppy road. RVers should take the internal road at a slow speed. The restooms are clean and very modern. However, the showers could benefit from a tile scrubbing, and some of the lights were not working when the campground was inspected. The laundry is spacious and clean. This is a very reasonable campground to spend several days in, and depending on which site you get, it may prove to be worthy of a longer stay.

BASICS

Operated By: Janet Park. **Open:** All year. **Site Assignment:** Assigned upon registration. Reservations require credit card in busy season; 24-hours cancellation policy. **Registration:** In office. (Late arrivals use drop box.) **Fee:** RV $20–23 depending on 30 or 50 amps (V, MC, AE, & D.) **Parking:** At site.

FACILITIES

Number of RV Sites: 41. **Number of Tent-Only Sites:** 0. **Hookups:** Water, sewer, electric (20, 30, 50 amps), cable. **Each Site:** Picnic table, grill, trash can. **Dump Station:** Yes. **Laundry:** Yes. **Pay Phone:** Yes. **Rest Rooms and Showers:** Yes. **Fuel:** No. **Propane:** Yes. **Internal Roads:** Dirt.

RV Service: No. **Market:** 5 mi. to Texarkana. **Restaurant:** 5 mi. to Texarkana. **General Store:** Yes. **Vending:** No. **Swimming:** Pool. **Playground:** Yes. **Other:** Small TV lounge, game room. **Activities:** Games, visiting museums, swimming. **Nearby Attractions:** Crater of Diamonds State Park, Dy Place Children's Museum. **Additional Information:** Texarkana Chamber of Commerce, (903) 792-7191.

Restrictions

Pets: On leash, cleaned up after, do not leave tied up. **Fires:** In grills. **Alcoholic Beverages:** At sites. **Vehicle Maximum Length:** None.

To Get There

From I-30, take Exit 7 to Mandeville. Go 0.2 mi. north on Hwy. 108 West, then take the first right onto the north service road and go 0.4 mi. straight into the campground.

VAN BUREN

Overland RV Park

1716 Fayetteville Hwy., Van Buren 72956. T: (501) 471-5474; olcrv@mail.cswnet.com.

RV ★★★ | Tent n/a

Beauty: ★	Site Privacy: ★★★
Spaciousness: ★★	Quiet: ★★★
Security: ★★★	Cleanliness: ★★★★
Insect Control: ★★★★	Facilities: ★★★

This RV park is part of an RV-oriented complex in a commercial area off a main road. The park is located next to a sales and service center, while a fence running around the park hides a supermarket, restaurants, and shops. Sites are laid out in three rows. The south row (even 2–32 and 33) contains back-ins of 40 × 22 feet and offers phone hookups. The north row (34–49) offers 50 amps service. pull-throughs are located in the north and middle rows. These sites are 65 feet in length, with a mixture of gravel and grass. 33 is slightly less desirable, as fencing on two sides seems to hem it in. The most desirable sites are in the north row, since they have the greatest amount of open space behind them, while the easternmost sites are furthest from the entrance. The shower facility is cleaner than the rest rooms, which are acceptable but not spectacular. At the time of our visit, the floors were utterly exhausted, and needed to be replaced. This campground is a reasonable overnight stay—and an extremely convenient one for those in need of RV servicing—but shouldn't make anyone's destination list.

Basics

Operated By: Richard Shilling. **Open:** All year. **Site Assignment:** First come, first served Credit card required for reservation; 24-hours cancellation policy. **Registration:** In RV at entrance, on right. If unattended, use mail slot. **Fee:** RV $17 (50 amps), $16 (30 amps) (checks, V, MC, & D). **Parking:** At site.

Facilities

Number of RV Sites: 49. **Number of Tent-Only Sites:** 0. **Hookups:** Water, sewer, electric (30, 50 amps), phone. **Dump Station:** Yes. **Laundry:** Yes. **Pay Phone:** Yes. **Rest Rooms and Showers:** Yes. **Fuel:** No. **Propane:** Yes. **Internal Roads:** Gravel. **RV Service:** Yes. **Market:** 1 block. **Restaurant:** 2 blocks. **General Store:** No. **Vending:** No. **Swimming:** No. **Playground:** No. **Other:** Pet walk area, pavilion. **Activities:** Railroad rides. **Nearby Attractions:** Arkansas & Missouri Railroad. **Additional Information:** Van Buren Visitors Center, (800) 332-5889.

Restrictions

Pets: On leash, cleaned up after. **Fires:** In grills. **Alcoholic Beverages:** At sites. **Vehicle Maximum Length:** None.

To Get There

From I-40 Exit 5, turn south onto Hwy. 59. On the south side of the highway crossover, go 0.1 mi. to the first left turn. Drive straight into the entrance.

WALDRON

Big Pine RV Park

1085 North Main St., Waldron 72958. T: (501) 420-5732 or (903) 665-8648; bjem@ipa.net.

RV ★★★ | Tent ★★★

Beauty: ★★	Site Privacy: ★★
Spaciousness: ★★★★	Quiet: ★★★
Security: ★★★	Cleanliness: ★★★
Insect Control: ★★★★	Facilities: ★★

This overnight park is located in a residential area, with little to enhance its beauty. Sites are grassy and open, and situated rather close to the road. (Sites 12–16 are especially close. Mainly unshaded, they are as open to the sun as they are to passer-by.) While sites are open-ended, anything larger than 60 feet or so seems unfeasible, especially if a number of sites are occupied. Sites 10 and 11 are perhaps the nicest, with a couple of trees around them to reduce the amount of direct sunlight that reaches them. Site 16 also has a tree, making it slightly better than the other roadside sites. Of the remaining sites, 1–8, are the better sites, being furthest from the highway. Perhaps a telling detail: a warning sign that reads "Not Responsible For Accidents" is displayed prominently in the campground, suggesting that entering and exiting the premises is somewhat difficult in traffic. But then, unless you are running late you probably won't want to bother to find out.

BASICS

Operated By: Billy & Esther Murphy. **Open:** All year. **Site Assignment:** First come, first served; verbal reservations OK. **Registration:** "Pick a spot & park." Register when someone is around. **Fee:** RV $12. **Parking:** At site.

FACILITIES

Number of RV Sites: 16. **Number of Tent-Only Sites:** Undesignated sites. **Hookups:** Water, sewer, electric (30, 50 amps). **Dump Station:** Yes. **Laundry:** Yes. **Pay Phone:** Yes. **Rest Rooms and Showers:** Yes. **Fuel:** No. **Propane:** No. **Internal Roads:** Gravel. **RV Service:** No. **Market:** 1 mi. south. **Restaurant:** 1 mile south. **General Store:** No. **Vending:** No. **Swimming:** No. **Playground:** No. **Activities:** Fishing, boating, swimming, hiking. **Nearby Attractions:** Ouachita National Forest, Blue Mountain Lake. **Additional Information:** Chamber of Commerce, (501) 637-2775.

RESTRICTIONS

Pets: On leash, cleaned up after. **Fires:** In grills. **Alcoholic Beverages:** At sites. **Vehicle Maximum Length:** 60 ft.

TO GET THERE

From the junction of Hwy. 71 and Hwy. 71 B north of town, turn south onto Hwy. 71B South, and go 0.7 mi. Turn left at the sign into the park.

WEST MEMPHIS

Trav-L-Park

7037 I-55, Marion 72364. T: (888) 857-4890 or (870) 739-4801; F: (870) 739-4801; www.tldirectory.com; tennpop@aol.com.

 ★★★★ 

Beauty: ★★★★
Site Privacy: ★★★★
Spaciousness: ★★★
Quiet: ★★★
Security: ★★★★
Cleanliness: ★★★★★
Insect Control: ★★★
Facilities: ★★★★★

West of the highway, with a cornfield to the north and an agricultural field to the south, this campground has attractive landscaping (using bushes at the ends of rows) and towering shade trees. Nearly all sites in the park are very well shaded, with a grass floor. Sites 1, 2, 4, and 9 are enormous (100-feet) pull-throughs, while 3 and 5–8 are 75-foot back-ins. End sites 16, 24, 32, 40, 48, and H have enormous leftover space at the ends of the rows. Sites 50–54 are 60-foot back-ins in a strip across from the office. Adjacent to these sites are sites 55–62, arranged in a semi-circle in the grass. These are undeveloped sites in a wooded area, with a very natural, almost wild, feel. (These sites can accommodate any size of rig, and can be pull-throughs if the adjacent area is clear.) Sites A–H face a residential area, and A and B are the least best sites in the campground, lacking shade trees. However, there is nary a truly bad site in the park. The rest rooms and showers are immaculate, well-lit, and tastefully decorated. The laundry is contained in its own cute little cabin, and is open 24 hrs. Located 15 miles to most attractions, and 22 miiles to Graceland, this park boasts very friendly management and is worth the drive out, especially given the state of other local campgrounds.

BASICS

Operated By: Joyce & Ramon Mitchell. **Open:** All year. **Site Assignment:** Assigned upon registration. Reservations require credit card or cell phone number, & are recommended; cancellation must be made 4 days before arrival. **Registration:** In office. (Late arrivals use drop box.) **Fee:** RV $22 (full), $18 (water, electric), tent $13. Winter RV rates are $18 & $16. **Parking:** At site, w/ plenty of visitor parking.

FACILITIES

Number of RV Sites: 125. **Number of Tent-Only Sites:** 3. **Hookups:** Water, sewer, electric (30, 50 amps). **Each Site:** Picnic table, grill. **Dump Station:** Yes. **Laundry:** Yes. **Pay Phone:** Yes. **Rest Rooms and Showers:** Yes. **Fuel:** No. **Propane:** Yes. **Internal Roads:** Gravel. **RV Service:** No. **Market:** 4 mi. south (Exit 10). **Restaurant:** 4 mi. south (Exit 10). **General Store:** Yes. **Vending:** No.

Swimming: Pool. **Playground:** Yes. **Other:** Dataport, rec room, pet walk area, horseshoes. **Activities:** Swimming, visiting museums, city tours, shopping. **Nearby Attractions:** Graceland, Sun Studio, Beale St., Pink Palace Museum, Rock 'n' Soul Museum, IMAX Theater. **Additional Information:** Visitor information Desk, (901) 543-5333.

Restrictions

Pets: On leash, cleaned up after. **Fires:** In grills. **Alcoholic Beverages:** At sites, no bottles. **Vehicle Maximum Length:** None. **Other:** No semis, operators prefer no large animals that must be kept outside of RVs.

To Get There

From I-55, take Exit 14. Take the first right (following the sign for Memphis). Follow the road around and take the right turn so that you are driving parallel to the interstate on the west service road. Go 0.2 mi. and turn right at the sign into the campground.

WYNNE

Village Creek State Park

201 CR 754, Wynne 72396. T: (870) 238-9406; F: (870) 238-9415; www.arkansasstateparks.com; villagecrk@arkansas.com.

RV ★★★★ | Tent ★★★★

Beauty: ★★★★	Site Privacy: ★★★★
Spaciousness: ★★★★	Quiet: ★★★★★
Security: ★★★★	Cleanliness: ★★★
Insect Control: ★★★	Facilities: ★★★★

This is a large campground divided up into three camping areas: South (1–41), West (42–73), and North (74–104), in order from the entrance. All sites are forested, and have a paved parking area for an RV or other vehicle. Most sites open to a grassy field that campers can use for recreation. The South Area consists of two loops in a figure 8, the more northernly of the two loops containing reservable sites. Sites 1 and 8 are set very close to the road, which makes them less desirable; while 7 is set back further than most, making it rather more private. Sites 23 and 24 are on either side of a hiking trail head, and may experience more foot traffic for this reason. Sites 25 and 26 together form a double. The West Area is close to Lake Dunn; sites 46–50 are the closest campsites to the swimming beach. Sites 53–57 back to the lake (with a strip of forest behind them), while 59 is close to the rest room facility. Sites 48 and 49 make a double, and 72 and 73 are very close to one another. 60–67 are located on a side street, making them slightly more private. Of these sites, 61 and 62 are the most remote. The North Area contains the most number of doubles, which will interest groups of campers. These include sites 75 and 76, 93 and 94, and 101 and 102. Site 74 is right at the entrance, but 85 and 86 are tucked away in a corner. This is a pleasant wilderness campground that will appeal to many campers for its quiet and natural setting.

Basics

Operated By: Arkansas Dept. of Parks & Tourism. **Open:** All year. **Site Assignment:** First come, first served. Reservations require deposit of one's night's stay, made 5 days in advance; cancellation requires 5-days notice; first night's deposit non-refundable. **Registration:** In Visitors Center. (Late arrivals select available site & register next morning after 8.) **Fee:** $14 (checks, V, MC, AE, & D). **Parking:** At site.

Facilities

Number of RV Sites: 104. **Number of Tent-Only Sites:** 0. **Hookups:** Water, electric (20, 30, 50 amps). **Each Site:** Picnic table, fire pit, tent pad. **Dump Station:** Yes. **Laundry:** No. **Pay Phone:** Yes. **Rest Rooms and Showers:** Yes. **Fuel:** No. **Propane:** No. **Internal Roads:** Paved. **RV Service:** No. **Market:** 7 mi. to Wynne. **Restaurant:** 7 mi. to Wynne. **General Store:** Yes. **Vending:** Yes. **Swimming:** Lake. **Playground:** Yes. **Other:** Cabins, auditorium. **Activities:** Golf, tennis, hiking. **Nearby Attractions:** Village Creek State Park, Parkin Arch State Park. **Additional Information:** Chamber of Commerce, (870) 238-2601.

Restrictions

Pets: On leash, cleaned up after, not in cabins. **Fires:** In grills. **Alcoholic Beverages:** At sites (preferably in a nondescript containers). **Vehicle Maximum Length:** None.

To Get There

From the junction of Hwy. 1 and Hwy. 64B/284, turn east onto Hwy. 64B/284, and go 1.9 mi., making sure to take the two turns within the first 0.7 mi. to stay on this highway. At the junction of Hwy. 64B and Hwy. 284, go 4.9 mi. south on Hwy. 284. Turn left at the sign into the park entrance.

Colorado

Colorado boasts what must be some of the best camping in the entire world. Mountains, rivers, forests, lakes, cliffs, wildlife, fishing, hiking, canoeing—Colorado has it all. Ranging from forested mountains to nearly desert plains, the geography and climate vary wildly from region to region and month to month. (Some would even say minute to minute.) It can be 80° in Denver with blizzard conditions in the mountains less than two hours away. For this reason, campers in the mountains should bring much warmer clothing than they would need in the city. Weather in the mountains changes quickly, and even summer nights can be downright cold.

Interstate 25 slices the state neatly into two vastly differing regions: the almost featureless grasslands of the east and the mountainous west, where the lion's share of exciting camping opportunities exist. **Bonny State Park** is an excellent welcome to visitors in search of outdoor recreation entering the state from Kansas. To the west, **Dinosaur National Monument** and the **Grand Mesa** area likewise show the state at its best. In fact, entering Colorado on nearly any road from the surrounding states quickly puts you in prime camping territory. And once you've made it to the center, opportunities for outdoor recreation abound.

With large tracts of national forest, plenty of state parks, and numerous private campgrounds, the mountains of Colorado provide endless possibilities for those who like to stretch their legs and breathe in clean mountain air. But let's not forget skiing! In some people's dictionaries, the entry for *snow skiing* says "see Colorado." **Vail, Aspen, Breckenridge, Steamboat Springs**—these are ski towns with nearly mythical status. All of these areas accommodate campers, whether they come in the largest RVs available or hike in with a tent. And every level of amenity is available, from the most basic primitive campgrounds with no running water to full-service resorts with a hot tub, Internet connection, and ice cream socials.

In-state attractions are nearly too numerous to mention, but **Mesa Verde National Park, Rocky Mountain National Park,** the **Great Sand Dunes National Monument, Telluride,** the **Durango and Silverton Narrow Gauge Railroad, Royal Gorge, Garden of the Gods, Denver, Boulder, Leadville, Cache La Poudre wilderness,** and **Central City** all deserve a mention—as well as a visit. Colorado is a camper's state, and boasts opportunities for any outdoor activity you can possibly imagine.

The following facilities accept payment in checks or cash only:

Cadillac Jack's Campground, Calhan
Camp Dick, Ward
Dakota Campground, Walsenburg
Horsetooth Reservoir (Stout Campground), Fort Collins
Hud's Campground, McClave
Kelly-Dahl Campground, Nederland
Lake Fork Campground & RV Resort, Lake City
Paonia State Park, Paonia
Parry Peak Campground, Twin Lakes
Ridgway State Park, Ridgway
Rifle Falls/Rifle Gap Campgrounds, Rifle
Stillwater Campground, Yampa

The following facilities feature 20 sites or fewer:

Hud's Campground, McClave
Paonia State Park, Paonia
Meadowlark Cafe, Motel & RV Park, Lindon
Mobile Manor RV Park, Monte Vista

Campground Profiles

ALAMOSA

Alamosa KOA

6900 Juniper Ln., Alamosa 81101. T: (800) 562-9157 or (719) 589-9757; www.koa.com.

RV ★★★★ Tent ★★★

Beauty: ★★★★ Site Privacy: ★★★
Spaciousness: ★★★ Quiet: ★★★★
Security: ★★★★ Cleanliness: ★★★★
Insect Control: ★★★★ Facilities: ★★★★

This campground, offering spectacular views of mountains to the east, has pull-through sites that average 60 × 22 feet in size—large enough to camp comfortably in almost any vehicle. End sites 16, 24, 32, and 42 have superb views, making them more attractive. Sites 41 and 42 are even longer (80-foot) pull-throughs, also with excellent views, although 42 shares space with a light standard. The last row of RV sites on Rd. 6 (sites 33–42) are arguably the nicest, as they are away from the office and closest to the grassy tent sites. (Of course, this row is also furthest from the rest rooms, so some campers may prefer not to take a site.) Tent sites on the north side of the campground have nice grass and great views, but no shade. (Tent sites at the northwest side have more trees, and are therefore a better bet for tenters.) The rest room and shower facilities are clean and spacious, although the showers share a cement floor, which is slightly less comfortable and clean-looking than tile. The laundry is clean, with loads of room.

Basics

Operated By: Private operator. **Open:** May 1–Oct. 25. **Site Assignment:** Assigned upon registration. Credit card required for reservation; 24-hour cancellation policy. $5 cancellation fee). **Registration:** In office. (Late arrivals use drop box.) **Fee:** RV $25 (full), $22 (water, electric), tent $19. **Parking:** At site.

Facilities

Number of RV Sites: 42. **Number of Tent-Only Sites:** 15. **Hookups:** Water, sewer, electric (30 amps). **Each Site:** Picnic table, grill. **Dump Station:** Yes. **Laundry:** Yes. **Pay Phone:** Yes. **Rest Rooms and Showers:** Yes. **Fuel:** No. **Propane:** No. **Internal Roads:** Gravel. **RV Service:** No. **Market:** 5 mi. west. **Restaurant:** 1 west. **General Store:** Yes. **Vending:** No. **Swimming:** No. **Playground:** Yes. **Other:** Pool table, video games, cabins, dog walk area. **Activities:** Hiking, viewing wildlife, volleyball, horseshoes. **Nearby Attractions:** Great Sand Dunes, Alamosa National Wildlife Refuge, San Luis Valley Alligator Farm. **Additional Information:** Alamosa County Chamber of Commerce, (800) 258-7597 or (719) 589-3681.

Restrictions

Pets: 1 per camper; on leash, cleaned up after. **Fires:** In community fire pit only. **Alcoholic Beverages:** At sites. **Vehicle Maximum Length:** 40 ft.

To Get There

From the junction of Hwy. 17 and Hwy. 160, go 3.2 mi. east on Hwy. 160. Turn north onto Juniper Ln., then take the first right into the campground. The office is on the left.

ALLENSPARK

Olive Ridge Campground

Boulder Ranger Office, 2140 Yarmouth Ave., Boulder 80301. T: (877) 444-6777 or (303) 444-6600 or (303) 747-2647; F: (303) 747-2647; www.reserveusa.com or www.fs.fed.us/arns.

RV ★★★★ Tent ★★★★

Beauty: ★★★★★	Site Privacy: ★★★★
Spaciousness: ★★★★	Quiet: ★★★★
Security: ★★★★	Cleanliness: ★★★★
Insect Control: ★★★★	Facilities: ★

Almost in the shadow of Long's Peak, this campground has very natural campsites scattered in a ponderosa pine forest. Sites average 40 feet, and all but 50 are back-ins. (Site 50 is a 45-foot "parallel-parking" site similar to a pull-through.) Sites 26 and 40 are oversized sites, roughly twice as large as a regular site. Sites 10, 42, 45, and 46 are reserved for campground hosts and administration. There is a hiking trail that starts by site 35, perhaps increasing foot traffic past this site. Water pumps are located near sites 2, 8, 16, 20, 30, 34, 36, and 49. Several sites have huge boulders that may either be seen as an encroachment on site space or as a source of shade and beauty. This is a slice of nature developed with a minimal impact, allowing campers to experience the beauty of nature. Facilities are limited to pit toilets, but the photos on the walls are an attempt to make the campground as comfortable as possible, considering its basic facilities. Tenters in particular may prefer this campground, but there is no reason why RVers willing to forego hookups for a night shouldn't enjoy it equally well.

Basics

Operated By: Thousand Trails Management. **Open:** May–Oct. (dates may vary). **Site Assignment:** First come, first served. Credit card required for reservation; 3-days cancellation policy. less $10.00 service fee; refunds must be requested within 30 days. **Registration:** At pay kiosk. (Camp Host will verify that campers have paid.) **Fee:** $12, $15 for oversized sites (checks, but no credit cards). **Parking:** At site.

Facilities

Number of RV Sites: 54. **Number of Tent-Only Sites:** 0. **Hookups:** None. **Each Site:** Picnic table, grill, fire pit. **Dump Station:** No. **Laundry:** No. **Pay Phone:** No. **Rest Rooms and Showers:** Rest rooms; no shower. **Fuel:** No. **Propane:** No. **Internal Roads:** Gravel/dirt. **RV Service:** No. **Market:** 12 mi. to Estes Park. **Restaurant:** 2 mi. to Allenspark. **General Store:** No. **Vending:** No. **Swimming:** No. **Playground:** Yes. **Other:** Amphitheater, 1 free picnic site. **Activities:** Fishing, hiking, mountain climbing, cross-country skiing. **Nearby Attractions:** Rocky Mountain National Park, Blackhawk, Central City Casinos. **Additional Information:** Thousand Trails Management, (303) 258-3610.

Restrictions

Pets: On leash, cleaned up after. **Fires:** In fire pits. **Alcoholic Beverages:** At sites. **Vehicle Maximum Length:** None.

To Get There

From the junction of Hwy. 72 and Hwy. 7, turn north onto Hwy. 7 and go 5.6 mi. Turn left at the sign into the entrance, then take the immediate left to go to the fee station.

ANTONITO

Josey's Mogote Meadow

34127 Hwy. 17, Antonito 81120. T: (719) 376-5774.

RV ★★★★ Tent ★★★★

Beauty: ★★★★	Site Privacy: ★★★★
Spaciousness: ★★★★	Quiet: ★★★★
Security: ★★★★	Cleanliness: ★★★★★
Insect Control: ★★★	Facilities: ★★★

This park consists of a large field that can take any-sized rig (except for sites 8–16, which are restricted to 55 feet in length). 40-feet wide sites are in a rural location with trees on all sides. (Some houses to the north belie the proximity to human habitation, but do not damage the scenery overly.) End site 27 is set slightly apart from the others, and has a large open space to the west. Sites 1–7 are situated along the entrance, and therefore receive more traffic than other sites. The laundry facility is slightly cramped and hot (it shares the building with a furnace and has no windows). The men's and women's rest rooms are separated—the men's being out in the middle of the park and the women's being in the same building as the laundry facility. These facilities are quite clean and comfortable. This is a fine campground in a great location.

BASICS

Operated By: Bob & Anne Josey. **Open:** May 1–Oct. 20. **Site Assignment:** Flexible depending on fullness; no reservations. **Registration:** In office. (Late arrivals select an available site & pay in the morning.) **Fee:** $16, tax (no credit cards, but checks). **Parking:** At site.

FACILITIES

Number of RV Sites: 45. **Number of Tent-Only Sites:** 0. **Hookups:** Water, sewer, electric (30, 50 amps). **Each Site:** Most have cement slab & large cottonwood. **Dump Station:** No (sewer at all sites). **Laundry:** Yes. **Pay Phone:** Yes. **Rest Rooms and Showers:** Yes. **Fuel:** No. **Propane:** Yes. **Internal Roads:** Gravel. **RV Service:** No. **Market:** 5 mi. to Antonito. **Restaurant:** 5 mi. to Antonito. **General Store:** Yes. **Vending:** No. **Swimming:** No. **Playground:** Yes. **Other:** Cabins, meeting hall. **Activities:** Fishing, volleyball, horseshoes, ping pong. **Nearby Attractions:** Scenic Byway, Cumbres & Toltect Scenic Railroad. **Additional Information:** Antonito Tourist Information Center & Chamber of Commerce, (719) 376-5441.

RESTRICTIONS

Pets: On leash, cleaned up after. **Fires:** No fires. **Alcoholic Beverages:** At sites. **Vehicle Maximum Length:** None.

TO GET THERE

From the junction of Hwy. 285 and Hwy. 17, go 4.8 mi. southwest on Hwy. 17. Turn right at the sign into the entrance. The office is immediately on the left.

ARBOLES

Pinon Park Campground and RV Resort

19 Lazy Ln., Arboles 81121. T: (970) 883-3636.

RV ★★★★ Tent ★★★★

Beauty: ★★★★
Site Privacy: ★★★★
Spaciousness: ★★★
Quiet: ★★★★
Security: ★★★★
Cleanliness: ★★★★★
Insect Control: ★★★
Facilities: ★★★★

This campground has just completed some renovations, and is therefore absolutely immaculate. The brand-new individual rest rooms are clean, spacious, and extremely comfortable, as is the new laundry facility. Anyone who frets over questionable rest rooms may want to stay an extra few days to luxuriate in the clean and comfortable facilities. The park itself is in a wilderness setting, not too far (0.5 miles) from Navajo State Park, which offers lake recreation. Both back-ins and pull-throughs are grassy but open sites 14–26 offer no shade at all, making them slightly less attractive. (There is not a lot of shade to begin with.) Tenters, on the other hand, will delight in the trees offered for the tenting area. All tent sites have water and a grill, and the sites are a mix of grass and dirt. Campers of either stripe (RV or tent) will be happy to stay in this park, which offers great views of the reservoir to the east. The RV experience would, however, be improved with the addition of more shade trees.

BASICS

Operated By: Nannette Colaizzy. **Open:** Apr.–Nov. **Site Assignment:** Assigned upon registration; flexible, depending on site availability. Credit card required for reservation; cancellation fees are $5 w/ 14-days notice & 50% of deposit within less than 14 days notice. **Registration:** In office. (Late arrivals use drop box.) **Fee:** RV $18.50 (full hookups), $14.50 (water, electric), tent $12 (V, MC, D). **Parking:** At site.

FACILITIES

Number of RV Sites: 35. **Number of Tent-Only Sites:** 30. **Hookups:** Water, sewer, electric (30, 50 amps). **Each Site:** Picnic table, grill. **Dump Station:** Yes. **Laundry:** Yes. **Pay Phone:** Yes. **Rest Rooms and Showers:** Yes. **Fuel:** No. **Propane:** No. **Internal Roads:** Primitive. **RV Service:** No. **Market:** 0.25 mi. to Arboles. **Restaurant:** 0.25 mi. to Arboles. **General Store:** Yes. **Vending:** Yes. **Swimming:** Reservoir. **Playground:** Yes. **Other:** RV rentals, pavillion, dog walk area, storage. **Activities:** 6 organized parties in summer. **Nearby Attractions:** San Juan National Forest, Vallecito Reservoir, Florida River, Mesa Verde National Park. **Additional Information:** Durango Chamber of Commerce, (800) 525-8855.

RESTRICTIONS

Pets: On leash, cleaned up after. **Fires:** Community

fire pit only. **Alcoholic Beverages:** At sites. **Vehicle Maximum Length:** 40 ft.

TO GET THERE

From Hwy. 151 in town, go 0.2 mi. north of Navajo State Park—look for the sign on the east side. Turn east into the driveway, then, at the T intersection, take the 2nd left into the campground. The office is the brown building ahead and to the right.

ASPEN

Aspen-Basalt Campground

Box 880 Aspen Hwy. 82, Aspen-Basalt Campground 81621. T: (800) KMP-ASPEN or (970) 927-3405; abc@soperis.net.

RV ★★★★ Tent n/a

Beauty: ★★★★ Site Privacy: ★★★★
Spaciousness: ★★★★ Quiet: ★★★
Security: ★★★★ Cleanliness: ★★★★★
Insect Control: ★★★★ Facilities: ★★★★★

With red hills to the southwest, forested hills to the east, south, and west, and loads of trees in and around the park, this campground is a comfortable location for an overnight or extended stay. Each site has at least one shade tree and a section of fence for increased privacy. Sites 1–6 are small (30-foot) back-ins and have no hookups. Sites 54–61, right next to these sites, are even smaller (25 feet in length), but have larger fences and are located in a beautiful, shaded corner. These are by far the most attractive sites, but very small. Sites 8–27 and 37–53 are 60-foot pull-throughs laid out in two rows. There are mobile homes located to the east of the row containing sites 8–27. Sites 28–36 to the south and 64–90 to the north (by the entrance) are reserved for monthly guests. These are 45-foot back-ins that back to trees and the road (in both areas). The rest rooms and showers are very clean, and the laundry is big and clean. This is an extremely pleasant destination located in a wonderful area.

BASICS

Operated By: Rich & Bonnie Nichols. **Open:** All year. **Site Assignment:** Assigned upon registration. Credit card required for reservation; 24-hours cancellation policy. **Registration:** In office. (Late arrivals use drop box.) **Fee:** $30 (full), $26 (water, electric, cable), $23 (no hookups) (checks, V, MC). **Parking:** At site.

FACILITIES

Number of RV Sites: 75. **Number of Tent-Only Sites:** 0. **Hookups:** Water, sewer, electric (20, 30, 50 amps), cable. **Each Site:** Picnic table. **Dump Station:** Yes. **Laundry:** Yes. **Pay Phone:** Yes. **Rest Rooms and Showers:** Yes. **Fuel:** No. **Propane:** Yes. **Internal Roads:** Gravel. **RV Service:** On-call. **Market:** 1 mi. north. **Restaurant:** 1 mi. north. **General Store:** Yes. **Vending:** Yes. **Swimming:** Pool & hot tub. **Playground:** Yes. **Other:** Dataport, game room. **Activities:** Movies, skiing, ATV riding, fishing, golfing, hunting, mountain biking, rafting, horseback riding, swimming, hiking. **Nearby Attractions:** Roaring Fork River, Aspen, golf courses. **Additional Information:** Aspen Chamber of Commerce, (970) 925-1940.

RESTRICTIONS

Pets: On leash, cleaned up after; no more than 2 pets. **Fires:** In grills. **Alcoholic Beverages:** At sites. **Vehicle Maximum Length:** None. **Other:** No smoking in buildings.

TO GET THERE

From the junction of Hwy. 133 and Hwy. 82, turn southeast onto Hwy. 82 and go 8.8 mi. Turn right, then take the immediate left and go straight into the campground.

BATTLEMENT MESA

Battlement Mesa RV Park

0095 Eldora Dr., P.O. Box 6000, Battlement Mesa 81635. T: (888) 828-0681 or (970) 285-7023 or (970) 285-9740; F: (970) 285-9721.

RV ★★★★ Tent ★★

Beauty: ★★★★ Site Privacy: ★★★
Spaciousness: ★★★ Quiet: ★★★★★
Security: ★★★★ Cleanliness: ★★★★★
Insect Control: ★★★★ Facilities: ★★★

This campground offers wonderous views of Battlement Mesa and other volcano-like peaks from any site. The location is very rural, and sites are level, grassy, and large. Super-long (70-foot) forked pull-throughs share a common entrance, but angle so that privacy is maximized given the site arrangment. Site 106 is next to a residence, and 139 and 144 are adjacent to electrical hardware, making these the least desirable sites. Sites 133, 145 have superior grass, bushes, and views, making these two highly desirable. Other coveted sites include odd numbers 101–109, which back to a dried river bed and forested hills and therefore receive less traffic and noise. The rest rooms and showers are very clean and modern, and Mr. Gibson is extremely affable, making the RV experience quite pleasant. However, tenters are at the mercy of the high winds or the occasional rainstorm, as there is absolutely no coverage to protect a tent. RVers should definitely check out this park, but tenters should consider moving on to Rifel, if possible.

Basics

Operated By: Charles Gibson. **Open:** All year. **Site Assignment:** Assigned upon registration; verbal reservations OK. **Registration:** In office. (Late arrivals go to 86 Partachute Way.) **Fee:** RV $22, tent $9.36 (checks, V, MC, AE, D, CB, DC). **Parking:** At site.

Facilities

Number of RV Sites: 135. **Number of Tent-Only Sites:** 12. **Hookups:** Water, sewer, electric (30, 50 amps), cable. **Each Site:** Picnic table. **Dump Station:** Yes. **Laundry:** Yes. **Pay Phone:** Yes. **Rest Rooms and Showers:** Yes. **Fuel:** No. **Propane:** Yes. **Internal Roads:** Paved. **RV Service:** No. **Market:** 2.5 mi. into Battlement Mesa. **Restaurant:** 2.5 mi. into Battlement Mesa. **General Store:** No. **Vending:** No. **Swimming:** No. **Playground:** No. **Other:** Dataport, dog walk, rec center (2.5 mi. away; free w/ park receipt). **Activities:** Skiing, fishing, swimming, golf, biking, horseshoes, tennis. **Nearby Attractions:** Aspen, Powederhorn, Vail, Grand Mesa, natural hot springs. **Additional Information:** Rifle Visitor Information Center, (970) 625-2085.

Restrictions

Pets: On 6-ft. leash, cleaned up after. **Fires:** Charcoal in grills. **Alcoholic Beverages:** At sites. **Vehicle Maximum Length:** None. **Other:** Call if late, no motorcycles or ATVs.

To Get There

From Hwy. I-70, take Exit 75, turn south, and go 0.75 mi. Turn right onto West Battlement Parkway, drive 1.5 mi., then turn right onto Stone Quarry Rd. Drive 2 mi., then turn right onto Thunderberg Trail. Take the 2nd left and keep straight to get to the office.

BRECKENRIDGE
Tiger Run RV Resort

85 Tiger Run Rd., Breckenridge 80424. T: (970) 453-9690; F: (970) 453-6782; www.tigerrunresort.com.

RV ★★★★★ Tent n/a

Beauty: ★★★★★ Site Privacy: ★★★★★
Spaciousness: ★★★★★ Quiet: ★★★★★
Security: ★★★★★ Cleanliness: ★★★★★
Insect Control: ★★★★★ Facilities: ★★★★★

The manager here calls this resort "its own little town," and this is not an exaggeration. With roughly 400 sites (70% of which are available to overnighters), tennis courts, indoor swimming pools, a recreation building with TV rooms and pool tables, laundry facilities, double-wide parking spaces, and chalet-style cabins on nearly each RV site, as well as incredible landscaping (lawns, trees, and brick walks), this resort feels more like a quiet suburban neighborhood than an overnight RV park. RVers who wish to use this resort as a travel park (as opposed to buying property) should speak to the manager about which sites are available, as some are privately owned or up for sale. Sites 122–129 and 147–151 are closest to the lake, while 1–7, 129–147, 204–243, and 345–367 are riverside sites. For those who like proximity to the facilities, sites 16–39 and 275–291 are closest to the recreation building. This is a top-notch RV park that deserves the title resort.

Basics

Operated By: The Whitt family. **Open:** All year. **Site Assignment:** Assigned upon registration Credit card required for reservation; 48-hours cancellation policy. **Registration:** In office 24 hours (Dial *9). **Fee:** RV $29–39 (checks, V, MC, AE, D, DC, CB; 10% cash discount). **Parking:** At site.

Facilities

Number of RV Sites: 358. **Number of Tent-Only Sites:** 0. **Hookups:** Water, sewer, electric (30, 50 amps), cable. **Each Site:** Picnic table, full-service cabin. **Dump Station:** No (sewer at all sites). **Laundry:** Yes. **Pay Phone:** Yes. **Rest Rooms and Showers:** Yes. **Fuel:** No. **Propane:** Yes. **Internal Roads:** Paved. **RV Service:** No. **Market:** 3.5 mi. to Breckenridge. **Restaurant:** 3.5 mi. to Breckenridge. **General Store:** Yes. **Vending:** Yes. **Swimming:** Pool & hot tub. **Playground:** Yes. **Other:** Cabins, dataport, TV room, pool table, free bus service, lake. **Activities:** Rafting, fishing, ping pong, biking, Wed. night free wine & cheese, Fri. night smores, live entertainment on weekends, tennis, rock climbing, GPS orienteering, teambuilding activities. **Nearby Attractions:** 14,000-ft.-plus mountains, Summit County. **Additional Information:** Breckenridge Resort Chamber, (970) 453-5579.

RESTRICTIONS

Pets: On leash, cleaned up after. **Fires:** In grills. **Alcoholic Beverages:** At sites. **Vehicle Maximum Length:** None. **Other:** No pop-ups or tents.

TO GET THERE

From Hwy. I-70 Exit 203, turn south onto Hwy. 9 and go 6.3 mi. Turn left at the sign onto the entrance (past MM 91) and turn left into the office complex.

BRUSH
Memorial Park

Mayor of Brush, P.O. Box 363, Brush 80723. T: (970) 842-5001; F: (970) 842-5909; www.brushcolo.com.

RV ★★★ Tent ★★★

Beauty: ★★★	Site Privacy: ★★★★
Spaciousness: ★★★★	Quiet: ★★★
Security: ★★★	Cleanliness: ★★★
Insect Control: ★★★★	Facilities: ★★★

A city park set in an urban environment with industrial and commercial lots around the perimeter, this park tries its best to present a comfortable stay to Brush visitors. Grassy areas and a cute schoolhouse definitely add to the attractiveness of the park, and visitors here should feel rather comfortable. (Especially knowing that their first night is free!) The sites are somewhat undistinguished, and can number more than the electrical boxes that dot the parking area, depending on how people park. There are rows of seemingly just 3–6 sites each, but the city employees who tend to the RV park insist that there are 50 possible sites. The south side of the park is conducive to pull-alongside sites, while the north is better suited to back-ins. The south side is slightly more industrial, and therefore less visibly attractive. All sites are located on the gravel interior road and do not have a picnic area in their immediate vicinity. Tenters can camp on the lush grass or the crushed gravel tent pads located at the entrance to the RV park. The facilities are city park–clean, and the shower is enormous. They are all open, lacking curtains or dividers of any kind. Overall, this is a rather comfortable city park

BASICS

Operated By: City of Brush. **Open:** All year. **Site Assignment:** First come, first served; no reservations. **Registration:** At pay station. **Fee:** first night free; $10, night thereafter (checks). **Parking:** At site.

FACILITIES

Number of RV Sites: 50. **Number of Tent-Only Sites:** Undesignated sites. **Hookups:** Electric (20, 30, 50 amps). **Each Site:** Picnic table, grill (tent pads at tent sites). **Dump Station:** Yes. **Laundry:** No. **Pay Phone:** Yes. **Rest Rooms and Showers:** Yes. **Fuel:** No. **Propane:** No. **Internal Roads:** Gravel. **RV Service:** No. **Market:** 0.5 mi. northwest. **Restaurant:** 0.5 mi. north. **General Store:** No. **Vending:** No. **Swimming:** Pool. **Playground:** Yes. **Other:** Covered picnic area, schoolhouse museum. **Activities:** Basketball, volleyball, baseball, swimming. **Nearby Attractions:** Brush Rodeo (July 1–4), buildings on National Historic Registry. **Additional Information:** Brush Chamber of Commerce, (970) 842-2666.

RESTRICTIONS

Pets: On leash, cleaned up after. **Fires:** In grills. **Alcoholic Beverages:** Beer only. **Vehicle Maximum Length:** None.

TO GET THERE

From Hwy. I-76 (Exit 90A), turn south onto Hwy. 1 and go 0.75 mi. Turn right onto Hwy. 34, then take the first left onto Clayton. Go 0.4 mi. Turn right at the sign into the entrance.

BUENA VISTA
Arkansas River Rim Campground and RV Park

33198 Hwy. 24 North, Buena Vista 81211. T: (719) 395-8883; www.coloradodirectory.com/arkansasriverrimcamp; www.arkriverrim@chaffee.net.

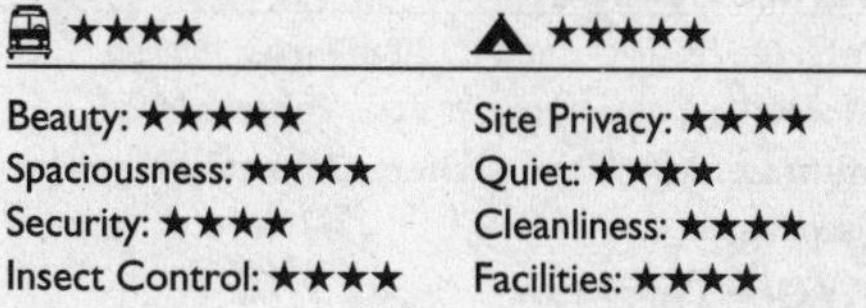

RV ★★★★ Tent ★★★★★

Beauty: ★★★★★	Site Privacy: ★★★★
Spaciousness: ★★★★	Quiet: ★★★★
Security: ★★★★	Cleanliness: ★★★★
Insect Control: ★★★★	Facilities: ★★★★

Located in a beautiful valley next to the Arkansas River, this campground offers comfortable sites with beautiful mountain views to the northeast. Sites 1–15 are 75-foot pull-throughs, and 16–24 are 40-foot back-ins located in the north part of the campground. Behind these sites are woods, and beyond those, distant mountains. Sites 25–31 are smaller back-ins (30-foot), while 28–32 are slightly larger (40-foot). Sites 30–32 back to a residence. Sites 33–36 are 60-foot pull-throughs, and 37 and 38, in the same row, are 42-foot pull-throughs. All sites are mostly open, although there is some shade throughout the park. Tent sites are located at the top of the embankment above the Arkansas River. These sites are wooded and very attractive in their natural state. The rest rooms and showers are located in a mobile home. The facilities aren't elaborate, but are comfortably clean. This is a very attractive campground in a stunning part of state—a worthwhile stop in a highly recommended area.

Basics

Operated By: Dale & Debbie Jantz. **Open:** All year. **Site Assignment:** Flexible, depending on site availability; reservations highly recommended in summer. Credit card required for reservation; call to cancel. **Registration:** In office. (Late arrivals select an available site & pay in the morning.) **Fee:** RV $20 (full), tent $15 (checks, V, MC, & D). **Parking:** At site.

Facilities

Number of RV Sites: 36. **Number of Tent-Only Sites:** 8. **Hookups:** Water, sewer, electric (30, 50 amps). **Each Site:** Picnic table. **Dump Station:** Yes. **Laundry:** Yes. **Pay Phone:** Yes. **Rest Rooms and Showers:** Yes. **Fuel:** No. **Propane:** No. **Internal Roads:** Gravel. **RV Service:** No. **Market:** 4.5 mi. south. **Restaurant:** 4 mi. south. **General Store:** Yes. **Vending:** No. **Swimming:** No. **Playground:** No. **Other:** Ice, fishing licenses. **Activities:** Fishing, gold panning, hiking, mountain climbing. **Nearby Attractions:** Classic auto show (July), ghost towns. **Additional Information:** Buena Vista Chamber of Commerce, (719) 395-6612.

Restrictions

Pets: On leash, cleaned up after. **Fires:** In grills. **Alcoholic Beverages:** At sites. **Vehicle Maximum Length:** None. **Other:** Children and groups discouraged.

To Get There

From the junction of Hwy. 285 and Hwy. 24, turn north onto Hwy. 24 and go 7 mi. Turn right at the sign into the entrance. The office is to the right.

BUFFALO CREEK
Kelsey Campground

P.O. Box 636, Woodland Park 80866. T: (800) 416-6992 or (877) 444-6777; www.fs.fed.us/r2/psicc/spl.

RV ★★★ Tent ★★★★

Beauty: ★★★★★	Site Privacy: ★★★★
Spaciousness: ★★★★	Quiet: ★★★★
Security: ★★★★	Cleanliness: ★★★★
Insect Control: ★★★★	Facilities: ★

Of the many campgrounds in the area, this is perhaps the best for RVers, as the sites are paved. Having said that, of course, there are no hookups, and some of the sites are quite severely sloped. A refined statement might read: this is the area's best campground for adventurous RVers in small rigs. Some of the sites (of which all are back-ins) are truly small: 1 is the smallest at 35 feet, 5 is 40 feet, and most of the rest range from 51 to 60 feet. Site 13 is by far the largest at 66 feet. Sites 8 and 9 are quite a bit less shaded than the rest of the sites. Sites 10, 11, and 13 are also somewhat unshaded, and are quite noticeably sloped. The best bets for RVers are 13 (for its size), 12 (level and close to the rest room), or one of the smaller sites 1–5. Tenters need not worry as much about the slope, as there is plenty of level ground to pitch a tent. In fact, this campground is practically a tenter's paradise, and the scenery is absolutely unbeatable. More adventurous RVers can also enjoy a foray into the wild at this campground.

Basics

Operated By: US Forest Service. **Open:** May 24–Sept. 1 (or later). **Site Assignment:** First come, first served. Credit card required for reservation; reservations can be made 4–240 days in advance. $8.65 reservation fee, $10 cancellation fee; cancellations within 3 days pay first night, no-shows pay $20 fee. (2-nights min. stay on weekends, 3-nights on holidays.) **Registration:** At pay station. **Fee:** $13. (checks). **Parking:** At site.

Facilities

Number of RV Sites: 17. **Number of Tent-Only Sites:** 0. **Hookups:** None. **Each Site:** Picnic table, grill. **Dump Station:** No. **Laundry:** No. **Pay Phone:** No. **Rest Rooms and Showers:** Pit toilets; no shower. **Fuel:** No. **Propane:** No. **Internal Roads:** Gravel. **RV Service:** No. **Market:** 18 mi. to Conifer. **Restaurant:** 9 mi. to Pine. **General Store:** No. **Vending:** No. **Swimming:** No. **Playground:** No. **Activities:** Hiking, mountain biking, fishing. **Nearby Attractions:** Arapaho National Forest. **Additional Information:** South Platte Peak Ranger District: (303) 275-5610.

RESTRICTIONS

Pets: On leash, cleaned up after. **Fires:** In grills. **Alcoholic Beverages:** At sites. **Vehicle Maximum Length:** None. **Other:** $4 per day park pass;$5 dollar 2nd vehicle fee. (2-nights min. stay on weekends, 3-nights on holidays.)

TO GET THERE

From the junction of Hwy. 285 and Hwy. 126, turn southeast onto Hwy. 126 and go 19.9 mi. (7.2 mi. from National Forest Service Buffalo Creek Work Center). Turn right at the sign into the entrance.

BURLINGTON

Bonny Lake State Park Campground

30010 Rd. 3, Idalia 80735. T: (800) 678-CAMP or (970) 354-7306; www.coloradoparks.org; bonny@plains.net.

RV: ★★★★	Tent: ★★★★
Beauty: ★★★★★	Site Privacy: ★★★★
Spaciousness: ★★★★	Quiet: ★★★★★
Security: ★★★	Cleanliness: ★★★★★
Insect Control: ★★★	Facilities: ★★★★

The best time to go to this campground, strung out along the perimeter of Lake Bonny, is in later spring or summer, when full facilities are provided and it's warm enough to tempt you into the water. Variety is the name of the game here: laid out in a series of loops, the campground offers sites both lakeside and further up the banks in the forest. (All sites are within a quarter mile of the lake.) There are both pull-throughs (average length 50 feet) and back-ins (average length 35 feet), all of which are grassy and mostly level. Tents or RVs can occupy any sites, although you may see primitive sites (without hookups) referred to as "tent sites". This forested campground has a secluded, wilderness feel to it, and is a fun destination for families who enjoy lake recreation. Campers should remember to bring along enough provisions for their stay, however, as the campground is a fair hike (25 miles) from the nearest full services. The marina inside the campground can, however, provide limited groceries, propane, and gasoline in proper containers.

BASICS

Operated By: Colorado State Parks. **Open:** All year (limitied services Oct.–mid-Apr.). **Site Assignment:** First come, first served. Reservations recommended in summer; credit card required. Cancellation fees are $12 w/ 14-days notice & $7 plus one night w/ less than 14 days notice. **Registration:** Check information board for reserved sites, select available campsite, then return to self-pay station to pay fee (in drop slot). **Fee:** Electric: $14, primitive: $10, plus $4 day pass (cash only for pay station). **Parking:** At site, some parking in lots.

FACILITIES

Number of RV Sites: 100. **Number of Tent-Only Sites:** 90. **Hookups:** Electric (30, 50 amps). **Each Site:** Picnic table, grill. **Dump Station:** Yes. **Laundry:** No. **Pay Phone:** Yes. **Rest Rooms and Showers:** Pit toilets; no shower. **Fuel:** Yes (marina). **Propane:** Yes (marina). **Internal Roads:** Paved/dirt. **RV Service:** No. **Market:** 25 mi. to Burlington. **Restaurant:** 25 mi. to Burlington. **General Store:** Marina. **Vending:** Yes. **Swimming:** Lake. **Playground:** No. **Other:** Boat ramp, amphitheater. **Activities:** Swimming, boating, fishing, ranger presentations. **Nearby Attractions:** Bonny Lake, wildlife viewing areas. **Additional Information:** Burlington Chamber of Commerce, (719) 346-8070.

RESTRICTIONS

Pets: On 6-ft. leash, cleaned up after. **Fires:** In fire pits. **Alcoholic Beverages:** Beer only. **Vehicle Maximum Length:** None. **Other:** Vehicle pass required.

TO GET THERE

From I-70, take Exit 437, then turn north onto Hwy. 385 and go 22 mi. Turn right at the sign (0.7 mi. after mile marker 209) onto CR-2, and follow the road 3.7 mi. to the park entrance. (You can also take CR-3, 1 mi. further north on Hwy. 385, to go directly to the north side of the lake.)

CALHAN

Cadillac Jack's Campground

1001 5th St., Calhan 80808. T: (719) 347-2000; F: (719) 347-2760.

RV ★★★ Tent ★★★

Beauty: ★★★ Site Privacy: ★★★
Spaciousness: ★★★ Quiet: ★★★
Security: ★★★★ Cleanliness: ★★★★
Insect Control: ★★★★ Facilities: ★★

Like most of eastern side of Colorado, this campground is largely barren and unshaded. It is, however, a comfortable place to camp, that offers several pull-throughs (1–6) able to accommodate a rig of any size, including a tow. Sites 7–16 (mostly unnumbered) are 30-foot back-ins that back to a row of large shrubs. These are the most shaded sites in the campground, but quite small. Larger sites (but not as large as 1–6) are laid out in a row along the northern edge of the campground. These sites are 33-foot (17–25) and 42-foot (26–37) pull-throughs that offer full hookups. Sites 15 and 16 deserve warning, as they are quite close to the highway that passes by the campground. The tent area is an open grassy space near the storage units in the southern part of the campground. Tenters will not enjoy this campground as much as self-contained RVs with shower and toilet, as there are no facilities for campers to use.

Basics

Operated By: Tom Covington. **Open:** All year. **Site Assignment:** First come, first served; no reservations. **Registration:** In A-frame kiosk in campground. **Fee:** RV $22 (full), $20 (water, electric), tent $10 (checks). **Parking:** At site, extra parking for tows.

Facilities

Number of RV Sites: 42. **Number of Tent-Only Sites:** 5. **Hookups:** Water, sewer, electric (30, 50 amps). **Dump Station:** No. **Laundry:** 1 block away. **Pay Phone:** Yes. **Rest Rooms and Showers:** No. **Fuel:** Next door. **Propane:** Across street. **Internal Roads:** Gravel. **RV Service:** No. **Market:** 20 mi. west. **Restaurant:** Across street. **General Store:** Next door. **Vending:** No. **Swimming:** No. **Playground:** No. **Other:** Covered pavilion, antique store, barber shop, bowling alley. **Activities:** Bowling, antique shopping. **Nearby Attractions:** Paint Mines, El Paso County Fair (late July), Colorado Springs. **Additional Information:** Colorado Springs Chamber of Commerce, (719) 635-1551.

Restrictions

Pets: On leash, cleaned up after. **Fires:** In grills. **Alcoholic Beverages:** At sites. **Vehicle Maximum Length:** None.

To Get There

From Hwy. 24, 0.75 mi. west of the town center on the north side of the street. (Look for the antique shop.)

CANON CITY

RV Campground

3120 East Main, Canon City 81212. T: (719) 275-4576.

RV ★★★ Tent ★★

Beauty: ★★★ Site Privacy: ★★★
Spaciousness: ★★★ Quiet: ★★
Security: ★★★★ Cleanliness: ★★★
Insect Control: ★★★★ Facilities: ★★

This is one of the few RV campgrounds in the area that is *not* a tacky theme park exploiting the Royal Gorge. Hwy. 50 is immediately to the north of this campground, and sites 1–10 are less desirable due to their proximity to this road. The sites to the south and east (11–16, 28–31, 36, and 40–48) have grass instead of gravel, and are therefore better picks. Best of these are 40–48, which are well away from the highway, grassy, and back to an open field to the south. Tent sites, along the interior road, are not very long (12-foot) but wide (45-foot). All tent sites but 50 have a tree, and all are right up against the fence along the border of the park. They are grassy but with bare patches. The rest rooms are clean but oldish, and the showers are not built-in but rather add-on units. All in all, this park is a decent stop for RVers, and not as cheesy as a lot of area parks.

Basics

Operated By: John & Conney Palmer. **Open:** All year. **Site Assignment:** Assigned upon registration. Check required for reservation; 24-hours cancellation policy. **Registration:** In office. (Late arrivals select an available site & pay in the morning.) **Fee:** RV $18.25 (full), tent $15 (checks, no credits cards). **Parking:** At site.

FACILITIES

Number of RV Sites: 47. **Number of Tent-Only Sites:** 9. **Hookups:** Water, sewer, electric (20, 30 amps). **Dump Station:** Yes. **Laundry:** No. **Pay Phone:** Yes. **Rest Rooms and Showers:** Yes. **Fuel:** No. **Propane:** No. **Internal Roads:** Dirt. **RV Service:** No. **Market:** Across street. **Restaurant:** Across street. **General Store:** No. **Vending:** Yes. **Swimming:** No. **Playground:** No. **Other:** Close to shopping. **Activities:** Rafting. **Nearby Attractions:** Rodeos in town, Royal Gorge, Museum of Colorado Prisons. **Additional Information:** Greater Canon City Chamber of Commerce, (800) 876-7922, (719) 275-2331.

RESTRICTIONS

Pets: On leash, cleaned up after. **Fires:** No fires. **Alcoholic Beverages:** At sites. **Vehicle Maximum Length:** 40 ft.

TO GET THERE

From the junction of Hwy. 115 and Hwy. 50, go 2.3 mi. east on Hwy. 50 (Royal Gorge Blvd. in town). Turn right at the Dozier St. light, and take the immediate left. Turn right at the sign and a then quick left into the campground.

CARBONDALE

BRB Crystal River Resort

7202 Hwy. 133, Carbondale 81623. T: (800) 963-2341 or (970) 963-2341; www.cabinscolorado.com; brbresort@cs.com.

RV ★★★★ Tent ★★★★

Beauty: ★★★★	Site Privacy: ★★★★
Spaciousness: ★★★	Quiet: ★★★★
Security: ★★★★	Cleanliness: ★★★★
Insect Control: ★★★	Facilities: ★★

This campground bills itself as the "ultimate resort," which isn't far from the truth. It is surrounded on three sides by towering hills and a mountain, and offers a relaxing rustic experience and wonderful views from any site. Sites K–O and 24–31, on the river's edge, are smaller (21-foot) back-ins for pop-ups. Site 25 looks a little cramped, but 26 and N have nice trees and grass. Sites A and B have tall trees, nice grass, and easy access. Tent sites are inside a loop, with excellent trees and wild grass (7–9, right off the highway, are less desirable). Sites E-J and V (all back-ins; there are no pull-throughs in the park) are a little too open and lacking in shade, are situated by the highway, and have more gravel than grass. The rest room and shower facility is a wooden structure that is rustic but cozy—probably chilly on a cold fall day but great in summer. A sign warns campers to keep the doors closed "due to bears". There is rather intimate space between the showers, but on the whole, the facility—as well as the park itself—is quite comfortable.

BASICS

Operated By: Omar Sultan. **Open:** Memorial Day–Oct. 31. **Site Assignment:** Flexible depending on availability. Credit card or check required for reservation; 24-hours cancellation policy. **Registration:** In office. (Late arrivals select an available site & pay in the morning.) **Fee:** RV $23, tent $15 (V, MC, D). **Parking:** At site.

FACILITIES

Number of RV Sites: 24. **Number of Tent-Only Sites:** 24. **Hookups:** Water, electric (30 amps). **Each Site:** Picnic table. **Dump Station:** Yes. **Laundry:** No. **Pay Phone:** Yes. **Rest Rooms and Showers:** Yes. **Fuel:** No. **Propane:** No. **Internal Roads:** Gravel. **RV Service:** No. **Market:** 5 mi. in Carbondale. **Restaurant:** 5 mi. in Carbondale. **General Store:** Yes. **Vending:** No. **Swimming:** Pool. **Playground:** Yes. **Other:** River, cabins. **Activities:** Volleyball, basketball, horseshoes, skiing, fishing, hunting. **Nearby Attractions:** McClure Pass, Hanging Lake. **Additional Information:** Glenwood Springs Chamber Resort Assoc.: (970) 945-6589.

RESTRICTIONS

Pets: On leash, cleaned up after. **Fires:** In fire pits. **Alcoholic Beverages:** At sites. **Vehicle Maximum Length:** None.

TO GET THERE

From the junction of Hwy. 82 and Hwy. 133, go 7 mi. south on Hwy. 133. The entrance is on the left, and the office to the right.

CASTLE ROCK
Castle Rock KOA

6527 South I-25, Castle Rock 80104. T: (800) KOA-3102 or (303) 681-3169; F: (303) 681-2592; www.koa.com.

RV ★★★★	Tent ★★★★
Beauty: ★★★★	Site Privacy: ★★★★★
Spaciousness: ★★★★★	Quiet: ★★★★
Security: ★★★★★	Cleanliness: ★★★★★
Insect Control: ★★★★	Facilities: ★★★★

A large campground with sites scattered over the side of a hill, this KOA offers extremely private sites separated from each other by large swaths of vegetation. Sites 1 and 2 are 75-foot pull-throughs right by the entrance. Sites 12, 14, 15, 17, and 19 are "pull-alongsides" that can accommodate 70 feet. Site 72 is an extra-long (100-foot) pull-through. Back-in sites in this area average 54 × 24 feet. Even sites 74–78 and 127 and 129 command a view to the northeast from the top of the hill, making these quite attarctive sites. Sites 85–89 are unshaded pull-throughs in the eastern section of the campground. Sites 174 and 175 have views of the volcano cones to the east. Sites 160–169 have approximately 45 feet of usable space (the rest has too much slope). Even 140–148 have views to the east, but are completely unshaded and are closest to the railroad tracks. Tent sites are mostly open and unshaded. These include walk-in sites T9–11 and sites T3–8, which are located on the side of the hill. This is quite an attractive campground with lots of vegetation. It is a very nice destination for both tenters and RVers.

Basics

Operated By: Private operator. **Open:** All year. **Site Assignment:** Assigned upon registration Credit card required for reservation; 24-hours cancellation policy. **Registration:** In office. (Late arrivals use drop box.) **Fee:** RV \$29.64 (full, 50 amps), \$26.62 (full, 30 amps), \$24.44 (water, electric), \$22.36 (electric), tent \$19.24 (checks, V, MC, D). **Parking:** At site.

Facilities

Number of RV Sites: 179. **Number of Tent-Only Sites:** 24. **Hookups:** Water, sewer, electric (30, 50 amps). **Each Site:** Picnic table, grill. **Dump Station:** Yes. **Laundry:** Yes. **Pay Phone:** Yes. **Rest Rooms and Showers:** Yes. **Fuel:** No. **Propane:** Yes. **Internal Roads:** Dirt. **RV Service:** No. **Market:** 8 mi. north. **Restaurant:** 8 mi. north. **General Store:** Yes. **Vending:** Yes. **Swimming:** Pool. **Playground:** Yes. **Other:** Snack bar, cabins, movie caboose, video games, dog walk. **Activities:** Shopping, swimming. **Nearby Attractions:** Castlewood Canyon State Park, outlet stores, Denver, Colorado Springs, Roxborough State Park. **Additional Information:** Castle Rock Chamber of Commerce, (303) 688-4597.

Restrictions

Pets: On leash, cleaned up after. **Fires:** In grills. **Alcoholic Beverages:** At sites. **Vehicle Maximum Length:** None. **Other:** No ATVs or motorcycles.

To Get There

From Hwy. I-25 (Exit 174), turn west onto Tomah Rd. and go across the railroad tacks. Take the first left into the campground parking lot.

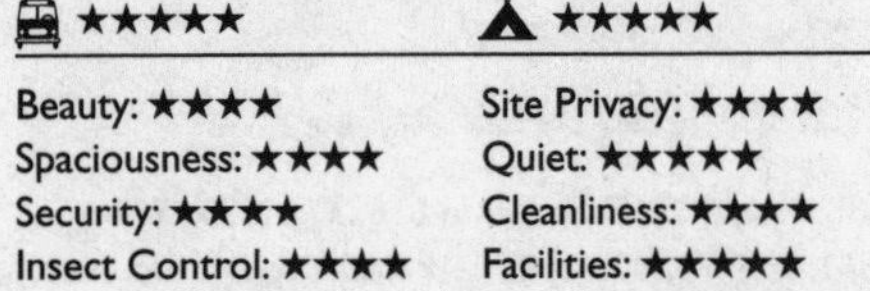

CEDAREDGE
Aspen Trails Campground and Resort

1997 Hwy. 65, Cedaredge 81413. T: (888) 856-1101 or (970) 856-6321.

RV ★★★★★	Tent ★★★★★
Beauty: ★★★★	Site Privacy: ★★★★
Spaciousness: ★★★★	Quiet: ★★★★★
Security: ★★★★	Cleanliness: ★★★★
Insect Control: ★★★★	Facilities: ★★★★★

This campground is beautifully landscaped with grass, trees lining the perimeter and dotting the park, and rocks demarking RV sites. (Sites 1–12 are clearly marked, but 13–22 as yet do not have numbers.) All pull-throughs are 72 × 28 feet. The RV site possibly numbered 13 (at any rate, the site southeast of 1) is closest to the road, although a fence does add some extra security. While there is no shade in the RV park, angling your vehicle can reduce direct sunlight dramatically—especially in conjunction with the use of an awning. The large tenting area to the west of the RV sites is wild and good: with lots of grass and tons of trees. Children should be careful of large rocks in the grass around the playground area near the tenting sites. The rest rooms have finely finished wood interiors with a Western theme. Showers share a partition and a drain, and the toilet stall doors are only 5 feet high—but otherwise, the facilities are quite comfortable. Located on a scenic byway, this campground is worth the drive up.

BASICS

Operated By: Dolly, Pat, & Tony Mercep. **Open:** Memorial Day–Nov 15. **Site Assignment:** Flexible depending on availability. Credit card required for reservation; 7-days cancellation policy, less one night's fee. **Registration:** In office. **Fee:** RV $19.50, tent $14 (V, MC, AE, D, checks). **Parking:** At site.

FACILITIES

Number of RV Sites: 22. **Number of Tent-Only Sites:** Undesignated sites. **Hookups:** Water, sewer, electric (30, 50 amps). **Each Site:** Picnic table, grill. **Dump Station:** Yes. **Laundry:** No. **Pay Phone:** Yes. **Rest Rooms and Showers:** Yes. **Fuel:** No. **Propane:** No. **Internal Roads:** Dirt/gravel. **RV Service:** No. **Market:** 2 mi. to Cedaredge. **Restaurant:** 2 mi. to Cedaredge. **General Store:** Yes. **Vending:** No. **Swimming:** No. **Playground:** Yes. **Other:** Ice cream & soda fountain, deli, cabins, pavillion, pet exercise area, groups welcome. **Activities:** Skiing, biking, hiking, fishing. **Nearby Attractions:** Grand Mesa, motorcycle rally (early Aug.). **Additional Information:** Delta Area Chamber of Commerce, (970) 874-8616.

RESTRICTIONS

Pets: On leash, cleaned up after; not allowed to chase deer. **Fires:** Depends on seasonal bans. **Alcoholic Beverages:** At sites. **Vehicle Maximum Length:** None.

TO GET THERE

From the Cedaredge town name signpost, go 2 mi. north. Turn west at the signs into the entrance.

CENTRAL CITY

Gambler's Edge RV Park

605 Lake Gulch Rd., Central City 80427. T: (877) 660-3465 or (303) 582-9345.

RV ★★★★★ | Tent n/a

Beauty: ★★★★★	Site Privacy: ★★★★
Spaciousness: ★★★★	Quiet: ★★★★★
Security: ★★★★★	Cleanliness: ★★★★★
Insect Control: ★★★★	Facilities: ★★★★

Still under construction, this campground did not offer all of the planned services at the time of review, but is already a very nice destination. Sites are uniform gravel back-ins 55 × 30 feet with exceptional landscaping. In addition to an attractive interior, this park benefits from stunning views to the east and northwest. Sites 1–10 back to a stone retaining wall and a beautiful view of Central City and the hills beyond. Sites 11–25 are laid out in two rows on the "island" inside the road that loops around the park. These are nice, but do not offer the views that most other sites enjoy. Sites 33–42 back to an open view to the east and are among the best sites in the park. While there are 80 sites planned for this park, work is still being done on about half. However, from the looks of the existing sites and facilities, this park promises to be a top-notch resort that is well worth a return trip.

BASICS

Operated By: Barb & Bob. **Open:** All year. **Site Assignment:** First come, first served; reservations recommended & preferred. Credit card required for reservation; 24-hours cancellation policy. **Registration:** In office. (Late arrivals come to office or use drop box). **Fee:** RV $28–30 (V, MC, D, checks). **Parking:** At site, next to huge parking lot.

FACILITIES

Number of RV Sites: 45. **Number of Tent-Only Sites:** 0. **Hookups:** Water, sewer, electric (30, 50 amps), telephone, dataport. **Dump Station:** No (sewer at all sites). **Laundry:** Yes. **Pay Phone:** Yes. **Rest Rooms and Showers:** Yes. **Fuel:** No. **Propane:** Yes. **Internal Roads:** Gravel. **RV Service:** No. **Market:** 8 mi. to Idaho Springs. **Restaurant:** 1 mi. to Central City. **General Store:** Yes. **Vending:** No. **Swimming:** No (hot tub). **Playground:** No. **Other:** Clubhouse. **Activities:** Rafting, hiking, mountain biking, skiing. **Nearby Attractions:** Ghost towns, Coors Brewery. **Additional Information:** Gilpin County Chamber of Commerce, (303) 582-5077.

RESTRICTIONS

Pets: On leash, cleaned up after. **Fires:** In grills. **Alcoholic Beverages:** At sites. **Vehicle Maximum Length:** None. **Other:** 1 vehicle only.

TO GET THERE

From I-70 (Exit 244), turn east onto Hwy. 6 and go 2.85 mi. Turn north onto Hwy. 119 and go 7.3 mi. Turn left onto Gregory St. and go 1 mi. Turn left onto Spring St. (turns into Hooper) and go 2 mi. Turn right onto Lake Gulch Rd. and go 0.15 mi. Turn left at the sign into the entrance.

CLARK

Steamboat Lake State Park

Box 750, Clark 80428. T: (800) 678-CAMP or (970) 879-7019 or (970) 879-3922; www.coloradoparks.org; steamboat.lake@state.co.us.

RV ★★★★ Tent ★★★★★

Beauty: ★★★★ Site Privacy: ★★★★
Spaciousness: ★★★★ Quiet: ★★★★★
Security: ★★★★ Cleanliness: ★★★★
Insect Control: ★★★★ Facilities: ★★★

This campground has forested campsites that include 60-foot back-ins and some 90-foot pull-throughs. (pull-throughs include 116, 118, 120, 121, 123, and 127.) Sites with electric hookups are limited to 116–165. All sites are laid out in loops, with the Baker Loop being slightly closer to the boat ramps and the swimming beach. Sites 131, 146, and 160 are all located at the end of roundabouts, and they are therefore more secluded than most others. Bridge Island is a separate section of the campground connected by the interior road. It contains sites 166–200, of which about half (181–200) are walk-in tent sites. The rest rooms and showers are large, clean, and comfortable. The showers cost 50 cents for three minutes. There are change machines in the rest rooms.

Basics

Operated By: Colorado State Parks. **Open:** All year. **Site Assignment:** First come, first served. Credit card required for reservation; 3-days cancellation policy. **Registration:** At pay station. **Fee:** RV $14 (electric), tent $10 (checks, no credits cards). **Parking:** At site.

Facilities

Number of RV Sites: 50. **Number of Tent-Only Sites:** 148. **Hookups:** Electric (20, 30, 50 amps). **Each Site:** Picnic table, grill, fire pit, tent pad. **Dump Station:** Yes (at Dutch Hill). **Laundry:** Yes (at Dutch Hill). **Pay Phone:** Yes (at Visitor Center). **Rest Rooms and Showers:** Yes (at Dutch Hill). **Fuel:** No. **Propane:** No. **Internal Roads:** Gravel. **RV Service:** No. **Market:** 26 mi. south. **Restaurant:** 26 mi. south. **General Store:** Marina. **Vending:** Yes. **Swimming:** Lake. **Playground:** No. **Other:** Boat ramp, fire wood, amphitheater, cabins, boat rentals, indoor picnic area. **Activities:** Fishing, boating, swimming, hiking. **Nearby Attractions:** Steamboat Springs. **Additional Information:** Steamboat Springs Chamber Resort Assoc., (970) 879-0880.

Restrictions

Pets: On leash, cleaned up after. **Fires:** In grills. **Alcoholic Beverages:** At sites. **Vehicle Maximum Length:** None. **Other:** $4 per vehicle for day-use fee.

To Get There

From the junction of Hwy. 40 and CR-129, turn north onto CR-129 and go 25 mi. to Visitor Center. Continue 0.9 mi. to first campground on the left.

COLORADO CITY

Pueblo South/Colorado City KOA

9040 I-25 South, Colorado City 81004. T: (800) 562-8646 or (719) 676-3376; www.koa.com; cocitykoa@juno.com.

RV ★★★★★ Tent ★★★★★

Beauty: ★★★★ Site Privacy: ★★★★
Spaciousness: ★★★★ Quiet: ★★★
Security: ★★★★★ Cleanliness: ★★★★
Insect Control: ★★★★ Facilities: ★★★★

This desert campground uses attractive indigenous plants and rocks in its landscaping, including at least one huge flowering cactus. RV sites are laid out in three rows, with tent sites occupying another distinct row. Row A, along the north side of the campground, has 60-foot back-ins that are mostly quite shady. (Sites 13 and 14 do not have shade trees.) Site A2 is next to the hot tub, which is convenient, but may attract more foot traffic. Site A9 has an extra large grassy site (27-foot wide), which makes it more desirable. Site A14, on the other hand, has "views" of a gas station and residences and backs to a mobile home, making it the least desirable site in the campground. Row B has grassy pull-throughs 60 × 18 feet. Sites B7–10 are especially shaded. Site B1 has a giant overhanging tree, and is closest to the rest rooms. Sites in Row C have views of an open field to the east, which is more attractive than, for example, A14's view. These sites are all grassy, and C7–10 are especially shaded. Site C16 has an electric pole and wires that encroach on its space. Tent sites are located along the south side of the campground. These sites have beautiful grass and loads of trees. There are also some very nice views of hills to the southwest. (Unfortunately, there is RV storage to the southeast.) Each of these spacious sites is separated by shrubs. The rest rooms are very nicely decorated, but had soap residue on the shower floors. Otherwise, the rest rooms were spotless. This is a very attractive campground that will appeal to most RV campers, and has excellent facilities for tenters.

Basics

Operated By: Tim & Elena Johnson. **Open:** All year. **Site Assignment:** Assigned upon registration Credit card required for reservation; 24-hours cancellation policy. **Registration:** In office. (Late arrivals use drop box.) **Fee:** RV $26, tent $18 (V, MC, D, checks). **Parking:** At site.

Facilities

Number of RV Sites: 67. **Number of Tent-Only Sites:** 16. **Hookups:** Water, sewer, electric (30, 50 amps). **Each Site:** Picnic table. **Dump Station:** Yes. **Laundry:** Yes. **Pay Phone:** Yes. **Rest Rooms and Showers:** Yes. **Fuel:** No. **Propane:** Yes. **Internal Roads:** Gravel. **RV Service:** No. **Market:** 2 mi. west. **Restaurant:** 0.25 mi. west. **General Store:** Yes. **Vending:** Yes. **Swimming:** No. **Playground:** Yes. **Other:** Mini golf, pavilion, pet walk, cabins. **Activities:** Basketball, fishing, offroad riding, swimming, boating. **Nearby Attractions:** Hollydot Golf Course, Bishop's Castle, Lake Beckweth, Lake Isabel. **Additional Information:** Visitor Information Center, (719) 543-1742.

Restrictions

Pets: On leash, cleaned up after. **Fires:** In fire pits. **Alcoholic Beverages:** At sites. **Vehicle Maximum Length:** 42 ft.

To Get There

From I-25 (Exit 74): from the south side of the exit, take the first right after the highway and go 0.25 mi. Turn left at the sign into the entrance.

COLORADO SPRINGS

Garden of the Gods Campground

3704 West Colorado Ave., Colorado Springs 80904. T: (800) 248-9451 or (719) 475-9450; www.coloradocampgrounds.com.

RV: ★★★★ Tent: ★★★★

Beauty: ★★★★	Site Privacy: ★★★
Spaciousness: ★★★	Quiet: ★★★
Security: ★★★★	Cleanliness: ★★★★
Insect Control: ★★★★	Facilities: ★★★★

This is a vast campground that offers a large selection of back-ins and pull-throughs, with some creekside spaces. Most sites are very well-shaded (the M, N, and O sites being one notable exception). Back-in sites range from 30 feet (A, B, and P sections), 45 feet (D, E, K, and S sections), to 60 feet (C section) long. pull-throughs are located in the F, G, M, N, and O sections. F and G sites are extra-long, 80-feet, sites used as end-to-end doubles, making each site roughly 40 feet. Longer single sites are located in sections M, N, and O, which are 60 feet in length. Creekside sites (indicated on the campground map by "CS") are located in the southwest corner. The tenting area is found on the west side of the campground, but there are also creekside tenting sites, marked on the map as "CRT." These are nice, shaded sites with some grass cover. Although they are closer to the road that passes by the campground, tenters may prefer these sites for their natural feel and the sound of the creek at night. The pool, the laundry, the rest rooms, and all other facilties are well-maintained, clean, and comfortable. This is a great campground to stay at while visiting the Garden of the Gods or any of the other numerous attractions in the area.

Basics

Operated By: Chuck Murphy. **Open:** All year. **Site Assignment:** Assigned upon registration Credit card required for reservation; 24-hours cancellation policy, less $5 fee. **Registration:** In office. (Late arrivals use drop box.) **Fee:** RV $37 (full, deluxe), $40 (full, creekside), $35 (full, standard), $32 (water, electric), tent $27 (checks, V, MC, D). **Parking:** At site.

Facilities

Number of RV Sites: 300. **Number of Tent-Only Sites:** 30. **Hookups:** Water, sewer, electric (30, 50 amps), phone. **Each Site:** Picnic table, grill. **Dump Station:** Yes. **Laundry:** Yes. **Pay Phone:** Yes. **Rest Rooms and Showers:** Yes. **Fuel:** No. **Propane:** No. **Internal Roads:** Paved. **RV Service:** No. **Market:** 0.5 mi. east. **Restaurant:** 1 block east. **General Store:** Yes. **Vending:** Yes. **Swimming:** Pool. **Playground:** Yes. **Other:** Clubhouse, jukebox, gift shop, coffee & donuts, pancake breakfasts, watermelon feasts, ice cream socials, fajitas, bus stop in front, cabins. **Activities:** Bus tours. **Nearby Attractions:** Garden of the Gods, Florissant Fossil Beds National Monument, Cripple Creek

& Victor Narrow Guage Railroad, Air Force Base Visitor Center, Mining Museum. **Additional Information:** Colorado Springs Chamber of Commerce, (719) 635-1551.

RESTRICTIONS

Pets: On leash, cleaned up after. **Fires:** In grills. **Alcoholic Beverages:** At sites. **Vehicle Maximum Length:** None.

TO GET THERE

From I-25 (Exit 141), turn west onto Hwy. 24 and go 2.6 mi. Turn north onto 31st St. and go 1 block. Turn left onto Colorado Ave. and go 0.8 mi. Turn right at the sign into the entrance.

CORTEZ

Cortez/Mesa Verde KOA

27432 East Hwy. 160, Cortez 81321. T: (800) 562-3901 or (970) 565-9301; F: (970) 565-2107; www.koa.com; cortezkoa@fone.net.

RV ★★★★ Tent ★★★★

Beauty: ★★★★	Site Privacy: ★★★★
Spaciousness: ★★★★	Quiet: ★★★
Security: ★★★★	Cleanliness: ★★★★★
Insect Control: ★★★★	Facilities: ★★★★★

This beautiful campground is surrounded on three sides by mountains, and has an excellent view of Sleeping Ute Mountain to the north. To the south are scrub-covered hills, and over everything looms big, open sky. RV sites are almost exclusively 70-foot pull-throughs, with a handful of 45-foot back-ins mostly used by long-term guests. Tent sites have both water and electric hookups. The tenting area is grassy, shaded, and very comfortable. The rest rooms and showers are spacious, comfortable, and absolutely spotless. The laundry room is bright and roomy, and all other facilities (pool, game room) are clean and tidy. This campground is centrally located for trips to Mesa Verde, Four Corners, and even further reaches such as Canyonlands or Monument Valley. Campers in tents or RVs will be pleased by this campground, which is worth making a destination on their itinerary.

BASICS

Operated By: Billy Sanders. **Open:** Apr 1–Oct. 15. **Site Assignment:** Assigned upon registration. **Registration:** In office. (Late arrivals use drop box.) **Fee:** RV $28 (full), $26 (water, electric), tent $20 (V, MC, D). **Parking:** At site.

FACILITIES

Number of RV Sites: 78. **Number of Tent-Only Sites:** 26. **Hookups:** Water, sewer, electric (30, 50 amps). **Each Site:** Picnic table, grill. **Dump Station:** Yes. **Laundry:** Yes. **Pay Phone:** Yes. **Rest Rooms and Showers:** Yes. **Fuel:** No. **Propane:** No. **Internal Roads:** Gravel. **RV Service:** No. **Market:** 1 mi. west. **Restaurant:** 0.25 mile west. **General Store:** Yes. **Vending:** Yes. **Swimming:** Pool. **Playground:** Yes. **Other:** Dataport, hot tub/sauna, firewood, game room, cabins, pet walk, teepees. **Activities:** Fishing, boating, swimming, golf, horseback riding, visiting ruins, volleyball, basketball. **Nearby Attractions:** Mesa Verde, Four Corners, Lake McPhee, Monument Valley, Canyonlands, Hovenweep National Monument. **Additional Information:** Cortez Area Chamber of Commerce, (800) 346-6526 or (970) 565-3414.

RESTRICTIONS

Pets: On leash, cleaned up after. **Fires:** In fire pits. **Alcoholic Beverages:** At sites. **Vehicle Maximum Length:** None.

TO GET THERE

From the junction of Hwy. 145 and Hwy. 160, turn east onto Hwy. 160 and go 0.4 mi. Turn right at the sign into the entrance.

COTOPAXI

Arkansas River KOA

21435 US Hwy. 50, Cotopaxi 81223. T: (800) 562-2686 or (719) 275-9308; F: (719) 275-2249; www.koa.com.

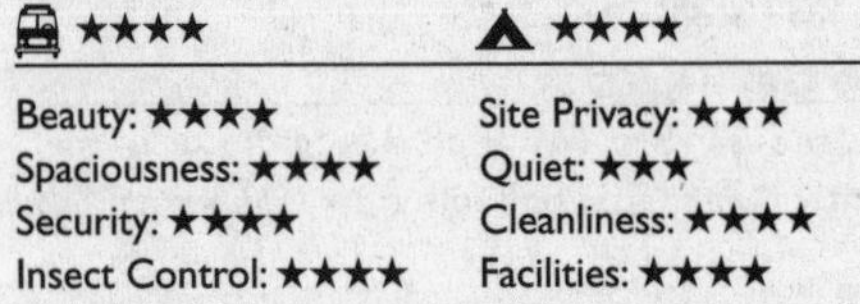

RV ★★★★ Tent ★★★★

Beauty: ★★★★	Site Privacy: ★★★
Spaciousness: ★★★★	Quiet: ★★★
Security: ★★★★	Cleanliness: ★★★★
Insect Control: ★★★★	Facilities: ★★★★

This riverside campground has three strips of pull-throughs (1–13, 14–29, and 30–49) between the highway and the river. These pull-through sites range from 60 feet to 80 feet in length. Sites with nice shade trees include 14, and 17–23. These sites also have beautiful vistas of the rocky hills across the river to the west. End site 30 is a slightly shorter (50-foot) pull-through, but has extra space around it. This site might be a tough spot to park in for a larger rig, due to its proximity to a cabin. Tent sites are back-ins, 35 × 18 feet, along the riverfront.

These sandy sites (51–80) have trees and vegetation, and they face the river and the woods on the far shore. These are excellent sites that tenters will be happy to occupy for a stay of any length. The rest rooms are clean, though slightly rundown, and appear to have been decorated in the 1970s. (There are additional porta-potties along the river for tenters' use.) Likewise, the laundry is dark and a little musty, but spacious and relatively clean. This is a pleasant campground in a beautiful setting that will appeal slightly more to tenters, but is still an excellent stay for RVers.

Basics

Operated By: Jim & Amy Burnham. **Open:** Apr. 15–Oct. 30. **Site Assignment:** Flexible, depending on site availability. Credit card required for reservation; cancellation by 4 p.m. same day. **Registration:** In office. (Late arrivals go to night registration at building to left of entrance.) **Fee:** RV $26 (full), $24 (water, electric), tent $20 (V, MC, D). **Parking:** At site.

Facilities

Number of RV Sites: 49. **Number of Tent-Only Sites:** 30. **Hookups:** Water, sewer, electric (30, 50 amps). **Each Site:** Picnic table, fire pit. **Dump Station:** Yes. **Laundry:** Yes. **Pay Phone:** Yes. **Rest Rooms and Showers:** Yes. **Fuel:** No. **Propane:** Yes. **Internal Roads:** Dirt. **RV Service:** No. **Market:** 25 mi. to Salida or Canon City. **Restaurant:** 25 mi. to Salida or Canon City. **General Store:** Yes. **Vending:** Yes. **Swimming:** Pool. **Playground:** Yes. **Other:** Pool table. **Activities:** Basketball, fishing, rafting, horseshoes, nightly hay ride, nightly kids movies, mini golf, tetherball, shuffleboard. **Nearby Attractions:** Royal Gorge. **Additional Information:** Canon City Chamber of Commerce, (719) 275-2331.

Restrictions

Pets: On leash, cleaned up after, $5 per pet. **Fires:** In fire pits. **Alcoholic Beverages:** At sites. **Vehicle Maximum Length:** None. **Other:** Protect trees, do not tie anything to trees.

To Get There

From the easternmost town name sign, go 1.3 mi. east on Hwy. 50 (just south of mi. marker 247). Turn left at the sign into the entrance. The office is on the right; night registration is to the left.

CRAIG

Craig KOA Kampground

2800 East US 40, Craig 81625. T: (970) 824-5105; www.koa.com.

RV ★★★ Tent ★★

Beauty: ★★★	Site Privacy: ★★★
Spaciousness: ★★★	Quiet: ★★★
Security: ★★★★	Cleanliness: ★★★★★
Insect Control: ★★★★	Facilities: ★★★★★

Just at the east end of town, and 2 miles from dowtown Craig, this campground has grassy fields and plenty of trees to the south and west. Its super-long (90-foot) double pull-throughs (sites 28–44) can be used by one long rig if the campground is not too full. Sites are level and grassy, averaging 27 feet wide. Sites 6–10 are wide open in the middle of the interior road with only two decent trees, thus they are the least desirable sites. Tent sites are located along the south fence, which presents one significant drawback: trains roll right past the park boundary by the fence. The rest room and shower facilities are spotless and well-lit. The laundry is spacious and clean, with a pleasant waiting area. Overall, the park is a decent place to stay, but tenters might have better luck elsewhere.

Basics

Operated By: Rocky Mt RV Park. **Open:** All year (monthly tenants only Dec 1–Apr 15). **Site Assignment:** Reservations recommended Apr. 1–Nov. 30; first come, first served Dec. 1–Mar. 31st. **Registration:** In store. (Late arrivals use drop box.) **Fee:** RV $27, tent $20 (V, MC, AE, D). **Parking:** At site only.

Facilities

Number of RV Sites: 83. **Number of Tent-Only Sites:** 20. **Hookups:** Water, sewer, electric (30, 50 amps). **Each Site:** Picnic table, tree. **Dump Station:** Yes. **Laundry:** Yes. **Pay Phone:** Yes. **Rest Rooms and Showers:** Yes. **Fuel:** No. **Propane:** Yes. **Internal Roads:** Gravel. **RV Service:** No. **Market:** 2 mi. west. **Restaurant:** 2 mi. west. **General Store:** Yes. **Vending:** Yes. **Swimming:** Pool. **Playground:** Yes. **Other:** 4 cabins, RV parts, dataport, pet walk area, hot tub, rec room, soccer field. **Activities:** Soccer, swimming, horseshoes, hiking. **Nearby Attractions:** Sandrocks Nature Trail & Petroglyphs, Museum of Northwest Colorado, Dinosaur National Monument. **Additional Infor-**

mation: Craig Chamber of Commerce, (800) 864-4405, (970) 824-5689.

Restrictions

Pets: On leash, cleaned up after. **Fires:** In fire pits; subject to seasonal bans. **Alcoholic Beverages:** At sites only. **Vehicle Maximum Length:** None.

To Get There

On Hwy. 40, go 0.5 mi. west of the easternmost Craig town name signpost. Turn south into the entrance. The office is straight ahead.

CREEDE

Mt. Views at River's Edge RV Resort

539 Airport Rd., Box 680, Creede 81130. T: (719) 658-2710; F: (719) 658-2711.

RV ★★★★★ Tent n/a

Beauty: ★★★ Site Privacy: ★★★★★
Spaciousness: ★★★★★ Quiet: ★★★★★
Security: ★★★★ Cleanliness: ★★★★★
Insect Control: ★★★★ Facilities: ★★★★★

This beautiful park is surrounded on all four sides by mountains and features all brand-new facilities. The laundry is spacious, clean, well-lit, and has lots of machines. The rest rooms are similarly brand-new and immaculate. (Management says that other new, unnamed, services will be added this year, making this park all the more luxurious.) There is truly a space for any rig of any size in this park: back-ins are 60 feet long, while pull-throughs are a lengthy 70 feet; both types are 40 feet wide, with a designated space for extra vehicles to the side of the main parking area. The best sites in this park (which is a difficult thing to judge!) are probably 107–110 on the north side, as they face nice pasture land, hills, and an attractive wooden fence, they are as long as anyone would need, and they are close to the rest rooms without being right next to them. Although shade trees—and perhaps a paved road—would improve this park, the location is so nice, the spaces so big, and the facilities so new and clean that it deserves top honors. This is a top-notch resort; make sure to get reservations, or you may not get in.

Basics

Operated By: Roland & Helen Zimmerman. **Open:** May–Oct. **Site Assignment:** Assigned upon registration. Reservations require deposit; $20 cancellation fee. **Registration:** In office. (Late arrivals use map on bulletin board to find available site, pay in the morning.) **Fee:** $21 (no credit cards). **Parking:** At site.

Facilities

Number of RV Sites: 100. **Number of Tent-Only Sites:** 0. **Hookups:** Water, sewer, electric (30, 50 amps). **Each Site:** Picnic table, sectioned-off picnic area. **Dump Station:** No (sewer at all sites). **Laundry:** Yes. **Pay Phone:** Yes. **Rest Rooms and Showers:** Yes. **Fuel:** No. **Propane:** Yes. **Internal Roads:** Gravel. **RV Service:** No. **Market:** 1.4 mi. west. **Restaurant:** 1.2 mi. west. **General Store:** Yes. **Vending:** No. **Swimming:** No. **Playground:** No. **Other:** Enclosed phone/dataport pavillion (5 units), group picnic/BBQ area, extremely large rec room, pool table, sofa, TV. **Activities:** Potlucks, Mexican-themed dinners, shared meat from hunting. **Nearby Attractions:** Creede Repertory Theater, Creede Underground Mining Museum. **Additional Information:** Creede-Mineral Chamber of Commerce, (800) 327-2102, or (719) 658-2374.

Restrictions

Pets: On leash, cleaned up after, no barking. **Fires:** In pavillion. **Alcoholic Beverages:** At sites. **Vehicle Maximum Length:** None.

To Get There

From the south edge of Creede, take Hwy. 149 0.75 mi. southwest. Turn south onto Airport Rd. (unmarked—look for blue trailer sign). Drive 0.5 mi. and take the first left into the gravel driveway. Continue straight ahead to get to the office.

CRIPPLE CREEK

Lost Burro

P.O. Box 614, Cripple Creek 80813. T: (719) 689-2345; www.lostburro.com; burrocamp@aol.com.

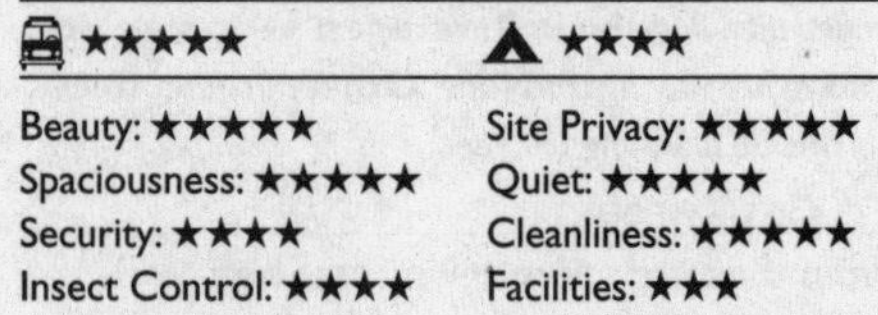

RV ★★★★★ Tent ★★★★

Beauty: ★★★★★ Site Privacy: ★★★★★
Spaciousness: ★★★★★ Quiet: ★★★★★
Security: ★★★★ Cleanliness: ★★★★★
Insect Control: ★★★★ Facilities: ★★★

Get lost in the pines! If you'd like to, you certainly can at the Lost Burro. Located in a small valley with wooded and rocky hills on all four sides, imposing cliffs to the north, and dense forest to the south, this campground feels truly "lost". Campsites are located in tiers up the hillside and down near the stream. Sites are well-spaced, and include some enormous pull-throughs (16 measures 100-feet), as well as long (60-foot) back-ins (8, 12, 13, 14, 15). RV site 11 is a long pull-through like the others, but only about 48 feet are level—the rest drop off quite quickly. Tents sites (by the stream) are mostly open, although sites 15 and 16 (up in the forest away from the stream) are wooded and separated from the rest, making them the best tent sites. The campground is wild and not overly built-up: sites are not much more than bulldozed strips in the woods, making them quite natural and beautiful. For some, the primitive sites, along with the lack of full hookups at every site, may represent too much of a step away from civilization. However, those savvy enough to realize that water spouts and a dump station make full hookups unnecessary will love this campground. Make sure you have reservations—once others "discover" the Lost Burro, it may be harder to get lost than you'd like.

Basics

Operated By: Kent Goza & Mary Eddleman. **Open:** All year. **Site Assignment:** Assigned upon registration. Credit card or check required for reservation; 24-hours cancellation policy. **Registration:** In office. (Late arrivals select an available site & pay in the morning.) **Fee:** RV $18, tent $14 (checks, V, MC, D). **Parking:** At site.

Facilities

Number of RV Sites: 13. **Number of Tent-Only Sites:** 23. **Hookups:** Electric (30, 50 amps). **Each Site:** Picnic table, fire pit. **Dump Station:** Yes. **Laundry:** No. **Pay Phone:** Yes. **Rest Rooms and Showers:** Yes. **Fuel:** No. **Propane:** No. **Internal Roads:** Dirt. **RV Service:** No. **Market:** 20 mi. to Woodland/Divide. **Restaurant:** 4 mi. to Cripple Creek. **General Store:** Yes. **Vending:** Yes. **Swimming:** No. **Playground:** No. **Other:** Stream, burgers. **Activities:** Hiking. **Nearby Attractions:** Casinos, Cripple Creek, Royal Gorge, Florissant Fossil Beds National Monument, Pike's Peak, Cripple Creek & Victor Narrow Gauge Railroad. **Additional Information:** Cripple Creek Chamber of Commerce, (719) 689-2169.

Restrictions

Pets: On leash, cleaned up after. **Fires:** In fire pits. **Alcoholic Beverages:** At sites. **Vehicle Maximum Length:** None. **Other:** Quiet at 9 p.m., no ATVs or motorcycles, no wood cutting or gathering.

To Get There

From the northwestern sign for the town of Cripple Creek on Carr Ave. (CR-Teller 1), go 3.2 mi. north. Turn left at the signs into the entrance. (Those coming from Canon City on CR-Teller 1 will find the campground on their right, just at the Open Air Chapel dome.) Follow the dirt drive down to the office on the right.

DELTA

Riverwood Inn

677 Hwy. 50 North, Delta 81416. T: (970) 874-5787; F: (970) 874-4872; www.riverwoodn.com; info@riverwoodn.com.

RV ★★★ Tent ★★★

Beauty: ★★★	Site Privacy: ★★★★
Spaciousness: ★★★	Quiet: ★★★
Security: ★★★	Cleanliness: ★★★
Insect Control: ★★★	Facilities: ★★★

This park, on the Gunnison River, has large back-ins (56–70-foot), and absolutely enormous pull-throughs (90–100-foot). Further more, there are loads of trees throughout the park, making shade a given for any site. Arguably the best sites are 5–7 in the northeast corner near the tenting area, with fine towering trees at the back, nice grass, and enough distance from the mobile homes to the west (behind 8–13) to allow increased privacy. The least desirable sites are 14 and 15, right along Hwy. 50 (with no fence at the perimiter), and sites 16 and 17, which back to the park entrance (again without a fence). The laundry facility is a little small (1 of each machine) and dingy. The tent sites are located on an "island" to the northeast of the RV sites. These are unmarked, virtually unlimited, and unkempt. While the wild grass and other vegetation, including lots of trees, is appealing to tenters, there was old wood and some cast away furniture littering the area during our inspection. Additionally, the only rest room on the "island" is a porta-potty. Disregarding this slight slap in the face to tenters, the actual tenting area is quite nice. Campers of all stripes will find it a reasonable stop, as it is easily accessed from Hwy. 50 or 92, and is quite close to town.

Basics

Operated By: Loren & Merced Pogue. **Open:** All year. **Site Assignment:** Assigned upon registration. Credit card required for reservation; 24-hours cancellation policy. **Registration:** In office. (Late arrivals select an available site & pay in the morning.) **Fee:** Pull-through: $21.50, back-in: $19.50, tent $11 (V, MC, D, DC, CB, check). **Parking:** At site.

Facilities

Number of RV Sites: 28. **Number of Tent-Only Sites:** Undesignated sites. **Hookups:** Water, sewer, electric (30, 50 amps). **Each Site:** Picnic table, grill; most have several trees & shrubs. **Dump Station:** No (sewer at all sites). **Laundry:** Yes. **Pay Phone:** Yes. **Rest Rooms and Showers:** Yes. **Fuel:** No. **Propane:** No. **Internal Roads:** Gravel. **RV Service:** No. **Market:** 0.5 mi. **Restaurant:** On site. **General Store:** No. **Vending:** No. **Swimming:** No. **Playground:** No. **Other:** River, 11-room hotel. **Activities:** Fishing, hiking, biking. **Nearby Attractions:** Grand Mesa, Fort Uncompahgre, Delta County Museum. **Additional Information:** Delta Area Chamber of Commerce, (970) 874-8616.

Restrictions

Pets: On leash, cleaned up after. **Fires:** In fire pits. **Alcoholic Beverages:** At sites. **Vehicle Maximum Length:** None.

To Get There

From the junction of Hwy. 92 and Hwy. 50, turn north onto Hwy. 50, go 0.5 mi., and turn right into the entrance.

DENVER

Delux RV Park

5520 North Federal Blvd., Denver 80221. T: (303) 433-0452.

RV ★★★ | Tent n/a

Beauty: ★★	Site Privacy: ★★★
Spaciousness: ★★★	Quiet: ★★★
Security: ★★★	Cleanliness: ★★★
Insect Control: ★★★★	Facilities: ★★★

Laid out in a horseshoe around the office and manager's residence, this campground features back-ins roughly 40 feet long, with a 30-foot cement slab at most sites. The campground is located in an urban residential area, and some of the sites lie next to houses and a lounge (18–22). Some of the sites are unnumbered, and the numbering scheme appears somewhat haphazard. Probably the nicest sites are 12–17, located on the inside of the internal road loop. Site 27 is less desirable, as it lies adjacent to the office parking lot. Sites 32–34 are even worse, as they lie right off of (busy) Federal Blvd. A number of the sites appear to be given over to long-term residents, especially those in the lower number (2–11) on the north side of the loop. The RV park, during our visit, was slightly run-down, but not uncomfortable. Being the only RV park in Denver proper, it is a convenient place to stay while checking out the sights in Denver.

Basics

Operated By: Tony Clemons. **Open:** All year. **Site Assignment:** Assigned upon registration. Credit card required for reservation; 24-hours cancellation policy. **Registration:** In office. (Late arrivals select an available site & pay in the morning.) **Fee:** RV $30 (V, MC, D). **Parking:** At site.

Facilities

Number of RV Sites: 31. **Number of Tent-Only Sites:** 0. **Hookups:** Water, sewer, electric (30, 50 amps), cable, phone. **Each Site:** Picnic table. **Dump Station:** Yes. **Laundry:** Yes. **Pay Phone:** Yes. **Rest Rooms and Showers:** Yes. **Fuel:** No. **Propane:** No. **Internal Roads:** Gravel. **RV Service:** No. **Market:** 2 mi. north. **Restaurant:** 1 mi. south. **General Store:** No. **Vending:** Yes. **Swimming:** No. **Playground:** No. **Other:** Dataport, 10 minutes to downtown Denver, Mile High Stadium, Civic Center, Elitch Gardens; 20 minutes to Denver Zoo, dataport. **Activities:** Visiting museums, sightseeing, amusement park. **Nearby Attractions:** Denver, Mile High Stadium, Civic Center, Elitch Gardens amusement park. **Additional Information:** Denver Chamber of Commerce, (303) 458-0220.

Restrictions

Pets: On leash, cleaned up after. **Fires:** In grills. **Alcoholic Beverages:** At sites. **Vehicle Maximum Length:** 39 ft.

To Get There

From the junction of Hwy. I-25 and Hwy. I-70, turn west onto Hwy. I-70 and go 2 mi. Turn north onto Federal Blvd and go 0.8 mi. Turn right at the sign into the entrance.

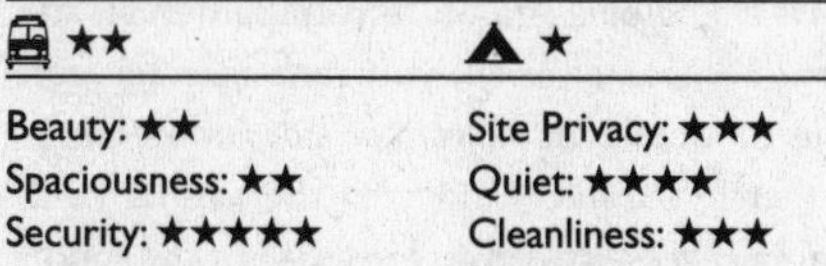

DINOSAUR

Blue Mountain Village

P.O. Box 7, Dinosaur 81610. T: (970) 374-2747; dinoma@nwco.quik.com.

★★ ▲ ★

Beauty: ★★	Site Privacy: ★★★
Spaciousness: ★★	Quiet: ★★★★
Security: ★★★★★	Cleanliness: ★★★
Insect Control: ★★★	Facilities: ★★

This fenced-in park has some views of mountains to the north, but is otherwise not much to look at, with few trees to speak of, gravel (not grassy) sites, and mobile homes at the front area of the RV park. However, that being said, this park is a middling palce to stay. The pull-throughs are long (85 feet), but narrow (16 feet). The pull-throughs in the southwest corner (70–80) are probably the nicest of the lot: they are well away from the road and have decent views to the south, west, and east. The laundry facility is clean and well-lit, but the showers are a little cramped. The rest rooms are otherwise reasonably clean and modern. Tent sites are located on a strip of grass along the fence at the south edge of the park. This strip is ratyher narrow, and provides no protection from the elements. Tenters would be advised to give the park a pass, while RVers could reasonably stay a couple of days—but not make a destination out of the park.

BASICS

Operated By: Jeanne & Jim. **Open:** Apr. 1–Nov. 1. **Site Assignment:** Assigned upon registration. Credit card required for reservation; 24-hours cancellation policy. **Registration:** In office. (Late arrivals ring doorbell.) **Fee:** RV $17.50, tent $11 (V, MC, many discounts honored). **Parking:** At site.

FACILITIES

Number of RV Sites: 88. **Number of Tent-Only Sites:** 12. **Hookups:** Water, sewer, electric (30, 50 amps). **Dump Station:** No (sewer at all sites). **Laundry:** Yes. **Pay Phone:** Yes. **Rest Rooms and Showers:** Yes. **Fuel:** No. **Propane:** No. **Internal Roads:** Gravel. **RV Service:** No. **Market:** 3 mi. to Vernal (mini market 0.5 mi.). **Restaurant:** 1 mi. **General Store:** No. **Vending:** No. **Swimming:** No. **Playground:** Yes. **Other:** Covered picnic shelter. **Activities:** Viewing dinosaur fossils, rafting. **Nearby Attractions:** Dinosaur National Monument. **Additional Information:** Dinosaur National Monument, (970) 374-3000.

RESTRICTIONS

Pets: On leash, cleaned up after. **Fires:** In fire pits. **Alcoholic Beverages:** At sites. **Vehicle Maximum Length:** None.

TO GET THERE

From the junction of Hwy. 40 and Hwy. 64, turn south onto Hwy. 64 (going east). Drive 0.5 mi. to 7th St. (go right at the fork in the road). Turn right onto Blue Mountain Village, then take the first left onto Morrison Ave. The office is at the end of the drive.

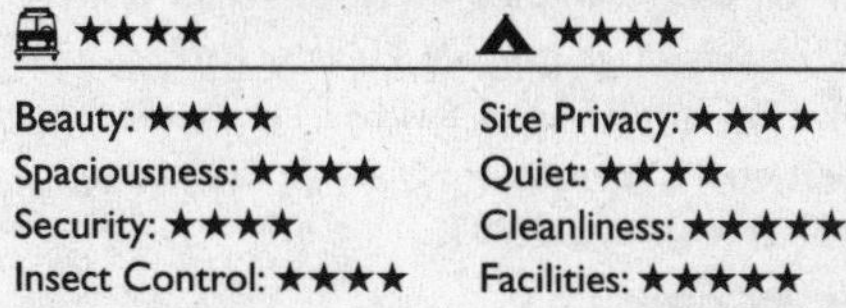

DURANGO

Durango East KOA

30090 US Hwy. 160, Durango 81303. T: (800) KOA-0793 or (970) 247-0783; F: (970) 247-3655; www.koa; 104117.3442@compuserve.com.

★★★★ ▲ ★★★★

Beauty: ★★★★	Site Privacy: ★★★★
Spaciousness: ★★★★	Quiet: ★★★★
Security: ★★★★	Cleanliness: ★★★★★
Insect Control: ★★★★	Facilities: ★★★★★

This campground, on the northeast side of town, has mostly back-ins, but of such large proportions (40–60 feet) that campers should not be put off by the prospect of not finding a pull-through. Indeed, the pull-throughs on the east side of the campground are less desirable than most back-ins due to the absence of any shade trees, and their "views" of nearby houses. Site 43 is a gigantic pull-through that will accommodate any rig, while 66 is a pull-through with a great view. Most sites have a row of trees and shrubs between them for an added sense of privacy. With the exception of the more open sites to the east, many spots have a lost-in-the-woods feel. The least desirable sites (1 and 2), however, are quite open and close to the propane storage, a separate storage unit, and the registration office; hopefully they are only used as overflow sites. This campground's ruggedness will appeal especially to tenters, who have lots of protection in a wilderness atmosphere. The rest rooms are clean, modern, and spacious, as is the laundry. This is a great campground in a wonderful location, and will suit both tenters and RVers.

BASICS

Operated By: Jay & Carol Coates. **Open:** May 1–Oct. 15. **Site Assignment:** Assigned upon registration. Reservations require deposit; 24-hours cancellation policy. **Registration:** In office. (Late arrivals use drop box.) **Fee:** RV $29 (full), $27 (water, electric), tent $22 (V, MC, checks). **Parking:** At site.

FACILITIES

Number of RV Sites: 60. **Number of Tent-Only Sites:** 24. **Hookups:** Water, sewer, electric (30, 50 amps), cable. **Each Site:** Picnic table, grill, trees. **Dump Station:** Yes. **Laundry:** Yes. **Pay Phone:** Yes. **Rest Rooms and Showers:** Yes. **Fuel:** No. **Propane:** Yes. **Internal Roads:** Gravel. **RV Service:** No. **Market:** 4 mi. southwest. **Restaurant:** 5 mi. southwest. **General Store:** Yes. **Vending:** No. **Swimming:** Pool. **Playground:** Yes. **Other:** Cabins, cottage, game room, TV lounge, group site, dataport, pool table, river. **Activities:** Mini golf, volleyball, fishing, ice cream socials, pancake breakfast, nightly movie. **Nearby Attractions:** Durango/Silverton Railroad, Mesa Verde. **Additional Information:** Durango Chamber of Commerce, (800) 525-8855.

RESTRICTIONS

Pets: On leash, cleaned up after; do not leave unattended. **Fires:** Subject to seasonal bans. **Alcoholic Beverages:** At sites. **Vehicle Maximum Length:** None.

TO GET THERE

From the northwest junction of Hwy. 550 and Hwy. 160/550 (at the western edge of town), go 2.7 mi. northeast on Hwy. 550. Turn right at the sign into the entrance. The office is straight ahead.

ESTES PARK

Estes Park KOA

2051 Big Thompson Ave., Estes Park 80517. T: (800) KOA-1887 or (970) 586-2888; F: (970) 577-0518; www.koa.com; estesparkkoa @compuserve.com.

RV: ★★★★ Tent: ★★★

Beauty: ★★★★★	Site Privacy: ★★★
Spaciousness: ★★★	Quiet: ★★★★
Security: ★★★★	Cleanliness: ★★★★★
Insect Control: ★★★★★	Facilities: ★★★★★

The fourth KOA campground ever built, this tiered campground is admittedly not for big rigs. Sites are somewhat cramped by today's standards (although the odd large 5th wheel can still be found, tucked in sideways), and space between sites is negligible. And yet the campground is still worth a visit—after all, you can't beat the gorgeous mountain views from all sides or the cooler weather in summer, and even the natural landscaping is very attractive. Sites 1–7 in the southwest corner along the highway are rather small back-ins (30 × 22 feet). Sites 8–29 are larger (40-foot) back-ins, as are 37–48 (40–42-feet). Sites 30–36 and 49–54 are longer (40–45-feet) "parallel parking" sites that resemble pull-throughs, and may be more convenient than a straight back-in. There are stairs between the tiered levels at sites 24,26, and 44, increasing the likelihood of foot traffic past these sites. Tent sites are located in the southeast corner (accessed on the road by cabins 9 and 12). Each tent site has at least one (two maximum) sides fenced in by a solid fence, with a wooden barricade on one other side, lending more privacy to these sites. There is one gravel pad and one astroturf pad per tent site. At 21 × 33 feet, the sites are medium-sized, but they are packed in one atop the other with little space between them. Despite the confined spaces, this is a beautiful campground and well worth a visit.

BASICS

Operated By: Wendy. **Open:** May 1–Oct. 20. **Site Assignment:** Assigned upon registration. Credit card required for reservation; 24-hours cancellation policy. **Registration:** In office. (Late arrivals use drop box.) **Fee:** RV $20 (full), $18 (water, electric), tent $10 (V, MC). **Parking:** At site.

FACILITIES

Number of RV Sites: 46. **Number of Tent-Only Sites:** 19. **Hookups:** Water, sewer, electric (30, 50 amps), cable. **Each Site:** Picnic table on wooden platform, grill. **Dump Station:** Yes. **Laundry:** Yes. **Pay Phone:** Yes. **Rest Rooms and Showers:** Yes. **Fuel:** No. **Propane:** Yes. **Internal Roads:** Dirt. **RV Service:** No. **Market:** 1.5 mi. west. **Restaurant:** 1.5 mi. west. **General Store:** Yes. **Vending:** No. **Swimming:** No. **Playground:** Yes. **Other:** 16 cabins, 7 cottages, teepees, gift shop, lounge, game room, across from lake. **Activities:** Fishing, boating, swimming, hiking, skiing, mountain climbing. **Nearby Attractions:** Rocky Mountain National Park, elk bugling, aspens turning. **Additional Information:** Estes Park Chamber of Commerce, (800) 443-7837 or (970) 586-4431.

RESTRICTIONS

Pets: On leash, cleaned up after. **Fires:** In fire pits. **Alcoholic Beverages:** At sites. **Vehicle Maximum Length:** 40 ft.

TO GET THERE

From the junction of Hwy. 36 and Hwy. 34, turn east onto Hwy. 34 and go 1.8 mi. Turn left at the sign into the entrance.

FAIRPLAY

Western Inn and RV Park

490 Hwy. 285 P.O. Box 187, Fairplay 80440. T: (877) 306-3037 or (719) 836-2026; F: (719) 836-0758; westerninn@chaffeee.net.

RV ★★★ Tent ★★★

Beauty: ★★ Site Privacy: ★★★★
Spaciousness: ★★★★ Quiet: ★★★
Security: ★★★★ Cleanliness: ★★★★
Insect Control: ★★★★ Facilities: ★★★

This is a small RV park operated in conjunction with a motel. The complex is located in a rural area with some industrial development especially towards the southeast. The RV sites are located on a gravel interior road. Each site contains a tree that is more decorative than shading. Sites 1–3 and 7–11 are open-ended pull-throughs that can easily accommodate 90 feet. Sites 4–6 are back-ins that can take approximately 55 feet. Tenters can pitch a tent to the southeast of the RV sites, pretty much wherever they can find room. The tenting area has sparse grass, and, like the RV section of the park, offers no shade. This campground is conveniently located clsoe to the town of Fairplay, and is a decent stop on the highway, but is not a destination in itself.

BASICS

Operated By: Jack & Linda Sanderson. **Open:** All year. **Site Assignment:** Flexible, depending on site availability. Credit card required for reservation; 24-hours cancellation policy. **Registration:** In office. (Late arrivals can call manager 24 hrs.) **Fee:** RV $20 (full), tent $10 (checks, V, MC, AE, D, DC). **Parking:** At site.

FACILITIES

Number of RV Sites: 11. **Number of Tent-Only Sites:** Undesignated sites. **Hookups:** Water, sewer, electric (30, 50 amps). **Each Site:** Picnic table. **Dump Station:** No (sewer at all sites). **Laundry:** 4 blocks. **Pay Phone:** Yes. **Rest Rooms and Showers:** Yes. **Fuel:** No. **Propane:** No. **Internal Roads:** Gravel. **RV Service:** No. **Market:** 6 blocks on Hwy. 9. **Restaurant:** Next door. **General Store:** No. **Vending:** Yes. **Swimming:** No (hot tub). **Playground:** Yes (in park 2 blocks away). **Other:** Some frozen foods in office. **Activities:** Hiking, hunting, skiing, fishing. **Nearby Attractions:** South Park city, 14,000-ft. mountains. **Additional Information:** Fairplay Chamber of Commerce, (719) 836-3410.

RESTRICTIONS

Pets: On leash, cleaned up after. **Fires:** In grills. **Alcoholic Beverages:** At sites. **Vehicle Maximum Length:** None.

TO GET THERE

From the junction of Hwy. 285 and Hwy. 9, turn north onto Hwy. 285 and go 0.2 mi. Turn left at the sign into the entrance.

FORT COLLINS

Horsetooth Campground (Stout Campground)

1800 South CR 31, Loveland 80537. T: (970) 679-4554; www.abouthorsetooth.com; info@abouthorsetooth.com.

RV ★★★★ Tent ★★★★★

Beauty: ★★★★★ Site Privacy: ★★★★★
Spaciousness: ★★★★★ Quiet: ★★★★
Security: ★★★★ Cleanliness: ★★★★
Insect Control: ★★★★ Facilities: ★★

Beautiful views of rocks, hills, and trees surround this park to the northeast and northwest. In addition to its beauty, the lake offers many recreational opportunities, including swimming, boating, and scuba diving. There are lots of trees throughout the park, and most sites are at least partially shaded. Site 1 is close to the entrance and the rest rooms. Site 8 is a 90-foot pull-through, and 14 and 15 are even longer (105-foot) pull-throughs. Sites 21, 26, 27, 29, and 30 are among the handful of back-ins in the park. Sites 32–42 are on a separate loop to the southeast of the main campground area. Site 37 has a water pump. Tent sites are walk-ins, with a central parking area for all sites. (There are a large number of tenting sites around the reservoir.) This campground is a decent stop for outdoor enthusiasts, and although it does not offer full services, many campers will enjoy a stay here.

Basics

Operated By: Larimer County. **Open:** All year. **Site Assignment:** First come, first served; no reservations. **Registration:** Ranger or Camp Host will collect fees. **Fee:** $10 (electric), tent $7. (checks). **Parking:** At site.

Facilities

Number of RV Sites: 42. **Number of Tent-Only Sites:** 0. **Hookups:** Electric (20, 30, 50 amps). **Each Site:** Picnic table, grill, tent pad. **Dump Station:** Yes. **Laundry:** No. **Pay Phone:** No. **Rest Rooms and Showers:** Pit toilets; no shower. **Fuel:** No. **Propane:** No. **Internal Roads:** Gravel. **RV Service:** No. **Market:** 6.5 mi. east. **Restaurant:** 6.5 mi. east. **General Store:** Yes. **Vending:** No. **Swimming:** Reservoir. **Playground:** No. **Other:** Boat ramp, covered picnic area. **Activities:** Fishing, boating, swimming, hiking, rock climbing, scuba diving, horseback riding. **Nearby Attractions:** Lory State Park, Horsetooth Mountain Park. **Additional Information:** Larimer City Parks & Open Lands Dept., (970) 679-4570.

Restrictions

Pets: On leash, cleaned up after. **Fires:** In grills. **Alcoholic Beverages:** Beer only. **Vehicle Maximum Length:** None. **Other:** Counter-clockwise boating only; $6 day pass for all vehicles.

To Get There

From I-25 (Exit 265), turn west onto Harmony Rd. and go 10.8 mi. Turn right at the sign into the entrance.

FRUITA

Monument RV Park

607 Hwy. 340, Fruita 81521. T: (888) 977-6777 or (970) 858-3155; F: (970) 858-4777.

RV ★★★ Tent ★★

Beauty: ★★	Site Privacy: ★★★
Spaciousness: ★★★	Quiet: ★★
Security: ★★★	Cleanliness: ★★★
Insect Control: ★★★	Facilities: ★★★

This is a functional jumping-off point to explore the Colorado National Monument, Devil's Canyon, and other destinations in Colorado or Utah. Despite the proximity of several gas stations and fast-food restaurants, the campground retains a semi-rural feel, with a horse pasture abutting the southeast corner. However, this rectangular campground is situated close to both the highway and the train tracks that run through town, and light-sleepers would be well-advised to bring earplugs. Likewise, the security floodlights are kept on all night, and (tent) campers may want to consider sleeping blinders. (No tent sites can escape the floodlights.) Travelers who do not wish to turn off of I-70 for lodging will find a reasonable place to spend the night here, but those who seek the wilder side would be advised to take the short drive up to Saddlehorn Campground at the Colorado National Monument.

Basics

Operated By: Lonnie & Angie. **Open:** All year. **Site Assignment:** First-come, first served. **Registration:** At office (Late arrivals select an available site & pay in the morning.) **Fee:** $24 (full), $21 (water, electric), $18 (tent). **Parking:** At site only.

Facilities

Number of RV Sites: 80. **Number of Tent-Only Sites:** 33. **Hookups:** Full. **Each Site:** Picnic table, some grills. **Dump Station:** Yes. **Laundry:** Yes. **Pay Phone:** Yes. **Rest Rooms and Showers:** Yes. **Fuel:** Yes. **Propane:** Yes. **Internal Roads:** Gravel, in good condition. **RV Service:** No (on-call mobile service). **Market:** 1.5 mi. **Restaurant:** No. **General Store:** Yes. **Vending:** Yes. **Swimming:** No. **Playground:** No. **Other:** Dog run, communal area. **Activities:** Fishing, hiking, boating. **Nearby Attractions:** Devil's Canyon, Colorado National Monument, Country Jam in nearby Mack (3rd weekend in June). **Additional Information:** Fruita Chamber of Commerce, (970) 858-3894.

Restrictions

Pets: On leash, cleaned up after. **Fires:** At sites only. **Alcoholic Beverages:** At sites. **Vehicle Maximum Length:** None.

To Get There

From I-70, take the Fruita exit (Exit 19), turn left onto Hwy. 340, and then left into the park.

GLENWOOD SPRINGS

Ami's Acres

50235 Hwy. 6 & 24, Glenwood Springs 81602. T: (970) 945-5340; F: (970) 947-9169; amisacres@yahoo.com.

RV ★★★★ Tent ★★★★

Beauty: ★★★★ Site Privacy: ★★★
Spaciousness: ★★ Quiet: ★★
Security: ★★★★ Cleanliness: ★★★★★
Insect Control: ★★★★ Facilities: ★★★

This terraced RV park on the slope of a hill facing gorgeous rock cliffs across the highway has long (90-foot) but narrow (15-foot) pull-throughs. Sites 51–56 are smaller back-ins for pop-ups, but back to a beautiful grassy hill, and are quite attractive sites. Tent sites are located up the slope from the RV sites, a nice distance from park traffic. These are nice, natural sites with plenty of tree coverage and soft dirt floor. The rest room and shower facilities are quite clean and modern, although the building they are housed in looks a little run-down. The laundry is small but clean. The landscaping is rather attractive, with plenty of trees and shrubs making a nice, natural setting. Another nice touch are the picnic tables, which are painted a variety of different colors. One downside is that the park is plagued by both train and traffic noise. However, if you can get past the minor inconvenience, this park is a nice stay.

Basics

Operated By: John & Roxanne Christner. **Open:** Mar 15– Nov. 1. **Site Assignment:** Assigned upon registration. Credit card required for reservation; 48-hours cancellation policy. **Registration:** In office. (Late arrivals use drop box.) **Fee:** RV $23, tent $16 (V, MC). **Parking:** At site.

Facilities

Number of RV Sites: 62. **Number of Tent-Only Sites:** 18. **Hookups:** Water, sewer, electric (30, 50 amps). **Each Site:** Picnic table, tree. **Dump Station:** No (sewer at all site). **Laundry:** Yes. **Pay Phone:** Yes. **Rest Rooms and Showers:** Yes. **Fuel:** No. **Propane:** No. **Internal Roads:** Gravel. **RV Service:** No. **Market:** 1 mi. east. **Restaurant:** 1 mi. east. **General Store:** No. **Vending:** No. **Swimming:** No. **Playground:** Yes. **Other:** Easy access from I-70. **Activities:** Rafting, hiking, biking, hunting, fishing, golf. **Nearby Attractions:** Glenwood Hot Springs Pool, Hanging Lake, Frontier Historical Museum, Yampa Spa & Vapour Cave. **Additional Information:** Glenwood Springs Chamber Resort Assoc., (970) 945-6589.

Restrictions

Pets: On leash, cleaned up after; no pets in tent sites. **Fires:** No wood fires. **Alcoholic Beverages:** At sites. **Vehicle Maximum Length:** None. **Other:** No ATVs or motorcycles.

To Get There

From I-70, take Exit 114, go 1 mi. west on the frontage road to the north of the highway. The entrance is on the right.

GOLDEN

Chief Hosa Campground

27661 Genesee Dr., Golden 80401. T: (303) 526-0242; F: (303) 526-2685; www.chiefhosa.com; info@chiefhosa.com.

RV ★★★ Tent ★★★★

Beauty: ★★★★ Site Privacy: ★★★★
Spaciousness: ★★★★ Quiet: ★★★★
Security: ★★★★ Cleanliness: ★★★★
Insect Control: ★★★★ Facilities: ★★

This is a giant campground that occupies both sides of the highway. (The western side of the campground closes on Sept. 1.) All of the sites in this campground are back-ins, averaging 40 feet in length. Sites 1–13 are 40-foot sites in a row along the northeast side. Sites 14–19 are located in the southeast, and 20–42 are in the central "island" of the park. Sites 43–48 are clustered around the bathhouse. There are numerous tent sites in this campground. The heavily forested sites are rough and natural. The road leading up to the hill on which sites 26–40 are located is very poorly maintained, and difficult to negotiate. Other tent sites are scattered around the park, and not quite as challenging to get to. The rest rooms and showers are located in a mobile home parked in the southwest corner. The facilities are quite clean, although the showers are slightly less so than the rest rooms. This is an enjoyable place to take the family for a camping outing, or just to get away for a weekend alone.

Basics

Operated By: City & County of Denver. **Open:** All year (limited services Labor Day–Memorial

Day). **Site Assignment:** Assigned upon registration. Credit card required for reservation; 24-hours cancellation policy. **Registration:** In office or use drop box. **Fee:** RV $20 (water, electric), tent $15 (V, MC, AE, D). **Parking:** At site.

FACILITIES

Number of RV Sites: 50. **Number of Tent-Only Sites:** 38. **Hookups:** Water, electric (30, 50 amps). **Each Site:** Picnic table. **Dump Station:** Yes. **Laundry:** No. **Pay Phone:** Yes. **Rest Rooms and Showers:** Yes. **Fuel:** No. **Propane:** No. **Internal Roads:** Gravel. **RV Service:** No. **Market:** 3.2 mi. west. **Restaurant:** 1 mi. east or west. **General Store:** No. **Vending:** No. **Swimming:** No. **Playground:** Yes. **Other:** Communal fire pit, dog walk. **Activities:** Volleyball, basketball, horseshoes. **Nearby Attractions:** Buffalo Bill's Grave, Buffalo Herd Overlook. **Additional Information:** Golden Chamber of Commerce, (303) 279-3113.

RESTRICTIONS

Pets: On leash, cleaned up after. **Fires:** In grills. **Alcoholic Beverages:** At sites. **Vehicle Maximum Length:** None.

TO GET THERE

From I-70 (Exit 253), on the southeast side of the highway, go straight on Genesee Rd. to campground entrance on right.

GOODRICH

Jackson Lake State Park Cove Campground

26363 Rd. 3, Orchard 80649. T: (877) 444-6777 or (970) 645-2551; F: (970) 645-1535; www.parks.state.co.us; jackson.lake@state.co.us.

RV ★★★	Tent ★★★★
Beauty: ★★★★	Site Privacy: ★★★
Spaciousness: ★★★★	Quiet: ★★★★
Security: ★★★★	Cleanliness: ★★★★
Insect Control: ★★★★	Facilities: ★★★

Seemingly its own little world, this state park offers water-oriented recreation in a wilderness setting. The sparse grass and low vegetation gives it a typical southwestern feel, and it is beautiful in its own way. There are several campgrounds with several hundred sites; those reviewed here are the Cove and Pelican Campgrounds, containing roughly 20 sites combined. Sites 1–4 in Cove Campground are unshaded 40-foot back-ins that do not provide much in the way of privacy. Sites 5 and 6 are 63-foot pull-throughs located near the amphitheater. Site 5 has much better shade than 1–4 or 6. There is an unnumbered, 60-foot "pull-alongside" near the swimming beach, and several possible campsites along the parking lot for the swim beach. (If the parking lot is full, there is no parking for these sites.) Sites 7–10 and 13–14 are 40-foot back-ins that back to woods. These sites have the best shade in the park. (Sites 15 and 16 are also well-shaded.) Sites 11 and 12 are much more open 45-foot back-ins. In the Pelican Campground, sites 5–10 are 60-foot pull-throughs that overlook the beach. There are also some tenting sites that are even closer to the edge of the beach. These are undoubtedly among the best tenting sites. The low shade trees and sandy cover make tent camping quite comfortable. This is a fun park for the entire family, whether in tents or an RV.

BASICS

Operated By: Colorado State Parks. **Open:** All year. **Site Assignment:** First come, first served. Credit card required for reservation; 3-days cancellation policy, less $10 service fee. **Registration:** At pay station. **Fee:** $14 (electric), tent $10. (checks). **Parking:** At site.

FACILITIES

Number of RV Sites: 250. **Number of Tent-Only Sites:** 0. **Hookups:** Electric (20, 30, 50 amps). **Each Site:** Covered picnic table, grill, fire pit. **Dump Station:** Yes. **Laundry:** No. **Pay Phone:** Yes. **Rest Rooms and Showers:** Yes. **Fuel:** No. **Propane:** No. **Internal Roads:** Paved/dirt. **RV Service:** No. **Market:** 18 mi. south in Wiggins. **Restaurant:** 18 mi. south in Wiggins. **General Store:** Marina. **Vending:** No. **Swimming:** Lake. **Playground:** No. **Other:** Boat ramp, ampitheater, hunting blinds, nature trails. **Activities:** Fishing, boating, swimming, hiking, ice skating, interpretive programs, hunting. **Nearby Attractions:** Riverside Reservoir, Pawnee National Grasslands. **Additional Information:** Fort Morgan Chamber of Commerce, (970) 867-6702.

RESTRICTIONS

Pets: On 6-ft. leash, cleaned up after. **Fires:** In grills. **Alcoholic Beverages:** Beer only. **Vehicle Maximum Length:** None. **Other:** $4 per day park pass; no cutting of firewood.

To Get There

From the junction of I-76 and Hwy. 39, turn north onto Hwy. 39 and go 7.65 mi. Turn west onto CR Y5 and go 2.4 mi. Turn right to go to the south end or continue straight to the north end and the office.

GOULD

North Park/Gould KOA

53337 Hwy. 14, Walden 80480. T: (800) 562-3596 or (970) 723-4310; www.koa.com.

RV ★★★★★ Tent ★★★★★

Beauty: ★★★★★	Site Privacy: ★★★★★
Spaciousness: ★★★★	Quiet: ★★★★★
Security: ★★★★	Cleanliness: ★★★★★
Insect Control: ★★★★	Facilities: ★★★★★

Ahhh . . . This is what camping is all about! Smack-dab in the middle of the forest in North Park, this campground is wooded, quiet, and clean. Now, campers should keep in mind the fact that North Park is 8,900 feet above sea level, and nights get pretty chilly here—even well into spring, when there can still be snow on the ground. Bring your long johns (especially tent campers) for cold nights and possible use during the day. Tenters should count on bringing more "winter woolies" and bed layers when camping at lower elevations. That said, this is a gorgeous campground that RVers and tenters alike will love. Back-in sites are quite long (50-foot), while pull-throughs are an incredible 90-foot—there's something for every rig here! Sites could be wider (they are just 22 feet), but should suffice for all but the widest RVs with slide-outs. Sites are well-spaced and private, located along a single giant loop. The only site that may present any incovneience is 30, which is located on the tip of the inner "island" of the loop, and may thus get a little more passing traffic than the others. All other sites are a camper's delight. The playground includes a neat wooden fort, and all of the facilities are spotless. There are a number of state, national, and private campgrounds in the area, but this campground is unequalled in services. If you are considering a trip to this region, by all means, plan to stop for a night at this KOA.

Basics

Operated By: The Vlasmans. **Open:** May 26–Nov 15. **Site Assignment:** Assigned upon registration. **Registration:** In office. (Late arrivals use drop box.) **Fee:** RV $25 (full), $22 (water, electric), tent $20. **Parking:** At site.

Facilities

Number of RV Sites: 30. **Number of Tent-Only Sites:** 7. **Hookups:** Water, sewer, electric (30 amps). **Each Site:** Picnic table. **Dump Station:** Yes. **Laundry:** Yes. **Pay Phone:** Yes. **Rest Rooms and Showers:** Yes. **Fuel:** Yes. **Propane:** Yes. **Internal Roads:** Gravel. **RV Service:** No. **Market:** 3 mi. to Gould. **Restaurant:** 3 mi. to Gould. **General Store:** Yes. **Vending:** No. **Swimming:** Lake. **Playground:** Yes. **Other:** Game room. **Activities:** Fishing, hiking, mountain biking, hunting, horseshoes, basketball. **Nearby Attractions:** North Park, North sandhills Recreation Area, Arapahoe National Wildlife Refuge. **Additional Information:** North Park Tourism Information Center, (970) 723-4344.

Restrictions

Pets: On leash, cleaned up after. **Fires:** In fire pits. **Alcoholic Beverages:** At sites. **Vehicle Maximum Length:** None.

To Get There

From the westernmost Gould town name signpost, drive 2.7 mi. west on Hwy. 14. Turn north at the sign into the campground entrance. The office is straight ahead.

GRANBY

Stillwater Campground

8590 US Hwy. 39, Granby 80446. T: (877) 444-6777 or (970) 887-0056; www.reserveusa.com.

RV ★★★★ Tent ★★★★

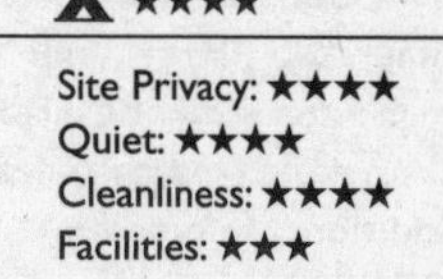

Beauty: ★★★★	Site Privacy: ★★★★
Spaciousness: ★★★	Quiet: ★★★★
Security: ★★★★	Cleanliness: ★★★★
Insect Control: ★★★★	Facilities: ★★★

Overlooking Lake Granby, this campground has a myriad of sites offering a combination of camping possibilities: great views, electrical hookups, facilities. One combination that does not seem possible, however, is an electric site with a superb view, as all of the electric sites are on the north side of the hill and the lake is further south. However, most sites are at least partially forested, and all seem very comfortable. Sites 1–4 accommodate tents only, as there is separate parking away from these sites. Electric sites include 12–14, 16–18, 20–23, and about half of the sites numbered in the 30s, 40s, and 50s. These sites range from 25-foot back-ins (12) to 42-foot back-ins (14). The only electric sites that have somewhat of a view are 12 and 23. Sites 61–92 offer spectacular views of the lake and the marina, but are entirely unshaded. Moreover, a number of these sites (76–83) do not permit tent camping. Loop C offers some great views—especially amongst the higher numbers—but is mostly unshaded. Tent sites include 24–28 and 32–35, which are walk-in sites overlooking the lake. The rest room is small and the showers made of crude cement, but they are otherwise modern and comfortable. This is a large and attractive campground that will appeal mostly to those interested in water recreational.

Basics

Operated By: Thousand Trails Management. **Open:** Memorial Day–early Sept. **Site Assignment:** First come, first served. Credit card required for reservation; 3-days cancellation policy, less $10 service fee. **Registration:** At pay station. **Fee:** $20 (water, electric), no hookups, $15. (checks). **Parking:** At site.

Facilities

Number of RV Sites: 20. **Number of Tent-Only Sites:** 128. **Hookups:** Water, electric (10, 20, 30, 50 amps). **Each Site:** Picnic table, fire pit. **Dump Station:** Yes. **Laundry:** No. **Pay Phone:** Yes. **Rest Rooms and Showers:** Yes. **Fuel:** No. **Propane:** No. **Internal Roads:** Gravel. **RV Service:** No. **Market:** 9 mi. south. **Restaurant:** 9 mi. south. **General Store:** No. **Vending:** No. **Swimming:** Lake. **Playground:** No. **Other:** Boat ramp, ampitheater. **Activities:** Fishing, boating, swimming, hiking, skiing. **Nearby Attractions:** Lake Granby. **Additional Information:** Forestry Office, (970) 887-4100.

Restrictions

Pets: On leash, cleaned up after. **Fires:** In grills. **Alcoholic Beverages:** At sites. **Vehicle Maximum Length:** None. **Other:** Max. 5 people per site.

To Get There

From the junction of Hwy. 40 and Hwy. 34, turn north onto Hwy. 34 and go 8.5 mi. Turn right at the sign into the entrance.

GRAND JUNCTION

RV Ranch at Grand Junction

3238 East I-70 Business Loop, Grand Junction 81520. T: (800) 793-0041 or (970) 434-6644; F: (970) 434-5681; www.rvranches.com; rvranch@gj.net.

RV ★★★★★ Tent ★★

Beauty: ★★★★ Site Privacy: ★★
Spaciousness: ★★★ Quiet: ★★★★
Security: ★★★★ Cleanliness: ★★★★★
Insect Control: ★★★★ Facilities: ★★★★★

This perfectly manicured, wonderfully clean park has loads of trees offering shade, nice landscaping, and long (75-foot) pull-throughs. The one downside is that sites are slightly narrow: the RVs with slide-outs on some of the 30-foot-wide spaces were practically touching on my visit. Besides this, however, it is hard to find a less-than-wonderful site in this park. (Although, 53 seems slightly chinsed on space and doesn't have a tree, and 54 is a little close to the basketball court.) Pull-throughs 44–52 and back-ins 23–35 are personal favorites due to their semi-isolated feeling and good trees. The rest rooms are immaculate and beautiful, with nice tiling and decorations. Showers have inner and outer doors for added privacy, and are spacious enough for anyone. A sign in the rest rooms asks guests to report any problems to management, and you can tell that these folks are on top of things. Tenters, unfortunately, don't fare quite as well, and the concrete slabs that pass for tent sites (ouch!) might as well be converted to RV sites for all they're worth. Tent campers should skip this park. However, anyone with an RV who is passing through Colorado should make a point to check out this park—it is what an RV park is supposed to be!

Basics

Operated By: RV Resorts Co. **Open:** All year. **Site Assignment:** Assigned upon registration. Credit card required for reservation; 24-hours cancellation policy. **Registration:** In office. (Late arrivals use drop box.) **Fee:** RV $26–33, tent $28 (V, MC, AE, D). **Parking:** At site.

Facilities

Number of RV Sites: 139. **Number of Tent-Only Sites:** 0. **Hookups:** Water, sewer, electric (20, 30, 50 amps). **Each Site:** Picnic table, grill. **Dump Station:** Yes. **Laundry:** Yes. **Pay Phone:**

Yes. **Rest Rooms and Showers:** Yes. **Fuel:** No. **Propane:** Yes. **Internal Roads:** Perfect paved. **RV Service:** Can call. **Market:** 0.5 mi. east. **Restaurant:** 0.5 mi. east (cafe on-site). **General Store:** Yes. **Vending:** Yes. **Swimming:** Pool. **Playground:** Yes. **Other:** Dog walk area, TV room, e-mail booth, exercise room, kitchen, nightly movies in summer, RV supplies. **Activities:** Hiking, wine-tasting, swimming, volleyball, horseshoes, pancake breakfasts, ice cream socials, fishing, golf, crafts. **Nearby Attractions:** Colorado National Monument, Dionosaur National Monument, Dinosaur Trail, Grand Mesa, wineries. **Additional Information:** Grand Junction Visitor & Convention Bureau, (800) 962-2547 or (970) 244-1480.

Restrictions

Pets: On leash, cleaned up after. **Fires:** In fire pits. **Alcoholic Beverages:** At sites. **Vehicle Maximum Length:** None. **Other:** No generators, no kennels, no clotheslines, no vehicle washing.

To Get There

From I-70, take Exit 30 onto the I-70 Business Loop. Go-0.75 mi. southwest, then turn right at the light onto F Rd. and take the first (sharp) right turn behind the Park-Ride. Drive 0.1 mi. and take the first left into the entrance.

GRAND LAKE

Elk Creek Campground

143 CR 48 (Golf Course Rd.) P.O. Box 549, Grand Lake 80447. T: (800) ELK-CREEK or (970) 627-8502; F: (970) 627-5456; www.coloradodirectory.com; elkcreek@rkymtnhi.com.

RV ★★★★ Tent ★★★★

Beauty: ★★★★	Site Privacy: ★★★★
Spaciousness: ★★★★	Quiet: ★★★★
Security: ★★★★	Cleanliness: ★★★★★
Insect Control: ★★★★	Facilities: ★★★★★

Located in a very rural area just outside of town, this campground has campsites laid out in a loop that extends almost into the forest. As a result, most sites are well-shaded. (Sites 1–3 and 27–33 are on the edge of a clearing and are therefore less shaded.) All sites are back-ins, averaging 45 feet in length, with little variation. Sites 20 and even numbers 34–40 are located at the foot of a forested hill, which makes these sites somewhat more attractive. Site 42 is by far the most secluded site, set well into the forest at the far end of the internal road loop. Tent sites are located across the Elk River opposite the playground. The management is planning to build more cabins, however, and these sites may no longer be available. The rec room is extremely cozy, and contains comfortable sofas as well as cable TV. The rest rooms are spic-and-span. The showers are individual unisex units just outside the rest rooms. While clean, they are extremely narrow, a little dark, and almost intimidating. Otherwise, this campground is a wonderful destination for any camper, along or with a family.

Basics

Operated By: Linda Stanley. **Open:** All year. **Site Assignment:** Assigned upon registration; reservations recommended. Credit card required for reservation; cancellation required by noon the day before a scheduled stay. **Registration:** In office. (Late arrivals select an available site & pay in the morning.) **Fee:** RV $25 (full), $23 (water, electric), tent $20 (checks, V, MC, D, AE). **Parking:** At site.

Facilities

Number of RV Sites: 50. **Number of Tent-Only Sites:** Undesignated sites. **Hookups:** Water, sewer, electric (30, 50 amps). **Each Site:** Picnic table, grill, fire pit. **Dump Station:** Yes. **Laundry:** Yes. **Pay Phone:** Yes. **Rest Rooms and Showers:** Yes. **Fuel:** No. **Propane:** Yes. **Internal Roads:** Gravel. **RV Service:** No. **Market:** 0.5 mi. toward Grand Lake. **Restaurant:** 0.75 mi. toward Grand Lake. **General Store:** Yes. **Vending:** No. **Swimming:** No. **Playground:** Yes. **Other:** 14 cabins, game room, rec room (w/ cable TV & pool table), dataport, RV supplies, fishing pond. **Activities:** Fishing, boating, swimming, hiking, golfing, horseback riding, hunting, snowmobiling, tennis, horseshoes, volleyball. **Nearby Attractions:** Rocky Mountain National Park. **Additional Information:** Grand Lake Chamber of Commerce, (970) 627-3402.

Restrictions

Pets: On leash, cleaned up after. **Fires:** In grills. **Alcoholic Beverages:** At sites. **Vehicle Maximum Length:** None. **Other:** No pets or food in game room or rec room.

To Get There

From the junction of Hwy. 278 and Hwy. 34, turn north onto Hwy. 34 and go 0.25 mi. Turn west onto CR 48 (Golf Course Rd.) and go 0.2 mi. Turn right at the sign into the entrance.

GREELEY

Greeley Campground and RV Park

501 East 27 St., Greeley 80631.T: (970) 353-6476; www.greeleyrvpark.com.

RV ★★★★ Tent ★★★

Beauty: ★★★★	Site Privacy: ★★★★
Spaciousness: ★★★★	Quiet: ★★★
Security: ★★★★	Cleanliness: ★★★★
Insect Control: ★★★★	Facilities: ★★★

Made up of uniform 65-foot pull-throughs, this campground offers many shaded sites and a comfortable environment. The western side of the campground is more shaded than the east. Many sites have a cement pad for picnicking, although some (especially towards the southwest) do not. Sites 2–12 along the north side face a row of vegetation, offering a very pleasant view. This row, and perhaps the row immediately to the south (60–71), is the nicest area in the park due to the large amount of shade and the view. There is a storage unit by sites 2 and 71 that makes these sites less desirable. Site 15, on the other hand, has exceptionally attractive landscaping (including flowers and a section of fence) that makes it the prettiest site in the park. The row containing sites 39–52 is closest to the highway, and therefore a less desirable place to camp. The tenting area is lcoated to the east of the office, and consists of a large grassy area with two huge shade trees. This area is even closer to the highway than the closest row of RV sites. The rest rooms and showers are aging slightly, but are very clean. This campground provides a pretty location for campers who wish to explore the Greeley area, and is very convenient for longer rigs.

BASICS

Operated By: Marlin & Shirley Ness. **Open:** All year. **Site Assignment:** Assigned upon registration Credit card required for reservation; 24-hours cancellation policy. **Registration:** In office. (Late arrivals use drop box.) **Fee:** RV $23.50 (full, 50 amps), $21.50 (full, 30 amps), tent $13 (checks, V, MC). **Parking:** At site, plenty of extra parking.

FACILITIES

Number of RV Sites: 95. **Number of Tent-Only Sites:** 10. **Hookups:** Water, sewer, electric (30, 50 amps). **Each Site:** Picnic table. **Dump Station:** No (sewer at all sites). **Laundry:** Yes. **Pay Phone:** Yes. **Rest Rooms and Showers:** Yes. **Fuel:** No. **Propane:** Yes. **Internal Roads:** Paved. **RV Service:** No. **Market:** 1 mi. west. **Restaurant:** 1 mi. west. **General Store:** Yes. **Vending:** Yes. **Swimming:** No. **Playground:** No. **Other:** RV parts, dataport, woodworking shop, dog walk area, cabins. **Activities:** Hiking, woodworking. **Nearby Attractions:** Pawnee Grasslands, Centennial Village, Greeley Independence Stampede (July 4th). **Additional Information:** Greeley/Weld Chamber of Commerce, (970) 352-3566.

RESTRICTIONS

Pets: On leash, cleaned up after, small pets only. **Fires:** In grills. **Alcoholic Beverages:** At sites. **Vehicle Maximum Length:** None. **Other:** Adult-oriented.

TO GET THERE

From the junction of Hwy. 85 and Hwy. 34 (Fort Morgan Exit), turn east onto Hwy. 34 and go 0.6 mi. Turn north at the blue trailer sign onto an unmarked road. Turn right at the sign into the entrance.

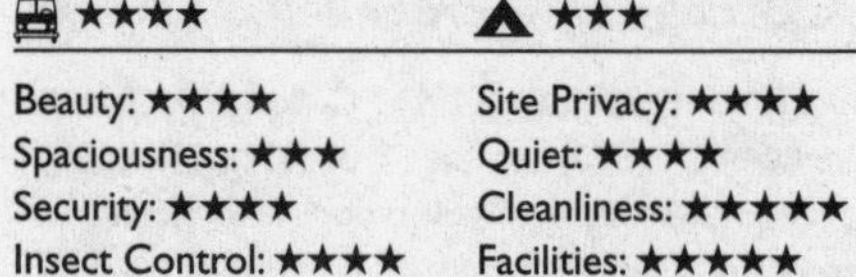

GUNNISON

Gunnison KOA

105 CR 50, Gunnison 81230.T: (800) 562-1248 or (970) 641-1358; F: (970) 641-5329; www.koa.com.

RV ★★★★ Tent ★★★

Beauty: ★★★★	Site Privacy: ★★★★
Spaciousness: ★★★	Quiet: ★★★★
Security: ★★★★	Cleanliness: ★★★★★
Insect Control: ★★★★	Facilities: ★★★★★

This campground on the southwest side of town features level, grassy sites laid out on two loops. The rural location and the attractive decor make for a pleasant camping experience. There is a farm to the southwest, and cars are greeted by curious geese upon entry. The interior spaces of the loops are large enough that vehicles of any size can park on the sites (which average 75 feet long). Except for the lack of shade, most sites are extremely nice. RV sites E-H are very close to the playground, which some campers may wish to avoid. Tent areas are grassy, with some large trees to the northeast. While the RV experience would be improved with more trees, this campground is pleasant enough to warrant a return visit. Tenters will likewise be pleased.

BASICS

Operated By: Norman & Karen. **Open:** Apr. 15–Nov. 1. **Site Assignment:** Assigned upon registration. Credit card required for reservation; 24-hours cancellation policy. **Registration:** In office. (Late arrivals use drop box.) **Fee:** RV $21–27, tent $18 (V, MC, AE, D). **Parking:** At site.

FACILITIES

Number of RV Sites: 126. **Number of Tent-Only Sites:** 0. **Hookups:** Water, sewer, electric (30, 50 amps). **Each Site:** Picnic table, grill. **Dump Station:** Yes. **Laundry:** Yes. **Pay Phone:** Yes. **Rest Rooms and Showers:** Yes. **Fuel:** No. **Propane:** Yes. **Internal Roads:** Gravel. **RV Service:** Can call. **Market:** 1.5 mi. **Restaurant:** 1 mi. **General Store:** Yes. **Vending:** Yes. **Swimming:** No. **Playground:** Yes. **Other:** Trout pond, covered picnic area, pet walk area, cabins. **Activities:** Fishing, golf, hunting, ATV riding. **Nearby Attractions:** Aspen trees at Kebler Pass, Curecanti National Recreation Area. **Additional Information:** Gunnison Chamber of Commerce, (800) 274-7580 or (970) 641-1501.

RESTRICTIONS

Pets: On leash, cleaned up after. **Fires:** In fire pits. **Alcoholic Beverages:** At sites. **Vehicle Maximum Length:** None. **Other:** No clotheslines, no vehicle washing/maintenance.

TO GET THERE

From the junction of Hwy. 135 and US 50, go 1.6 mi. west on Hwy. 50. Turn south onto CR 38 (just east of the bridge across the street). Go 0.5 mi., then turn right after the sign. Take the first right into the entrance. The office is on the right.

HOTCHKISS

Mountain Valley Meadows RV Park

1083 Hwy. 133 P.O. Box 893, Hotchkiss 81419. T: (800) 782-4037 or (970) 872-2351; F: (970) 872-4961; www.mountainvalleymeadows.com; mrvpark@aol.com.

RV ★★★ Tent ★★

Beauty: ★★★	Site Privacy: ★★★
Spaciousness: ★★★★	Quiet: ★★★★
Security: ★★★★	Cleanliness: ★★★
Insect Control: ★★★★	Facilities: ★★

This campground offers 54-foot grassy back-ins in a loop, with a 40-foot space at each site for an extra vehicle. Sites 15–17 at the end of the loop back to woods to the west and a fence to the rear. They feel slightly apart from the other sites, and have an incomparable view of the mountains to the east (as do 28–30). Sites 21 and 24 are at the corner of two internal roads, and may receive more traffic due to this location. Long-term residents occupy several of the RV sites. Tent sites are to the southeast of the RV sites in a strip, on either side of the internal road. While these sites have gorgeous grass, there is no shade to protect from the sun or rain. Site T2 is less desirable due to a dumpster that encroaches on it. The rest rooms have composting, non-flush toilets and curtained-off showers that are extremely clean. This is a worthwhile campground for either tenters or RVers, although RVers may find it slightly more comfortable.

BASICS

Operated By: Private operator. **Open:** All year. **Site Assignment:** First come, first served. **Registration:** In office. (Late arrivals use drop box.) **Fee:** RV $18.90 (full), $15.75 (water, electric), tent $10.50 (V, MC, D). **Parking:** At site.

FACILITIES

Number of RV Sites: 30. **Number of Tent-Only Sites:** 5. **Hookups:** Water, sewer, electric (30, 50 amps). **Each Site:** Picnic table, fire ring. **Dump Station:** Yes. **Laundry:** Yes. **Pay Phone:** Yes. **Rest Rooms and Showers:** Yes. **Fuel:** No. **Propane:** No. **Internal Roads:** Gravel/dirt. **RV Service:** No. **Market:** No. **Restaurant:** No. **General Store:** No. **Vending:** No. **Swimming:** No. **Playground:** Yes. **Other:** Well water. **Activities:** Hiking, fishing, hunting, boating, swimming. **Nearby Attractions:** Gunnison National Forest, Crawford State Park, Gunnison Gorge National Conservation Area. **Additional Information:** Delta Chamber of Commerce, (970) 874-8616.

RESTRICTIONS

Pets: On leash, cleaned up after. **Fires:** In fire pits. **Alcoholic Beverages:** At sites. **Vehicle Maximum Length:** None.

TO GET THERE

From the junction of Hwy. 92 and Hwy. 133, turn east onto Hwy. 133 and go 1 mi. Turn left at the sign into the entrance. The office is the first building on the left.

HUDSON
Pepper Pod KOA

P.O. Box 445, Hudson 80642. T: (303) 536-4763 or (303) 536-9554; www.koa.com; koahudson@qwest.net.

RV ★★★★ Tent ★★★

Beauty: ★★ Site Privacy: ★★★★
Spaciousness: ★★★★ Quiet: ★★
Security: ★★★★ Clealiness: ★★★★
Insect Control: ★★★★ Facilities: ★★★★

Laid out as a square with rows on the inside and sites ringing the perimter, this campground is adjacent to some industrial and commercial areas, and it has a definite urban feel. There is a railroad that passes to the east of the campground. Sites to the northwest (especially 19 and 29) have the most industrial views, and are less attractive as a result. Sites 2–10 are 30-foot back-ins on thick grass that is even better than the grass in the tenting area. Site 2 is directly next to the trash dumpster and the RV dump, and is the least desirable site. The row containing 32–39 is perhaps the nicest section, as it is furthest from the highway and the residences around the park. Sites 42 and 52 are adjacent to the manager's residence, and sites 52–59 border an external residential area. The tenting area occupies the entire western side of the campground. There is sparse vegetation covering the ground, and little shade except in the northwest corner. The camper kitchen did not have running water at the time of this review. This is an acceptable overnight campground, but neither the area nor the campground itself present any reason to make a special trip out.

BASICS

Operated By: Neal Pontius. **Open:** All year. **Site Assignment:** Assigned upon registration Credit card required for reservation; 24-hours cancellation policy. **Registration:** In office. (Late arrivals use drop box.) **Fee:** RV $27 (full), $23 (water, electric), tent $18 (checks, V, MC, D). **Parking:** At site.

FACILITIES

Number of RV Sites: 65. **Number of Tent-Only Sites:** 10. **Hookups:** Water, sewer, electric (20, 30, 50 amps). **Each Site:** Picnic table, grill. **Dump Station:** Yes. **Laundry:** Yes. **Pay Phone:** Yes. **Rest Rooms and Showers:** Yes. **Fuel:** No. **Propane:** Yes. **Internal Roads:** Gravel. **RV Service:** No. **Market:** 18 mi. to Brighton. **Restaurant:** 1 block. **General Store:** Yes. **Vending:** No. **Swimming:** Pool. **Playground:** Yes. **Other:** 2 cabins, game room, pet walk, dataport, community building. **Activities:** Swimming, meetings, volleyball, touring Denver. **Nearby Attractions:** Denver. **Additional Information:** Fort Lupton Chamber of Commerce, (303) 857-4474.

RESTRICTIONS

Pets: On leash, cleaned up after. **Fires:** In grills. **Alcoholic Beverages:** At sites. **Vehicle Maximum Length:** 65 ft.

TO GET THERE

From I-76 (Exit 33), turn east onto Hwy. 52 and go 0.1 mi., then turn right and go 0.2 mi. Turn left at the sign into the entrance. The office is on the right.

KREMMLING
Red Mountain RV Park

P.O. Box 1267, Kremmling 80459. T: (970) 724-9593 or (877) 375-9593; www.redmtnrvpark.com.

RV ★★★ Tent ★★★

Beauty: ★★★ Site Privacy: ★★★
Spaciousness: ★★★ Quiet: ★★★★
Security: ★★★★ Cleanliness: ★★★★★
Insect Control: ★★★★ Facilities: ★★★★

The presence or abscence of trees in this park will make or break your stay—at least in summer. Sites 1–10 are shaded 54-foot gravel pull-throughs laid out horizontally to the highway. The dump station is right at site 10, making this site less desirable. The rest of the sites, however, are entirely unshaded. In effect, this park consists of hookups set around a large, open gravel space. To the north are long-term residents and RV storage. There is a baseball field to the east and a large antenna to the west. The sites that have grass (mostly towards the north) are in large part overgrown. The tent area is a cordoned-off section of thick grass that has two covered picnic tables. This area is nice, but only large enough to comfortably fit about 6 tents. The rest rooms and showers are very clean and roomy enough. They are often used by hunters who only pass through for a shower. For campers who wish to stay and explore the area, this park is a pleasant stay.

Basics

Operated By: Jeff & Sara Miller. **Open:** All year. **Site Assignment:** Flexible, depending on site availability. Credit card required for reservation; 24-hours cancellation policy. **Registration:** In office. (Late arrivals select an available site & pay in the morning.) **Fee:** RV $19 (full), tent $12 (checks, V, MC, & D). **Parking:** At site.

Facilities

Number of RV Sites: 45. **Number of Tent-Only Sites:** Undesignated sites. **Hookups:** Water, sewer, electric (30, 50 amps). **Each Site:** Picnic table. **Dump Station:** Yes. **Laundry:** Yes. **Pay Phone:** Yes. **Rest Rooms and Showers:** Yes. **Fuel:** No. **Propane:** Yes. **Internal Roads:** Gravel. **RV Service:** No. **Market:** 1 mi. west. **Restaurant:** 1 mi. west. **General Store:** Yes. **Vending:** Yes. **Swimming:** No. **Playground:** Yes. **Other:** Dataport, lounge, RV storage. **Activities:** Hunting, fishing, hiking. **Nearby Attractions:** Rocky Mountain National Park, Steamboat Springs. **Additional Information:** Kremmling Area Chamber of Commerce, (970) 724-3472.

Restrictions

Pets: On leash, cleaned up after. **Fires:** In grills. **Alcoholic Beverages:** At sites. **Vehicle Maximum Length:** None.

To Get There

From the junction of Hwy. 9 and Hwy. 40, turn east onto Hwy. 40 and go 1 mi. Turn north onto CR 22 and go 1 block. Turn right at the sign into the entrance.

LA JUNTA

La Junta KOA

26680 West Hwy. 50, La Junta 81050. T: (800) 562-9501 or (719) 384-9580; F: (719) 384-5221; www.koa.com.

RV ★★★★ Tent ★★★

Beauty: ★★	Site Privacy: ★★★
Spaciousness: ★★★★	Quiet: ★★★
Security: ★★★★	Cleanliness: ★★★★
Insect Control: ★★★★	Facilities: ★★★★

Pull-throughs in this campground range from 30 feet to 60 feet in length, and all are very level, grassy, and open. End sites 31, 41, and 49 are at the small end of this scale, making them slightly less desirable. The best RV site is 25, as it contains large shade trees on both sides. This is an important consideration, as most sites (and most campgrounds in the area) have very little shade. Site 49 comes in second thanks to a single towering shade tree. Tenters have it a little nicer with regards to shade. The strip of tent sites at the north end of the campground (just off the highway, unfortunately) and to the west of the pool have a line of overarching trees that protect tenters from the sun's rays. The earth is quite hard here, however, and the sites receive a fair amount of traffic noise. The group tenting area at the extreme south end of the campground does not have shade trees like the strip at the north end, and is therefore not quite as nice. The rest room facility is a little small but quite clean. The shower curtains and floors look dated, but the facility is otherwise comfortable. The laundry room is clean and roomy, and open 24 hours. RVers will enjoy this campground, but tenters may want to push on.

Basics

Operated By: Hank & Margy Rogers. **Open:** All year. **Site Assignment:** Assigned upon registration Credit card required for reservation; 24-hours cancellation policy. **Registration:** In office. (Late arrivals). **Fee:** RV $24.50 (full, 30 amps), $26.50 (full, 50 amps), $23.50 (water, electric), tent $18 (V, MC, D). **Parking:** At site; additional lots.

Facilities

Number of RV Sites: 52. **Number of Tent-Only Sites:** 5. **Hookups:** Water, sewer, electric (30, 50 amps), cable. **Each Site:** Picnic table, tree or shrub. **Dump Station:** Yes. **Laundry:** Yes. **Pay Phone:** Yes. **Rest Rooms and Showers:** Yes. **Fuel:** No. **Propane:** Yes. **Internal Roads:** Gravel. **RV Service:** No. **Market:** 0.2 mi. west (limited on site). **Restaurant:** 0.2 mi. west. **General Store:** Yes. **Vending:** Yes. **Swimming:** Pool. **Playground:** Yes. **Other:** Meeting room, dog walk area, pool table, covered patio, dataport. **Activities:** Fishing, golf, boating, horseshoes, video games. **Nearby Attractions:** Bent's Fort. **Additional Information:** La Junta Chamber of Commerce, (719) 384-7411.

Restrictions

Pets: On leash, cleaned up after, max. of 2 (small) dogs. **Fires:** In grills only. **Alcoholic Beverages:** At sites. **Vehicle Maximum Length:** None.

To Get There

From the junction of Hwy. 10 and Hwy. 50, go 1.5 mi. west on Hwy. 50. Turn left at the sign into the entrance. Keep straight to enter the campground. The office is on the left.

LA VETA

Circle the Wagons RV Park and Motel

124 North Main St., P.O. Box 122, La Veta 81055. T: (719) 742-3233.

RV ★★ Tent ★

Beauty: ★★	Site Privacy: ★★★
Spaciousness: ★★★	Quiet: ★★
Security: ★★★★	Cleanliness: ★★★
Insect Control: ★★★	Facilities: ★★★

This campground is divided into two parks, with a much different experience depending on which campground you stay at. The main campground (where the office is located) has much more of an urban feel to it. The pull-throughs near the office are 75 feet long, while the internal road is so wide that any rig can manoeuvre within it, and even stick out from any site. End sites 63 and 56 have trees and grass in a strip that effectively adds 10–15 feet to their site width. (Most other sites have neither grass nor trees.) Back-ins 49–53 back to undeveloped land with hills in the distance, making them more scenic, while 42–48 back to a residential area, which lessens their appeal. 55, by the bathhouse, is a pull-through that could take a rig of any size and has grass and extra width. The facilities are clean but unremarkable. Now for the park's better half. The west campground is much prettier and even cleaner than the east campground. All sites are grassy, the campground is surrounded by trees, and there are views of hills and distant peaks. The best of these 60-foot back-ins are probably 10 and 12, which are near the pond, with decent trees, and even 1, which is by the entrance but has great trees and perhaps a little more space. The rest rooms and laundry facilities are much nicer, and there is even a small sitting area with books in the same building. Unless a pull-through is absolutely necessary, be sure to get a space in the western campground. The road leading in is on the rough side (drive slowly!), but once you're in, you'll be happier than in the east side park.

Basics

Operated By: Lonnie Hawkins. **Open:** All year. **Site Assignment:** First come, first served; verbal reservations OK. **Registration:** In office; inform management if staying multiple nights. (Late arrivals ring bell.) **Fee:** Pull-through: $20, tent $12 (V, MC, AE, D, DC, CB). **Parking:** At site.

Facilities

Number of RV Sites: 63. **Number of Tent-Only Sites:** 0. **Hookups:** Water, sewer, electric (30, 50 amps), cable. **Each Site:** Picnic table. **Dump Station:** No (sewer at all sites). **Laundry:** Yes. **Pay Phone:** Yes. **Rest Rooms and Showers:** Yes. **Fuel:** No. **Propane:** No. **Internal Roads:** Gravel. **RV Service:** Small repairs possible. **Market:** Next door. **Restaurant:** On site. **General Store:** No. **Vending:** Yes. **Swimming:** No. **Playground:** No. **Other:** Dance hall, children's fishing pond, gift shop, clubhouse, special events room. **Activities:** Scenic drives, horseracing, horseshoes. **Nearby Attractions:** La Mesa horse track, Royal Gorge, Highway of Legends Scenic Byway, Great Sand Dunes National Monument. **Additional Information:** La Veta/Cuchara Chamber of Commerce, (719) 742-3676.

Restrictions

Pets: On leash, cleaned up after. **Fires:** In fire rings. **Alcoholic Beverages:** At sites. **Vehicle Maximum Length:** None.

To Get There

From the junction of Hwy. 160 and Hwy. 12, go 4.3 mi. south on Hwy. 12, turn right at the sign into the entrance. (The entrance to the second part of the campground is on the left side of Main St., south of 1st St.)

LAKE CITY

Lake Fork Campground and RV Resort

P.O. Box 1086, Lake City 81235. T: (970) 944-9519 or (970) 944-2217.

RV ★★★ Tent ★★★

Beauty: ★★★★	Site Privacy: ★★★★
Spaciousness: ★★★	Quiet: ★★★★
Security: ★★★★	Cleanliness: ★★★
Insect Control: ★★★	Facilities: ★★★

Beautiful views of mounatins to the southwest, a river to the east, and plenty of trees around and inside the park make this campground a serene rural escape. The proximity to downtown makes it a convenient stop for motorists who wish to relax in town for a day or an evening. While sites are a little on the narrow side (20 feet wide), some are doubles that can pass as super-long (90-foot) pull-throughs if the opposite site is unoccupied. The rest rooms are clean, spacious, and still comfortable, though old. Showers have a curtained off changing area that adds to the privacy, although accessing the second shower stall requires walking through the first. The best RV sites are 21–24 on the east side, facing trees, a garden, and wooded hills. These sites also have lots of trees and are close to the rest room facilities. Tent sites would be better if they were grassy, not gravel. Please note that this campground has recently come under new management, and some policies (such as reservations and cancellations) had not been established before we went to press.

Basics

Operated By: Charles Sansing, Cecil Bergerson. **Open:** June–Sept. 6. **Site Assignment:** Flexible, depending on availability. Check required for reservation. **Registration:** In office. (Late arrivals settle in morning.) **Fee:** RV $22, tent $17.50 (checks, no credit cards). **Parking:** At site.

Facilities

Number of RV Sites: 23. **Number of Tent-Only Sites:** 3. **Hookups:** Water, sewer, electric (30 amps). **Each Site:** Overturned cable spool for table, fencing, tree. **Dump Station:** No (sewer at all sites). **Laundry:** Yes. **Pay Phone:** Yes. **Rest Rooms and Showers:** Yes. **Fuel:** No. **Propane:** No. **Internal Roads:** Gravel. **RV Service:** No. **Market:** 2 block (limited). **Restaurant:** 1 block. **General Store:** No. **Vending:** Yes. **Swimming:** No. **Playground:** No. **Activities:** Fishing, mountain climbing, hiking, cross-country skiing. **Nearby Attractions:** Uncompahgre Peak, Lake San Cristobal, Lake Fork. **Additional Information:** Lake City Chamber of Commerce, (800) 569-1874 or (970) 944-2527.

Restrictions

Pets: On leash, cleaned up after. **Fires:** In fire pits. **Alcoholic Beverages:** At sites. **Vehicle Maximum Length:** 40 ft.

To Get There

From Hensen Creek Bridge at the south edge of town, go 1 block north on Hwy. 149. Turn right at the sign for the museum onto 2nd St. Take the first right onto Hensen St., and follow the signs to the office at the south end of the park.

LAKEWOOD

Bear Creek Lake Campground

15600 West Morrison Rd., Morrison 80465. T: (303) 697-6159.

RV ★★★★ Tent ★★★★

Beauty: ★★★★	Site Privacy: ★★★★
Spaciousness: ★★★★	Quiet: ★★★★
Security: ★★★★	Cleanliness: ★★★★
Insect Control: ★★★	Facilities: ★★★★

Almost appearing out of place, this campground is in a desert-like field with few trees and low, sparse vegetation. Sites are mostly dirt, with some vegetation cover. The campground is at the far southeast end of the park. The electric sites (more suitable for RVs) are on a hill overlooking the primitive sites. Sites are laid out in rows of roughly five units. Sites 13–16 are closest to the railroad that passes by the park, and are therefore less desirable. Of the primitive sites, 45–49 are extremely long (100–105-foot) pull-throughs. Others are quite long (65–70-foot) back-ins. Sites 65–70 are located just off the internal raod, making them more susceptible to passing vehicular traffic. Walk-in tent sites are found to the northeast of the RV sites. These are surrounded by both fences and trees. This is a nice, wild campground located surprisingly close to the highway to Denver. It is a welcome relief from the busy city, that most campers should enjoy.

Basics

Operated By: Lakewood Community Resources. **Open:** Apr. 1–Oct. 31. **Site Assignment:** First come, first served; no reservations. **Registration:** At pay station. **Fee:** Electric: $10, primitive: $7 (checks). **Parking:** At site.

Facilities

Number of RV Sites: 52. **Number of Tent-Only Sites:** 0. **Hookups:** Electric (20, 30, 50 amps). **Each Site:** Picnic table, grill, fire pit. **Dump Station:** No. **Laundry:** No. **Pay Phone:** Yes. **Rest Rooms and Showers:** Yes. **Fuel:** No. **Propane:** No. **Internal Roads:** Paved/gravel. **RV Service:** No. **Market:** 3 mi. east. **Restaurant:** 0.5 mi. into Morrison. **General Store:** Marina. **Vending:** No. **Swimming:** Lake. **Playground:** Yes. **Other:**

Amphitheater, swim beach, picnic areas, horse rentals, archery range, boat rentals, boat ramp, yurt. **Activities:** Fishing, boating, swimming, hiking, volleyball. **Nearby Attractions:** Denver. **Additional Information:** Denver Chamber of Commerce, (303) 458-0220.

Restrictions

Pets: On 6-ft. leash, cleaned up after. **Fires:** In grills. **Alcoholic Beverages:** At sites. **Vehicle Maximum Length:** None. **Other:** $3/vehicle/day.

To Get There

From the junction of Hwy. 470 (Bear Creek Lake Exit), turn east onto Hwy. 8. Go 1 mi. Turn right at the sign into the entrance.

LAMAR

Lamar KOA

5385 Hwy. 50, Lamar 81052. T: (800) KOA-7626 or (719) 336-7625; www.koa.com.

RV ★★★★ Tent ★★★

Beauty: ★★★ Site Privacy: ★★★
Spaciousness: ★★★ Quiet: ★★★
Security: ★★★★ Cleanliness: ★★★★
Insect Control: ★★★★ Facilities: ★★★★

This campground has all pull-throughs laid out in rows, with level grassy sites. Like other campgrounds in the area, the sites are open with little shade. There is, however, a row of dense trees to the north that blocks off views of a residential area, and provides some shade to campers in those sites. Otherwise, there are very few trees or bushes in the campground itself. Sites average 24 feet wide and 60–70 feet in length. The best sites for RVers are the end sites 10, 16, and 21. These sites are significantly wider than the others, are closest to the row of trees, and furthest from the highway. (End sites 31 and 43 are also wide, but not as close to the trees.) Tent sites are located in Row A and the southwest section of Row F. Row A is wide open, with no shade at all. These are less desirable sites than those in Row F. Sites in Row F (33–37) have a decent grass covering and, even more important, a half-covering over the picnic tables, which affords campers at these sites more shade than nearly any other sites. The rest rooms and showers are very clean, well-lit, and modern, as is the laundry facility. This is probably the nicest campground in the area, and campers should make a note to head here when in southeast Colorado.

Basics

Operated By: Bill Rich. **Open:** All year (limited facilities in winter). **Site Assignment:** Flexible, depending on availability. Credit card required for reservation; same-day cancellation policy. **Registration:** In office. (Late arrivals use drop box.) **Fee:** RV $25 (full), $23 (water, electric), tent $18. **Parking:** At site.

Facilities

Number of RV Sites: 28. **Number of Tent-Only Sites:** 15. **Hookups:** Water, sewer, electric (20, 30 amps). **Each Site:** Picnic table (half are covered), grill. **Dump Station:** Yes. **Laundry:** Yes. **Pay Phone:** Yes. **Rest Rooms and Showers:** Yes. **Fuel:** No. **Propane:** Yes. **Internal Roads:** Gravel. **RV Service:** No. **Market:** 5 mi. southeast. **Restaurant:** 1 mi. southeast. **General Store:** Yes. **Vending:** No. **Swimming:** Pool. **Playground:** Yes. **Other:** Mini golf, dog walk area, cabin, outdoor patio. **Activities:** Hunting, fishing, golf, video games. **Nearby Attractions:** Big Timbers Museum, Madonna of the Trail, Arkansas River, Bent's Old Fort. **Additional Information:** Lamar Chamber of Commerce, (719) 336-4379.

Restrictions

Pets: On leash, cleaned up after. **Fires:** In grills only. **Alcoholic Beverages:** At sites. **Vehicle Maximum Length:** None. **Other:** Children under 7 must be accompanied by an adult in the swimming pool.

To Get There

From the junction of Hwy. 50 and Hwy. 287 (Olive and Main Sts. in town), go 4.3 mi. northwest on Hwy. 50/287. Turn right at the sign into the entrance. The office is on the left.

LEADVILLE

Leadville RV Corral

135 West 2nd St., Leadville 80461. T: (719) 486-3111.

RV ★★★ Tent ★★★

Beauty: ★★ Site Privacy: ★★★
Spaciousness: ★★★ Quiet: ★★★
Security: ★★★★ Cleanliness: ★★★★
Insect Control: ★★★★ Facilities: ★★★

Within walking distance to downtown, this campground offers a convenient place to stay the night while visiting the Leadville area. However, spacious and beautifully landscaped it is not. This is a rather urban overnighter, with uniform 45-foot spaces laid out in a ring around the perimeter, surrounded by residences and semi-industrial lots surrounding it. All sites are gravel, but most have a grassy strip for picnicking located next to the drive. (Sites 1 and 2 do not.) Sites 1–8 are back-ins; all the rest of the sites are pull-throughs. Sites 17 and 33 are located along an external road, and are less deisrable for this fact. Sites 1 and 2 double as the entrance and exit, which raises the question of how to get in or out when they are occupied. A tenting area is located next to the office. This is an open, grassy, but rather small area. Three tents could reasonably stay there, and five could probably squeeze in, especially if they were together. The facilities are clean, and the management quite friendly, making this an acceptable location for a stay of a night or two.

Basics

Operated By: Rudy Klucik, Steve Anerson. **Open:** All year. **Site Assignment:** Flexible, depending on site availability. Credit card required for reservation; 24-hours cancellation policy. **Registration:** In office. (Late arrivals use drop box.) **Fee:** RV $23.94 (full), tent $16.32 (checks, V, MC). **Parking:** At site.

Facilities

Number of RV Sites: 33. **Number of Tent-Only Sites:** 5. **Hookups:** Water, sewer, electric (30, 50 amps), cable. **Each Site:** Picnic table, grill. **Dump Station:** Yes. **Laundry:** Yes. **Pay Phone:** Yes. **Rest Rooms and Showers:** Yes. **Fuel:** No. **Propane:** No. **Internal Roads:** Gravel. **RV Service:** No. **Market:** 2 mi. north. **Restaurant:** 2 mi. north. **General Store:** Planned. **Vending:** Yes. **Swimming:** No. **Playground:** No. **Other:** Walking distance to downtown. **Activities:** Fishing, hunting, hiking. **Nearby Attractions:** Boom Days (first weekend in Aug.), 100-mile footrace. **Additional Information:** Leadville Chamber of Commerce, (719) 486-3900.

Restrictions

Pets: No dogs outside. **Fires:** In grills. **Alcoholic Beverages:** At sites. **Vehicle Maximum Length:** 45 ft.

To Get There

From the junction of Hwy. 24 (Harrison) and West 2nd St., turn west onto West 2nd St. and take 2nd parking lot entrance.

LIMON
Limon KOA

575 Colorado Ave., Limon 80828. T: (719) 775-2151; www.koa.com.

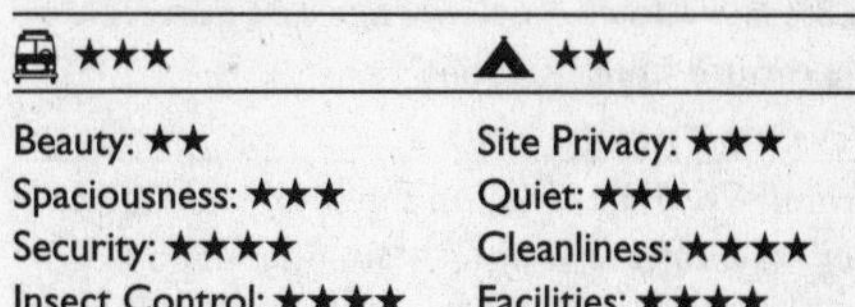

RV ★★★ Tent ★★

Beauty: ★★ Site Privacy: ★★★
Spaciousness: ★★★ Quiet: ★★★
Security: ★★★★ Cleanliness: ★★★★
Insect Control: ★★★★ Facilities: ★★★★

Hunkered down in the middle of nowhere, this campground serves mainly overnighters and is not close to any specific attractions for tourists. The land it is located on is likewise mainly devoid of trees and grass, and sites in the campground mostly lack shade. There are residences to the southwest of the campground and storage units to the west, making the area surrounding the campground less than attractive. The row of sites to the north consists of 33-foot back-ins (43–46) and 75-foot pull-throughs (47–59). The row of pull-throughs to the south (1–26) consists of 70-foot sites that face out to the residences and storage facility. Tenting sites in the west end of the park are entirely unshaded, although two sites have shaded picnic tables.

Basics

Operated By: Private operator. **Open:** All year (services are weather-dependent). **Site Assignment:** Assigned upon registration. Credit card required for reservation; 24-hours cancellation policy, less $5 fee. **Registration:** In office. (Late arrivals use drop box.) **Fee:** RV $24.95 (full), $22.95 (water, electric), tent $18.95 (checks, V, MC). **Parking:** At site.

Facilities

Number of RV Sites: 50. **Number of Tent-Only Sites:** 10. **Hookups:** Water, sewer, electric (30, 50 amps), cable. **Each Site:** Picnic tables, grills. **Dump Station:** Yes. **Laundry:** Yes. **Pay Phone:** Yes. **Rest Rooms and Showers:** Yes. **Fuel:** No. **Propane:** No. **Internal Roads:** Dirt. **RV Service:** No. **Market:** Small market 1 mi. east. **Restaurant:** 0.25 mi. towards I-40. **General Store:** Yes. **Vending:** No. **Swimming:** Pool. **Playground:** Yes. **Other:** Cabins, RV supplies, dataport, dog walk. **Activities:** Swimming, fishing (at Bonny State Park), volleyball, basketball. **Nearby Attractions:** Denver, Colorado Springs, Burlington. **Additional Information:** Limon Chamber of Commerce, P.O. Box 101, Limon, Colorado, 80828.

RESTRICTIONS

Pets: On leash, cleaned up after; no horses. **Fires:** In fire pits. **Alcoholic Beverages:** At sites. **Vehicle Maximum Length:** None.

TO GET THERE

From I-70 (Exit 361), on the south side of the highway, turn west onto Main St. and go 0.2 mi. Turn right onto Hwy. 24/40/287 and go 0.2 mi. Turn left at the sign into the entrance.

LINDON

Meadowlark Cafe, Motel and RV Park

12120 CR South, Lindon 80740. T: (970) 383-2298.

RV ★★★ Tent ★★

Beauty: ★★ Site Privacy: ★★★
Spaciousness: ★★★★ Quiet: ★★★★★
Security: ★★★★ Cleanliness: ★★★★
Insect Control: ★★★★ Facilities: ★★

This part of Colorado does not, unfortunately, lend itself to tourism in general, and camping specifically. There are no attractions in the immediate area, and this campground (if it can be called that) offers little more than a place to park an RV for the night. (Bonny State Park, the nearest area for recreation, is a good 50 miles distant.) The park consists of one row of hookups in a large, open grassy field, with two other sites located to the east of this row. None of the sites offers shade, but on the positive side, all of these sites can accommodate a rig of any size. There are open fields to the north, west, and east, and a motel and a row of bushes to the south and east. The grain silos to the immediate north are at least something to look at, but many campers here may want to catch up on their reading or television-watching. Outside of such activities, there is, alas, little else to do in this campground.

BASICS

Operated By: Doug or Dwayne Bowers. **Open:** All year. **Site Assignment:** Assigned upon registration; verbal reservations OK. **Registration:** In office. (Late arrivals register at night office.) **Fee:** RV $15 (full), tent $8 (checks, V, MC, AE, D). **Parking:** At site.

FACILITIES

Number of RV Sites: 12. **Number of Tent-Only Sites:** Undesignated sites. **Hookups:** Water, sewer, electric (20, 50 amps). **Dump Station:** Yes. **Laundry:** Yes. **Pay Phone:** Yes. **Rest Rooms and Showers:** Yes. **Fuel:** No. **Propane:** No. **Internal Roads:** Gravel. **RV Service:** No. **Market:** 6 mi. northeast/northwest. **Restaurant:** On site. **General Store:** No. **Vending:** No. **Swimming:** No. **Playground:** No. **Other:** Cafe, motel rooms, pet walk. **Activities:** Swimming, fishing, boating, hunting. **Nearby Attractions:** Bonny State Park. **Additional Information:** Limon Chamber of Commerce, P.O. Box 101, Limon, Colorado, 80828.

RESTRICTIONS

Pets: On leash, cleaned up after. **Fires:** In fire pits. **Alcoholic Beverages:** At sites. **Vehicle Maximum Length:** None.

TO GET THERE

From the easternmost town sign on Hwy. 36, go 0.1 mi. west, and take first right onto the dirt road. Follow the road 0.15 mi. to the entrance on the right.

LONGMONT

Barbour Ponds State Park

4995 Weld CR 24 1/2, Longmont 80504. T: (303) 678-9402; www.coloradoparks.org.

RV ★★★ Tent ★★★

Beauty: ★★★ Site Privacy: ★★★★
Spaciousness: ★★★★ Quiet: ★★★
Security: ★★★★ Cleanliness: ★★★
Insect Control: ★★★★ Facilities: ★★★

Divided into the North, West, and East campgrounds, this park offers rather undeveloped sites with both back-ins and pull-throughs. The North Campground is located quite close to I-25, and cannot be recommended due to the amount of traffic noise it receives. Sites in this campground include 40-foot (57–60) to 66-foot back-ins (48–50, 52–54), and 70-foot pull-throughs (46, 47, 51). Many of these sites are well-shaded. The West Campground has 45–54-foot back-ins that lie closest to the water. Some of these sites are right on the banks of the ponds. Furthest west, the unattractive view of mines to the south opens up. The views to the north, however, are much nicer. The East Campground has several tent sites in a stand of trees right at the entrance (site 28). Other sites are 45-foot back-ins, and many of these are unshaded. Facilities are limited to pit toilets (no showers). This is a pleasant but rather small state park that attracts mostly fishermen and does not offer much in terms of facilities or activities.

BASICS

Operated By: Colorado State Parks. **Open:** All year. **Site Assignment:** First come, first served; reservations available Memorial Day–Labor Day. Credit card required for reservation; 3 days cancellation policy. **Registration:** At pay kiosk. **Fee:** $10 (checks, no credits cards). **Parking:** At site, lots of extra parking.

FACILITIES

Number of RV Sites: 60. **Number of Tent-Only Sites:** 0. **Hookups:** None. **Each Site:** Picnic table, grill, fire pit, tent pad. **Dump Station:** No. **Laundry:** No. **Pay Phone:** No. **Rest Rooms and Showers:** Rest rooms; no shower. **Fuel:** No. **Propane:** Rest rooms, but no showers. **Internal Roads:** Dirt. **RV Service:** No. **Market:** less than 10 mi. to 17th & Pace Sts. **Restaurant:** 3 mi. to I-25. **General Store:** No. **Vending:** No. **Swimming:** No. **Playground:** Yes. **Other:** Firewood, nature trails, wildlife, views of Rocky Mountains, covered picnic areas. **Activities:** Non-motorized boating, fishing. **Nearby Attractions:** Denver, Boulder, Rocky Mountain National Park. **Additional Information:** Boulder CVB, (303) 442-2911.

RESTRICTIONS

Pets: On 6-ft. leash, cleaned up after. **Fires:** In fire pits. **Alcoholic Beverages:** At sites. **Vehicle Maximum Length:** None. **Other:** Pack out trash, $4 entrance fee, no swimming, no bills larger than $20.

TO GET THERE

From the junction of Hwy. I-25 (Exit 240), turn west onto Hwy. 179 and go 1.1 mi. Turn right onto Rd. 7 and go 1.3 mi. to the entrance.

LOVELAND

Carter Valley Campground

1326 North Carter Lake Rd., Loveland 80537. T: (970) 663-3131.

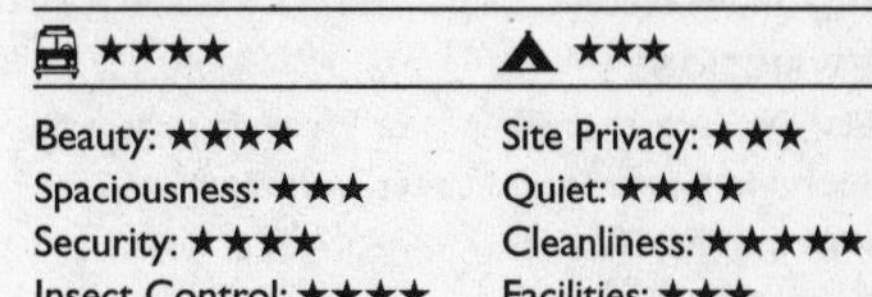

RV ★★★★ Tent ★★★

Beauty: ★★★★ Site Privacy: ★★★
Spaciousness: ★★★ Quiet: ★★★★
Security: ★★★★ Cleanliness: ★★★★★
Insect Control: ★★★★ Facilities: ★★★

Sites in this campground are laid out in rows on three tiers up a hillside. The campground is surrounded by farms, and there are forests and mountains to the northwest. Sites around the office are open-ended back-ins that can accommodate a vehicle of about 40 feet Sites 15–25 on the second tier are 40-foot angled back-ins with parking in front of the sites. Sites 53–62 measure 25 × 35 feet and are laid out by the highway. These sites are somewhat cramped and (although well-shaded) rather undesirable. The top tier, adjacent to a large grassy hill, contains long-term residents. This is probably the nicest section of the park. Sites 37–40 are located along the south edge, perpendicular to the rows on the three tiers. There is RV storage to the west of site 37, making this area less attractive. Tent sites are located on the second tier, above the office. These are grassy but unshaded sites. This campground is in an attractive area and close to a number of recreation opportunities. It is a pleasant stay for RVers or tenters.

BASICS

Operated By: Tammy Johnson. **Open:** All year. **Site Assignment:** Assigned upon registration; verbal reservations OK. **Registration:** In office. (Late arrivals ring bell.) **Fee:** RV $20 (full), $18 (water, electric), tent $10 (checks, V, MC, D). **Parking:** At site.

FACILITIES

Number of RV Sites: 58. **Number of Tent-Only Sites:** 6. **Hookups:** Water, sewer, electric (30, 50 amps). **Each Site:** Picnic table. **Dump Station:** Yes. **Laundry:** Yes. **Pay Phone:** Yes. **Rest Rooms and Showers:** Yes. **Fuel:** No. **Propane:** No. **Internal Roads:** Gravel. **RV Service:** No. **Market:** 4 mi. east. **Restaurant:** 2.5 mi. east. **General Store:** Yes. **Vending:** Yes. **Playground:** Yes. **Other:** Potlucks every 2 weeks, rec room w/ pool table & TV. **Activities:** Skiing, hiking, rock climbing, fishing, boating, swimming, bicycling, mountain climbing. **Nearby Attractions:** Golf courses, Rocky Mountain National Park, flea markets, antique malls. **Additional Information:** Loveland Visitor Center: (970) 667-5728.

Restrictions

Pets: On leash, cleaned up after. **Fires:** In grills. **Alcoholic Beverages:** At sites. **Vehicle Maximum Length:** 42 ft.

To Get There

From the junction of Hwy. 287 and Hwy. 34, turn west onto Hwy. 34 and go 7.25 mi. Turn left onto Carter Lake Rd. and go 0.45 mi. Turn left at the sign into the entrance.

MANITOU SPRINGS

Pike's Peak RV Park and Campground

320 Manitou Dr., Manitou Springs 80829. T: (719) 685-9459.

RV ★★★★ Tent ★★★

Beauty: ★★★★	Site Privacy: ★★★
Spaciousness: ★★	Quiet: ★★★
Security: ★★★★	Cleanliness: ★★★★
Insect Control: ★★★★	Facilities: ★★★

Laid out in a giant loop that rings the entire campground, RV sites are a tight 19 feet wide and a maximum of 40 feet in length. Sites 1–19 back to woods along the northern edge of the campground. Besides 24–27, which are quite near the basketball court and may find games there disruptive, these are among the best sites due to the natural scenery. Sites 26–47 back to the creek, which would make these the nicest sites, except the highway lies just beyond, bringing traffic noise to these sites. Sites 48–58 are in the middle of the park. Sites 58 and 59 are close by a private residence, but definitely the most spacious sites. Tent sites are on a crushed gravel drive. Sites 70 and 71 are wide open to the sun, but 72–74 are very well-shaded. All of these sites are just off the highway.

Basics

Operated By: Allen & Jackie Branine. **Open:** Apr. 1–Oct. 31. **Site Assignment:** Assigned upon registration. Credit card required for reservation; 24-hours cancellation policy. **Registration:** In office. (Late arrivals select an available site & pay in the morning.) **Fee:** RV $26 (full), $26 (water, electric), tent $20 (checks, V, MC). **Parking:** At site.

Facilities

Number of RV Sites: 60. **Number of Tent-Only Sites:** 6. **Hookups:** Water, sewer, electric (30, 50 amps). **Each Site:** Picnic table. **Dump Station:** No. **Laundry:** Yes. **Pay Phone:** Yes. **Rest Rooms and Showers:** Yes. **Fuel:** No. **Propane:** No. **Internal Roads:** Gravel. **RV Service:** On-call. **Market:** less than 0.25 mi. **Restaurant:** Across street. **General Store:** Yes. **Vending:** Yes. **Swimming:** Pool. **Playground:** No. **Other:** Dataport, next door to city park & pool, central location, fishing in creek. **Activities:** Swimming, fishing, sightseeing, mountain climbing, hiking, tours. **Nearby Attractions:** Garden of the Gods, Pike's Peak. **Additional Information:** Manitou Springs Chamber of Commerce, (719) 685-5089.

Restrictions

Pets: On leash, cleaned up after. **Fires:** In grills. **Alcoholic Beverages:** At sites. **Vehicle Maximum Length:** 40 ft.

To Get There

From the junction of Hwy. 24 and Hwy. Business 24 (Manitou Ave.), turn west onto Manitou Ave. and go 0.25 mi. Turn right at the sign into the entrance.

McCLAVE

Hud's Campground

29995 Hwy. 50, McClave 81057. T: (719) 829-4344.

RV ★★★ Tent ★★★

Beauty: ★★★	Site Privacy: ★★★★
Spaciousness: ★★★★	Quiet: ★★★
Security: ★★★★	Cleanliness: ★★★
Insect Control: ★★★★	Facilities: ★★★★

This rural campground consists of a large open field. There is a mobile home to the west of the park, which is slightly unattractive, and the highway is just off the east edge. A big plus in this campground is that sites are defined by width, but not by length. Therefore, pull-throughs measure 30 × 60 feet or longer. Rigs of any size can easily park here. Sites are open, grassy spaces situated in rows. The campground contains only sparse bushes, and, as a result, not much shade. The best sites, at the northern edge of the campground, are slightly larger but situated right on the internal road. Tenting sites, to the south of the pool, are also quite open, but the grass is rather thick, making for a decent ground covering. The shower and rest room facility is a large concrete building, reminiscent of a public swimming pool changing room. The floor needed painting during our inspection, and the showers, while certainly adequate, were due for a good scrubbing.

Basics

Operated By: Bob & Patty Boyer. **Open:** All year (limited facilities in winter). **Site Assignment:** First come, first served; verbal reservations OK. **Registration:** In store. (Late arrivals select an available site & settle in the morning.) **Fee:** RV $14, tent $11. **Parking:** At site.

Facilities

Number of RV Sites: 20. **Number of Tent-Only Sites:** 5. **Hookups:** Water, sewer, electric (30 amps). **Each Site:** Some picnic tables. **Dump Station:** No (sewer at all sites). **Laundry:** Yes. **Pay Phone:** Yes. **Rest Rooms and Showers:** Yes. **Fuel:** No. **Propane:** No. **Internal Roads:** Gravel. **RV Service:** No. **Market:** 15 mi. into Lamar. **Restaurant:** 15 mi. into Lamar. **General Store:** Yes. **Vending:** No. **Swimming:** Pool. **Playground:** Yes. **Other:** RV parts, horseshoes, lake (7 mi. away). **Activities:** Swimming, fishing. **Nearby Attractions:** John Martin Lake. **Additional Information:** Lamar Chamber of Commerce, (719) 336-4379.

Restrictions

Pets: On leash, cleaned up after. **Fires:** In fire pits. **Alcoholic Beverages:** At sites. **Vehicle Maximum Length:** None. **Other:** No BB guns.

To Get There

At the junction of Hwy. 50 and Hwy. 196, on the southwest side.

MEEKER

Stagecoach Campground

39084 Hwy. 13, Meeker 81641. T: (970) 878-4334.

RV ★★★★ Tent ★★★

Beauty: ★★★★	Site Privacy: ★★★★
Spaciousness: ★★★★★	Quiet: ★★★★
Security: ★★★★	Cleanliness: ★★★
Insect Control: ★★★	Facilities: ★★

This is a beautiful campground with lush grass and giant cottonwoods surrounded by natural scenery on all sides: grassy hills to the south and west, a rocky hill to the north, and wetlands to the east. Sites 30–34 are long enough (120 feet) to be used as doubles, but, surprisingly, are not. Sites are a generous 45 feet wide, grassy, and forested. Sites 11–18C may require some manoeuvering to park in, but are still excellent places to camp. RV sites 1–10 are shorter (36-foot) back-ins, much more cramped than the humongous pull-throughs. Tent sites are on a strip of thick grass to the west of the RV sites, but there is only one fire pit, under a cottonwood by the river. Whoever can grab that one spot has quite possibly the best tenting space for 20 miles around! The laundry is small, and the rest rooms are small and darkish, with sealant flaking off the cement floors. Showers are spacious, but one light didn't work when inspected. These facilities are rough, but not uncomfortable. Don't let the less-than-perfect toilet facilities put you off: this is a park to return to again and again!

Basics

Operated By: Gerry Meislohn. **Open:** May 1–Nov. 15. **Site Assignment:** Flexible, depending on fullness; verbal reservations OK. **Registration:** In office. (Late arrivals knock on door or use drop box). **Fee:** RV $20 (full), $18 (water, electric), tent $5 per person (max. $10), (V, MC). **Parking:** At site.

Facilities

Number of RV Sites: 31. **Number of Tent-Only Sites:** Undesignated sites. **Hookups:** Water, sewer, electric (20, 30, 50 amps). **Each Site:** Picnic table, fire ring. **Dump Station:** Yes. **Laundry:** Yes. **Pay Phone:** Yes. **Rest Rooms and Showers:** Yes. **Fuel:** No. **Propane:** No. **Internal Roads:** Gravel. **RV Service:** No. **Market:** 2 mi. into town. **Restaurant:** 2 mi. into town. **General Store:** No. **Vending:** No. **Playground:** No. **Other:** River, meat-hanging area for hunters, cottonwoods, wildlife. **Activities:** Fishing, hunting, skiing, backpacking, snowmobiling. **Nearby Attractions:** White River Museum, White River National Forest, Meeker Classic Sheepdog Trials (Sep.). **Additional Information:** Meeker Chamber of Commerce, (970) 878-5510.

Restrictions

Pets: On leash, cleaned up after. **Fires:** In fire rings/pits. **Alcoholic Beverages:** At sites. **Vehicle Maximum Length:** None.

To Get There

On the south side at the junction of Hwy. 13 and Hwy. 64 (2 mi. out of town). The office is on the left of the driveway.

MONTE VISTA

Mobile Manor RV Park

2830 US Hwy. 160 West, Monte Vista 81144. T: (719) 852-5921; F: (719) 852-0122.

RV: ★★ Tent: n/a

Beauty: ★★ Site Privacy: ★★★★
Spaciousness: ★★★★ Quiet: ★★★
Security: ★★★ Cleanliness: ★★★★
Insect Control: ★★★★ Facilities: ★

This RV park is a wide-open gravel parking area with two rows of six RV sites. As a result, a rig of any size could park in any of the sites, but the park itself is not very appealing. While it is true that there are nice views on three sides (woods and mountains), the park lacks any kind of landscaping or trees. Furthermore, the adjacent motel occupies the view to the southeast, and a drive-in movie screen picks up where the motel leaves off. The higher-numbered sites in both rows are progressively further away from the motel and drive-in, and it is recommended that campers who stay the night here use one of these sites. Tents need not apply.

Basics

Operated By: George Kelloff. **Open:** All year. **Site Assignment:** First come, first served. **Registration:** In motel office. **Fee:** RV $18 (full; by reservation only), $15 (water, electric), $12 (electric) (checks, V, MC, D). **Parking:** At site.

Facilities

Number of RV Sites: 12. **Number of Tent-Only Sites:** 0. **Hookups:** Water, sewer, electric (30, 50 amps). **Each Site:** Picnic table. **Dump Station:** No. **Laundry:** No. **Pay Phone:** Yes. **Rest Rooms and Showers:** Yes. **Fuel:** No. **Propane:** No. **Internal Roads:** Gravel. **RV Service:** No. **Market:** 2 mi. east. **Restaurant:** On site. **General Store:** No. **Vending:** No. **Swimming:** No. **Playground:** No. **Other:** Drive-in movies. **Activities:** Hiking, watching wildlife. **Nearby Attractions:** Monte Vista National Wildlife Reserve. **Additional Information:** Alamosa County Chamber of Commerce, (800) BLU-SKYS or (719) 589-3681.

Restrictions

Pets: On leash, cleaned up after. **Fires:** In fire pits. **Alcoholic Beverages:** At sites. **Vehicle Maximum Length:** None. **Other:** Full hookups by reservation only.

To Get There

From the junction of Hwy. 285 and Hwy. 160, turn west onto Hwy. 160 and go 2.9 mi. Turn left at the sign into the entrance (next to the drive-in movies).

MONTROSE

Montrose RV Resort (formerly KOA)

200 North Cedar Ave., Montrose 81401. T: (888) 249-9554 or (970) 249-9177.

RV: ★★★★ Tent: ★★★

Beauty: ★★★ Site Privacy: ★★★★
Spaciousness: ★★★★ Quiet: ★★★★★
Security: ★★★★ Cleanliness: ★★★★★
Insect Control: ★★★★ Facilities: ★★★★★

All sites are level and grassy here and the landscaping makes this an attractive park. (Storage units to the south detract a little from the beauty.) Sites 1–7 are 36-foot back-ins; although 4 does not have a shade tree, making it less desirable. Sites 8–13 and 18–23 are 56-foot pull-throughs with a shared covered picnic area separated by a wooden divider. 24–31 are slightly larger (66 × 24 feet). Tent sites are in a fenced-off area to the north of the RV sites and west of the cabins. Beyond this, there is an open grassy field with trees at the far end and views of distant hills to the north and west. (43 has the only shade tree among the tent sites.) The rest rooms and showers are spotless, modern, and spacious. There is a bench running along one side for towels and toiletries as well as a clothes rack. Note that the door locks are is a little complicated to use. The laundry is spacious and clean. All in all, this is quite a nice park—especially for RVers.

Basics

Operated By: Ray & Angeline Wells. **Open:** All year. **Site Assignment:** Flexible, depending on availability. Credit card required for reservation; 24-hours cancellation policy. **Registration:** In office. (Late arrivals use drop box.) **Fee:** RV

$23.95 (full), $21.95 (water, electric), tent $18.50 (V, MC, AE, D). **Parking:** At site.

Facilities

Number of RV Sites: 26. **Number of Tent-Only Sites:** 17. **Hookups:** Water, sewer, electric (30, 50 amps). **Each Site:** Picnic table, grill. **Dump Station:** Yes. **Laundry:** Yes. **Pay Phone:** Yes. **Rest Rooms and Showers:** Yes. **Fuel:** No. **Propane:** Yes. **Internal Roads:** Nice gravel. **RV Service:** No. **Market:** 1 mi. into town. **Restaurant:** 1 mi. into town. **General Store:** Yes. **Vending:** No. **Swimming:** Pool. **Playground:** Yes. **Other:** Dog walk area, nightly movies on large screen TV, covered pavillion, cabins. **Activities:** Basketball, movies, swimming, hunting, hiking, biking, rafting, boating. **Nearby Attractions:** Montrose County Historical Museum, Ute Indian Museum & Ouray Memorial Park. **Additional Information:** Montrose Chamber of Commerce, (800) 923-5515 or (970) 249-5000, (970) 249-5515.

Restrictions

Pets: On leash, cleaned up after. **Fires:** In grills. **Alcoholic Beverages:** At sites. **Vehicle Maximum Length:** None.

To Get There

From the junction of Hwy. 50 and Hwy. 550, go 0.8 mi. east on Hwy. 50 (Main St. in town), then 0.2 mi. north on Cedar Ave. Turn right at the sign into the entrance.

NEDERLAND

Kelly-Dahl Campground

Boulder Ranger Office, 2140 Yarmouth Ave., Boulder 80301. T: (877) 444-6777, (800) 280-2267, or (303) 444-6600; www.reserveusa.com or www.fs.fed.us/arns; pmdelong@yahoo.com.

RV ★★★★ | Tent ★★★★

Beauty: ★★★★	Site Privacy: ★★★★
Spaciousness: ★★★★	Quiet: ★★★★
Security: ★★★★	Cleanliness: ★★★
Insect Control: ★★★★	Facilities: ★

The campgrounds in this area of the Roosevelt National Forest unfortunately do not include hookups. RVers wishing to camp here therefore has to make a bit of a sacrifice. However, this sacrifice may well be worth it, as the forest and the surrounding area is beautiful and wonderfully peaceful. This campground is laid out in three loops, with site driveways ranging from 20 feet (site 39) to 45 feet (site 30) in length. Average length is between 35 feet and 40 feet Site 11 is a 72-foot quasi pull-through (that actually requires parallel parking). The rest of the sites are straightforward back-ins. Sites 16, 18, and 20 have a hill that provides a view when climbed. Both the Aspen Loop and the Pine Loop are quite forested. The Fir Loop is more open. Reservable sites are located in the Fir and Pine Loops. Site 30 (in the Pine Loop) is located extremely close to the playground, which may make it less desirable to some campers. The toilets are typical pit toilets, with no running water or showers. This campground offers the chance to get close to nature, which, of course, entails giving up some modern conveniences.

Basics

Operated By: Thousand Trails Management. **Open:** May–Oct. (dates may vary). **Site Assignment:** First come, first served. Credit card required for reservation; 3-days cancellation policy, less $10 fee. **Registration:** At pay kiosk. (Camp Host will verify that campers have paid.) **Fee:** $12. (checks, no credit cards). **Parking:** At site.

Facilities

Number of RV Sites: 46. **Number of Tent-Only Sites:** 0. **Hookups:** None. **Each Site:** Picnic table, grill, fire pit. **Dump Station:** No. **Laundry:** No. **Pay Phone:** No (in Rollingsville). **Rest Rooms and Showers:** Rest rooms; no shower (showers in downtown Nederland mall). **Fuel:** No. **Propane:** No. **Internal Roads:** Gravel/dirt. **RV Service:** No. **Market:** 3.5 mi. to Nederland. **Restaurant:** 3.5 mi. to Nederland. **General Store:** No. **Vending:** No. **Swimming:** No. **Playground:** Yes. **Other:** Firewood for sale. **Activities:** Hiking, gambling, horseback riding, mountain biking. **Nearby Attractions:** Rocky Mountain National Park, Blackhawk, Central City. **Additional Information:** Thousand Trails Management, (303) 258-3610.

Restrictions

Pets: On leash, cleaned up after. **Fires:** In fire pits. **Alcoholic Beverages:** At sites. **Vehicle Maximum Length:** None.

To Get There

From the junction of Hwy. 72 and Hwy. 119, turn south onto Hwy. 119/72 and go 3 mi. Turn left at the sign into the entrance and follow the dirt road to the pay kiosk.

OURAY

4J+1+1 Trailer Park

P.O. Box F, Ouray 81427. T: (970) 325-4418.

RV ★★★★ Tent ★★★★

Beauty: ★★★★ Site Privacy: ★★★★
Spaciousness: ★★★★ Quiet: ★★★★
Security: ★★★★ Cleanliness: ★★★★
Insect Control: ★★★★ Facilities: ★★★★

Located in an outstandingly beautiful part of Colorado, this campground offers spectacular scenes from any site. This rural park has level gravel sites close to the river as well as further back. "R" sites are back-ins by the river. 1–6 are quite small (24 feet long), but 7–13 get progressively longer: 27 feet to 45 feet. The pull-throughs in the middle of the park (14–19) are 55–60 feet long and contain shade trees, making them the best pull-through sites. Tent sites are along the western edge of the park right at the base of the mountain. (No worry about rockfall, though, as the mountain side is all trees.) The least appealing spot is 15, which is located next to a concrete slab as well as a telephone pole and dumpster. The rest of the tent sites are quite nice, however, and 6–10 are all the nicer for the overhanging trees they contain. Tent sites 1–4 have attractive wooden fencing for added privacy, and it appears as though all tent sites will soon have this added feature. The rest rooms are clean but rather cramped—so much so, in fact, that only 1 of 4 stalls has a door, and only 1 of 3 showers has a curtain—which may make for an awkward bathroom experience. The playground is located across a road, and, while it is fenced in, it would be wise to keep an eye on children playing there. The RV experience here would be improved with more trees, and tenters would enjoy more grass, but either experience is quite satisfactory in this campground.

BASICS

Operated By: Jack & Jackie Clark & Family. **Open:** May 15–Oct. 15 (fully self-contained units may come before & after these dates). **Site Assignment:** Flexible, depending on site availability. Credit card required for reservation; 24-hours cancellation policy, 72-hours for 4th of July.) **Registration:** In office. (Late arrivals park & register in the morning.) **Fee:** RV $26 (Full), tent $18 (V, MC). **Parking:** At site.

FACILITIES

Number of RV Sites: 55. **Number of Tent-Only Sites:** 10. **Hookups:** Water, sewer, electric (30, 50 amps). **Each Site:** Picnic table, grill. **Dump Station:** Yes. **Laundry:** Across street. **Pay Phone:** Yes. **Rest Rooms and Showers:** Yes. **Fuel:** No. **Propane:** No. **Internal Roads:** Paved. **RV Service:** No. **Market:** 3 blocks. **Restaurant:** 1 block. **General Store:** No. **Vending:** Yes. **Swimming:** No. **Playground:** Yes. **Other:** River, conveniently located near downtown & hot springs. **Activities:** Jeep tours, hiking, mountain biking, skiing (Telluride). **Nearby Attractions:** Hot springs, historic district. **Additional Information:** Ouray Chamber Resort Assoc.: (800) 228-1876 or (970) 325-4746.

RESTRICTIONS

Pets: On leash, cleaned up after. **Fires:** In fire pits. **Alcoholic Beverages:** At sites. **Vehicle Maximum Length:** None.

TO GET THERE

From Hwy. 550 in town, turn west onto 7th Ave. Drive 2 blocks to the end (just past the river), then turn right at the end of 7th Ave. onto Oak St. Take the first right into the entrance. The office is on the left.

PAGOSA SPRINGS

Cool Pines RV Park

1501 West Hwy. 160, Pagosa Springs 81147. T: (970) 264-9130; coolpinesrv@frontier.net.

RV ★★★★ Tent ★★★

Beauty: ★★★★ Site Privacy: ★★★★
Spaciousness: ★★★ Quiet: ★★★★
Security: ★★★★ Cleanliness: ★★★★★
Insect Control: ★★★ Facilities: ★★★★

This attractive park is surrounded by "cool pines," and offers some mountain views from within. Terraced sites are situated on a loop with a grassy patch between each site. Pull-throughs are 60 feet long, while back-ins are only slightly smaller (50–55 feet long). There is one unmarked RV site directly by the office, which may get more traffic, but also has a better view of the mountains. Tent sites are unmarked on a grassy patch behind the shops to the north, which could comfortably fit five or so tents. (There are only 3 trees to provide coverage, however, and one fire ring.) The rest rooms are individual units, which can be locked when in use. They are all very clean and spacious. The rec room, which houses the rest rooms, is likewise very clean and comfortable. RVers should definitely make a point to come to Cool Pines. Tenters will also be comfortable, but would benefit from more coverage, and more fire rings or pits and some tables. This is a peaceful, wilderness location with convenient proximity both to the highway and to town.

Basics

Operated By: The Robinsons. **Open:** Mid-Apr.–mid-Nov. **Site Assignment:** Flexible depending on fullness. Credit card required for reservation; 3-days cancellation policy. **Registration:** In office. (Late arrivals come to office.) **Fee:** RV $24, tent $16 (V, MC). **Parking:** At site.

Facilities

Number of RV Sites: 22. **Number of Tent-Only Sites:** Undesignated sites. **Hookups:** Water, sewer, electric (30, 50 amps), cable. **Each Site:** Picnic table, several trees. **Dump Station:** Yes. **Laundry:** Yes. **Pay Phone:** Yes. **Rest Rooms and Showers:** Yes. **Fuel:** No. **Propane:** No. **Internal Roads:** Gravel. **RV Service:** No. **Market:** 1 mi. **Restaurant:** 1 mi. **General Store:** No. **Vending:** No. **Swimming:** No (hot tub). **Playground:** Yes. **Other:** Handicap accessible. **Activities:** Hiking, mountain biking, river rafting, fishing. **Nearby Attractions:** Chimney Rock. **Additional Information:** Pagosa Springs Area Chamber of Commerce, (800) 252-2204, (970) 264-2360.

Restrictions

Pets: On leash, cleaned up after. **Fires:** In grills. **Alcoholic Beverages:** At sites. **Vehicle Maximum Length:** 42 ft.

To Get There

From the junction of Hwy. 84 and Hwy. 160, go 2.5 mi. west on Hwy. 160. Turn right at the sign, and drive down behind the store fronts to get to the RV park.

PAONIA

Paonia State Park

Paonia State Park, P.O. Box 147, Crawford 81415. T: (800) 678-2267 or (303) 470-1144; www.parks.state.co.us.

RV ★★★ Tent ★★★★

Beauty: ★★★★★	Site Privacy: ★★★★
Spaciousness: ★★★★	Quiet: ★★★★
Security: ★★★★	Cleanliness: ★★★★
Insect Control: ★★★★	Facilities: ★

Of the two campgrounds in this state park, Hawsapple Campground is the closest to the reservoir boat and swimming access areas. Sites 1–3 are scrunched together at the end of the roundabout, near a pit toilet. These are 27 feet long, but have ample parking space, as they are 25 feet wide. Site 0 is a "pull-alongside" that can accommodate 42–45 feet If you turn left at the entrance, you continue on to sites 4–7. Of these, 4–6 are large pull-throughs, measuring 84–90 feet each. Site 7 is a 54-foot shaded back-in. The reservoir access area is a mile further up this road. Spruce Campground is located just off Hwy. 133, and contains sites 8–15. Sites 8–12 are located together by the entrance, and sites 8 and 10 seem to be sharing parking spaces as do 11 and 12. Site 13 is a smallish back-in (36 feet long), but extremely well-shaded. Site 15 is a 60-foot "pull-alongside" with an open picnic area down by the edge of the river. The two campgrounds in this state park offer a variety of recreational opportunities related to the reservoir, and campers of all stripes will enjoy an adventurous stay here.

Basics

Operated By: Colorado State Parks. **Open:** Apr. 1–Sept. 30. **Site Assignment:** First come, first served. Credit card or check required for reservation; 24-hours cancellation policy. **Registration:** At pay station. **Fee:** $6, plus $4 day use fee (checks). **Parking:** At site.

Facilities

Number of RV Sites: 15. **Number of Tent-Only Sites:** 0. **Hookups:** None. **Each Site:** Picnic table, grill. **Dump Station:** No. **Laundry:** No. **Pay Phone:** No. **Rest Rooms and Showers:** Pit toilets; no shower. **Fuel:** No. **Propane:** No. **Internal Roads:** Gravel. **RV Service:** No. **Market:** 16 mi.

to Paonia. **Restaurant:** At bottom of reservoir. **General Store:** No. **Vending:** No. **Swimming:** Reservoir. **Playground:** No. **Other:** Boat ramp, picnic area. **Activities:** Fishing, boating, swimming, hiking. **Nearby Attractions:** Gunnison National Forest. **Additional Information:** Gunnison National Forest (970) 921-5721.

Restrictions

Pets: On 6-ft. leash, cleaned up after. **Fires:** In grills. **Alcoholic Beverages:** At sites. **Vehicle Maximum Length:** None.

To Get There

From the junction of Hwy. 133 and CR2 (at the sign for Paonia State Park), turn left and cross the bridge. (A 2nd campground is 0.1 mi. south on Hwy. 133, on the left.) Take the first right and go 0.5 mi. Turn right into the campground.

PONCHA SPRINGS

Monarch Spur RV Park and Campground

18989 West Hwy. 50, P.O. Box 457, Poncha Springs 81242. T: (888) 814-3001 or (719) 530-0341; www.monarchspurrvpark.com; jerry@monarchspurRVPark.com.

RV ★★★★ Tent ★★★★

Beauty: ★★★★	Site Privacy: ★★★★
Spaciousness: ★★★★	Quiet: ★★★★
Security: ★★★★	Cleanliness: ★★★
Insect Control: ★★★★	Facilities: ★★★

Billing itself as a "big rig park", this campground makes good on its promise with decent 60-foot sites. This park uses its natural setting to its best advantage, employing rows of large rocks to designate site boundaries, and setting tent sites (and some RV sites) in the thick forest and on the grassy hills that encompass the park. RV sites are arranged in two rows of sites sixe 60 × 30 feet. All pull-throughs are level with a grass and gravel mix. Unmarked tent sites are scattered along the river on grassy patches. These are fairly wild sites with good grass, lots of trees, and the constant sound of the river (which helps drown out traffic noise). The owner is apparently building many new sites in the forest, which should be ready by summer 2002. Of the current sites, 22–31 are scattered up in the forest, making them slightly more isolated and definitely more shaded. However, accessing these sites requires navigating a very primitive road that leads up a slight hill; sites 1–21 are definitely easier to pull into. The laundry room is clean and spacious, as are the rest rooms. The showers are, however, slightly dingy. Tucked away on Hwy. 50, this campground can be a little difficult to locate. However, if you call, the staff will help you locate the park and even come out and get you.

Basics

Operated By: Jerry Gunkel. **Open:** All year. **Site Assignment:** Flexible, depending on site availability. Credit card required for reservation; 48-hours cancellation policy, less $5 fee. **Registration:** In office. (Late arrivals select an available site & pay in the morning.) **Fee:** RV $22, tent $17. **Parking:** At site.

Facilities

Number of RV Sites: 30. **Number of Tent-Only Sites:** 20. **Hookups:** Water, sewer, electric (20, 30, 50 amps). **Each Site:** Picnic table, grass strip. **Dump Station:** No (sewer at all sites). **Laundry:** Yes. **Pay Phone:** Yes. **Rest Rooms and Showers:** Yes. **Fuel:** No. **Propane:** Yes. **Internal Roads:** Gravel/dirt. **RV Service:** No. **Market:** 10 mi. to Salida. **Restaurant:** 7 mi. to Poncha Springs. **General Store:** Yes. **Vending:** Yes. **Swimming:** No. **Playground:** No. **Other:** ATV rentals, picnic deck. **Activities:** Hiking, ATV trails, horseshoes, swimming, hunting. **Nearby Attractions:** San Isabel National Forest, San Juan National Forest. **Additional Information:** Heart of the Rockies Chamber of Commerce, (877) 772-5432 or (719) 539-2068.

Restrictions

Pets: On leash, cleaned up after. **Fires:** In fire pits; subject to seasonal bans. **Alcoholic Beverages:** At sites. **Vehicle Maximum Length:** 60 ft. **Other:** Read policy sheet.

To Get There

From the junction of Hwy. 285 and Hwy. 50 in Salida, go 8.2 mi. west on Hwy. 50. Turn south at the sign onto a dirt road and follow it to the office.

PUEBLO

Pueblo KOA

4131 I-25 North, Pueblo 81008. T: (800) 562-7453 or (719) 542-2273; www.koa.com; pueblokoa@juno.com.

RV ★★★★ Tent ★★★

Beauty: ★★★★	Site Privacy: ★★★
Spaciousness: ★★★★	Quiet: ★★★
Security: ★★★★★	Cleanliness: ★★★★★
Insect Control: ★★★★	Facilities: ★★★★

This campground in a desert setting has scattered rows of sites, each designated by a letter. Row A has pull throughs measuring 60 × 18 feet that are separated from each other by a row of bushes. Sites A5 and A6 share a large shade tree. Towards the south are Rows N and P. Row N has pull-throughs of 45 × 30 feet, and is separated from Row P by a hedge. All sites are well-shaded. Row P, at the southern edge of the campground, has 40-foot back-ins. Sites P1 and P2 are separated from each other by a wooden fence, which offers these sites more privacy than practically any others. They back to the hedge and open to the pool and a dirt road. There is a private residence next to P6. On the other side of P6 is a hedge that separates it from P5, making this latter site very private. In the middle and northern side of the campground, Rows B, C, D, and E have unshaded pull-throughs that average 60 feet in length. (Row C has some slightly shorter pull-throughs, 42–57 feet long) Rows F, G, and H are primitive sites good for tenting and possibly a pop-up. These sites are nicer, in fact, than the designated tent area between Rows C and D, which has completely open sites on sparse grass set amongst a number of RV sites. The rest rooms are pristine; the showers are a little worn but still acceptable. This is a beautiful campground for those who appreciate the austere beauty of the desert.

Basics

Operated By: Mark & Alexis Whitworth. **Open:** All year. **Site Assignment:** Assigned upon registration. Credit card required for reservation; 24-hours cancellation policy. **Registration:** In office. (Late arrivals use drop box.) **Fee:** RV $26 (full), $24 (water, electric), tent $18 (Colorado checks, V, MC, AE, D). **Parking:** At site.

Facilities

Number of RV Sites: 60. **Number of Tent-Only Sites:** 25. **Hookups:** Water, sewer, electric (50 amps). **Each Site:** Picnic table. **Dump Station:** Yes. **Laundry:** Yes. **Pay Phone:** Yes. **Rest Rooms and Showers:** Yes. **Fuel:** No. **Propane:** Yes. **Internal Roads:** Gravel. **RV Service:** No. **Market:** 8 mi. south to Hwy. 50. **Restaurant:** 2 mi. north. **General Store:** Yes. **Vending:** Yes. **Swimming:** Pool. **Playground:** Yes. **Other:** Rec room (pool table, video games), dataport, dog walk, nature trail. **Activities:** Swimming, hiking, mountain climbing, boating, swimming, caving. **Nearby Attractions:** Lake Pueblo State Park, Royal Gorge Bridge, Pikes Peak, Seven Falls, Cave of the Winds, Garden of the Gods, Manitou Cliff Dwellings. **Additional Information:** Visitor Information Center: (719) 543-1742.

Restrictions

Pets: On leash, cleaned up after; or must stay inside at night. **Fires:** Charcoal only. **Alcoholic Beverages:** At sites. **Vehicle Maximum Length:** None.

To Get There

From I-25 (Exit 108): on the west side of the highway, take the first right and go 0.6 mi. straight into the campground. (From northbound I-25, there is a single lane underpass 13 ft. 6 in. high to negotiate. The owner assures there has never been a rig that can't pass through.)

RED FEATHER

Dowdy Lake Campground

Red Feather Lakes, Bellevue 80512. T: (877) 444-6777; www.reserveusa.com/nrrs/co/dowd.

RV ★★ Tent ★★★★

Beauty: ★★★★★	Site Privacy: ★★★
Spaciousness: ★★★	Quiet: ★★★★
Security: ★★★★	Cleanliness: ★★★★
Insect Control: ★★★	Facilities: ★

This National Forest campground is divided up into Loops A–E, each containing a varying number of campsites. The average size of a site is 24 × 18 feet, which, of course, limits the number of RVs that can camp here. As there are no RV hookups, the campground is more geared towards tenters. However, RVers who don't mind roughing it for a night or two will also enjoy the natural beauty and the quiet this campground has to offer. Sites 1–3 in Loop A are spacious and quite close to the lake (3 is closest) and some neat rock formations. These are quite possibly the best sites in the campground, as they boast terrific views of the lake, are close to the camp hosts, and aren't bothered by too much passing traffic. Sites right on the water include 27, 28, 30–32, 35, and 37. Sites 33 and 34 are very close together, and they may be best for a group that is camping together. Group sites that require a double fee include 44–46, 50, 53, and 54. These are aimed at groups of 10 people or more. Sites 52 and 57 are outside the woods that most of the other sites are located in. The rest rooms are pit toilets, and, unfortunately, there are no showers. Some RVers may hesitate to camp in a park without hookups, but those hardy enough to do so will join adventurous tenters in an excellent wilderness of woods, grass, wildflowers, rock outcroppings, and gorgeous lake views.

Basics

Operated By: Thousand Trails. **Open:** May 15–Sept. **Site Assignment:** First come, first served; reservations can be made 5–240 days in advance. Credit card required for reservation; 24-hours cancellation policy. **Registration:** Self-pay station. **Fee:** $11 (checks, no credits cards). **Parking:** At site, Loop C parking lot.

Facilities

Number of RV Sites: 48. **Number of Tent-Only Sites:** 14. **Hookups:** None. **Each Site:** Picnic table, grill, flat tent space. **Dump Station:** No. **Laundry:** No. **Pay Phone:** No. **Rest Rooms and Showers:** Toilets; no shower. **Fuel:** No. **Propane:** No. **Internal Roads:** Dirt. **RV Service:** No. **Market:** 35 mi. west to Wellington. **Restaurant:** 3 mi. west. **General Store:** No. **Vending:** No. **Swimming:** No. **Playground:** No. **Other:** Boat ramp, no fee day use. **Activities:** Fishing, boating, hiking, cycling. **Nearby Attractions:** Dowdy Lake, North Park. **Additional Information:** Red Feather Lakes Tourist Council, (800) 462-5870.

Restrictions

Pets: On leash, cleaned up after. **Fires:** In fire pits. **Alcoholic Beverages:** At sites. **Vehicle Maximum Length:** 40 ft. **Other:** Wakeless boating, no swimming, do not fill water reserves, no ATVs.

To Get There

From the junction of Prairie Divide Rd. and Red Feather Lakes Rd. (74 East), go 1 mi. east on 74 East. Turn north onto Dowdy Lake Rd. and go 1 mi. (keep right on Dowdy Rd.) to pay station.

RIDGWAY

Ridgway State Park

28555 Hwy. 50, Ridgway 81432. T: (800) 678-2267/(303) 470-1144 or (970) 626-5822; www.coloradoparks.org/ridgway.

RV ★★★★ Tent ★★★★

Beauty: ★★★★	Site Privacy: ★★★★
Spaciousness: ★★★	Quiet: ★★★★★
Security: ★★★★	Cleanliness: ★★★★
Insect Control: ★★★	Facilities: ★★

This state park includes three separate campgrounds (Elk Ridge, Dakota Terraces, and Pa-Co-Chu-Puk), each offering a slightly different experience. All campgrounds are organized in loops, offering back-ins that range from 25-foot backins for pop-ups to 65-foot pull-throughs for longer RVs. The first campground on the way in from the entrance and the Visitor Center, Dakota Terraces is also closest to the swimming beach at the reservoir (especially sites 56–79 in Loop C). Elevated wooden tent decks are offered at sites 10 and 50, while shade shelters can be found at 4, 6, 8–10, 79, and others (indicated on the state park map). This campground has many trees, and is the best bet for those who want to take advantage of the reservoir. Elk Ridge Campground is located on top of a hill overlooking the reservoir. It is thus a little further from the water than Dakota Terraces, as well as more open. The most remote, and thus most private, sites are odd numbers 139–149 in Loop E, as well as 184–187. Wooden tent decks are provided at sites 99–103 (and others), while improved tent sites include 80, 83, 87, 123, 124, 165, 170 and others. Most difficult to pronounce, Pa-Co-Chu-Pak (also known as "Cow Creek") offers full hookups (sites 200–280) and walk-in tent sites (281–295). This campground is the most remote, and possibly the best for tenters—as long as they don't mind parking first and trekking in with their stuff. This campground offers two fishing ponds and almost exclusively pull-throughs. The most private sites include 200–208 in Loop F and 251, 254, and 257 in Loop G. This is a rare example of a state park offering full hookups, and those campers who enjoy getting out into the wild a little should definitely take advantage of these campgrounds.

Basics

Operated By: Colorado State Parks. **Open:** All year (closed during bad weather; limited facilities in winter). **Site Assignment:** First come, first served; reservations can be made 3–90 days in advance. Credit card required for reservation. **Registration:** At self-pay kiosk. **Fee:** $14–16 ($10 for tent walk-in sites), $4 park pass (checks, no credit card). **Parking:** At site.

Facilities

Number of RV Sites: 267. **Number of Tent-Only Sites:** 15. **Hookups:** Water, sewer, electric (50 amps). **Each Site:** Picnic table, grill. **Dump Station:** Yes. **Laundry:** Yes. **Pay Phone:** Yes. **Rest Rooms and Showers:** Yes. **Fuel:** No. **Propane:** No. **Internal Roads:** Paved. **RV Service:** No. **Market:** 6 mi. in Ridgway. **Restaurant:** 6 mi. in Ridgway. **General Store:** Yes. **Vending:** Yes. **Swimming:** Lake. **Playground:** Yes. **Other:** Marina. **Activities:** Hiking, swimming, biking, hunting, fishing. **Nearby Attractions:** Ridgway Reservoir. **Additional Information:** Ridgway Visitor Center, (970) 626-5868.

Restrictions

Pets: On 6-ft. leash, cleaned up after. **Fires:** In fire pits/grills. **Alcoholic Beverages:** Beer only. **Vehicle Maximum Length:** 65 ft. **Other:** No gathering firewood.

To Get There

From the junction of Hwy. 62 and Hwy. 550, go 4.6 mi. north on Hwy. 550. Turn northwest at "Dutch Charlie" sign into the entrance. Go 0.4 mi. to the pay station or to the park HQ.

RIFLE

Rifle Falls/Rifle Gap

0050 CR 219, Rifle 81650. T: (800) 678-2267 or (303) 470-1144 or (970) 625-1607; F: (970) 625-4327; www.coloradoparks.org; rifle.gap.park@state.co.us.

 ★★★★ 

Beauty: ★★★★★ Site Privacy: ★★★★
Spaciousness: ★★★★ Quiet: ★★★★★
Security: ★★★ Cleanliness: ★★★★★
Insect Control: ★★★ Facilities: ★★★★

The Rifle Falls/Rifle Gap State Park Camping area consists of five small campgrounds—four in Rifle Gap, one in rifle Falls—each of which is described below. The Cottonwood Campground in Rifle Gap has absolutely huge pull-throughs that can accommodate a rig of any size. These sites, which average 100 × 100 feet, are scattered around the lake edge—some right up to the water, which would allow for an easy morning dip or an afternoon cast. This is the first campground one would approach from the main entrance, and well worth occupying for the night. Next in line is Cedar Campground, which contains mostly back-ins (average 48 feet in length), and one single pull-through. Also close to the water, this campground is better for smaller RVs, such as pop-ups or vans. Sage Campground, as the name implies, is "dry"—that is, has no direct water access. There are, however, 100-foot pull-throughs in a loop along the road, each with a large covered picnic area—ideal for landlubbers who only want to dip once or twice in the lake. Pinion Campground is perhaps the prettiest, crowded as it is with pinions and juniper. Like Cedar Campground, sites are smaller, and best suited for small vehicles or tents. (Tenters won't be thrilled by the gravel bed in each site, however.) Rifle Falls Campground, which offers easy access to the falls and caves that accompany them, has back-ins and pull-throughs that range in length from 28 feet to 120 feet. Tent sites are walk-ins to the south of the RV sites. The more remote sites, while offering better privacy, also require lugging equipment several hundred feet. Campers in tents or RVs will enjoy the beautiful sites—and sights—of Rifle Falls, and should definitely consider making a stop here.

Basics

Operated By: Colorado State Parks. **Open:** All year. **Site Assignment:** First come, first served. **Registration:** At pay kiosk. **Fee:** $10, $4 park pass (checks). **Parking:** At site.

Facilities

Number of RV Sites: 60. **Number of Tent-Only Sites:** 7. **Hookups:** Electric (30, 50 amps). **Each Site:** Picnic table, grill. **Dump Station:** Yes. **Laundry:** No. **Pay Phone:** No (at golf course). **Rest Rooms and Showers:** Pit toilets; no shower. **Fuel:** No. **Propane:** No. **Internal Roads:** Gravel. **RV Service:** No. **Market:** 10 mi. to Rifle. **Restaurant:** 10 mi. to Rifle. **General Store:** No. **Vending:** No. **Swimming:** Lake. **Playground:** No. **Other:** Creek, lake, falls. **Activities:** Boating, swimming, fishing, water skiing, scuba diving, ice skating, golf, caving, hiking, windsurfing. **Nearby Attractions:** Rifle Falls, Rifle Gap Reservoir. **Additional Information:** Rifle Visitor Information Center/ Chamber of Commerce, (970) 625-2085.

Restrictions

Pets: On 6-ft. leash, cleaned up after. **Fires:** In fire pits. **Alcoholic Beverages:** Beer only. **Vehicle Maximum Length:** None. **Other:** No removing of plants or artifacts; cell phones may not work.

To Get There

From the junction of Hwy. 13 and Hwy. 325, go 6 mi. northeast on Hwy. 325. At the fork, stay on the paved road to reach the campground. (You can take the dirt road to the park office.) Turn left at the sign into the Rifle Gap Reservation, or continue for another 4 mi. to get to Rifle Falls.

RUSTIC
Glen Echo Resort

31503 Poudre Canyon Dr./Hwy. 14, Rustic 80512. T: (800) 348-2208 or (970) 881-2208; F: (970) 881-2066.

RV ★★★★ Tent ★★★

Beauty: ★★★★	Site Privacy: ★★★
Spaciousness: ★★	Quiet: ★★★★★
Security: ★★★★	Cleanliness: ★★★★★
Insect Control: ★★★	Facilities: ★★★

Situated on scenic Hwy. 14, this campground delivers on the beauty promised by the scenic drive to get there. Hills surround the campground on all four sides, and a river runs at the back, behind the cabins. The air is fresh, birds sing constantly, and there is green everywhere you look. Even the wood and stone buildings blend in well with the natural surroundings. Now, for the sites themselves. The best sites by far are those in the south portion of the park, which is divided by a retaining wall running east-west down the middle. Unfortunately, nearly half of the sites in the park (including, you guessed it, the choicest south sites) are occupied by long-term residents. There are still some very nice sites available (pull-throughs 64–68 are 80 feet long and have good tree coverage), but chances are good that you will end up on the north side, in a back-in facing to the highway. Not that that's a bad place to be. Sites are level, grassy, and for the most part, shaded by numerous trees. (Sites 14–21 one row in from the highway have no shade to speak of and are therefore less desirable.) The rest room and shower facilities (both in the main living and laundry complex and the secondary building to the south) are immaculate and brand-spanking new. The laundry is likewise clean and comfortable, with a sofa and bookshelf stocked with loaners. Note that the "playground" consists of one merry-go-round, but since most of the residents are retirees, there probably isn't call for much more than that. There is a fine group picnic shelter that even has electric outlets. Living up to the name of the town, this campground is "rustic," and makes a scenic as well as comfortable destination. Make a special trip to come out!

Basics

Operated By: Lloyd & Gaile Rowe. **Open:** All year. **Site Assignment:** First come, first served. **Registration:** In store until 7 p.m. (Late arrivals not allowed.) **Fee:** RV $25, tent $16 (V, MC). **Parking:** At site.

Facilities

Number of RV Sites: 77. **Number of Tent-Only Sites:** 2. **Hookups:** Water, sewer, electric (30, 50 amps). **Each Site:** Picnic table, trees. **Dump Station:** No (sewer at all sites). **Laundry:** Yes. **Pay Phone:** Yes. **Rest Rooms and Showers:** Yes. **Fuel:** Yes, including diesel. **Propane:** Yes. **Internal Roads:** Dirt, in good condition. **RV Service:** No. **Market:** Limited on-site (full, 40 mi. east to La Porte). **Restaurant:** Yes. **General Store:** Yes. **Vending:** No. **Swimming:** No. **Playground:** Yes. **Other:** 9 cabins, 2 duplex cabins, group picnic shelter. **Activities:** Special dinner on Mother's Day, hiking, driving. **Nearby Attractions:** Roosevelt National Forest, Cache La Poudre Scenic Byway.

Additional Information: North Park Chamber of Commerce, (970) 723-4600.

Restrictions

Pets: On leash. **Fires:** In grills. **Alcoholic Beverages:** No alcohol permitted. **Vehicle Maximum Length:** None.

To Get There

On Hwy. 14, just west of the Rustic town name sign and mile marker 91.

SALIDA
Four Seasons RV Park

4305 East US Hwy. 50, Salida 81201. T: (888) 444-3626 or (719) 539-3084; fourseasons@amigo.net.

RV: ★★★★★ Tent: n/a

Beauty: ★★★★	Site Privacy: ★★★★★
Spaciousness: ★★★★★	Quiet: ★★★★
Security: ★★★★	Cleanliness: ★★★★★
Insect Control: ★★★★	Facilities: ★★★★★

This two-tiered campground offers sites just off the highway as well as sites down by the river. All of the long back-ins in the B row are gorgeous, and most river sites are equally nice. (R15 has exceptionally great shade.) The D row, one in from the river, is also quite pleasant, with lush grass, two pull-throughs (in addition to the lengthy back-ins), and fencing between sites. Most sites in the park have one side to either the river or to an embankment, adding privacy and security, and a shade tree of considerable size. The exceptions to this are 11–13 by the river, which lack grass as well as shade and are undoubtedly the least desirable sites. The rest rooms are immaculate and spacious, as is the laundry. There is also a community room with microwave, fridge, books, and nine tables. Although big rigs will have to unhook, you really can't go wrong with any site in the D or R rows. Ask for a site on the lower tier by the river, and you will be pleased with virtually any site you get.

Basics

Operated By: Paul & Candy Draper. **Open:** May–Oct. 1. **Site Assignment:** Assigned upon registration. Credit card required for reservation. 72-hours to 1-week cancellation policy, depending on legth of stay. **Registration:** In office. (Late arrivals use drop box.) **Fee:** Full: $23, water, electric: $18.50 (V, MC, D). **Parking:** At site.

Facilities

Number of RV Sites: 67. **Number of Tent-Only Sites:** 0. **Hookups:** Water, sewer, electric (30, 50 amps). **Each Site:** Picnic table. **Dump Station:** No (sewer at all sites). **Laundry:** Yes. **Pay Phone:** Yes. **Rest Rooms and Showers:** Yes. **Fuel:** No. **Propane:** Yes. **Internal Roads:** Dirt. **RV Service:** No. **Market:** 2 mi. west to Salida. **Restaurant:** 2 mi. west to Salida. **General Store:** No. **Vending:** Yes. **Swimming:** No. **Playground:** Yes. **Other:** Meeting room, storage. **Activities:** Rafting, horseshoes, shuffleboard, fishing, Jeep tours, hiking, mountain biking, skiing, golf, hunting, rock-hounding. **Nearby Attractions:** Hot springs pools, ghost towns, kayaking competition. **Additional Information:** Heart of the Rockies Chamber of Commerce, (877) 772-5432 or (719) 539-2068.

Restrictions

Pets: On leash, cleaned up after. **Fires:** No open fires. **Alcoholic Beverages:** At sites. **Vehicle Maximum Length:** None.

To Get There

From the junction of Hwy. 291 and Hwy. 50, go 1.4 mi. east on Hwy. 50. Turn north at the sign into the entrance. The office is on the right.

SEIBERT
Shadey Grove Campground

306 Colorado St., Seibert 80834. T: (970) 664-2218; F: (970) 664-2222.

RV: ★★★★ Tent: ★★★★

Beauty: ★★★★	Site Privacy: ★★★★
Spaciousness: ★★★★	Quiet: ★★★★
Security: ★★★★	Cleanliness: ★★★★
Insect Control: ★★★★	Facilities: ★★★

This campground is split up into three separate areas. The two main camping areas are on either side of the office. On the north side, there are 12 50-foot pull-throughs with cable TV hookups. These sites are mainly open, with some trees. The 2nd main area is on the south side of the office. There are 11 60-foot pull-throughs in this area (without cable). This area is more heavily forested, and most every site is shaded. The third area, for overflow, consists of an open grassy field with six 70-foot back-ins. These sites are completely unshaded and do not offer any facilities (other than electric hookups).

The town and surrounding area are devoid of attractions.

BASICS

Operated By: Linda & Jerry Starks. **Open:** Apr–Oct. **Site Assignment:** Assigned upon registration; verbal reservations OK. **Registration:** In office. (Late arrivals use drop box.) **Fee:** RV $20 (full), tent $11 (checks, no credits cards). **Parking:** At site.

FACILITIES

Number of RV Sites: 29. **Number of Tent-Only Sites:** Undesignated sites. **Hookups:** Water, sewer, electric (20, 30, 50 amps), cable. **Dump Station:** No (sewer at all sites). **Laundry:** Yes. **Pay Phone:** Yes. **Rest Rooms and Showers:** Yes. **Fuel:** No. **Propane:** No. **Internal Roads:** Gravel. **RV Service:** No. **Market:** Less than 0.25 mi. north. **Restaurant:** Less than 1 mi. south. **General Store:** No. **Vending:** No. **Swimming:** No. **Playground:** No. **Activities:** Fishing, boating, swimming, hiking. **Nearby Attractions:** Bonny State Park. **Additional Information:** Burlington Chamber of Commerce, (719) 346-8070.

RESTRICTIONS

Pets: On leash, cleaned up after. **Fires:** In grills. **Alcoholic Beverages:** At sites. **Vehicle Maximum Length:** None.

TO GET THERE

From I-70 (Exit 405), turn north onto Hwy. 59 and go 0.2 mi. Turn right onto 4th St. and go 0.2 mi. Turn right onto Colorado and go 1 block to the office on the right.

SILVERTON

Silver Summit

640 Mineral St., P.O. Box 656, Silverton 81433. T: (800) 352-1637 or (970) 387-0240; F: (970) 387-5495; www.silverton.org/silversummit; slvrsmmt@frontier.net.

RV ★★★★ Tent ★★★

Beauty: ★★★★	Site Privacy: ★★★
Spaciousness: ★★★	Quiet: ★★★★★
Security: ★★★★	Cleanliness: ★★★★★
Insect Control: ★★★★	Facilities: ★★★★

At the southern edge of town, this campground is surrounded on all four sides by mountains (including Kendell Mountain to the east). There are beautiful vistas from anywhere inside this campground, making it a wonderful place to stop and relax. While there are no shade trees around the park, summers do not get overly hot and the park remains quite comfortable. End site 23 is an open pull-through that could accommodate a rig of any size. All other sites (pull-throughs and back-ins) range from 50 feet to 55 feet. Tents are allowed on any of the RV spaces, which are all level, grassy, and open, making them a fine place to set up a tent. The rest rooms are fantastically clean, and there is plenty of space in the showers. The laundry room is also quite clean and spacious. This is a very pretty campground with unbeatable vistas that both tenters and RVers will enjoy.

BASICS

Operated By: Denny & Sigrun Martin. **Open:** May 15–Oct. 15. **Site Assignment:** Assigned upon registration. Credit card required for reservation; 48-hours cancellation policy. **Registration:** In office. (Late arrivals select an available site & pay in the morning.) **Fee:** RV $22, tent $17 (V, MC, AE, D). **Parking:** At site.

FACILITIES

Number of RV Sites: 39. **Number of Tent-Only Sites:** 0. **Hookups:** Water, sewer, electric (30, 50 amps). **Each Site:** Picnic table, grill. **Dump Station:** Yes. **Laundry:** Yes. **Pay Phone:** Yes. **Rest Rooms and Showers:** Yes. **Fuel:** No. **Propane:** No. **Internal Roads:** Gravel. **RV Service:** No. **Market:** 1 block. **Restaurant:** 6 blocks. **General Store:** Yes. **Vending:** No. **Swimming:** No (hot tub). **Playground:** No. **Other:** Jeep rentals. **Activities:** Jeeping, hiking, fishing, horseback riding, guided tours, gold mining tours. **Nearby Attractions:** Ghost towns, railroad, scenic byway, national historic district, wild flowers, native crafts, museum. **Additional Information:** Silverton Chamber of Commerce, (800) 752-4494 or (970) 387-5654.

RESTRICTIONS

Pets: On leash, cleaned up after. **Fires:** In fire pits. **Alcoholic Beverages:** At sites. **Vehicle Maximum Length:** 42 ft.

TO GET THERE

From the junction of Hwy. 550 and Hwy. 110, go 0.2 mi. north on Hwy. 110. Turn east onto East 7th St. Turn right onto Mineral St. The office is on the left.

SOUTH FORK

Grandview Cabins and RV

P.O. Box 189, South Fork 81154. T: (719) 873-5541.

RV ★★★★ Tent n/a

Beauty: ★★★ Site Privacy: ★★★
Spaciousness: ★★★ Quiet: ★★★★
Security: ★★★★ Cleanliness: ★★★★
Insect Control: ★★★ Facilities: ★★★★

This campground has quite attractive sites in the southern part, but more open and unshaded sites to the north. There are level grassy pull-throughs as well as back-ins, which average 35 × 25 feet. Back-ins in the southwest (16–24) back to a wall of trees that makes these sites quite attractive. Sites 25–34 are larger (40 × 27 feet), but do not have as many trees. Sites 51–54 are very nice back-ins with shade trees and nice landscaping that back to an attractive fence. Site 48, next to the cabins, is also quite a nice spot, with several trees in the corner. The laundry, which shares a room with a furnace and water tanks, is a little hot and cramped and in need of a paint job, but has quite a few machines. The rest rooms are housed individually, and are very clean and comfortable.

BASICS

Operated By: Gary & Maria Hodges. **Open:** All year. **Site Assignment:** Assigned upon registration. Credit card required for reservation; 1-week cancellation policy. **Registration:** In office. (Late arrivals park by the river & settle in the morning). **Fee:** $16–18 (V, MC, D). **Parking:** At site.

FACILITIES

Number of RV Sites: 92. **Number of Tent-Only Sites:** 0. **Hookups:** Water, sewer, electric (30 amps). **Each Site:** Picnic table. **Dump Station:** Yes. **Laundry:** Yes. **Pay Phone:** Yes. **Rest Rooms and Showers:** Yes. **Fuel:** No. **Propane:** No. **Internal Roads:** Gravel. **RV Service:** No. **Market:** 0.5 mi. to South Fork. **Restaurant:** 0.5 mi. to South Fork. **General Store:** No. **Vending:** No. **Swimming:** No (hot tub). **Playground:** No. **Other:** Fish cleaning station, cabins, meeting room, free RV storage, kitchenette. **Activities:** Hunting, fishing, Jeep tours, evening camp fires, skiing, snow mobiling, rafting, hiking, country & western dancing, potlucks, ice cream socials. **Nearby Attractions:** Great Sand Dunes, Creede, Silver Thread Scenic Byway, Mesa Verde, Rio Grande River, Durango-Silverton RR, Royal Gorge Bridge. **Additional Information:** Durango Chamber of Commerce, (800) 525-8855.

RESTRICTIONS

Pets: Only in north RV sites; on leash, cleaned up after. **Fires:** In fire rings. **Alcoholic Beverages:** At sites. **Vehicle Maximum Length:** None.

TO GET THERE

From the junction of Hwy. 148 and Hwy. 160, go 0.6 mi. northwest on Hwy. 149. Turn left at the sign onto a dirt road. Keep straight and follow the signs to the office.

STEAMBOAT SPRINGS

Steamboat Campground

3603 Lincoln Ave., Steamboat Springs 80487. T: (800) 562-7549; skitownkoa@springsips.com.

RV ★★★★ Tent ★★★★

Beauty: ★★★★ Site Privacy: ★★★
Spaciousness: ★★★ Quiet: ★★★
Security: ★★★★ Cleanliness: ★★★★
Insect Control: ★★★★ Facilities: ★★★★★

At the very western tip of town, this campground is split in half by the Yampa River: RVs on the north side, tents on the south. There are stunning mountain views from practically anywhere in the campground. However, Hwy. 40 is just a stone's throw away, and noise can be heard as far away as in the tent sites. The grounds are clean, with immaculately manicured, lush grass. The rest room facilities are clean and modern, as is the laundry, although the latter is a little cramped. Some of the best sites (36–39, 41, 42) are back-ins, that may exclude some larger rigs, but they sport nice trees along the southwest fence. Another drawback to this area are the mobile homes parked along this strip—some of which look quite run-down. Other RV sites are laid out in a grid, with decent-sized pull throughs among them (73 × 28 feet). (Back-in spaces run 42 feet in length and a comparable width.) The RV section of the park is mostly open, and all sites are level and grassy. The tent area is a whole different ballgame, left nicely wild with loads of trees and grass. Some tent sites (99A–106) are right on the river's edge, while the rest have a more forested feel. In all, this park offers a very nice stay in a location that can't be beat.

Basics

Operated By: the Sabia family. **Open:** All year. **Site Assignment:** Assigned upon registration. **Registration:** In office. (Late arrivals use drop box.) **Fee:** RV $30 (full), $25 (water, electric), tent $20 (V, MC, D). **Parking:** At site.

Facilities

Number of RV Sites: 104. **Number of Tent-Only Sites:** 36. **Hookups:** Water, sewer, electric (30, 50 amps). **Each Site:** Picnic table, grill. **Dump Station:** Yes. **Laundry:** Yes. **Pay Phone:** Yes. **Rest Rooms and Showers:** Yes. **Fuel:** No. **Propane:** Yes. **Internal Roads:** Paved, gravel to tent area. **RV Service:** No. **Market:** 2 mi. into town. **Restaurant:** 2 mi. into town. **General Store:** Yes. **Vending:** Yes. **Swimming:** Pool. **Playground:** Yes. **Other:** TV room w/ pool table, RV parts, mini golf, free local bus service, cabins, river, dataport, hot tub, breakfast patio, snack bar, pet walk area. **Activities:** Volleyball, horseshoes, fishing, hiking, skiing. **Nearby Attractions:** Steamboat Springs ski area, Routt National Forest, Fish Creek Falls, Haymaker Golf Course, Flat Tops Wilderness Area, Tread of Pioneers Museum. **Additional Information:** Steamboat Springs Chamber Resort Assoc., (970) 879-0880.

Restrictions

Pets: On leash, cleaned up after use pet walk area. **Fires:** In fire ring only. **Alcoholic Beverages:** At sites. **Vehicle Maximum Length:** None. **Other:** In winter, only open to monthly rentals.

To Get There

0.1 mi. from the western town name signpost on Hwy. 40. Entrance is on the south side.

STERLING

Yogi Bear's Jellystone Camp Resort

22018 Hwy. 6, Sterling 80751. T: (970) 522-2233 or (970) 522-6701; www.gocampingamerica.com/yogisterling/index.html; ranger@campjellystonepark.com.

RV ★★★★ Tent ★★★★

Beauty: ★★★	Site Privacy: ★★★
Spaciousness: ★★★	Quiet: ★★★★
Security: ★★★★★	Cleanliness: ★★★★
Insect Control: ★★★★	Facilities: ★★★★

This family-oriented campground offers lots of activities within the park itself, with facilities from a swimming pool to volleyball nets to meeting rooms. There are two separate RV areas, offering very different experiences. Sites E1–E14 are laid out in two wings along a central row, and are entirely unshaded. These are, of course, electric sites only, and lack of other hookups and shade trees makes them less desirable than sites in the main camping area. The main camping area contains both RV sites (laid out in a large loop) and tenting sites (occupying the middle of the loop). These 47 RV sites are uniformly forested, and all of them are pull-throughs. Sites average 75 feet in length—easily large enough for any vehicle, even with a tow. About half of these sites are large enough for double slide-outs, but all sites are certainly roomy enough for pleasant family camping. Sites with the highest numbers (40–47) are closest to the pool and the office, while those in the 20s and 30s are furthest away from the action. The tenting area is likewise well-shaded, and very comfortable. The rest rooms and showers are exceptionally clean and comfrotable. This is a family-oriented campground that offers enough in the way of recreation opportunities to be a destination in itself.

Basics

Operated By: "Ranger" Bill. **Open:** All year. **Site Assignment:** Assigned upon registration. **Registration:** In office. (Late arrivals use drop box.) **Fee:** RV $27.74 (full), $25.57 (water, electric), tent $21.22 (checks, V, MC). **Parking:** At site.

Facilities

Number of RV Sites: 61. **Number of Tent-Only Sites:** Undesignated sites. **Hookups:** Water, sewer, electric (20, 30 amps). **Each Site:** Picnic table, grill. **Dump Station:** Yes. **Laundry:** Yes. **Pay Phone:** Yes. **Rest Rooms and Showers:** Yes. **Fuel:** No. **Propane:** Yes. **Internal Roads:** Gravel. **RV Service:** No. **Market:** 5 mi. to Sterling. **Restaurant:** 0.5 mi. to I-76. **General Store:** Yes. **Vending:** Yes. **Swimming:** Pool. **Playground:** Yes. **Other:** Mini golf, game room, meeting room, pet walk. **Activities:** Volleyball, swimming, planned activities, horseshoes, basketball, fishing, boating. **Nearby Attractions:** North Sterling State Park, North Sterling Reservoir. **Additional Information:** Logan County Chamber of Commerce, (800) 544-8609 or (970) 522-5070.

Restrictions

Pets: On leash, cleaned up after. **Fires:** In fire pits. **Alcoholic Beverages:** At sites. **Vehicle Maximum Length:** None.

To Get There

From Hwy. I-76 (Exit 125), turn east onto Hwy. 6 and go 0.5 mi. Turn right at the sign into the entrance.

THORNTON

Denver North Campground and RV Park

16700 North Washington St., Broomfield 80020. T: (800) 851-6521 or (303) 452-4120; F: (303) 452-4156; campdenver@aol.com.

★★★★ ★★★★

Beauty: ★★★★	Site Privacy: ★★★★
Spaciousness: ★★★★	Quiet: ★★★★
Security: ★★★★★	Cleanliness: ★★★★★
Insect Control: ★★★★	Facilities: ★★★★★

Just off the highway and offering easy on and off access, this campground has plenty of long pull-throughs for larger rigs with tows. Laid out in 5 rows, sites 1–60 are pull-throughs in the middle of the campground. Sites 1–24 are 54 feet in length, while 25–60 are 40 feet. To the east, sites in the 100s and 200s are more open (with fewer shade trees) and closer to the highway. However, these sites include the longest (75-foot) pull-throughs. Close to the entrance are 45-foot back-ins reserved for long-term residents. This area also contains the tenting sites, which offer wooden partitions for increased privacy and sand tent pads for increased comfort. However, these sites are just off the road and may suffer from passing traffic noise. The rest rooms are small but clean. They are housed in a mobile home that seems to be showing its age slightly. The showers are individual units, and very clean. This is a quite decent stop for tenters or RVers who wish to stay in the area for several days.

Basics

Operated By: Steve & Chris Hennings. **Open:** All year. **Site Assignment:** Assigned upon registration Credit card required for reservation; cancellation requires same-day notice by 10 a.m. **Registration:** In office. (Late arrivals use drop box.) **Fee:** RV $29.50 (full, 50 amps), $27.90 (full, 30 amps), $26.50 (water, electric), tent $21 (checks, V, MC, D). **Parking:** At site.

Facilities

Number of RV Sites: 140. **Number of Tent-Only Sites:** 15. **Hookups:** Water, sewer, electric (30, 50 amps). **Each Site:** Picnic table, grill. **Dump Station:** Yes. **Laundry:** Yes. **Pay Phone:** Yes. **Rest Rooms and Showers:** Yes. **Fuel:** No. **Propane:** Yes. **Internal Roads:** Paved/dirt. **RV Service:** No. **Market:** 5 mi. south. **Restaurant:** 5 mi. south. **General Store:** Yes. **Vending:** Yes. **Swimming:** Pool. **Playground:** Yes. **Other:** 2 cabins, dataport, meeting room, game room, dog walk. **Activities:** Pancake corral (Memorial Day–Labor Day), swimming. **Nearby Attractions:** Denver, Boulder, Rocky Mountain National Park. **Additional Information:** Denver Chamber of Commerce, (303) 458-0220.

Restrictions

Pets: On leash, cleaned up after. **Fires:** In grills. **Alcoholic Beverages:** At sites. **Vehicle Maximum Length:** None.

To Get There

From I-25 (Exit 229), on the east side of the highway, take the first right turn and go 0.2 mi. Turn left at the sign into the entrance.

TRINIDAD

Summit Inn Motel and RV Park

9800 Santa Fe Trail, Trinidad 81082. T: (719) 846-2251; F: (719) 846-2251.

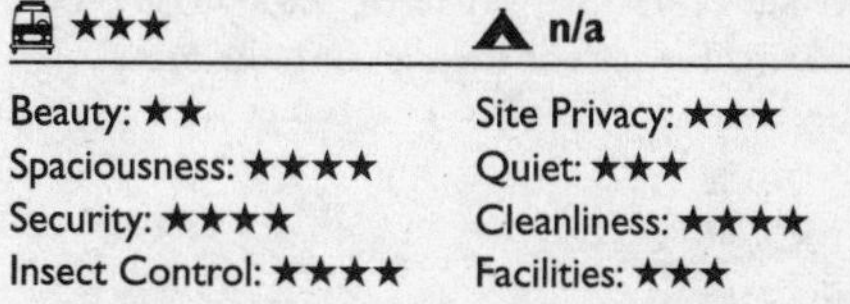

★★★ n/a

Beauty: ★★	Site Privacy: ★★★
Spaciousness: ★★★★	Quiet: ★★★
Security: ★★★★	Cleanliness: ★★★★
Insect Control: ★★★★	Facilities: ★★★

RV sites are located behind this motel. To the east and south are woods-covered hills, giving rise to the motel's claim of "great views". There are two rows of RV sites, with back-ins on the north side and pull-throughs on the south side. Each site has a gravel strip and cement pad. pull-throughs are 75 × 33 feet, back-ins are 70 × 33 feet. The best sites are to the east, as these have the best views, and are furthest away from the entrance and the highway. Sites 9–12 are closest to the motel and slightly apart from the others. Site 10 is just off the parking lot, while 9 is actually on the parking lot behind the motel. This motel/RV park is an acceptable overnighter for RVers, and close enough to Trinidad State Park to make day recreation at the lake possible. Tenters, however, will have to move on, either to Walsenburg or on into New Mexico.

Basics

Operated By: JoAnn Tortorelli. **Open:** All year. **Site Assignment:** First come, first served; verbal reservations OK. **Registration:** In office. **Fee:** RV $23 (full), $19 (water, electric) (checks, V, MC, D). **Parking:** At site.

Facilities

Number of RV Sites: 32. **Number of Tent-Only Sites:** 0. **Hookups:** Water, sewer, electric (20, 30, 50 amps). **Each Site:** Table. **Dump Station:** Yes. **Laundry:** Yes. **Pay Phone:** Yes. **Rest Rooms and Showers:** Yes. **Fuel:** No. **Propane:** No. **Internal Roads:** Gravel, paved. **RV Service:** No. **Market:** At Exit 11. **Restaurant:** At Exit 11. **General Store:** No. **Vending:** No. **Swimming:** Pool & indoor spa. **Playground:** No. **Other:** Free continental breakfast. **Activities:** Soaking in spa, boating, fishing, hiking, wildlife watching. **Nearby Attractions:** Trinidad State Park. **Additional Information:** Trinidad Chamber of Commerce, (719) 846-9285.

Restrictions

Pets: On leash, cleaned up after. **Fires:** In fire pits. **Alcoholic Beverages:** At sites. **Vehicle Maximum Length:** None.

To Get There

From I-25 Exit 11, take the first right on the east side of the highway (Santa Fe Trail) and go 0.25 mi. Turn left at the sign into the motel entrance.

TWIN LAKES

Parry Peak Campground

2015 North Poplar, Leadville 80461. T: (800) 416-6992; F: (719) 395-9022.

RV: ★★★★ Tent: ★★★★

Beauty: ★★★★★	Site Privacy: ★★★★
Spaciousness: ★★★★	Quiet: ★★★★
Security: ★★★★	Cleanliness: ★★★★
Insect Control: ★★★★	Facilities: ★

At the foot of a large mountain and by a river, this campground offers a very natural escape from the world. Unfortunately, that world drives past quite close to the campground, and no site is immune to passing traffic noise. Sites 1, 3–5, 7, and 9 back to the highway and receive the worst traffic noise. Most of the sites are 50–54-foot back-ins, although there are large pull-throughs, including 6 (78-foot) and 8 (70-foot), as well as an oversized back-in (site 26 measures 30 × 36 feet) and at least one smaller site (5 is a 30-foot back-in). While most sites in this forested campground are well-shaded, 12 is an exception, and many campers may wish to avoid this site for that reason. Sites 16–26, located across a small bridge from the main campground area, also offer tent pads at each site. Some of these sites (17–21 especially) are among the quietest sites, as they are furthest from the highway. Although there are no hookups in this campground, drinking water is found at several sites, including 10 and between 17 and 18. Besides the RV sites and the sites with tent pads, tenters can also choose from several extremely attractive walk-in sites. These are just off the road (no fear of dragging your gear for hundreds of yards), and three are located just off the river. While lacking hookups, this campground offers a great escape for those willing to give up luxury for a night or two.

Basics

Operated By: National Forest Service. **Open:** Memorial Day–after Labor Day. **Site Assignment:** First come, first served; reservations can be made 4–240 days in advance. Credit card required for reservation; $8.65 reservation fee, $10 cancellation fee; cancellations within 3 days pay first night, no-shows pay $20 fee. 2-nights min. stay on weekends, 3-nights on holidays. **Registration:** At pay station. **Fee:** $10 (checks). **Parking:** At site.

Facilities

Number of RV Sites: 26. **Number of Tent-Only Sites:** 4. **Hookups:** None. **Each Site:** Picnic table, grill. **Dump Station:** No. **Laundry:** No. **Pay Phone:** No. **Rest Rooms and Showers:** Pit toilets; no shower. **Fuel:** No. **Propane:** No. **Internal Roads:** Gravel. **RV Service:** No. **Market:** 22 mi. to Leadville. **Restaurant:** 2.8 mi. to Twin Lakes. **General Store:** No. **Vending:** No. **Swimming:** Lake. **Playground:** No. **Other:** Firewood. **Activities:** Fishing, boating, swimming, hiking. **Nearby Attractions:** Leadville, Rocky Mountains, San Isabel National Forest. **Additional Information:** Leadville Chamber of Commerce, (719) 486-3900.

Restrictions

Pets: On leash, cleaned up after. **Fires:** In grills. **Alcoholic Beverages:** At sites. **Vehicle Maximum Length:** None. **Other:** $3 day use fee.

To Get There

From the junction of Hwy. 24 and Hwy. 82, turn west onto Hwy. 82 and go 9 mi. Turn left at the sign into the entrance.

WALDEN

Roundup Motel

365 Main, Walden 80480. T: (970) 723-4680; F: (970) 723-4959; www.roundupmotel.com; bobbie@roundupmotel.com.

RV ★★★ | Tent n/a

Beauty: ★★★ | Site Privacy: ★★★
Spaciousness: ★★★ | Quiet: ★★★★
Security: ★★★★ | Cleanliness: ★★★★
Insect Control: ★★★★ | Facilities: ★★★

Recently opened as an RV park, the Roundup Motel has only a few spaces available, but these are the only full hookups within several miles of town. (There are two other pull-through sites with full hookups at the North Park Motel, also on Main.) The "park" consists of five back-ins, 25 feet wide and virtually as long as you want. On the opposite side of the fence that runs around the park are mobile homes, and the surrounding area has a destinct small town feel. The sites are a mix of gravel and grass. The middle sites are slightly more desirbale, as they do not abut a residence. The advantage of this park over the National Forest campgrounds in the surrounding area is twofold: full hookups (as opposed to electrical or none) and proximity to town. Everything in town is within walking distance of this park. Tenters can pitch a tent in the town park or continue on to one of the National Forest parks. This RV park is extremely small but convenient.

Basics

Operated By: Mark & Bobbie Scott. **Open:** All year. **Site Assignment:** First come, first served. Credit card required for reservation; 24-hours cancellation policy. **Registration:** In office. (Late arrivals ring manager's number on phone.) **Fee:** RV $20 (checks, V, MC, D, AE). **Parking:** At site.

Facilities

Number of RV Sites: 5. **Number of Tent-Only Sites:** 0. **Hookups:** Water, sewer, electric (20, 30 amps), cable. **Dump Station:** No (sewer at all sites). **Laundry:** No (in town). **Pay Phone:** Yes. **Rest Rooms and Showers:** Yes. **Fuel:** No. **Propane:** No. **Internal Roads:** Gravel. **RV Service:** No. **Market:** Less than 1 mi. north. **Restaurant:** 1 block south. **General Store:** Across street. **Vending:** Across street. **Swimming:** No. **Playground:** No. **Other:** Motel rooms. **Activities:** Fishing, boating, swimming, hiking, cross-country skiing, hunting. **Nearby Attractions:** Steamboat Springs, Laramie, wildlife, natural sand dunes, Big Creek Lakes, North Platte River, Routt National Forest. **Additional Information:** North Park Chamber of Commerce, (970) 723-4600.

Restrictions

Pets: On leash, cleaned up after. **Fires:** In grills. **Alcoholic Beverages:** At sites. **Vehicle Maximum Length:** None.

To Get There

From the junction of Hwy. 14 and Hwy. 125, Turn right at the sign into the entrance.

WALSENBURG

Dakota Campground

P.O. Box 206, Walsenburg 81089. T: (719) 738-9912.

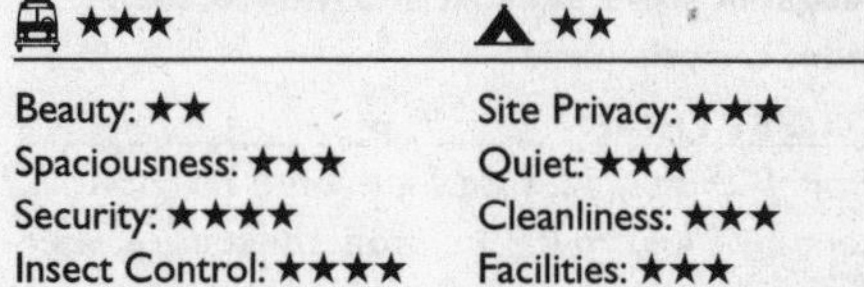

RV ★★★ | Tent ★★

Beauty: ★★ | Site Privacy: ★★★
Spaciousness: ★★★ | Quiet: ★★★
Security: ★★★★ | Cleanliness: ★★★
Insect Control: ★★★★ | Facilities: ★★★

Next to an RV service shop, dry storage, and mobile homes, this campground is surrounded by commercial/industrial space, and only the trees along the west liven it up slightly. Sites are grassy and unshaded 90-foot and 100-foot pull-throughs. Sites 1–22 are mobile homes along the south. RV sites 23–34, located behind the office, measure 90 × 16 feet. Rigs with slide-outs will feel the squeeze in these sites, especially if situated next to one another. Sites 35–46 are longer (100 feet), and include the best sites: 35–37 and 44–46, which are away from the office and playground, have views of the trees to the west. Sites 47–68 are 100-foot sites close to a commercial area and the highway, making them less desirable. The tenting area is located ot the north, adjacent to a shed. Grass and a few tables make this area acceptable, but it is far from a haven for tenters. The rest rooms are reasonably clean, but showing their age. This campground is a reasonable stop—especially for

RVs—but won't likely make anyone's destination list.

Basics

Operated By: George & Mikell Birrer. **Open:** All year. **Site Assignment:** Assigned upon registration; verbal reservations OK. **Registration:** In office. (Late arrivals go to house.) **Fee:** RV $20 (full), tent $10 (no checks, no credit cards). **Parking:** At site.

Facilities

Number of RV Sites: 72. **Number of Tent-Only Sites:** 10. **Hookups:** Water, sewer, electric (30, 50 amps). **Each Site:** Picnic table. **Dump Station:** Yes. **Laundry:** Yes. **Pay Phone:** Yes. **Rest Rooms and Showers:** Yes. **Fuel:** No. **Propane:** Yes. **Internal Roads:** Gravel. **RV Service:** Yes. **Market:** 1 mi. north. **Restaurant:** 0.5 mi. north. **General Store:** Yes. **Vending:** No. **Swimming:** No. **Playground:** Yes. **Activities:** Boating, fishing, golf. **Nearby Attractions:** Lathrop State Park. **Additional Information:** Huerfano County Chamber of Commerce, (719) 738-1065.

Restrictions

Pets: On leash, cleaned up after. **Fires:** In fire pits. **Alcoholic Beverages:** At sites. **Vehicle Maximum Length:** None.

To Get There

From I-25 Exit 52, turn south onto Business Loop I-25 and go 0.3 mi. from the south side of the highway. Turn right at the sign into the entrance.

WARD

Camp Dick

Boulder Ranger Office, 2140 Yarmouth Ave., Boulder 80301. T: (877) 444-6777 or (303) 444-6600; www.reserveusa.com or www.fs.fed.us/arns.

RV ★★★ | Tent ★★★★★

Beauty: ★★★★★	Site Privacy: ★★★★
Spaciousness: ★★★★	Quiet: ★★★★★
Security: ★★★★	Cleanliness: ★★★
Insect Control: ★★★★	Facilities: ★

Nature lovers will enjoy this campground, but those who rely on campground facilities may have mixed feelings. The beauty of this location is undeniable: the entire campground is surrounded by forested hills and most of the sites are at least partially forested. On the downside, of course, is the lack of RV hookups and narrow road in—hopefully, two giant 5th wheels will never meet on this road. Most of the sites are 40-foot back-ins, but there are exceptions to this. Site 16 is a large (75-foot) pull-through, and sites 7 and 21 are oversized sites—large enough for two vehicles and much wider than ordinary sites. Sites to the north (10, 12, and 13–16) back to a lovely stream, making these more desirable sites. Sites 26 and 28, on the other hand, are totally unshaded, making them less desirable. Site 35 offers more privacy, located as it is at the end of a roundabout. Sites 30–38 offer somewhat more seclusion, as they are located on a separate road from the other sites. The facilities include pit toilets but no showers or running water. Hardier campers will enjoy the chance to be close to nature, but those who prefer to be pampered will want to look elsewhere.

Basics

Operated By: Thousand Trails Management. **Open:** May–Oct. (dates may vary). **Site Assignment:** First come, first served. Credit card required for reservation; 3-days cancellation policy, less $10.00 service fee. **Registration:** At pay kiosk. (Camp host will verify that campers have paid.) **Fee:** $12, $15 for oversized sites (checks, no credit cards). **Parking:** At site.

Facilities

Number of RV Sites: 41. **Number of Tent-Only Sites:** 0. **Hookups:** None. **Dump Station:** No. **Laundry:** No. **Pay Phone:** No. **Rest Rooms and Showers:** Rest rooms; no shower. **Fuel:** No. **Propane:** No. **Internal Roads:** Paved. **RV Service:** No. **Market:** 12 mi. (in Nederland). **Restaurant:** 5 mi. north (in town). **General Store:** No. **Vending:** No. **Swimming:** No. **Playground:** No. **Activities:** Fishing, hiking, mountain climbing, cross-country skiing, gambling. **Nearby Attractions:** Rocky Mountain National Park, Blackhawk, Central City. **Additional Information:** Thousand Trails Management, (303) 258-3610.

Restrictions

Pets: On leash, cleaned up after. **Fires:** In fire pits. **Alcoholic Beverages:** At sites. **Vehicle Maximum Length:** None.

To Get There

From the junction of Hwy. 7 and Hwy. 72, turn south onto Hwy. 72 and go 4.1 mi. Turn right at the sign into the entrance. Pass through Peaceful Valley Campground to get to Camp Dick.

WELLINGTON

Fort Collins/Wellington KOA

P.O. Box 130, Wellington 80549. T: (800) KOA-8142 or (970) 568-7486; www.koa.com.

RV ★★★★ Tent ★★★★

Beauty: ★★★★ Site Privacy: ★★★★
Spaciousness: ★★★★ Quiet: ★★★★
Security: ★★★★ Cleanliness: ★★★★★
Insect Control: ★★★★ Facilities: ★★★★★

With the exception of a small row of back-ins for long-term guests, this campground offers all pull-throughs. Sites average 70 feet (60 feet in Row Cougar). The sites consist of gravel and sparse grass, and have only limited amounts of shade from small trees. The views to the west are best enjoyed from sites A12, B14, C10, and D10. These end sites are also the furthest from the entrance (especially in rows Antelope, Buffalo, and Cougar) and the office. The 50-amp sites are in the southeast corner of the RV sites (A 1–5 and B 1–5). There are 19 tent sites on a semi-circle to the southeast. These sites are also sparsely shaded at best. The rest rooms and showers are very clean and spacious. There are four individual units inside the office complex that are open during business hours. These are equally spotless. This campground is a pleasant place to stay, whether visiting the Ft. Collins area or continuing on to the Poudre valley.

Basics

Operated By: Guenter Kippschull, Helmut Roy. **Open:** All year. **Site Assignment:** Credit card required for reservation; 24-hours cancellation policy, less $4 fee. **Registration:** In office. (Late arrivals use drop box.) **Fee:** RV $25 (full), $23 (water, electric), tent $19 (checks, V, MC, AE). **Parking:** At site.

Facilities

Number of RV Sites: 75. **Number of Tent-Only Sites:** 19. **Hookups:** Water, sewer, electric (30, 50 amps). **Each Site:** Picnic table. **Dump Station:** Yes. **Laundry:** Yes. **Pay Phone:** Yes. **Rest Rooms and Showers:** Yes. **Fuel:** No. **Propane:** Yes. **Internal Roads:** Gravel. **RV Service:** No. **Market:** 12 mi. south to Fort Collins. **Restaurant:** 12 mi. south to Fort Collins. **General Store:** Yes. **Vending:** No. **Swimming:** Pool. **Playground:** Yes. **Other:** Pavilion, rec room (w/ TV), dog walk, storage, patio, bicycle rentals. **Activities:** Rafting, fishing, swimming. **Nearby Attractions:** Cache La Poudre, Fort Collins, Budweiser Brewery, Cheyenne Days Rodeo (July). **Additional Information:** Fort Collins CVB, (970) 491-3388.

Restrictions

Pets: On leash, cleaned up after; monthly guests must pay deposit. **Fires:** In grills. **Alcoholic Beverages:** At sites. **Vehicle Maximum Length:** None. **Other:** No speeding (5 mph limit).

To Get There

From I-25 (Exit 281), turn east onto CR 70 and go 0.3 mi. Turn into 2nd driveway (to the east) and continue to the office.

WESTCLIFFE

Grape Creek RV Park

56491 Hwy. 69, Westcliffe 81252. T: (888) 783-CAMP or (719) 783-2588; grapecreekrv@rmi.net.

RV ★★★★★ Tent ★★★

Beauty: ★★★★ Site Privacy: ★★★★
Spaciousness: ★★★★ Quiet: ★★★★★
Security: ★★★★ Cleanliness: ★★★★★
Insect Control: ★★★★ Facilities: ★★★★

A destination for peace, quiet, and, in the words of Mr. Latham, "some of the most beautiful sunsets you've ever seen," this campground has beautiful sites with lush grass and gorgeous views of snow-capped peaks to the west. Pretty much all sites are wonderful, although 25–32 are closest to the offices and may get a little more passing traffic than other sites. Sites 1–12 and end site 24 have the best views of the mountains and the valley, and are therefore more desirable. All RV sites are grassy pull-throughs averaging 50 × 30 feet. The rest rooms and showers are immaculate, spacious, and modern, as is the laundry room. Tenting is possible to the west of the RV sites or below the park by the river. Either location has beautiful grass but no cover. In fact, pretty much the only conceivable complaint anyone could have here is the lack of shade. But why complain when you're in such a beautiful site? Sit back, relax, and enjoy the quiet and scenery!

Basics

Operated By: Zane & Diana Latham. **Open:** May 10–Oct. 1. **Site Assignment:** Assigned upon registration. Credit card required for reservation;

30-days cancellation policy. **Registration:** In office. (Late arrivals come to office.) **Fee:** RV $24 (full), water, electric: $20, tent $14. **Parking:** At site.

FACILITIES

Number of RV Sites: 34. **Number of Tent-Only Sites:** 10. **Hookups:** Water, sewer, electric (30, 50 amps). **Each Site:** Bushes between sites, space for extra vehicle. **Dump Station:** Yes. **Laundry:** Yes. **Pay Phone:** Yes. **Rest Rooms and Showers:** Yes. **Fuel:** No. **Propane:** No. **Internal Roads:** Gravel. **RV Service:** No. **Market:** 2 mi. to Westcliffe. **Restaurant:** 2 mi. to Westcliffe. **General Store:** No. **Vending:** No. **Swimming:** No. **Playground:** No. **Other:** Cabins. **Activities:** Fishing, mountain climbing, mountain biking, hunting. **Nearby Attractions:** Bishop Castle, Kit Carson Mountain, Carson Mountain, Crestone Peak, Crestone Needle, Humboldt Peak, Grape Creek. **Additional Information:** Custer County Chamber of Commerce, (719) 783-9163.

RESTRICTIONS

Pets: On leash, cleaned up after. **Fires:** In rings (not at sites). **Alcoholic Beverages:** At sites. **Vehicle Maximum Length:** 45 ft.

TO GET THERE

From the junction of Hwy. 96 and Hwy. 69, go 2 mi. south on Hwy. 69. Turn right at the sign onto a dirt lane and follow it into the campground.

WHEAT RIDGE

Prospect RV Park

11600 West 44th Ave., Wheat Ridge 80033. T: (800) 344-5702 or (303) 424-4414.

RV ★★★★ | Tent n/a

Beauty: ★★★★	Site Privacy: ★★★
Spaciousness: ★★★	Quiet: ★★★★
Security: ★★★★★	Cleanliness: ★★★★★
Insect Control: ★★★★	Facilities: ★★★★

Although this campground is located in an urban residential area, it abuts a park and a lake, so it feels much more like a hideaway. The red barn and horses in the southwest corner only add to this feeling. Sites consist of shaded gravel spaces a uniform 24 feet wide. pull-throughs average 50 feet in length, and back-ins average 35 feet. Sites 5–10 have a very nice view of the neighboring lake. Sites 21–35 and 42–47 are quite attractive back-ins that back to a hedge that runs along the perimeter of the manager's residence. Sites 49–71 are laid out in three rows. These pull-throughs are somewhat smaller than the others in the park (30–42 feet). Sites 41 and 55 have the nicest views of the farmland to the southwest, but 64 has the least desirable view (a storage shed). The rest rooms are bright, modern, and absolutely immaculate. This campground offers urban convenience, but the surprise it holds up its sleeve is the quiet, pretty retreat it creates in the middle of the city.

BASICS

Operated By: Nancy Laird. **Open:** All year. **Site Assignment:** Assigned upon registration. Credit card required for reservation; call to cancel. **Registration:** In office. (Late arrivals select an available site & pay in the morning.) **Fee:** RV $28 (full), $24 (water, electric) (checks, V, MC). **Parking:** At site.

FACILITIES

Number of RV Sites: 71. **Number of Tent-Only Sites:** 0. **Hookups:** Water, sewer, electric (30, 50 amps). **Each Site:** Picnic table on concrete slab. **Dump Station:** Yes. **Laundry:** Yes. **Pay Phone:** Yes. **Rest Rooms and Showers:** Yes. **Fuel:** No. **Propane:** No. **Internal Roads:** Gravel. **RV Service:** On-call. **Market:** 6 blocks west. **Restaurant:** 3 blocks west. **General Store:** No. **Vending:** Yes. **Swimming:** No. **Playground:** Yes (next door). **Other:** Pet walk, dataport. **Activities:** Fishing, biking, hiking. **Nearby Attractions:** Prospect Park, Prospect Lake. **Additional Information:** Denver Chamber of Commerce, (303) 458-0220.

RESTRICTIONS

Pets: On leash, cleaned up after, some problem breeds not allowed. **Fires:** In grills. **Alcoholic Beverages:** At sites. **Vehicle Maximum Length:** None.

TO GET THERE

From the junction of I-25 and I-70, take Exit 214A and turn west onto I-70. Go 8.1 mi. to Exit 266, then turn south onto Ward Rd. and go 1 block south. Turn east onto 44th Ave. and go 0.6 mi. (past the RV service center). Turn right at the sign into the entrance. The office is on the right.

WINTER PARK

Idlewild Campground

9 Ten Mile Rd., Granby 80446. T: (970) 887-4100 www.fs.fed.us/recreation; hmcolburn@fs.fed.us.

RV ★★★ Tent ★★★★★

Beauty: ★★★★	Site Privacy: ★★★★
Spaciousness: ★★★★	Quiet: ★★★★
Security: ★★★★	Cleanliness: ★★★★
Insect Control: ★★★★	Facilities: ★

Laid out in two levels, the majority of sites here are located on the upper level. The lower level is mainly given over to a cycling path, and the right turn immediately at the bottom of the (steep) road between levels leads to a dead end where only bicycles can continue. All sites in this campground are well shaded, but there is not much grass growing below the pines. On the lower level, site 3 is dedicated to the camp host. Several sites (including 4 and 16) can accommodate two vehicles. Site 18 is a 70-foot pull-through located close to the rest rooms. On the upper level, site 5 is a 90-foot pull-through and 8 is a 60-foot "parallel parking" site to the side of the road. Sites 9–11 are located by the rest room in a small, secluded area. Of these sites, 11 backs to the internal road, making it much less private than 9 or 10. Near the exit, site 13 is an extremely sloped 30-foot back-in. This campground is as natural and wild as they come. It will appeal to tenters and RVers who have both a sense of adventure and a toilet and shower facility.

BASICS

Operated By: Fraser Valley Lion's Club. **Open:** May to Sept. 15. **Site Assignment:** First come, first served; no reservations. **Registration:** At pay station. **Fee:** $10 (checks). **Parking:** At site.

FACILITIES

Number of RV Sites: 26. **Number of Tent-Only Sites:** 0. **Hookups:** None. **Each Site:** Picnic table, grill. **Dump Station:** No. **Laundry:** No. **Pay Phone:** No. **Rest Rooms and Showers:** Pit toilets; no shower. **Fuel:** No. **Propane:** No. **Internal Roads:** Gravel. **RV Service:** No. **Market:** 1.5 mi. north. **Restaurant:** 1.5 mi. north. **General Store:** No. **Vending:** No. **Swimming:** No. **Playground:** No. **Other:** Firewood for sale. **Activities:** Hiking, biking, hunting, skiing. **Nearby Attractions:** Arapaho National Forest, Berthoud Pass. **Additional Information:** Sulpher Ranger District: (970) 887-4100.

RESTRICTIONS

Pets: On leash, cleaned up after. **Fires:** In grills. **Alcoholic Beverages:** At sites. **Vehicle Maximum Length:** None. **Other:** No fireworks.

TO GET THERE

From the junction of Hwy. 40 and Vasquez Rd. (the southernmost traffic light in town), turn south onto Hwy. 40 and go 1.2 mi. Turn left at the sign into the entrance.

WRAY

Hitchin' Post RV Park

34172 Hwy. 385, Wray 80758. T: (970) 332-3128; www.plains.net//hitchinpost; hitchinpost@plains.net.

RV ★★★★ Tent ★★★★

Beauty: ★★★	Site Privacy: ★★★★
Spaciousness: ★★★★	Quiet: ★★★★
Security: ★★★★	Cleanliness: ★★★★
Insect Control: ★★★★	Facilities: ★★★

This campground consists solely of two rows of pull-throughs. These unshaded gravel sites can accommodate RVs of any size. There is a third row of back-ins/tent sites to the south of the RV sites. These back-ins, (which can also be used by tents), are located on a lush grassy field. Sites are 40 feet in length. While the sites themselves do not offer any facilities, the campground has attractive landscaping that uses flowers, trees, and white fencing. The rest rooms are perfectly clean, and the showers only slightly less so. This is a pleasant campground that will appeal equally well to tenters and to RVers.

BASICS

Operated By: Noble & Virgene Burns. **Open:** All year. **Site Assignment:** Assigned upon registration; verbal reservations OK. **Registration:** In office. (Late arrivals select an available site & pay in the morning.) **Fee:** RV $20 (full), tent $10 (checks, no credits cards). **Parking:** At site.

FACILITIES

Number of RV Sites: 19. **Number of Tent-Only Sites:** Undesignated sites. **Hookups:** Water, sewer, electric (15, 30, 50 amps). **Each Site:** Hitchin' Post RV Park. **Dump Station:** Yes. **Laundry:** Yes. **Pay Phone:** Yes. **Rest Rooms and Showers:** Yes. **Fuel:** No. **Propane:** Yes. **Internal**

Roads: Gravel. **RV Service:** No. **Market:** 1 mi. north. **Restaurant:** 1 mi. north. **General Store:** No. **Vending:** No. **Swimming:** No. **Playground:** No. **Other:** Dog pen. **Activities:** Fishing, boating, swimming. **Nearby Attractions:** Bonny State Park. **Additional Information:** Chamber of Commerce, (970) 332-4609.

RESTRICTIONS

Pets: On leash, cleaned up after. **Fires:** In grills. **Alcoholic Beverages:** At sites. **Vehicle Maximum Length:** None. **Other:** See rule sheet.

TO GET THERE

From the junction of Hwy. 34 and Hwy. 385, turn south onto Hwy. 385 and go 1.1 mi. Turn left at the sign into the entrance, then right towards the office.

YAMPA

Stillwater Campground

P.O. Box 7, 300 Roselawn Ave., Yampa 80483. T: (970) 879-1722.

 ★★★★ ▲ ★★★★

Beauty: ★★★★★	Site Privacy: ★★★★★
Spaciousness: ★★★★★	Quiet: ★★★★★
Security: ★★★★	Cleanliness: ★★★
Insect Control: ★★★★	Facilities: ★

The long but beautiful drive in to this campground is worth the effort once you are there, as this campground offers spectacular views of lakes and the mountains that rise above them. The recreational opportunities for outdoor enthusiasts are also limitless. The campground itself is very small (7 sites), but there are a number of campsites along the road in. Some of these (including 28, just across from the campground, and 33, a pull-through overlooking Bear Lake) are at the tops of hills, allowing a view overlooking the entire area. Site 1 in the campground is right by the entrance, and may be less desirable for this location. Sites 2–4 are 45–50-foot back-ins; of these, 3 has the best views to the southeast. Site 5 is an 80-foot back-in, and 6 and 7 are 75-foot pull-throughs. All of these sites are at least partially forested and some (2 and 4) are completely lost in trees. Come to this campground in Sept., when the aspens are turning. You will see a startle of yellow aspens among the stately deep-green ponderosa pines. This campground offers wonderful scenic and recreational opportunities but next to nothing in the way of facilities. As such, it may appeal most to tenters and RVers with a sense of adventure.

BASICS

Operated By: US Forest Service. **Open:** All year. **Site Assignment:** First come, first served; no reservations. **Registration:** At pay station. **Fee:** Site in campground: $10, developed campsites along road: $3 (checks). **Parking:** At site.

FACILITIES

Number of RV Sites: 29. **Number of Tent-Only Sites:** 0. **Hookups:** None. **Each Site:** Picnic table, fire pit. **Dump Station:** No. **Laundry:** No. **Pay Phone:** No. **Rest Rooms and Showers:** Toilets; showers in town. **Fuel:** No. **Propane:** No. **Internal Roads:** Dirt. **RV Service:** No. **Market:** 16 mi. northeast. **Restaurant:** 16 mi. northeast. **General Store:** No. **Vending:** No. **Swimming:** Reservoir. **Playground:** No. **Activities:** Fishing, boating, swimming, hiking, hunting, horseback riding. **Nearby Attractions:** Stillwater Reservoir, Yamcolo Reservoir, Bear Lake, Devil's Causeway, Stagecoach State Park. **Additional Information:** Yampa Ranger District, (970) 638-4516.

RESTRICTIONS

Pets: On leash, cleaned up after. **Fires:** In grills. **Alcoholic Beverages:** At sites. **Vehicle Maximum Length:** None. **Other:** $3 per vehicle day use pass, no cutting firewood.

TO GET THERE

From the junction of Hwy. 131 and Moffat Ave. (by gas station complex at southeastern edge of town), turn southwest onto Moffat Ave. and go 0.4 mi. to Main St. Cross over Main and continue on CR 7 (which becomes unpaved FR 900) for 13.3 mi. to Bear Lake Campground. The campground is on the left.

Kansas

Kansas isn't what you might think: cornfield and tornado country with nothing to see. While there are cornfields and twisters, there's also much more available to visitors than you might guess by looking over the guardrail as you speed down I-70. If you slow down and turn off the main routes, you'll find an honest vision of America struggling in the face of same-as-everywhere megamarts and fast-food chains.

Kansas is a small-town state. But that is good news for campers, as this makes for a lot of quiet rural camping. While Kansas has its share of overnighters, many campgrounds are in rural areas where you're as likely to encounter a horse as a human being. For outdoor enthusiasts, nearly every county has a state fishing lake open to anglers and campers alike.

For a look at what Kansas was like in the nineteenth century, go to **Dodge City** or **Meade** or **Coffeyville.** The museums that remain offer tourists a chance to relive history. You will see why lawmakers in Clint Eastwood movies shook in their boots when they heard talk of dreaded Kansas.

To see Kansas as it faces the future, visit the large cities of **Wichita, Kansas City,** and **Topeka.** These make convenient destinations (or even just stopping points) on a cross-Kansas trip. Spend a few days in these urban centers to soak up some culture, then venture forth into the special small places Kansas has to offer—such as the Amish community of **Yoder,** the weird rock formations at **Monument Rocks National Landmark,** or "the living ghost town" of **Elk Falls.** One highway slogan sums it up: "Drive through Kansas and you'll miss it."

The following facilities accept payment in checks or cash only:

Bourquin's RV Park, Colby
Circle-O, Meade
Crawford State Park, Girard
Elk City State Park, Independence
Homewood RV Park, Ottawa-Williamsburg
Prairie Dog State Park, Norton
Tarrant Overnight Camping, El Dorado
Tuttle Creek State Park, Manhattan

The following facilities feature 20 sites or fewer:

Pleasant View Motel & Overnight RV Park, Greensburg
Evergreen Inn & RV Park, Pratt
Payne Oil CO, Newton
Country Squire Motel & RV Park, Hiawatha

ABILENE

Covered Wagon RV Resort

803 South Buckeye, Abilene 67410. T: (800) 864-4053 or (785) 263-2343.

RV ★★★★★ Tent ★★★★★

Beauty: ★★★★ Site Privacy: ★★★★
Spaciousness: ★★★★ Quiet: ★★★★
Security: ★★★ Cleanliness: ★★★★
Insect Control: ★★★★ Facilities: ★★★★

Two dramatically different experiences await RVers at this park, depending on which portion of the park you find yourself parked in. Those parked close to the house will find a forested campsite with level, grassy sites and plenty of (deciduous) tree coverage. Sites 26–31 at the edge of the park are treed-off from the rest of the sites and face a grassy field under a canopy of trees. Site 7 would make a particularly nice tent site due to the protection of trees. However, sites 52–57 sit on an open gravel/grassy strip at the edge of the property with no coverage whatsoever. Adding insult to injury, a row of storage units faces this landing strip, degrading the visual aesthetic even further. For an enjoyable stay, insist on a site closer to the house.

BASICS

Operated By: Richard & Cathy Osborn. **Open:** All year. **Site Assignment:** Upon registration, reservations OK, credit card to hold, must cancel within 24 hours. **Registration:** In house, late arrivals use drop box. **Fee:** $15–$21; V, MC, D, $1 discount for cash or check. **Parking:** At site.

FACILITIES

Number of RV Sites: 40. **Number of Tent-Only Sites:** 0. **Hookups:** Water, sewer, electric (30, 50 amp), phone. **Each Site:** Picnic table, tree. **Dump Station:** Yes. **Laundry:** Yes. **Pay Phone:** Yes. **Rest Rooms and Showers:** Yes. **Fuel:** No. **Propane:** No. **Internal Roads:** Yes. **RV Service:** No. **Market:** 1 mi. **Restaurant:** 0.25 mi. **General Store:** Yes. **Vending:** No. **Swimming:** Pool. **Playground:** Yes. **Other:** Accepts horses, makes reservations for lunch/dinner in town or for tours, horseshoes. **Activities:** Swimming, basketball, tennis, volleyball at nearby Eisenhower Park. **Nearby Attractions:** Dwight D. Eisenhower Presidential Center, Greyhound Hall of Fame, antique doll museum. **Additional Information:** Abilene Chamber of Commerce, (913) 263-1770.

RESTRICTIONS

Pets: On leash only. **Fires:** In grills. **Alcoholic Beverages:** At sites. **Vehicle Maximum Length:** None.

TO GET THERE

From I-70, take Exit 275, then turn south onto Hwy. 15, then drive 2.3 mi. The entrance is on the right. Park behind the house to go to the office.

ATWOOD

Linis Park at Lake Atwood

4th St. & Lake Rd., Atwood 67730. T: (785) 626-3020 or (785) 626-9503.

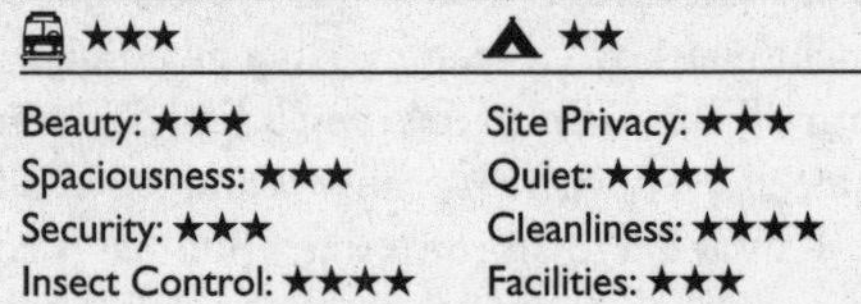

RV ★★★ Tent ★★

Beauty: ★★★ Site Privacy: ★★★
Spaciousness: ★★★ Quiet: ★★★★
Security: ★★★ Cleanliness: ★★★★
Insect Control: ★★★★ Facilities: ★★★

Campsites are located in a strip a few hundred feet away from the edge of the lake. With the lake to the northwest, a cute pavillion, and a romantic lit walkway around the circumference of the lake, the campground is pretty, with a quiet, small-town park atmosphere. Sites 1–4 are situated on the paved parking lot (with grass behind), while 5–9 are all grass. All sites are open back-ins with full hookups. Tent sites are located between the RV sites and the lake, in a large, open grassy field with virtually unlimited sites. Be forewarned of the hot-rod rally that occurs May 18–20, as sites fill up quickly. Site 1, being an end site, has much more space than all the others except 9, the other end site. (There is a 10th water hookup and space for another vehicle next to site 9 that isn't rented out, but it seems hard to believe someone might not take advantage of it in the busy season.) While the restroom and showers are in the park, other all services (such as phone and vending) are located at the Vista mart.

BASICS

Operated By: Lion's Club. **Open:** All year. **Site Assignment:** First come, first served. **Registration:** In Vista mart 6 a.m.–midnight. **Fee:** RV $15, $5 refundable key deposit, tents free. **Parking:** At site.

FACILITIES

Number of RV Sites: 9. **Number of Tent-Only Sites:** Undesignated sites. **Hookups:** Water, sewer, electric (20, 30, 50 amp). **Each Site:** Grill, picnic table, tree. **Dump Station:** No (sewer at all sites). **Laundry:** No. **Pay Phone:** Yes. **Rest Rooms and Showers:** Yes. **Fuel:** Yes. **Propane:** No. **Internal Roads:** Paved. **RV Service:** No. **Market:** 6 blocks. **Restaurant:** 2 blocks. **General Store:** Yes. **Vending:** Yes. **Swimming:** No. **Playground:** Yes. **Other:** Fishing lake, lit walkway around lake. **Activities:** Fishing, 9-hole golf, softball, basketball, volleyball, boating. **Nearby Attractions:** Lake Atwood 10 mi. race, Hayden Nature Trail, Atwood Country Club & Golf Course. **Additional Information:** Atwood Chamber of Commerce, (785) 626-9630.

Restrictions

Pets: On leash. **Fires:** In grills. **Alcoholic Beverages:** At sites. **Vehicle Maximum Length:** None.

To Get There

From Hwy. 36 and 4th St. in town, turn north onto 4th St. At the end of the block, turn left onto Lake Rd., then take the immediate right into the park. Select a spot, then walk to the Coastal/Vista gas station on the south side of Hwy. 36 and 4th St. to register.

BELLEVILLE

Evergreen Acres RV Park

1880 Elm Rd., Belleville 66935. T: (785) 987-5544.

RV ★★★★ Tent ★★★★

Beauty: ★★★★★ Site Privacy: ★★★
Spaciousness: ★★★ Quiet: ★★★★★
Security: ★★★★ Cleanliness: ★★★★★
Insect Control: ★★★★ Facilities: ★★★★

This isolated campground offers an authentic farm experience in a beautiful pastoral setting. Traffic noise is supplanted by the croaking of frogs, the calling of birds, and the sighing of the wind. Large mature evergreens shield the campground from the road and add to the verdant beauty. The campground is divided into two sections: one near the house, one barely a quarter mile away by the lake. (To get to the second section, continue on the road just past the authentic, functional barn with the authentic, functional cows, take the first left turn, then again the immediate left turn onto the white gravel driveway.) The lake is located at the second section, but in fact, the better sites are closer to the house. Sites near the lake (1–10) are a little more tightly crammed together and are lined up in a single row. Sites at the house are more scattered (offering more privacy) and contain more trees. All sites are grassy and level pull-throughs, however, and the least desirable site is located in the campground you have to go to when all the spaces at Evergreen Acres are full.

Basics

Operated By: Henry & Mildred Blecha. **Open:** All year (lake area may close for winter). **Site Assignment:** Upon registration. **Registration:** In office. **Fee:** RV $10, tent $6; checks OK, no credit cards. **Parking:** At site.

Facilities

Number of RV Sites: 15. **Number of Tent-Only Sites:** Undesignated sites. **Hookups:** Water, sewer, electric (30 amp). **Each Site:** Picnic table. **Dump Station:** No (sewer at all sites). **Laundry:** No. **Pay Phone:** Yes. **Rest Rooms and Showers:** Yes. **Fuel:** No. **Propane:** No. **Internal Roads:** Gravel. **RV Service:** No. **Market:** 4 mi. north to Chester, Nebraska. **Restaurant:** 4 mi. North to Chester, Nebraska. **General Store:** No. **Vending:** No. **Swimming:** No. **Playground:** Yes. **Other:** Lake. **Activities:** Fishing. **Nearby Attractions:** Pawnee Indian museum. **Additional Information:** Belleville Chamber of Commerce, (913) 527-5519.

Restrictions

Pets: On leash, cleaned up after. **Fires:** Stoves only. **Alcoholic Beverages:** At sites. **Vehicle Maximum Length:** None.

To Get There

From the junction of Hwy. 36 and Hwy. 81, travel North on Hwy. 81 for 9.5 mi., then turn East onto a gravel road. Follow this road 0.8 mi., then turn left at the sign into the entrance. Keep left to go to the office.

COLBY

Bourquin's RV Park

155 East Willow, I-70 Frontage Rd., Colby 67701. T: (785) 462-3300; www.colby.ixks.com; shirleyb@colby.ixks.com.

RV ★★★ Tent ★★

Beauty: ★★★ Site Privacy: ★★
Spaciousness: ★★ Quiet: ★★★★
Security: ★★★ Cleanliness: ★★★
Insect Control: ★★★ Facilities: ★★

Conveniently close (half a mile) to town, this campground is still far enough removed to avoid most of the lights and noise. Most sites are back-in, with the possibility of pull-throughs in the inner circle of the loop (requiring pulling out over a strip of grass that looks like it can take it—and has.) Sites are not well shaded, so the summer sun could prove a little overwhelming—as could a strong spring rain or windstorm. The Prairie Art Museum to the north offers a cute view of a miniaturized church, barn, and windmill. Unmarked tent sites are off in the northwest corner, next to a charming red one-room schoolhouse with several large shrubs, but are equally unprotected and sit next to a road. Tenters might optimally give this campground a miss and continue on to Oakley or Goodland. The best RV sites are 19–36, which lie on the outside of the loop away from town-side, and next to open land and a pond to the east. The least desirable sites are 37–48, which are a little squashed together and share tables and grills.

Basics

Operated By: Shirley Bourquin. **Open:** Apr. 15–Sept. 30. **Site Assignment:** First come, first served. **Registration:** In office, late arrivals use drop box; verbal reservations OK. **Fee:** RV $18, coach $20, van/pop-up $16, tent $12. **Parking:** At site.

Facilities

Number of RV Sites: 50. **Number of Tent-Only Sites:** Undesignated sites. **Hookups:** Water, sewer, electric (20, 30, 50 amp). **Each Site:** Some tables, grills, trees. **Dump Station:** Yes. **Laundry:** No. **Pay Phone:** Yes. **Rest Rooms and Showers:** Yes. **Fuel:** No. **Propane:** No. **Internal Roads:** Gravel, good condition. **RV Service:** No. **Market:** 0.5 mi. to Colby. **Restaurant:** On site. **General Store:** Yes. **Vending:** No. **Swimming:** No. **Playground:** No. **Other:** Homemade organic foods. **Activities:** Bluegrass festival in July. **Nearby Attractions:** Prairie Art Museum. **Additional Information:** Prairie Museum of Art & History, Northwest Research Extension Center.

Restrictions

Pets: On leash, cleaned up after. **Fires:** In grills. **Alcoholic Beverages:** At sites. **Vehicle Maximum Length:** None.

To Get There

From I-70, take Exit 53 and turn north. Take the first right onto the frontage road along I-70. Follow the road 0.5 mi. to the entrance.

CONCORDIA

Brome Ridge RV Park

RR1 Box 149, Concordia 66901. T: (785) 243-4539.

RV ★★★★★ Tent ★★★★

Beauty: ★★★★ Site Privacy: ★★★
Spaciousness: ★★★ Quiet: ★★★
Security: ★★★★ Cleanliness: ★★★★
Insect Control: ★★★★ Facilities: ★★★★

This campground is charming and pictoresque. Along the drive into the campground are several items of country kitsch ("Coyote Crossing" sign, animal statuettes) that are—surprisingly—tastefully done. Trees line the drive half of the way down, while the rest of the grounds open up to reveal scenes of rural Kansas: rolling hills, farms, cows, and a large pond. Indeed, the entire park feels like it's on a farm. All RV sites are level and grassy pull-throughs situated on a giant loop. While it is hard to think of a "least desirable site" in the campground, site 1 does sit right at the tip of the loop, and may therefore receive more internal traffic than a camper would care for. But it's still not bad! Sites 18–20 are slightly nicer than others due to their size and proximity to a large open field. Please note that the hot and cold water knobs were inverted—there really is hot water, you just have to turn it to maximum blue (cold) instead of red (hot).

Basics

Operated By: Stan & Maxine Van Meter. **Open:** All year. **Site Assignment:** First come, first served. **Registration:** At self-pay station. **Fee:** RV $14 full, $8 dry; tent $5. **Parking:** At site.

Facilities

Number of RV Sites: 21. **Number of Tent-Only Sites:** Undesignated sites. **Hookups:** Water, sewer, electric (30, 50 amp). **Each Site:** Picnic table, deciduous shrub. **Dump Station:** No (sewer at all sites). **Laundry:** Yes. **Pay Phone:** No. **Rest Rooms and Showers:** Yes. **Fuel:** No. **Propane:** No. **Internal Roads:** Gravel, in good condition. **RV Service:** No. **Market:** 7 mi. to Concordia. **Restaurant:** 7 mi. to Concordia. **General Store:** No. **Vending:** Yes. **Swimming:** No. **Playground:** Yes. **Other:** Storm shelter, cabins, pond, catering, club house w/ kitchenette. **Activities:** Hunting, fishing. **Nearby Attractions:** Brown Grand Theatre, Cloud County Historical Museum, Republican

River. **Additional Information:** Concordia Chamber of Commerce, (785) 243-4290.

Restrictions

Pets: On leash, cleaned up after. **Fires:** In grills. **Alcoholic Beverages:** At sites. **Vehicle Maximum Length:** None.

To Get There

From Hwy. 81, drive 7 mi. south of Concordai. Between mile markers 195 and 196, turn west at the sign into the entrance. Follow the drive to the self-pay station.

COUNCIL GROVE

Council Grove Lake

RT2 Box 110, Council Grove 66846. T: (877) 444-6777 or (316) 767-5195; F: (620) 767-6919; www.reserveusa.com.

RV ★★★★★ Tent ★★★★★

Beauty: ★★★★★	Site Privacy: ★★★★
Spaciousness: ★★★★★	Quiet: ★★★★★
Security: ★★★★	Cleanliness: ★★★★
Insect Control: ★★	Facilities: ★★★

Eight different campgrounds surround the lake, with sites ranging from lakeside higher ground. All sites are spacious, level, and grassy, with some as big as 100 × 100 feet. Although there are too many campsites to enumerate, several distinguish themselves as particularly nice. Sites 21–26 on the penninsula in Ritchie Cove and 1–13 on a strip by the waterfront, for example, have spectacular views of the sunset. All campgrounds have a wilderness feel, and if you come on a weekday in spring, you may get the whole place to yourself! A wonderful destination for a fun-filled stay of any length.

Basics

Operated By: U.S. Army Corps of Engineers. **Open:** All year. **Site Assignment:** First come, first served; reservations OK, need credit card to hold, $10 cancellation fee, first-night's-use fee if not cancelled within 3 days of arrival date. **Registration:** Self-pay station. **Fee:** RV $14, tent $10. **Parking:** At site, additional parking available.

Facilities

Number of RV Sites: 180. **Number of Tent-Only Sites:** 0. **Hookups:** Water, sewer, electric (30, 50 amp). **Each Site:** Covered picnic table, fire pit/grill, trees. **Dump Station:** Yes. **Laundry:** No. **Pay Phone:** No. **Rest Rooms and Showers:** Yes. **Fuel:** No. **Propane:** No. **Internal Roads:** Paved. **RV Service:** No. **Market:** 2 mi. to Council Grove. **Restaurant:** 2 mi. to Council Grove. **General Store:** Yes. **Vending:** Yes. **Swimming:** Yes (lake). **Playground:** Yes. **Activities:** Fishing, swimming, boating, waterskiing, hunting. **Nearby Attractions:** July 4th fireworks in town, Kay Mission State Historic Site. **Additional Information:** Council Grove Chamber of Commerce, (316) 767-5413.

Restrictions

Pets: On leash. **Fires:** In fire rings only. **Alcoholic Beverages:** At sites. **Vehicle Maximum Length:** None. **Other:** No fireworks.

To Get There

From the junction of Hwy. 56 & Hwy. 57/177 in town, take Hwy. 57/177 2 mi. north, then turn left at the sign for Council Grove Lake. Follow the road 1.3 mi. across the lake, then cross the intersection to arrive at the office. (You may also go to any campsite & then to a self-pay station.)

DODGE CITY

Watersports Campground

500 East Cherry St., Dodge City 67801. T: (316) 225-8044 or (316) 225-9003; F: (316) 225-4407; www.gocampingamerica.com.

RV ★★★★ Tent ★★★

Beauty: ★★★	Site Privacy: ★★★
Spaciousness: ★★★	Quiet: ★★★★
Security: ★★★★	Cleanliness: ★★★★
Insect Control: ★★★	Facilities: ★★★★

This popular RV park sits just west of the lake from which its name derives. (The RV park on the east side of the lake is for members only.) Sites 31–52 have an attractive view of the lake, but 51 and 52 are very close to the playground. Full hookup pull-throughs 1–10 face open grassy land with an attractive row of trees at the far end. Site 31 has extra space to the north side, while site 38 is known among visitors as "the best site," presumably for its commanding view of the lake. Sites may be a little cramped for larger rigs (45–50 feet long), and spare vehicles may have to be parked crosswise in a space. Tents can be pitched on the well-manicured lawn that extends between the RV park and the lake.

Basics

Operated By: Deana Vogel. **Open:** All year. **Site Assignment:** At registration, verbal reservations OK except for holidays. **Registration:** In office, late arrivals use slot in door. **Fee:** $15, $1 utility (water free); no credit cards. **Parking:** At site.

Facilities

Number of RV Sites: 56. **Number of Tent-Only Sites:** Undesignated sites. **Hookups:** Water, sewer, electric (30, 50 amp). **Each Site:** Tree. **Dump Station:** Yes. **Laundry:** Yes. **Pay Phone:** Yes. **Rest Rooms and Showers:** Yes. **Fuel:** No. **Propane:** Yes. **Internal Roads:** Dirt/gravel. **RV Service:** No. **Market:** 4 blocks. **Restaurant:** 10 blocks. **General Store:** Yes. **Vending:** Yes. **Swimming:** Yes (lake). **Playground:** Yes. **Other:** Courtesy van to Boot Hill, lifeguard, walking path. **Activities:** Swimming, fishing, pool table, video games, self-guiding tours. **Nearby Attractions:** Boot Hill, Fort Dodge, Home of Stone. **Additional Information:** Dodge City Chamber of Commerce, (316) 227-3119.

Restrictions

Pets: "We do not like rotweilers, dobermans, or pit bulls." **Fires:** In fire pits only. **Alcoholic Beverages:** At sites. **Vehicle Maximum Length:** 45 ft.

To Get There

From the junction of Hwy. 50 and 2nd Ave. in town, turn south at the light onto 2nd Ave., then drive 0.5 mi. and turn left onto Cherry St. Take Cherry St. 0.4 mi. to the end, and follow the dirt road to the right to go to the office.

EL DORADO

Tarrant Overnight Camping

RR2 Box 272, El Dorado 67042. T: (316) 321-6272.

RV ★★★ | Tent n/a

Beauty: ★★★	Site Privacy: ★★★
Spaciousness: ★★	Quiet: ★★★
Security: ★★★	Cleanliness: ★★
Insect Control: ★★★	Facilities: ★★★

Vehicle length is not a problem in this campground, but even according to management, width can pose problems. Sites are laid out in two rows of 18 sites, 1–18 being doubled-up pull-throughs parked back-to-back, 19–36 being back-ins. Sites 32–26 look quite cramped, while 20 has a telephone pole that encroaches, and 19 (next to the rest rooms) has a patch of tulips that enlivens the site but also clips a corner. The best sites are 13–18, closest to the forested southeast corner, with the convenience of a pull-through. The restroom facilities are less than thrilling: the shower stalls share a curtain divider and floor, and the toilet is not enclosed, making for inconvenient use of the toilet while someone else is showering. This campground is the only one in the immediate area this is open during the winter season, making it a convenient—or perhaps necessary—stop, but not a haven to plan around.

Basics

Operated By: Doug & Sharon Varner. **Open:** All year. **Site Assignment:** Assigned when getting full, verbal reservations OK. **Registration:** In office, late arrivals use drop box. **Fee:** Under 35 ft. $15, 35 ft. or longer $17. **Parking:** At site.

Facilities

Number of RV Sites: 36. **Number of Tent-Only Sites:** 0. **Hookups:** Water, sewer, electric (30, 50 amp). **Each Site:** Picnic table, mature shade tree. **Dump Station:** No. **Laundry:** No. **Pay Phone:** No. **Rest Rooms and Showers:** Yes. **Fuel:** No. **Propane:** No. **Internal Roads:** Gravel. **RV Service:** Across street. **Market:** 4 mi. to El Dorado. **Restaurant:** 2.5 mi. to El Dorado. **General Store:** No. **Vending:** No. **Swimming:** No. **Playground:** No. **Other:** Storm shelter, notary public. **Activities:** Swimming, fishing, shopping, visiting museums. **Nearby Attractions:** State lake (4 mi.), Wichita, art museum, historical museum, antique stores. **Additional Information:** El Dorado Chamber of Commerce, (316) 321-3150.

Restrictions

Pets: On leash, cleaned up after. **Fires:** In grill or stove. **Alcoholic Beverages:** At sites. **Vehicle Maximum Length:** None. **Other:** No vehicle washing.

To Get There

From the junction of Hwy. 35 and Hwy. 254, take Exit 71 onto Hwy. 254 and go east (after 0.3 mi., Hwy. 254 becomes Hwy. 54). Stay on Hwy. 54 going east for 3 mi., then turn right into the entrance, half block west of the El Dorado State Lake Park entrance. Follow the drive to the back of the park and to the office straight ahead.

EMPORIA

Emporia RV Park

4601 West Hwy. 50, Emporia 66801. T: (316) 343-3422; F: (316) 341-0105; www.gocampingamerica.com/emporia; emprv@valu-line.com.

RV ★★★ Tent ★★★

Beauty: ★★ Site Privacy: ★★★
Spaciousness: ★★★ Quiet: ★★★
Security: ★★★★ Cleanliness: ★★★★★
Insect Control: ★★★★ Facilities: ★★★

The proximity to the highway to the north and east detracts slightly from the ambiance, but adds greatly to the convenience of the campsite. A forested area to the east/southeast and to the west helps create a rural feel in the campground, as does the fish pond to the northwest. Each site has at least one tree, but some are too small to afford any real shade. Sites are pull-throughs laid out in two strips. Sites 20 and 39 on the ends are slightly shortchanged for space, and odd numbers 21–39 face the highway. The better sites are odd numbers 1–19, which face the woods on the western border of the property. Average site size is 75 × 27 feet, large enough for a big rig with slide-outs.

BASICS

Operated By: Paul & Charlotte Pinick. **Open:** All year. **Site Assignment:** Upon registration, reservations OK, credit card to hold, must cancel within 24 hours. **Registration:** In office, late arrivals use drop box. **Fee:** RV $20, tent $18. **Parking:** At site.

FACILITIES

Number of RV Sites: 39. **Number of Tent-Only Sites:** Undesignated sites. **Hookups:** Water, sewer, electric (20, 30, 50 amp), cable. **Each Site:** Picnic table, tree. **Dump Station:** Yes. **Laundry:** Yes. **Pay Phone:** Yes. **Rest Rooms and Showers:** Yes. **Fuel:** No. **Propane:** Yes. **Internal Roads:** Gravel. **RV Service:** No. **Market:** 0.5 mi. to Emporia. **Restaurant:** 0.5 mi. to Emporia. **General Store:** Yes. **Vending:** No. **Swimming:** No. **Playground:** Yes. **Other:** Fishing pond, rec room, dog walk area, skate ramp. **Activities:** Fishing, skating, boating, swimming in nearby reservoirs. **Nearby Attractions:** Tallgrass Prairie National Preserve, farmer's market. **Additional Information:** Emporia Chamber of Commerce, (316) 342-1600.

RESTRICTIONS

Pets: On leash, not tied up. **Fires:** None. **Alcoholic Beverages:** On sites only. **Vehicle Maximum Length:** 70 ft.

TO GET THERE

From the junction of I-35 (Exit 127C) and Hwy. 50, turn west onto Hwy. 50 and begin to merge left as soon as possible. The entrance is on the left, barely 0.5 mi. from the junction.

FARLINGTON

Crawford State Park

1 Lake Rd., Farlington 66734. T: (620) 362-3671.

RV ★★★★★ Tent ★★★★★

Beauty: ★★★★★ Site Privacy: ★★★★★
Spaciousness: ★★★★★ Quiet: ★★★★★
Security: ★★★ Cleanliness: ★★★★★
Insect Control: ★★★ Facilities: ★★★

Campsites around this lake are enormous (some 100 × 100 feet) and vary from waterfront to higher up and set into woods. There are four separate camping areas, several nature trails, a mountain biking/hiking trail, as well as scads of picnic and water-use areas. Some of these areas (evening Breeze Point, Osage Bluff, Cherokee Landing, Lonesome point) offer primitive camping (and toilets) only. All RV sites are back-in only, but spacious and private enough to make up for this small inconvenience. Washrooms are surprisingly clean but sparse—possibly a drive away from some campsites. This campground is a great destination to bring the kids.

BASICS

Operated By: Kansas Dept. of Wildlife & Parks. **Open:** All year. **Site Assignment:** First come, first served. **Registration:** At office or self-pay station. **Fee:** $7–$18, $5/day vehicle permit. **Parking:** At site.

FACILITIES

Number of RV Sites: 72. **Number of Tent-Only Sites:** 35. **Hookups:** Water, electric (30 amp); no water Oct. 15–Apr. 1. **Each Site:** Picnic table, fire pit/grill, trees. **Dump Station:** Yes. **Laundry:** Yes. **Pay Phone:** Yes. **Rest Rooms and Showers:** Yes. **Fuel:** No. **Propane:** No. **Internal Roads:** Paved. **RV Service:** No. **Market:** 10 mi. to Farlington. **Restaurant:** 10 mi. to Farlington. **General Store:** Yes. **Vending:** Yes. **Swimming:** Yes (lake). **Playground:** Yes. **Other:** Boat ramp, amphitheater. **Activities:** Boating, swimming, fishing, hiking. **Nearby Attractions:** Fort Scott. **Additional Information:** Girard Chamber of Commerce, (620) 724-4715.

Restrictions

Pets: On leash. **Fires:** In fire pits; subject to seasonal bans. **Alcoholic Beverages:** Beer only. **Vehicle Maximum Length:** None. **Other:** 1 vehicle/site, boat registration.

To Get There

From the junction of Hwy. 57 and Hwy. 7, turn north onto Hwy. 7 and drive 8.7 mi. Turn right at the sign onto 710 Ave. and continue 1 mi. to the entrance.

FORT SCOTT

Fort Scott Campground

2162 Native Rd., Fort Scott 66701. T: (800) 538-0216 or (620) 223-3440; F: (620) 223-4950.

RV ★★★★★ Tent ★★★★

Beauty: ★★★★	Site Privacy: ★★★
Spaciousness: ★★★	Quiet: ★★★★
Security: ★★★	Cleanliness: ★★★★★
Insect Control: ★★★	Facilities: ★★★

A very cute, tidy campground with 40 pull-throughs and 10 back-ins. An average site measures 24 × 70 feet, leaving a potentially restricted area around some bigger rigs. However, the ambiance is virtually unbeatable, more than making up for possible space shortages. This is the kind of campground you want to take a walk around as soon as you arrive, just to take in the natural beauty. Sites are very clearly labeled with attractive wooden signs. Many sites have two or more trees, increasing the impression of privacy. Site 33 is slightly encroached upon by signs, and 34 (which may not be assigned) appears to be part of a through-road. Any other sites really can't be beat. As an added bonus, end site 42 seems to have inherited some extra space, and 16 (closest to the fishing pond and cow pasture) has a wide-open east side. One glaring exception to this pristine idyll is the swingsets, which are rusted and unstable looking. A safer bet for kids are the other swings, teeter-totter, and merry-go-round. The tent site to the north of the office offers thick grass, mature shade trees, and almost unlimited number of spaces. A sure bet for campers of any stripe!

Basics

Operated By: Jack & Ruth Jaro. **Open:** All year (limited services Nov. 16–Feb. 28). **Site Assignment:** Fist come, first served or assigned upon registration, verbal reservations OK, cancel within 48 hours. **Registration:** In office, late arrivals use drop box. **Fee:** RV $19 full, $17 water/ electric, $12 winter; checks, V, MC, AE. **Parking:** At site.

Facilities

Number of RV Sites: 50. **Number of Tent-Only Sites:** 15. **Hookups:** Water, sewer, electric (30, 50 amp). **Each Site:** Picnic table, trees. **Dump Station:** Yes. **Laundry:** Yes. **Pay Phone:** No. **Rest Rooms and Showers:** Yes. **Fuel:** No. **Propane:** No. **Internal Roads:** Gravel. **RV Service:** No. **Market:** 4 mi. in Fort Scott. **Restaurant:** 0.25 mi. **General Store:** Yes. **Vending:** No. **Swimming:** Pool. **Playground:** Yes. **Other:** Stocked fishing pond, free firewood, 1 cabin, central fire ring, pet walk area, video games. **Activities:** Fishing, volleyball, horseshoes, pool. **Nearby Attractions:** Fort Scott. **Additional Information:** Fort Scott Chamber of Commerce, (316) 223-3566.

Restrictions

Pets: On leash, always attended, cleaned up after. **Fires:** In fire ring or grill. **Alcoholic Beverages:** Prefer cans (due to pool). **Vehicle Maximum Length:** 70 ft. **Other:** Some pool restrictions.

To Get There

From the junction of Hwy. 69 and Hwy. 54, take Hwy. 64 west for 0.5 mi., turn north immediately at the sign. Follow the road 0.4 mi., then turn right into the entrance and take the second right to the office.

GARDEN CITY

Garden City KOA Kampground

4100 East Hwy. 50, Garden City 67846. T: (800) KOA-8613 or (620) 276-9741; F: (620) 276-1987.

RV ★★★★ Tent ★★

Beauty: ★★★	Site Privacy: ★★★
Spaciousness: ★★★	Quiet: ★★★
Security: ★★★★★	Cleanliness: ★★★★★
Insect Control: ★★★★	Facilities: ★★★★★

This is a clean, respectable campground packed with facilities. All RV sites are pull-throughs arranged in a grid, and can accommodate a 60-foot rig. All sites are grassy, level, 25-feet wide, and most have 50 amp electrical. There are lots of shade trees except where they are most sorely needed: in the tening area. (The tent area benefits from a fence to the back, but no other real protection.) RV sites 68, 70, 72, and 76 and tent site 5 are extremely close to the playground. Site 87 is carved into part of the internal road. A mobile-home park to the north and one to the east are potential sources of loud music, but otherwise, most sites are pleasant and quiet. Shower and toilet facilities are clean, modern, and well lit. The tenting experience would improve with more and larger trees, as well as more distance from the campground road. Security is not an issue, as there are frequent sheriff patrols.

Basics

Operated By: Paul Foster. **Open:** All year. **Site Assignment:** Assigned until 9 p.m, verbal reservations OK. **Registration:** In office, late arrivals use drop box. **Fee:** RV $20–$22, tent $15. **Parking:** At site.

Facilities

Number of RV Sites: 60. **Number of Tent-Only Sites:** 20. **Hookups:** Water, sewer, electric (30, 50 amp), cable. **Each Site:** Picnic table, grill, tree. **Dump Station:** Yes. **Laundry:** Yes. **Pay Phone:** Yes. **Rest Rooms and Showers:** Yes. **Fuel:** Yes. **Propane:** Yes. **Internal Roads:** Paved/dirt. **RV Service:** Yes. **Market:** 2.5 mi. in Garden City. **Restaurant:** 2.5 mi. in Garden City. **General Store:** Yes. **Vending:** Yes. **Swimming:** Pool. **Playground:** Yes. **Other:** Cabins, dog walk area. **Activities:** Shuffleboard, horseshoes, basketball. **Nearby Attractions:** Finnup Park & Lee Richardson Zoo, Finney Game Refuge. **Additional Information:** Garden City Chamber of Commerce, (316) 276-3264.

Restrictions

Pets: On leash, cleaned up after. **Fires:** In grills. **Alcoholic Beverages:** At sites. **Vehicle Maximum Length:** 60 ft. **Other:** Quiet after 9 p.m.

To Get There

From the junction of Hwy. 83 (*not* the business loop of Hwy. 83) and Hwy. 50 (Fulton St. in town), go 1 mi. east on Hwy. 50. Turn right into the entrance.

GOODLAND

Goodland KOA

1114 East Hwy. 24, Goodland 67735. T: (800) 562-5704 or (785) 899-5701; www.koa.com; goodl&koa@nwkansas.com.

RV: ★★★★ Tent: ★★★

Beauty: ★★ | Site Privacy: ★★★
Spaciousness: ★★★ | Quiet: ★★★
Security: ★★★ | Cleanliness: ★★★★
Insect Control: ★★★★ | Facilities: ★★★★★

Located just off the highway, this campground is an easy-on, easy-off stop. Most campsites have at least two trees, with other trees scattered around the campground, lending a back-to-nature feel. Back-in sites 66–71 have a more than normal number of trees, which gives them woodsy feel. The east side of the campground is partitioned off from neighboring land by dense vegetation, and an open grassy field lies to the north. In addition, cute landscaping using shrubs, flower beds, and several tree trunk carvings liven up the grounds. On the downside, there is unattractive commercial development to the west, but not enough to detract terribly from the environment. Laundry and restroom/shower facilities are large, well lit, and immaculate. Some sites in the 28–42 area are not clearly marked, making their location a minor hassle. Overall, however, this is a convenient and enjoyable stay.

Basics

Operated By: Dale & Wally Neill. **Open:** Mar. 15–Nov. 1. **Site Assignment:** Upon registration, reservations with credit card or check to hold, must cancel within 24 hours for refund. **Registration:** At office, late arrivals use drop box. **Fee:** RV $21–$26, tent $15. **Parking:** At site only.

Facilities

Number of RV Sites: 51. **Number of Tent-Only Sites:** 17. **Hookups:** Water, sewer, electric (30, 50 amp), cable. **Each Site:** Picnic table, some fire grills. **Dump Station:** Yes. **Laundry:** Yes. **Pay Phone:** Yes. **Rest Rooms and Showers:** Yes. **Fuel:** No. **Propane:** No. **Internal Roads:** Gravel/dirt. **RV Service:** No. **Market:** 1.5 mi. (into Goodland). **Restaurant:** 0.25 mi. (into Goodland). **General Store:** Yes. **Vending:** No. **Swimming:** Pool. **Playground:** Yes. **Other:** 4 cabins, dog walk area. **Activities:** Mini golf, horseshoes, basketball.

Nearby Attractions: 18-hole golf course, Goodland High Plains Museum. **Additional Information:** Goodland Chamber of Commerce, (913) 899-7130.

RESTRICTIONS

Pets: On leash only. **Fires:** Grills only. **Alcoholic Beverages:** At sites. **Vehicle Maximum Length:** None.

TO GET THERE

From I-70, take exit 19, turn North onto Hwy. 24 and follow it for 0.8 mi. The entrance is on the right.

GREENSBURG

Pleasant View Motel and Overnight RV Park

800 West Kansas Ave., Greensburg 67054. T: (316) 723-2105.

RV ★★ Tent ★

Beauty: ★ Site Privacy: ★★★
Spaciousness: ★★★ Quiet: ★★★
Security: ★★★ Cleanliness: ★★★
Insect Control: ★★★ Facilities: ★★★

The name says it all for this campground—it is certainly an overnight stop devoid of attractions to warrant a longer stay. The campground is a large, open dirt parking lot in an urban setting. All sites (nine back-ins, six pull-throughs) are in extremely level rows. Tenting is possible on grassy spots to both the east and the west of the RV park. This is a reasonable stop on the way to Dodge City, Wichita, or Oklahoma. The proprietors are, however, quite friendly, making this stop a little nicer.

BASICS

Operated By: Lila. **Open:** All year. **Site Assignment:** Upon registration, reservations OK, credit card to hold if spaces filling up. **Registration:** In motel office, late arrivals ring bell. **Fee:** Varies; V, MC, AE, D. **Parking:** At site.

FACILITIES

Number of RV Sites: 15. **Number of Tent-Only Sites:** Undesignated sites. **Hookups:** Water, sewer, electric (30, 50 amp). **Dump Station:** No (sewer at all sites). **Laundry:** No. **Pay Phone:** Yes. **Rest Rooms and Showers:** Yes. **Fuel:** No. **Propane:** No. **Internal Roads:** Dirt. **RV Service:** No. **Market:** 0.5 mi. **Restaurant:** Next door. **General Store:** No. **Vending:** No. **Swimming:** No. **Playground:** No. **Other:** Storage room, 24 hour gas station within 100 yards. **Activities:** Fishing, swimming, wildlife-viewing (at nearby Kiowa State Fishing Lake). **Nearby Attractions:** Big Well, Pallasite Meteorite. **Additional Information:** Greensburg Chamber of Commerce, (316) 723-2261.

RESTRICTIONS

Pets: On leash only. **Fires:** In (own) grill. **Alcoholic Beverages:** At sites. **Vehicle Maximum Length:** None.

TO GET THERE

From the junction of Hwy. 183 and Hwy. 54, go 1 mi. east on Hwy. 54. Going west on Hwy. 54, drive to the west end of town, 0.5 mi. west of Main St. Turn at the motel sign (across the street from the John Deere dealership).

HAYS

Sunflower Creek RV Park and Campground

6th & Vine, Hays 67601. T: (785) 623-4769 or (785) 625-7518; www.kansasrvroads.com; jshaver@comlinkusa.net.

RV ★★★ Tent ★

Beauty: ★★ Site Privacy: ★★★★
Spaciousness: ★★★★ Quiet: ★★★
Security: ★★★★ Cleanliness: ★★★
Insect Control: ★★★ Facilities: ★★★★

This park was converted from a mobile-home park, so sites are ultra-wide, situated on one island and one row. The tent area is sectioned off by a chain-link fence on a grassy, but slightly uneven, area. One large shade tree provides protection from the sun for several tents, but there is no protection in the case of rain. Further, the area to the north is wide open to passing pedestrians and motorists, although set back about 100 feet from the sidewalk. (There is no fence around the perimeter of the property.) RV sites 7 and 8 abut a neighboring mobile-home park. Better sites are 1–5, which are located away from both the mobile homes and the road. This park offers the convenience of many services within walking distance, and owners John and Nancy promise many changes in their second year of operation.

Basics

Operated By: John & Nancy Shaver. **Open:** All year. **Site Assignment:** Upon registration. **Registration:** In office, late arrivals use drop box. **Fee:** RV $16–$18, tent or no hookups $15. **Parking:** At site.

Facilities

Number of RV Sites: 28. **Number of Tent-Only Sites:** 25. **Hookups:** Water, sewer, electric (30, 50 amp). **Each Site:** Some picnic tables, some trees. **Dump Station:** Yes. **Laundry:** Yes. **Pay Phone:** No. **Rest Rooms and Showers:** Yes. **Fuel:** No. **Propane:** No. **Internal Roads:** Gravel. **RV Service:** No. **Market:** 2 mi. into Hays. **Restaurant:** 1 block. **General Store:** No. **Vending:** Yes. **Swimming:** No. **Playground:** No. **Other:** Produce stand. **Activities:** Old Fort Hays Days. **Nearby Attractions:** Fort Hays, Sternberg Museum of Natural History, Aqua park. **Additional Information:** Hays Chamber of Commerce, (913) 628-8201.

Restrictions

Pets: On leash, cleaned up after. **Fires:** In grills. **Alcoholic Beverages:** At sites. **Vehicle Maximum Length:** None.

To Get There

From the junction of I-70 and Hwy. 183, turn south onto Hwy. 183 (which becomes Vine St.) and go 2.5 mi. through town to 6th St. Turn right onto 6th Ave. then take the immediate left at the sign.

HIAWATHA

Country Squire Motel and RV Park

2000 West Oregon St., Hiawatha 66434. T: (785) 742-2877.

RV ★★★ Tent ★★

Beauty: ★★★	Site Privacy: ★★★
Spaciousness: ★★★	Quiet: ★★★
Security: ★★★★	Cleanliness: ★★★★★
Insect Control: ★★★★	Facilities: ★★★★

Despite its proximity to urban amenities, this campground has a definite rural feel. Trees line the east and west perimeters and block off most of the road to the south. In addition, a visually appealing chunk of pine forest blocks view of the office from the RV park. To the west is a large, open grassy field. The north is slightly less attractive, with a ball park that can become noisy during games. Campsites are situated on a loop, with back-in sites around the perimiter. All sites are grassy and level, with trees close to the edges. Two exceptions to this are sites 15 and 16, which are not close to any trees and consequently have an open, almost vulnerable feel. The most favorable is site 1 (which is surrounded on two sides by trees), followed by odd-number sites 3–11 (which are away from both the road and the ball park and face a grassy field with trees at the opposite end). Tucked behind the motel buildings, the campground is well away from motel traffic. Tenting sites occupy the tip of the island, with enough space to comfortbaly fit 10–12 tents. Five large trees (four deciduous) provide enough shelter for a comfortable tent stay.

Basics

Operated By: Leland & Carla Oplinger. **Open:** All year. **Site Assignment:** Depends on availability. **Registration:** In office, late arrivals ring bell. **Fee:** RV $10 no hookups, $2 hookup, $1 cable; tent $5–$7. **Parking:** At site.

Facilities

Number of RV Sites: 16. **Number of Tent-Only Sites:** 10. **Hookups:** Water, sewer, electric (30, 50 amp), cable. **Each Site:** Picnic table. **Dump Station:** Yes. **Laundry:** No. **Pay Phone:** Yes. **Rest Rooms and Showers:** Yes. **Fuel:** No. **Propane:** No. **Internal Roads:** Gravel. **RV Service:** No. **Market:** 1 mi. **Restaurant:** 1 mi. **General Store:** No. **Vending:** Yes. **Swimming:** No. **Playground:** No. **Other:** Free coffee, golf course. **Activities:** Mini golf. **Nearby Attractions:** Old town clock, Davis Memorial, flea markets, casinos. **Additional Information:** Hiawatha Chamber of Commerce, (785) 742-7136.

Restrictions

Pets: On leash. **Fires:** Stove or grill only. **Alcoholic Beverages:** At sites. **Vehicle Maximum Length:** None.

To Get There

From Hwy. 36, turn north onto Oregon St. (West Exit). Continue 0.3 mi. on Oregon St.—the entrance is on the right-hand side, slightly east (and across the road) from the water tower.

HUTCHINSON

Melody Acres Campground

1009 East Blanchard, Hutchinson 67501. T: (316) 665-5048; F: (316) 663-4134.

★★★★ ★★★★

Beauty: ★★★★ Site Privacy: ★★★★
Spaciousness: ★★★★ Quiet: ★★★
Security: ★★★ Cleanliness: ★★★
Insect Control: ★★★ Facilities: ★★★

This cute campground is lined by cedars on the east, is forested to the west, and has a line of mature shade trees to the north, which gives it a real forested feel. Most camping sites have at least one tree, although some too small to provide any real shade. Tent sites, by contrast, are right in the middle of the treed area providing lots of overhead protection and an honest middle-of-the-forest ambiance. While the campgrounds themselves are clean, the rest room/shower facility is a little dingey. The unfinished cement floors and peeling paint make the facilities feel more like a storage area than a comfortble washroom. The most convenient sites are the pull-throughs (1–10 and others in the bizarrely-numbered scheme) in the middle of the loop, while the prettiest are the back-ins (8–19 and A–G) that abut the forested area. All sites are level and grassy, with pull-throughs an enormous 45 × 100 feet. (The back-ins are equally wide but not as long.) Sites C and D have a particularly pleasing mulberry tree overhanging them.

BASICS

Operated By: Judy Mitchell. **Open:** All year. **Site Assignment:** First come, first served; verbal reservations OK. **Registration:** In office, late arrivals pay in morning. **Fee:** RV $18, tent $10; no credit cards. **Parking:** At site.

FACILITIES

Number of RV Sites: 32. **Number of Tent-Only Sites:** Undesignated sites. **Hookups:** Water, sewer, electric (30, 50 amp). **Dump Station:** Yes. **Laundry:** Yes. **Pay Phone:** No. **Rest Rooms and Showers:** Yes. **Fuel:** No. **Propane:** No. **Internal Roads:** Dirt. **RV Service:** No. **Market:** 1 mi. to Hutchinson. **Restaurant:** 1 mi. to Hutchinson. **General Store:** No. **Vending:** No. **Swimming:** No. **Playground:** No. **Other:** Storm shelter. **Activities:** Viewing IMAX films, visiting museums. **Nearby Attractions:** Kansas Cosmosphere & Space Center, Reno County Museum. **Additional Information:** Hutchinson Chamber of Commerce, (316) 662-3391.

RESTRICTIONS

Pets: No dogs over 20 lbs in park. **Fires:** Subject to seasonal bans. **Alcoholic Beverages:** At sites. **Vehicle Maximum Length:** 70 ft.

TO GET THERE

From the junction of Hwy. 61 and Hwy. 50, go 0.25 mi. west on Hwy. 50. Take the first right turn into the entrance and drive through the campground to the office.

INDEPENDENCE

Elk City State Park

P.O. Box 945, Independence 67301. T: (316) 331-6295.

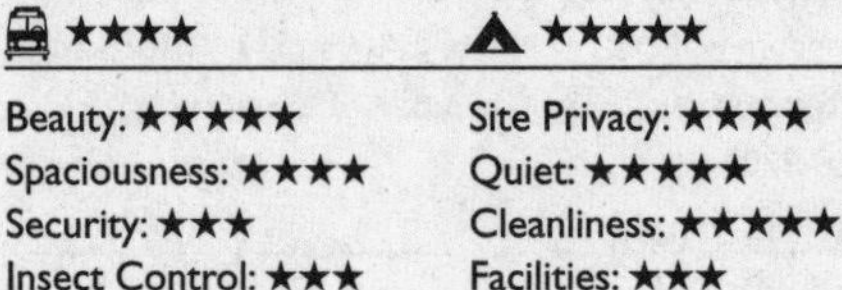
★★★★ ★★★★★

Beauty: ★★★★★ Site Privacy: ★★★★
Spaciousness: ★★★★ Quiet: ★★★★★
Security: ★★★ Cleanliness: ★★★★★
Insect Control: ★★★ Facilities: ★★★

This campground is another of the many attractive state parks in Kansas. Sites are well-groomed, located close to the water's edge, as well as further away. Those further away tend to be more open, with more trees closer to the edge of the lake. (For this reason, tenters may want to consider a site close to the water for the increased shelter.) Most sites are back-ins, with a limited number of pull-throughs. Sites fill up quickly for major holidays (Memorial Day, July 4th, Labor Day), so get there early in the day to ensure a spot for yourself.

BASICS

Operated By: Kansas Dept. of Wildlife & Parks. **Open:** All year. **Site Assignment:** First come, first served. **Registration:** In office. **Fee:** $7–$18, $5/day vehicle permit; no credit cards. **Parking:** At site, plenty of additional parking.

FACILITIES

Number of RV Sites: 150. **Number of Tent-Only Sites:** 56. **Hookups:** Water, sewer, electric (30, 50 amp). **Each Site:** Picnic table, fire pit/grill, trees. **Dump Station:** Yes. **Laundry:** No. **Pay Phone:** Yes. **Rest Rooms and Showers:** Yes. **Fuel:** No. **Propane:** No. **Internal Roads:** Paved. **RV Service:** No. **Market:** 5 mi. to Independence. **Restaurant:** 5 mi. to Independence. **General**

Store: No. **Vending:** Yes. **Swimming:** Yes (lake). **Playground:** Yes. **Other:** Wildlife. **Activities:** Fishing, swimming, boating, waterskiing, hiking, hunting. **Nearby Attractions:** Little House on the Prairie, Riverside Park. **Additional Information:** Independence Chamber of Commerce, (316) 331-1890.

RESTRICTIONS

Pets: On leash only. **Fires:** In fire ring. **Alcoholic Beverages:** At sites. **Vehicle Maximum Length:** None.

TO GET THERE

From the junction of Hwy. 75 and Hwy. 160 (Main St. and 10th St. in town), go west on Hwy. 160 for 1.7 mi. Turn right onto Peter Pan Rd. Go 1 mi. north on this road (which turns into CR 3525), then turn left onto CR 4800. Continue west to the office or to a pay station.

KINSLEY

Four Aces RV Campground and Mobile Home

104 South Massechusettes Ave., Kinsley 67547.
T: (620) 659-2060.

RV ★★★ Tent ★★

Beauty: ★★★ Site Privacy: ★★
Spaciousness: ★★★ Quiet: ★★★★
Security: ★★★ Cleanliness: ★★
Insect Control: ★★★ Facilities: ★★★

This campground lies in an open rural setting with woods to the south and east and agricultural land to the west. Detracting a little are houses to the north and several white buildings and tanks to the west that stand out sharply. Sites are level pull-throughs with large concrete slabs and a dirt/grass mixture beteen spaces. The ground is relatively barren, and there are no shade trees within the park. While the campground itself is clean enough with somewhat pretty surroundings, it could benefit from renovated rest rooms. The rest room and shower facilities are shared men/women, and toilets are separated by wooden sides that do not enclose each stall from floor to ceiling. Despite somewhat off-putting toilet facilities, this campground is an agreeable stay.

BASICS

Operated By: Private operator. **Open:** All year. **Site Assignment:** First come, first served. **Registration:** In office, late arrivals use drop box. **Fee:** $16. **Parking:** At site.

FACILITIES

Number of RV Sites: 20. **Number of Tent-Only Sites:** Undesignated sites. **Hookups:** Water, sewer, electric (20, 30, 50 amp). **Dump Station:** Yes. **Laundry:** Yes. **Pay Phone:** No. **Rest Rooms and Showers:** Yes. **Fuel:** No. **Propane:** No. **Internal Roads:** Dirt. **RV Service:** No. **Market:** 1 mi. into Kinsley. **Restaurant:** 1 mi. into Kinsley. **General Store:** No. **Vending:** Yes. **Swimming:** No. **Playground:** No. **Activities:** None on site. **Nearby Attractions:** Edwards County Historical Museum. **Additional Information:** Kinsley Chamber of Commerce, (316) 659-3642.

RESTRICTIONS

Pets: On leash only, cleaned up after. **Fires:** In grills. **Alcoholic Beverages:** At sites. **Vehicle Maximum Length:** None.

TO GET THERE

From the junction of Hwy. 183 and Hwy. 50, go 3 blocks west on Hwy. 50, turn left onto Massachusettes Ave., and follow the dirt road into the entrance.

LAWRENCE

Lawrence/Kansas City KOA

1473 Hwy. 40, Lawrence 66044. T: (800) 562-3708 or (785) 842-3877; F: (785) 312-9186; www.lawrencekoa.com.

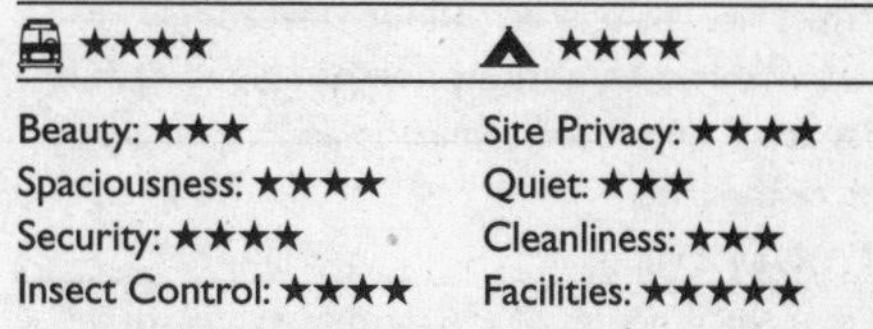

RV ★★★★ Tent ★★★★

Beauty: ★★★ Site Privacy: ★★★★
Spaciousness: ★★★★ Quiet: ★★★
Security: ★★★★ Cleanliness: ★★★
Insect Control: ★★★★ Facilities: ★★★★★

A little messy due to renovations (scheduled for completion in 2002) but otherwise attractive, this campground is surrounded by seven acres of undeveloped land to the north and a sod farm with lush green grass to the east. Flowering trees and flowers planted in surprising nooks add color and charm to the grounds. All sites are grassy, level pull-throughs located on loops that are separated by rows of trees. Already packed with features, this campground promises exciting additional services when the renovations are completed. The best time to come is when the flowers and trees are in bloom. Keep in mind, however, the NASCAR schedule and be sure to cancel well in advance, if necessary, to avoid losing your deposit during these busy times.

Basics

Operated By: Ralph & Kim Newell. **Open:** All year. **Site Assignment:** Upon registration, credit card for reservation; must cancel 24 hours in advance, except for race weekends, when cancellation must be made 1 week in advance for refund. **Registration:** In store, late arrivals select site from map & use drop box. **Fee:** RV $26, tent $20. **Parking:** At site, additional parking available.

Facilities

Number of RV Sites: 69. **Number of Tent-Only Sites:** 26. **Hookups:** Water, sewer, electric (30, 50 amp). **Each Site:** Picnic table, fire pit, trees. **Dump Station:** Yes. **Laundry:** Yes. **Pay Phone:** Yes. **Rest Rooms and Showers:** Yes. **Fuel:** No. **Propane:** Yes. **Internal Roads:** Paved/dirt. **RV Service:** Yes. **Market:** 2 mi. into Lawrence. **Restaurant:** 0.5 mi. into Lawrence. **General Store:** Yes. **Vending:** Yes. **Swimming:** Pool. **Playground:** Yes. **Other:** Game room, cabins, group meeting room, dog walk area, cycling/running trail. **Activities:** Volleyball, basketball, badminton, canoe trips, tetherball. **Nearby Attractions:** NASCAR track, golf course, Kansas City. **Additional Information:** Lawrence Chamber of Commerce, (913) 865-4411.

Restrictions

Pets: On leash, not left outside, cleaned up after. **Fires:** Fire pits only. **Alcoholic Beverages:** At sites. **Vehicle Maximum Length:** None. **Other:** Pay attention to speed limits, no parking on grass; no clotheslines.

To Get There

From the junction of I-70 and Hwy. 59, drive 0.5 mi. north on 59, veer right (east) onto Hwy. 24, and follow Hwy. 24 for 0.2 mi. Take the first right at the KOA sign into the entrance. Follow the driveway to the end to register at the store.

LIBERAL

B&B Overnite RV Camp

Rte. 1 Box 66, Liberal 67901. T: (620) 624-5581; bbonc@midusa.net.

RV ★★ Tent ★★

Beauty: ★★ Site Privacy: ★★★
Spaciousness: ★★★ Quiet: ★★
Security: ★★★ Cleanliness: ★★
Insect Control: ★★★★ Facilities: ★★★★

Just on the outskirts of town, this campground has the potential to be quite attractive, but requires some renovations and beautification to achieve this goal. Sites are of a decent size (average 24 × 55 feet), with some quite lengthy pull-throughs (over 100 feet). Sites 23–25 offer good shade, while sites 28–30 in the southeast corner (the best sites) have good tree shade and abut the vegetation along the perimeter of the property. The east side of the property boasts a row of trees, and behind that, undeveloped land. However, there are some unsightly vehicles parked on the neighboring land in the southwest corner. One shower stall was quite clean, but the remaining two were less so. Additionally, dog waste was a problem in several campsites. Overall, this campground is a reasonable stopover, but not yet a destination in itself.

Basics

Operated By: Betty Booth. **Open:** All year. **Site Assignment:** First come, first served; verbal reservations OK. **Registration:** In office, late arrivals use drop box. **Fee:** RV $21, tent $16. **Parking:** At site.

Facilities

Number of RV Sites: 30. **Number of Tent-Only Sites:** 8. **Hookups:** Water, sewer, electric (30, 50 amp), cable. **Each Site:** Tree; most have picnic tables. **Dump Station:** Yes. **Laundry:** Yes. **Pay Phone:** Yes. **Rest Rooms and Showers:** Yes. **Fuel:** No. **Propane:** No. **Internal Roads:** Gravel. **RV Service:** No. **Market:** 5 mi. (into Liberal). **Restaurant:** Less than 0.25 mi. **General Store:** Yes. **Vending:** Yes. **Swimming:** No. **Playground:** Yes. **Other:** RV parts. **Activities:** Visit museums. **Nearby Attractions:** Mid-America Air Museum, Dorothy's House/Coronado Museum. **Additional Information:** Liberal Chamber of Commerce, (316) 624-3855.

Restrictions

Pets: On leash, not tied up, cleaned up after. **Fires:** In grills only. **Alcoholic Beverages:** At sites. **Vehicle Maximum Length:** None. **Other:** No generators.

To Get There

From the junction of Hwy. 54 and Western Ave. in town (last light on western edge of town), go 2.5 mi. west on Hwy. 54. Turn left at the sign into the entrance.

MANHATTEN

Tuttle Creek State Park

5800A River Pond Rd., Manhatten 66502. T: (785) 539-7941; www.wp.state.ks.us; tuttlecreeksp@wp.state.ks.us.

RV ★★★★★ Tent ★★★★★

Beauty: ★★★★ Site Privacy: ★★★★★
Spaciousness: ★★★★★ Quiet: ★★★★★
Security: ★★★★ Cleanliness: ★★★★★
Insect Control: ★★★ Facilities: ★★★★

Located to the northwest of Manhatten, this humungous state park (1,100-plus acres) offers four camping areas with grassy sites on large loops. Like other state parks, this campground offers a variety of sites, from waterfront to woodsy. The River Pond campground, for example, offers some spacious, well-groomed pull-throughs, although the back-ins (sites 71–104) are a little more pressed together. Tenters should be aware that some sites offer no protection in case of rain. The best time of year to come is after the spring rains, when the deciduous trees are in leaf. Regardless of your tastes and preferences, there is certain to be something for everyone.

Basics

Operated By: Kansas Dept. of Wildlife & Parks. **Open:** All year. **Site Assignment:** First come, first served; 10 reservable sites, must have credit card to hold, no refunds. **Registration:** At office or self-pay station. **Fee:** Varies, $5/day vehicle permit, add $2 for prime sites indicated by red. **Parking:** At site.

Facilities

Number of RV Sites: 116. **Number of Tent-Only Sites:** 500. **Hookups:** Water, electric (30, 50 amp). **Each Site:** Picnic table, fire pit, trees. **Dump Station:** Yes. **Laundry:** No. **Pay Phone:** Yes. **Rest Rooms and Showers:** Yes. **Fuel:** No. **Propane:** No. **Internal Roads:** Paved. **RV Service:** No. **Market:** 3 mi. to Manhatten. **Restaurant:** 3 mi. to Manhatten. **General Store:** Yes. **Vending:** Yes. **Swimming:** Yes (lake). **Playground:** Yes. **Other:** Boat ramp, group picnic shelters, fish cleaning station, canoe rentals. **Activities:** Swimming, boating, waterskiing, windsurfing, cycling, hiking, softball, hunting. **Nearby Attractions:** Flint Hills, Riley County Historical Museum, Wonder Workshop. **Additional Information:** Manhatten CVB, (800) 759-0134.

Restrictions

Pets: On 10-ft. leash. **Fires:** In rings or grills. **Alcoholic Beverages:** Beer only. **Vehicle Maximum Length:** None. **Other:** $5 per day vehicle permit.

To Get There

From the junction of Hwy. 24 and Hwy. 13, turn east onto Hwy. 13 and drive 1.8 mi. Take the tricky right turn at the sign (this may be problematic for larger rigs) and follow the road 1 mi. to the office or self-pay station. Alternately, take Hwy. 24 0.5 mi. east from the junction with Hwy. 13, and turn left at the sign. This takes you away from the office, but avoids the hair-brained/hair-pin turn.

MEADE

Circle-O Motel and RV Park

P.O. Box 203, Meade 67864. T: (620) 873-2405 or (620) 873-2543.

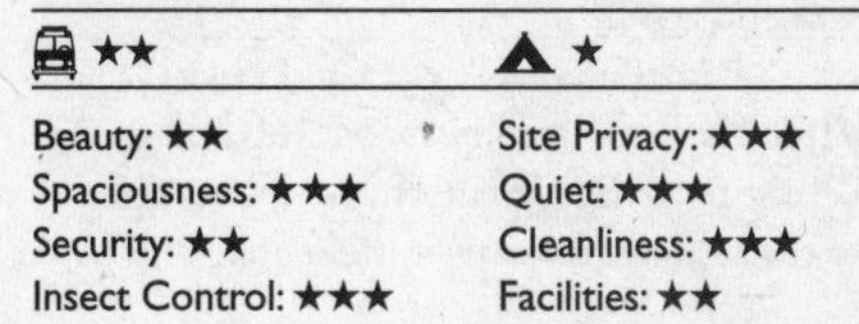

RV ★★ Tent ★

Beauty: ★★ Site Privacy: ★★★
Spaciousness: ★★★ Quiet: ★★★
Security: ★★ Cleanliness: ★★★
Insect Control: ★★★ Facilities: ★★

This campground has an urban feel, with motor homes occupying the northwest corner, a residential area to the north, a commercial area to the south, and a total paucity of shade trees throughout the campground. A residential back alley runs through the campground, and sites 25 and 31 occupy a portion of it. The average site is 25-feet wide, but there are some absolutely humungous pull-throughs (sites 35 and 36). Shower facilities are slightly cramped but reasonably clean. The least desirable sites are 15–17, which are just off the back alley and next to the dump station. Better sites are 26, 32, and 33, close to the grassy tent area. (The tent area is a well-mowed lawn, but lacking the protection of trees.) Circle-O Motel is a reasonable place to spend a night, and if you are lucky, you can hit on a choice spot. Beware the lack of shade in the summer, however. Tenters: move on!

BASICS

Operated By: Mick & Pat Ohnick. **Open:** All year. **Site Assignment:** First come, first served; assigned during busy season. **Registration:** In motel office, late arrivals use honor system to settle in the morning. **Fee:** Varies depending on vehicle; no credit cards. **Parking:** At site.

FACILITIES

Number of RV Sites: 24. **Number of Tent-Only Sites:** Undesignated sites. **Hookups:** Water, sewer, electric (30, 50 amp). **Dump Station:** Yes. **Laundry:** No. **Pay Phone:** Yes. **Rest Rooms and Showers:** Yes. **Fuel:** Next door. **Propane:** No. **Internal Roads:** Gravel/dirt. **RV Service:** No. **Market:** 7 blocks. **Restaurant:** 6 blocks. **General Store:** Across the street. **Vending:** No. **Swimming:** No. **Playground:** Yes. **Other:** Pet area. **Activities:** Visiting museums. **Nearby Attractions:** Dalton Gang Hideout, Meade County Historical Society Museum. **Additional Information:** Meade Economic Development, (316) 873-8795.

RESTRICTIONS

Pets: On leash only. **Fires:** In grills. **Alcoholic Beverages:** At sites. **Vehicle Maximum Length:** None. **Other:** No vehicle washing.

TO GET THERE

From the junction of Hwy. 23 and Hwy. 54/160, turn east onto Hwy. 54/160 and go 0.4 mi. Turn north onto State St., then turn right into the second driveway at the motel.

NEWTON

Payne Oil Co. RV Park

Rte. 2, Junction I-135 & K-15, Exit 34, Newton 67114. T: (316) 283-5530.

RV ★★★ Tent ★

Beauty: ★★ Site Privacy: ★★★
Spaciousness: ★★★ Quiet: ★★
Security: ★★ Cleanliness: ★★★★
Insect Control: ★★★ Facilities: ★★★★

This small RV park located next to the highway is a convenient stop for those requiring RV parts or servicing or too tired to push on. Part gas station, part RV service, part campground, Payne Oil Co. makes up in services what it lacks in beauty. (Note that the rest room and shower facilities are located within the office and are unavailable outside office hours. The park does supply a porta-potty for campers' use.) Laid out as spokes radiating from a central road, sites are open and grassy, with 15 pull-thrus and 5 back-ins. The average site size is 30 × 100 feet. The most advantageous sites (10, 20) are located on the end closest to the golf course, where the park abuts a large grassy field. The gas station to the northwest and storage units and the highway to the west conspire to make the scenery rather unattractive, although a sparse number of small trees do their best to liven up the grounds. Seemingly any number of tents can be pitched on the grassy area to the south of the RV sites. This is a great service stop, but not a destination in itself.

BASICS

Operated By: Rick & Maura Payne. **Open:** All year. **Site Assignment:** First come, first served. **Registration:** At gas station, late arrivals use drop box under picnic shelter. **Fee:** RV $15, tent $5; V, MC, AE, D. **Parking:** At site.

FACILITIES

Number of RV Sites: 20. **Number of Tent-Only Sites:** Undesignated sites. **Hookups:** Water, sewer, electric (30, 50 amp). **Dump Station:** Yes. **Laundry:** Yes. **Pay Phone:** No. **Rest Rooms and Showers:** Yes. **Fuel:** Yes. **Propane:** Yes. **Internal Roads:** Dirt. **RV Service:** Yes. **Market:** 2 mi. in Newton. **Restaurant:** 2 mi. in Newton. **General Store:** No. **Vending:** No. **Swimming:** No. **Playground:** No. **Other:** 9-hole golf course. **Activities:** Jogging, cycling, golf. **Nearby Attractions:** Kauffman Museum. **Additional Information:** Newton Chamber of Commerce, (316) 283-2560.

RESTRICTIONS

Pets: On leash only. **Fires:** In grills. **Alcoholic Beverages:** At sites. **Vehicle Maximum Length:** None.

TO GET THERE

From I-135, take Exit 34 and turn east onto Hwy. 15. Drive 0.1 mi. on Hwy. 15 and turn right into the gas-station entrance.

NORTON

Prairie Dog State Park

RR 431, Norton 67654. T: (785) 877-2953.

RV ★★★★ Tent ★★★★★

Beauty: ★★★★ Site Privacy: ★★★★
Spaciousness: ★★★★★ Quiet: ★★★★★
Security: ★★★★ Cleanliness: ★★★★
Insect Control: ★★★ Facilities: ★★★

Named for the prairie dog town at the entrance, this park is renowned for the excellent fishing it provides in the Sebelius Reservoir. Best in the spring or fall, the park is extremely crowded during the summer, and especially so for the holidays. Sites are grassy and open, averaging 60-feet long and up to 65-feet wide, with both back-ins and pull-throughs. Despite the number of new trees planted, sites do not benefit from their shade. Branded Cedar sites W1–W6 have a commanding view of the lake and proximity to the showers, while Medowlark campsites have fire pits and are situated right on the lake. Tenting areas are separated from the RV sites and also offer fire pits. This park is a beautiful alternative to the overnight RV spots in town, with only slightly fewer facilities.

Basics

Operated By: Camp Hosts Ray & Leta Koel. **Open:** All year. **Site Assignment:** First come, first served; 8 reservable sites. **Registration:** At office or self-pay stations. **Fee:** $7–$18, $5/day vehicle permit; no credit cards. **Parking:** At site.

Facilities

Number of RV Sites: 58. **Number of Tent-Only Sites:** 139. **Hookups:** Water, electric (30, 50 amp). **Each Site:** Picnic table, tree, some lantern poles. **Dump Station:** Yes. **Laundry:** No. **Pay Phone:** Yes. **Rest Rooms and Showers:** Yes. **Fuel:** Yes. **Propane:** Yes. **Internal Roads:** Paved/gravel. **RV Service:** No. **Market:** 6 mi. to Norton. **Restaurant:** 6 mi. to Norton. **General Store:** Yes. **Vending:** No. **Swimming:** Yes (lake). **Playground:** Yes. **Other:** Boat ramp, renovated adobe home, one-room schoolhouse, marina concessions, picnic shelters, some free firewood. **Activities:** Fishing, boating, swimming, waterskiing, archery, wildlife-watching, fireworks over lake on July 4th w/ free watermelon. **Nearby Attractions:** Gallery of Also Rans (First State Bank building). **Additional Information:** Norton Chamber of Commerce, (785) 877-2501.

Restrictions

Pets: On leash only. **Fires:** In grills. **Alcoholic Beverages:** None (kegs w/ a permit). **Vehicle Maximum Length:** None. **Other:** No washing of vehicles or boats.

To Get There

From the junction of Hwy. 283 and Hwy. 36, turn west onto Hwy. 36 and drive 4.3 mi. through the town of Norton. Turn right at the sign for the park onto Hwy. 261 and drive 1 mi. to the office or to a self-pay station.

OAKLEY

Camp Inn RV Park

462 US 83, Oakley 67748. T: (785) 672-4440.

RV ★★★★ Tent ★★★★

Beauty: ★★★★ Site Privacy: ★★★
Spaciousness: ★★★ Quiet: ★★★★
Security: ★★★ Cleanliness: ★★★★
Insect Control: ★★★★ Facilities: ★★★

Despite its proximity to the commercial area of Oakley (half a mile), this campground retains a secluded feel. Laid out on loops, sites are spacious, open, and grassy, with both back-ins and pull-throughs. Average sites are 30-feet wide, although several (M1, M10, M11, D12) seem short-changed for space. Sites M1–M10 feel slightly as if they were in a fishbowl for all to look at, but M12–M20 are more removed and private. The best sites are D13–17 and E13–17, which are more secluded but have a convenient proximity to facilities. The tent area is fenced-off from the RV sites, next to a large open field. Although the unmarked sites lack overhead protection, this campground is a better bet for tenters than the campground in nearby Colby.

Basics

Operated By: Marvin Huelsmann. **Open:** All year. **Site Assignment:** First come, first served (unless close to full). **Registration:** In office, late arrivals use drop box. **Fee:** Summer (Apr. 15–Oct. 15) $20, winter $15. **Parking:** At site.

Facilities

Number of RV Sites: 86. **Number of Tent-Only Sites:** Undesignated sites. **Hookups:** Water, sewer, electric (30, 50 amp). **Each Site:** Picnic table, shade tree. **Dump Station:** No (sewer at all sites). **Laundry:** Yes. **Pay Phone:** Yes. **Rest Rooms and Showers:** Yes. **Fuel:** Yes. **Propane:** No. **Internal Roads:** Gravel. **RV Service:** No. **Market:** 1 mi. in Oakley. **Restaurant:** Next door. **General Store:** Yes. **Vending:** No. **Swimming:** Pool (Memorial Day–Labor Day). **Playground:** Yes. **Other:** Mini-golf, ATM, discount at Conoco gas station w/ valid RV park receipt. **Activities:** Golf, horseshoes, volleyball, video games. **Nearby Attractions:** Monument Rocks, Fick Fossil & History Museum, Prairie Dog Town. **Additional Infor-**

mation: Oakley Chamber of Commerce, (913) 672-4862.

Restrictions

Pets: On leash only. **Fires:** In grills. **Alcoholic Beverages:** At sites. **Vehicle Maximum Length:** None.

To Get There

From I-70, take Exit 70, then turn south onto Hwy. 83. Drive 0.2 mi. on Hwy. 83 and take the first right after the I-70 junction. Go straight into the entrance.

PRATT

Evergreen Inn and RV Park

20001 West US 54, Pratt 67124. T: (800) 456-6424 or (620) 672-6431.

RV: ★★★ Tent: ★★★

Beauty: ★★★ Site Privacy: ★
Spaciousness: ★ Quiet: ★★★
Security: ★★★ Cleanliness: ★★★★
Insect Control: ★★★ Facilities: ★★★

This is a fairly attractive park with decent services, but a little cramped. The south side is bordered by an open grassy field with dogwood, fir, and deciduous trees at the far end, while the building complex is somewhat shielded by large shade trees. Spaces, however, are a meager 15-feet wide, posing potential difficulties for larger rigs with slide-outs. Sites 13 and 14 are situated well away from the rest of the sites and from each other and can accommodate a larger-sized vehicle. Site 13 is particularly nice, tucked away under mature shade trees and sided by an open grassy field and a wooden fence. Sites 1 and 12 also benefit from an extra bit of grassy space. There is plenty of extra space at the head of the sites to park an extra vehicle. The shower and rest room facilities are quite clean, but can accommodate only one person at a time. Tent space is located between the RV park and the motel on a grassy area with a fair number of shade trees.

Basics

Operated By: Mike. **Open:** All year. **Site Assignment:** First come, first served; reservations only after 4 p.m. & with credit card, cancel before 4 p.m. same day for refund. **Registration:** In motel office, late arrivals ring doorbell. **Fee:** RV $16, tent $10; V, MC, AE, D. **Parking:** At site.

Facilities

Number of RV Sites: 14. **Number of Tent-Only Sites:** Undesignated sites. **Hookups:** Water, sewer, electric (30 amp). **Dump Station:** Yes. **Laundry:** Yes. **Pay Phone:** No. **Rest Rooms and Showers:** Yes. **Fuel:** No. **Propane:** No. **Internal Roads:** Gravel. **RV Service:** No. **Market:** 2 mi. to Pratt. **Restaurant:** Next door. **General Store:** No. **Vending:** Yes. **Swimming:** Pool. **Playground:** Yes. **Other:** Trampoline. **Activities:** Basketball. **Nearby Attractions:** Kansas State Fish Hatchery. **Additional Information:** Pratt Chamber of Commerce, (316) 672-5501.

Restrictions

Pets: On leash only. **Fires:** No. **Alcoholic Beverages:** Not in pool. **Vehicle Maximum Length:** 60 ft.

To Get There

From the junction of Hwy. 281 and Hwy. 54, go 2 mi. west on Hwy. 54, then turn left at the sign into the entrance.

RUSSELL

Triple J Campground

187 Edwards, Russell 67665. T: (785) 483-4826; F: (785) 483-4826.

RV: ★★★★ Tent: ★★★

Beauty: ★★★ Site Privacy: ★★★★
Spaciousness: ★★★★ Quiet: ★★★
Security: ★★★ Cleanliness: ★★★★
Insect Control: ★★★★ Facilities: ★★★★

This campground has pull-throughs that could accommodate all but the largest monster rig on the road without unhooking. Average site size is 40 ¥ 60 feet. The grounds are spacious and open, with a rural feel; an open field and horses in the west corner add to the ambiance. Unmarked tent sites are on a grassy strip that is set away from the RV sites. Trees provide a natural barricade to the neighboring land to the north, and the best sites (even numbers 34–38 and odd numbers 39–47) face this direction. The least favorable sites—still nowhere near a bad spot to end up—are on the east side, facing the distant shopping complex. (The campground is quite removed from this complex, and these sites are offset from the entrance, which gives them extra space and privacy.) RVers will be happy with any available spot; tenters, however, fare a little worse, being closer to the highway and its attendant noise.

Basics

Operated By: Lana Zorn. **Open:** All year. **Site Assignment:** First come, first served. **Registration:** In office. **Fee:** RV $18, tent $12; no credit cards. **Parking:** At site.

Facilities

Number of RV Sites: 52. **Number of Tent-Only Sites:** Undesignated sites. **Hookups:** Water, sewer, electric (30, 50 amp). **Each Site:** Picnic table; grill & tree at most sites. **Dump Station:** No (sewer at all sites). **Laundry:** Yes. **Pay Phone:** Yes. **Rest Rooms and Showers:** Yes. **Fuel:** No. **Propane:** No. **Internal Roads:** Paved/gravel. **RV Service:** No (within 1 block). **Market:** 1 block. **Restaurant:** 1 block. **General Store:** Yes. **Vending:** Yes. **Swimming:** No. **Playground:** Yes. **Other:** Storm shelter, dataport hookups. **Activities:** Mini-golf, horseshoes, video games. **Nearby Attractions:** Sternberg Museum, Cathedral of the Plains, Garden of Eden sculptures. **Additional Information:** Russell CVB, (800) 658-4686.

Restrictions

Pets: On leash only, cleaned up after. **Fires:** In grills only. **Alcoholic Beverages:** At sites. **Vehicle Maximum Length:** None.

To Get There

From I-70, turn north onto Hwy. 281 and follow it for 1 block. The entrance is on the left. Follow the driveway around to the right; the office is across from the mini-golf.

SCOTT CITY

Camp Lakeside

520 West Scott Lake Dr., Scott City 67871. T: (620) 872-2061; scottsp@wp.state.ks.us.

RV: ★★★★ Tent: ★★★★★

Beauty: ★★★★ Site Privacy: ★★★★
Spaciousness: ★★★★ Quiet: ★★★★
Security: ★★★ Cleanliness: ★★★★★
Insect Control: ★★★ Facilities: ★★★

The Scott Lake campgrounds are divided into several campgrounds around the lake, with sites close to the water (Lakeside campground) as well as further up the embankment, with a more woodsy feel (Elm Grove). Sites are laid out on a series of loops, with both pull-throughs and back-ins. All sites are spacious and level, and the lake offers a variety of activities for a day, a week, or even just an afternoon. Rocky outcrops around part of the lake add to the natural beauty, but the lack of water facilities in winter may make this campground too natural for some campers. Those who don't mind roughing it a little (in winter only) should definitely make a point to stop here—and bring the kids.

Basics

Operated By: Kansas Dept. of Wildlife & Parks. **Open:** All year. **Site Assignment:** First come, first served. **Registration:** At office or self-pay stations. **Fee:** $7–$18, $5/day vehicle permit. **Parking:** At site.

Facilities

Number of RV Sites: 60. **Number of Tent-Only Sites:** 170. **Hookups:** Electric, water (no water Oct.–Apr.). **Each Site:** Grill. **Dump Station:** Yes. **Laundry:** No. **Pay Phone:** Yes. **Rest Rooms and Showers:** Yes. **Fuel:** No. **Propane:** No. **Internal Roads:** Paved/gravel. **RV Service:** No. **Market:** 14 mi. to Scott City (limited market on site). **Restaurant:** 14 mi. to Scott City. **General Store:** Yes. **Vending:** Yes. **Swimming:** Yes (lake). **Playground:** Yes. **Other:** Boat ramp, canoe/boat rentals. **Activities:** Boating, fishing, cycling, hiking, horseback riding, hunting. **Nearby Attractions:** El Cuartelego pueblo ruins. **Additional Information:** Scott City Chamber of Commerce, (316) 872-3525.

Restrictions

Pets: On leash only. **Fires:** In grills only. **Alcoholic Beverages:** Beer only. **Vehicle Maximum Length:** None.

To Get There

From the junction of Hwy. 83 and Hwy. 95, turn north onto Hwy. 95. To go to the office (or a pay station), follow Hwy. 95 to West Scott Lake Drive, and turn left into the office parking lot. To get to other pay stations and campsites, turn right onto East Scott Lake Drive and drive 2.5 mi.

STOCKTON

Webster State Park

1210 Nine Rd., Stockton 67669. T: (785) 425-6775; F: (785) 425-6180; webstersp@wp.state.ks.us.

RV ★★★★ Tent ★★★

Beauty: ★★★★ Site Privacy: ★★★★
Spaciousness: ★★★★ Quiet: ★★★★★
Security: ★★★ Cleanliness: ★★★★
Insect Control: ★★★ Facilities: ★★★

Sites in this campground vary from water's edge to further up the embankment. Thus the camper can experience woods, beach, and park all in one. All sites are level and grassy, averaging 50 × 60 feet in size (some pull-throughs are even longer), situated on a series of large loops and some grid sites. The reservoir itself is surrounded by reeds (at the water's edge) and fields with short pines. Sites close to the water generally have more trees, while those away from the water are more open. While parking is available at each of the sites, there is enough additional parking (for day use) to accommodate extra vehicles. Facilities are clean but a hike away from some campsites. Overall, this is a fun, family-oriented destination with plenty of activities for kids and grandparents alike.

BASICS

Operated By: Kansas department of Wildlife & Parks. **Open:** All year. **Site Assignment:** First come, first served; 18 reservable sites, can be reserved 2 weeks in advance by check or credit card or 1 week in advance in person, no refunds. **Registration:** At station or self-pay sites (Apr. 1–Sept. 30 self-pay only). **Fee:** Campsite $7, 1 utility $17, 2 utilities $18, 3 utilities $20, add $2 for prime sites marked red. **Parking:** At site.

FACILITIES

Number of RV Sites: 72. **Number of Tent-Only Sites:** 100. **Hookups:** Water, electric (20, 30, 50 amp). **Each Site:** Picnic table, fire pit, trees; some lantern poles, some free firewood. **Dump Station:** Yes. **Laundry:** No. **Pay Phone:** Yes. **Rest Rooms and Showers:** Yes. **Fuel:** No. **Propane:** No. **Internal Roads:** Paved. **RV Service:** No. **Market:** 9 mi. to Stockton. **Restaurant:** 9 mi. to Stockton. **General Store:** Yes. **Vending:** Yes. **Swimming:** Yes (lake). **Playground:** Yes. **Other:** Picnic shelters, fishing dock, fish cleaning station, wildlife. **Activities:** Swimming, fishing, baseball, boating, hiking, volleyball, horseshoes. **Nearby Attractions:** Webster Reservation Wildlife Area. **Additional Information:** Stockton Chamber of Commerce & Economic Development: (785) 425-6162.

RESTRICTIONS

Pets: On leash only. **Fires:** In grills or pits. **Alcoholic Beverages:** Beer only. **Vehicle Maximum Length:** 60 ft.

TO GET THERE

From the junction of Hwy. 183 and Hwy. 24, turn north onto Hwy. 24 and drive 9 mi. The entrance is on the left (past the overpass). Follow the road to the office or to a self-pay station. (The turn-off for Webster Reservoir onto Hwy. 283 leads to the Goose Flats camping area.)

TOPEKA

Topeka KOA

3366 KOA Rd., Topeka 66429. T: (800) 562-8717 or (785) 246-3419; www.koa.com.

RV ★★★★★ Tent ★★★

Beauty: ★★★★ Site Privacy: ★★★
Spaciousness: ★★★ Quiet: ★★★★
Security: ★★★★ Cleanliness: ★★★★★
Insect Control: ★★★★ Facilities: ★★★★★

This campground has the feeling of being lost in the woods. The land in front of the office is undeveloped, and Area A (in back) is surrounded on three sides by undeveloped land. There is, accordingly, no highway noise; however, trains pass close enough to be heard from all over the campground. Sites are grassy, with level pull-throughs in Area B. Area A, has some slope—all sites but end site 26 seemed to require jacks. However, this is the nicer area of the campground if you can tolerate some slope. Area B has longer but narrower sites: 25 feet vs. 30 feet in Area A. Area B is also open to office, road, and pool traffic. The best sites are 25 and 26 in Area A, as they are level and in the prettiest part of the park. Sites 1 and 2 are the least desirable, being close to the office, to the parking lot, and to a garbage dumpster. The tent area is a long strip of grass at the front of the property. Sites are separated by a small length of wooden fencing providing better privacy. Although located a fair distance outisde of the metroplois of Topeka, this campground is worth the trip and offers a relaxing, quiet stay in the middle of the woods.

BASICS

Operated By: Private operator. **Open:** Apr. 1–Nov. 15 (otherwise limited services). **Site Assignment:** Upon registration; credit card to reserve site, cancel before 4 p.m. the day before arrival for refund. **Registration:** In office, late arrivals use drop box. **Fee:** RV $20 full, $19 water/ electric, tent $16. **Parking:** At site.

FACILITIES

Number of RV Sites: 36. **Number of Tent-Only Sites:** 11. **Hookups:** Water, sewer, electric (20, 30, 50 amp). **Each Site:** Picnic table, grill or fire pit, tree. **Dump Station:** Yes. **Laundry:** Yes. **Pay Phone:** No. **Rest Rooms and Showers:** Yes. **Fuel:** No. **Propane:** No. **Internal Roads:** Gravel. **RV Service:** No. **Market:** 2 mi. to Topeka. **Restaurant:** 2 mi. to Topeka. **General Store:** Yes. **Vending:** Yes. **Swimming:** Pool. **Playground:** Yes. **Other:** Pond, cabins, rec room, antique shop. **Activities:** Golf, shopping, visiting museums, sightseeing, swimming. **Nearby Attractions:** Combat Air Museum, Gage Park, Kansas Center for Historical Research, State Capitol, Ward-Meade Park, golf course, antique malls, casinos. **Additional Information:** Topeka CVB, (800) 235-1030.

RESTRICTIONS

Pets: On leash only, cleaned up after. **Fires:** In fire ring. **Alcoholic Beverages:** At sites. **Vehicle Maximum Length:** None.

TO GET THERE

From the junction of I-70 and Hwy. 75, take Exit 358 and drive 9 mi. to Hwy. 24. Take the Hwy. 24 east Exit, then turn left at the KOA sign (at mile marker 374) onto KOA Rd. Follow the gravel drive 1.3 mi. through a residential area and over the bridge. The entrance is on the right, north of 31st St.

WAKEENEY

Wakeeney KOA Kampground

P.O. Box 235, Wakeeney 67672. T: (800) 562-2761 or (785) 743-5612.

RV ★★★★ Tent ★★★

Beauty: ★★★ Site Privacy: ★★★★
Spaciousness: ★★★★ Quiet: ★★★
Security: ★★★★ Cleanliness: ★★★★★
Insect Control: ★★★ Facilities: ★★★★★

This campground features modern, clean, and tastefully decorated facilities. All sites are level and grassy, the majority (all except those in C area) being pull-throughs. Sites and rows are clearly marked, and site sizes average 30 × 62 feet (up to 80 feet). The playground and pool facilities are well away from camping sites. Tent sites are likewise separated from the RV sites by the internal road and from each other by a half-length of wood fencing. The back-ins in the C area face a screen of trees, but are closest to the highway. Site 75 in the southeast corner faces two unattractive sheds and a slightly crumbling fence. Besides this minor insult to the senses, you really can't go wrong with any site, nor can the facilities be beat. There is definitely a site to fit all preferences: large shade tree, proximity to the restroom facilities, to the pool, etc.

BASICS

Operated By: Fred & Sue Wallace. **Open:** Mar. 15–Nov. 15. **Site Assignment:** Upon registration, reservations w/ credit card, cancel same day. **Registration:** In office, late arrivals use drop box. **Fee:** RV $20–$22, tent $16. **Parking:** At site.

FACILITIES

Number of RV Sites: 79. **Number of Tent-Only Sites:** 13. **Hookups:** Water, sewer, electric (30, 50 amp). **Each Site:** Picnic table, tree. **Dump Station:** Yes. **Laundry:** Yes. **Pay Phone:** Yes. **Rest Rooms and Showers:** Yes. **Fuel:** No. **Propane:** Yes. **Internal Roads:** Dirt/gravel. **RV Service:** No. **Market:** 1 mi. to Wakeeney. **Restaurant:** 2 blocks. **General Store:** No. **Vending:** Yes. **Swimming:** Pool. **Playground:** Yes. **Other:** 3 cabins. **Activities:** Volleyball. **Nearby Attractions:** Cedar Bluff State Park, Castle rock. **Additional Information:** Wakeeney Chamber of Commerce, (913) 743-2077.

RESTRICTIONS

Pets: On leash. **Fires:** In grills. **Alcoholic Beverages:** At sites. **Vehicle Maximum Length:** None.

TO GET THERE

From I-70, take Exit 127 and turn south onto Hwy. 283. Go 100 yards on Hwy. 283 onto the frontage road, which dead-ends at the KOA entrance.

WELLINGTON
Wheatland RV Park

R.R. 1 Box 227, Wellington 67152. T: (877) 914-6114 or (620) 326-6114.

RV ★★★ Tent ★★★

Beauty: ★★★ Site Privacy: ★★★
Spaciousness: ★★★ Quiet: ★★★★
Security: ★★★ Cleanliness: ★★
Insect Control: ★★★ Facilities: ★★★★★

A little unkempt and ragged around the edges, this campground suffers from a few shortcomings that could easily be set right to turn the park around. Bordered on the south and east by wooded land and to the west by a grassy field, it offers quite a good deal of shade. Trees and shrubs around the office and driveway give a secluded feeling. Tent sites are in a row among the shrubs around the periphery of the campsite. From here, however, the campground slides downhill: a mobile-home park abuts the south western side, longer rigs (55 feet) will stick out from both ends, there seems to be lax enforcement of the leash law, and the curve in the road near sites 38–43 and 25–27 seems prone to flooding after a rain. (The dirt road had dried into a choppy, difficult mess after a recent rain, with no obvious attempts to smooth it out.) Sites include both back-ins and pull-throughs, all of which are both level and grassy. End site 27 seems to have been invaded by the road. Other less desriable sites include 15–20 (trees severely cut back) and 25–26 (trees too young for shade). The best sites are 21–24, followed closely by odd numbers 51–55—these are pull-throughs that face the shrubbery to the east and rest under a canopy of shade trees.

Basics

Operated By: Richard D. McCue. **Open:** All year. **Site Assignment:** Upon registration or first come, first served; verbal reservations OK. **Registration:** In office, late arrivals use drop box. **Fee:** RV $22, tent $16; V, MC, AE, D; 10% discount for KOA, Good Sam, or AARP membership or cash. **Parking:** At site.

Facilities

Number of RV Sites: 72. **Number of Tent-Only Sites:** 15. **Hookups:** Water, sewer, electric (30, 50 amp). **Each Site:** Picnic table, grill, tree; every other tent site has a fire pit. **Dump Station:** Yes. **Laundry:** Yes. **Pay Phone:** Yes. **Rest Rooms and Showers:** Yes. **Fuel:** No. **Propane:** Yes. **Internal Roads:** Dirt. **RV Service:** No. **Market:** 5 mi. into Wellington. **Restaurant:** 0.5 mi. into Wellington. **General Store:** Yes. **Vending:** No. **Swimming:** Pool. **Playground:** Yes. **Other:** 1 cabin, hot tub, video games, dog walk. **Activities:** Swimming, visiting museums. **Nearby Attractions:** Chisholm Trail Museum. **Additional Information:** Wellington Chamber of Commerce, (316) 326-7466.

Restrictions

Pets: On leash only. **Fires:** In fire ring or grill. **Alcoholic Beverages:** At sites. **Vehicle Maximum Length:** None.

To Get There

From the junction of I-35 and Hwy. 160, go west on 160 for 1.5 mi. Turn left into the entrance at the sign.

WICHITA
USI RV Park

2920 East 33rd North, Wichita 67219. T: (800) 782-1531 or (316) 838-8699 or (316) 838-0435; F: (316) 838-1193.

RV ★★★★ Tent n/a

Beauty: ★★ Site Privacy: ★★
Spaciousness: ★★★ Quiet: ★★★
Security: ★★★★ Cleanliness: ★★★★★
Insect Control: ★★★★ Facilities: ★★★★

This popular park consists of gravel and grassy sites laid out in strips 25-feet wide and long enough to accommodate almost any rig. Most sites are pull-throughs with very little grass—there is slightly more grass at the sites around the perimeter. The most favorable sites are in the A area, which boasts trees (sites 6–8 are especially nice), more grass, and proximity to the rest rooms. Sites 13–14 are jammed between the office and a garage and seem to have been added as an afterthought. All facilities are fantastically clean, and there are separate phone and dataport rooms, which give excellent privacy. While the wooden fence around the west side does a fine job of blocking out the view of neighboring land, there is a storage area to the southeast and a large radio antenna due north that detract from the setting.

Basics

Operated By: Sheila Wagner. **Open:** All year. **Site Assignment:** Upon registration, reservations strongly recommended, credit card to hold site; for shorter stay, cancel within 24 hours; for longer stay, within 5 days. **Registration:** In office, late arrivals use drop box. **Fee:** $21–$23. **Parking:** At site.

Facilities

Number of RV Sites: 75. **Number of Tent-Only Sites:** 0. **Hookups:** Water, sewer, electric (30, 50 amp). **Each Site:** Picnic table, tree. **Dump Station:** Yes. **Laundry:** Yes. **Pay Phone:** Yes. **Rest Rooms and Showers:** Yes. **Fuel:** No. **Propane:** Yes. **Internal Roads:** Gravel. **RV Service:** No. **Market:** 3 mi. east. **Restaurant:** 3 mi. east. **General Store:** Yes. **Vending:** Yes. **Swimming:** No. **Playground:** No. **Other:** Dataports, rec room, storm shelter. **Activities:** Sightseeing, shopping. **Nearby Attractions:** Wichita Grdens, Sedgwick County Zoo, Indian Center Museum, Wichita Art Museum, Wichita Center for the Arts, Omnisphere & Science Center, Wichita Greyhound Park. **Additional Information:** Wichita Chamber of Commerce, (316) 265-7771, Wichita CVB, (800) 288-9424.

Restrictions

Pets: 2 pets per vehicle; must sign pet agreement. **Fires:** None. **Alcoholic Beverages:** No kegs. **Vehicle Maximum Length:** None. **Other:** 10-year age limit of vehicle.

To Get There

From Hwy. 135 (southbound Exit 10, northbound Exit 10A), turn east onto Hwy. 96 and go 1 mi. Take the Hillside Exit and turn left onto Hillside Rd., then make an immediate left after the overpass onto 33rd St. Drive 1 block and turn right at the sign.

WILLIAMSBURG

Homewood RV Park

2161 Idaho Rd., Williamsburg 66095. T: (785) 242-5601.

RV: ★★★★ Tent: ★★★

Beauty: ★★★★	Site Privacy: ★★★
Spaciousness: ★★★	Quiet: ★★★
Security: ★★★	Cleanliness: ★★★★
Insect Control: ★★★	Facilities: ★★★★

This campground, one corner of a 55-acre farm, is a very pretty and convenient stopover from the highway, and proprietor Betty is friendly and full of life. (If interested, ask to see historical family photos.) The park is ringed on all sides by trees, some of them flowering. There is a small picnic area in a stand of woods bordering the farmland, and an unused (and somewhat unattractive) pond to the north. The audible traffic noise is quickly forgotten in the natural surroundings. Sites 1–3, 10–13, and 17 have particularly nice rustic views, while sites 16, 16b (unmarked), and 17 are off the main loop and back into woods, beyond which lies only farmland. Slightly less desirable sites are 1 (a little too close to the rest rooms) and 15 (tip of an island in the loop, and slightly cut off). Tent sites are unmarked, but adequate both in number and in overhead protection.

Basics

Operated By: Larry & Betty Shaffer. **Open:** All year. **Site Assignment:** Upon registration. **Registration:** In office, verbal reservations OK. **Fee:** Pull-through $16, back-in $15, tent $12. **Parking:** At site.

Facilities

Number of RV Sites: 24. **Number of Tent-Only Sites:** Undesignated sites. **Hookups:** Water, sewer, electric (30, 50 amp), some phone. **Each Site:** Trees, some picnic tables. **Dump Station:** Yes. **Laundry:** Yes. **Pay Phone:** Yes. **Rest Rooms and Showers:** Yes. **Fuel:** No. **Propane:** No. **Internal Roads:** Gravel. **RV Service:** No. **Market:** 8 mi. to Ottawa. **Restaurant:** 8 mi. to Ottawa. **General Store:** No. **Vending:** No. **Swimming:** No. **Playground:** No. **Other:** Walking trail, library, dogwalk area, country & western singer. **Activities:** Impromptu dinners. **Nearby Attractions:** Rail Trail, architecture, antique stores in Ottawa. **Additional Information:** Ottawa Chamber of Commerce, (913) 242-1000.

Restrictions

Pets: No rottweilers or pit bulls. **Fires:** In grills or fire ring. **Alcoholic Beverages:** At sites. **Vehicle Maximum Length:** 70 ft. **Other:** No hunting, no swimming in pond, no children near pond, children must be accompanied by an adult at all times.

To Get There

From I-35, take Exit 176, then turn north and go 1 block to the entrance on the right. Keep left to go to the office.

Missouri

Missouri is a state with history—there's no mistaking it. The Pony Express was headquartered here, Lewis and Clark took a little trip through the state, and Kansas City hosted the Dred Scott slavery trial that triggered the Civil War. Along with the American Indian roots of the state, all of this adds up to a wealth of reasons to visit Missouri. And the growing number of tourists is reflected in the number of campgrounds and RV parks built to serve their needs.

For RVers seeking top-notch resorts, the **Kansas City** area is the place to go. Many visitors come to Kansas City for the casinos, amusement parks, or a dash of culture. Others may pine for a photo of the Arch in **St. Louis.** And for some, Missouri means **Branson**—home to dozens of theaters that host big-name entertainers in extravagant shows. These are all legitimate destinations, but so much more of Missouri lies in the natural places—and you don't have to tunnel underground in The Cave State to find them.

Rockhounds and fortune-seekers alike will want to visit **Crater of Diamonds State Park,** where visitors can keep whatever gems they uncover. The **Trail of Tears State Park** near **Cape Girardeau** is *de rigeur* for anyone wishing to understand the state's history. And if you really *do* want to visit a cave, **Meramec State Park** near **Sullivan** is a fine place to look for hidden adventure.

One not-so-hidden treasure is the **Mark Twain National Forest,** which covers much of the southeastern part of the state. Similarly evident is the **Ozark Mountains** region, where scenic hills offer free roller-coaster rides. The **Harry S. Truman Reservoir** is an enormous complex of lakes that will appeal to water sports enthusiasts, anglers, and campers. You don't have to go to the big cities in Missouri to enjoy this state; its green places have as much to offer as its metropolitan centers.

The following facilities accept payment in checks or cash only:

- Ballard's Campground, Carthage
- Glenwood Park, Branson
- McCullough Park Campground, Chillicothe
- Missouri Park Campground, Mountain Grove
- Peculiar Park Place, Peculiar
- Pine Trails RV Ranch, Monett
- Stadium RV Park, Independence
- Thousand Hills State Park, Kirksville
- Traveler's Park Campground, Springfield

The following facilities feature 20 sites or fewer:

- Pheasant Acres Campground, St James

BRANSON
Glenwood Park

1550 Fall Creek Rd., Branson 65616. T: (417) 334-7024.

RV ★★★ Tent ★★★

Beauty: ★★★ Site Privacy: ★★★
Spaciousness: ★★ Quiet: ★★★★
Security: ★★★★ Cleanliness: ★★★★
Insect Control: ★★★★ Facilities: ★★★

Laid out in a figure eight, this campground packs in a lot of sites (mostly back-ins) and at times suffers from a lack of room. The inner side of the first loop (sites in 10s–30s) feels cramped: although there are some long sites (75 feet), the width is restricted to 24 feet. An unsightly storage shed impinges on the space of sites 38 and 39, making them less desirable. Sites 42–44 are very petite sites (25 × 25 feet) in the southeast corner. Sites 49–54, by contrast, are larger (75 feet) back-ins that feel roomier. These are undoubtedly the sites de choix, being nicely shaded and secluded feeling. Sites 55–61 in the same corner are the same size as these latter sites, but can accommodate only about 45 feet because of the angle at which an RV has to back in. Hidden in their own little clearing in the woods, sites 65–67 are cute but large enough only for a van or a pop-up. Despite the cramped feel of a number of sites, this is a decent stop for anyone visiting Branson for even a couple of days. The campground is within a short drive of many of the attractions and has shaded sites that can keep summer campers cool.

Basics

Operated By: Carol & Kyle Taylor. **Open:** Mar. 15–Nov. 15. **Site Assignment:** Depending on site availability; verbal reservations OK w/ a contact phone number. **Registration:** In office; late arrivals select available site & pay in the morning. **Fee:** RV $22 (full), $20 (water, electric); tent $16; checks, V, MC, D. **Parking:** At site.

Facilities

Number of RV Sites: 62. **Number of Tent-Only Sites:** Undesignated sites. **Hookups:** Water, sewer, electric (30, 50 amp). **Each Site:** Picnic table. **Dump Station:** Yes. **Laundry:** Yes. **Pay Phone:** Yes. **Rest Rooms and Showers:** Yes. **Fuel:** No. **Propane:** No. **Internal Roads:** Paved. **RV Service:** No. **Market:** 1.25 mi. west. **Restaurant:** Across street. **General Store:** No. **Vending:** Yes. **Swimming:** No. **Playground:** No. **Other:** Close to attractions, easy access. **Activities:** Fishing, boating, swimming, hiking, wine-tasting, shows, tours, train rides. **Nearby Attractions:** Bull Shoals Lakes, Table Rock, Taneycomo, Branson Scenic Railway, Silver Dollar City, Talking Rocks Cavern, wineries. **Additional Information:** Branson Chamber of Commerce, (417) 334-4136, (417) 334-4137.

Restrictions

Pets: On leash only, cleaned up after. **Fires:** In grills. **Alcoholic Beverages:** At sites. **Vehicle Maximum Length:** None.

To Get There

From the junction of Hwy. 65 and Hwy. 76, turn west onto Hwy. 76 (Main St.) and go 1.1 mi. Turn left onto Fall Creek Rd. The campground is on the left.

CAMDENTON
Heavenly Days Resort and Campground

Rte. 71 Box 799, Camdenton 65020. T: (573) 873-5325; www.funlake.com/accommodations/heavenlydays; heavenlycg@socket.net.

RV ★★★★ Tent ★★★★

Beauty: ★★★★★ Site Privacy: ★★★
Spaciousness: ★★★ Quiet: ★★★★
Security: ★★★★ Cleanliness: ★★★★
Insect Control: ★★★ Facilities: ★★★

This lakeside campground has tiered sites with attractive stone and cement retaining walls, as well as nice grass and trees. All RV sites have cement tracks to drive onto. Site 1 really is *the one* site, located on a promontory overlooking the lake. Sites 2–4 are very nice 60-foot back-ins. Sites 5–14 are back-ins that range from 30 to 45 feet. Of these, 5–9 are in the parking area for the office, and 14 is adjacent to a trash dumpster, making it least desirable. Sites 17–22, located on a tier above the tenting area, are 60-foot back-ins. The road leading down to sites 24–31 is very steep and in poor condition. However, the drive is worth the effort, as these sites rival site 1 in quality. Situated right on the water, they are extremely attractive. The problem with this area is the lack of space: sites seem stacked one upon the other. However, if you can tolerate the lack of space, these sites are very pleasant. The tenting area is an open grassy field. There are a couple of tall shade trees for protection. The rest rooms are very clean and spacious but, oddly, have windows (and no curtains) at eye-level running the entire length of the front. This may put off campers who prefer more privacy. Overall, Heavenly Days has some excellent sites for both tenters and RVers, and can be an exceptional stay for either.

BASICS

Operated By: Chip. **Open:** Apr.–Oct. **Site Assignment:** Depending on site availability; reservations require check deposit, 2 weeks cancellation policy. **Registration:** In office; late arrivals ring bell. **Fee:** RV $21–$23, tent $19; checks, V, MC, D. **Parking:** At site.

FACILITIES

Number of RV Sites: 29. **Number of Tent-Only Sites:** 4. **Hookups:** Water, sewer, electric (30 amp). **Each Site:** Picnic table, fire pit. **Dump Station:** No (sewer at all sites). **Laundry:** Yes. **Pay Phone:** Yes. **Rest Rooms and Showers:** Yes. **Fuel:** No. **Propane:** No. **Internal Roads:** Gravel. **RV Service:** No. **Market:** 3 mi. to Greenview. **Restaurant:** 3 mi. to Greenview. **General Store:** No. **Vending:** No. **Swimming:** Yes (lake). **Playground:** Yes. **Other:** Shuffleboard, arcade games, picnic area, pavilion. **Activities:** Fishing, boating. **Nearby Attractions:** Bridal Cave. **Additional Information:** Camdenton Area Chamber of Commerce, (800) 769-1004, (573) 346-2676.

RESTRICTIONS

Pets: On leash, cleaned up after. **Fires:** In grills. **Alcoholic Beverages:** At sites. **Vehicle Maximum Length:** 50 ft.

TO GET THERE

From the junction of Hwy. 54 and Hwy. 5/7, go north on Hwy. 5/7 8.8 mi. Turn left onto Hwy. 7 and go 0.6 mi. Turn left onto Hwy. EE and go 3.1 mi. Stay to the left at the fork in the road and go 2.8 mi. Turn right at the sign into the entrance.

CAMERON

Down Under Camp Resort

8074 Northeast County Hwy. H, Turney 64493. T: (800) 221-6056 or (816) 632-3695; www.campdownunder.com.

▲ ★★★★★

Beauty: ★★★★ Site Privacy: ★★★
Spaciousness: ★★★ Quiet: ★★★★★
Security: ★★★★★ Cleanliness: ★★★★
Insect Control: ★★★★ Facilities: ★★★★

Sites in this huge campground are scattered, undeveloped spaces with grass-and-gravel mix and a fair number of trees. Sites A1–A5, north of Kanga Lake, are full-hookup back-ins. Site 27 is a large (90 feet) pull-through, while 28–28 are much smaller (30–45 feet). These sites are mostly open, without the cover of shade trees. Sites 60–69 are 70-foot pull-throughs with little shade. A small gazebo lies next to site 65. Sites 70–74, 81, and 82 are 30-foot back-ins that lie right next to the pool. These sites see a large amount of foot traffic. The best sites in the campground are 87–100 and 120, which are located right on the lake. They are grassy and without much shade (except for 96 and 97). These sites are 45-foot back-ins, although a larger rig could overhang slightly, due to the sites' open end. Sites 104–110 are open grassy sites that face lush vegetation. They are very nice, but the grassy strip they lie on suffers from some degree of slope, and campers will have to take time to level their rig. The nicest tent sites are T3–T5, which lie right on the lake (but also on the entrance road). The grass here is very suitable for tenting. The showers are clean and spacious, if a little primitive. The rest rooms are also clean, and, on the whole, the facilities are quite comfortable. A fun campground that offers activities for the whole family in a pleasant environment.

BASICS

Operated By: Bonnie Beck. **Open:** All year (limited services Apr.–Nov.). **Site Assignment:** Upon registration; reservations recommended, credit card or check required for reservation more than 7 days (lose $5 to cancell); less than 7 days, lose one night's deposit. **Registration:** In office; late arrivals use drop box. **Fee:** RV $25 (full), $23 (water, electric), $20 (electric); tent $18; checks, V, MC. **Parking:** At site.

FACILITIES

Number of RV Sites: 120. **Number of Tent-Only Sites:** 26. **Hookups:** Water, sewer, electric (20, 30, 50 amp). **Each Site:** Picnic table, grill. **Dump Station:** Yes. **Laundry:** Yes. **Pay Phone:**

Yes. **Rest Rooms and Showers:** Yes. **Fuel:** No. **Propane:** Yes. **Internal Roads:** Gravel. **RV Service:** No. **Market:** 8 mi. west. **Restaurant:** 8 mi. west. **General Store:** Yes. **Vending:** Yes. **Swimming:** Pool. **Playground:** Yes. **Other:** RV parts, modem, lake, mini-golf, pavilion, snack bar, game room, cabin on lake. **Activities:** Fishing, paddle boating, swimming, shuffleboard. **Nearby Attractions:** Worlds of Fun. **Additional Information:** Cameron Chamber of Commerce, (816) 632-2005.

Restrictions

Pets: On leash, cleaned up after. **Fires:** In grills. **Alcoholic Beverages:** At sites. **Vehicle Maximum Length:** None. **Other:** No fireworks, children under 14 years in pool must be supervised by adult within pool fence.

To Get There

From Hwy. I-35 (Exit 48), turn east onto Hwy. 69 and go 2.5 mi. Turn right onto H and go 1.1 mi. Turn right at the sign into the entrance.

CAPE GIRARDEAU

Trail of Tears State Park

429 Moccasin Springs, Jackson 63755. T: (573) 334-1711.

RV ★★★★ Tent ★★★★★

Beauty: ★★★★	Site Privacy: ★★★★
Spaciousness: ★★★★	Quiet: ★★★★★
Security: ★★★★★	Cleanliness: ★★★
Insect Control: ★★★★	Facilities: ★★★

This state parks contains the only campground in Missouri that lies on the Mississippi River (named, appropriately, Mississippi River Campground), as well as one primitive campground (Boutin Campground). The Mississippi River Campground has electric sites close to the river bank. Sites 4–10 back to the river. Site 13 is a handicapped site that lies in a corner against a forested backdrop. Sites 14–19 back to woods as well, and are all well-shaded. There is only one unisex toilet in this campground and the bathhouse is within 0.25 mi. Boutin Campground has forested primitive sites. Site 20 is by far the longest pull-through (140 feet). Site 30 is located across from the bathhouse and the Camp Hosts, which is normally a benefit, but the dump station is also right next to it. Sites 47, 51, 52, and 54 are more isolated, being located at the end of a roundbout in the internal road. Boutin is a wonderful campground with a historical element that families will appreciate, and with plenty of recreational facilities appreciated by any camper.

Basics

Operated By: Missouri Dept. of Natural Resources. **Open:** All year. **Site Assignment:** First come, first served; no reservations. **Registration:** In office; fees also collected by Camp Hosts. **Fee:** RV $15 (full), $12 (water, electric); tent $7; checks, V, MC, D. **Parking:** At site.

Facilities

Number of RV Sites: 18. **Number of Tent-Only Sites:** 35. **Hookups:** Water, sewer, electric (30 amp). **Each Site:** Picnic table, fire pit. **Dump Station:** Yes. **Laundry:** Yes. **Pay Phone:** Yes. **Rest Rooms and Showers:** Yes. **Fuel:** No. **Propane:** No. **Internal Roads:** Paved. **RV Service:** No. **Market:** 15 mi. south. **Restaurant:** 15 mi. south. **General Store:** No. **Vending:** No. **Swimming:** Yes (lake). **Playground:** Yes. **Other:** Boat ramp, exhibits. **Activities:** Fishing, boating, swimming, hiking, tours. **Nearby Attractions:** Trail of Tears, Bollinger Mill State Historic Site, Cape Rock. **Additional Information:** Cape Girardeau CVB, (800) 777-0068, (573) 335-1631.

Restrictions

Pets: On leash, cleaned up after. **Fires:** In grills. **Alcoholic Beverages:** At sites. **Vehicle Maximum Length:** None. **Other:** Gates locked at 10 p.m.

To Get There

From the junction of Broadway and Hwy. 177 in town, turn north onto Hwy. 177 and go 11.8 mi. (Be sure to turn right at tyhe 11.7 mi. mark.) Take first right into park.

CARTHAGE

Ballard's Campground

13965 Ballard Loop, Carthage 64836. T: (417) 359-0359; F: (417) 359-0359; wswwgoff@yahoo.com.

RV ★★★ Tent ★★★

Beauty: ★★★★	Site Privacy: ★★★★
Spaciousness: ★★★★	Quiet: ★★★
Security: ★★★★★	Cleanliness: ★★★★
Insect Control: ★★★★	Facilities: ★★★

While the highway passes on one side of this campground, the other three sides are surrounded by forest, giving it a natural, almost wilderness, feel. Ballard's is arranged in three rows of paired sites that are slightly tiered but level. Sites 1–6, 13–18, and 21–26 are 85-foot pull-throughs, while 7–12 and 19–20 are 75-foot pull-throughs. Most sites are very well shaded, but 10 and 25 are exceptions. Outside sites 12, 22, 24, and 26 seem a little short on space. They require parking at the edge of the internal road and sharing the picnic space on the far side of the neighboring site. Site 7 is close to the fishing pond, and site 12 is at the edge of the property, which makes it a little more private. The nicest site is probably 21—everything just seems to coalesce nicely here: it is well-shaded, grassy, far from the entrance, and facing mostly forest. The tent area is in a large open space next to the pond, with trees around the perimeter. The grass is very nice, but there is little shade or protection from the elements. The rest rooms are spacious and mostly clean, with modern facilities. A nice campground that feels further away from it all than its convenient location belies.

BASICS

Operated By: William & Wanda Goff. **Open:** All year. **Site Assignment:** Depending on availability; no reservations. **Registration:** In office; late arrivals pay in morning. **Fee:** RV $12 (full), $11 (water, electric); tent $10; no credit cards, but check. **Parking:** At site.

FACILITIES

Number of RV Sites: 30. **Number of Tent-Only Sites:** Undesignated sites. **Hookups:** Water, sewer, electric (30 amp). **Each Site:** Picnic table, fire pit. **Dump Station:** Yes. **Laundry:** Yes. **Pay Phone:** Yes. **Rest Rooms and Showers:** Yes. **Fuel:** No. **Propane:** Yes. **Internal Roads:** Gravel. **RV Service:** No. **Market:** 5 mi. northeast. **Restaurant:** 2 mi. south. **General Store:** Yes. **Vending:** Yes. **Swimming:** No. **Playground:** No. **Other:** Fishing pond w/ pavilion. **Activities:** Fishing (catch & release). **Nearby Attractions:** Precious Moments Chapel. **Additional Information:** Carthage CVB, (417) 358-2373.

RESTRICTIONS

Pets: On leash only, cleaned up after. **Fires:** In grills. **Alcoholic Beverages:** At sites. **Vehicle Maximum Length:** None.

TO GET THERE

From Hwy. I-44, take Exit 18A. On the south side of the highway overpass, go 0.3 mi. on Hwy. Alt 71.

CHARLESTON

Sams Camping

Beasly Park Rd., P.O. Box 357, Charleston 63834. T: (573) 683-6362 or (573) 683-6415.

RV ★★★ Tent ★★

Beauty: ★★	Site Privacy: ★★★
Spaciousness: ★★★	Quiet: ★★★
Security: ★★★★	Cleanliness: ★★★
Insect Control: ★★★★	Facilities: ★★★

This campground has grassy/gravel pull-through sites laid out in strips. Sites A–T are in two rows that run perpendicular to the road. J and T are right on the road and closest to the entrance. J has a large sign, light post, and fire hydrant that encroach on its space. Sites A–G are well shaded, particularly D–F, but not B. Sites 1–8 are in a strip along the south edge of the campground, facing an agricultural field. Contiguous with 1–8, sites 9–16 run along the eastern edge, facing truck parking and commercial buildings. Site 16 is closest to the road, but not as close as J and T. All of these sites are 72 × 21-foot pull-throughs. Tenting is permitted in a field of open grass, but is not overly comfortable. The rest rooms are clean, but could use some brightening up. An acceptable overnight stay, but not comfortable enough to warrant a special trip.

BASICS

Operated By: Donald Sams. **Open:** All year. **Site Assignment:** Depending on site availability; no reservations. **Registration:** In office; late arrivals use drop box. **Fee:** 2 people $15, 4 people $17, 6 people $19. **Parking:** At site.

FACILITIES

Number of RV Sites: 36. **Number of Tent-Only Sites:** Undesignated sites. **Hookups:** Water, sewer, electric (20, 30, 50 amp). **Dump Station:** No (sewer at all sites). **Laundry:** No. **Pay Phone:** Yes. **Rest Rooms and Showers:** Yes. **Fuel:** No. **Propane:** No. **Internal Roads:** Gravel. **RV Service:** No. **Market:** Less than 0.25 mi. north. **Restaurant:** Less than 0.25 mi. north. **General Store:** No. **Vending:** Yes. **Swimming:** No.

Playground: No. **Other:** Fish in city lake across street. **Activities:** Fishing. **Nearby Attractions:** Big Oak Tree State Park. **Additional Information:** Charleston Chamber of Commerce, (573) 683-6509.

RESTRICTIONS

Pets: On leash, cleaned up after. **Fires:** In grills. **Alcoholic Beverages:** At sites. **Vehicle Maximum Length:** None.

TO GET THERE

From Hwy. 57 (Exit 10), turn south and take the first left after the off-ramp onto Beasly Park Rd. Go 0.2 mi. and then turn right at the sign into the entrance.

CHILLICOTHE

McCullough Park Campground

13248 Liv 216, Chillicothe 64601. T: (816) 646-2735.

RV ★★★★ Tent ★★★★

Beauty: ★★★★★	Site Privacy: ★★★★
Spaciousness: ★★★★★	Quiet: ★★★★★
Security: ★★★★★	Cleanliness: ★★★★
Insect Control: ★★★★★	Facilities: ★★★

Most sites in this campground are forested, making for cooler summer days. The main campground is in the wooded area to the north of the office. This is a slice of forest with a farm flavor. (None of the sites are designated by anything other than an open area with an electrical outlet for several sites, and the owners often provide extention cords for additional electric sites, so a description of individual sites is neither possible nor helpful in this case.) The undeveloped sites to the east of the office are tenter or pop-up heaven, but not convenient for large rigs or tows. Larger RVs should head towards the "big rig section" on the hill to the northwest of the office. It's an open field with trees around the perimeter and huge sites with room for wide turns. Again, the sites are not numbered, but are indicated by the presence of the hookups. Tenting is unlimited in lush, beautiful grass and a thick forest canopy overhead. The rest room is smallish but comfortable and clean. With the exception of the bluegrass festival held here every year, this is a quiet campground secluded in the woods. It is absolutely a haven for tenters, and the section for large RVs ensures that all campers can enjoy their stay here.

BASICS

Operated By: Don McCullough. **Open:** All year (limited service Nov.–Mar.). **Site Assignment:** Upon registration; verbal reservations OK. **Registration:** In office; late arrivals select available site & pay in the morning. **Fee:** RV $18 (full), $15 (water, electric); tent $12; no credits cards, but checks. **Parking:** At site.

FACILITIES

Number of RV Sites: 300. **Number of Tent-Only Sites:** 30. **Hookups:** Water, sewer, electric (30 amp). **Each Site:** Can get table from owners. **Dump Station:** Yes. **Laundry:** No. **Pay Phone:** Yes. **Rest Rooms and Showers:** Yes. **Fuel:** No. **Propane:** No. **Internal Roads:** Gravel. **RV Service:** No. **Market:** 4 mi. south. **Restaurant:** 4 mi. south. **General Store:** No. **Vending:** No. **Swimming:** No. **Playground:** No. **Other:** Firewood. **Activities:** Special events (including bluegrass festival), old-time harvest. **Nearby Attractions:** Pershing State Park, Poosey Conservation Area, Bunch Hollow Conservation Area. **Additional Information:** Chillicothe Area Chamber of Commerce, (660) 646-4050.

RESTRICTIONS

Pets: On leash only, cleaned up after. **Fires:** In grills. **Alcoholic Beverages:** At sites, restricted during events. **Vehicle Maximum Length:** None.

TO GET THERE

From the junction of Hwy. 36 and Hwy. 65, turn north onto Hwy. 65 and go 7.4 mi. Turn right onto the gravel road and go 0.3 mi. Turn left at the sign into the entrance.

CLINTON

Harry S. Truman Dam and Reservoir (Sparrowfoot Park)

150 Southeast 450 Rd., Clinton 64735. T: (877) 444-6777, or Visitor's center (660) 438-2216, or park (660) 885-7546; www.reserveusa.com.

RV ★★★★ Tent ★★★★

Beauty: ★★★★	Site Privacy: ★★★★
Spaciousness: ★★★	Quiet: ★★★★
Security: ★★★★	Cleanliness: ★★★★
Insect Control: ★★★★	Facilities: ★★★

A lakeside campground, this park has sites laid out in two large loops. Loop A itself has two loops in a figure 8. Most sites in this loop are somewhat shaded, but not forested. Sites on the inside of the loop back to dense vegetation, while sites on the outside back to more open vegetation. Sites A13 and A14 are entirely unshaded. Prime sites closest to the lake include A15–A21, of which A17–A19 have the best views. Site A22, a 90-foot pull-through, is just across from A20 and A21 but does not include the prime-site price tag. Site 33 is just as close to the toilets as 32, but likewise does not cost as much as the more expensive site. Sites 28–48 back to other sites and are thus less private. Sites along the northeast edge and 16–21 do not back to any other sites. Site A50 is a 105-foot pull-through, and sites A59–62 are closest to the rest rooms in the second loop of Loop A. In Loop B, site B1 is a prime site due to its proximity to the rest rooms, but is much too close to the road for comfort. Even-numbers 2–16 back to dense vegetation, which makes them very attractive. Sites B15, 18, and 20 are just as close to the water access area as B16, 17, and 19, but are not priced like prime sites. Sites B19 and 20 may, in fact, suffer from an inordinate amount of passing foot traffic. The rest rooms and showers are basic but functional. During off-season, only pit toilets are available—no showers, flush toilets, or laundry. Overall, an attractive campground that offers plenty of recreation facilities and pleasant spots for campers.

Basics

Operated By: Army Corps of Engineers. **Open:** All year (limited services Oct. 16–Apr. 14). **Site Assignment:** First come, first served; no reservations. **Registration:** In office; late arrivals select available site from sign-in sheet in booth & pay in the morning. **Fee:** RV $16 (prime), $14 (electric); tent $10, off-season $6; V, MC, AE, D, DC. **Parking:** At site.

Facilities

Number of RV Sites: 93. **Number of Tent-Only Sites:** 19. **Hookups:** Electric (20, 30 amp). **Each Site:** Picnic table, fire pit, lantern pole. **Dump Station:** Yes. **Laundry:** Yes. **Pay Phone:** No. **Rest Rooms and Showers:** Yes. **Fuel:** No. **Propane:** No. **Internal Roads:** Paved. **RV Service:** No. **Market:** 5 mi. to Clinton. **Restaurant:** 5 mi. to Clinton. **General Store:** No. **Vending:** No. **Swimming:** Yes (lake). **Playground:** Yes. **Other:** Picnic area, beach. **Activities:** Fishing, boating, swimming, ATV riding. **Nearby Attractions:** Henry County Museum & Cultural Arts Center. **Additional Information:** Clinton Chamber of Commerce, (660) 885-8168.

Restrictions

Pets: On leash only, cleaned up after. **Fires:** In grills. **Alcoholic Beverages:** At sites. **Vehicle Maximum Length:** None.

To Get There

From the junction of Hwy. 7 and Hwy. 13 by hospital, turn south onto Hwy. 13 and go 7 mi. Turn left onto southeast 450 and go 1.2 mi. Turn right at the sign into the entrance.

COLUMBIA

Cottonwoods RV Park

5170 Oakland, Columbia 65202. T: (573) 474-2747; F: (573) 474-0946; cottonwoodrv@aol.com.

RV ★★★★★ Tent ★★★★

Beauty: ★★★★	Site Privacy: ★★★★
Spaciousness: ★★★★	Quiet: ★★★★
Security: ★★★★★	Cleanliness: ★★★★★
Insect Control: ★★★★	Facilities: ★★★★★

Like most RV parks in the area, Cottonwoods does not offer much shade. This is where the similarity with most other campgrounds ends, however, as this is a fantastic, upscale resort that will appeal to all RV campers. It features extremely well-tended landscaping, with grass and trees on three sides and buildings to the east. Strips of grassy sites run east to west, with monthlies (1–23) located at the southern end. All sites are 27 feet wide, and overnight spaces are 60–65 feet. pull-throughs. (Sites 70–97 are doubles that meet end to end and measure 110 feet—slightly less than the rest of the sites.) Although it is difficult to pick a "best" site, campers may prefer the middle area (roughly 32–43, 52–63, 74–80, 87–93), as it is furthest from the entry road, does not face any buildings, has very nice trees and grass, and is close to the rest rooms. Tent sites are at the entrance of the park. They have beautiful grass but—again—no shade, and feel somewhat like an afterthought in an RV park. Rest rooms and showers are exceptionally clean and comfortable. This RV park caters to the upscale urban camper. It is extremely comfortable by any standards, and campers of any kind will enjoy a stay here.

BASICS

Operated By: Buster & Loretta Candle (owners), Gary Lynch (mgr.). **Open:** All year. **Site Assignment:** Upon registration; credit card required for reservation, 24-hours cancellation policy. **Registration:** In office; late arrivals use drop box. **Fee:** RV $25 (50 amp), $22 (30 amp), $20 (water, electric); tent $18; checks, V, MC, D. **Parking:** At site.

FACILITIES

Number of RV Sites: 100. **Number of Tent-Only Sites:** 6. **Hookups:** Water, sewer, electric (20, 30, 50 amp). **Each Site:** Picnic table. **Dump Station:** Yes. **Laundry:** Yes. **Pay Phone:** Yes. **Rest Rooms and Showers:** Yes. **Fuel:** No. **Propane:** Yes. **Internal Roads:** Gravel. **RV Service:** No. **Market:** 4 mi. south. **Restaurant:** 2 mi. south. **General Store:** Yes. **Vending:** Yes. **Swimming:** Pool. **Playground:** Yes. **Other:** Meeting room, game room, antique mall, gift shop, modem, pool table, exercise equipment, pet walk, small & large pavilions. **Activities:** Biking, hiking, basketball, horseshoes, swimming. **Nearby Attractions:** Katy Trail State Park, Rockbridge State Park. **Additional Information:** Columbia Chamber of Commerce, (573) 875-1231.

RESTRICTIONS

Pets: On leash only, cleaned up after. **Fires:** In grills. **Alcoholic Beverages:** At sites. **Vehicle Maximum Length:** None. **Other:** No refunds, see rule sheet.

TO GET THERE

From Hwy. I-70 (Exit 128A), turn north onto PP and take entrance to Hwy. 63. Go 3 mi., then turn right onto Oakland Gravel Rd. Turn right off the ramp, then left onto Starke Ln. Go 0.4 mi., then turn right at the sign into the entrance.

DANVILLE

Kan-Do Kampground RV Park

99 Hwy. TT, Montgomery City 63361. T: (573) 564-7993; kando@ktis.net.

RV ★★★★★ Tent ★★★★★

Beauty: ★★★★	Site Privacy: ★★★★
Spaciousness: ★★★★	Quiet: ★★★★
Security: ★★★★	Cleanliness: ★★★★★
Insect Control: ★★★★	Facilities: ★★★★

This campground is laid out in a loop, with all sites on the outside and a large grassy field on the inside. All sites are pull-throughs, some of them enormous (11 is 140 feet, 2–9 and 15–26 are 120 feet), and all well shaded. In fact, you really can't go wrong with any site in the park. Sites with full hookups are located along the south side of the campground. Sites 1 and 27–29 are seasonal. Tent sites are equally well shaded and have a mix of grass, gravel, and dirt. The rest room is small but immaculate. Kan-Do is a campground that all campers will enjoy, and spacious enough to meet the demands of any sized rig.

BASICS

Operated By: Debbie & Randy Bohnsac. **Open:** Apr. 15–Oct. 15 (otherwise limited services). **Site Assignment:** Upon registration; credit card required for reservation, 4-days cancellation policy. **Registration:** In office; late arrivals use drop box. **Fee:** RV $20 (50 amp), $17 (30 amp), $13 (water, electric); tent $11. **Parking:** At site.

FACILITIES

Number of RV Sites: 35. **Number of Tent-Only Sites:** 12. **Hookups:** Water, sewer, electric (30, 50 amp). **Each Site:** Picnic table, fire pit. **Dump Station:** No (sewer at all sites). **Laundry:** Yes. **Pay Phone:** Yes. **Rest Rooms and Showers:** Yes. **Fuel:** No. **Propane:** Yes. **Internal Roads:** Gravel. **RV Service:** No. **Market:** 7 mi. northeast. **Restaurant:** 5 mi. east. **General Store:** Yes. **Vending:** No. **Swimming:** Pool. **Playground:** Yes. **Other:** Fishing pond, recreation fields, pavilion. **Activities:** Volleyball, swimming, fishing. **Nearby Attractions:** Graham Cave State Park. **Additional Information:** Columbia Chamber of Commerce, (573) 874-1132.

RESTRICTIONS

Pets: On leash, cleaned up after. **Fires:** In grills. **Alcoholic Beverages:** At sites. **Vehicle Maximum Length:** None. **Other:** Visitors must purchase day pass.

TO GET THERE

From Hwy. I-70 (Exit 170), turn north onto Hwy. 161 and then take the first left onto West Service Rd. at the dead-end sign. Go 1 mi., then turn right at the sign into the entrance.

DONIPHAN

Rocky River Resort

304 West Jefferson, Doniphan 63935. T: (800) 748-7672 or (573) 996-7171; F: (573) 996-4018.

★★★★ ★★★★

Beauty: ★★★★	Site Privacy: ★★★★
Spaciousness: ★★★★	Quiet: ★★★
Security: ★★★★★	Cleanliness: ★★★
Insect Control: ★★★★	Facilities: ★★★

Hidden in the forest, Doniphan has wooded, grassy back-ins and pull-throughs, as well as a tenting area. This campground abuts the Current River, and the focus is squarely on float trips. Sites 1–18 are 60 × 55-foot back-ins along the entrance road. Sites 6–9 are located across from a play area, and 13–15 are across from a pavilion, which may increase traffic past these sites. Sites 19–34 are situated around the "Teardrop" area. These are 50-foot back-ins, best for tenters or smaller RVs (such as pop-ups), as the dirt road can be difficult to navigate. Closest to the river access area are sites 23–27. The rest of the sites (35–51) are forested, comfortable, and spacious. Site 35, across from the Snack Shack, has one open side that is not forested. The tenting area is secluded and close to the river on the western edge of the campground. The rest rooms are reasonably modern and clean, aside from paint flaking off the floors. There are several porta-potties throughout the campground in addition to the rest rooms. A fun campground geared towards floating on the river; a great destination for families.

Basics

Operated By: Bill & Virginia. **Open:** All year. **Site Assignment:** Upon registration; credit card or check deposit for reservation (credit, but no refunds, given). **Registration:** In office; late arrivals select available site & pay in the morning. **Fee:** RV $17, tent $4/person; checks, V, MC, AE, D. **Parking:** At site.

Facilities

Number of RV Sites: 51. **Number of Tent-Only Sites:** 6. **Hookups:** Water, sewer, electric (30, 50 amp), cable. **Each Site:** Picnic table, fire pit. **Dump Station:** Yes. **Laundry:** No. **Pay Phone:** No. **Rest Rooms and Showers:** Yes. **Fuel:** No. **Propane:** No. **Internal Roads:** Gravel. **RV Service:** No. **Market:** 0.25 mi. east. **Restaurant:** 0.25 east. **General Store:** Yes. **Vending:** No. **Swimming:** No. **Playground:** Yes. **Other:** Tube rentals. **Activities:** Tubing. **Nearby Attractions:** Current River. **Additional Information:** Doniphan Chamber of Commerce: (573) 996-2212.

Restrictions

Pets: On leash, cleaned up after, no pit bulls or rottweilers. **Fires:** In grills. **Alcoholic Beverages:** At sites, no bottles. **Vehicle Maximum Length:** None. **Other:** 2 vehicles per site, visitors must check in.

To Get There

From the junction of Hwy. 21 and Hwys. 142 and 160, go 0.85 mi. west on 21/142/160. Take last left turn on east side of bridge and go 0.35 mi. on Jefferson (which is not signed). Turn right at the sign into the entrance.

EAGLEVILLE

I-35 RV Park

Exit 106, P.O. Box 56, Eagleville 64442. T: (660) 867-3377; F: (660) 867-3377; theoasis@grm.net.

★★★ ★★★

Beauty: ★★★	Site Privacy: ★★★
Spaciousness: ★★	Quiet: ★★★
Security: ★★★★	Cleanliness: ★★★
Insect Control: ★★★★	Facilities: ★★

Sites in this campground are laid out in one big loop, with pull-throughs in a strip on the west side, and back-ins in a strip on the east side. Pull-through sites range 75–85 feet in length and average 22 feet in width. Back-ins are 45 feet long before the site begins to slope. Site 1 is next to the office, and may receive registration traffic passing by. Sites 7 and 8 are closest to the rest rooms, while 9 and 10 are closest to the entrance. The nicest site is 18, closest to a tree with a seat below it. The tenting area is to the south, near the rest rooms. There is good grass cover for these sites, and a communal fire pit. The rest rooms are primitive but decent. The shower is a cement room with plastic sheeting that renders it waterproof. Some campers may find this setup a little bizarre and uncomfortable. With residences to the west and north and a semi-industrial area to the east, this campground has a slightly urban feel, but the pretty farmland to the south makes up somewhat for the lacking beauty. Overall, an acceptable stay but not an important destination.

Basics

Operated By: Michael & Betty Sanchez. **Open:** All year. **Site Assignment:** First come, first served; verbal reservations OK. **Registration:** In office;

late arrivals use drop box. **Fee:** RV $15 (pull-through), $13 (back-in); tent $8, checks. **Parking:** At site.

FACILITIES

Number of RV Sites: 22. **Number of Tent-Only Sites:** Undesignated sites. **Hookups:** Water, sewer, electric (20, 30, 50 amp). **Dump Station:** Yes. **Laundry:** No. **Pay Phone:** Yes. **Rest Rooms and Showers:** Yes. **Fuel:** No. **Propane:** No. **Internal Roads:** Gravel. **RV Service:** No. **Market:** 3 mi. east. **Restaurant:** 3 blocks east. **General Store:** No. **Vending:** No. **Swimming:** No. **Playground:** No. **Other:** Snack shop, RV supplies, close to town square, covered picnic pavilion. **Activities:** Horseshoes. **Nearby Attractions:** Grand Trace Conservation Area. **Additional Information:** Cameron Chamber of Commerce, (816) 632-2005.

RESTRICTIONS

Pets: On leash, cleaned up after. **Fires:** In communal fire ring. **Alcoholic Beverages:** At sites. **Vehicle Maximum Length:** None. **Other:** Pay before occupying site.

TO GET THERE

From Hwy. I-35 (Exit 106), turn west and go 0.4 mi. Turn left at the sign into the entrance.

EMINENCE

Jacks Fork Campground

P.O. Box 188, Eminence 65466. T: (800) 333-5628 or (800) 365-2537 or (800) 522-5736; www.currentrivercanoe.com.

RV ★★★★ Tent ★★★★★

Beauty: ★★★★	Site Privacy: ★★★★
Spaciousness: ★★★★★	Quiet: ★★★
Security: ★★★★	Cleanliness: ★★★
Insect Control: ★★★	Facilities: ★★★★

This natural campground lies along a river and is geared towards floating and canoe trips. Sites 1–21 are in a forested strip along the entrance road. These grassy sites have water and electricity, and back to lush vegetation. Along the same entrance road, sites 22–29 are much more open and not quite as nice as the first 21 sites. Grassy sites with no hookups, sites 37–40, 46, and 47 lie along the river. They contain lots of vegetation and a fair number of trees, which makes them quite comfortable. One row back from the river, sites 41–45 are spacious and with lots of shade. Similar to these are sites 50–55 in another row further back. Pull-through sites with river access include 41–45. Sites 102–129 are in a loop at the north end of the campground. Of these, sites 105–108 are right on the river, 114–115 are in a shaded corner, while 129 contains a little stand of young trees that give some amount of shade. Right at the entrance to the loop are sites 102, 127, and 128. They are right under a number of shade trees, but all other sites in this loop are very open. The rest rooms are in an aging wooden building, the showers are coin-operated. Jacks Fork makes for a decent stay for RVers who can snag a site with hookups (or don't mind going without electricity and using their facilities), and is a great place for tenters to camp.

BASICS

Operated By: Gene & Eleanor Maggard. **Open:** Apr. 15–Oct. 15. **Site Assignment:** Depending on site availability; credit card required for reservations (credit certificates given but no refunds). **Registration:** In office; late arrivals pick available site & settle in the morning. **Fee:** Sun.–Thu. $5/person, Fri.–Sat. $6/person, electricity $5/night. **Parking:** At site.

FACILITIES

Number of RV Sites: 133. **Number of Tent-Only Sites:** 0. **Hookups:** Water, electric (30, 50 amp). **Each Site:** Picnic table, grill, trees. **Dump Station:** Yes. **Laundry:** No. **Pay Phone:** No. **Rest Rooms and Showers:** Yes. **Fuel:** No. **Propane:** No. **Internal Roads:** Gravel. **RV Service:** No. **Market:** 0.5 mi. to Eminence. **Restaurant:** 0.5 mi. to Eminence. **General Store:** Yes. **Vending:** Yes. **Swimming:** Yes (river). **Playground:** Yes. **Other:** Cabins, pavilion. **Activities:** Swimming, canoeing, volleyball, fishing. **Nearby Attractions:** Angenvine Conservation Area, Peck Ranch Conservation Area, Ozarck National Scenic Riverways, Mark Twain National Forest. **Additional Information:** Eminence Chamber of Commerce, (573) 226-3318.

RESTRICTIONS

Pets: On leash, cleaned up after. **Fires:** In grills. **Alcoholic Beverages:** At sites. **Vehicle Maximum Length:** None. **Other:** Campground divided into noisy & quiet sections.

TO GET THERE

From the junction of Hwy. 19 and Hwy. 106, go 0.4 mi. east on Hwy. 106. Turn left at the sign into the campground.

GRAVOIS MILLS

Gravois Creek Campground

P.O. Box 167, Gravois Mills 65037. T: (800) 573-CAMP or (573) 372-3211; F: (573) 372-3212; www.gravoiscreek.com; camp@gravoiscreek.com.

RV ★★★★ Tent ★★★★★

Beauty: ★★★★★	Site Privacy: ★★★
Spaciousness: ★★★	Quiet: ★★★★
Security: ★★★★★	Cleanliness: ★★★★
Insect Control: ★★★★	Facilities: ★★★★

Gravois Creek is a rural campground with a wilderness feel and very attractive landscaping, including grape vines on a trellis in front of the rest rooms, flowering trees, and woods on all four sides. The creek lies to the northeast and is accessible from the campground. Most sites are shaded, making this an exceptional camping area. Sites 1–4 are 75-foot pull-throughs, 7–13 are larger (85 feet) and well shaded, and 15–22 are even bigger (90 feet) and hidden amidst trees. Down by the creek are sites suitable for tents or pop-ups. Sites furthest to the east are electric sites wrapped by bushes and hidden under shade trees. For tenters and those RVs that can fit, this is an excellent place to camp. The area to the north of the office—a beautiful grassy field with loads of shade—is strictly for tents (no cars allowed). The showers are individual units, and the rest rooms are small but very clean. This campground is a shade-lovers paradise (a rare thing in the area).

Basics

Operated By: Johnny Keller. **Open:** Mar.–Nov. **Site Assignment:** Depending on site availability; credit card required for reservation, 48-hours cancellation policy. **Registration:** In office; late arrivals use drop box. **Fee:** RV $18 (full), $16 (water, electric); tent $11; checks, V, MC, D. **Parking:** At site.

Facilities

Number of RV Sites: 35. **Number of Tent-Only Sites:** Undesignated sites. **Hookups:** Water, sewer, electric (20, 30, 50 amp), cable. **Each Site:** Picnic table, grill or fire pit. **Dump Station:** Yes. **Laundry:** Yes. **Pay Phone:** Yes. **Rest Rooms and Showers:** Yes. **Fuel:** No. **Propane:** No. **Internal Roads:** Gravel. **RV Service:** No. **Market:** 2 mi. south. **Restaurant:** 1 mi. south. **General Store:** Yes. **Vending:** No. **Swimming:** Yes (stream). **Playground:** Yes. **Other:** Cabins, firewood, pet area, creek. **Activities:** Fishing, swimming. **Nearby Attractions:** Free public boat ramp. **Additional Information:** Lake of The Ozarks West Chamber of Commerce, (573) 374-5500.

Restrictions

Pets: On leash, cleaned up after, not in cabins. **Fires:** In grills. **Alcoholic Beverages:** At sites. **Vehicle Maximum Length:** None. **Other:** No fireworks.

To Get There

From the north city limits, go 1.7 mi. north on Hwy. 5. Turn right at the sign into the entrance.

HANNIBAL

Injun Joe Campground

14113 Clemens Dr., New London 63459. T: (573) 985-3581.

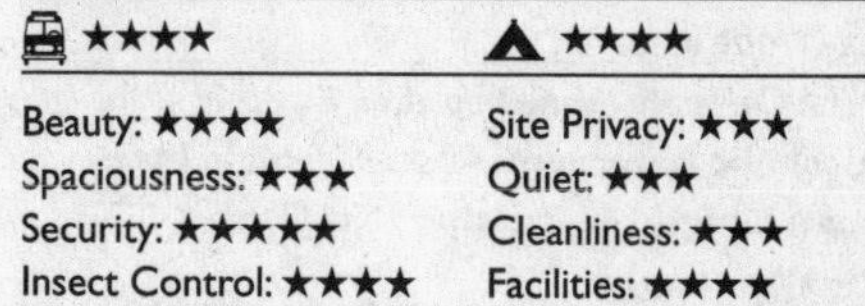

RV ★★★★ Tent ★★★★

Beauty: ★★★★	Site Privacy: ★★★
Spaciousness: ★★★	Quiet: ★★★
Security: ★★★★★	Cleanliness: ★★★
Insect Control: ★★★★	Facilities: ★★★★

A sure hit with families, Injun Joe offers swimming, go karts, plays, and many more recreation facilities. Most sites are back-ins, with an average size of 55 feet. Sites 8–35 are laid out in a loop and back to woods as do sites 101–107. Sites 130–133 are located along the entrance road and may receive more passing traffic. Site 107 is in the furthest corner, with pleasant views to two sides. Sites 139–144 back to sites 1–7 so closely that detract from the privacy of both sets of sites. The tenting area is a large field with quite a number of trees. There is a picnic shelter and decent grass covering. Most natural and woodsy is the area to the southwest. The rest room is extremely small for such a large campground, with one toilet for every 45 RV campers. It is clean and modern, but you may have to wait in line for a while during the morning rush hour. It is hard not to have a great time in Injun Joe, and families would do well to spend a few days enjoying the recreation facilities on offer.

Basics

Operated By: Clarence & Ann Steinman. **Open:** All year. **Site Assignment:** Upon registration; credit card or check required for reservation, 2-weeks cancellation policy. **Registration:** In office.

Fee: RV $19 (full), $17 (water, electric); tent $15; checks, V, MC, D. **Parking:** At site.

Facilities

Number of RV Sites: 168. **Number of Tent-Only Sites:** Undesignated sites. **Hookups:** Water, sewer, electric (20, 30, 50 amp). **Each Site:** Picnic table on concrete slab, grill. **Dump Station:** Yes. **Laundry:** Yes. **Pay Phone:** Yes. **Rest Rooms and Showers:** Yes. **Fuel:** No. **Propane:** No. **Internal Roads:** Gravel. **RV Service:** No. **Market:** 2 mi. south. **Restaurant:** On site. **General Store:** Yes. **Vending:** No. **Swimming:** Pool. **Playground:** Yes. **Other:** Dog walk, lakes, go karts, water slide, mini-golf, batting cage, amphitheater, game room. **Activities:** Fishing, swimming, plays, go-karting. **Nearby Attractions:** Mark Twain Cave, Sawyer's Creek Fun Park, Riverview Park, Mark Twain Outdoor Theater. **Additional Information:** Hannibal CVB, (573) 221-2477.

Restrictions

Pets: On leash, cleaned up after. **Fires:** In grills. **Alcoholic Beverages:** At sites. **Vehicle Maximum Length:** 40 ft. **Other:** No ATVs.

To Get There

From the junction of Hwy. 36 and Hwy. 61, turn south onto Hwy. 61 and go 6.5 mi. Turn right. (Look for the statue and sign for Clemens Landing.) Go 2 blocks past the residences into the campground.

HAYTI

Hayti-Portageville KOA

2824 MO State East Outer Rd., Portageville 63873. T: (800) KOA-0965 or (573) DJW-1580; F: (573) DJW-0965; www.koa.com.

RV ★★★★ Tent ★★★★

Beauty: ★★★ Site Privacy: ★★★★
Spaciousness: ★★★★ Quiet: ★★★
Security: ★★★★ Cleanliness: ★★★★★
Insect Control: ★★★★ Facilities: ★★★★★

This campground is surrounded on three sides by agricultural land (with the highway on the fourth side), which lends it a rural feel. A large number of trees throughout the park make the sites comfortable, even when the sun is boring down. Situated in five rows, sites are a combination of gravel and grass, with a predominance of pull-throughs. Sites 1–7 are 45-foot back-ins close to the playground area. The rest of the sites are 70–75-foot pull-throughs, whose desirability more or less depends on personal taste (proximity to rest rooms, etc.). Several exceptionally good sites are the end sites (31, 41, 39, 49) of the last two rows, as these are furthest from the highway and seem to have more space. The tent sites are located in the southwest corner on grassy ground cover and have loads of trees. The tenting area is so spacious that each tent can be pitched under a different tree. The laundry is small but clean and contains an exercise bike. The rest rooms are very clean, and the showers (individual units) are immaculate and have air conditioning. A very comfortable campground with great facilities.

Basics

Operated By: Dan & Joyce Webb. **Open:** All year. **Site Assignment:** Upon registration; credit card required for reservations, $20 non-refundable deposit. **Registration:** In office; late arrivals use drop box. **Fee:** RV $24 (full), $22 (water, electric); tent $19. **Parking:** At site.

Facilities

Number of RV Sites: 49. **Number of Tent-Only Sites:** 20. **Hookups:** Water, sewer, electric (30, 50 amp). **Each Site:** Picnic table, grill. **Dump Station:** Yes. **Laundry:** Yes. **Pay Phone:** Yes. **Rest Rooms and Showers:** Yes. **Fuel:** No. **Propane:** Yes. **Internal Roads:** Gravel. **RV Service:** No. **Market:** 7 mi. north or south. **Restaurant:** 7 mi. north or south. **General Store:** Yes. **Vending:** Yes. **Swimming:** Pool. **Playground:** Yes. **Other:** Cabins, game room, snack bar, kitchen, modem. **Activities:** Swimming. **Nearby Attractions:** Mississippi River. **Additional Information:** Hayti Chamber of Commerce, (573) 359-0632.

Restrictions

Pets: On leash, cleaned up after, no vicious breeds (pit bulls, rottweilers) outside of vehicles. **Fires:** In fire rings. **Alcoholic Beverages:** At sites. **Vehicle Maximum Length:** None. **Other:** No smoking in buildings.

To Get There

From Hwy. I-55, take Exit 27. Turn onto the service road on the east side of the highway (East Outer Rd.) and go 3 mi. Turn left at the sign into the campground.

INDEPENDENCE
Stadium RV Park

10021 East US Hwy. 40, Independence 64055. T: (816) 353-0242; F: (816) 358-4226.

RV ★★★ Tent n/a

Beauty: ★★ Site Privacy: ★★★
Spaciousness: ★★ Quiet: ★★★
Security: ★★★★ Cleanliness: ★★★
Insect Control: ★★★★ Facilities: ★★★

A renovated mobile-home park, this campground still has a few scattered tenants (mostly on the east side), although the management is slowly converting to all RVs. Stadium is surrounded by residential areas and has a definite urban feel. Sites are not consistently numbered, and finding any one particular spot is difficult. Most sites are 30–36 feet long and 25 feet wide. Two sites on the south edge can take vehicles of at least 45 feet in length, but not with tows. Sites feel a little cramped, especially for rigs with slide-outs. The laundry is old and in need of a good scrubbing and paint job. The rest rooms are likewise a little past prime, though acceptable. Larger rigs in particular might want to skip this campground altogether.

Basics

Operated By: Sarah Donahue. **Open:** All year. **Site Assignment:** Upon registration; check deposit required for reservation, 24-hours cancellation policy. **Registration:** In office; late arrivals go to house. **Fee:** RV $20. **Parking:** At site.

Facilities

Number of RV Sites: 58. **Number of Tent-Only Sites:** 0. **Hookups:** Water, sewer, electric (30, 50 amp). **Dump Station:** No (sewer at all sites). **Laundry:** Yes. **Pay Phone:** No. **Rest Rooms and Showers:** Yes. **Fuel:** No. **Propane:** No. **Internal Roads:** Gravel. **RV Service:** No. **Market:** 0.5 mi. east or west. **Restaurant:** In front. **General Store:** No. **Vending:** Yes. **Swimming:** No. **Playground:** Yes. **Activities:** Tours of KC, visiting museums, golf, theater, shopping. **Nearby Attractions:** Harry S. Truman Coutroom & Office, Kansas City. **Additional Information:** Independence Dept. of Tourism, (816) 325-7111.

Restrictions

Pets: On leash, cleaned up after, keep indoors. **Fires:** In grills. **Alcoholic Beverages:** At sites. **Vehicle Maximum Length:** None.

To Get There

From Hwy. I-70 (Exit 10), turn north onto Sterling Ave. and go 0.2 mi. Turn right onto Hwy. 40 and go 0.8 mi. Turn left at the sign into the entrance. (Beware of the hard curb.) The office is on the left.

KIRKSVILLE
Thousand Hills State Park

Rte. 3 Box 126, Kirksville 63501. T: (660) 665-6995; www.mostateparks.com.

RV ★★★★ Tent ★★★★

Beauty: ★★★★ Site Privacy: ★★★
Spaciousness: ★★★ Quiet: ★★★★
Security: ★★★★ Cleanliness: ★★★★
Insect Control: ★★★★ Facilities: ★★★

Although there are currently three campgrounds in this state park, campground 2 is slated to be remodeled and will be closed in 2002. Campground 1 has grassy sites (mostly back-ins) that back to forest. This is a large, popular place, and sites go quickly during high season. They range from 30 feet to more than 80 feet. Sites 28–35 are located on a separate road from the others, affording a little more privacy. Sites 36, 48, 50, 57, and 58 are paved pull-throughs. Site 66 is closest to the bathhouse. Campground 3 is smaller and not quite as popular.However, with the closing of campground 2, it is likely to be just as packed. Site 13 is located right at the entrance, which makes it less desirable. Contrary to this, sites 15–17 are located on a separate road and are thus more private. Site 18 is a large pull-through. The rest room here is less developed than the bathhouse in campground 1, but still decent. This campground makes a wonderful destination for RVers and campers who wish to recreate on the water or learn about the local natural environment.

Basics

Operated By: Missouri Dept. of Natural Resources. **Open:** All year (limited services Nov.–Mar.). **Site Assignment:** First come, first served, no reservations. **Registration:** Ranger will collect fees at site. **Fee:** RV $15 (full), $12 (water, electric); tent $7; checks, but no credit cards. **Parking:** At site.

Facilities

Number of RV Sites: 50. **Number of Tent-Only Sites:** 8. **Hookups:** Electric (30, 50 amp). **Each Site:** Picnic table, grill, lantern post. **Dump Station:** Yes. **Laundry:** Yes. **Pay Phone:** Yes. **Rest Rooms and Showers:** Yes. **Fuel:** No. **Propane:** No. **Internal Roads:** Paved. **RV Service:** No. **Market:** Junction of Hwy. 6 & 63. **Restaurant:** Junction of Hwy. 6 & 63. **General Store:** Yes. **Vending:** Yes. **Swimming:** Yes (lake). **Playground:** Yes. **Other:** Amphitheater, cabins, petroglyphs, picnic area, mountain-biking trails, boat rentals, fishing licenses. **Activities:** Fishing, boating, swimming, hiking, mountain biking, nature activities. **Nearby Attractions:** Still National Osteopathic Museum, Big Creek, Sugar Creek. **Additional Information:** Kirksville Area Chamber of Commerce: (660) 665-3766.

Restrictions

Pets: On leash, cleaned up after. **Fires:** In grills. **Alcoholic Beverages:** At sites. **Vehicle Maximum Length:** None.

To Get There

From the junction of Hwy. 63 and Hwy. 6, turn west onto Hwy. 6 and go 3.3 mi. Turn left onto Hwy. 157. Go 1.7 mi. to first campground.

LAMAR

Lamar KOA

240 Southeast 1st Ln., Lamar 64739. T: (417) 682-9600; F: (417) 682-3504; www.camplamar.com; lamarmo@mykoa.com.

RV ★★★★ Tent ★★★

Beauty: ★★★ Site Privacy: ★★★★★
Spaciousness: ★★★★★ Quiet: ★★★★
Security: ★★★★ Cleanliness: ★★★★★
Insect Control: ★★★★ Facilities: ★★★★★

Although Lamar KOA is surrounded to the south and east by woods, there are few trees within the campground itself. Those that are inside the campground are young and offer little shade. All sites are grassy pull-throughs with gravel drives, averaging 75 × 50 feet—a decent size by any standard. Sites with the best views of the woods and the pond are 9, 16, 20, and 25. Site 9, in the southeast corner, is the overall nicest, being closest to the pond and furthest from the entrance and pool traffic. Tent spaces are completely open—no shade at all. The sites are crushed gravel pads that include a lantern pole. There is a very nice kitchen (and grills) in the pavilion for tenters' use. The rest rooms and showers are individual units by the pool. They are modern and extremely clean and spacious—some of the nicest rest rooms that can be found on the road. Lamar KOA is a relatively new campground, and some work is still underway. It promises to be an excellent stay in the future. One consideration to keep in mind, especially if travelling in summer, is the lack of shade trees.

Basics

Operated By: Bill & Shari Emmerling. **Open:** Mar. 1–Nov. 1. **Site Assignment:** Depending on site availability; credit card required for reservation, 24-hours cancellation policy. **Registration:** In office; late arrivals use drop box. **Fee:** RV $25 (full), $22 (water, electric), $20 (electric); tent $18; checks for small amounts, V, MC, AE, D. **Parking:** At site.

Facilities

Number of RV Sites: 31. **Number of Tent-Only Sites:** 6. **Hookups:** Water, sewer, electric (50 amp). **Each Site:** Picnic table, fire pit. **Dump Station:** Yes. **Laundry:** Yes. **Pay Phone:** Yes. **Rest Rooms and Showers:** Yes. **Fuel:** No. **Propane:** Yes. **Internal Roads:** Gravel. **RV Service:** No. **Market:** 3 mi. north. **Restaurant:** 2 mi. north. **General Store:** Yes. **Vending:** Yes. **Swimming:** Pool. **Playground:** Yes. **Other:** Fishing pond, pavilion w/ kitchen, communal fire ring. **Activities:** Volleyball, fishing. **Nearby Attractions:** Harry S. Truman Birthplace State Historic Site. **Additional Information:** Lamar Chamber of Commerce, (417) 682-3595.

Restrictions

Pets: On leash, cleaned up after, not in cabins. **Fires:** In grills. **Alcoholic Beverages:** At sites. **Vehicle Maximum Length:** None.

To Get There

From the junction of Hwy. I-44 and Hwy. 160, turn east onto Hwy. 160 and go to first set of traffic lights. Trun right onto Outer Rd. and go 1.9 mi. Turn left at the sign into the entrance.

LEBANON

Lebanon KOA

18376 Campground Rd., Phillipsburg 65722. T: (800) KOA-3424 or (417) 532-3422; F: (417) 588-7084; www.koa.com; lebanonkoa@socket.net.

★★★★ ★★★★

Beauty: ★★★★ Site Privacy: ★★★★
Spaciousness: ★★★ Quiet: ★★★★
Security: ★★★★ Cleanliness: ★★★★★
Insect Control: ★★★★ Facilities: ★★★★★

Long pull-throughs are the name of the game in this campground. There is no need to unhook any towed vehicles, as there is sure to be a site that can accommodate the longest rigs on the road. Sites 16–19B (RV sites start at 16) are 70 feet long, while the neighboring ones (in the 20s–40s) average 75 feet. Sites 50–52 are the "big boys" of the campground, measuring 100–120 feet. Site 52—the longest and very well shaded—is the nicest in the entire campground. Site 50 is unshaded and therefore less desirable. Tent sites have crushed gravel inside a tent pad surrounded by logs, and nice thick grass. Unfortunately, there is little shade offered to tent sites. (Tent sites T1–T3, along the entrance road, are shaded, but receive all of the incoming and outgoing traffic from the campground.) Billing itself as an "overnight park," this campground with easy on/off access from the highway offers much more than what that label might suggest. In fact, it's nice enough for an extended stay for either RVers or tenters.

Basics

Operated By: Dennis & Kelly Szymanski. **Open:** Mar. 31–Dec. 31. **Site Assignment:** Upon registration; credit card required for reservation, 24-hours cancellation policy (by 4 p.m. the day before). **Registration:** In office; late arrivals use drop box. **Fee:** RV $26 (full), $21 (water, electric); tent $18; checks, V, MC, D. **Parking:** At site.

Facilities

Number of RV Sites: 48. **Number of Tent-Only Sites:** 5. **Hookups:** Water, sewer, electric (50 amp). **Each Site:** Picnic table, fire pit. **Dump Station:** Yes. **Laundry:** Yes. **Pay Phone:** Yes. **Rest Rooms and Showers:** Yes. **Fuel:** No. **Propane:** Yes. **Internal Roads:** Gravel. **RV Service:** Next door. **Market:** 7 mi. east. **Restaurant:** 4 mi. east. **General Store:** Yes. **Vending:** No. **Swimming:** Pool. **Playground:** Yes. **Other:** Cabins, video games, modem, fishing hole. **Activities:** Basketball, volleyball, ping pong, breakfasts & dinners, ice cream socials on weekends, fishing. **Nearby Attractions:** Branson, Springfield, Mansfield, Meramec Caverns, Laura Ingalls Wilder Home, Bennett Springs State Park. **Additional Information:** Lebanon Chamber of Commerce, (417) 588-3256.

Restrictions

Pets: On leash, cleaned up after. **Fires:** In grills. **Alcoholic Beverages:** At sites. **Vehicle Maximum Length:** None.

To Get There

From Hwy. I-44 (Exit 123), turn south and take the first left after the highway ramp onto Outer Rd. East. Go 3 mi. and turn right at the sign into the entrance.

LESTERVILLE

Parks Bluff Campground

P.O. Box 24, Lesterville 63654. T: (573) 637-2290; F: (573) 637-2342.

★★★ ★★★★

Beauty: ★★★★ Site Privacy: ★★★
Spaciousness: ★★★ Quiet: ★★★★★
Security: ★★★★★ Cleanliness: ★★★★
Insect Control: ★★★★ Facilities: ★★★

Campers looking for fun on the river or in an ATV have come to the right place, but those who are looking for a quiet time should probably look elsewhere. (One indication of this is that quiet time begins at midnight.) Sites 1–4 and A–K are located in an open field surrounded by bushes and trees. These sites can accommodate a rig of any size, but cannot be pulled through unless the campground were completely empty. Most other electric sites are in a forested patch just off the Mud Pit (used for 4-wheeling). Sites 23–30 are 60-foot back-ins adjacent to the pit. Across the internal road are loads of tenting spaces. These are mostly dirt with some grass, and back thick vegetation. Many of the sites have short paths that lead to the river. There is also unlimited tenting possible along the southeast edge of the property by the river's edge. The restroom building is primitive, but the facilities are decent; the three showers are all open. Parks Bluff is geared more towards tenters than RVs (view the lack of hookups other than electric), but anyone in search of fun on the river will enjoy their stay here.

Basics

Operated By: Jayme Parks. **Open:** May–Sept. **Site Assignment:** RV sites upon registration, tent sites first come, first served; credit card or check deposit for reservation, 7-days cancellation policy. **Registration:** In office; late arrivals check in w/ guard at gate. **Fee:** $3 adult, $2 child, $3 hookup; checks, V, MC, D. **Parking:** At site.

Facilities

Number of RV Sites: 30. **Number of Tent-Only Sites:** Undesignated sites. **Hookups:** Electric (30 amp). **Each Site:** Picnic table, fire pit. **Dump Station:** No. **Laundry:** No. **Pay Phone:** Yes. **Rest Rooms and Showers:** Yes. **Fuel:** No. **Propane:** No. **Internal Roads:** Dirt. **RV Service:** No. **Market:** 9 mi. to Centerville. **Restaurant:** Less than 1 mi. west. **General Store:** Yes. **Vending:** No. **Swimming:** Yes (river). **Playground:** No. **Activities:** Floating, 4-wheeling, volleyball. **Nearby Attractions:** Black River, Johnsons Shut-Ins State Park, Taum Sauk State Park. **Additional Information:** Missouri Dept. of Natural Resources, (800) 334-6946.

Restrictions

Pets: On leash, cleaned up after. **Fires:** In grills. **Alcoholic Beverages:** At sites, no glass. **Vehicle Maximum Length:** None. **Other:** No vehicles in river.

To Get There

From the junction of Hwy. 49 North and Hwy. 21/49/72, turn east onto Hwy. 21/49/72 and go 2.8 mi. Turn right at the sign into the entrance.

LIBERTY

Miller's Kampark

145 1/2 North Stewart Rd., Liberty 64068. T: (800) 272-7578 or (816) 781-7724.

RV: ★★★ Tent: n/a

Beauty: ★★	Site Privacy: ★★★
Spaciousness: ★★	Quiet: ★★
Security: ★★★★	Cleanliness: ★★★
Insect Control: ★★★★	Facilities: ★★★

A number of towns in the Kansas City area have campgrounds. This one has the advantage of being relatively close to the city; however, it is really only an overnighter, and not a great place for tenters. (Tent sites are possible in 25 and 26, which are gravel sites; 25 is at least shaded.) The inner strip in the park has 60-foot pull-throughs. A strip along the south has 45-foot back-ins that back to trees and a fence. There are 30-foot back-ins on the east side of the park as well as a strip along the north side. The laundry facility is clean and roomie, and the rest rooms and showers are somewhat primitive but clean. The floors are untrated cement, and the stalls only contain half doors. This RV park is a middling stop for RVers, but tenters will want to move on. There is some amount of choice in the area, including campgrounds in Independence, Kansas City, and Oak Grove, that may be more suited for tenters.

Basics

Operated By: Richard & Barb Gercken. **Open:** All year. **Site Assignment:** Upon registration; credit card required for reservation, 24-hours cancellation policy. **Registration:** In office; late arrivals use drop box. **Fee:** RV $21 (50 amp), $20 (30 amp), $18 (water, electric); checks, V, MC, D. **Parking:** At site.

Facilities

Number of RV Sites: 48. **Number of Tent-Only Sites:** 0. **Hookups:** Water, sewer, electric (30, 50 amp). **Each Site:** Picnic tables. **Dump Station:** Yes. **Laundry:** Yes. **Pay Phone:** Yes. **Rest Rooms and Showers:** Yes. **Fuel:** No. **Propane:** Yes. **Internal Roads:** Gravel. **RV Service:** No. **Market:** 0.25 mi. west. **Restaurant:** 0.25 mi. west. **General Store:** Yes. **Vending:** Yes. **Swimming:** Pool. **Playground:** Yes. **Other:** Rec hall, close to Wal-Mart. **Activities:** Basketball, swimming, horseshoes. **Nearby Attractions:** Kansas City, Historic Liberty Jail, Jesse James Bank Museum, casinos, Worlds of Fun. **Additional Information:** CVB of Greater Kansas City, (800) 767-7700, (816) 221-5242.

Restrictions

Pets: On leash, cleaned up after. **Fires:** In grills. **Alcoholic Beverages:** At sites. **Vehicle Maximum Length:** None.

To Get There

From Hwy. I-35 (Exit 17), turn south onto Hwy. 291 and go 1 mi. Turn right onto Stewart Rd. and go 0.25 mi. Turn left, then right at the sign into the entrance.

MACON

Long Branch Lake State Park

30174 Visitor Center Rd., Macon 63552. T: (660) 385-2108.

RV: ★★★★ Tent: ★★★★★

Beauty: ★★★★★	Site Privacy: ★★★★
Spaciousness: ★★★★	Quiet: ★★★★★
Security: ★★★★★	Cleanliness: ★★★★
Insect Control: ★★★★	Facilities: ★★★★

Sites in this campground are divided between electric and primitive. Those with electrical hookups are numbered 1–40, and those without any hookups, 41–83. Most sites are 65-foot back-ins. Sites located on the outside of the loop are open, while those on the inside are more forested. Site 1 is right next to the entrance, 10 is next to the restrooms. Sites 12 and 13 and 19 and 20 are doubles. The nicest site is 52, which is located at the end of a roundabout, surrounded by lush vegetation, and offers views of the lake. Site 53, also secluded, is adjacent to a lake access area, and 78–80 are next to a boat access area. Sites 54–62 are walk-in tent sites hidden in thick woods. Site 30 is a long (120 feet) pull-through located next to the entrance for easy access. Site 40, all on its own, is located near the entrance and the RV dump. The rest rooms and showers are clean, roomy, and modern. This is a great campground for campers who like to get out into the wild a bit, but it also offers modern amenities for maximum comfort.

Basics

Operated By: Missouri Dept. of Natural Resources. **Open:** All year (limited facilities Nov.–Mar. 31). **Site Assignment:** First come, first served; no reservations. **Registration:** On-season, fees collected at sites; off-season, register in visitor center; late arrivals select available site & pay in the morning. **Fee:** RV $15 (full), $12 (water, electric); tent $7; checks, V, MC, D. **Parking:** At site.

Facilities

Number of RV Sites: 40. **Number of Tent-Only Sites:** 43. **Hookups:** Water, electric (30 amp). **Each Site:** Picnic table, fire pit, lantern pole. **Dump Station:** Yes. **Laundry:** No. **Pay Phone:** No. **Rest Rooms and Showers:** Yes. **Fuel:** No. **Propane:** No. **Internal Roads:** Paved. **RV Service:** No. **Market:** 4.5 mi. east. **Restaurant:** 3 mi. east. **General Store:** Yes. **Vending:** Yes. **Swimming:** Yes (lake). **Playground:** Yes. **Activities:** Fishing, boating, swimming, hiking. **Nearby Attractions:** Thomas Hill Reservoir. **Additional Information:** Macon Economic Development Corporation, (660) 385-5627.

Restrictions

Pets: On 6-ft. leash, cleaned up after. **Fires:** In grills. **Alcoholic Beverages:** At sites. **Vehicle Maximum Length:** None. **Other:** Max. 6 people/site.

To Get There

From the junction of Hwy. 63 and Hwy. 36, turn west onto Hwy. 36 and go 2.1 mi. Exit to the right at the sign, then take the first left onto Visitor Center Rd. Go 2.6 mi., then turn right into the campground.

MARSHALL

Lazy Days Campground

Rte. 1 Box 66, Marshall 65340. T: (660) 879-4411; F: (660) 879-4396.

RV ★★★ Tent ★★★

Beauty: ★★★	Site Privacy: ★★★
Spaciousness:0★★★	Quiet: ★★
Security: ★★★★	Cleanliness: ★★★★
Insect Control: ★★★★	Facilities: ★★★

This rural campground is surrounded on three sides by woods, with some residences to the north, and some commercial buildings to the southwest. There are three sections: the 30-amp sites (1–20), the 50-amp sites (21–35), and the tent area. Sites 1–4 are 60-foot pull-throughs in the 30-amp section, site 5 is a little shorter (50 feet). Sites 6–14, 17, and 18 are 75-foot pull-throughs, while 19 and 20 are shorter (50 feet). Sites 8, 12, 14, 16, and 17 have nice shade trees. The 50-amp section is a large open field that can accommodate rigs of any size. (Sites 31 and 32 share a shed that limits them to about 50 feet.) All of these sites are pull-throughs. The tent sites are likewise in a huge open field. While it offers lush grass to all tent campers, there are only two trees and two picnic tables. The rest rooms are fairly clean, but the showers are much less comfortable—the flaking paint and stained walls during our visit were a bit of a shock. The cement building that houses them looks somewhat worn. As it is, this campground is adequate, though not very quiet.

Basics

Operated By: The Younger Family. **Open:** All year. **Site Assignment:** Depending on site availability; verbal reservations OK. **Registration:** In office; late arrivals use drop box. **Fee:** RV $15 (full), tent $10; checks, V, MC, AE, D. **Parking:** At site.

Facilities

Number of RV Sites: 35. **Number of Tent-Only Sites:** 55. **Hookups:** Water, sewer, electric (30, 50 amp). **Each Site:** Picnic table, grill. **Dump Station:** Yes. **Laundry:** Yes. **Pay Phone:** Yes. **Rest Rooms and Showers:** Yes. **Fuel:** No. **Propane:**

Yes. **Internal Roads:** Gravel. **RV Service:** No. **Market:** 8 mi. north. **Restaurant:** Onsite. **General Store:** Yes. **Vending:** Yes. **Swimming:** Pool. **Playground:** Yes. **Other:** Modem, rec room, video games, fish pond, breakfasts. **Activities:** Fishing, basketball, Fri. night prime rib night. **Nearby Attractions:** Van Meter State Park. **Additional Information:** Marshall Chamber of Commerce, (660) 886-3324.

RESTRICTIONS

Pets: On leash, cleaned up after. **Fires:** In grills. **Alcoholic Beverages:** At sites. **Vehicle Maximum Length:** None.

TO GET THERE

From Hwy. I-70 (Exit 78B), follow off-ramp onto Hwy. 65, and take the first right. Go 0.6 mi. and turn right at the sign into the entrance.

MOBERLY
Thompson Campground

Rothwell Park Rd., Moberly 65270. T: (660) 670-4522 or (660) 263-6757.

RV ★★★	Tent ★★★
Beauty: ★★★★	Site Privacy: ★★★
Spaciousness: ★★★	Quiet: ★★★★★
Security: ★★★★★	Cleanliness: ★★★
Insect Control: ★★★★	Facilities: ★★★

This park has RV sites in a strip of 12 spaces, with two RVs designated per site. None of the sites are numbered. Sounds confusing? The setup is apparently just as confusing to the people who run the park, as they are not even sure of the number of RVs that the park can accommodate. However, this is a nice little park surrounded on three sides by woods, and is worth the minor hassle the site numbers may cause. Although sites are 90 feet in length, the slope from which nearly all of them suffer cuts the usable length down to about 70 feet. (Sites to the south are more level, but are adjacent to stored equipment and piles of miscellaneous stuff.) The tenting area is just as confusing as the RV section. In fact, there is no indication anywhere of the location of the tent area. It is, for the record, just to the north of the internal road, facing the RV sites. The thick grass and tree coverage make for comfortable camping, but the primitive toilet and lack of sink and showers is a severe drawback for tenters—as are the almost inescapable security lights. (Still, at this price, who can complain?) Police and ranger patrols ensure that the campground is secure throughout the night. Thompson is nicer for RVs than for tents, although the cheap price makes it worthwhile for any camper on a budget.

BASICS

Operated By: City of Moberly. **Open:** All year. **Site Assignment:** First come, first served; no reservations. **Registration:** Wait for ranger to collect fees. **Fee:** $8 (water, electric), $3 tent; checks. **Parking:** At site.

FACILITIES

Number of RV Sites: 24. **Number of Tent-Only Sites:** Undesignated sites. **Hookups:** Water, electric (30 amp). **Each Site:** Picnic table. **Dump Station:** Yes. **Laundry:** No. **Pay Phone:** No. **Rest Rooms and Showers:** Rest rooms; no shower. **Fuel:** No. **Propane:** No. **Internal Roads:** Gravel. **RV Service:** No. **Market:** 1 mi. northeast. **Restaurant:** 1 mi. northeast. **General Store:** No. **Vending:** No. **Swimming:** Pool. **Playground:** Yes. **Other:** Jogging trails, group shelters, lake, pool, recreation field, boat ramp. **Activities:** Fishing, boating, swimming, field sports, basketball, archery. **Nearby Attractions:** Mark Twain Birthplace State Historic Area. **Additional Information:** Chamber of Commerce Moberly Area, (660) 263-6070.

RESTRICTIONS

Pets: On leash, cleaned up after. **Fires:** In grills. **Alcoholic Beverages:** At sites, subject to public drinking ordinance if outside sites. **Vehicle Maximum Length:** None.

TO GET THERE

From the junction of Hwy. 63 and Hwy. 24, turn west on Hwy. 24 and go 3 mi. Turn right onto Rothwell Park Rd. Turn right at the sign into the entrance.

MONETT
Pine Trails RV Ranch

40 Hwy. 60, Monett 65708. T: (417) 235-8682.

RV ★★★★	Tent n/a
Beauty: ★★★★	Site Privacy: ★★★★★
Spaciousness: ★★★★	Quiet: ★★★★
Security: ★★★★★	Cleanliness: ★★★★★
Insect Control: ★★★★	Facilities: ★★

This small RV park in the pine trees has 80 × 33-foot pull-throughs laid out in two rows. To the northeast is forest, and to the northwest are open fields creating a very quiet and peaceful atmosphere. Site 1 is slightly easier to get in and out of. (This is true of the lower numbers in general.) Site 21 has a larger grassy area than other sites, but, in general, all the sites are of a uniform quality. Unabashedly oriented towards older folks, this campground provides a very low-key and quiet place to camp. Note the lack of rest rooms, which disqualifies tents and RVs that are not self-contained.

Basics

Operated By: Frank & Sandy Theser. **Open:** All year. **Site Assignment:** Upon registration; verbal reservations OK. **Registration:** In office; late arrivals use drop box. **Fee:** RV $19 (50 amp), $17 (30 amp); no credits cards, but checks. **Parking:** At site.

Facilities

Number of RV Sites: 21. **Number of Tent-Only Sites:** 0. **Hookups:** Water, sewer, electric (30, 50 amp). **Each Site:** Picnic table. **Dump Station:** Yes. **Laundry:** No. **Pay Phone:** No. **Rest Rooms and Showers:** No. **Fuel:** No. **Propane:** No. **Internal Roads:** Gravel. **RV Service:** No. **Market:** 3 mi. west. **Restaurant:** 3 mi. west. **General Store:** No. **Vending:** No. **Swimming:** No. **Playground:** No. **Other:** Modem, picnic area, close to attractions, pet walk area. **Activities:** Hiking, shows (in Branson), fishing, boating. **Nearby Attractions:** Roaring River State Park, Mark Twain National Forest, Branson, Springfield. **Additional Information:** Monett Chamber of Commerce, (417) 235-7919.

Restrictions

Pets: On leash, cleaned up after. **Fires:** In common fire ring. **Alcoholic Beverages:** At sites. **Vehicle Maximum Length:** None. **Other:** Keep satellite dish on gravel.

To Get There

From the junction of Hwy. 37 and Hwy. 60, turn east onto Hwy. 60 and go 3 mi. Turn left at the sign into the entrance.

MOUNTAIN GROVE

Missouri Park Campground

2325 Missouri Park Dr., Mountain Grove 65711.
T: (417) 926-4104 or (417) 926-6237; mopark@getgoin.net.

RV: ★★★★ Tent: ★★★★

Beauty: ★★★★	Site Privacy: ★★★★
Spaciousness: ★★★	Quiet: ★★★★
Security: ★★★★	Cleanliness: ★★★★
Insect Control: ★★★★	Facilities: ★★★★

This campground has a combination of overnight RV spaces and mobile homes. Sites 1–9 are right at the entrance. These are 90-foot gravel pull-throughs just south of the mobile-home area. Site 2 has some shade, but the others in this strip are all open. The rest of the RV sites lie west, in a forested area, with sites 1–10 being the most forested. Sites 2, 4, and 6 are 95–120-foot pull-throughs; 16 and 18 are also very long. The back-ins in this area range from 35 to 45 feet in length. (Most of the sites are not numbered, which makes it difficult to find the proper site, especially in the nothern part of the loop, 12–18.) The tenting area is a large grassy field that can take any number of tents. The grass cover is healthy, but because the area is slightly sloped, tenting in some areas becomes difficult; there is also a lack of shade in the entire field. The rest rooms are clean and comfortable, with air conditioning, new countertops, and brand-new tile laid on the floor. A woodsy, comfortable campground.

Basics

Operated By: Paul & Christine Gasperson. **Open:** All year (limited services Jan.–Feb.). **Site Assignment:** Depending on site availability; verbal reservations OK. **Registration:** In office; late arrivals use drop box. **Fee:** RV $20 (full), $15 (water, electric); tent $12; no credits cards, but checks. **Parking:** At site.

Facilities

Number of RV Sites: 30. **Number of Tent-Only Sites:** Undesignated sites. **Hookups:** Water, sewer, electric (30, 50 amp). **Dump Station:** No (sewer at all sites). **Laundry:** Yes. **Pay Phone:** Yes. **Rest Rooms and Showers:** Yes. **Fuel:** No. **Propane:** No. **Internal Roads:** Gravel. **RV Service:** No. **Market:** 3 mi. to Exit 95. **Restaurant:** 3 mi. to Exit 95. **General Store:** Yes. **Vending:** No.

Swimming: Pool. **Playground:** No. **Other:** Fishing lake, game room w/ pool table. **Activities:** Swimming, fishing, hiking. **Nearby Attractions:** Laura Ingles Wilder's Home, Mark Twain National Forest. **Additional Information:** Mountain Grove Chamber of Commerce, (417) 926-4135.

RESTRICTIONS

Pets: On leash, cleaned up after. **Fires:** In grills. **Alcoholic Beverages:** At sites. **Vehicle Maximum Length:** None.

TO GET THERE

From Hwy. 65 (Business 60 Hwy. Exit, which is Mountain Grove's westernmost exit), go north over the highway overpass and take the service road 1.2 mi. Turn right onto Missouri Park Dr. and then left into the campground.

NOEL

Elk River Floats Wayside Campground

P.O. Box 546, Noel 64854. T: (417) 475-3230 or (417) 475-3561; www.missouri2000.net/wayside; wayside@netins.net.

RV ★★★ Tent ★★★★

Beauty: ★★★★★	Site Privacy: ★★
Spaciousness: ★★★	Quiet: ★★★
Security: ★★★★★	Cleanliness: ★★★
Insect Control: ★★★★	Facilities: ★★★

The "open camping" policy of this campground means that once you pay for a site, you can go and pick any site you want to occupy. Therefore, sites are not numbered, as they are not assigned. You can also camp as close to the water as you like. The first designated sites are near the office, on the southwest edge. These are gravel/grass full hookup sites with some shade. Open-ended, they can take rigs of any size but are restricted to a tight 16 -foot width. Sites along the western edge are the best—level, grassy, and shady. The downside is that the highway lies just on the other side of a wooded strip from these sites. Other full hookup sites are found on the penninsula. They are rather open and receive a fair amount of passing traffic, but are close to the water. The tip of the penninsula is a more secluded area that is great for such groups as family reunions. Tenters can pitch a tent anywhere they like, right up to the water's edge, if they prefer. The rest rooms are a little rough, made of cement and wood and lacking both windows and external doors. Showers are located only in the red office building. These are spacious cement stalls that remind one of YMCA showers—minus the lockers. Elk River is a water fun–oriented campground, geared more towards a younger crowd. It is definitely a destination for groups, although couples will also enjoy a stay here. Those looking for a quiet time should look elsewhere. One note of caution: the highway coming into the park has overhanging cliffs that could present a danger to large rigs.

BASICS

Operated By: Rod & Rence Lett. **Open:** Apr.–Oct. **Site Assignment:** First come, first served; no reservations. **Registration:** In office; late arrivals select site & pay in the morning during the week, see person at the gate on weekends. **Fee:** RV $16 (full), $6 person, $3 electric, $6 RV hookups; V, MC, D, no checks. **Parking:** At site.

FACILITIES

Number of RV Sites: 98. **Number of Tent-Only Sites:** Undesignated sites. **Hookups:** Water, sewer, electric (30 amp). **Each Site:** Picnic tables at some sites. **Dump Station:** Yes. **Laundry:** No. **Pay Phone:** At motel next door. **Rest Rooms and Showers:** Yes. **Fuel:** No. **Propane:** No. **Internal Roads:** Gravel. **RV Service:** No. **Market:** 0.25 mi. east. **Restaurant:** 0.25 mi. west. **General Store:** No. **Vending:** No. **Swimming:** Yes (river). **Playground:** Yes. **Other:** Boat rentals, paddleboats, tubes. **Activities:** Floating, boating, swimming, fishing. **Nearby Attractions:** Grand Lake (OK), Bluff Dwellers Cave, Branson, Table Rock Lake, Bass Pro Shop. **Additional Information:** Joplin Area Chamber of Commerce, (417) 624-1996.

RESTRICTIONS

Pets: On leash, cleaned up after, prefer no large breeds. **Fires:** In grills. **Alcoholic Beverages:** At sites, no glass or styrofoam on river. **Vehicle Maximum Length:** None. **Other:** No fireworks.

TO GET THERE

From the junction of Hwy. 59 and Hwy. 90, turn wast onto Hwy. 90 and go 0.1 mi. Take first right into campground.

OAK GROVE

Kansas City East KOA

303 Northeast 3rd St. P.O. Box 191, Oak Grove 64075. T: (800) 562-7507 or (816) 690-6660; F: (816) 690-6660; www.koa.com; kckoa@yahoo.com.

RV ★★★★ Tent ★★★

Beauty: ★★★ Site Privacy: ★★★
Spaciousness: ★★★ Quiet: ★★★
Security: ★★★★ Cleanliness: ★★★★
Insect Control: ★★★★ Facilities: ★★★★

Under new management, this campground may introduce new services or procedures than those described below. As of today, it has several rows of large pull-throughs: 1–10 are unshaded 70-foot sites, 18–26 are unshaded 54-foot sites, and 27–33 are shaded 90-foot sites. Sites 42–47 are head-to-head pull-throughs along the east edge. These sites are well shaded, but as a consequence of being doubles, they offer less room and privacy. Sites 54–68 along the south edge are back-ins that back to trees and other vegetation. These are mostly well-shaded sites. Sites 71–73 are located in the shaded northwest corner and are comfortable and grassy. Sites T1 and T2 are located in the southeast corner, and back to a hedge. They have decent grass and cool shade. Other tent sites (38–41) are located to the north of sites 42–43. The rest rooms and showers are somewhat old but still clean and comfortable. Although slightly better for RVers than for tents, this campground is a decent stay with loads of facilities for all.

Basics

Operated By: Mary & Melvin Lueck. **Open:** All year. **Site Assignment:** Depending on site availability; credit card required for reservation but not charged. **Registration:** In office; late arrivals use drop box in laundry. **Fee:** RV $28 (full), $25 (water, electric); tent $20; checks, V, MC, D. **Parking:** At site.

Facilities

Number of RV Sites: 73. **Number of Tent-Only Sites:** 14. **Hookups:** Water, sewer, electric (30, 50 amp). **Each Site:** Picnic table, fire pit. **Dump Station:** Yes. **Laundry:** Yes. **Pay Phone:** Yes. **Rest Rooms and Showers:** Yes. **Fuel:** No. **Propane:** Yes. **Internal Roads:** Gravel. **RV Service:** No. **Market:** Less than 1 mi. southwest. **Restaurant:** Less than 1 mi. southwest. **General Store:** Yes. **Vending:** Yes. **Swimming:** Pool. **Playground:** Yes. **Other:** Mini golf, dog walk, cabins, game room, pool table, horseshoes. **Activities:** Volleyball, basketball, swimming. **Nearby Attractions:** Worlds of Fun, Truman Library, Truman Home, casinos. **Additional Information:** CVB of Greater Kansas City, (800) 767-7700, (816) 221-5242.

Restrictions

Pets: On leash, cleaned up after. **Fires:** In grills. **Alcoholic Beverages:** At sites. **Vehicle Maximum Length:** None.

To Get There

From Hwy. I-70 (Exit 28), turn north onto H and go 0.25 mi. Turn right onto 3rd St. and go 2 blocks to the entrance on the right.

OZARK

Ozark RV Park

320 North 20th St., Ozark 65721. T: (417) 581-3203; chickenfoot@pcis.net.

RV ★★ Tent n/a

Beauty: ★ Site Privacy: ★★★
Spaciousness: ★★★ Quiet: ★★★
Security: ★★★ Cleanliness: ★★★★
Insect Control: ★★★★ Facilities: ★

Ozark RV park is surrounded by commercial development, which unfortunately detracts heavily from the environment. These unshaded sites are all grassy pull-throughs ranging from 60 feet (21–28) to 70 feet (1–14), laid out in three rows. As the park is surrounded by roads on three sides, the least desirable sites are closest to the edges. Better sites are somewhere in the middle (9–13). Site 14 has the largest strip of grass, but is closest to the external road to the south. There are no rest rooms or showers, so self-contained vehicles are the only kind possible. The one advantage that the park has is proximity to restaurants and other commercial sites. As such, it makes a fair overnight stop.

Basics

Operated By: Jeanne Siler. **Open:** All year. **Site Assignment:** Upon registration; credit card required for reservation, 24-hours cancellation policy. **Registration:** Use drop box. **Fee:** RV $18 (full), $15 (water, electric). **Parking:** At site.

Facilities

Number of RV Sites: 28. **Number of Tent-Only Sites:** 0. **Hookups:** Water, sewer, electric (30, 50 amp), cable. **Dump Station:** No. **Laundry:** No. **Pay Phone:** No. **Rest Rooms and Showers:** No. **Fuel:** No. **Propane:** No. **Internal Roads:** Gravel. **RV Service:** No. **Market:** Less than 0.5 mi. east. **Restaurant:** Less than 0.25 mi. east. **General Store:** No. **Vending:** Yes. **Swimming:** No. **Playground:** No. **Activities:** Musical shows, shopping, hiking. **Nearby Attractions:** Springfield, Branson, Mark Twain National Forest. **Additional Information:** Ozark Chamber of Commerce, (417) 581-6139.

Restrictions

Pets: On leash, cleaned up after. **Fires:** In grills. **Alcoholic Beverages:** At sites. **Vehicle Maximum Length:** None.

To Get There

From Hwy. 65 (Nixa/Hwy. 14 Exit), turn west onto Hwy. 14. Go through the light and take the first left, then an immediate left into the park.

PECULIAR

Peculiar Park Place

22901 Southeast Outer Rd., Peculiar 64078. T: (816) 779-6300; F: (816) 779-6303.

RV ★★★★★ | Tent n/a

Beauty: ★★★★ | Site Privacy: ★★★★
Spaciousness: ★★★★ | Quiet: ★★★
Security: ★★★★★ | Cleanliness: ★★★★★
Insect Control: ★★★★ | Facilities: ★★★★

Although only open since August 2000, this RV park is already a beautiful place to camp. The landscaping includes rocks, plants, trees, brick and wood on the office building, and a bricked patio and stenciled cement table for each site. Sites 1–10 are 75-foot pull-throughs that have a very nice view of the highway and the woods beyond. Sites 11 and 12 are located in a beautiful grassy spot with an attractive rock retaining wall behind, while 13–18 back to woods, also with very pleasant landscaping. Sites 19–28 are 90-foot unshaded pull-throughs that overlook sites 1–10 and share the same view. Sites 29–34 are 70-foot pull-throughs, 39–51 are 90-foot pull-throughs. Like 13–18, 35–38 also back to some nice woods. Planned improvements to the park include a paved road, as well as many recreation facilities. The rest rooms are absolutely top-notch—some of the best of any campground on the road. They are tiled, modern, and at least as comfortable as at home. Although tenters will have to find another place to camp, RVers would be well advised to mark this park on their itinerary. It is the nicest RV park in the Kansas City area, and is destined only to get better.

Basics

Operated By: Frosty & Gail. **Open:** All year. **Site Assignment:** Upon registration; verbal reservations OK. **Registration:** In office; late arrivals call phone number on door 24 hrs. **Fee:** RV $24 (50 amp), $22 (30 amp); checks OK, no credit cards. **Parking:** At site.

Facilities

Number of RV Sites: 61. **Number of Tent-Only Sites:** 0. **Hookups:** Water, sewer, electric (20, 30, 50 amp). **Each Site:** Picnic table, brick patio, fire pit. **Dump Station:** Yes. **Laundry:** Yes. **Pay Phone:** Yes. **Rest Rooms and Showers:** Yes. **Fuel:** No. **Propane:** Yes. **Internal Roads:** Gravel. **RV Service:** No. **Market:** 2 mi. west. **Restaurant:** 2 mi. west. **General Store:** No. **Vending:** No. **Swimming:** No. **Playground:** No. **Other:** Pet walk, gift shop, gazebo; planned facilities include pavilion, bandstand, putting green, dance floor, hot tub. **Activities:** Wildlife-viewing, hiking, potlucks. **Nearby Attractions:** Branson, Kansas City. **Additional Information:** CVB of Greater Kansas City, (800) 767-7700, (816) 221-5242.

Restrictions

Pets: On leash, cleaned up after, small or medium-sized dogs only. **Fires:** In grills. **Alcoholic Beverages:** At sites. **Vehicle Maximum Length:** None.

To Get There

From Hwy. 71 (Peculiar Exit), turn east onto J and take first right after highway off-ramp onto East Outer Rd. Go 1.5 mi. and turn left at the sign into the entrance.

PERRYVILLE

Perryville/Cape Girardeau KOA

89 KOA Ln., Perryville 63775. T: (800) 562-5304 or (573) 547-8303; F: (573) 547-7422; www.koa.com.

Beauty: ★★★★ Site Privacy: ★★★★
Spaciousness: ★★★ Quiet: ★★★
Security: ★★★★ Cleanliness: ★★★★★
Insect Control: ★★★★ Facilities: ★★★★★

Sites in this campground are arranged in rows A–K. All rows but A and B are hidden amongst shade trees which makes them more desirable. Row A contains 65-foot pull-throughs, rows B–J have 72-foot pull-throughs. Sites A1 and B1 are next to a residence, and C1 and D1 are next to an unattractive shed. Sites J4 and J5 and F1 have large pieces of electrical hardware that encroach on their space. Sites F8 and F9 and E9 and E10 are less shaded than others around them. Aside from these few shortcomings, you really can't go wrong with any of the sites in this park. For a more wilderness feel, try rows H–K. They are less developed and are further back in the woods. Row K has 52-foot back-ins that back to the forest surrounding the campground. The best sites in any row (especially C–J) are close to the middle (for example, 3–6). Tent sites are 45 feet wide, with plenty of depth, grassy, and forested—ideal for a tenter. The rest rooms are clean, spacious, and very private. This campground is comfortable for any style of camping and offers plenty to do. A great place to bring kids.

BASICS

Operated By: Mary Ann Abernathy. **Open:** All year. **Site Assignment:** Depending on site availability; verbal reservations OK. **Registration:** In office; late arrivals use drop box. **Fee:** RV $25 (full), $23 (water, electric); tent $19; checks, V, MC, AE, D. **Parking:** At site.

FACILITIES

Number of RV Sites: 92. **Number of Tent-Only Sites:** 10. **Hookups:** Water, sewer, electric (30, 50 amp). **Each Site:** Picnic table, grill. **Dump Station:** Yes. **Laundry:** Yes. **Pay Phone:** Yes. **Rest Rooms and Showers:** Yes. **Fuel:** No. **Propane:** Yes. **Internal Roads:** Gravel. **RV Service:** No. **Market:** 1 mi. east. **Restaurant:** 1 mi. east. **General Store:** Yes. **Vending:** Yes. **Swimming:** Pool. **Playground:** Yes. **Other:** Mini-golf, cabins, tipis, pavilions, pet walk, game room, sun deck, accommodates groups, fishing pond. **Activities:** Campfires, Sat. kids' events, Chirstmas in July, fishing (catch & release). **Nearby Attractions:** Hometown of Popeye the Sailor (Chester, IL), Hostoric St. Genevieve (oldest town west of the Mississippi), St. Mary's seminary. **Additional Information:** Perryville Chamber of Commerce, (573) 547-6062.

RESTRICTIONS

Pets: On leash, cleaned up after. **Fires:** In grills. **Alcoholic Beverages:** At sites. **Vehicle Maximum Length:** None. **Other:** Catch & release fishing.

TO GET THERE

From Hwy. I-55 (Exit 129), turn west onto Hwy. 51 and take the first right after the highway overpass (Outer Rd. North). Go 1.4 mi., then turn left at the sign into the entrance.

PLATTE CITY

Basswood Country Inn and RV Resort

15880 Interurban Rd., Platte City 64079. T: (800) 242-2775 or (816) 858-5556; F: (816) 858-5556; www.basswoodresort.com; info@basswoodresort.com.

RV ★★★★★ Tent ★★★★

Beauty: ★★★★ Site Privacy: ★★★
Spaciousness: ★★★ Quiet: ★★★★
Security: ★★★★★ Cleanliness: ★★★★★
Insect Control: ★★★★ Facilities: ★★★★★

Rarely does an RV "resort" live up to the excellence its name promises. However, Basswood is an exception; it's a smooth operation and a guaranteed great stay for both RVers and tenters. Besides the usual facilites, there are stocked fishing lakes, modem access, and room at the inn for those who need a change of pace. The two areas named "Tent A" and "Tent B" on the map handed out to you are misleading—these are all RV spaces. Tent A has 51-foot cement slabs in pull-throughs sites, while Tent B has 30-foot gravel back-ins. Of these sites, 8 and 21 are particularly well shaded. South of this is the real tenting area. These are grassy, shaded sites, very comfortable for tents. Site A is above the lake and across the interior road, B and C are right on the lake. These are the best tent sites, as they are closest to the lake and more isolated. Sites D–T are in rows to the west of this area. These are grass-and-dirt sites but lack any real shade. (There are only decorative trees and shrubs.) Sites D–L on the east side are 33 × 45 feet, while

M–T are 25 × 36 feet. The big-rig area is located to the extreme west, in a hollow surrounded by trees and dirt cliffs. Sites 75 and 76 are 35-foot back-ins, but the rest of the sites are much larger. Sites 77–97 and 120–129 are 75 × 30-foot gravel pull-throughs. The rest rooms are individual units with shower, toilet, and sink. They are all very modern, extremely comfortable, and with air conditioning.

Basics

Operated By: John Pottie. **Open:** All year. **Site Assignment:** Upon registration; credit card required for reservation, 7-days cancellation policy. **Registration:** In office; late arrivals knock on night window. **Fee:** RV $26 (full), tent $18. **Parking:** At site.

Facilities

Number of RV Sites: 58. **Number of Tent-Only Sites:** 20. **Hookups:** Water, sewer, electric (30, 50 amp), phone. **Each Site:** Picnic table, grill, fire pit. **Dump Station:** No (sewer at all sites). **Laundry:** Yes. **Pay Phone:** Yes. **Rest Rooms and Showers:** Yes. **Fuel:** No. **Propane:** Yes. **Internal Roads:** Gravel/paved. **RV Service:** On-call. **Market:** 6 mi. west. **Restaurant:** 5 mi. west. **General Store:** Yes. **Vending:** Yes. **Swimming:** Pool. **Playground:** Yes. **Other:** Athletic field, meeting facilities, fishing lakes, games, cottage, inn, trails, covered picnic shelter, modem. **Activities:** Fishing, boating, swimming, hiking. **Nearby Attractions:** Alldredge Orchards, Guy B. Park Conservation Area, Platte Falls Conservation Area, "Pumpkins, Etc.", Fulk's Tree Farm, Shiloh Springs Golf Course. **Additional Information:** Platte City Chamber of Commerce: www.plattecitymo.com.

Restrictions

Pets: On leash, cleaned up after. **Fires:** In grills. **Alcoholic Beverages:** At sites. **Vehicle Maximum Length:** None. **Other:** No washing or working on vehicles.

To Get There

From Hwy. I-29 (Exit 18), turn east onto Hwy. 92 and go 3.5 mi. Turn left onto Winan Ave. and go 1.7 mi. to the stop sign. Turn left onto Interurban Hwy. and go 0.3 mi. Turn left at the sign onto Basswood Lake Rd. and drive up to the office.

REVERE

Battle of Athens State Historical Site Campground

RR 1 Box 26, Revere 63465. T: (660) 877-3871; F: (600) 877-1202.

RV ★★★★ Tent ★★★★

Beauty: ★★★★ Site Privacy: ★★★★
Spaciousness: ★★★★ Quiet: ★★★★
Security: ★★★★ Cleanliness: ★★★★
Insect Control: ★★★★ Facilities: ★★

Located southwest of the historical site, this campground has all forested sites located in lush vegetation. Sites are back-ins that average 65–75 feet. Sites 1–4 are located on a separate road that branches off the main road right at the entrance. Sites 1 and 4 are the nicest in the campground, as they are more secluded than the others. Sites 14 and 18 are very close together and lack privacy. Sites 26 and 27 are doubles, best suited for groups that need two adjacent sites. The three rest rooms in the campground all have pit toilets and no showers or running water. An attractive campground, but rather short on facilities—especially for tent campers.

Basics

Operated By: Missouri Dept. of Natural Resources. **Open:** All year. **Site Assignment:** First come, first served; no reservations. **Registration:** Camp Host will collect fees at sites. **Fee:** RV $15 (full), $12 (water, electric); tent $7; checks, V, MC, D. **Parking:** At site.

Facilities

Number of RV Sites: 15. **Number of Tent-Only Sites:** 14. **Hookups:** Electric (30 amp). **Each Site:** Picnic table, fire pit. **Dump Station:** No. **Laundry:** No. **Pay Phone:** Yes. **Rest Rooms and Showers:** Rest rooms; no shower. **Fuel:** No. **Propane:** No. **Internal Roads:** Paved. **RV Service:** No. **Market:** 10 mi. to Farmington. **Restaurant:** 10 mi. to Farmington. **General Store:** No. **Vending:** No. **Swimming:** No. **Playground:** Yes. **Other:** Lake. **Activities:** Fishing, boating, hiking. **Nearby Attractions:** Des Moines River, Mark Twain Birthplace Museum, Thousand Hills. **Additional Information:** Kirksville Chamber of Commerce, (660) 665-3766.

Restrictions

Pets: On leash, cleaned up after. **Fires:** In grills. **Alcoholic Beverages:** At sites. **Vehicle Maximum Length:** None.

To Get There

From the junction of Hwy. 81 and Hwy. CC, turn east onto Hwy. CC and go 4 mi. Turn left onto gravel road and continue to park entrance.

SEDALIA

Countryside Adult/Senior RV Park

5464 South Limit Ave., Sedalia 65301. T: (660) 827-6513 or (660) 827-3735; F: (660) 826-9471; rvpark@murlin.com.

RV ★★★ Tent n/a

Beauty: ★★★★ Site Privacy: ★★★
Spaciousness: ★★★ Quiet: ★★★
Security: ★★★★ Cleanliness: ★★★★
Insect Control: ★★★★ Facilities: ★★★

The owners of this campground are normally out during the day, but sites available for overnighters are posted on the door to the office. Sites 19–22, 27, and 28 are (at least nominally) pull-throughs. It is, however, difficult to see how sites 21–25 could be pull-throughs without driving over the grassy patch that borders them on one side (and looks more like landscaping than a driveway). Sites are on a large gravel area and measure 100 feet in length. Sites 1–13, on the east side, back to woods and residences. Sites 14–20 are against the southern edge and back to woods and the office. The large open field to the northwest that looks so enticing is used only during the summer fair in Sedalia. Overnighters must select from open sites on the gravel. The rest rooms are individual units that include showers. These are all very clean and comfortable. This campground is a decent stop for overnighters, although many may wish they could camp out on the grass instead.

Basics

Operated By: Linda Alcorn. **Open:** All year. **Site Assignment:** First come, first served; reservations required for more than 5 days. **Registration:** In house. **Fee:** RV $19 (full), $17 (water, electric). **Parking:** At site.

Facilities

Number of RV Sites: 27. **Number of Tent-Only Sites:** 0. **Hookups:** Water, sewer, electric (30, 50 amp), cable. **Each Site:** Picnic table. **Dump Station:** Yes. **Laundry:** Yes. **Pay Phone:** Yes. **Rest Rooms and Showers:** Yes. **Fuel:** No. **Propane:** No. **Internal Roads:** Gravel. **RV Service:** No. **Market:** Less than 5 mi. north. **Restaurant:** Less than 5 mi. north. **General Store:** No. **Vending:** Yes. **Swimming:** No. **Playground:** No. **Other:** Modem hookup, pavilion. **Activities:** Self-guiding tours. **Nearby Attractions:** Bothwell Lodge, Silver Dollar City. **Additional Information:** Sedalia Area Chamber of Commerce, (800) 827-5295, (660) 826-2222.

Restrictions

Pets: On leash, cleaned up after. **Fires:** In grills. **Alcoholic Beverages:** At sites. **Vehicle Maximum Length:** None.

To Get There

From the junction of Hwy. 50 and Hwy. 65, turn south onto Hwy. 65 and go 2.8 mi. Turn right at the sign into the entrance and follow the gravel drive around to the house.

SIKESTON

Hinton Park

2860 East Malone, Sikeston 63801. T: (800) 327-1457 or (573) 471-1457.

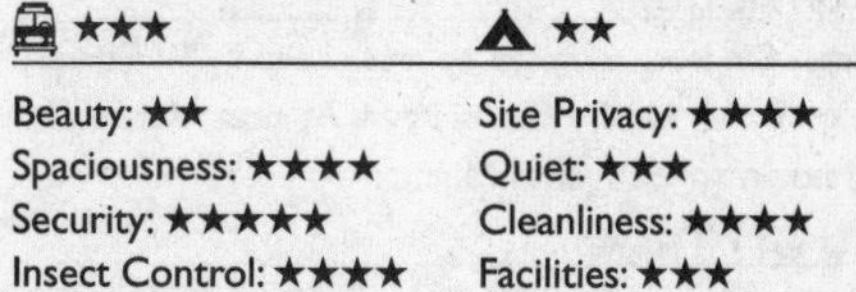

RV ★★★ Tent ★★

Beauty: ★★ Site Privacy: ★★★★
Spaciousness: ★★★★ Quiet: ★★★
Security: ★★★★★ Cleanliness: ★★★★
Insect Control: ★★★★ Facilities: ★★★

Hinton Park has long pull-throughs laid out in rows of gravel and grassy sites. Sites 1–26, located on the east edge of the property, are 90 × 30 feet. They are sandwiched between mobile homes to the west and an industrial field to the east. Site 1 is slightly shorter (75 feet), but is adjacent to a pleasant agricultural field to the south. Other sites, some unnumbered, lie in rows to the southwest of the office. As they are in a large open field, there is no size restriction to the vehicles that can occupy these sites. Site 16 has a nice shade tree, and 8 and 13 are next to a row of pretty bushes. Tenting is possible on a large grassy field off the highway. While there is plenty of room, the location is not conducive to quiet. The rest-room facilities are clean and modern, but the walls and floors are unattractive cement. (Tile would help the appearance of cleanliness.) This is a fine campground, but better suited for RVers than tenters.

Basics

Operated By: Mark Hinton. **Open:** All year. **Site Assignment:** Upon registration; check deposit required for reservation, 24-hours cancellation policy. **Registration:** In office; late arrivals use drop box. **Fee:** RV $17, tent $9; checks, V, MC. **Parking:** At site.

Facilities

Number of RV Sites: 46. **Number of Tent-Only Sites:** Undesignated sites. **Hookups:** Water, sewer, electric (30, 50 amp), cable. **Each Site:** Picnic table. **Dump Station:** Yes. **Laundry:** Yes. **Pay Phone:** Yes. **Rest Rooms and Showers:** Yes. **Fuel:** No. **Propane:** Yes. **Internal Roads:** Gravel. **RV Service:** No. **Market:** 3 mi. west. **Restaurant:** 0.6 mi. west. **General Store:** No. **Vending:** No. **Swimming:** No. **Playground:** No. **Other:** Modem/phone at every site, free shuttle to Lambert's Cafe (home of the "throwed roll"). **Activities:** Hiking, fishing. **Nearby Attractions:** Big Oak Tree State Park. **Additional Information:** Charleston Chamber of Commerce, (573) 683-6509.

Restrictions

Pets: On leash, cleaned up after, keep in RV. **Fires:** In grills. **Alcoholic Beverages:** At sites. **Vehicle Maximum Length:** None.

To Get There

From the junction of Hwy. I-55 and Hwy. 62, turn east onto Hwy. 62 and go 0.4 mi. Turn right at the sign into the entrance.

SPRINGFIELD

Travelers Park Campground

425 South Trailview Rd., Springfield 65802. T: (417) 866-4226.

RV ★★★★ Tent ★★★★

Beauty: ★★★★★ Site Privacy: ★★★★
Spaciousness: ★★★★★ Quiet: ★★★
Security: ★★★★ Cleanliness: ★★★★
Insect Control: ★★★★ Facilities: ★★★

This campground is surrounded by trees, and some of the sites have tree cover, providing desirable shade in the summer months. Sites are unnumbered, making it a little hard to figure out which site is which. Four RV sites in the northwest corner are completely forested, which makes them very desirable. On the north side of the campground are 72-foot back-ins that back to fields with a natural, "wild," feel. Five sites in the middle of the campground are 90–110-foot pull-throughs with loads of space. The two westernmost sites are well shaded and are some of the most desirable sites in the entire park. In the southeast corner are RV sites in an open field that can accommodate rigs of any size. In the same corner are tent sites with exceptionally nice grass and a number of large shade trees.

Basics

Operated By: Winfred & Maxine Short. **Open:** All year. **Site Assignment:** Upon registration; verbal reservations OK. **Registration:** In office; late arrivals select available site & pay in the morning or use drop box. **Fee:** RV $19 (full), tent $14; no credits cards, but checks. **Parking:** At site.

Facilities

Number of RV Sites: 33. **Number of Tent-Only Sites:** Undesignated sites. **Hookups:** Water, sewer, electric (30 amp). **Each Site:** Picnic table. **Dump Station:** No (sewer at all sites). **Laundry:** Yes. **Pay Phone:** No. **Rest Rooms and Showers:** Yes. **Fuel:** No. **Propane:** No. **Internal Roads:** Gravel. **RV Service:** Next door. **Market:** 4 mi. east. **Restaurant:** 4 mi. east. **General Store:** Yes. **Vending:** No. **Swimming:** Pool. **Playground:** No. **Other:** Game room. **Activities:** Golf. **Nearby Attractions:** Bass Pro Shop, golf course, tours, Dy Center, Fantastic Caverns, Japanese Stroll Garden. **Additional Information:** Springfield CVB Tourist Information Center, (800) 678-8767, (417) 881-5300.

Restrictions

Pets: On leash, cleaned up after. **Fires:** In grills. **Alcoholic Beverages:** At sites. **Vehicle Maximum Length:** 42 ft. **Other:** See rule sheet.

To Get There

From Hwy. I-44 (Exit 72), on west side of Hwy. overpass, take the first left onto Outer Rd. and go 0.5 mi. The campground is at the end of this dead-end road.

ST. JAMES

Pheasant Acres

20279 Hwy. 8, St. James 65559. T: (573) 265-5149; F: (573) 265-6900; pheasant@tigernet.missouri.org.

RV ★★★★ Tent ★★★★

Beauty: ★★★★★	Site Privacy: ★★★★★
Spaciousness: ★★★★	Quiet: ★★★★★
Security: ★★★★★	Cleanliness: ★★★★★
Insect Control: ★★★★	Facilities: ★★

RV sites in this campground are back-ins that range from 36 to 54 feet in length and are 35 feet wide. Sites 1–10 are in a strip along the west side. These sites are well shaded and back to a line of trees. In front of these spaces is a grassy field with some lovely flowers, bushes, and other vegetation. Site 10 has a large amount of space and is furthest from the entrance. Sites 12–18 are located on the inner loop of the internal road. All of these sites are quite decent. Sites 19–21 lie between the rest rooms and a barn. They are a little less roomy, but back to woods and are otherwise comfortable. The tenting area lies under magnificent oaks and has a thick grass cover. The area is surrounded on two sides by woods, but, on the downside, there is some slope. The rest rooms are located in a mobile home near the tenting area. It is very clean and comfortable, and the showers even have a large dry area for clothes and a towel.

BASICS

Operated By: Chuck & Diana Kesler. **Open:** All year. **Site Assignment:** Depending on site availability; verbal reservations OK. **Registration:** In office; late arrivals use drop box. **Fee:** RV $15 (full), $12 (electric); tent $10. **Parking:** At site.

FACILITIES

Number of RV Sites: 20. **Number of Tent-Only Sites:** 5. **Hookups:** Water, sewer, electric (30 amp). **Each Site:** Picnic table, grill. **Dump Station:** No (sewer at all sites). **Laundry:** No. **Pay Phone:** No. **Rest Rooms and Showers:** Yes. **Fuel:** No. **Propane:** No. **Internal Roads:** Gravel. **RV Service:** No. **Market:** 5 mi. west. **Restaurant:** 2 mi. east or west. **General Store:** No. **Vending:** No. **Swimming:** No. **Playground:** No. **Other:** Borders conservation area, wood, pavilion. **Activities:** Hiking, float trips, basketball. **Nearby Attractions:** Wineries, Maramec Spring Park, Maramec Museum. **Additional Information:** Rolla Chamber of Commerce, (573) 364-3577.

RESTRICTIONS

Pets: On leash, cleaned up after. **Fires:** In grills. **Alcoholic Beverages:** At sites. **Vehicle Maximum Length:** 40 ft. **Other:** Quiet enforced.

TO GET THERE

From Hwy. I-44 (Exit 195), turn south and go 5.5 mi. east. Turn left at the sign into the entrance. (Campers would be advised to drive slowly, as the sign is small and the entrance a little narrow.)

ST. JOSEPH

AOK Overnite Kampground

12430 CR 360, St. Joseph 64505. T: (816) 324-4263 or (816) 324-7808; jhun213@aol.com.

RV ★★★ Tent ★★★

Beauty: ★★★	Site Privacy: ★★★
Spaciousness: ★★★	Quiet: ★★★
Security: ★★★★	Cleanliness: ★★
Insect Control: ★★★★	Facilities: ★★★

Laid out in a giant loop, this campground has RV and tent sites near a fishing lake. The nicest rows of RV sites are the closest to the lake (1–6 and 7–14). The lower-numbered row contains 75-foot pull-through sites, while one row in from the lake contains 60-foot pull-throughs. Sites with nice shade trees include 5–8, 10, 12, and 14. Sites 15–22 range from 60 to 90 feet, with lower numbers being larger sites. Sites 23–28 are adjacent to a mobile-home park making them less desirable. The row of sites to the east (43–50) consists of grassy 75-foot back-ins that back to woods and residences. The tent area has very thick grass, which is excellent for tenting, but there are no shade trees. The rest rooms and shower appear neglected. This is too bad, as the campground would benefit from a nicer rest room. As it is, this campground is adequate if you need to spend a night near St. Joseph.

BASICS

Operated By: Jody & Jan Hundley. **Open:** All year. **Site Assignment:** Upon registration; no reservations. **Registration:** In office; late arrivals use drop box. **Fee:** RV $15, tent $10; checks, V, MC, AE, D. **Parking:** At site.

Facilities

Number of RV Sites: 50. **Number of Tent-Only Sites:** Undesignated sites. **Hookups:** Water, sewer, electric (20, 30, 50 amp). **Each Site:** Picnic table. **Dump Station:** Yes. **Laundry:** Yes. **Pay Phone:** Yes. **Rest Rooms and Showers:** Yes. **Fuel:** No. **Propane:** No. **Internal Roads:** Gravel. **RV Service:** No. **Market:** 3 mi. south. **Restaurant:** 3 mi. south. **General Store:** No. **Vending:** Yes. **Swimming:** Pool. **Playground:** Yes. **Other:** Lake, limited groceries, pavilion. **Activities:** Fishing, volleyball, horseshoes. **Nearby Attractions:** Jesse James Museum, St. Joseph Museum, Pony Express Stables Museum, casinos. **Additional Information:** St. Joseph CVB, (800) 785-0360, (816) 233-6688.

Restrictions

Pets: On leash, cleaned up after. **Fires:** In grills. **Alcoholic Beverages:** At sites. **Vehicle Maximum Length:** 45 ft.

To Get There

From Hwy. 29/71 (Exit 53), turn north onto 71 Business and go 0.3 mi. to the second left (across the highway) onto the (gravel) Rd. 360. Go 0.4 mi. to the campground. The office is on the left.

ST. LOUIS

St. Louis RV Park

900 North Jefferson P.O. Box 7663, St. Louis 63106. T: (800) 878-3330 or (314) 241-3330; F: (314) 241-4823; www.stlouisrvpark.com.

RV ★★★ | Tent n/a

Beauty: ★★	Site Privacy: ★★★
Spaciousness: ★★	Quiet: ★★★
Security: ★★★★★	Cleanliness: ★★★★★
Insect Control: ★★★★	Facilities: ★★★

Some like it paved. St. Lous RV park consists entirely of a paved lot, with a hedge running around the perimeter. Three rows of 55 × 20-foot pull-throughs lie in the middle of the park (1–15, 16–31, and 32–48). The lower numbers of each row have the best view of downtown and the Arch. The rest of the sites are back-ins in a ring around the campground. These sites are 36 × 20 feet, with the possibility of rigs sticking out somewhat due to the large amount of space in the interior road. Most of these sites back to the hedge. Sites 81 and 82 in the northwest corner are two of the most desirable, containing a grassy patch, bushes, and even a shade tree. Sites 59 and 60 in the northeast corner come close, but do not have a tree on the grass patch they share. Probably the single nicest site, however, is 97 in the southwest corner. This site has extra space, a shade tree, and a flower pot, and is close to the rest rooms, which are absolutely immaculate. Showers are self-contained units that are a bit older than the rest rooms and contain no fan, but are otherwise comfortable. This is a decent RV park for folks who like ultra-developed parks. It offers nice views of the Arch, but the addition of shade trees would improve it immensely.

Basics

Operated By: Mary & George Hudson. **Open:** Mar. 1–Nov. 15. **Site Assignment:** Upon registration; credit card required for reservation, 24-hours cancellation policy. **Registration:** In office; late arrivals must call in advance to get into the security gate. **Fee:** RV $31 (50 amp), $29 (30 amp). **Parking:** At site.

Facilities

Number of RV Sites: 100. **Number of Tent-Only Sites:** 0. **Hookups:** Water, sewer, electric (30, 50 amp). **Dump Station:** Yes. **Laundry:** Yes. **Pay Phone:** Yes. **Rest Rooms and Showers:** Yes. **Fuel:** No. **Propane:** No. **Internal Roads:** Paved. **RV Service:** No. **Market:** 2 mi. southwest. **Restaurant:** 1 mi. southeast. **General Store:** Yes. **Vending:** No. **Swimming:** Pool. **Playground:** No. **Other:** Meeting room, observation deck, e-mail access, dog walk area, close to downtown (15 blocks), view of Arch. **Activities:** Visiting museums, shopping, tours, riverboat cruises, theater. **Nearby Attractions:** St. Louis Art Museum, St. Louis Zoo, Forest Park, Gateway Arch, St. Louis Science Center. **Additional Information:** St. Louis Visitors Center: (314) 241-1764.

Restrictions

Pets: On leash, cleaned up after. **Fires:** In grills. **Alcoholic Beverages:** At sites. **Vehicle Maximum Length:** None.

To Get There

From Hwy. I-55 (Exit 207C: Lafayette Ave.), turn left at the light. Go 0.6 mi., then turn right onto Jefferson. Go 1.7 mi. on Jefferson, then turn right onto Dr. Martin Luther King, left onto 23rd St., then right at the sign into the entrance.

SULLIVAN

Native Experience Adventure Campground

1451 East Springfield, Sullivan 63080. T: (573) 468-8750.

RV ★★★★ Tent ★★★★★

Beauty: ★★★★	Site Privacy: ★★★★
Spaciousness: ★★★★	Quiet: ★★★★
Security: ★★★★★	Cleanliness: ★★★★★
Insect Control: ★★★★	Facilities: ★★★★★

More than just a campground, Native Experience is a philosophy. New proprietor Keith Campbell envisions creating a natural and ecologically-sustainable campground where travelers and adventurers converge for shared experiences. (However, as the campground is new, many of the services proposed are not yet in operation.) The campground is situated on Historic Rte. 66 and close to a number of recreation areas, which attracts travelers and adventurers alike. All sites are well shaded, with grassy sites laid out in a loop. Sites 1–17 are 75–100-foot pull-throughs (the largest are sites 10–17). Sites 19 and 20 are even longer, at 120 feet and 80 feet respectively. Running in a row from north to south, sites 24–36 are 50 × 36-foot back-ins. (Sites 22 and 23 can pull through if the opposite site is vacant.) The tenting area is north of RV site 36. Surrounded on all sides by woods, the area is also well forested and protects tenters from both sun and rain. All tent sites are located on the inside of the looped interior road. Campers are encouraged to enjoy a "native experience" in Sullivan, and should feel free to ask the knowledgeable owner about natural recreation opportunities in the area.

Basics

Operated By: Keith Campbell. **Open:** All year. **Site Assignment:** Depending on site availability; verbal reservations OK. **Registration:** In office; late arrivals use drop box. **Fee:** RV $20 (full), $18 (electric); tent $15. **Parking:** At site.

Facilities

Number of RV Sites: 36. **Number of Tent-Only Sites:** 10. **Hookups:** Water, sewer, electric (30 amp). **Each Site:** Picnic table, fire pit. **Dump Station:** Yes. **Laundry:** Yes. **Pay Phone:** Yes. **Rest Rooms and Showers:** Yes. **Fuel:** No. **Propane:** Yes. **Internal Roads:** Gravel. **RV Service:** No. **Market:** 2 mi. west (at I-44). **Restaurant:** 2 mi. west (at I-44). **General Store:** Yes. **Vending:** No. **Swimming:** Pool. **Playground:** Yes. **Other:** Dog walk, cabin, adventure tours. **Activities:** Caving, swimming, hiking, kayaking, biking. **Nearby Attractions:** Meremac State Park, Rte. 66. **Additional Information:** Sullivan Area Chamber of Commerce, (573) 468-3314.

Restrictions

Pets: On leash, cleaned up after. **Fires:** In grills. **Alcoholic Beverages:** At sites. **Vehicle Maximum Length:** None. **Other:** No ATVs/dirt bikes, no generators.

To Get There

From Hwy. I-44 (Exit 226), turn south onto Hwy. 185 and go 0.25 mi. Turn left onto Service Rd. (first left after gas station complex) and go 1.4 mi. Turn left at the sign into the entrance.

WILLIAMSVILLE

Lake Wappapello State Park

HC 2 Box 2349, Williamsville 63966. T: (573) 222-8139 or (573) 222-8773 or (573) 222-8562.

RV ★★★★ Tent ★★★★★

Beauty: ★★★★★	Site Privacy: ★★★★★
Spaciousness: ★★★★★	Quiet: ★★★★★
Security: ★★★★★	Cleanliness: ★★★★
Insect Control: ★★★	Facilities: ★★★★

This state park offers two campgrounds—one by the lake and the other perched on a ridge in the woods. All sites in the lakeside campground are grassy, shaded sites with cement slabs and a view of the lake. Closest to the lake are 57, 58, 63, 65, and 67–73. Sites 55 and 74 are furthest from the lake and have more of a forested feel than a lakeside feel. Sites 65, 71, 74, and 79 are 75-foot pull-throughs. Sites 61 and 62 are 60-foot doubles. The ridgeside campground has 60-foot gravel back-ins that back to forest as well as some collossal (110 feet) pull-throughs, such as 38. The east side of this campground has a partial view of the lake, while the west side is pure forest. Sites 7 and 8 are doubles. The remotest sites are 23 and 24, which are located at the end of a roundabout. Lake Wappapello State Park offers the best of both worlds: forest and lakeside sites.

Both those wishing to play in the water and those wishing to relax in the shade will find it an appealing campsite.

Basics

Operated By: Missouri Dept. of Natural Resources. **Open:** All year (limited services Nov.–Mar.). **Site Assignment:** First come, first served; currently no reservations, may begin reservation system in 2002. **Registration:** Fees will be collected by ranger. **Fee:** $12 (water, electric), $7 tent; checks, V, MC, D. **Parking:** At site, do not park on grass (boat or trailer OK).

Facilities

Number of RV Sites: 37. **Number of Tent-Only Sites:** 43. **Hookups:** Electric (30 amp). **Each Site:** Picnic table, grill, lantern post. **Dump Station:** Yes. **Laundry:** Yes. **Pay Phone:** Yes. **Rest Rooms and Showers:** Yes. **Fuel:** No. **Propane:** No. **Internal Roads:** Paved. **RV Service:** No. **Market:** 16 mi. to Poplar Bluff. **Restaurant:** 5 mi. to Chaonia Landing. **General Store:** No. **Vending:** No. **Swimming:** Yes (lake). **Playground:** Yes. **Other:** 3 boat ramps, 8 cabins, amphitheater, firewood, picnic shelters, horse trails, hiking trails. **Activities:** Fishing, boating, swimming, horseback riding, hiking. **Nearby Attractions:** Lake Wappapello. **Additional Information:** Poplar Bluff Chamber of Commerce, (573) 785-7761.

Restrictions

Pets: On leash, cleaned up after. **Fires:** In grills. **Alcoholic Beverages:** At sites, no glass bottles. **Vehicle Maximum Length:** None. **Other:** No fireworks, no digging, no metal detectors, no hunting, visitors must leave by 10 p.m., no breaking of tree limbs.

To Get There

From the junction of Hwy. 67 and Hwy. 172, turn east onto Hwy. 172 and go 8 mi. Turn left at the T in the road at the 4.4 mile mark, and right at the 5.5 mile mark.) The office is on the left.

New Mexico

Lucky are those about to visit New Mexico for the first time. The epitome of the Southwest, New Mexico presents a striking, sun-baked beauty that peeks out in a bloom of purple flowers in the desert, in the shocking red of dried chilies hanging from a brown adobe house, or in the reds, yellows, and blacks of Indian blankets on sale in the marketplace. Just look at Georgia O'Keefe's life work for a glimpse into this living gallery. You practically expect to see cattle skulls bleaching by the highway as you pass.

But it's not all desert. **Taos** hosts world-class skiing, the railroad in **Chama** winds through sheer mountains, and the forest around **Gila National Monument** looks like a lost slice of Colorado. The extremes of Mother Nature's handiwork can be found in New Mexico—**Carlsbad Caverns, White Sands, Capulin Volcano National Monument**—as well as some very impressive manmade creations—the **Very Large Assembly** radio telescope at **Datil,** the **Gila Cliff Dwellings,** and of course, the (perhaps *space*man-made) attractions in **Roswell.** RVers will be happy to note that these attractions are generally served by well-maintained roads, and camping opportunities abound.

Camping in New Mexico is a pleasure. Prices are much more reasonable than at many resorts in Arizona, and the bounty of attractions makes an exciting destination possible at the end of practically every travel day. In addition to the numerous places to see within the state, many visitors use New Mexico as a stepping stone to the country for which it was named. **Las Cruces** is a convenient stop on the way down I-25 toward **El Paso** and points more foreign. But you don't need to travel to a foreign country to find a meaningful travel experience. Whether you stay for a week or a winter, New Mexico will surprise you like those chilies in your green sauce.

The following facilities accept payment in checks or cash only:

Bluewater Lake State Park, Prewitt
Bosque Birdwatcher's RV Park, San Antonio
Buckhorn RV Park, Buckhorn
Capulin RV Park, Capulin
Casas Adobes RV Park, Mimbres
Ideal RV Park, Clovis
Manzano's RV Park, Silver City
Ramblin' Rose RV Park, Santa Rosa
Rodeo RV Park, Rodeo
Summerlan RV Park, Raton
Trail's End RV Park, Jemez Springs
Ute Lake State Park, Logan
Vado RV Park, Vado
Wagon Wheel RV Park, Deming
Wagon Wheel RV Park, Portales
West Lake RV Park, Eagle Nest

The following facilities feature 20 sites or fewer:

Buckhorn RV Park, Buckhorn
Casas Adobes RV Park, Mimbres
Coyote Creek State Park, Angelfire
Manzano Mountains State Park, Mountainair
Rodeo RV Park, Rodeo
Trail's End RV Park, Jemez Springs

Campground Profiles

ABIQUIU

Riana Campground

Abiquiu Lake Project Office P.O. Box 290, Abiquiu 87510. T: (505) 685-4371; F: (505) 685-4647; www.spa.usace.army.mil/abiquiu; cespa-od-ab@spa02.usace.army.mil.

RV ★★★★ Tent ★★★★★

Beauty: ★★★★★ Site Privacy: ★★★★
Spaciousness: ★★★★ Quiet: ★★★★★
Security: ★★★★ Cleanliness: ★★★★
Insect Control: ★★★★ Facilities: ★★

Laid out in several loops, Riana offers sites above the reservoir—some with excellent views. Sites 1–15 are mostly 60–75-foot back-ins with electric hookups. These sites have extra space for a boat or second vehicle. Sites 9 and 10 are pull-throughs (actually "pull-alongsides") that are 90 feet in length. Sites 13 and 15 have the best views, but are just above the playground. Sites 16–30 are located in a fenced-in parking area. Each site is 36 × 30 feet with a camping area beside. The fences make it difficult for larger rigs to back into some of these sites (such as 25–30). Sites 16 and 17 are pull-throughs similar to 9 and 10. Sites 18–20 have the best views. The remaining sites are primitive or walk-in sites. The RV sites are 45–55-foot back-ins with wonderful views of the reservoir. Sites 40–54 are walk-in tent sites inside a fenced-in area. Each site has a 12 × 12-foot crushed gravel pad for a tent. Sites 47–50 have nice desert views. There are porta-potties for tenters' use in this area. Riana is a pretty (but rather primitive) campground that offers lake recreation and fun for the entire family.

BASICS

Operated By: US Army Corps of Engineers. **Open:** All year. **Site Assignment:** First come, first served; reservations made through ReserveAmerica (www.reserveusa.com, (877) 444-6777). **Registration:** At gate; camp host will come around to sites in morning in case of late arrivals. **Fee:** $17 (water, electric), primitive $10, walk-in tent $5; checks, V, MC, AE, D. **Parking:** At site, overflow parking.

FACILITIES

Number of RV Sites: 39. **Number of Tent-Only Sites:** 15. **Hookups:** Electric (30, 50 amp). **Each Site:** Covered picnic table, grill, lantern pole. **Dump Station:** Yes. **Laundry:** No. **Pay Phone:** Yes. **Rest Rooms and Showers:** Yes. **Fuel:** No. **Propane:** No. **Internal Roads:** Paved. **RV Service:** No. **Market:** 8 mi. south to Abiquiu. **Restaurant:** 8 mi. south to Abiquiu. **General Store:** No. **Vending:** No. **Swimming:** Yes (reservoir). **Playground:** Yes. **Other:** Picnic area. **Activities:** Fishing, boating, swimming, hiking. **Nearby**

Attractions: Ghost Ranch Conference Center, Georgia O'Keefe house in Abiquiu. **Additional Information:** Española Chamber of Commerce, (505) 753-2831.

RESTRICTIONS

Pets: On leash, cleaned up after. **Fires:** In grills. **Alcoholic Beverages:** At sites. **Vehicle Maximum Length:** None.

TO GET THERE

From the junction of Hwy. 84 and Hwy. 96 (about 7 mi. north of town), turn west onto Hwy. 96 and go 1.3 mi. Turn right at the sign into the entrance.

ALAMOGORDO

Alamogordo KOA

412-24th St., Alamogordo 88310. T: (800) KOA-3992 or (505) 437-3003; F: (505) 437-1493.

RV ★★★★★ Tent ★★★

Beauty: ★★★★	Site Privacy: ★★★★★
Spaciousness: ★★★★	Quiet: ★★★★
Security: ★★★★	Cleanliness: ★★★★
Insect Control: ★★★★	Facilities: ★★★★★

This campground boasts beautiful landscaping as well as mountain vistas to the east (especially sites 48–63). A small section of ratty fencing to the south that conceals a mobile-home park does insult the view, but can be mostly ignored. Pull-throughs are level and long (60 × 30 feet), while back-ins are a spacious 32 × 30 feet. The smaller back-ins close to the pool (65–67) have nice grass and trees and are still pleasant spots to camp. Tent sites are away from the RV sites, along the southwest side of the office on a strip of grass with plenty of tree coverage. However, parking is directly behind the sites, where a row of RVs in storage compete for space. The laundry facility is large, clean, and modern, with lots of machines, loads of space, and a raft of magazines. Rest rooms are also large, clean, well lit, and tastefully decorated. Playground facilities are well maintained and safe. Overall, this is a great destination in a great location for visiting the White Sands National Monument, and even Carlsbad Caverns and Mexico.

BASICS

Operated By: Ken and Judy Bonnell. **Open:** All year. **Site Assignment:** Upon registration; credit card required for reservation, must cancel within 24 hours for refund. **Registration:** In office; late arrivals use drop box. **Fee:** RV up to $30 (depending on hookups), tent $18. **Parking:** At site.

FACILITIES

Number of RV Sites: 65. **Number of Tent-Only Sites:** 10. **Hookups:** Water, sewer, electric (15, 30, 50 amp), cable. **Each Site:** Cement table, cement privacy wall, tree, lamp, grill. **Dump Station:** Yes. **Laundry:** Yes. **Pay Phone:** Yes. **Rest Rooms and Showers:** Yes. **Fuel:** No. **Propane:** Yes. **Internal Roads:** Paved. **RV Service:** No. **Market:** 1 mi. **Restaurant:** 2 blocks. **General Store:** Yes. **Vending:** No. **Swimming:** Pool. **Playground:** Yes. **Other:** 2 cabins, pool open May 15–Sept. 15. **Activities:** Swimming. **Nearby Attractions:** White Sands National Monument, White Sands Missle Range/Trinity site, Texas, Mexico. **Additional Information:** Alamogordo Chamber of Commerce, (800) 826-0294, (505) 437-6120.

RESTRICTIONS

Pets: On leash. **Fires:** None. **Alcoholic Beverages:** At sites. **Vehicle Maximum Length:** None.

TO GET THERE

From Hwy. 54/70 (White Sands Blvd.), turn east onto 24th St. in town. Go 0.2 mi. on 24th St., then turn right at the sign into the entrance. The office lies straight ahead.

ALBUQUERQUE

Albuquerque Central KOA

12400 Skyline Rd. Northeast, Albuquerque 87123. T: (505) 296-2729; F: (505) 296-3354; www.koa.com; albuquerque@koa.net.

RV ★★★★ Tent ★★★

Beauty: ★★★	Site Privacy: ★★★
Spaciousness: ★★★	Quiet: ★★★
Security: ★★★★	Cleanliness: ★★★★★
Insect Control: ★★★★	Facilities: ★★★★★

This is an enormous campground with rows and rows of RV sites. Sites 1–15 are 35-foot sites that back to a fence and residential area. D row, which contains the best sites (28–44), is in the middle of the campground, away from the road and the highway on the other side. Sites 33–36 are close to the rest rooms, and 35 is well shaded. The rows containing sites 45–74 are in the second-best area. West of this area is a sea of RVs:

five rows of RV sites (81–169) packed in together. Sites 81–88, along the southwest fence, are 60-foot back-ins. Sites 98–148 are 70 × 33-foot pull-throughs—large enough for any rig, but placed like dozens of pawns on a chessboard. Sites 149–169 are 30-foot back-ins along the west wall that back to apartments close by. End sites on the north side (113 and 130) are close to both the pet run and the highway, and are therefore less desirable. The "Tent Village" is a fenced-in dirt area with one shade tree. While it might work out if a large group were camping together, it feels cramped for campers who do not know each other. There are, in fact, two tenting areas, one of which has a shaded bench and table per tent site, and one that does not. Neither is particularly roomy, and campers may feel hemmed in by the fencing. This is a gigantic campground, and one may feel somewhat like an anonymous log moving through a sawmill. The facilities, however, are clean and comfortable, and the campground offers a safe and comfortable (if crowded) environment.

BASICS

Operated By: Frank De Turo. **Open:** All year. **Site Assignment:** Upon registration; credit card required for reservation, 24-hours cancellation policy. **Registration:** In office; late arrivals use drop box. **Fee:** RV $39 (full, 50 amp), $37 (full, 30 amp), $34 (water, electric); tent $26; V, MC, AE, D. **Parking:** At site.

FACILITIES

Number of RV Sites: 206. **Number of Tent-Only Sites:** 25. **Hookups:** Water, sewer, electric (30, 50 amp). **Each Site:** Picnic table. **Dump Station:** Yes. **Laundry:** Yes. **Pay Phone:** Yes. **Rest Rooms and Showers:** Yes. **Fuel:** No. **Propane:** Yes. **Internal Roads:** Paved. **RV Service:** Mobile. **Market:** 0.25 mi. north. **Restaurant:** 0.25 mi. north. **General Store:** Yes. **Vending:** Yes. **Swimming:** Pool. **Playground:** Yes. **Other:** Cabin, modem, 1 phone site, rec hall, mini-golf, video games, RV rentals. **Activities:** Swimming, golf. **Nearby Attractions:** Balloon Fiesta (first Sun. in Oct.). **Additional Information:** Albuquerque Chamber of Commerce, (505) 764-3700.

RESTRICTIONS

Pets: On leash, cleaned up after. **Fires:** In grills. **Alcoholic Beverages:** At sites. **Vehicle Maximum Length:** None.

TO GET THERE

From Hwy. I-40 (Exit 166), turn south onto Juan Tabo Blvd. and go 0.25 mi. Turn left onto Skyline Rd. and go 0.35 mi. Turn left at the sign into the entrance.

ANGEL FIRE

Sierra Bonita Cabins and RV Park

P.O. Box 963, Angel Fire 87710. T: (800) 942-1556 or (505) 387-5508; www.sierrabonita.com; sierrabonita@bigfoot.com.

RV ★★★★ Tent ★★★★

Beauty: ★★★★★ Site Privacy: ★★★
Spaciousness: ★★★ Quiet: ★★★★
Security: ★★★★ Cleanliness: ★★★★★
Insect Control: ★★★★ Facilities: ★★★

This park consists of one strip of open-ended back-ins. The open field in which these sites are located allows for any size of rig. Most sites are 22 feet wide and back to the road about 50 feet away. Site 1, in the northwest corner, is closest to the bathhouse. Site 11 in the southwest corner seems a little cramped (there is a fence on one side). The park is located in a valley, which means that sunrise is slightly later and sunset slightly earlier—this may make for a chilly morning or evening. The location is absolutely gorgeous, with forested hills on all sides. The park abuts a fishing area that guests may use. The showers are individual unisex units that are very clean and comfortable. The rest rooms are also individual units, and likewise very clean. This park is much more secluded than the RV park in town, although it requires longer drive to get to. However, the drive is absolutely worth the extra effort, and this is a campground that many people return to year after year.

BASICS

Operated By: Dale Powell. **Open:** May 15–Oct. 15. **Site Assignment:** First come, first served; credit card required for reservation, 1 week cancellation policy. **Registration:** In office; late arrivals select available site and pay in the morning. **Fee:** $13 (water, electric); checks, V, MC, D. **Parking:** At site.

FACILITIES

Number of RV Sites: 11. **Number of Tent-Only Sites:** 0. **Hookups:** Water, electric (20, 30 amp). **Each Site:** Picnic table, fire pit. **Dump Station:** Yes. **Laundry:** Yes. **Pay Phone:** Yes. **Rest Rooms and Showers:** Yes. **Fuel:** No. **Propane:** No. **Internal Roads:** Dirt. **RV Service:** No. **Market:** 17 mi. north or south. **Restaurant:** 17 mi. north or south. **General Store:** Yes. **Vending:** No. **Swimming:** No. **Playground:** No. **Other:** Cabins, group shelter. **Activities:** Fishing, scenic drives through Coyote Creek Canyon. **Nearby Attractions:** Harold Brock fishing area, Coyote Creek State Park. **Additional Information:** New Mexico State Parks Division, (888) NM-PARKS.

RESTRICTIONS

Pets: On leash, cleaned up after. **Fires:** In grills. **Alcoholic Beverages:** At sites, not in group shelter. **Vehicle Maximum Length:** None.

TO GET THERE

From the junction of Hwy. 64 and Hwy. 434, turn south onto Hwy. 434 and go 10.8 mi. Turn right at the junction with Hwy. 120 to stay on Hwy. 434 and go a further 8.2 mi. The office is on the right, up a flight of stairs.

ARTESIA

Artesia RV Park

201 West Hermosa Dr., Artesia 88210. T: (505) 746-6184; www.artesiarv.com; artesiarv@swcinternet.net.

RV: ★★★★ Tent: ★★★

Beauty: ★★	Site Privacy: ★★★★★
Spaciousness: ★★★★★	Quiet: ★★★★
Security: ★★★★★	Cleanliness: ★★★★★
Insect Control: ★★★★	Facilities: ★★★

This is a rather simple but comfortable campground with open gravel spaces divided into undefined rows. Sites 1–5 to the northwest average 45 × 34 feet. Sites 6–13 (in two rows) are also 45 feet in length. Site 13 is located against a shed, which makes it less desirable, but 10 has a trellis with plants growing up it, and 9 and 12 have trees. (The trees that dot the park are not large enough to provide shade, but add to the overall attractiveness.) Sites B1–10 and A1–10 in the middle of the park are doubles about 75 feet long but only 12 feet wide. End sites A6 and B10 are the widest (30 feet), since they do not share a site. Site 14 in the southwest corner is adjacent to a wooden storage shed, and is thus less desirable. Sites 16–21 along the southern edge are for long-term residents. The tent area is a grassy strip to the east of the RV sites. While there are a few covered tables and two grills, it is obvious that this park is more RV- than tent-oriented. The horseshoes at one end of the tent area could make for a rude awakening to an unlucky tent camper on that side. The rest rooms and showers are wonderfully clean and extremely spacious. This is a park that RVers will enjoy thoroughly, although tenters may wish to move on.

BASICS

Operated By: Ken, Wayne, and Mary Floyd. **Open:** All year. **Site Assignment:** Upon registration; verbal reservations OK. **Registration:** In office; late arrivals use drop box. **Fee:** RV $18 (full), tent $15; checks, V, MC. **Parking:** At site.

FACILITIES

Number of RV Sites: 42. **Number of Tent-Only Sites:** 10. **Hookups:** Water, sewer, electric (30, 50 amp), cable, phone. **Dump Station:** Yes. **Laundry:** Yes. **Pay Phone:** Yes. **Rest Rooms and Showers:** Yes. **Fuel:** No. **Propane:** No. **Internal Roads:** Gravel. **RV Service:** No. **Market:** 3 mi. west. **Restaurant:** 0.25 mi. south. **General Store:** No. **Vending:** No. **Swimming:** No. **Playground:** No. **Other:** Modem, pet walk. **Activities:** Fishing, boating, swimming, hiking, tours to Carlsbad Caverns, horseshoes. **Nearby Attractions:** Brantly Lake State Park, Carlsbad Caverns, Roswell. **Additional Information:** Artesia Chamber of Commerce, (505) 746-2744.

RESTRICTIONS

Pets: On leash, cleaned up after. **Fires:** In grills. **Alcoholic Beverages:** At sites. **Vehicle Maximum Length:** 40 ft.

TO GET THERE

From the junction of Hwy. 82 and Hwy. 285, turn south onto Hwy. 285 and go 1 mi. to Hermosa Drive. Turn right onto Hermosa Dr. and go 0.1 mi. Turn left at the sign into the entrance.

AZTEC

Aztec Ruins RV Park

312 Ruins Rd., Aztec 87410. T: (505) 334-3160; F: (505) 334-3160; rrrv@outbounds.net.

RV ★★ Tent ★★★

Beauty: ★★★ Site Privacy: ★★★
Spaciousness: ★★★ Quiet: ★★★★
Security: ★★★★ Cleanliness: ★★★
Insect Control: ★★★ Facilities: ★

Like many RV parks in this area, Aztek Ruins does not offer many services: there are no rest rooms, no laundry, no phone. In fact, there is not much to this park than a place to spend a night. However, the trees around the park (and the few inside), as well as the grassy sites, make it slightly nicer than the RV parks in the neighboring towns of Farmington and Kirtland. (This RV park abuts a trailer park to the north, which seems quiet enough and should not pose a problem to RVers.) As an added bonus, the pull-through sites are 85 feet long, with a possibility of sticking out even further, since the internal road is so wide. Tenters have it a little better. The tent sites are on an "island" by the river that has loads of trees, grass, and other vegetation. (Be sure to take the hill down into the tenting area slowly—it's steep.) The tenting experience would benefit from rest rooms and showers, but otherwise the park is a wild, comfortable place to tent. (Tenters in need of a potty might consider the Aztec Public Library at 201 West Chaco St.)

BASICS

Operated By: Dave Hare. **Open:** All year. **Site Assignment:** Depending on site availability. **Registration:** In office; late arrivals knock on door of resident manager. **Fee:** RV $15, tent $6. **Parking:** At site.

FACILITIES

Number of RV Sites: 24. **Number of Tent-Only Sites:** 5. **Hookups:** Water, sewer, electric (30, 50 amp). **Dump Station:** Yes. **Laundry:** No. **Pay Phone:** No. **Rest Rooms and Showers:** No. **Fuel:** No. **Propane:** No. **Internal Roads:** Dirt. **RV Service:** No. **Market:** 2 mi. into Aztec. **Restaurant:** 2 mi. into Aztec. **General Store:** No. **Vending:** No. **Swimming:** No. **Playground:** No. **Activities:** Sightseeing, swimming, boating, fishing. **Nearby Attractions:** Aztec Ruins National Monument, Navajo Lake (23 mi.). **Additional Information:** Aztec Chamber of Commerce and Visitors Center, (505) 334-9551.

RESTRICTIONS

Pets: On leash, cleaned up after; ask about other restrictions. **Fires:** In grills; subject to seasonal bans. **Alcoholic Beverages:** At sites. **Vehicle Maximum Length:** None.

TO GET THERE

From the junction of Hwy. 550 and Hwy. 516 (Main St. in town), go 0.6 mi. southwest on 550. Turn right onto Ruins Rd. Go 0.3 mi., then turn right at the sign into the campground. The office is on the left.

BERNARDO

Kiva RV Park and Horse Motel

21 Old Hwy. 60 West, Bernardo 87006. T: (877) 374-KIVA or (505) 861-0693; kivarv@juno.com.

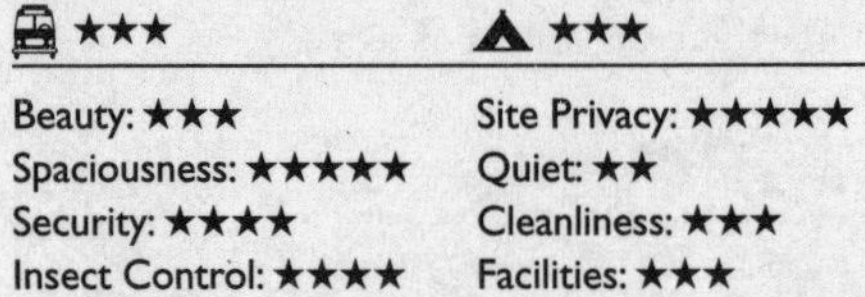

RV ★★★ Tent ★★★

Beauty: ★★★ Site Privacy: ★★★★★
Spaciousness: ★★★★★ Quiet: ★★
Security: ★★★★ Cleanliness: ★★★
Insect Control: ★★★★ Facilities: ★★★

Smack dab in the middle of wildlife sanctuaries, this campground emphasizes horses and horseback riding. These unnumbered sites are gravel pull-throughs that are designated as 56 feet long, but can accommodate much larger rigs than this. Sites are very wide (40 feet), with a logged-in patch of grass and bushes between each site. Eastern end sites are not defined on the east side and are therefore extremely large. There is a beautiful desert rock garden at the west edge of the campground, containing flagstones, trellises with grapes, and a fountain. The rest rooms are almost Zen-like in simplicity, but very clean (other than the chipped linoleum and cement floor). Tenting is possible on grassy areas around the park. The best area is in the northeast corner, where there are two stone pads sunk into the ground. This is a fairly nice campground, but geared more towards horse enthusiasts than your average overnighter.

BASICS

Operated By: Bob and Diane Wiltshire. **Open:** All year. **Site Assignment:** First come, first served; credit card required for reservation, 24 hours cancellation policy. **Registration:** In office; late arrivals use drop box. **Fee:** RV $18 (full), tent $5; checks,V, MC, D. **Parking:** At site.

FACILITIES

Number of RV Sites: 26. **Number of Tent-Only Sites:** Undesignated sites. **Hookups:** Water, sewer, electric (20, 30, 50 amp). **Dump Station:** No (sewer at all sites). **Laundry:** Yes. **Pay Phone:** Yes. **Rest Rooms and Showers:** Yes. **Fuel:** No. **Propane:** Yes. **Internal Roads:** Gravel. **RV Service:** No. **Market:** 5 mi. into town. **Restaurant:** 5 mi. into town. **General Store:** No. **Vending:** No. **Swimming:** No. **Playground:** No. **Other:** Horse facilities. **Activities:** Horseback riding, next to 280,000 acres of wildlife reserve. **Nearby Attractions:** Riley Ghost Town. **Additional Information:** Socorro Chamber of Commerce, (505) 835-0424.

RESTRICTIONS

Pets: On leash, cleaned up after. **Fires:** In grills. **Alcoholic Beverages:** At sites. **Vehicle Maximum Length:** None.

TO GET THERE

From Hwy. I-25 (Exit 175): on the north side of the highway, take the first left turn and then turn left into the campground.

BUCKHORN

Buckhorn RV Park

7656 Hwy. 180 West, Buckhorn 88025. T: (505) 535-2995.

RV ★★★★ Tent ★★★

Beauty: ★★★ Site Privacy: ★★★
Spaciousness: ★★★ Quiet: ★★★★
Security: ★★★★ Cleanliness: ★★★★
Insect Control: ★★★★ Facilities: ★★

Sites in this campground are laid out in two rows and numbered 1–10 and A–I. All sites in this field are open-ended, roughly 90 feet long. There are mobile homes around the entire perimeter of this campground. Sites on the east side (A–I) are 24 feet wide pull-throughs under willow trees. Site I is next to a mobile home. The nicest sites are A–C, as they are closest to the rest rooms and away from the mobile homes. On the west side, sites 1–10 are open-ended, 20-foot-wide back-ins. These sites are entirely unshaded and not as nice as the pull-through spaces. Site 10 lies next to some buildings. The rest rooms are small but clean and comfortable. This is a decent stop for a short stay, and is conveniently located near some interesting areas, such as the Catwalk.

BASICS

Operated By: Dave and Polli Morgan. **Open:** All year. **Site Assignment:** First come, first served; verbal reservations OK. **Registration:** In house or store; late arrivals use drop box at manager's house. **Fee:** RV $15 (full), tent $10; checks, but no credits cards. **Parking:** At site.

FACILITIES

Number of RV Sites: 19. **Number of Tent-Only Sites:** Undesignated sites. **Hookups:** Water, sewer, electric (30, 50 amp). **Dump Station:** No (sewer at all sites). **Laundry:** Yes. **Pay Phone:** Yes. **Rest Rooms and Showers:** Yes. **Fuel:** No. **Propane:** No. **Internal Roads:** Gravel. **RV Service:** No. **Market:** 10 mi. to Gila. **Restaurant:** Next door. **General Store:** Yes. **Vending:** Yes. **Swimming:** No. **Playground:** No. **Activities:** Bird-watching, fishing, hiking. **Nearby Attractions:** Mogollon ghost town, Glenwood Catwalk, Bill Evans Lake, Silver City. **Additional Information:** Silver City Grant County Chamber of Commerce, (505) 538-3785.

RESTRICTIONS

Pets: On leash, cleaned up after. **Fires:** In grills. **Alcoholic Beverages:** At sites. **Vehicle Maximum Length:** None.

TO GET THERE

From Hwy. 180, 0.25 mi. west of the town sign, on the south side of the highway.

CAPULIN

Capulin Camp and RV Park

P.O. Box 68, Capulin 88414. T: (505) 278-2921.

RV ★★★ Tent ★★★

Beauty: ★★★ Site Privacy: ★★★
Spaciousness: ★★ Quiet: ★★★
Security: ★★★★ Cleanliness: ★★★★
Insect Control: ★★★★ Facilities: ★★★

This campground has one row of back-ins and one row of pull-throughs. Sites 1–10 are 60-foot back-ins along the north edge that back to trees behind which is the highway. Sites 11–29 are 50-foot pull-throughs that can pull in sideways for extra space if one site is not large enough. Eastern end site 11 has the most space (33 feet wide) compared to the others (15 feet wide). Sites 13 and 14 and 15 and 16 share large shade trees. All other pull-through sites are unshaded, except for 29, which is right up against a copse of trees. (In fact, it is so close that the space is somewhat cramped because of its location.) Tenting is possible wherever there is grass (which is mostly to the south or east, next to sites 11 or 12). While the grass cover is quite adequate, the campground itself is not really tent-oriented, and there are no other facilities (such as table or fire pit) for tenters' use. The rest rooms are clean and comfortable. This campground is a very nice spot to stay at for a few days, and the Capulin Volcano National Monument is well worth checking out.

BASICS

Operated By: Donna Shewbert. **Open:** All year. **Site Assignment:** First come, first served; verbal reservations OK. **Registration:** In office; late arrivals use drop box. **Fee:** RV $18 (50 amp), $16 (30 amp), tent $10; checks, but no credits cards. **Parking:** At site.

FACILITIES

Number of RV Sites: 29. **Number of Tent-Only Sites:** Undesignated sites. **Hookups:** Water, sewer, electric (30, 50 amp). **Dump Station:** Yes. **Laundry:** Yes. **Pay Phone:** 1 block. **Rest Rooms and Showers:** Yes. **Fuel:** No. **Propane:** No. **Internal Roads:** Gravel. **RV Service:** No. **Market:** 0.25 mi. east. **Restaurant:** 0.25 mi. east. **General Store:** No. **Vending:** No. **Swimming:** No. **Playground:** No. **Other:** Cards and picnicking in the garage. **Activities:** Cards, hiking, swimming, boating, fishing. **Nearby Attractions:** Sugarite Canyon State Park, Capulin Volcano National Monument, Folsom Man Site, Clayton Lake State Park. **Additional Information:** Clayton Chamber of Commerce, (505) 374-9253.

RESTRICTIONS

Pets: On leash, cleaned up after. **Fires:** In grills. **Alcoholic Beverages:** At sites. **Vehicle Maximum Length:** None.

TO GET THERE

From the junction of Hwy. 325 and Hwy. 64/87, turn east onto Hwy. 64/87 and go 0.1 mi. Turn right at the sign into the entrance.

CARLSBAD

Carlsbad RV Park and Campground

4301 National Parks Hwy., Carlsbad 88220. T: (505) 885-6333; F: (505) 885-0784; www.carlsbadrvpark.com; camping@cavement.net.

RV ★★★★ Tent ★★★

Beauty: ★★★ Site Privacy: ★★★★
Spaciousness: ★★★★ Quiet: ★★★★
Security: ★★★★ Cleanliness: ★★★★★
Insect Control: ★★ Facilities: ★★★★★

Located on the southwest side of town (towards the caverns as you leave Carlsbad), this campground has got it all: pool, laundry, RV servicing, and activities galore. On top of that, facilities are super-clean and spacious. Sites are level and long (60 feet), with some extra-wide spaces (45 feet) for slideouts. Most RV sites have trees, with the exception of A4–A6. End site B31 is perhaps the most desirable site, with a large shade tree, extra space, and an easy in/out. Tent sites are level, but with a thin grass coverage. Tent sites 33 and 39 have good, large trees, and the unmarked site in the extreme northeast corner has extra room, being on the end of a row and backing onto a grassy field. Normal tent sites are 40 × 40 feet, a comfortable size. However, tent sites would be greatly improved if the trees were away from the road instead of right up against it. Owners of large dogs will be happy with the 3 acre off-leash area, where horses have even been let out to roam! Large camping groups can likewise be accommodated with the meeting room that can hold over one hundred people and includes a kitchen. Carlsbad makes a wonderful stop for those exploring the caverns or making their way to Texas or even Mexico.

BASICS

Operated By: Eddie and Sammie Herrington. **Open:** All year. **Site Assignment:** Upon registration; verbal reservations OK, necessary in summer; cancel within 24 hours for refund. **Registration:** In office; late arrivals use drop box. **Fee:** RV $20, tent $15. **Parking:** At site.

FACILITIES

Number of RV Sites: 96. **Number of Tent-Only Sites:** 36. **Hookups:** Water, sewer, electric (30, 50 amp), cable. **Each Site:** Tent sites: picnic table, grill. **Dump Station:** Yes. **Laundry:** Yes. **Pay Phone:** Yes. **Rest Rooms and Showers:** Yes. **Fuel:** No. **Propane:** No. **Internal Roads:** Gravel, in good condition. **RV Service:** Yes. **Market:** 1.5 mi. in Carlsbad. **Restaurant:** 3 blocks north. **General Store:** Yes. **Vending:** Yes. **Swimming:** Pool (heated indoor). **Playground:** Yes. **Other:** Cabins, tipi, rec room, group meeting room (100-plus person) w/ kitchen, dog walk, free charcoal and gas grills, RV storage, juke box. **Activities:** Holiday potlucks in summer, ping pong, video games, swimming, air hockey. **Nearby Attractions:** Carlsbad Caverns, Sitting Bull Falls, Living Desert. **Additional Information:** Carlsbad CVB, (800) 221-1224, (505) 887-6516.

Restrictions

Pets: On leash. **Fires:** In fire rings or grills. **Alcoholic Beverages:** Prefer none. **Vehicle Maximum Length:** 60 ft.

To Get There

From the junction of Hwy. 62/180 and Hwy. 285, go 1.7 mi. south on Hwy. 62/180. Turn west at the sign into the campground. The office is straight ahead.

CARRIZOZO

Sands RV Park and Motel

South Hwy. 54, P.O. Box 957, Carrizozo 88301. T: (800) 81SANDS or (505) 648-2989; F: (505) 648-4029.

RV ★★★ Tent ★★

Beauty: ★★★ Site Privacy: ★★
Spaciousness: ★★ Quiet: ★★
Security: ★★★★ Cleanliness: ★★★
Insect Control: ★★★★ Facilities: ★★★

Laid out in two rows, these RV sites are located close to a railway, and it gets very noisy when a train passes (just across the road). All sites are open-ended pull-throughs 15 feet wide and 75 feet (or so) long. Site 14 is blocked by a tree, so there is no way to pull through. End site 18 is also blocked by a tree, but has loads more space than any other site. The nicest site in the park is 15, which is very well shaded. Sites 19–21, situated to the west at 90° from the other sites, have cement slabs to park on, and are divided by short cement walls. The rest room is one unisex unit that is clean and comfortable. This park, under new management, makes a decent overnight stop, but need not make anyone's destination list.

Basics

Operated By: Steve and Gwen Dunne. **Open:** All year. **Site Assignment:** First come, first served; no reservations. **Registration:** In office, 24 hours. **Fee:** RV $15; checks, V, MC, AE, CB. **Parking:** At site.

Facilities

Number of RV Sites: 21. **Number of Tent-Only Sites:** Undesignated sites. **Hookups:** Water, sewer, electric (30, 50 amp), cable. **Dump Station:** No (sewer at all sites). **Laundry:** Yes. **Pay Phone:** No. **Rest Rooms and Showers:** Yes. **Fuel:** No. **Propane:** No. **Internal Roads:** Gravel. **RV Service:** No. **Market:** 0.1 mi. north. **Restaurant:** less than 0.25 mi. north. **General Store:** No. **Vending:** Yes. **Swimming:** No. **Playground:** No. **Other:** Rec center within walking distance. **Activities:** Fishing, boating. **Nearby Attractions:** Benito Lake, Valley of Fires, Ruidoso. **Additional Information:** Ruidoso Chamber of Commerce, (505) 257-7395.

Restrictions

Pets: On leash, cleaned up after. **Fires:** In grills. **Alcoholic Beverages:** At sites. **Vehicle Maximum Length:** None.

To Get There

From the junction of Hwy. 380 and Hwy. 54, turn south onto Hwy. 54 and go 0.8 mi. Turn right at the sign into the entrance.

CHAMA

Rio Chama RV Park

182 North State Hwy. 17, P.O. Box 706, Chama 87520. T: (505) 756-2303.

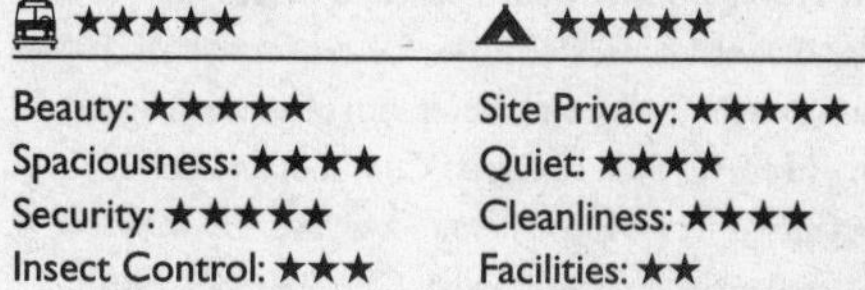

RV ★★★★★ Tent ★★★★★

Beauty: ★★★★★ Site Privacy: ★★★★★
Spaciousness: ★★★★ Quiet: ★★★★
Security: ★★★★★ Cleanliness: ★★★★
Insect Control: ★★★ Facilities: ★★

This lovely campground is loaded with trees, sits next to the Rio Chama River, and has beautiful RV and tent sites. The Cumbres and Toltec Scenic Railway passes within a stone's throw of the east border—which may or may not be an attraction to some campers. (There is only one run per day, entailing two passes of the campground.) Pretty much any site is highly desirable, with the possible exception of A6, which is right at the entrance. Site 39 has no shade tree but receives shade from the trees in neighboring sites. Pull-throughs are a good 65 feet in length, while back-ins average 42 feet. All sites are nearly 30 feet in width, which makes them comfortably spacious. The tenting area is absolutely gorgeous: it contains lush grass, large sites, and plenty of trees. A barbed-wire fence runs the length of the area, making it quite secure. Site 5 is the least desirable, as it contains a telephone pole and the communal wash basin. Any other tent site is well worth the price of admission. This campground is a popular destination—many seniors return year after year to meet old friends—and justifiably so.

Basics

Operated By: Harry and Kathy Tate. **Open:** May–Oct. **Site Assignment:** Upon registration; for reservations, write to the campground between Oct. and May, call between May and Oct. **Registration:** In office; late arrivals wake up manager for site assignment. **Fee:** RV $20 (full, 50 amp), $18 (full, 30 amp), $16 (water, electric); tent $12; V, MC. **Parking:** At site.

Facilities

Number of RV Sites: 98. **Number of Tent-Only Sites:** 14. **Hookups:** Water, sewer, electric (30, 50 amp). **Each Site:** Picnic table, fire ring/grill, many trees. **Dump Station:** Yes. **Laundry:** No. **Pay Phone:** Yes. **Rest Rooms and Showers:** Yes. **Fuel:** No. **Propane:** No. **Internal Roads:** Gravel. **RV Service:** No. **Market:** 2 mi. into Chama. **Restaurant:** 0.25 mi. **General Store:** No. **Vending:** Limited in office. **Swimming:** No. **Playground:** No. **Other:** Rio Chama River, covered shelter and stage, RV storage, notice board, railroad passes park (twice daily). **Activities:** Pot lucks, ice-cream socials, coffee and doughnuts on weekends, horseback riding, fishing. **Nearby Attractions:** Cumbres and Toltec Scenic Railroad, Rio Chama River. **Additional Information:** Chama Valley Chamber of Commerce, (800) 477-0149, (505) 756-2306.

Restrictions

Pets: On leash, cleaned up after, always attended outside. **Fires:** In ring/grill between 4–10 p.m. **Alcoholic Beverages:** At sites. **Vehicle Maximum Length:** None. **Other:** No generators.

To Get There

From the junction of Hwy. US 84/64 and Hwy. 17, go 1.8 mi. north on Hwy. 17. Turn right (east) at the sign into the campground entrance. The office is in a boxcar on the right.

CIMARRON
Ponil Campground

P.O. Box 323, Cimarron 87714. T: (505) 376-2700; F: (505) 376-2700.

RV ★★★★ Tent ★★★

Beauty: ★★★★ Site Privacy: ★★★
Spaciousness: ★★★ Quiet: ★★★★
Security: ★★★★★ Cleanliness: ★★★★★
Insect Control: ★★★★ Facilities: ★★★★

There is a tangible feeling of community amongst campers in Ponil. The sites in this park contribute to this feeling, as they are not all clearly delineated, and there is not a lot of space between them. However, there are spaces to accommodate a rig of any size. Sites in the northeast corner (in a somewhat separated nook) are very well shaded. Sites along the north and northwest edge back to trees. Sites in the southwest (along the entrance) back to an open grassy field where deer and elk are seen in the morning. These sites can pull through. The space around them is enough for each camper to do his or her own thing, but also lends itself to meeting and interacting with neighbors—one of the best reasons to travel. Tenting is possible in the open field in front of the house. There is one large tree and a hedge along the perimeter of the property that blocks out the road. This is a favorite destination for cub scouts and for RVers who wish to meet other campers in a lovely and quiet setting.

Basics

Operated By: Butch and Lawana Whitten. **Open:** All year. **Site Assignment:** Depending on site availability; verbal reservations OK. **Registration:** At manager's trailer; late arrivals select available site and pay in the morning. **Fee:** RV $15 (full), tent $10; checks, but no credits cards. **Parking:** At site.

Facilities

Number of RV Sites: 36. **Number of Tent-Only Sites:** Undesignated sites. **Hookups:** Water, sewer, electric (30 amp). **Dump Station:** Yes. **Laundry:** Yes. **Pay Phone:** Yes. **Rest Rooms and Showers:** Yes. **Fuel:** No. **Propane:** No. **Internal Roads:** Gravel. **RV Service:** No. **Market:** 1.5 mi. south. **Restaurant:** 1 mi. south. **General Store:**

No. **Vending:** No. **Swimming:** No. **Playground:** Yes. **Other:** Rec room. **Activities:** Singing twice weekly, hiking, wildlife-viewing. **Nearby Attractions:** Cimarron Canyon State Park, Maxwell National Wildlife Reserve, Ponil River at edge of campground. **Additional Information:** Cimarron Chamber of Commerce, (505) 376-2417.

RESTRICTIONS

Pets: On leash, cleaned up after. **Fires:** In grills. **Alcoholic Beverages:** At sites. **Vehicle Maximum Length:** None.

TO GET THERE

From the junction of Hwy. 58 and Hwy. 64, turn east onto Hwy. 64 and go 1 mi. Turn left at the sign into the entrance.

CLAYTON

Meadowlark KOA

P.O. Box 366, Clayton 88415. T: (800) 562-9507 or (505) 374-9508.

RV ★★★★ Tent ★★★★

Beauty: ★★★★	Site Privacy: ★★★★
Spaciousness: ★★★★	Quiet: ★★★★
Security: ★★★★	Cleanliness: ★★★★★
Insect Control: ★★★★	Facilities: ★★★★

The sites in Meadowlark KOA are enormous (easily 100 feet in length) and are able to accommodate a rig of any size. They are level, open, and grassy, with decent space (30 feet) between each one. The campground is surrounded by trees (except to the south), but there are not a lot of shade trees within the campground itself. The best RV sites are end sites 7, 14, 21, 27, and 33, which are endowed with larger trees and much more space. The least desirable sites are the back-ins along the eastern edge—not only because they are smaller (24 × 30 feet) and require backing in, but because they are close to the dog walk area. Indeed, sites 109 and 110 (100 and 101 on the map) are right on top of the dog walk area and contain a pooper scooper and trash bin. Sites 50–80 to the north are also less desirable, as they contain unsightly stumps (one has to wonder why the trees were cut down!) and are closer to the manager's house and the office buildings. Tent sites along the western edge are situated in front of a row of trees (which supply a canopy of shade), and are a roomy 24 × 40 feet. Those tent sites at the north side of the campground have much smaller trees, and back to a residential area, which makes them not nearly as nice as the former. The rest room and showers are modern, spacious, and spotless. They are simply, but nicely, decorated. The laundry is likewise clean and roomy. This is a campground that is worthwhile finding, whether camping in an RV or a tent.

BASICS

Operated By: Chuck and Sue Richardson. **Open:** Mar. 1–Oct. 31. **Site Assignment:** Upon registration; credit card required for reservation, 24 hours cancellation policy. **Registration:** In office; late arrivals use drop box. **Fee:** RV $20 (full), tent $16. **Parking:** At site.

FACILITIES

Number of RV Sites: 65. **Number of Tent-Only Sites:** 12. **Hookups:** Water, sewer, electric (30, 50 amp), cable. **Each Site:** Picnic table, grill, shrubs for privacy. **Dump Station:** Yes. **Laundry:** Yes. **Pay Phone:** Yes. **Rest Rooms and Showers:** Yes. **Fuel:** No. **Propane:** Yes. **Internal Roads:** Gravel. **RV Service:** No. **Market:** 8 blocks northwest. **Restaurant:** 6 blocks northwest. **General Store:** Yes. **Vending:** No. **Swimming:** No. **Playground:** Yes. **Other:** 2 cabins, game room, pet walk area. **Activities:** Hiking, tetherball. **Nearby Attractions:** Clayton State Park, Capulin Mountain National Monument, dinosaur tracks. **Additional Information:** Clayton Chamber of Commerce, (505) 374-9253.

RESTRICTIONS

Pets: On leash, cleaned up after. **Fires:** In grills. **Alcoholic Beverages:** At sites. **Vehicle Maximum Length:** None.

TO GET THERE

From the junction of Hwy. 56/64/412 and Hwy. 87, go 0.7 mi. south on Hwy. 87 (East). Turn left at the sign onto Spruce, and go 0.35 mi. to the entrance. Turn right at the sign.

CLOVIS

Ideal RV Park

1051 NM 311, Clovis 88101. T: (505) 791-3177 or (505) 799-2315; F: (505) 791-3177; idealrv@zianet.com.

RV ★★★ Tent n/a

Beauty: ★★★	Site Privacy: ★★★
Spaciousness: ★★★★	Quiet: ★★★★
Security: ★★★	Cleanliness: ★★★
Insect Control: ★★★	Facilities: ★★★

Ideal is a shady campground with loads of trees: there are trees at nearly every site, and a row of trees along the north perimeter, beyond which lies agricultural land. The downside are the mobile homes to the east and along part of the south side—they detract about as much as the trees add. Sites are 60-foot long pull-throughs, 33 feet wide, level and grassy. However, most sites are not clearly marked: only those closest to the laundry have numbers. The laundry facility is large and well-lit, with a cute row of flowers planted around the outside. The rest rooms within are clean except for the floors (including inside the showers), which, during our visit, were peeling paint and in need of a scrub. The site that could be 14 (6 sites east of the laundry on the north side) has a nice tree and a little extra space. The least desirable sites are on the ends closest to the mobile homes—again, unnumbered. According to its proprietor, the park is only in its second year of operation and hopefully it will see some improvement in the coming years. As it stands today, it is a campground of extremes, with its deficiencies offsetting its attributes.

BASICS

Operated By: Rickey and Mindy Boddy. **Open:** All year. **Site Assignment:** First come, first served; verbal reservations OK. **Registration:** In office; late arrivals use drop box. **Fee:** $14. **Parking:** At site.

FACILITIES

Number of RV Sites: 20. **Number of Tent-Only Sites:** 0. **Hookups:** Water, sewer, electric (30, 50). **Each Site:** Tree. **Dump Station:** No (sewer at all sites). **Laundry:** Yes. **Pay Phone:** No. **Rest Rooms and Showers:** Yes. **Fuel:** No. **Propane:** No. **Internal Roads:** Gravel. **RV Service:** No. **Market:** 7 mi. east to Clovis. **Restaurant:** 7 mi. east to Clovis. **General Store:** No. **Vending:** No. **Swimming:** No. **Playground:** No. **Other:** Close to Cannon Air Force Base. **Activities:** Clovis Music Festival. **Nearby Attractions:** Blackwater Draw Museum. **Additional Information:** Clovis/Curry County Chamber of Commerce, (505) 763-3435.

RESTRICTIONS

Pets: On leash. **Fires:** In grills/pits (unless burn ban in effect). **Alcoholic Beverages:** At sites. **Vehicle Maximum Length:** None.

TO GET THERE

From the junction of Hwy. 70 and Hwy. 60/84, turn west onto Hwy. 60/84 (first street north of the bridge) and drive 7.2 mi. to Hwy. 311. Turn right onto Hwy. 311 and drive 0.5 mi., then turn right at the sign into the entrance. The office is on the right.

COLUMBUS

Pancho Villa State Park

P.O. Box 450, Columbus 88029. T: (505) 531-2711; F: (505) 531-2115.

RV ★★★★★ Tent ★★★★

Beauty: ★★★★★	Site Privacy: ★★★★★
Spaciousness: ★★★★★	Quiet: ★★★★
Security: ★★★★	Cleanliness: ★★★★
Insect Control: ★★★★	Facilities: ★★★

Columbus is a small town, and despite proximity to the highway and the town, the park still retains a desert-wilderness feel. On top of this, the park management obviously puts a lot of work into maintenance, which brings out the beauty of the natural environment. Large rigs will love this park, as all but four sites are pull-throughs—and those four are large enough (60 feet) to "parallel park" instead of backing in, if so desired. Sites 1–4 are 150-foot pull-throughs along the eastern edge of the campground (by the highway). Sites 22–25 are the same, but across an internal drive, and 26–34 are further south. Sites 5–10 are located on a gigantic, open gravel road that can fit any rig in practically any direction. Sites 10–16 are nicer than the eastern side, since they are further from the highway. Sites 58–61 are developed back-in sites (no electricity) that measure 60 × 60 feet. The best area to camp in is the western side, as it is further from the highway and the entrance. However, any site in this park is a beautiful place to camp. Tent sites are located on a patch of thick grass that looks rather out of place in this desert campground, but offers nice camping. The rest rooms are attractively modeled and both clean and spacious. This is a wonderful campground with natural sites that tenters and RVers will enjoy.

BASICS

Operated By: New Mexico State Park Division. **Open:** All year. **Site Assignment:** First come, first served; reservations by credit card or check, no refunds. **Registration:** At pay station. **Fee:** Primitive site $8, developed site $10, water, electric $14; checks, but no credit cards. **Parking:** At site.

FACILITIES

Number of RV Sites: 80. **Number of Tent-Only Sites:** Undesignated sites. **Hookups:** Electric (20, 30 amp). **Each Site:** Picnic table, fire pit. **Dump Station:** Yes. **Laundry:** No. **Pay Phone:** Yes. **Rest Rooms and Showers:** Yes. **Fuel:** No. **Propane:** No. **Internal Roads:** Paved. **RV Service:** No. **Market:** 0.25 mi. north. **Restaurant:** 0.25 mi. north. **General Store:** No. **Vending:** No. **Swimming:** No. **Playground:** Yes. **Other:** Rec hall, picnic pavilion, botanical gardens, museum. **Activities:** Tours to Mexico, rock-hounding. **Nearby Attractions:** Mexico, El Paso, Rockhound State Park. **Additional Information:** New Mexico State Parks Division, (888) NM-PARKS.

RESTRICTIONS

Pets: On leash, cleaned up after. **Fires:** In grills. **Alcoholic Beverages:** At sites. **Vehicle Maximum Length:** None.

TO GET THERE

From the junction of Hwy. 11 and Hwy. 9, turn southwest onto Hwy. 9 and go 0.1 mi. Turn left at the sign into the entrance.

DATIL

Eagle Guest Ranch

P.O. Box 68, Datil 87821. T: (505) 772-5612.

RV: ★★★★ Tent: ★★

Beauty: ★★★★
Spaciousness: ★★★★
Security: ★★★★
Insect Control: ★★★★
Site Privacy: ★★★★
Quiet: ★★★★
Cleanliness: ★★★
Facilities: ★★

This RV park is located behind a cafe, motel, gas station, and crafts store. The campground is very undeveloped, with grass and dirt spaces. Some of the sites (especially 1–4) are overgrown with weeds, and the campground itself needs a good picking-up. Sites 1–14 are 45-foot back-ins laid out along the highway. Sites 1–3 are very well shaded, site 10 is unshaded, and sites 7 and 8 are used by long-term residents. Pull-throughs include 15 and 16 (40 feet) and 20–22 (150 feet). Sites 12 and 14 and 17 and 18 can be used as pull-throughs if the accompanying site is unoccupied. Sites 24 and 25 are 75-foot back-ins, and 26 is a well shaded 45-foot pull-through. Both 25 and 26 have a rather rough road. Tenting is possible wherever there is grass (which is pretty much anywhere around the campground), but a shade tree is hard to come by. As there are no showers, tenters will have a rougher time than self-contained units. Likewise, the rest rooms in the store are closed from 9 p.m. and all day Sunday. There are many campgrounds in the area, but they do not offer hookups. In fact, this may very well be the only campground within 50 miles to offer hookups of any kind. Tenters may have a better stay at a National Forest campground, as these are sure to provide showers.

BASICS

Operated By: Carol Coker. **Open:** All year. **Site Assignment:** First come, first served; no reservations. **Registration:** In store; late arrivals select available site and pay in the morning. **Fee:** RV $12 (full), tent $6; V, MC, AE, D, DC, CB. **Parking:** At site.

FACILITIES

Number of RV Sites: 25. **Number of Tent-Only Sites:** Undesignated sites. **Hookups:** Water, sewer, electric (20, 50 amp). **Dump Station:** No. **Laundry:** No. **Pay Phone:** Yes. **Rest Rooms and Showers:** No (rest rooms in store). **Fuel:** Yes. **Propane:** No. **Internal Roads:** Dirt. **RV Service:** No. **Market:** 34 mi. to Magdalena. **Restaurant:** On-site. **General Store:** Yes. **Vending:** No. **Swimming:** No. **Playground:** No. **Other:** Cafe, motel. **Activities:** Rock-climbing, fishing, boating, hunting. **Nearby Attractions:** Thompson Canyon, VLA, Quemado Lake. **Additional Information:** Socorro Chamber of Commerce, (505) 835-0424.

RESTRICTIONS

Pets: On leash, cleaned up after. **Fires:** In grills. **Alcoholic Beverages:** At sites. **Vehicle Maximum Length:** None.

TO GET THERE

Located at the intersection of Hwy. 12 and Hwy. 60 in Datil.

DEMING

Wagon Wheel RV Park

2801 East Motel Dr., Deming 88030. T: (505) 546-8650.

RV ★★★★ Tent ★★★

Beauty: ★★★ Site Privacy: ★★★
Spaciousness: ★★★★ Quiet: ★★★
Security: ★★★★ Cleanliness: ★★★
Insect Control: ★★★★ Facilities: ★★★

Laid out in three rows of sites, this campground has very attractive landscaping using bushes, trees, and flowers. Sites 1–11 are 45-foot back-ins in the southeast corner. Site 12 is secluded by trees and a fence and has good shade. In the eastern row, sites 13–28 are 60-foot pull-throughs. Sites in the northern section (21–28) are bare gravel. Sites 29–51 in the middle row are open-ended pull-throughs averaging 60 × 21 feet. Site 29, in front of the office, may receive registration traffic. Sites 31, 34, and 39 are very well shaded. Sites in the northern section (44–51) are bare gravel. The western row (sites 56–72) has back-ins along the fence (sites 56–63) and 60-foot pull-throughs (64–72). All sites can be used for tenting, although 1–12 are probably the best. The rec room and jacuzzi are comfortable, although the campground gets crowded in winter, and you may have to wait to use these facilities. The rest rooms are OK, but could use a deep cleaning. Priding itself on being the least expensive campground in a row of RV parks, this is a very nice destination for RVers for a short stay or even over the winter.

BASICS

Operated By: Dan Wagner. **Open:** All year. **Site Assignment:** Depending on site availability; verbal reservations OK. **Registration:** In office; late arrivals use drop box. **Fee:** RV $11 (full), tent $11; no credits cards, but checks. **Parking:** At site.

FACILITIES

Number of RV Sites: 73. **Number of Tent-Only Sites:** 0. **Hookups:** Water, sewer, electric (20, 30, 50 amp), cable, phone. **Each Site:** Picnic table. **Dump Station:** No (sewer at all sites). **Laundry:** Yes. **Pay Phone:** Yes. **Rest Rooms and Showers:** Yes. **Fuel:** No. **Propane:** No. **Internal Roads:** Gravel. **RV Service:** No. **Market:** 1.25 mi. west. **Restaurant:** Less than 0.25 mi. west. **General Store:** No. **Vending:** Yes. **Swimming:** No (Jacuzzi). **Playground:** No. **Other:** RV supplies, clubhouse w/ kitchen, game room, movies, gift shop, modem. **Activities:** Planned activities in winter, rock-hounding, hiking. **Nearby Attractions:** Rockhound State Park, City of Rocks State Park. **Additional Information:** Deming Chamber of Commerce, (505) 546-2674.

RESTRICTIONS

Pets: On leash, cleaned up after. **Fires:** In grills. **Alcoholic Beverages:** At sites (not in clubhouse). **Vehicle Maximum Length:** None.

TO GET THERE

From Hwy. I-10 (Exit 85), turn south onto Motel Dr. and go 1.2 mi. Turn right at the sign into the entrance.

DWYER

Faywood Hot Springs

165 Hwy. 61, HC 71 Box 1240, Dwyer 88034. T: (505) 536-9663; www.faywood.com.

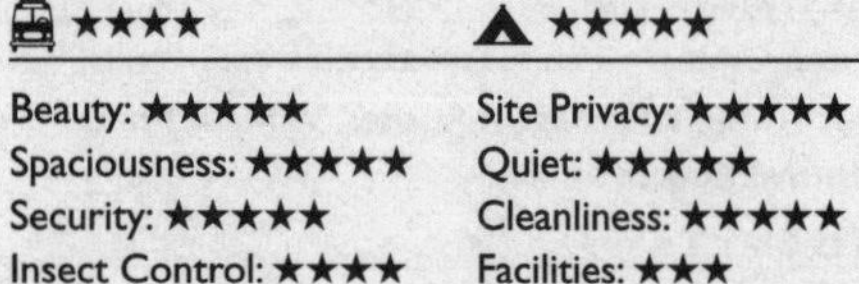

RV ★★★★ Tent ★★★★★

Beauty: ★★★★★ Site Privacy: ★★★★★
Spaciousness: ★★★★★ Quiet: ★★★★★
Security: ★★★★★ Cleanliness: ★★★★★
Insect Control: ★★★★ Facilities: ★★★

Let's put this out upfront: this natural campground in the desert wilderness will most likely appeal to folks with an adventurous heart. The public clothing-optional areas are certainly not for everyone. That being said, it's a wonderful campground with beautiful, if undeveloped, sites somewhat scattered about the property. Site 7–16 are pull-throughs located along the northern edge. Site 7 is located next to the caretaker's mobile home. Site 10 is extra wide (40 feet compared to 21 feet). One of the nicest spots, 18, lacks shade but is an extremely large back-in that commands a gorgeous view. Sites

23–26 in the southwest corner are surrounded by vegetation and are therefore very private. Tent sites 4–6 are sandy sites surrounded by vegetation. These are the nicest, most private sites. The other tent sites are mixed in amongst the RV sites. The rest rooms are pit toilets scattered around the campground, and the shower is outdoors, only partially concealed. This campground may appeal most to tenters and the adventurous Airstream crowd, but is a beautiful slice of desert wilderness that should not be missed.

Basics

Operated By: Elon Yurwit and Wanda Fuselier. **Open:** All year. **Site Assignment:** First come, first served; credit card required for reservation, 2 days cancellation policy. **Registration:** In office; no late arrivals, gate locked at 10 p.m. **Fee:** RV $27 (full), tent $15; V, MC. **Parking:** At site.

Facilities

Number of RV Sites: 21. **Number of Tent-Only Sites:** 12. **Hookups:** Water, sewer, electric (20, 30, 50 amp). **Dump Station:** Yes. **Laundry:** No. **Pay Phone:** No. **Rest Rooms and Showers:** Yes. **Fuel:** No. **Propane:** No. **Internal Roads:** Gravel. **RV Service:** No. **Market:** Convenience store 12 mi. north to Hurley, supermarket 24 mi. north or south. **Restaurant:** 12 mi. north to Hurley. **General Store:** No. **Vending:** No. **Swimming:** No (hot springs). **Playground:** No. **Other:** 1,200 acres of hiking, drinks and some grocery items, cabins, tipi, shaded picnic pavilion, clothing required/optional areas. **Activities:** Horseback riding, birding, hiking, biking, stargazing. **Nearby Attractions:** City of Rocks State Park, Gila National Monument, Las Cruces. **Additional Information:** Deming Chamber of Commerce, (505) 546-2674.

Restrictions

Pets: On leash, cleaned up after. **Fires:** In grills. **Alcoholic Beverages:** At sites. **Vehicle Maximum Length:** None.

To Get There

From the junction of Hwy. 180 and Hwy. 61, go north on Hwy. 61 1.6 mi. Turn left onto a very nondescript gravel road (with small sign) and follow it to the office.

EAGLE NEST

West Lake RV Park

HCR 71 Box 6, Eagle Nest 87718.T: (505) 377-PARK; gplenz@afweb.com.

RV ★★★★ Tent n/a

Beauty: ★★★★	Site Privacy: ★★★
Spaciousness: ★★	Quiet: ★★★★
Security: ★★★★	Cleanliness: ★★★★★
Insect Control: ★★★★	Facilities: ★

This campground is located in a valley surrounded by mountains, with lake views and access to lake. Sites are laid out in a semi-circle around the perimeter of the property. Sites are open-ended back-ins, but limited to about 45 × 25 feet. Sites 1–12 are located along the wooden fence to the north. Site 1 is quite small (30 × 25 feet), and 11–13, in the corner, seem somewhat hemmed in. Sites 13–18 are laid out along the east side, overlooking the lake. These sites (minus 13 and 18) are the nicest sites. Sites 19–28, along the south side, overlook fields, cabins, and the lake. Site 18 and 19 are slightly blocked by one another. In an area with a number of RV parks, this campground offers nice lake views. Any one of the RV parks in the area are a great place to be when the weather elsewhere is climbing into the 90s, as this place stays cool all year.

Basics

Operated By: Phil and Glenda Lenz. **Open:** May 1–Oct. 31. **Site Assignment:** Depending on site availability; verbal reservations OK. **Registration:** In office; late arrivals select available site and pay in the morning. **Fee:** RV $19; checks, but no credits cards. **Parking:** At site.

Facilities

Number of RV Sites: 28. **Number of Tent-Only Sites:** 0. **Hookups:** Water, sewer, electric (30, 50 amp). **Each Site:** Covered picnic table. **Dump Station:** No (sewer at all sites). **Laundry:** Yes. **Pay Phone:** No. **Rest Rooms and Showers:** No. **Fuel:** No. **Propane:** No. **Internal Roads:** Gravel. **RV Service:** No. **Market:** 12 mi. to Angel Fire. **Restaurant:** 1.5 mi. east. **General Store:** No. **Vending:** No. **Swimming:** No. **Playground:** No. **Other:** Covered pavilion, views, cool weather. **Activities:** Fishing, boating, fish fry Fri., potlucks. **Nearby Attractions:** Cimarron Canyon State Park, DAV Vietnam Veterans National Memorial.

Additional Information: Eagle Nest Chamber of Commerce, (505) 377–2420.

Restrictions

Pets: On leash, cleaned up after. **Fires:** In common grill. **Alcoholic Beverages:** At sites. **Vehicle Maximum Length:** 42 ft.

To Get There

From the junction of Hwy. 38 and Hwy. 64, turn west onto Hwy. 64 and go 1.5 mi. Turn left at the sign into the entrance.

EDGEWOOD

Red Arrow Edgewood RV Park

P.O. Box 1750, Edgewood 87015. T: (505) 281-0893.

RV ★★★ Tent ★★

Beauty: ★★★	Site Privacy: ★★★
Spaciousness: ★★★	Quiet: ★★★
Security: ★★★★	Cleanliness: ★★★
Insect Control: ★★★★	Facilities: ★★★

Basically a large, open desert area, Red Arrow Edgewood has a natural, back-to-earth feel. There is an attractive garden with bench and fountain at the entrance. However, the campground itself is in need of some attention. While most visitors (especially RVers) may not even notice, those who poke around a little (or use the tenting area) will soon begin to find the stored equipment, piles of wood and tree limbs. The RV section itself is mainly clean. Consisting of lettered rows of sites, this park has long back-ins and pull-throughs that can accommodate most rigs—even with tows. Rows A and M have 75-foot pull-throughs. While row A is unshaded, a few sites in row M (11 and 12) are shaded. Rows B, BD, and P have 60-foot back-ins. Rows B and BD are a little nicer; P abuts a junky yard. The tent area to the northwest is—to say the least—a disappointment. The nicest site has a good view of a billboard, while the other tent sites are located next to piles of wood and other debris. The rest rooms, likewise, need only a few basic repairs to be of better service. While the campground itself has the potential to be utterly charming, the lack of maintenance detracts from the experience.

Basics

Operated By: Jerry and Lory Veckert. **Open:** All year. **Site Assignment:** Upon registration; verbal reservations OK. **Registration:** In office; late arrivals use drop box. **Fee:** RV $22 (full), tent $15; checks, V, MC, AE, D. **Parking:** At site.

Facilities

Number of RV Sites: 40. **Number of Tent-Only Sites:** 5. **Hookups:** Water, sewer, electric (30, 50 amp). **Each Site:** Some tables. **Dump Station:** Yes. **Laundry:** Yes. **Pay Phone:** Yes. **Rest Rooms and Showers:** Yes. **Fuel:** No. **Propane:** No. **Internal Roads:** Gravel. **RV Service:** No. **Market:** 0.25 mi. west. **Restaurant:** 0.5 mi. west. **General Store:** No. **Vending:** No. **Swimming:** Pool. **Playground:** Yes. **Activities:** Tours to Albuquqrque. **Nearby Attractions:** Rte. 66. **Additional Information:** Albuquerque Chamber of Commerce, (505) 764-3700.

Restrictions

Pets: On leash, cleaned up after. **Fires:** In grills. **Alcoholic Beverages:** At sites. **Vehicle Maximum Length:** None.

To Get There

From Hwy. I-40 (Exit 187), turn south onto Hwy. 334 and go 1 block to the 4-way stop. Turn left onto Historic Rte. 66 (Hwy. 333E) and go 0.5 mi. east on Hwy. 333. Turn left at the sign into the entrance.

EL MORRO

El Morro RV Park

Rte. 2 Box 44, Ramah 87321. T: (505) 783-4612; www.elmorrow-nm.com; elmorrow@elmorrow-nm.com.

RV ★★★ Tent ★★★★

Beauty: ★★★★	Site Privacy: ★★★
Spaciousness: ★★★★	Quiet: ★★★★
Security: ★★★★	Cleanliness: ★★★
Insect Control: ★★★★	Facilities: ★★★

This is a wilderness campground with the highway directly to the north. Sites are not all numbered, and the only distinction between a tent or RV site is the existence or lack of hookups. Sites 1 and 3 are 60-foot back-ins that back slightly into the woods. Sites 2 and 4 are 45-foot back-ins that are slightly sloped. Sites on the inside of the loop are 54-foot back-ins (including 7). The site furthest west on the outside of the loop (possibly 9) is a 65-foot back-in. Site 10 is the largest, at 75 feet. This is a dirt back-in with trees around the site, but the site itself is not shaded. Sites 15 and 16 are overgrown with weeds. Sites that back to the highway include 10, 16, and 19, as well as some unnumbered sites on the north side of the loop. Tent sites include three in the southwest corner, on the inside of the loop. Tent site 35 is the best, as it offers a space under a tree. Neither the roads nor the sites themselves are in especially good condition. The sites are mostly dirt, and many are overgrown. On the plus side, there are excellent views of a rocky outcropping, and the campground is located only one mile from the El Morro National Monument.

Basics

Operated By: Louis Gross. **Open:** All year. **Site Assignment:** First come, first served; no reservations. **Registration:** In cafe; late arrivals select available site and pay in the morning. **Fee:** RV $10 (full), tent $7; V, MC. **Parking:** At site.

Facilities

Number of RV Sites: 27. **Number of Tent-Only Sites:** 6. **Hookups:** Water, sewer, electric (20, 30 amp). **Each Site:** Picnic table. **Dump Station:** No. **Laundry:** No. **Pay Phone:** Yes. **Rest Rooms and Showers:** Yes. **Fuel:** No. **Propane:** No. **Internal Roads:** Gravel/dirt. **RV Service:** No. **Market:** Small, 5 mi. southwest; large, 15 mi. to Vine Hill. **Restaurant:** 15 mi. to Vine Hill. **General Store:** No. **Vending:** No. **Swimming:** No. **Playground:** No. **Other:** Cafe, cabins, trails. **Activities:** Hiking, caving. **Nearby Attractions:** El Morro National Monument, Bandera Crater and Ice Caves, Cibola National Forest. **Additional Information:** Grants Chamber of Commerce, (505) 287-4802.

Restrictions

Pets: On leash, cleaned up after. **Fires:** In grills. **Alcoholic Beverages:** At sites. **Vehicle Maximum Length:** None.

To Get There

From Hwy. I-40 (Exit 81), turn southwest onto Hwy. 53 and go 40 mi. Turn left at the sign (near mile marker 46) into the entrance.

ELEPHANT BUTTE

Lakeside RV Park

107 Country Club Blvd., P.O. Drawer 981, Elephant Butte 87935. T: (800) 808-5848 or (505) 744-5996; F: (505) 744-4903; www.lakeside.com; lakeside@riolink.com.

RV: ★★★★★ Tent: n/a

Beauty: ★★★★	Site Privacy: ★★★★★
Spaciousness: ★★★★★	Quiet: ★★★★
Security: ★★★★★	Cleanliness: ★★★★★
Insect Control: ★★★★	Facilities: ★★★★

This RV park is not only the closest park to the lake, but is a beautiful place to camp to boot. Laid out in three tiers, the park uses natural desert landscaping (rocks, cacti) to beautiful effect. In the lowest tier, sites 2–8 are open-ended back-ins (roughly 55 ¥ 22 feet) situated around the office. The uppermost tier contains sites large enough for a vehicle and boat. These open-ended pull-throughs (sites 20–26 and 36–41) are about 70 ¥ 30 feet. Sites 27–30 are 45-foot back-ins. Sites 42–50 deserve special mention, as they are located around the Native Garden, a gorgeous display of alow, rocks, and cacti. Of these sites, 44 and 47 have the best shade. These are by far the most beautiful sites in the park. In the middle tier are 54-foot back-ins that back to either a fence and the first tier (on the west side) or to a hedge and the road (on the east side). Two hosts live in the campground, ensuring that the park remains secure at all times. The rest rooms are absolutely spotless and nicely decorated. The showers are likewise clean and very comfortable. This is an RV park that deserves a special visit, not only for the surrounding beauty, but for the care and maintenance given to the park itself.

Basics

Operated By: Mary and Dave Amaral. **Open:** All year. **Site Assignment:** Upon registration; credit card required for reservation, no refunds. **Registration:** In office; late arrivals select available site and pay in the morning. **Fee:** Back-ins $20, pull-throughs $22–26; checks, V, MC, D. **Parking:** At site.

Facilities

Number of RV Sites: 50. **Number of Tent-Only Sites:** 0. **Hookups:** Water, sewer, electric (30, 50 amp), cable. **Dump Station:** Yes. **Laundry:**

Yes. **Pay Phone:** Yes. **Rest Rooms and Showers:** Yes. **Fuel:** No. **Propane:** No. **Internal Roads:** Gravel. **RV Service:** No. **Market:** 5 mi. to Truth or Consequences. **Restaurant:** 0.5 mi. to Elephant Butte. **General Store:** No. **Vending:** No. **Swimming:** Yes (lake). **Playground:** No. **Other:** Lounge, phone hookups, BBQ pits. **Activities:** Organized activities (in winter), potlucks, doughnuts on Wednesday morning, boating, fishing, swimming. **Nearby Attractions:** Ghost towns, Truth or Consequences, Elephant Butte State Park. **Additional Information:** Elephant Butte Chamber of Commerce, (505) 744-9101.

Restrictions

Pets: On leash, cleaned up after, no barking. **Fires:** In grills. **Alcoholic Beverages:** At sites. **Vehicle Maximum Length:** None.

To Get There

From Hwy. I-25 (Exit 83): from the east side of the highway, go straight east on Hwy. 95 for 3.6 mi. Turn right onto Country Club Blvd., and go 0.1 mi. Turn right onto Water Ave. and take the first right into the park.

ESPAÑOLA

Cottonwood RV Park

Rte. 3 Box 245, Española 87532. T: (505) 753-6608; F: (505) 753-3858.

RV ★★★ | Tent ★★★

Beauty: ★★★★	Site Privacy: ★★★
Spaciousness: ★★★	Quiet: ★★★★
Security: ★★★★★	Cleanliness: ★★★
Insect Control: ★★★★	Facilities: ★★★

RV sites in this campground are laid out in one continuous row from the entrance at the south end to the furthest site to the north. They are, however, broken up into three tiers, with a fourth tier for tents right at the entrance. Sites 1–12 on the first tier are 30-foot sites (1–6 are pull-throughs, 7–12 are back-ins). All spaces are 25 feet wide. Sites 2 and 10 are well shaded, site 12 lies next to and above a house. On the second tier, site 13 is used by a long-term guest, and 14 is the smallest site at 40 feet. The rest of the sites are 70-foot pull-throughs. Sites 17–20 have the best shade. Site 22 has only 45 feet of usable space before it begins to slope. On the lowest tier, 23 requires an excruciatingly tight turn on the sloped road from the second tier and should be avoided by larger rigs. Sites 30–33 share a large shade tree, and 30 is the overall nicest (and shadiest) site. Site 32 looks unusable, and the tree there prevents 31 from being a true pull-through. This level is the nicest area, as it is surrounded by vegetation and offers the most shade. The tent sites are located in a dirt area sheltered by tree. There is one BBQ and a cement fire pit with seats for communal use. The rest rooms need a good cleaning, and the stalls (at least in the men's room) do not have doors. This campground is equally nice for tenters as for RVers.

Basics

Operated By: Art Martinez. **Open:** All year. **Site Assignment:** Upon registration; credit card required for reservation, 48 hours cancellation policy. **Registration:** In restaurant; late arrivals select available site and pay in the morning. **Fee:** RV $19 (full), tent $15; checks, V, MC, D. **Parking:** At site.

Facilities

Number of RV Sites: 37. **Number of Tent-Only Sites:** Undesignated sites. **Hookups:** Water, sewer, electric (30, 50 amp). **Dump Station:** No (sewer at all sites). **Laundry:** Yes. **Pay Phone:** Yes. **Rest Rooms and Showers:** Yes. **Fuel:** No. **Propane:** No. **Internal Roads:** Gravel. **RV Service:** No. **Market:** 2 mi. north. **Restaurant:** On-site. **General Store:** No. **Vending:** No. **Swimming:** No. **Playground:** No. **Other:** Discount on meal or free margarita upon registration. **Activities:** Fishing, gambling, visiting pueblos. **Nearby Attractions:** Pueblos, Santa Fe Opera, casinos. **Additional Information:** Española Chamber of Commerce, (505) 753-2831.

Restrictions

Pets: On leash, cleaned up after. **Fires:** In grills. **Alcoholic Beverages:** At sites. **Vehicle Maximum Length:** None.

To Get There

From the junction of Hwy. 30 and Hwy. 84/285, turn east onto Hwy. 84/285 and go 2 mi. Turn left into the restaurant complex and register in the restaurant.

FARMINGTON

Dad's RV Park

202 East Pinon St., Farmington 87401. T: (888) 326-DADS or (505) 564-2222.

RV ★★ | Tent n/a

Beauty: ★ | Site Privacy: ★★★
Spaciousness: ★★★ | Quiet: ★★★
Security: ★★★★★ | Cleanliness: ★★★
Insect Control: ★★★★ | Facilities: ★

This RV park is an enclosed gravel area in the middle of an urban setting. The fence is locked at night for added security. The park is close to services that a traveler might need, and its proximity makes it a popular place to stay for visitors to the city's hospital. However, there is little else to recommend here. The sites are flat and open. There is one tree in the park, shared by sites 8 and 9. These two sites, along with 10, are clustered together and slightly set apart from the rest of the sites, which makes them slightly more private. The rest of the sites are located in a strip. They all are pull-throughs designed for self-contained units. The laundry, in the red "barn" by the manager's house, is small but comfortable and clean. Dad's would benefit from shade trees and rest room facilities. RVers who are not equipped (or willing) to stay in a park without rest rooms or shade trees should press on—possibly to Aztec.

BASICS

Operated By: Regina Ingram. **Open:** All year. **Site Assignment:** Upon registration; credit card or check required for reservation, 8–12 hours cancellation policy. **Registration:** In office at back of park, 24 hours. **Fee:** RV $15; V, MC, D. **Parking:** At site.

FACILITIES

Number of RV Sites: 13. **Number of Tent-Only Sites:** 0. **Hookups:** Water, sewer, electric (30 amp). **Each Site:** Picnic table. **Dump Station:** No (sewer at all sites). **Laundry:** Yes. **Pay Phone:** Yes. **Rest Rooms and Showers:** No. **Fuel:** No. **Propane:** No. **Internal Roads:** Gravel. **RV Service:** No. **Market:** 9 blocks. **Restaurant:** 4 blocks. **General Store:** No. **Vending:** No. **Swimming:** No. **Playground:** No. **Activities:** Golf, sightseeing. **Nearby Attractions:** Aztec Ruins National Monument, Bisti/De-Na-Zin Wilderness Area. **Additional Information:** Farmington CVB, (800) 448-1240, (505) 326-7602.

RESTRICTIONS

Pets: On leash, cleaned up after. **Fires:** None. **Alcoholic Beverages:** None. **Vehicle Maximum Length:** 45 ft.

TO GET THERE

From the junction of Hwys. 64 (Murray St.) and 371 (Pinon St.), go 1 mi. east on Pinon. Turn left at the sign into the entrance. The office is at the very back of the park.

FORT SUMNER

Valley View Mobile Home and RV Park

Rte. 1 Box 36, 1401 East Sumner, Fort Sumner 88119. T: (505) 355-2380; www.billythekid.nv.switchboard.net; btkmuseum@plateautel.net.

RV ★★ | Tent n/a

Beauty: ★★ | Site Privacy: ★★★
Spaciousness: ★★★★ | Quiet: ★★★
Security: ★★ | Cleanliness: ★★★
Insect Control: ★★★ | Facilities: ★★

Valley View has super-long sites (80-foot pull-throughs and back-ins), but, alas, little else for which to recommend it. The trees visible from the campground help elevate the beauty of this park from its urban setting, but the mobile homes inside detract in equal measure. The three (unnumbered) back-ins in the southeast corner have a hedge along the east side, and there is a row of trees along the south side, making these three back-ins much nicer than the rest of the sites. The pull-throughs in the middle of the park are long, level, and grassy, but quite open. They are, however, clearly numbered, which is not the case for the back-ins. The least desirable site is undoubtedly 19, barely 30 feet from a mobile home to the south. Other sites are a good 40 feet wide. Be advised that there are no showers, no toilets, no dump station. Drivers of long rigs may welcome the spacious sites, but those looking for more than a parking space should look elsewhere. Tenters might consider nearby Lake Sumner.

BASICS

Operated By: Don and Lula Sweet. **Open:** All year. **Site Assignment:** First come, first served; verbal reservations OK, please call to cancel. **Registration:** Wait for someone to collect fee, after 10 p.m. use drop box. **Fee:** $15, subject to change without notice. **Parking:** At site.

FACILITIES

Number of RV Sites: 37. **Number of Tent-Only Sites:** 0. **Hookups:** Water, sewer, electric (30, 50 amp), cable. **Each Site:** 1–2 trees. **Dump Station:** No (sewer at all sites). **Laundry:** No. **Pay Phone:** No. **Rest Rooms and Showers:** No. **Fuel:** No. **Propane:** No. **Internal Roads:** Dirt. **RV Service:** No. **Market:** 1 mi. west. **Restaurant:** Across street. **General Store:** No. **Vending:** No. **Swimming:** No. **Playground:** No. **Activities:** Visiting sites/museums. **Nearby Attractions:** Billy the Kid Museum, Billy the Kid's Grave. **Additional Information:** Da Baca/Ft. Sumner County Chamber of Commerce, (505) 355-7705.

RESTRICTIONS

Pets: On leash. **Fires:** In own grills. **Alcoholic Beverages:** Prefer none, but in RV unit OK. **Vehicle Maximum Length:** None.

TO GET THERE

From the junction of Hwy. 60 and Hwy. 84, go 0.8 mi. east on Hwy. 60/84 and turn right at the sign. Take the immediate left into the campground and select a spot.

GALLUP

Gallup KOA

2925 West Hwy. 66, Gallup 87301. T: (505) 865-5021; F: (505) 865-5021; www.koa.com; koagallup@cnetco.com.

RV ★★★★ Tent ★★★

Beauty: ★★★	Site Privacy: ★★★★
Spaciousness: ★★★★	Quiet: ★★★★
Security: ★★★★★	Cleanliness: ★★★★★
Insect Control: ★★★★	Facilities: ★★★★★

This campground is laid out in five rows of pull-throughs with two rows of tent sites behind them, and one row of back-ins along the eastern wall. Sites 1–12 and 15–30 are 70-foot gravel sites, slightly shorter (60 feet) on the ends. Sites 31–48 are 65-foot sites, while 49–69 and 70–91 are slightly shorter (54 feet and 60 feet). Back-ins 122–141 are 30-foot sites, best suited for pop-ups or vans. The best RV sites are those on the eastern edge (1, 15, 31, 49, and 70), as these face into trees and hills beyond. The tent sites at the end of the park are 24 × 27-foot open sites. Trees are mostly small and scarce. The best tent sites are 23 and 25, which share a larger tree. The rest rooms and showers are exceptionally clean and comfortable. The electric eye at the gate alerts the owners of all incoming guests, ensuring the safety of the park. A very comfortable campground that campers of all types will enjoy.

BASICS

Operated By: Charles Diaz. **Open:** All year. **Site Assignment:** Upon registration; verbal reservations OK. **Registration:** In office. **Fee:** RV $27 (full), $25 (water, electric); tent $21; checks, V, MC, D. **Parking:** At site.

FACILITIES

Number of RV Sites: 120. **Number of Tent-Only Sites:** 16. **Hookups:** Water, sewer, electric (30, 50 amp). **Each Site:** Picnic table. **Dump Station:** Yes. **Laundry:** Yes. **Pay Phone:** Yes. **Rest Rooms and Showers:** Yes. **Fuel:** No. **Propane:** Yes. **Internal Roads:** Paved. **RV Service:** No. **Market:** 1 mi. west. **Restaurant:** On-site. **General Store:** Yes. **Vending:** No. **Swimming:** Pool. **Playground:** Yes. **Other:** Cabins, modem. **Activities:** Swimming, rodeos, American Indian dances. **Nearby Attractions:** Historic Rte. 66, Red Rock State Park, Inter-Tribal Indian Ceremonial. **Additional Information:** Gallup Mc Kinley City Chamber, (505) 722-2228.

RESTRICTIONS

Pets: On 6-ft. leash, cleaned up after, use dog walk. **Fires:** In grills. **Alcoholic Beverages:** At sites. **Vehicle Maximum Length:** None. **Other:** No groups.

TO GET THERE

From Hwy. I-40 (Exit 16), turn east onto Historic Rte. 66 and go 1 mi. Turn right at the sign into the entrance.

GRANTS

Lavaland RV Park

1901 East Santa Fe Ave., Grants 87020. T: (505) 287-8665; F: (505) 285-5181; lavaland@7cities.net.

RV ★★★★ Tent ★★★

Beauty: ★★★★	Site Privacy: ★★★★
Spaciousness: ★★★★	Quiet: ★★★
Security: ★★★★	Cleanliness: ★★★★
Insect Control: ★★★★	Facilities: ★★★

Sites in Lavaland are laid out in four rows. Sites are 60 feet long and 30 feet wide. Sites 1–11 are back-ins along the western edge that back to a retaining wall with trees and a fence. Sites 11 and 12 at the end do not have shade trees. In the middle of the campground, sites 12–27 and 28–39 are pull-throughs. Site 39 is located next to the dump station and is thus less desirable. On the east side, sites 40–51 face the highway and hills in the distance. These pull-throughs as well as the road they lie on are rougher in spots (especially 48) than the other rows of pull-throughs. The tenting area is in the southeast corner by the entrance. These dirt sites have nice desert views, and some are shaded. The rest rooms and showers are clean, but there is no window, so the room is pitch black when the light is not on. (Be sure to turn on the light before the door closes!) Lavaland is an attractive campground that will appeal to many campers—a little better to RVers than to tenters.

Basics

Operated By: Fidel and Leticia Duenas. **Open:** All year. **Site Assignment:** Upon registration; credit card required for reservation, 48 hours cancellation policy. **Registration:** In office; late arrivals use drop box. **Fee:** RV $16 (full), tent $14; V, MC, D. **Parking:** At site.

Facilities

Number of RV Sites: 51. **Number of Tent-Only Sites:** Undesignated sites. **Hookups:** Water, sewer, electric (30, 50 amp). **Each Site:** Picnic table, grill. **Dump Station:** Yes. **Laundry:** Yes. **Pay Phone:** Yes. **Rest Rooms and Showers:** Yes. **Fuel:** No. **Propane:** No. **Internal Roads:** Gravel. **RV Service:** No (minor repairs). **Market:** 0.25 mi. at I-40. **Restaurant:** 0.25 mi. at I-40. **General Store:** No. **Vending:** Yes. **Swimming:** No. **Playground:** No. **Other:** Studio rooms, gift shop. **Activities:** Caving, hiking. **Nearby Attractions:** Visitor center within walking distance, Mine Museum, ice caves, Acoma Sky City, Cibola Natioanl Forest. **Additional Information:** Grants Chamber of Commerce, (505) 287-4802.

Restrictions

Pets: On leash, cleaned up after, no big dogs outside. **Fires:** In grills. **Alcoholic Beverages:** At sites. **Vehicle Maximum Length:** 60 ft.

To Get There

From Hwy. I-40 (Exit 85), from the south side of the highway, turn south and take the first right onto Jurassic Ct., then take the first right into the campground.

HOBBS

Harry McAdams Park

5000 Jack Gomez Blvd., Hobbs 88240. T: (505) 392-5845.

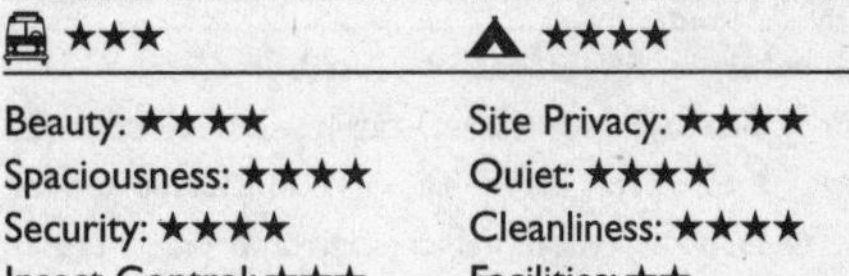

RV ★★★ Tent ★★★★

Beauty: ★★★★ Site Privacy: ★★★★
Spaciousness: ★★★★ Quiet: ★★★★
Security: ★★★★ Cleanliness: ★★★★
Insect Control: ★★★ Facilities: ★★

Six miles northwest of Hobbs, near the College of the Southwest, the Harry McAdams Park is divided into north and south, each with a different flavor. The north campground is more primitive with regards to hookups (only three sites have full hookups), but contains the rest room facilities and sits on prettier grounds. Sites are 54-foot back-ins with enough space on all sides to accommodate a large family with children. Sites inside the loop share an interior common grounds, while those on the outside of the loop back onto an expansive grassy area. Site 9 on the outside loop is situated somewhat away from the rest and backs onto a field that runs toward the day area a few hundred yards away. The grass is lush and extremely well maintained—be forewarned that crews get under way early to avoid the hot sun of afternoon. The rest room facilities are acceptably clean and spacious, with showers in a separate curtained-off area. The south campground is an open field with a strip of sites down a central road. The field is humongous, but does receive some airplane noise. Campsites here are more minimalist, with a table and young tree that does not provide shade. (An exception is the tree in sites 21/23.) These pull-through sites, virtually unlimited in size, are not your traditional pull-throughs: when leaving, you pull out into the field, turn around, and come back through your site. The south campground rates lower on beauty and quiet, and would rate higher on facilities due to the hookups, although the rest rooms are a block away in the north campground. For those seeking a quiet escape (and can forego full hookups for a night), Harry McAdams (especially the north side) is an extremely pleasant and comfortable place to stay.

Basics

Operated By: Rudy and Lorraine. **Open:** All year. **Site Assignment:** First come, first served. **Registration:** At self-pay station. **Fee:** Site $7, electricity $11. **Parking:** At site.

Facilities

Number of RV Sites: 62. **Number of Tent-Only Sites:** 0. **Hookups:** Water, sewer, electric (30 amp). **Each Site:** North campground: Picnic shelter w/ table, trees, grill; South campground: picnic table. **Dump Station:** Yes. **Laundry:** No. **Pay Phone:** Yes. **Rest Rooms and Showers:** Yes. **Fuel:** No. **Propane:** No. **Internal Roads:** Paved, in perfect condition. **RV Service:** No. **Market:** 6 mi. to Hobbs. **Restaurant:** 2 mi. towards Hobbs. **General Store:** No. **Vending:** Yes. **Swimming:** No. **Playground:** Yes. **Other:** 2 trout-stocked ponds, day use area. **Activities:** Volleyball, horseshoes, fishing. **Nearby Attractions:** Blackwater Draw Museum, Old Fort Sumner Museum, Billy the Kid Museum. **Additional Information:** Hobbs Chamber of Commerce, (800) 658-6291, (505) 397-3202.

Restrictions

Pets: On leash. **Fires:** In grills. **Alcoholic Beverages:** At sites. **Vehicle Maximum Length:** None. **Other:** No generators, 1 camp vehicle, plus 1 other vehicle per site.

To Get There

From Hwy. 18 (between Hobbs and Lovington), turn west onto Jack Gomez. (Much more visible than the street sign are the two signs at the street entrance on the west side for the Hobbs Industrial Air Park.) Go 0.8 mi. on Jack Gomez behind a police station, then turn right into the campground. All guests must register at the pay station here. To get to the south campground, continue on Jack Gomez through the stop sign and into the area marked Hobbs Army Air Base. Make the first left into the campground, then return to the north campground to register.

JEMEZ SPRINGS

Trail's End RV Park

37695 Hwy. 126, Jemez Springs 87025. T: (505) 829-4072; F: (505) 829-4072; trailsendrv@hotmail.com.

RV: ★★★★★ Tent: ★★★★★

Beauty: ★★★★★	Site Privacy: ★★★★★
Spaciousness: ★★★★★	Quiet: ★★★★★
Security: ★★★★★	Cleanliness: ★★★★★
Insect Control: ★★★★★	Facilities: ★★

Trail's End offers the only full hookups in the area. But even if that weren't the case, it would well be worth a visit. The area is gorgeous, and the campground takes full advantage of the forest where it lies. Sites are left in a natural condition, and there are flowers planted amongst the pines. Sites 1–7 are gravel back-ins located upslope from the office. Site 1 is one of the longest, at 55 feet. Smaller sites (30 feet) include 3–9. Sites 8–17 are located along the southern side. Of these, 11 is a 70-foot pull-through (of which only 60 feet are usable, due to the slope), and 17 is likewise quite long (65 feet). Sites 12, 13, and 15 are 45-foot back-ins. Closest to the entrance (which makes for the easiest in and out), but also located just off the highway is site 16, which is a 60-foot pull-through. (Some of the sites have a slightly smaller usable length due to the slope.) Tenting is possible in sites 18 and 19, but, with 50,000 acres of national forest surrounding the campground and offering free camping, even the owner asks why a tenter would pay to camp. The rest room, although small, is brand-spanking new, with further facilities under construction. An absolutely gorgeous campground that is not to be missed by RVers.

Basics

Operated By: Steve McMahon. **Open:** All year. **Site Assignment:** Upon registration; verbal reservations OK. **Registration:** In office; no arrivals after 9 p.m. **Fee:** RV $22 (full), $20 (water, electric); tent $12; checks, but no credits cards. **Parking:** At site.

Facilities

Number of RV Sites: 14. **Number of Tent-Only Sites:** 2. **Hookups:** Water, sewer, electric (30 amp). **Each Site:** Picnic table, grill. **Dump Station:** No (sewer at all sites). **Laundry:** No. **Pay Phone:** No. **Rest Rooms and Showers:** Toilet; no shower.

Fuel: No. **Propane:** No. **Internal Roads:** Gravel. **RV Service:** No. **Market:** 1 mi. south. **Restaurant:** 1 mi. south. **General Store:** No. **Vending:** No. **Swimming:** No. **Playground:** Yes. **Other:** Surrounded by national forest. **Activities:** Fishing, hiking, horseback riding, hunting. **Nearby Attractions:** Soda Dam, Santa Fe, Albuquerque, hot springs, Fenton Lake State Park, Santa Fe National Forest, Jemez Pueblo, Zia Pueblo. **Additional Information:** Los Alamos Chamber of Commerce, (505) 662-8105.

Restrictions

Pets: On leash, cleaned up after. **Fires:** In grills. **Alcoholic Beverages:** At sites. **Vehicle Maximum Length:** 38 ft.

To Get There

From the junction of Hwy. 550 and Hwy. 4, turn north onto Hwy. 4 and go 26.5 mi. (8.1 mi. north of Jemez Springs National Monument). Turn left onto Hwy. 126 and go 5 mi. to the campground.

KIRTLAND

Paramount RV Park

4336 US Hwy. 64, Kirtland 87417. T: (505) 598-9824; F: (505) 598-6515.

RV: ★★ Tent: n/a

Beauty: ★	Site Privacy: ★★★
Spaciousness: ★★★	Quiet: ★★
Security: ★★★★★	Cleanliness: ★★★★
Insect Control: ★★★★	Facilities: ★

This RV park is a large gravel area with no defined sites (other than hookups). As a result, both back-ins and pull-throughs can accommodate a rig of any size, which, along with the security fence and gate, is pretty much the main draw to this park. You know you can get any vehicle inside, and you won't be bothered once there. Apart from this, the park does not stand out, save for some distant views of buttes to the south. Back-ins 1–8 have some low shrubs and so could be called a little prettier, but they back directly to the highway, which makes them closer to the traffic noise. Site 25 is right next to the office and seems more cramped and busy because of this. All sites are level but very open—RVers will have to roll out the awning here.

Basics

Operated By: James and Darlene Stewart. **Open:** All year. **Site Assignment:** Depending on site availability; check required for reservation, 24 hours cancellation policy. **Registration:** In office; late arrivals use drop box. **Fee:** RV $16 (full, cable), $12 (water, electric); no credits cards, but checks. **Parking:** At site.

Facilities

Number of RV Sites: 24. **Number of Tent-Only Sites:** 0. **Hookups:** Water, sewer, electric (30, 50 amp). **Dump Station:** No. **Laundry:** No. **Pay Phone:** No. **Rest Rooms and Showers:** No. **Fuel:** No. **Propane:** No. **Internal Roads:** Gravel. **RV Service:** No. **Market:** 1 mi. **Restaurant:** 1 mi. **General Store:** No. **Vending:** No. **Swimming:** No. **Playground:** No. **Other:** Dog walk. **Activities:** Sightseeing. **Nearby Attractions:** Navajo Reservation, Aztec Ruins, Four Corners. **Additional Information:** Farmington Chamber of Commerce, (505) 325-0279.

Restrictions

Pets: On leash, cleaned up after. **Fires:** In grills; subject to seasonal bans. **Alcoholic Beverages:** At sites. **Vehicle Maximum Length:** None.

To Get There

From the junction of Hwy. 64 and the only stop light in town, go 1.3 mi. east on Hwy. 64. Turn left into the entrance. (Look for the sign at the top of the hill.) Turn into paved road, follow it to the back of the park, then take the first left at the sign into the campground. The office is on the right.

LAS CRUCES

Best View RV Park

814 Weinrich Rd., Las Cruces 88005. T: (800) 526-6555 or (505) 526-6555; F: (505) 526-9421; www.bestviewrvpark.com; bvrvpark@zianet.com.

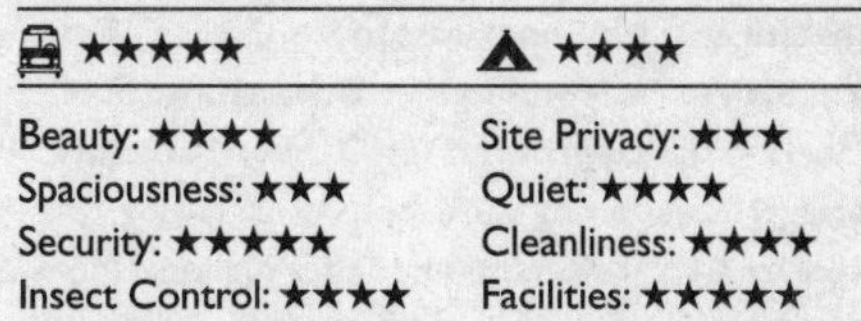

RV: ★★★★★ Tent: ★★★★

Beauty: ★★★★	Site Privacy: ★★★
Spaciousness: ★★★	Quiet: ★★★★
Security: ★★★★★	Cleanliness: ★★★★
Insect Control: ★★★★	Facilities: ★★★★★

Southwest of Las Cruces and toward the airport, this campground commands a view of the town with its agricultural areas, plentiful trees, and the Organ Pipe Mountain behind that really lives up to its name. The campground is laid out in a giant "L" shape, with back-ins around the perimeter and pull-throughs inside. Pull-throughs average 62 feet in length, with sites 60–61 slightly longer (65 feet), which makes them among the best sites available—certainly for longer rigs. Back-ins are roughly the same length as pull-throughs, although there are some much smaller sites to accommodate vans/pop-ups near the tent and cabin area. All sites are level and mostly open. The tent area is short of tables and grills, with only a bare ground covering of grass. (Grass does not grow well in the area.) However, there are enough trees for ample protection from above. Tent sites are generally flat, with a slight slope in sites 75 and 80. The second tent (and RV) area near the cabins is close to the road, with the attendant traffic sounds. The southwest corner above the cabins contains a slightly scruffy residence, but that is the only detraction from the beauty of this campground. The rest room and shower facilities are quite clean. Overall, this is a great camping experience for both RVers and tenters, with a "best view" from nearly all of the sites.

Basics

Operated By: Steve and Keri Perry. **Open:** All year. **Site Assignment:** Upon registration; reservations require credit card, cancel up to 7 p.m. day of arrival. **Registration:** In office; late arrivals use drop box. **Fee:** Full $22, water, electric $17.50, tent $14.50. **Parking:** At site.

Facilities

Number of RV Sites: 84. **Number of Tent-Only Sites:** 14. **Hookups:** Water, sewer, electric (30, 50 amp). **Each Site:** Picnic table, grill, tree. **Dump Station:** Yes. **Laundry:** Yes. **Pay Phone:** Yes. **Rest Rooms and Showers:** Yes. **Fuel:** No. **Propane:** Yes. **Internal Roads:** Paved. **RV Service:** No. **Market:** 5 mi. northeast to Las Cruces. **Restaurant:** 5 mi. northeast to Las Cruces. **General Store:** Yes. **Vending:** Yes. **Swimming:** Pool (May–Sept.). **Playground:** Yes. **Other:** 4 acres RV storage, 4 cabins, dog walk. **Activities:** Hiking. **Nearby Attractions:** White Sands National Monument, Mesilla, City of Rocks State Park. **Additional Information:** Las Cruces CVB, (800) 343-7827, (505) 541-2444.

Restrictions

Pets: On leash, cleaned up after. **Fires:** In grills. **Alcoholic Beverages:** At sites. **Vehicle Maximum Length:** None.

To Get There

From I-25, take Exit 6B, turn west onto Main St., and drive 2.4 mi. to Picachio St. Turn right onto Picachio and drive 5.2 mi. Turn left at the sign, then take the second immediate left into the campground. The office is right at the entrance.

LAS VEGAS

Vegas RV Overnite Park

504 Harris Rd., Las Vegas 87701. T: (505) 425-5640; vegasrv@zialink.com.

RV ★★★ Tent ★★

Beauty: ★	Site Privacy: ★★★★
Spaciousness: ★★★	Quiet: ★★★
Security: ★★★	Cleanliness: ★★★★
Insect Control: ★★★★	Facilities: ★★★

Take it from the business card of this park: this is a storage business with an RV park attached. There are storage units to the north and east, mobile homes to the west, and residences and commercial development to the south. None of these add to the attractiveness of the campground. Sites are laid out in four rows. Sites in row A are 54 × 33 feet, sites in row B are 65 × 33 feet, and sites in row C are 70 × 33 feet. All of these are pull-throughs. Back-ins in Row D are 48 × 30 feet. These sites are right next to the storage units. Tenting sites are also located in this area. While there is decent grass cover, there is no shade—a problem endemic to the entire park. There is also very little landscaping, aside from the bench and vegetation next to C1—which prevents the use of a grill at this site. The northeast corner (sites C6–11) is the nicest section, as it is furthest from the office and road. End site C11 is right off the road, and can therefore accommodate larger rigs but does get more passing traffic. The rest rooms are clean, but the showers do not have a lip to hold back the water. As a result, the entire rest room gets drenched with every shower.

Basics

Operated By: Mark Shubert. **Open:** All year. **Site Assignment:** Upon registration; credit card required for reservation, 24 hours cancellation policy. **Registration:** In office; late arrivals use drop box. **Fee:** RV $18 (full), $13 (water, electric); tent $11; checks, V, MC. **Parking:** At site.

FACILITIES

Number of RV Sites: 40. **Number of Tent-Only Sites:** 0. **Hookups:** Water, sewer, electric (30 amp), cable. **Dump Station:** No (sewer at all sites). **Laundry:** No. **Pay Phone:** Yes. **Rest Rooms and Showers:** Yes. **Fuel:** No. **Propane:** No. **Internal Roads:** Gravel. **RV Service:** No. **Market:** Less than 0.25 mi. south. **Restaurant:** Less than 0.25 mi. south. **General Store:** No. **Vending:** No. **Swimming:** No. **Playground:** No. **Other:** Phone hookups for long-term guests. **Activities:** Fishing, boating, swimming, hiking. **Nearby Attractions:** Storrie Lake State Park, historic downtown, Pecos National Monument, Santa Fe Trail, Ft. Union. **Additional Information:** Las Vegas Chamber of Commerce, (505) 425-8631.

RESTRICTIONS

Pets: On leash, cleaned up after. **Fires:** In grills. **Alcoholic Beverages:** At sites. **Vehicle Maximum Length:** 58 ft.

TO GET THERE

From Hwy. I-25 (Exit 347), turn south onto Grand Ave. and go 1.2 mi. Turn right onto Mills Ave. and go 0.7 mi. Turn right onto 7th St. and go 1.1 mi. north. Turn right before the sign and take the second left into the campground.

LOGAN

Ute Lake State Park

P.O. Box 52, Logan 88426. T: (877) 664-7787 or (888) NM-PARKS or (505) 487-2284; www.icampnm.com.

RV ★★★ Tent ★★★

Beauty: ★★★	Site Privacy: ★★★★★
Spaciousness: ★★★★★	Quiet: ★★★★
Security: ★★★★	Cleanliness: ★★★
Insect Control: ★★★	Facilities: ★★

There are two campgrounds (Zia and Yucca) in this desert-setting state park. Zia Campground is closest to the office and contains the reservable sites. The outside of this looped campground contains 95-foot pull-throughs (all odd numbers), while the inside contains 35-foot back-ins (all even numbers), which are separated one from the other by large boulders and trees. Sites with the best lake views are 11, 13, and 15. Those closest to the rest rooms are 17, 18, 20, and 21. To the south of this loop is an area of primitive sites that offer sheltered picnic tables and grills. The southernmost sites are grassy, shaded, and open to the lake. (The rest of the sites are open to the blazing sun.) Yuccan Campground has absolutely the largest pull-throughs you'll ever see (165 × 65 feet)—obviously built with the boater in mind. Sites are in two rows along a gravel drive. Sites on the south side (57–72) have a view of the lake and are closest to the lake access area (by 72), but there is no boat ramp there. Instead, this road provides access to the dispersed tent camping along the bank of the lake. While there is no shade nor grass, the upside is that you can practically roll out of your tent into the lake if you want. The bathhouse, located east of Yucca Campground, is clean, comfortable, and very spacious. There are further campgrounds on the north and south sides of the lake, but the two described are easier to access and enjoyable by anyone looking for fun on a lake.

BASICS

Operated By: New Mexico State Park Division. **Open:** May 15–Sept. 15. **Site Assignment:** First come, first served; reservations by credit card or check, no refunds. **Registration:** At pay station. **Fee:** Primitive site $8, developed site $10, hookup $4; checks, V, MC, D. **Parking:** At site.

FACILITIES

Number of RV Sites: 77. **Number of Tent-Only Sites:** 57. **Hookups:** Water, electric (30 amp). **Each Site:** Picnic table, grill, fire pit. **Dump Station:** Yes. **Laundry:** No. **Pay Phone:** Yes. **Rest Rooms and Showers:** Yes. **Fuel:** No. **Propane:** No. **Internal Roads:** Paved. **RV Service:** No. **Market:** 2.5 mi. east. **Restaurant:** 2.5 mi. east. **General Store:** Yes. **Vending:** No. **Swimming:** Yes (lake). **Playground:** Yes. **Other:** Trails, boat ramp, baseball field. **Activities:** Fishing, boating, swimming, hiking. **Nearby Attractions:** Ute Lake. **Additional Information:** State Park Office, (505) 487-2284.

RESTRICTIONS

Pets: On leash, cleaned up after. **Fires:** In grills. **Alcoholic Beverages:** At sites. **Vehicle Maximum Length:** None.

TO GET THERE

From the junction of Hwy. 54 and Hwy. 540, turn west onto Hwy. 540 and go 2.4 mi. Turn left at the sign into the entrance.

LORDSBURG

Lordsburg KOA

1501 Lead St., Lordsburg 88045. T: (800) 562-5772 or (505) 542-8003; www.koa.com.

RV ★★★★ Tent ★★★★

Beauty: ★★★	Site Privacy: ★★★★★
Spaciousness: ★★★★★	Quiet: ★★★
Security: ★★★★	Cleanliness: ★★★★★
Insect Control: ★★★★	Facilities: ★★★★★

This campground with mountain views in all directions offers all 60-foot (or larger) pull-throughs laid out in eight rows. Rows 1 and 2 (sites 1–4 and 14–17) are open-ended sites that can easily accommodate 60 feet, and are 33 feet wide. These sites are closest to the facilities. Rows 4–7 are slightly larger than 60 feet and contain the remotest sites to the southwest. (The single remotest site is 54 in row 7.) Row 8 runs perpendicular to rows 1–7 on the south edge of the property. The longest pull-throughs (90 feet) are located in this row. Of these sites, the least desirable are 5 (faces a mobile home) and 9 (faces a dumpster). Sites 58–63, along the north edge, are electric sites only. These are grassier, however, and quite nice. Tent sites occupy sites 1–3 of row 3, and T4 of row 4. These walled-in sites are 33 × 22 feet and offer a square of dirt for a tent. Site 3 has the communal wash basin and trash recepticle. There is also group tenting along the north edge by the cabins. A camping kitchen for tenters is located next to the basketball court. Lordsburg is a very nice campground that both RVers and tenters will enjoy.

BASICS

Operated By: Marin and Naty. **Open:** All year. **Site Assignment:** Upon registration; credit card required for reservation, 24 hours cancellation policy. **Registration:** In office; late arrivals use drop box. **Fee:** RV $22 (full), $20 (water, electric); tent $17; checks, V, MC, D. **Parking:** At site.

FACILITIES

Number of RV Sites: 62. **Number of Tent-Only Sites:** 5. **Hookups:** Water, sewer, electric (30, 50 amp). **Each Site:** Picnic table (tent sites: picnic table, grill, lantern pole). **Dump Station:** Yes. **Laundry:** Yes. **Pay Phone:** Yes. **Rest Rooms and Showers:** Yes. **Fuel:** No. **Propane:** No. **Internal Roads:** Gravel. **RV Service:** No. **Market:** Less than 0.25 mi. on Main St. **Restaurant:** Less than 0.25 mi. on Main St. **General Store:** Yes. **Vending:** Yes. **Swimming:** Pool. **Playground:** Yes. **Other:** Dog walk, cabins, covered pavilion, rec room. **Activities:** Swimming, basketball, badminton, horseshoes, hiking, visiting ghost towns. **Nearby Attractions:** Shakespeare Ghost Town, Gila National Forest. **Additional Information:** Lordsburg-Hidalgo Chamber of Commerce, (505) 542-9864.

RESTRICTIONS

Pets: On leash, cleaned up after. **Fires:** In grills. **Alcoholic Beverages:** At sites. **Vehicle Maximum Length:** None.

TO GET THERE

From Hwy. I-10 (Exit 22), from the south side of the highway, go 1 block south on Main to Maple St. and turn right. Follow Maple (which curves to the left) and go 0.3 mi. Continue straight on into the campground.

MAYHILL

Rio Penasco RV Camp

P.O. Box 47, Mayhill 88339. T: (505) 687-3715; ejnutt@pvtnetworks.net.

RV ★★★★★ Tent ★★★★

Beauty: ★★★★	Site Privacy: ★★★
Spaciousness: ★★★	Quiet: ★★★★★
Security: ★★★★	Cleanliness: ★★★★★
Insect Control: ★★★	Facilities: ★★★★

Just to the south of Mayhill, Rio Penasco is surrounded on all sides by trees and verdant hills along the entire eastern perimeter. Laid out as a giant circle with rows cut inside, the campground boasts gigantic (70 feet long) pull-throughs as well as a few back-ins around the office area. (These are the least desirable sites, assigned last when the park is full. Sites 3 and 4 are especially prone to registration traffic, being smack dab in front of the office.) The best site by a long shot is 13, which is a huge pull-through well apart from the rest, under an enormous willow, and open to the hills and creek to the east. Second place goes to 9, which is similar in every way to 13, but is sided by site 8, which detracts only slightly from its desirability. Sites are all a level grassy/gravel mix, long enough to accommodate pretty much anything, but a little on the narrow side (22 feet wide). Should this concern you at all, however, the rest room and laundry facilities will ease your mind a hundredfold. These are the nicest rest room facilities you are likely to find on your journey—no matter where you are destined. Tastefully decorated with handicrafts, they are carpeted, immaculate, and as comfortable as those at home. Likewise, the laundry facility is spacious and clean, and contains a small, carpeted rec room with sofa, table, games, puzzles, magazines, and more handicrafts. Situated in a gorgeous setting in the tiny mountain town of Mayhill near Cloudcroft, this campground is a splendid destination for return visits.

Basics

Operated By: John and Emily Nutt. **Open:** All year. **Site Assignment:** Depending on availability; credit card or check for reservations, reservations required June–Aug. **Registration:** In office; late arrivals use drop box or settle in morning. **Fee:** RV $13.50, tent $10. **Parking:** At site.

Facilities

Number of RV Sites: 32. **Number of Tent-Only Sites:** Undesignated sites. **Hookups:** Water, sewer, electric (30 amp). **Each Site:** Picnic table. **Dump Station:** No (sewer at all sites). **Laundry:** Yes. **Pay Phone:** Yes. **Rest Rooms and Showers:** Yes. **Fuel:** No. **Propane:** Yes. **Internal Roads:** Gravel, in good condition. **RV Service:** No. **Market:** 1 mi. to Mayhill. **Restaurant:** 1 mi. to Mayhill. **General Store:** Yes. **Vending:** No. **Swimming:** No. **Playground:** No. **Other:** RV supplies, creek, pavilion, rec room. **Activities:** Nightly entertainment in pavilion, fishing, games. **Nearby Attractions:** Cloudcroft, Weed (historic logging town). **Additional Information:** Cloudcroft Chamber of Commerce, (505) 682-2733.

Restrictions

Pets: On leash, cleaned up, no barking. **Fires:** In grills or fire ring in pavilion. **Alcoholic Beverages:** None. **Vehicle Maximum Length:** None. **Other:** Christian atmosphere (no swearing).

To Get There

From the junction of Hwy. 82 and Hwy. 130 (Rio Penasco Rd.), turn west onto Rio Penasco Rd., cross bridge and take the first left at the sign into the campground. (This turn may be a little tricky for large rigs. For those wishing to avoid the turn, there is another entrance/exit just to the west of this one.) The office is to the right of the first entrance.

MIMBRES

Casas Adobes RV Park

Rte. 15 Box 2540, Mimbres 88049. T: (505) 536-9599.

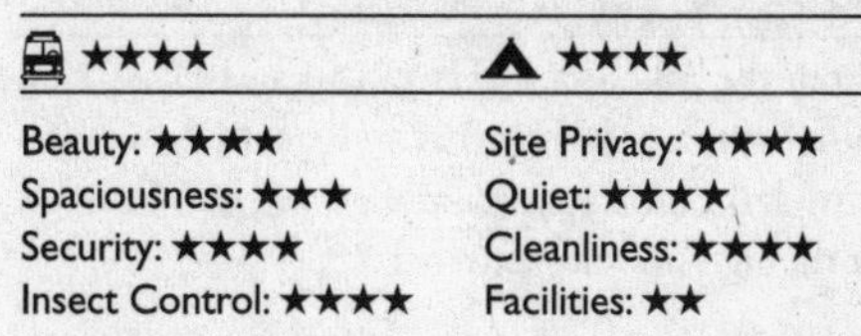

★★★★ ★★★★

Beauty: ★★★★ Site Privacy: ★★★★
Spaciousness: ★★★ Quiet: ★★★★
Security: ★★★★ Cleanliness: ★★★★
Insect Control: ★★★★ Facilities: ★★

All sites in this campground are 72 × 24-foot pull-throughs laid out in a straight line bordering the highway 60 feet away. There are mountain views to the north and south. Most sites are quite well-shaded. Site 3 is extra wide to accommodate a long-term guest. Site 11 is closest to the bath house. There are Camp Hosts in sites 8 and 9. End site 20 is next to mobile homes, but end site 1 has a fence, extra space, and larger trees, making it the most desirable site. Tenting is possible in sites 12 and 13, which are roped off from RVs. These sites have fine gravel and sparse grass, and loads of shade from trees. There is also an open tenting area to the southwest. The rest rooms and showers are in a carpeted mobile home, and are both clean and very comfortable. This campground makes a very nice stop for both RVers and tenters.

Basics

Operated By: Aaron and Wandra Emerson. **Open:** All year. **Site Assignment:** First come, first served; verbal reservations OK. **Registration:** Pay station at entrance. **Fee:** RV $12 (full), tent $6; checks, but no credits cards. **Parking:** At site.

Facilities

Number of RV Sites: 19. **Number of Tent-Only Sites:** Undesignated sites. **Hookups:** Water, sewer, electric (50 amp), phone. **Each Site:** Garbage can. **Dump Station:** No (sewer at all sites). **Laundry:** No (within 0.5 mi.). **Pay Phone:** No. **Rest Rooms and Showers:** Yes. **Fuel:** No. **Propane:** No (within 0.25 mi.). **Internal Roads:** Gravel. **RV Service:** No. **Market:** 25 mi. to Silver City. **Restaurant:** 0.5 mi. north. **General Store:** No. **Vending:** No. **Swimming:** No. **Playground:** No. **Activities:** Hiking, scenic drives. **Nearby Attractions:** Gila Cliff Dwellings National Monument, Gila National Forest. **Additional Information:** Silver City Grant County Chamber of Commerce, (505) 538-3785.

RESTRICTIONS

Pets: On leash, cleaned up after. **Fires:** In grills. **Alcoholic Beverages:** None. **Vehicle Maximum Length:** None.

TO GET THERE

From the junction of Hwy. 180 and Hwy. 152, turn north onto Hwy. 152 and go 14.3 mi. east. Turn left onto Hwy. 35 and go 1.5 mi. Turn left at the sign into the entrance.

MOUNTAINAIR

Manzano Mountains State Park

HC 66 Box 202, Mountainair 87036. T: (505) 847-2820.

RV ★★★★	Tent ★★★★
Beauty: ★★★★★	Site Privacy: ★★★★★
Spaciousness: ★★★★	Quiet: ★★★★★
Security: ★★★★	Cleanliness: ★★★★★
Insect Control: ★★★★	Facilities: ★★

Laid out in a loop, this small campground is located in a forest at the foot of the Manzano Mountains. Sites are all back-ins, ranging from 30 feet (1 and 3) to 70 feet (6). Some sites (1, 6, 7, 10, and 12) have covered shelters, while others (11–16) offer electrical hookups. Site 7 seems particularly spacious, as does 16. Sites 9 and 10 are next to the access for overflow camping, which is normally closed, but may increase traffic by these two sites when open. Site 8 is a 60-foot site, completely hidden in trees. Sites 4 and 5 are tent-only sites, but a tenter would be happy at any of these sites. Although the sites are not grassy, nearly all offer overhanging tree cover, making tenting comfortable in this park. The rest rooms are clean and modern. The nearby Red Canyon National Forest campground (accessed by turning right at the entrance to this state park) is only slightly larger at around 50 sites, but offers no hookups. Tenters may find it an acceptable alternative, but RVers will prefer the Manzano Mountains campground due to the electrical hookups.

BASICS

Operated By: New Mexico State Park Division. **Open:** All year. **Site Assignment:** First come, first served; reservations by credit card or check, no refunds. **Registration:** At pay station. **Fee:** Primitive site $8, developed site $10, water, electric $14; checks, but no credit cards. **Parking:** At site.

FACILITIES

Number of RV Sites: 18. **Number of Tent-Only Sites:** 0. **Hookups:** Electric (20, 30 amp). **Each Site:** Picnic table, grill, fire pit. **Dump Station:** Yes. **Laundry:** No. **Pay Phone:** In office. **Rest Rooms and Showers:** Yes. **Fuel:** No. **Propane:** No. **Internal Roads:** Gravel. **RV Service:** No. **Market:** Small: Mountainair (16 mi.); large: Sturgess (26 mi.). **Restaurant:** 16 mi. to Mountainair. **General Store:** No. **Vending:** No. **Swimming:** No. **Playground:** No. **Other:** Group shelter, backs to national forest. **Activities:** Hiking, visiting ruins, horseshoes. **Nearby Attractions:** Salinas Pueblo Ruins. **Additional Information:** New Mexico State Parks Division, (888) NM-PRKS.

RESTRICTIONS

Pets: On leash, cleaned up after. **Fires:** In grills. **Alcoholic Beverages:** At sites. **Vehicle Maximum Length:** None.

TO GET THERE

From the junction of Hwy. 60 and Hwy. 55, turn north onto Hwy. 55 and go 12.4 mi. Turn left onto Hwy. 31 and go 2.4 mi. Continue straight ahead to enter the park.

PORTALES

Wagon Wheel RV Park

42699 US 70, Portales 88130. T: (505) 356-3700.

RV ★★★	Tent ★★
Beauty: ★★★	Site Privacy: ★★★
Spaciousness: ★★★	Quiet: ★★★
Security: ★★★★	Cleanliness: ★★★★
Insect Control: ★★★	Facilities: ★★★

On the wall outside the rest rooms is a collage of notes from previous satisfied customers attesting to their contentment with this quiet and "peaseful" campground. The grounds are quite clean and peaceful, although some traffic noise from the highway does reach the park. The campground is laid out in two rows, the lettered strip sporting more grass and thus being generally a little nicer. While most trees are too thin to provide shade, the tree at sites 7 and 8 is an exception. Sites are level pull-throughs that vary in length from 45 to 56 feet. Site 11 is at the shortest extreme (45 feet) and has no tree, making it the least desirable RV site. Tent sites in the southeast corner have good grass, and the possible use of a row of small trees along the back fence. Behind these sites is a pleasant farm with geese and a pond. The rest rooms are reasonably clean and comfortable with a nice wood decor. The campground, likewise, is comfortable and clean, but may not quite live up to the letters it boasts on the walls.

BASICS

Operated By: Birl and Sue Gray. **Open:** All year. **Site Assignment:** First come, first served. **Registration:** In office; late arrivals use drop box (most often no one in office); verbal reservations OK. **Fee:** RV $16, tent $14; checks are OK, but no credit cards. **Parking:** At site.

FACILITIES

Number of RV Sites: 21. **Number of Tent-Only Sites:** 4. **Hookups:** Water, sewer, electric (20, 30, 50 amp). **Each Site:** Most have trees, some picnic tables. **Dump Station:** Yes. **Laundry:** Yes. **Pay Phone:** No. **Rest Rooms and Showers:** Yes. **Fuel:** No. **Propane:** No. **Internal Roads:** Gravel, in good condition. **RV Service:** No. **Market:** 2.5 mi. southwest. **Restaurant:** 5 mi. southwest. **General Store:** No. **Vending:** No. **Swimming:** No. **Playground:** No. **Other:** Basketball hoop. **Activities:** Basketball. **Nearby Attractions:** Blackwater Draw Museum. **Additional Information:** Roosevelt County Chamber of Commerce, (800) 635-8036, (505) 356-8541.

RESTRICTIONS

Pets: On leash, cleaned up, no barking, not tied up outside. **Fires:** Talk to manager. **Alcoholic Beverages:** At sites. **Vehicle Maximum Length:** 55 ft. **Other:** No generators; do not park vehicle next to RV.

TO GET THERE

From the junction of Hwy. 70 and Hwy. 206 in town, drive 4.2 mi. north on Hwy. 70. Turn east at the sign (at mile marker 427) into the campground. The office is at the entrance.

PREWITT

Bluewater Lake State Park

Lake Rte. Box 3419, Prewitt 87045. T: (505) 876-2391 or (505) 876-2318.

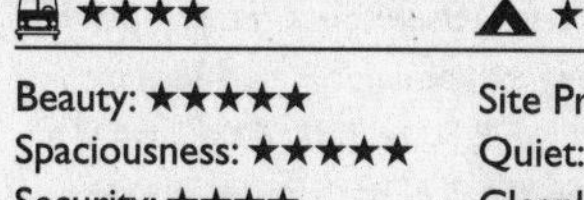

Beauty: ★★★★★ Site Privacy: ★★★★
Spaciousness: ★★★★★ Quiet: ★★★★★
Security: ★★★★ Cleanliness: ★★★★
Insect Control: ★★★★ Facilities: ★★★

There are four major campgrounds in this state park (Canyonside, Lakeside, Northpoint, and Creek Overlook), offering everything from waterfront camping to hillside sites with a view. Canyonside Campground, to the southeast of the ranger station, has the only electric sites in the park. Reservable sites are E1–E6, which are 57-foot back-ins. The Campground host is located at E7. Sites E9 and E10 are doubles (75 feet and 60 feet), while E11 and E13 are huge (100-foot and 150-foot) pull-throughs. This campground also has the only showers. Lakeside Campground (which ought really to be called "Lake Overlook") has primitive sites with a view (although Pinon Cliff Campground is better). The road in is rough and steep—no place for a large RV. Northpoint Campground likewise has primitive sites and a rough road that ends at the lake. There is no real road between sites. For the best views (but, again, primitive sites), go to Creek Overlook Campground. This campground offers dirt sites amidst trees. There are beautiful vistas of rocky bluffs, the grassy creek area, and woods below. The rest rooms and showers (in Canyonside Campground) are clean and decently large. This state park caters to tenters, but RVers who don't mind forgoing water and sewer hookups (let alone cable!) will enjoy the beautiful views and outdoor recreation opportunities this park affords.

BASICS

Operated By: New Mexico State Park Division. **Open:** All year. **Site Assignment:** First come, first served; reservations by credit card or check, no refunds. **Registration:** At pay station. **Fee:** Primitive site $8, developed site $10, electric $14; checks, but no credit cards. **Parking:** At site.

FACILITIES

Number of RV Sites: 14. **Number of Tent-Only Sites:** 106. **Hookups:** Electric (20, 30 amp).

Each Site: Picnic table, fire pit. **Dump Station:** Yes. **Laundry:** No. **Pay Phone:** Yes. **Rest Rooms and Showers:** Yes. **Fuel:** No. **Propane:** No. **Internal Roads:** Gravel. **RV Service:** No. **Market:** 25 mi. Grants. **Restaurant:** 25 mi. Grants. **General Store:** No. **Vending:** No. **Swimming:** No. **Playground:** Yes. **Other:** Boat ramp. **Activities:** Fishing, boating, swimming, hiking. **Nearby Attractions:** Red Rock State Park. **Additional Information:** New Mexico State Parks Division, (888) NM-PARKS.

Restrictions

Pets: On leash, cleaned up after. **Fires:** In grills. **Alcoholic Beverages:** At sites. **Vehicle Maximum Length:** None.

To Get There

From Hwy. I-40 (Exit 63), turn south onto Hwy. 412 and go 5.9 mi. to the entrance of the park.

RATON

Summerlan RV Park

1900 South Cedar St., Raton 87740. T: (505) 445-9536; F: (505) 445-9536.

RV ★★★★ Tent ★★★

Beauty: ★★★	Site Privacy: ★★★
Spaciousness: ★★★	Quiet: ★★★
Security: ★★★★	Cleanliness: ★★★★
Insect Control: ★★★★	Facilities: ★★★★

Sites in this campground are laid out in Rows A, B, and C. Western end sites (A1 and 2, B1 and 2, C1 and 2) share large shade trees. Sites B9, C5–8, and C15 are well shaded, but A4–8 are mostly unshaded. Rows A and B are pull-throughs, while Row C has only back-ins. Tenting is possible behind the RV sites. (There is a bridge between the two areas at site C9.) There is thick grass, but not much shade. There is, however, a covered pavilion for tenters' use. The rest rooms are simple, with painted cement walls, but quite clean and spacious. This is a decent campground for a short stay, and there is long-term RV storage for those who do not want to haul their rig back home at the end of the season. Tenters will also enjoy this campground, although the addition of shade trees would make the tenting experience much better.

Basics

Operated By: Buddy, Linda, and Tim Bryant. **Open:** All year. **Site Assignment:** Upon registration; credit card required for reservation, 24 hours cancellation policy. **Registration:** In office; late arrivals use drop box. **Fee:** RV $21.50 (full), tent $14.50; checks, but no credits cards. **Parking:** At site.

Facilities

Number of RV Sites: 45. **Number of Tent-Only Sites:** Undesignated sites. **Hookups:** Water, sewer, electric (30, 50 amp), cable. **Each Site:** Picnic table. **Dump Station:** No (sewer at all sites). **Laundry:** Yes. **Pay Phone:** Yes. **Rest Rooms and Showers:** Yes. **Fuel:** No. **Propane:** Yes. **Internal Roads:** Gravel. **RV Service:** Yes. **Market:** 0.75 mi. west. **Restaurant:** Across street. **General Store:** No. **Vending:** No. **Swimming:** No. **Playground:** Yes. **Other:** Storage, covered pavilion. **Activities:** Horseshoes, hiking. **Nearby Attractions:** Sugarite Canyon State Park, Capulin Volcano National Monument. **Additional Information:** Cimarron Chamber of Commerce, (505) 376-2417.

Restrictions

Pets: On leash, cleaned up after. **Fires:** In grills. **Alcoholic Beverages:** At sites. **Vehicle Maximum Length:** None.

To Get There

From Hwy. I-25 (Exit 451), from the east side of the highway, take the immediate right into 1900 Cedar St. and go 0.2 mi. Turn right at the sign into the entrance.

RODEO

Rodeo RV Park and Country Store

P.O. Box 80, Rodeo 88056. T: (505) 557-2266.

RV ★★★ Tent ★★

Beauty: ★★★	Site Privacy: ★★★
Spaciousness: ★★★★	Quiet: ★★★★
Security: ★★★★★	Cleanliness: ★★★★
Insect Control: ★★★★	Facilities: ★★★

This campground consists of an open gravel lot next to a residence and a store. Sites are open-ended pull-throughs that can accommodate a rig of any length, but are only 18 feet wide. Laid out in a single row, site 9 lies closest to the entrance (next to a fence and stored equipment), while site 1 is furthest from the entrance. There is a number of vehicles, along with stored equipment, scattered around the campground, making it less attractive than it would otherwise be. Tenting is possible anywhere, as there is crushed gravel all around the campground. This campground is OK for an overnight stay for RVers, but the motel right next door (that also has RV spaces) might be better for tenters. It is only slightly more expensive ($1 more for tenters, $2 more for RVers), and of roughly the same quality.

Basics

Operated By: Marianne and Edward Gullot. **Open:** All year. **Site Assignment:** First come, first served; verbal reservations OK. **Registration:** In store; late arrivals select available site and pay in the morning. **Fee:** RV $10 (full), tent $5; checks, but no credits cards. **Parking:** At site.

Facilities

Number of RV Sites: 9. **Number of Tent-Only Sites:** Undesignated sites. **Hookups:** Water, sewer, electric (20, 30 amp). **Dump Station:** No (sewer at all sites). **Laundry:** No. **Pay Phone:** No. **Rest Rooms and Showers:** Yes. **Fuel:** No. **Propane:** No. **Internal Roads:** Gravel. **RV Service:** No (some small repairs). **Market:** 0.25 mi. north. **Restaurant:** 0.1 mi. north. **General Store:** Yes. **Vending:** No. **Swimming:** No. **Playground:** No. **Activities:** World-class bird-watching, hiking, hunting. **Nearby Attractions:** Chiracahua Gallery, Wachuka Mountains, Geronimo Surrender Monument, Wonderland of Rock, Natural History Museum Research Center. **Additional Information:** Lordsburg-Hidalgo Chamber of Commerce, (505) 542-9864.

Restrictions

Pets: On leash, cleaned up after. **Fires:** In grills. **Alcoholic Beverages:** At sites. **Vehicle Maximum Length:** None.

To Get There

From the junction of Hwy. 9 and Hwy. 80, turn south onto Hwy. 80 and go 5.8 mi. into Rodeo. Turn left at the sign into the entrance.

ROSWELL

Trailer Village RV Campground

1706 East 2nd, Roswell 88201. T: (505) 623-6040; F: (505) 623-6040.

 ★★★  ★★★

Beauty: ★★★	Site Privacy: ★★★
Spaciousness: ★★★★	Quiet: ★★★★
Security: ★★★★	Cleanliness: ★★★★
Insect Control: ★★★★	Facilities: ★★★

Laid out in an L-shape this campground has back-ins all along the perimeter, and a row of pull-throughs in the middle. Sites 1–13 back against a fence and residences. All of these but 5 are well-shaded. Sites 14–19 turn the corner towards the southwest. These are 42-foot back-ins against the fence. Sites 20–27 back to a fence along the south side, beyond which lies a farm. Site 27 is a little narrower than other sites, and fenced on three sides. Sites 29–45 are smaller back-ins (30 feet) that back to a field beyond the fence. Of these, 30 has the most shade. The pull-throughs sites in the middle of the park all have a shade tree except 48. End site 46 has a larger grassy area than the other sites. The tent sites are the same as RV sites 1–5. These offer a thin grass covering and little shade. As the name suggests, this "campground" is RV-oriented, but it is not really a camping destination.

Basics

Operated By: Private Operator. **Open:** All year. **Site Assignment:** Depending on site availability; credit card required for reservation, 24 hours cancellation policy. **Registration:** In office; late arrivals use drop box. **Fee:** RV $17.50 (full), tent $17.50; V, MC, D. **Parking:** At site.

Facilities

Number of RV Sites: 53. **Number of Tent-Only Sites:** 5. **Hookups:** Water, sewer, electric (30, 50 amp), cable. **Dump Station:** No (sewer at all sites). **Laundry:** Yes. **Pay Phone:** Yes. **Rest Rooms and Showers:** Yes. **Fuel:** No. **Propane:** No. **Internal Roads:** Gravel. **RV Service:** No. **Market:** 8 blocks west. **Restaurant:** 14 blocks west. **General Store:** No. **Vending:** No. **Swimming:** No. **Playground:** No. **Other:** Modem. **Activities:** Swimming, visiting museums, boating, watching wildlife. **Nearby Attractions:** Bitter Lake National Wildlife Reserve, Bottomless Lakes State Park, International UFO Museum and Research Center. **Additional Information:** Roswell Chamber of Commerce, (505) 623-5695.

Restrictions

Pets: On leash, cleaned up after, 2 pets of max. 20 lbs/RV. **Fires:** In grills. **Alcoholic Beverages:** At sites. **Vehicle Maximum Length:** None. **Other:** See rule sheet.

To Get There

From the junction of Hwy. 285 and Hwy. 70/380, turn east onto Hwy. 380 (2nd St. in town) and go 1.4 mi. Turn right at the sign into the entrance.

RUIDOSO

Tall Pines RV Park

1800 Sudderth Dr., Ruidoso 88345. T: (877) 957-5233 or (505) 257-5233; F: (505) 630-0712; www.tallpinesrv.com; info@tallpinesrv.com.

RV ★★★★ Tent n/a

Beauty: ★★★★ Site Privacy: ★★★
Spaciousness: ★★★ Quiet: ★★★
Security: ★★★★ Cleanliness: ★★★★
Insect Control: ★★★★ Facilities: ★★★★

This campground is divided into three sections: an upper, middle, and lower tier. The lower tier is located on the same level as the office and entrance. Lower-numbered sites back to woods on the west side, and to a fence on the south side. Sites 17–32 are 60-foot back-ins that also back to woods. Sites 33–38 are 45-foot back-ins, and 39–43 are 78-foot pull-throughs. In the middle tier, sites 49 and 50 are slightly secluded in a wooded patch along the road. Site 61, to the west, is also slightly secluded. The sites in this section 61–76) are 75-foot pull-throughs. The lower level is coated by the river, and is the nicest area to camp in. Sites 51–57 back to sites in the middle tier, but sites 58–60 back to the river, making these the most desirable sites in the park. The rest room in the rec building is a decent facility, but if you happen to find the one in the laundry, you will not be as pleased. That rest room seems to be an afterthought, stuck in an old furnace room, with one toilet and no sink. This campground is a popular spot for campers, and choice sites may be occupied by guests staying for several weeks. However, it is definitely worth the trip.

Basics

Operated By: Private operator. **Open:** All year. **Site Assignment:** Upon registration; credit card required for reservation, 48 hours cancellation policy. **Registration:** In office; late arrivals use drop box. **Fee:** RV $37 (33 w/ discount); checks, V, MC, AE, D. **Parking:** At site, lots of extra parking.

Facilities

Number of RV Sites: 74. **Number of Tent-Only Sites:** 0. **Hookups:** Water, sewer, electric (30, 50 amp), cable. **Dump Station:** Yes. **Laundry:** Yes. **Pay Phone:** Yes. **Rest Rooms and Showers:** Toilets; no shower. **Fuel:** No. **Propane:** No. **Internal Roads:** Gravel. **RV Service:** No. **Market:** 1.5 mi. west. **Restaurant:** Across street. **General Store:** No. **Vending:** Yes. **Swimming:** No. **Playground:** No. **Other:** Downtown within walking distance, modem, rec building. **Activities:** Fishing, golf. **Nearby Attractions:** Casinos, horse races. **Additional Information:** Ruidoso Chamber of Commerce, (505) 257-7395.

Restrictions

Pets: On leash, cleaned up after. **Fires:** In grills. **Alcoholic Beverages:** At sites. **Vehicle Maximum Length:** 45 ft.

To Get There

From the junction of Hwy. 70 and Hwy. 48 (Sudderth Dr. in town), turn west onto Sudderth Dr. and go 2.1 mi. Turn right at the sign into the entrance.

SAN ANTONIO

Bosque Birdwatcher's RV Park

1481 NM Rd. 1, San Antonio 87832. T: (505) 835-1366.

RV ★★★ Tent ★★

Beauty: ★★★ Site Privacy: ★★★★
Spaciousness: ★★★★ Quiet: ★★★★★
Security: ★★★★★ Cleanliness: ★★★★
Insect Control: ★★★★ Facilities: ★★★

Surrounded by national wildlife refuge land, this campground has undeveloped (mostly dirt) sites and natural gardens and landscaping, using rocks and local plants. Sites around the house are unnumbered and finding them can be at times a confusing task. There is one small site behind the house under a shade tree, and one long pull-through under a row of shade trees to the south of the house. These sites are the nicest, as they are very well-shaded and have character. The rest of the sites are in a gravel clearing to the west of the house. The south row has 60 × 30-foot pull-throughs, while the north row has larger (90 × 30 feet) sites. The north row has some amount of shade at each site, but the south row is unshaded. Tenting is possible along the north edge of the gravel lot. There is sparse grass and no shade, making for rather barren camping. The rest rooms are rather simple but spotless and very comfortable. This is a reasonable stop for RVers, and a great convenience for bird-watchers, but tenters will likely want to move on.

Basics

Operated By: Jackie and Billy Trujillo. **Open:** All year. **Site Assignment:** Upon registration; verbal reservations OK. **Registration:** In office; late arrivals select available site and pay in the morning. **Fee:** RV $17.50 (full), tent $10; no credits cards, but checks. **Parking:** At site.

Facilities

Number of RV Sites: 30. **Number of Tent-Only Sites:** Undesignated sites. **Hookups:** Water, sewer, electric (20, 30, 50 amp). **Dump Station:** No (sewer at all sites). **Laundry:** No. **Pay Phone:** No. **Rest Rooms and Showers:** Yes. **Fuel:** No. **Propane:** No. **Internal Roads:** Gravel. **RV Service:** No. **Market:** 13 mi. north. **Restaurant:** 3 mi. north. **General Store:** No. **Vending:** No. **Swimming:** No. **Playground:** No. **Other:** 2 phone hookups, modem. **Activities:** Bird-watching. **Nearby Attractions:** Bosque del Apache National Wildlife Refuge. **Additional Information:** Socorro Chamber of Commerce, (505) 835-0424.

Restrictions

Pets: On leash, cleaned up after. **Fires:** In grills. **Alcoholic Beverages:** At sites. **Vehicle Maximum Length:** None.

To Get There

From Hwy. I-40 (Exit 139), turn east onto Hwy. 380 from the east side of the highway, and go 0.55 mi. Turn right onto Hwy. 1 and go 3.1 mi. (Go 0.1 mi. past the billboard.) Turn right at the sign into the entrance.

SAN JOSE

Pecos River Campground

HCR 73 Box 30, San Jose 87565. T: (505) 421-2211; F: (505) 421-3660; campground@pleateautel.net.

 ★★★★ 

Beauty: ★★★★
Site Privacy: ★★★
Spaciousness: ★★★★
Quiet: ★★★★★
Security: ★★★★★
Cleanliness: ★★★★
Insect Control: ★★★★
Facilities: ★★★

This wilderness campground with a typical "southwest" flavor is pretty in a somewhat austere way. There is sparse grass and low trees, but also beautiful mountain views. An additional plus: all sites are long pull-throughs. Sites in the middle row average 65 feet, while those in the west row average 70 feet and those in the east row 78 feet. Sites 3, 5, 7, 10, and 12 are double width. Site 1 has somewhat more space, but is not as large as a double-width site. There are some really nice views of national forest in the west row, and other views from sites 12, 36, and 37. The tenting area is located in the northeast corner. This area has sparse grass cover but loads of juniper bushes and a scenic overlook to the north. The nicest site, at the very northern tip, has a covered picnic table and great views. This is an attractive campground that tenters and RVers alike will enjoy.

Basics

Operated By: Glen and Nina Post. **Open:** All year. **Site Assignment:** Depending on site availability; verbal reservations OK. **Registration:** In office; late arrivals use drop box. **Fee:** $10, $15, $20, depending on site size. **Parking:** At site.

Facilities

Number of RV Sites: 37. **Number of Tent-Only Sites:** 10. **Hookups:** Water, sewer, electric (30, 50 amp). **Dump Station:** No (sewer at all sites). **Laundry:** Yes. **Pay Phone:** Yes. **Rest Rooms and Showers:** Yes. **Fuel:** No. **Propane:** No. **Internal Roads:** Gravel. **RV Service:** No. **Market:** 24 mi. north. **Restaurant:** 5 mi. southeast. **General Store:** Yes. **Vending:** Yes. **Swimming:** No. **Playground:** Yes. **Other:** Meeting room, 1000-plus videos for rental, hunting and fishing licenses, borders national forest. **Activities:** Fishing, ATV riding, hiking. **Nearby Attractions:** Rte. 66, Pecos River. **Additional Information:** Las Vegas Chamber of Commerce, (505) 425-8631.

Restrictions

Pets: On leash, cleaned up after. **Fires:** In grills. **Alcoholic Beverages:** At sites. **Vehicle Maximum Length:** None. **Other:** See rule sheet.

To Get There

From Hwy. I-25 (Exit 319), on the north side of

the highway, take the first left. Turn left at the sign into the entrance.

SANTA FE

Santa Fe Skies RV Park

14 Browncastle Ranch, Santa Fe 87505. T: (877) 565-0451; www.santafeskiesrvpark.com; sfskysrv@swcp.com.

RV: ★★★★★ Tent: n/a

Beauty: ★★★★★	Site Privacy: ★★★★
Spaciousness: ★★★★	Quiet: ★★★★★
Security: ★★★★	Cleanliness: ★★★★★
Insect Control: ★★★★	Facilities: ★★★★

Although this campground is brand-new and still under construction, one thing that will not change as new facilities are added are the gorgeous 360-degree views for which the campground is named. There are, in essence, two mini-campgrounds contained in this park. The first has an RV park feel to it, with sites laid out in rows of gravel strips with a small strip of vegetation. These are 70 × 25-foot pull-throughs. Sites 1–10 are back-ins along the western edge. The second section of this park lies on Yucca, and has a more "campground" feel to it. Sites are 45–54 × 42-foot back-ins separated by wild-growing bushes. Sites 1–22 back to a wooden fence. The sites with the best views face north on top of a slight hill on Yucca: 24–28, J, and K. The rest rooms are provisionally located in a mobile home, but the new bathhouse was already under construction in 2001. The existing rest rooms are individual unisex units that are absolutely immaculate and very comfortable. Hopefully, these units herald what is to come. Even with construction still underway, this campground promises to be a destination to return to annually, and the owners will hopefully maintain their current level of quality.

BASICS

Operated By: John Brown. **Open:** All year. **Site Assignment:** Upon registration; credit card required for reservation (July-Oct.), 48 hours cancellation policy. **Registration:** In office; late arrivals select available site and pay in the morning. **Fee:** RV $25 (full), $20 (water, electric); checks, V, MC. **Parking:** At site.

FACILITIES

Number of RV Sites: 98. **Number of Tent-Only Sites:** 0. **Hookups:** Water, sewer, electric (30, 50 amp), instant phone. **Dump Station:** Yes. **Laundry:** Yes. **Pay Phone:** Yes. **Rest Rooms and Showers:** Yes. **Fuel:** No. **Propane:** No. **Internal Roads:** Gravel. **RV Service:** On-call. **Market:** 5 mi. north. **Restaurant:** 5 mi. north. **General Store:** Yes. **Vending:** No. **Swimming:** No. **Playground:** No. **Other:** Modem, views. **Activities:** Tours, shopping, opera, music. **Nearby Attractions:** Hyde Memorial State Park, Tesuque Pueblo, galleries, Georgia O'Keefe Museum. **Additional Information:** Santa Fe CVB, (800) 777-CITY, (505) 984-6760.

RESTRICTIONS

Pets: On leash, cleaned up after. **Fires:** In grills. **Alcoholic Beverages:** At sites. **Vehicle Maximum Length:** None.

TO GET THERE

From Hwy. I-25 (Southbound Exit 276, Northbound Exit 276A): on the north side of the highway, follow the signs for Hwy. 14, then cross Hwy. 14 and go 0.5 mi. Turn left at the sign into the entrance.

SANTA ROSA

Ramblin' Rose RV Park

602 Black St., Santa Rosa 88435. T: (505) 472-3820.

RV: ★★★ Tent: n/a

Beauty: ★★	Site Privacy: ★★★
Spaciousness: ★★★	Quiet: ★★
Security: ★★★★	Cleanliness: ★★★★
Insect Control: ★★★★	Facilities: ★★

This is an urban RV park with a bit of an unfortunate location. To the east is ugly industrial area, and the train passes very close by on the west side, making for both unattractive and noisy surroundings. In addition, the site numbers are either out of whack or missing, making for a confusing time in finding a particular site. Sites 1–3, in the southwest corner by the office, are 60-foot back-ins. There is a strip of 6 sites along the south side that are approximately 60-foot pull-throughs. In the middle of the park, sites 6–12 are 45-foot sites, while 12 is 30 feet. These sites are right in front of the office, and are not very attractive. The unnumbered site at the tip of the "island" in the parking lot in front of the office is arguably the most spacious site, but not very private. Look to 6–12 or 5–10 by the train for more privacy. This RV park is an acceptable overnighter. Tenters will have to look elsewhere for camping regardless.

BASICS

Operated By: Rosie Pruitt. **Open:** All year. **Site Assignment:** First come, first served; no reservations. **Registration:** In office; late arrivals select available site and pay in the morning or use drop box. **Fee:** RV $15; no credits cards, but checks. **Parking:** At site.

FACILITIES

Number of RV Sites: 32. **Number of Tent-Only Sites:** 0. **Hookups:** Water, sewer, electric (30, 50 amp), cable. **Dump Station:** No (sewer at all sites). **Laundry:** No. **Pay Phone:** Yes. **Rest Rooms and Showers:** Yes. **Fuel:** No. **Propane:** No. **Internal Roads:** Gravel/paved. **RV Service:** No. **Market:** 6 blocks north. **Restaurant:** 6 blocks north. **General Store:** No. **Vending:** No. **Swimming:** No. **Playground:** No. **Activities:** Fishing, boating, swimming, hiking. **Nearby Attractions:** Santa Rosa Lake State Park. **Additional Information:** Santa Rosa Chamber of Commerce, (505) 472-3763.

RESTRICTIONS

Pets: On leash, cleaned up after. **Fires:** In grills. **Alcoholic Beverages:** At sites. **Vehicle Maximum Length:** None.

TO GET THERE

From Hwy. I-40 (Exit 275), turn west onto Hwy. 54/84 and to 1.3 mi. Turn left at the sign for Vaughn onto Hwy. 54 and go 0.2 mi. Turn right at the sign into the entrance.

SILVER CITY

Manzano's RV Park

103 Flury Ln., Silver City 88061. T: (505) 538-0918.

RV: ★★★★★ | Tent: n/a

Beauty: ★★★★★ | Site Privacy: ★★★★★
Spaciousness: ★★★★★ | Quiet: ★★★★★
Security: ★★★★★ | Cleanliness: ★★★★★
Insect Control: ★★★★ | Facilities: ★★★

In this campground, natural beauty reigns. There are flowers, trees, native plants, and rocks, and the campground itself is surrounded by trees. Site 1, a 90-foot back-in by the entrance, is nicely mostly hidden by bushes. Site 2 is smaller (75 feet) and more open, but has attractive landscaping. Sites 4 and 6 and 5 and 7 are pull-throughs that flow into each other, and are easily 80 feet each. Sites 8–13 are 60–80-foot back-ins. In the middle island, site 14 (on the west side) is laid out along the internal road, and can accommodate a rig of any size. In the southwest corner of the island, site 15 is easily the widest site (45 feet wide), but only 40 feet in length. 16, on the other hand, is the shortest pull-through, at 40 feet. Sites 17 and 18, located behind the office, are 60-foot back-ins that are situated quite close together. This is a delightfully natural campground that RVers will enjoy much more than the nearby competition. (Tenters, however, may find the KOA the best choice, as Manzano's does not take tents.)

BASICS

Operated By: E.C. Manzano. **Open:** All year. **Site Assignment:** First come, first served; verbal reservations OK. **Registration:** In house; late arrivals select an available site and pay in the morning. **Fee:** RV $16; no credits cards, but checks. **Parking:** At site.

FACILITIES

Number of RV Sites: 18. **Number of Tent-Only Sites:** 0. **Hookups:** Water, sewer, electric (20, 30, 50 amp). **Each Site:** Picnic table. **Dump Station:** No (sewer at all sites). **Laundry:** Yes. **Pay Phone:** Yes. **Rest Rooms and Showers:** Yes. **Fuel:** No. **Propane:** No. **Internal Roads:** Gravel. **RV Service:** No. **Market:** 1 mi. towards Silver City. **Restaurant:** 1 mi. towards Silver City. **General Store:** No. **Vending:** No. **Swimming:** No. **Playground:** No. **Other:** Quiet, views. **Activities:** Hiking. **Nearby Attractions:** City of Rocks State Park, Gila National Forest. **Additional Information:** Old West Country Chamber of Commerce, (505) 538-0061.

RESTRICTIONS

Pets: On leash, cleaned up after. **Fires:** In grills. **Alcoholic Beverages:** At sites. **Vehicle Maximum Length:** 45 ft. **Other:** Pick up cigarette butts.

TO GET THERE

From the junction of Hwy. 90 and Hwy. 180, turn east onto Hwy. 180 and go 3.8 mi. Turn left onto Kirkland Rd. and go 0.3 mi. to Flury Ln. Turn right and go 0.4 mi. straight into the campground.

TAOS

Monte Bello RV Park

24819 Hwy. 64 West, El Prado 87529. T: (505) 751-0774; F: (505) 751-0675; www.taosmontebello rvpark.com; monte@taosnet.com.

RV ★★★★ Tent ★★★

Beauty: ★★★★★ Site Privacy: ★★★★
Spaciousness: ★★★★★ Quiet: ★★★
Security: ★★★★ Cleanliness: ★★★★★
Insect Control: ★★★★ Facilities: ★★★★

This is a brand new campground with parts still under construction. There are three rows of unshaded sites, but with wonderful views of the mountains and spectacular sunrises and sunsets. Both the campground and the sites themselves are left in a natural state, without being overly developed. All sites are 80 × 40-foot pull-throughs. End site 7 (to the north) has extra space to the side, as does 14, but this latter is next to the playground. Site 19 is next to the tenting sites. The best sites are on the northern or eastern end (7 and 19), as they are furthest from the highway and have the best views. The tent sites to the northeast are 25 × 40-foot spaces of dirt and sparse grass. Although there are currently only 4 tent sites, more are planned for the future. This campground looks like it will become a top-notch campground when all of the facilities are in place. It is already a very nice place to stay.

BASICS

Operated By: John and Concha Torres. **Open:** All year. **Site Assignment:** Depending on site availability; credit card required for reservation, $10 deposit, no refund. **Registration:** In store; late arrivals select available site and pay in the morning. **Fee:** RV $25 (full), $21 (water, electric); tent $13; V, MC. **Parking:** At site.

FACILITIES

Number of RV Sites: 19. **Number of Tent-Only Sites:** 4. **Hookups:** Water, sewer, electric (20, 30, 50 amp). **Each Site:** Picnic table. **Dump Station:** Yes. **Laundry:** Yes. **Pay Phone:** Yes. **Rest Rooms and Showers:** Yes. **Fuel:** No. **Propane:** No. **Internal Roads:** Gravel. **RV Service:** No. **Market:** 5 mi. to Taos. **Restaurant:** 3 mi. to Taos. **General Store:** Yes. **Vending:** No. **Swimming:** No. **Playground:** Yes. **Other:** Dog walk, walking trail, modem, sunrises/sunsets. **Activities:** Children's activities, skiing, scenic drives, mountain biking, rafting, walking tours, galleries. **Nearby Attractions:** Taos, Rio Grande Gorge Bridge, Taos Pueblo, Kit Carson State Historic Park. **Additional Information:** Taos Chamber of Commerce, (505) 758-3873.

RESTRICTIONS

Pets: On leash, cleaned up after. **Fires:** In grills. **Alcoholic Beverages:** At sites. **Vehicle Maximum Length:** None.

TO GET THERE

From the junction of Hwy. 522, 150, and 64, turn west onto Hwy. 64 and go 2.25 mi. Turn right at the sign into the entrance.

TUCUMCARI

Mountain Rd. RV Park

1700 Mountain Rd., Tucumcari 88401. T: (505) 461-9628.

RV ★★★ Tent ★★★

Beauty: ★★★ Site Privacy: ★★★
Spaciousness: ★★★ Quiet: ★★★★
Security: ★★★★ Cleanliness: ★★★★
Insect Control: ★★★★ Facilities: ★★★

This campground has 4 rows of open-ended pull-throughs. Sites are only about 45 × 28 feet, although rigs can stick out somewhat from there. Sites are mostly of a uniform quality, without much to distinguish one from the other. Site 59 is given over to long-term residents. Site 60 is a little cramped compared to the other sites. The best sites are 50–55, which face mostly fields, and are located away from the entrance and the mobile homes. The tent sites are in an area to the southwest. This area has a decent grass covering and two large shade trees for protection from the sun. The adjacent fields make for attractive surroundings. This campground makes for an agreeable overnight stay, and is fine for even longer.

BASICS

Operated By: Jackie O'Brien. **Open:** All year. **Site Assignment:** Depending on site availability; no reservations. **Registration:** In office; late arrivals use drop box. **Fee:** RV $18 (full), tent $10; checks, V, MC, D. **Parking:** At site.

FACILITIES

Number of RV Sites: 60. **Number of Tent-Only Sites:** 6. **Hookups:** Water, sewer, electric

(30, 50 amp). **Each Site:** Picnic table. **Dump Station:** No (sewer at all sites). **Laundry:** Yes. **Pay Phone:** Yes. **Rest Rooms and Showers:** Yes. **Fuel:** No. **Propane:** No. **Internal Roads:** Gravel. **RV Service:** No. **Market:** less than 8 mi. to Tucumcari. **Restaurant:** less than 8 mi. to Tucumcari. **General Store:** No. **Vending:** No. **Swimming:** No. **Playground:** Yes. **Other:** RV supplies. **Activities:** Fishing, boating, swimming, hiking, visiting museums, cheese sampling. **Nearby Attractions:** Mesalands Dinosaur Museum, Tucumcari Historical Museum, Tucumcari Mountain Cheese Museum, Conchas Lake State Park. **Additional Information:** Tucumcari Chamber of Commerce, (505) 461-1694.

RESTRICTIONS

Pets: On leash, cleaned up after. **Fires:** In grills. **Alcoholic Beverages:** At sites. **Vehicle Maximum Length:** None.

TO GET THERE

From Hwy. I-40 (Exit 333), from the north side of the highway, turn north onto Hwy. 54 and go 0.3 mi. Turn left at the sign into the entrance.

VADO

Vado RV Park

16201 Las Alturas Ave., Vado 88072. T: (505) 233-2573.

RV ★★★ Tent ★

Beauty: ★★★	Site Privacy: ★★★
Spaciousness: ★★★	Quiet: ★★★★
Security: ★★★★	Cleanliness: ★★★
Insect Control: ★★★★	Facilities: ★★★★

Laid out in 7 strips of pull-throughs with plenty of space at the back, this campground can accommodate vehicles of any length. The average size of a site is 30 × 45 feet, but the internal road is quite wide and can allow for longer vehicles. (As a last resort, super-long vehicles such as semis can be parked in the back, but without hookups.) There is a potential for some very attractive landscaping in the front that seems, unfortunately, to have been abandoned. The views at the back of the park (to the east) are also very nice, but sabotaged by a storage shed and miscellaneous equipment parked or piled around it. The proximity of the highway to row G makes these sites the least desirable, but not drastically so. End sites (those with the highest numbers) in all rows are also less desirable, due to their "view" of the storage unit. The most favorable sites are those along row A, as they are furthest from the highway and abut a desert with views of the mountains. Tent sites are located in a small enclosed section in front of the laundry facility at the end of row D. There is enough space to fit 6–8 tents comfortably, but only one table and no fire pit or grill. The rest room facilities are slightly shabby (cracked mirror, unsightly fly-strip, paper on the floor) but comfortable. A huge convenience for guests is the clubhouse at the east boundary of the property. Open to guests, the clubhouse has a full kitchen (including fridge and microwave), sofas, board games, free coffee, and TV. This is a worthwhile visit made all the more comfortable by its numerous facilities.

BASICS

Operated By: Ruth and Shane Brisco. **Open:** All year. **Site Assignment:** Upon registration; verbal reservations OK. **Registration:** In office; late arrivals use drop box. **Fee:** RV $16, tent $6; no credit cards, checks OK. **Parking:** At site.

FACILITIES

Number of RV Sites: 73. **Number of Tent-Only Sites:** Undesignated sites. **Hookups:** Water, sewer, electric (20, 30 amp). **Each Site:** Picnic table, 1–2 trees, concrete slab. **Dump Station:** Yes. **Laundry:** Yes. **Pay Phone:** Yes. **Rest Rooms and Showers:** Yes. **Fuel:** No. **Propane:** No. **Internal Roads:** Dirt. **RV Service:** No. **Market:** 1 mi. into town. **Restaurant:** 0.5 mi. into town. **General Store:** Yes. **Vending:** Yes. **Swimming:** Pool. **Playground:** No. **Other:** Pet walk area, clubhouse. **Activities:** Board games, TV. **Nearby Attractions:** Organ Mountains, City of Rocks State Park, White Sands National Monument, Mexico. **Additional Information:** Las Cruces CVB, (800) 343-7827, (505) 541-2444.

RESTRICTIONS

Pets: On leash. **Fires:** In grills. **Alcoholic Beverages:** At sites. **Vehicle Maximum Length:** None.

TO GET THERE

From I-10, take Exit 155 and turn east. Turn right onto the frontage road and drive 0.4 mi. Turn left at the sign into the campground. The office is straight ahead.

WHITE'S CITY

AAA White's City RV Park

17 Carlsbad Caverns Highway, White's City 88268. T: (800) CAVERNS or (505) 785-2291; www.whitescity.com (keyword "caverns").

RV ★★★ Tent ★★

Beauty: ★★★	Site Privacy: ★★★
Spaciousness: ★★★	Quiet: ★★★★
Security: ★★★★	Cleanliness: ★★★
Insect Control: ★★★★	Facilities: ★★★

Located a block west of the Registration Lobby, this campground is made up of blocks of individual campgrounds, making effectively four different campgrounds. The RV sites closest to the road are average 32 ¥ 36 feet in size, for both back-ins and pull-throughs. (Longer sites further south and west can accommodate vehicles up to 60 feet in length.) Sites are open and level on a gravel lot. Sites J–P sit atop a bit of an embankment, but are otherwise level. Sites around the perimeter abut a dried stream bed filled with cacti and bushes, and most benefit from a mature shade tree, making these sites (127–142) most desirable. The least desirable sites (R–Y) are situated along the road and exit, and are not clearly labeled. Site R is particularly open to road traffic. Rest room facilities are unisex rooms with an open toilet and shower. The laundry facility is modern and clean, with a counter for folding clothes and table and bench for killing time while your clothes get done. Tent sites, separated from the RV sites by 100 yards, are located on a loop with a grassy field on the interior. Sites on the inside of the loop have ample tree coverage and those in the middle back to the common area, making them potentially double the size of end sites. Tent sites on the outside of the loop have no trees, and are restricted to 30 × 40 feet. The rest room facilities here are less modern and less clean, and the shower is not closed off. The playground area occupies the most lush patch of grass in the entire park, with several large trees providing enough shade for families to picnic while the children play. Tenters may be green with envy at the sight of this patch of grass, but RVers will find this an acceptable base of operations for tours into Carlsbad, or a jumping-off point to Texas and beyond.

BASICS

Operated By: Tom Dugger. **Open:** All year. **Site Assignment:** First come, first served. **Registration:** In registration lobby; late arrivals ring bell. **Fee:** RV/tent $22. **Parking:** At site.

FACILITIES

Number of RV Sites: 92. **Number of Tent-Only Sites:** 40. **Hookups:** Water, sewer, electric (30 amp). **Each Site:** Picnic table, grill, shared shelter, most have trees. **Dump Station:** Yes. **Laundry:** Yes. **Pay Phone:** Yes. **Rest Rooms and Showers:** Yes. **Fuel:** Yes. **Propane:** No. **Internal Roads:** Paved, gravel. **RV Service:** No. **Market:** Yes. **Restaurant:** Yes. **General Store:** Yes. **Vending:** Yes. **Swimming:** Pool. **Playground:** Yes. **Other:** Security gate, post office, shops. **Activities:** Tennis, volleyball, basketball. **Nearby Attractions:** Carlsbad Caverns. **Additional Information:** Carlsbad CVB, (800) 221-1224, (505) 887-6516.

RESTRICTIONS

Pets: On leash. **Fires:** In grills/pits. **Alcoholic Beverages:** At sites. **Vehicle Maximum Length:** None. **Other:** Water park is not part of RV park. No overnight parking within 5 mi. radius (if not in campground).

TO GET THERE

From Hwy. 62/180, turn west onto Carlsbad Caverns Highway, then take the first left into the Old West complex. Resister in the Registration Lobby.

Oklahoma

Oklahoma is a real slice of American bread. There's nobody more down-to-earth than a native Oklahoman working the land, having coffee with friends before a hard day's work, or going to church to start the week. And nobody's more hospitable. This is wave-at-your-neighbor-as-you-drive-past country, and strangers are greeted with the same friendly wave.

Many of Oklahoma's visitor-friendly towns line I-35, which bisects the state. The panhandle of Oklahoma (from the New Mexico border to about Canton Lake) does not offer much to travelers, and any Oklahoman will tell you: *nobody* comes to Oklahoma in the dead of summer. July and August are months for exploring the other 49 states. But spring and fall are beautiful—and popular—times to visit. **Tulsa** is a modern city with a history, **Bartlesville** is home to a 3,500-acre wildlife preserve, **Grove** has a reconstructed village from the nineteenth century, and you can still get your kicks on (Historic) **Route 66.**

And of course, there's **Oklahoma City.** Oklahoma City lies at the crossroads of I-35, I-40, and I-44, ensuring that visitors from any surrounding state can get there. And well they should. Oklahoma City might strike you at first as the fitting home of the **National Cowboy Hall of Fame,** but promenade through the skywalks of downtown for another view. Take in the **Air Space Museum,** the **Crystal Bridge at Myriad Gardens,** the **Civic Center** that spans six blocks in the heart of downtown, and the touching **Oklahoma City National Memorial.** The impression you take with you of the city—and quite likely the state for which it was named—will be of a complex embroidery waiting to be unraveled. Don't believe the Board of Tourism signs that claim, "Oklahoma is OK!" It's much better than that.

The following facilities accept payment in checks or cash only:

Big Cedar RV Park, Big Cedar
Big Cedar RV Park, Big Cedar
Bridgeport RV Park, Eufaula
Elk Run RV Park, Elk City
Moneka Park, Waurika
Rockin' Horse RV Park, Spiro
Sawyer RV Park, Sawyer
Simmons RV Park, Durant
Wink's RV Park, Clinton
Woodland Camper Park, Tonkawa

The following facilities feature 20 sites or fewer:

Oak Hill RV Park, Davis
Sawyer RV Park, Sawyer
Cherokee Riverside Campground, Disney
Corky's Get & Go, Woodward

ANADARKO

Indian City USA

P.O. Box 695, Anadarko 73005. T: (405) 247-5661; F: (405) 247-2467; www.indiancityusa.com; indiancty@aol.com.

RV ★★★ Tent ★★★

Beauty: ★★★	Site Privacy: ★★★
Spaciousness: ★★★★	Quiet: ★★★★★
Security: ★★★★	Cleanliness: ★★
Insect Control: ★★★	Facilities: ★★

This campground is set up in two tiers. The top tier is an open gravel lot surrounded on the perimeter by trees, but containing a row of only 4 shade trees down the middle. The (unnumbered) sites that have shade trees are the more desirable sites. The lower tier to the west is a nicer area, but requires negotiating a tight hairpin turn just where the road is most damaged. These are all grassy sites with cement one-piece picnic tables. While still quite open, there are more shade trees here than in the upper tier. (Be sure to drive carefully on the lower tier, as the grass is rather choppy and uneven.) There are unlimited tenting possibilities in the grassy field to the west of the RV park, and even in the woods around it. The grass is great for tents, but there are no trees whatsoever in the field. The rest room itself is clean, but appears rather old and worn. The floors are stained and could use a re-tiling. One gets the impression of a very nice campground that only needs a helping hand to make it really sparkle. As it is, it's a decent place to spend the night, and offers touristy attractions for those interested in Native American culture.

BASICS

Operated By: George Moran. **Open:** All year. **Site Assignment:** First some, first served; verbal reservations OK. **Registration:** In Indian City. (Late arrivals select an available site & settle in the morning.) **Fee:** RV $13.12, tent $9.98. **Parking:** At site.

FACILITIES

Number of RV Sites: 65. **Number of Tent-Only Sites:** Undesignated sites. **Hookups:** Water, sewer, electric (30 amps). **Each Site:** Picnic tables on lower tier. **Dump Station:** Yes. **Laundry:** No. **Pay Phone:** No. **Rest Rooms and Showers:** Yes. **Fuel:** No. **Propane:** No. **Internal Roads:** Paved, but in disrepair. **RV Service:** No. **Market:** 2 mi. in Anadarko. **Restaurant:** 1 block. **General Store:** No. **Vending:** Yes. **Swimming:** Pool. **Playground:** Yes. **Other:** None. **Activities:** Guided tours of American Indian villages. **Nearby Attractions:** Indian City USA, Indian City Museum, American Indian dancing, National Hall of Fame for Famous American Indians, Anadarko Philomathic Pioneer Museum, Southern Plains Indian Museum & Crafts Center. **Additional Information:** Anadarko Chamber of Commerce, (405) 247-6651.

RESTRICTIONS

Pets: On leash, cleaned up after. **Fires:** In grills. **Alcoholic Beverages:** At sites. **Vehicle Maximum Length:** None.

TO GET THERE

From the junction of Hwys. 8, 9, and 62, go 2.3 mi. south on Hwy. 8. Turn left at the sign onto the paved road and go 0.3 mi. Turn right into the campground or continue up the road 0.2 mi. to register in Indian City.

ARDMORE

Ardmore/Marietta KOA

Rte. 1 Box 640, Ardmore 73448. T: (800) KOA-5893 or (580) 276-2800.

RV ★★★★ Tent ★★★★

Beauty: ★★★★	Site Privacy: ★★★★
Spaciousness: ★★★★	Quiet: ★★★
Security: ★★★★	Cleanliness: ★★★★★
Insect Control: ★★★★	Facilities: ★★★★

Built on a slope, this campground has levelled pull-throughs 84 × 25 feet in size. There is a distinct farm feeling on the campground, and it is surrounded on the south by a farm, on the west by trees, and the north by an open field with trees in the distance. The most desirable sites are 15, 16, and 21–26, which all have shade trees. The other sites are in the open to a greater or lesser extent. Tenting is possible on the grassy field to the west of the RV sites, or—better yet—in the field to the north, where a handful of shade trees provide coverage. The rest rooms and showers are extremely clean, although the floor is slightly peeling (but not dirty). The laundry room is equally clean and spacious, and very well decorated. This is a small but very nice campground. Tenters and RVers alike will enjoy a stay here.

Basics

Operated By: Jery Burns. **Open:** All year. **Site Assignment:** Assigned upon registration; credit card required for reservation. **Registration:** In office. (Late arrivals use drop box in laundry.) **Fee:** RV $22 (full), $20 (water, electric), tent $16. **Parking:** At site.

Facilities

Number of RV Sites: 26. **Number of Tent-Only Sites:** Undesignated sites. **Hookups:** Water, sewer, electric (30, 50 amps). **Each Site:** Picnic table, grill. **Dump Station:** Yes. **Laundry:** Yes. **Pay Phone:** Yes. **Rest Rooms and Showers:** Yes. **Fuel:** No. **Propane:** Yes. **Internal Roads:** Gravel. **RV Service:** No. **Market:** 6 mi. south to Marietta. **Restaurant:** 6 mi. south to Marietta. **General Store:** Yes. **Vending:** No. **Swimming:** No. **Playground:** Yes. **Other:** Game room, 2 cabins. **Activities:** Volleyball, fishing, boating. **Nearby Attractions:** Arbuckle Mountains, Eliza Cruce Hall Doll Collection, Tucker Tower Nature Center, Charles B. Goddard Center for the Visual & Performing Arts. **Additional Information:** Ardmore Chamber of Commerce, (580) 223-7765.

Restrictions

Pets: On leash, cleaned up after. **Fires:** In grills. **Alcoholic Beverages:** At sites. **Vehicle Maximum Length:** None.

To Get There

From I-35, take Exit 21. Turn west onto Oswalt and go 0.1 mi. Turn left at the sign onto the dirt entrance road.

BARTLESVILLE

Riverside RV Resort

1211 Southeast Adams Blvd., Bartlesville 74003. T: (888) 572-1241 or (918) 336-6431; F: (918) 336-3892; riversidervrst@aol.com.

RV ★★★ Tent ★★★

Beauty: ★★★ Site Privacy: ★★★
Spaciousness: ★★ Quiet: ★★★★
Security: ★★★★ Cleanliness: ★★★
Insect Control: ★★★★ Facilities: ★★★

Located in a residential area, this campground features some attractive landscaping using flowers, bricks around some of the sites, and a fountain, but it also looks a little run-down. Sites 1–14 are in the northwest corner, along the entrance. These sites (especially 1–8) are closest to the pool. Sites 15–19, in the middle of the campground, are pull-throughs 65 × 21 feet, and 20–23, in the same area, are pull-throughs 60 × 21 feet. All of these sites but 21 are well-shaded. Other 65-foot pull-throughs are 49–53 in the southeast corner. Sites 55–60, also in the southeast corner, are slightly shorter, at 60 feet. Any of these are a decent stay, depending on the length of site required for your vehicle. These sites are closest to the river, but are still up and off the bank. Tenting is allowed along the river bank. While shaded, these sites do not have abundant room for a tent—let alone recreating or relaxing at your site. The rest rooms and showers, individual units located in the office building, are tidy and nicely decorated. Both the rest rooms and the (small) laundry are clean. While adequate, this park is, as the name implies, better for RVs than tents—although it hardly lives up to the title "resort."

Basics

Operated By: Dave & Joyce Butler. **Open:** All year. **Site Assignment:** Assigned upon registration; verbal reservations OK. **Registration:** In office. (Late arrivals pay in morning.) **Fee:** RV $16 (full), tent $6 (checks, no credit cards). **Parking:** At site.

Facilities

Number of RV Sites: 70. **Number of Tent-Only Sites:** Undesignated sites. **Hookups:** Water, sewer, electric (20, 30, 50 amps), cable. **Dump Station:** Yes. **Laundry:** Yes. **Pay Phone:** Yes. **Rest Rooms and Showers:** Yes. **Fuel:** No. **Propane:** Yes. **Internal Roads:** Gravel. **RV Service:** No. **Market:** Less than 0.5 mi. west. **Restaurant:** 1.5 mi. east. **General Store:** No. **Vending:** Yes. **Swimming:** Pool. **Playground:** No. **Other:** Dataport, pavilion, river. **Activities:** Swimming, fishing. **Nearby Attractions:** Caney River, Woolaroc Ranch Museum. **Additional Information:** Bartlesville Area CVB, (800) 364-8708 or (918) 336-8708.

Restrictions

Pets: On leash, cleaned up after. **Fires:** In grills. **Alcoholic Beverages:** Inside RV only. **Vehicle Maximum Length:** 70 ft. **Other:** None.

To Get There

From the junction of Hwy. 75 and Hwy. 60 West (Pawhuska/Ponca City Exit), turn west onto Hwy. 60 and go 1.6 mi. to Quapaw Ave. Turn left onto Quapaw Ave. and take the first left into the campground.

BEAVER

Beaver Dunes State Park

P.O. Box 1190, Beaver 73932. T: (405) 625-3373; F: (405) 625-3525; www.otrd.state.ok.us; rstrpark@otrd.state.ok.us.

RV ★★★ Tent ★★★★

Beauty: ★★★★
Site Privacy: ★★★
Spaciousness: ★★★★
Quiet: ★★★★
Security: ★★★
Cleanliness: ★★★★
Insect Control: ★★
Facilities: ★★★

Just a mile and a half north of town, this campground offers primitive sites and electrical hookups for campers who like to get close to nature. There are campsites right at the water's edge (although no swimming is permitted), as well as furth up on shore. (Sites are not numbered.) There are seven huge pull-throughs (85 feet long) to the north of the "comfort station" (rest rooms and showers), which are the best bet for anything longer than 22 feet. There are, however, no shade trees in these sites. Following the one-way road, you come across three 27-foot back-ins that have covered picnic tables. One of these sites has water. Just to the southeast of the comfort station are four primitive sites: two are right on the lake, while the other two are on either side of the building. These are attractive sites, with nice tree coverage and good views of the lake and the bridge. However, they receive foot traffic to and from the rest rooms and cars drive past to reach other campsites. Perhaps the nicest campsite of all is the first one you see when you enter the campground. It is right on the water, has soft sand (on a bit of a slope), and some tree shade. The biggest drawback is that you must park above the site on the road, and walk down to the campsite, making RV parking at this site impossible. The "comfort station" is very spacious and clean, although the cement building itself seems a little old. This is a fine campground for those seeking to sleep out in nature, and has enough variety to satisfy pretty much any tastes.

BASICS

Operated By: Oklahoma State Parks. **Open:** All year. **Site Assignment:** First come, first served; no reservations. **Registration:** In office, or ranger will collect at site. **Fee: Hookups:** $13, primitive: $7 (V & MC). **Parking:** At (or near) site.

FACILITIES

Number of RV Sites: 7. **Number of Tent-Only Sites:** 10. **Hookups:** Water, electric (30 amps). **Each Site:** Picnic table, grill/pit. **Dump Station:** Yes. **Laundry:** No. **Pay Phone:** In office (collect or calling card only). **Rest Rooms and Showers:** Yes. **Fuel:** No. **Propane:** No. **Internal Roads:** Paved. **RV Service:** No. **Market:** 1 mi. to Beaver. **Restaurant:** 1 mi. to Beaver. **General Store:** No. **Vending:** No. **Swimming:** No. **Playground:** Yes. **Other:** Picnic pavillion, wildlife. **Activities:** Hiking, ATV riding, volleyball, horseshoes, children's fishing. **Nearby Attractions:** Sand dunes, lake. **Additional Information:** Beaver County Chamber of Commerce, (580) 625-4726.

RESTRICTIONS

Pets: On leash, cleaned up after. **Fires:** In grills; subject to bans. **Alcoholic Beverages:** Beer only. **Vehicle Maximum Length:** None. **Other:** No swimming, ATV regulations.

TO GET THERE

From the junction of Hwy. 64/270 and Hwy. 23, turn right onto Hwy. 23/270, and go 4.9 mi. south. Turn right at the sign into the campground, or left to get to the office.

BIG CEDAR

Big Cedar RV Park

0.3 mi. west of US Hwy. 259 on SH63, Big Cedar 74939. T: (918) 651-3271; www.big-cedar.net; rlsand50@yahoo.com.

RV ★★★★ Tent ★★★

Beauty: ★★★★
Site Privacy: ★★★★
Spaciousness: ★★★★
Quiet: ★★★★★
Security: ★★★★★
Cleanliness: ★★★★★
Insect Control: ★★★
Facilities: ★★★

This rural campground is surrounded by lush woods and forested hills to the north and east. It has a down-home, farmy atmosphere and grassy pull-through sites laid out in rows. Sites are a lengthy 75 feet and a uniform 24 feet wide. The most desirable sites are the lowest in number

(1–6), as these are furthest from the highway and closest to the "Bath Barn". Site 1 contains a tree, but is not itself shaded. Sites 12 and 13 share a small shed that impinges slightly on their space. The tenting area is an open field on the south and east sides of the RV sites. There is a very nice grass cover, which will appeal to tenters, and one large tree, but otherwise the tenting area is quite open. The laundry is very spacious and clean and contains two small showers (normally not used). The facilities in the "Bath Barn" are self-contained units that include nicely decorated rest rooms with a vanity and showers. All facilities are kept immaculate. Although this is a small campground, it is worthy as a destination, and its family-run atmosphere will make all visitors feel comfortable.

Basics

Operated By: Bob & Carolyn Sanders. **Open:** All year. **Site Assignment:** First come, first served; verbal reservations OK. **Registration:** In office. (Late arrivals use drop box.) **Fee:** RV (30 amps) or tent $10, RV (50 amps): $12 (checks, no credit cards). **Parking:** At site.

Facilities

Number of RV Sites: 21. **Number of Tent-Only Sites:** Undesignated sites. **Hookups:** Water, sewer, electric (30, 50 amps). **Each Site:** Picnic table. **Dump Station:** Yes. **Laundry:** Yes. **Pay Phone:** No (0.3 mi. away). **Rest Rooms and Showers:** Yes. **Fuel:** No (0.3 mi. away). **Propane:** No (0.3 mi. away). **Internal Roads:** Gravel. **RV Service:** No. **Market:** 30 mi. to Taliniha. **Restaurant:** 5 mi. in Big Cedar. **General Store:** No. **Vending:** No. **Swimming:** No. **Playground:** No. **Other:** None. **Activities:** Hiking, scenic drives, wildlife watching. **Nearby Attractions:** Winding Stair National Wildlife Reserve. **Additional Information:** Talihina Chamber of Commerce, (918) 567-3434.

Restrictions

Pets: On leash, cleaned up after. **Fires:** In grills. **Alcoholic Beverages:** At sites. **Vehicle Maximum Length:** None.

To Get There

From the junction of Hwy. 63 and Hwy. 259, go 0.35 mi. west on Hwy. 63. Turn left at the sign into the entrance. The office is the green building on the left.

BROKEN BOW

Reiger RV Park

Rte. 4 Box 27, Hwy. 259 North, Broken Bow 74728. T: (800) 550-6521 or (580) 494-6553; F: (580) 494-6553; www.hochatownjunction.com; HJ-Resorts @pine-net.com.

RV: ★★★ Tent: n/a

Beauty: ★★★★ Site Privacy: ★★★★
Spaciousness: ★★★ Quiet: ★★★
Security: ★★★★ Cleanliness: ★★★★
Insect Control: ★★★★ Facilities: ★★

This campground is carved into the forest, and the road into the campground is as rough as you might expect. However, the campground itself is quite pretty and worth the cautious drive. Sites are grassy and basically level, although longer pull-throughs are shortened from 95 feet to a useable 50 feet by a slope at both ends (1–6). The nicest sites include 20, which is in a shaded corner to the northeast; 24, which is in a shaded corner separated from all other sites by a wall of pines; and 25–27, which are in a clearing surrounded by lush vegetation. These sites are all 75-foot back-ins. Sites 4–6 along the south strip are also nice and long. (Note that you must drive around the entire campground to get to these spaces.) The least desirable sites are 1–3, 7–9, and an unnumbered site by the shed, at all of which campers may find the noise from the nearby go-carts annoying. This is a very nice campground located on some beautiful land, and only needs a rest room to come very highly recommended.

Basics

Operated By: Stan Zimmerman. **Open:** All year. **Site Assignment:** Flexible, depending on availability. Credit card required for reservation; refund requires 24-hours notice. **Registration:** In store. (Late arrivals find on-site manager.) **Fee:** $12 (checks, V, MC, AE, D). **Parking:** At site.

Facilities

Number of RV Sites: 27. **Number of Tent-Only Sites:** 0. **Hookups:** Water, sewer, electric (35 amps). **Dump Station:** No (sewer at all sites). **Laundry:** No. **Pay Phone:** Yes. **Rest Rooms and Showers:** No. **Fuel:** No. **Propane:** No. **Internal Roads:** Dirt/gravel. **RV Service:** No. **Market:** 6 mi. south. **Restaurant:** Less than 1 mi. south. **Gen-**

eral Store: No. **Vending:** Yes. **Swimming:** No. **Playground:** No. **Other:** Go carts, mini golf, cabins, fly shop, casting pond. **Activities:** Scuba diving, fishing, swimming, golf. **Nearby Attractions:** Broken Bow Lake. **Additional Information:** Broken Bow Chamber of Commerce, (800) 528-7337 or (580) 584-3393.

RESTRICTIONS

Pets: On leash, cleaned up after. **Fires:** In grills. **Alcoholic Beverages:** At sites. **Vehicle Maximum Length:** None. **Other:** No fireworks.

TO GET THERE

From the junction of Hwy. 70 and Hwy. 259, go 6.4 mi. north on Hwy. 259. Turn left into "The Cedar Chest" complex. Register in the store.

CLAYTON

Clayton Lake State Park

Rte. 1 Box 33-10, Clayton 74536. T: (918) 569-7981; www.touroklahoma.com/Pages/stateparks/parks/cllspbig.html; rsrtpark@otrd.state.ok.us.

RV ★★★ Tent ★★★★★

Beauty: ★★★★ Site Privacy: ★★★★
Spaciousness: ★★★ Quiet: ★★★★
Security: ★★★★ Cleanliness: ★★★
Insect Control: ★★★ Facilities: ★★

This state park is divided up into 2 Areas. Area 1 has a boat ramp and lake access, with RV sites to the north. RVers should take note that the road is steep and broken in places, and drivers should take it slowly. As you drive in, it can be a little confusing as to where the RV sites are (look for the sign that says "RV Area"), but note that the tent sites (to the southeast of the office) are all forested and have some degree of slope to them, whereas the RV sites are all on a level, open strip. These sites are all large back-ins with an open area to pull in, allowing a rig of any size to park here. There is only one (unnumbered) site that has a table, grill, and tree—the rest do not have these features. Area 2 is designated the "assigned camping" area. These are also large (75-foot) back-ins that any RV should be able to fit into. The first site is right at the entrance, and is therefore less desirable. Further from the water, but with excellent views, are sites E3 and E4. There is a small gated area away from the rest of the sites that has gravel sites and 50-foot back-ins. The sites in this area are all open but surrounded by forest. The rest room facilities are clean and modern, as are the showers. This park offers a nice getaway on a lake, with shaded spots that are fine for RVs and ideal for tents.

BASICS

Operated By: Oklahoma State Parks. **Open:** All year. **Site Assignment:** Assigned upon registration; verbal reservations OK. **Registration:** In office. (Late arrivals select an available site & pay in the morning.) **Fee:** RV $14 (water, electric), tent $7. **Parking:** At site.

FACILITIES

Number of RV Sites: 55. **Number of Tent-Only Sites:** 0. **Hookups:** Water, electric. **Each Site:** Picnic table, grill. **Dump Station:** Yes. **Laundry:** No. **Pay Phone:** No. **Rest Rooms and Showers:** Yes. **Fuel:** No. **Propane:** No. **Internal Roads:** Paved. **RV Service:** No. **Market:** 5 mi. north. **Restaurant:** 2 mi. north. **General Store:** No. **Vending:** No. **Swimming:** Lake. **Playground:** Yes. **Other:** Covered pavilion. **Activities:** Swimming, boating, fishing, hiking, wildlife watching. **Nearby Attractions:** Talimena State Park, McGee Creek State Park. **Additional Information:** Choctaw County Chamber Of Commerce, (580) 326-7511.

RESTRICTIONS

Pets: On leash, cleaned up after. **Fires:** In grills. **Alcoholic Beverages:** At sites. **Vehicle Maximum Length:** None.

TO GET THERE

From the junction of Hwy. 2 and Hwy. 271, turn south onto Hwy. 271 and go 4.4 mi. Turn right at the sign into the entrance. Area 1 is to the right, Area 2 lies straight ahead.

CLINTON

Wink's RV Park

1410 Neptune, Clinton 73601. T: (580) 323-1664.

RV ★★★★ Tent ★★★★

Beauty: ★★★★ Site Privacy: ★★★★
Spaciousness: ★★★★ Quiet: ★★★★
Security: ★★★★ Cleanliness: ★★★★★
Insect Control: ★★ Facilities: ★★★

This campground is divided into 3 tiers, providing a very different experience in the top tier than in the bottom two. The top tier contains all open back-ins averaging 40 × 18 feet. These sites are all level, but do not have shade, picnic tables, or grills. This makes for an unmistakably "urban" camping experience. However, the lower two tiers have beautiful campsites with huge shade trees and beautiful grass. These sites are all pull-throughs that average 35 feet in length, although there are much larger ones on the lower tier. The best sites are 11–13 and 33–39, as they are practicall enveloped in shade trees and face a nice grassy area. Less nice is site 14, which seems clipped and looks out over junked autos in the neighboring yard. Sites 49 and 50 are the largest, as they are not delineated in size, but are rather spaces in a grassy field that could accommodate a rig of any size. These sites are separated from the others, as are sites 43–45, which offers more privacy. The rest rooms and showers are spacious and clean, but have two flaws: the toilets are only separated by a curtain, and there is no space to hold clothes inside each individual shower. These are rather small faults, however, and the overall camping experience is excellent.

Basics

Operated By: Winston & Ruthelma Hoffman. **Open:** All year. **Site Assignment:** Assigned upon registration; verbal reservations OK. **Registration:** In office. (Late arrivals use drop box.) **Fee:** RV, tent (2 people): $18, tent (1 person): $10. **Parking:** At site.

Facilities

Number of RV Sites: 65. **Number of Tent-Only Sites:** 0. **Hookups:** Water, sewer, electric (20, 30, 50 amps). **Dump Station:** No (sewer at all sites). **Laundry:** Yes. **Pay Phone:** Yes. **Rest Rooms and Showers:** Yes. **Fuel:** No. **Propane:** No. **Internal Roads:** Gravel. **RV Service:** No. **Market:** 0.75 mi. north. **Restaurant:** 0.5 mi. north. **General Store:** No. **Vending:** No. **Swimming:** No. **Playground:** Yes. **Other:** Basketball net. **Activities:** Visiting museums, basketball. **Nearby Attractions:** Oklahoma Rte. 66 Museum. **Additional Information:** Clinton Chamber of Commerce, (800) 759-1397 or (580) 323-2222.

Restrictions

Pets: On leash, cleaned up after. **Fires:** In grills. **Alcoholic Beverages:** At sites. **Vehicle Maximum Length:** None.

To Get There

From the junction of I-40 (Exit 65A) and Historic Rte. 66, go 0.3 mi. south on Rte. 66. Turn right at the sign into the campground. The office is on the right.

COLBERT

Sherrard RV and KOA Kampground

411 Sherrard St., Colbert 74733. T: (800) KOA-2485 or (580) 296-2485.

RV ★★★★ Tent ★★★★

Beauty: ★★★★	Site Privacy: ★★★★
Spaciousness: ★★★★	Quiet: ★★★
Security: ★★★★	Cleanliness: ★★★★
Insect Control: ★★★★	Facilities: ★★★★

Half RV sales and servicing, half campground, the Sherrard complex has much to offer the RV camper. The sites open to overnighters are on the west side of the park. (The sites to the north, 1–50 and 107–111 are reserved for monthly customers.) These sites are all 75-foot grassy pull-throughs arranged in rows (61–98) and two small groups on their own (53–56 and 101–106). Most every site is well-shaded, although 64, 65, and 76 are not, and sites 101 and 104 have a single shade tree at the edge of their space. Sites 102, 103, 105, and 106 have several large shade trees each. The row numbered in the 80s has the most developed sites, with cement slabs, and the best sites in the park are on this row: 86–88. These three sites face a row of trees (that cover an RV storage area), and are furthest from the service building. Sites 66–68 are also very nice—they are closest to the attractive tenting area. The least desirable sites are 51–56, which are out in a field by the cabins and the park entrance. 54 and 56 are so close to the RVs for sale in the adjacent lot that you could put your hand out your window and touch them. Sites 51 and 52 are also less nice, being located on the parking lot next to the office. The tenting area is just west of the pool in a very well-shaded area with good grass. The rest rooms are clean and modern, but a touch "used" looking. This is a superb RV park that has much to offer the RVer, and is fine for the tent camper, too.

Basics

Operated By: Carolyn Work. **Open:** All year. **Site Assignment:** Assigned upon registration; verbal reservations OK. **Registration:** In office. (Late arrivals use drop box.) **Fee:** RV $17.50 (full), $15.50 (electric), tent $13.95. **Parking:** At site.

Facilities

Number of RV Sites: 48. **Number of Tent-Only Sites:** 6. **Hookups:** Water, sewer, electric (30, 50 amps). **Each Site:** Picnic table, tree. **Dump Station:** Yes. **Laundry:** Yes. **Pay Phone:** Yes. **Rest Rooms and Showers:** Yes. **Fuel:** Yes. **Propane:** Yes. **Internal Roads:** Paved. **RV Service:** Yes. **Market:** 1 mi. to Colbert. **Restaurant:** 1 mi. to Colbert. **General Store:** Yes. **Vending:** No. **Swimming:** Pool. **Playground:** Yes. **Other:** TV lounge, pet walk area, recreation room with pool table. **Activities:** Fishing, swimming, boating. **Nearby Attractions:** Denison Dam, boat shows, antique shops, Lake Texoma State Park. **Additional Information:** Durant Chamber of Commerce, (580) 924-0848.

Restrictions

Pets: On leash, cleaned up after. **Fires:** In grills. **Alcoholic Beverages:** At sites. **Vehicle Maximum Length:** None. **Other:** Rule sheet on back of site map.

To Get There

From the junction of Hwy. 75/69 and Hwy. 91, turn west onto Hwy. 91 and take the first right onto Sherrard Dr. Go 0.25 mi. and turn left at the sign into the entrance. Follow the road straight ahead to the office.

DAVIS

Oak Hill RV Park

P.O. Box 515, Davis 73030. T: (580) 369-5270.

RV ★★★ Tent ★★

Beauty: ★★★	Site Privacy: ★★★
Spaciousness: ★★★★	Quiet: ★★★
Security: ★★★★	Cleanliness: ★★★
Insect Control: ★★★★	Facilities: ★★

Despite its location immediately behind a gas station and store, this park has some nice landscaping (flowers and trees) that liven up what would otherwise be an open grassy field. While surrounded by the highway to the east, by the store to the south, and a lumber company to the west, this campground has a definite "get-away" feel, enhanced by the trees that surround it in the distance. The best thing about this park, though, is the size of its sites. There are eleven back-ins 70 × 34 feet and five 115-foot pull-throughs. Of the back-ins, the best are sites 5, 8 and 9, which have large shade trees (which the others lack). For those who require pull-throughs, site 13 has the only shade trees, and has them in spades. All the other pull-throughs are open to the sun. (Site 13 is also close to a grassy section of field and abuts a thicket of vegetation, making it an attractive RV site.) Tenting is possible, they say, but not worth the price unless you are hard-pressed for a spot. For RVers, don't let the proximity of the gas station scare you off—this is a nice, hidden RV park that offers a decent overnight stay.

Basics

Operated By: Rick McElhaney. **Open:** All year. **Site Assignment:** First come, first served; no reservations. **Registration:** In store. (Late arrivals select an available site & settle in the morning.) **Fee:** $14 (V, MC, AE, D). **Parking:** At site.

Facilities

Number of RV Sites: 16. **Number of Tent-Only Sites:** 0. **Hookups:** Water, sewer, electric (30 amps). **Dump Station:** Yes. **Laundry:** No. **Pay Phone:** Yes. **Rest Rooms and Showers:** Yes (no shower). **Fuel:** Yes. **Propane:** No. **Internal Roads:** Gravel. **RV Service:** No. **Market:** 2.5 mi. east (limited on-site). **Restaurant:** 2.5 mi. east (limited on-site). **General Store:** Yes. **Vending:** Yes. **Swimming:** No. **Playground:** No. **Other:** 2 picnic tables. **Activities:** Hiking, swimming. **Nearby Attractions:** Arbuckle Wilderness, Turner Falls Park. **Additional Information:** Davis Chamber of Commerce, (580) 369-2402.

Restrictions

Pets: On leash, cleaned up after. **Fires:** In grills. **Alcoholic Beverages:** At sites. **Vehicle Maximum Length:** None.

To Get There

From the junction of I-35 (Exit 55) and Hwy. 7, go west on Hwy. 7 to the first right (into the gas station/store). The campground is behind the store.

DISNEY
Cherokee State Park (Riverside Campground)

P.O. Box 220, Disney 74340. T: (918) 782-9830.

RV ★★★ | Tent ★★★★★

Beauty: ★★★★★ | Site Privacy: ★★★★
Spaciousness: ★★★★★ | Quiet: ★★★★★
Security: ★★★★★ | Cleanliness: ★★
Insect Control: ★★★ | Facilities: ★★★

As the name implies, Riverside Campground lies along the banks of the Grand River, where fishing is the name of the game. The campground is situated on a penninsula, surrounded on three sides by water. Packed-dirt RV sites are on the east side of the campground, on the inside of the internal looped road. While all sites are technically back-ins, it is possible to pull through on 3, which the camp host encourages for larger rigs. This site, like 2 and 4, is 100 feet in length. (Not all site numbers are visible. Starting at the camp host site, RV sites increase in number counterclockwise.) Sites 17 and 18 are next in size (90 feet), while 10 is still a generous 75 feet. The rest of the sites average 65 feet in length. Of these, 12 and 13 are very close together, and can be used by groups who wish to camp close together. The RV sites with the best views of the river are 2–10; higher numbers look out over the "inland" portion of the river between the campground and shore. Tent sites are located to the west, by the boat ramp. These sites are also mostly dirt, but they have excellent tree cover. Tent sites right on the banks of the river tend to be grassier. Site 26 is particularly secluded. The rest room at the entrance is quite simple and "state park–clean". The bathhouses at the west end are old and peeling, and probably do not benefit from regular maintenance. However, this should not discourage those who enjoy state parks, as this one is quite nice—especially for fishermen.

Basics

Operated By: Oklahoma State Parks. **Open:** All year. **Site Assignment:** First come, first served; no reservations. **Registration:** With camp host. (Late arrivals see camp host in morning.) **Fee:** RV $14 (water, electric), tent $7 (checks, V, MC, AE, D). **Parking:** At site.

Facilities

Number of RV Sites: 18. **Number of Tent-Only Sites:** 50. **Hookups:** Water, electric (30 amps). **Each Site:** Picnic table, grill, fire pit. **Dump Station:** Yes. **Laundry:** No. **Pay Phone:** No. **Rest Rooms and Showers:** Yes. **Fuel:** No. **Propane:** No. **Internal Roads:** Paved. **RV Service:** No. **Market:** 2.5 mi. to Langley. **Restaurant:** less than 1 mi. to Disney. **General Store:** No. **Vending:** No. **Swimming:** Lake. **Playground:** Yes (at Lakeside campground). **Other:** Boat ramp, golf course, pavilions. **Activities:** Swimming, boating, fishing, tours of dam. **Nearby Attractions:** Grand River, Pensacola Dam, Har-Ber Village, Will Rogers Memorial Rodeo. **Additional Information:** Grove Area Chamber of Commerce, (918) 786-9079.

Restrictions

Pets: On leash, cleaned up after. **Fires:** In grills. **Alcoholic Beverages:** Beer only. **Vehicle Maximum Length:** None. **Other:** Prefer no glass containers.

To Get There

From Hwy. 28, cross the dam to the west of Disney (into Langley). Veer left after the large Grand River Dam (Langley side). Take the first left after the electric station (where Hwy. 82A ends). Turn left onto Broadway Ave. and go 1.5 mi. Turn left at the sign into the entrance.

DURANT
Simmons RV Park

Rte. 1 Box 50, Mead 74701. T: (580) 924-3091; coysimmons@hotmail.com.

RV ★★★ | Tent ★★★

Beauty: ★★★★ | Site Privacy: ★★★
Spaciousness: ★★ | Quiet: ★★
Security: ★★★★ | Cleanliness: ★★★
Insect Control: ★★★ | Facilities: ★★★

This is a cute urban park on a residential property with very attractive landscaping. Flowers, bushes, some trees, and rustic farm equipment perk up the grounds. Sites are in strips along the outside of the internal road. All sites are open, grassy, and very level. Sites 1–9E on the east side are all 45-foot back-ins with no shade. Sites in row C are 60-foot pull-throughs by the laundry, and are quite good sites due to their length and location. Less desirable sites are 1–5W, which are just off the highway. The best sites are 8–11, which have the most amount of shade and are furthest from the highway.

Basics

Operated By: Coy Simmons. **Open:** All year. **Site Assignment:** Assigned upon registration; verbal reservations OK. **Registration:** In office. (Late arrivals settle in the morning). **Fee:** RV $12 (full), tent $12. **Parking:** At site.

Facilities

Number of RV Sites: 34. **Number of Tent-Only Sites:** Undesignated sites. **Hookups:** Water, sewer, electric (20, 30 amps). **Dump Station:** Yes. **Laundry:** Yes. **Pay Phone:** Yes. **Rest Rooms and Showers:** Yes. **Fuel:** No. **Propane:** No. **Internal Roads:** Gravel. **RV Service:** No. **Market:** 3.5 mi. east. **Restaurant:** 3.5 mi. east. **General Store:** No. **Vending:** No. **Swimming:** No. **Playground:** No. **Other:** Covered pavilion w/ BBQ grill, patio. **Activities:** Basketball, swimming, boating. **Nearby Attractions:** Lake Texacoma Recreational Area. **Additional Information:** Durant Chamber of Commerce, (580) 924-0848.

Restrictions

Pets: On leash, cleaned up after. **Fires:** In grills. **Alcoholic Beverages:** At sites. **Vehicle Maximum Length:** None.

To Get There

From Hwy. 75/69, take the Hwy. 70 exit. Turn west onto Hwy. 70 and go 3.8 mi. Turn left at the sign (somewhat difficult to see). The office is in the house at the back.

EL RENO

Best Western

2701 South Country Club Rd., El Reno 73036. T: (800) 263-3844 or (405) 262-6490; F: (405) 262-3844.

RV ★★★★ Tent n/a

Beauty: ★★★	Site Privacy: ★★★
Spaciousness: ★★★	Quiet: ★★★★
Security: ★★★★	Cleanliness: ★★★★★
Insect Control: ★★★★	Facilities: ★★★★

This RV park contains three rows of sites, the first two of which (sites 1–9 and 10–18) are 60-foot pull-throughs, and the final row of which contains 80-foot pull-throughs (19–23) and 40-foot pull-throughs (24–26). All sites are cement with a strip of grass and bushes in between them. Although mostly concrete, the park is quite attractive: there are 2 flowering bushes and a large rock at the end of each of the grassy strips. The park itself is bordered on the east and south by large bushes (although there is less attractive commercial development to the north and west). Although there is not a large amount of room between most sites (which average 18 feet wide), there are a few extra-wide spaces that are 21 feet wide. The best sites are in the north/northeast corner (especially 9, 18, and 26, which have extra grassy space and a tree). Site 18 has the largest grassy section. The less desirable sites are 10 and (especially) 19, which are next to a commercial building. The laundry, rest rooms, and showers are all very clean and spacious, making this a very decent stop that only needs a little more room between sites to make for an even better stay.

Basics

Operated By: Sadhna Kelly. **Open:** All year. **Site Assignment:** Assigned upon registration. Reservations can be made using credit card; cancel before 6 p.m. the day of arrival. **Registration:** In office (24 hours). **Fee:** RV $22 (checks, V, MC, AE, D, DC). **Parking:** At site.

Facilities

Number of RV Sites: 26. **Number of Tent-Only Sites:** 0. **Hookups:** Water, sewer, electric (30, 50 amps), cable. **Each Site:** Picnic table. **Dump Station:** No (sewer at all sites). **Laundry:** Yes. **Pay Phone:** Yes. **Rest Rooms and Showers:** Yes. **Fuel:** Next door. **Propane:** No. **Internal Roads:** Gravel. **RV Service:** No. **Market:** Less than 0.25 mi. **Restaurant:** Across street. **General Store:** No. **Vending:** Yes. **Swimming:** Pool. **Playground:** Yes. **Other:** Dataport. **Activities:** Fishing, boating, swimming. **Nearby Attractions:** Downtown trolley, antique stores, Lake El Reno, golf course, Lucky Star Casino, Oklahoma City. **Additional Information:** El Reno Chamber of Commerce, (405) 262-1188.

Restrictions

Pets: On leash, cleaned up after. **Fires:** In grills. **Alcoholic Beverages:** At sites. **Vehicle Maximum Length:** None.

To Get There

From I-40 (Exit 123): on the south side of the highway, turn left into the Best Western complex.

ELK CITY

Elk Run RV Park

Rte. 1 Box 161, Elk City 73644. T: (580) 225-4888.

RV ★★★ Tent ★★★

Beauty: ★ Site Privacy: ★★★★
Spaciousness: ★★★★ Quiet: ★★★
Security: ★★★★ Cleanliness: ★★★★
Insect Control: ★★★★ Facilities: ★★★

Unfortunately for this campground, the panhandle of Oklahoma does not have many pretty features to make it an attractive destination, and this park reflects that reality all too well. The commercial development to the south and a parking lot and building to the east make for less-than-spectacular views. The sites themselves are rather roomy, which makes up somewhat for the surroundings. Row A, to the south by the office, has 2 60-foot back-ins and 3 90-foot back-ins. Row B, sites 7–18 to the east, has 105-foot back-ins, while Rows C–E contain 90-foot pull-throughs. None of the sites has a real shade tree, although there are a few smaller trees and bushes around the park. Tenters can camp anywhere on the open grass (mostly to the east) at the back of the park. These sites, like the RV sites, have no shade, and they are situated next to a chain link fence that surrounds a parking lot on the other side. The rest room and showers are very clean, but the toilet in the men's room does not have a curtain or separator of any kind, which can make some campers feel awkward. The park is an acceptable overnight stay, but if you are after a scenic campground, you'll have to push on.

Basics

Operated By: Ed Tremblay. **Open:** All year. **Site Assignment:** Assigned upon registration; verbal reservations OK. **Registration:** In office. (Late arrivals select an available site & pay in the morning.) **Fee:** RV $16 (full), tent $6 (checks, no credits cards). **Parking:** At site.

Facilities

Number of RV Sites: 39. **Number of Tent-Only Sites:** 20. **Hookups:** Water, sewer, electric (30, 50 amps), cable. **Dump Station:** No (sewer at all sites). **Laundry:** Yes. **Pay Phone:** Yes. **Rest Rooms and Showers:** Yes. **Fuel:** Next door. **Propane:** No. **Internal Roads:** Gravel. **RV Service:** No. **Market:** 2 mi. south. **Restaurant:** Across street. **General Store:** No. **Vending:** Yes. **Swimming:** No. **Playground:** No. **Other:** Easy on/off from highway, close to gasoline & restaurants. **Activities:** Hiking. **Nearby Attractions:** National Rte. 66 Museum, Elk City Old Town Museum Complex, Black Kettle National Grasslands. **Additional Information:** Elk City Chamber of Commerce, (800) 280-0207 or (580) 225-0207.

Restrictions

Pets: On leash, cleaned up after. **Fires:** In grills. **Alcoholic Beverages:** At sites. **Vehicle Maximum Length:** None. **Other:** See rule sheet.

To Get There

From I-40 (Exit 41), turn north at the light onto Hwy. 34 and then turn right just past the gas station complex. The drive leads straight into the park.

ENID

High Point RV Park

2700 North Van Buren Box 0, Enid 73703. T: (580) 234-1726; F: (580) 234-5081; highpoint@characterlink.net.

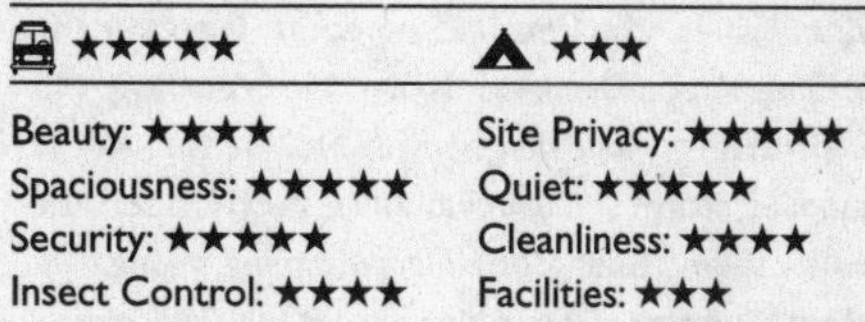

RV ★★★★★ Tent ★★★

Beauty: ★★★★ Site Privacy: ★★★★★
Spaciousness: ★★★★★ Quiet: ★★★★★
Security: ★★★★★ Cleanliness: ★★★★
Insect Control: ★★★★ Facilities: ★★★

This RV park contains sites in three distinct locations. Closest to the office is the "Custer Circle"—a unique and really neat way of parking RVs: in a circle. Pull-through sites 73–92 form the inner circle, with 35–72 (all long-term sites) forming an outside ring. These pull-throughs are 105 × 45 feet—large enough for the largest rigs with slide-outs. In addition, all sites are separated by rows of hedges and have shade trees, making them both private and comfortable. These sites are by far the best in the entire park. The two other locations are to the west of the office, outside the main park entrance. On the south side are 18 102-foot back-ins that are enclosed by hedges. These sites are somewhat shaded, but many are occupied by long-term residents and mobile homes. The final area is to the northwest of the office. Laid out in two rather indistinct rows, these sites are shaded, gravel pull-throughs of varying lengths. Sites 2–6 are the largest at 105 feet, while 9–18 are 54 feet in length. Sites 17 and 18 are close to the road and share an oil pump, which makes these sites distinctly less desirable. Tenters can camp in an open grassy space in this last area. There is not much shade to protect tenters, and the grass is likewise rather sparse. This is much more of an RV-oriented park, and those who can "circle the wagons" will pass an extremely enjoyable stay here.

BASICS

Operated By: Robert Stewart. **Open:** All year. **Site Assignment:** Assigned upon registration; verbal reservations OK. **Registration:** In office. (Late arrivals use drop box or pay in morning.) **Fee:** RV $17 (full), tent $5 (checks, V, MC, AE, D, DC.) **Parking:** At site.

FACILITIES

Number of RV Sites: 60. **Number of Tent-Only Sites:** Undesignated sites. **Hookups:** Water, sewer, electric (30, 50 amps), instant phone. **Dump Station:** Yes. **Laundry:** Yes. **Pay Phone:** Yes. **Rest Rooms and Showers:** Yes. **Fuel:** End of block. **Propane:** No. **Internal Roads:** Gravel. **RV Service:** Call-in. **Market:** 0.25 mi. south. **Restaurant:** 0.25 mi. south. **General Store:** No. **Vending:** No. **Swimming:** No. **Playground:** No. **Other:** RV supplies, storm shelter, clubhouse. **Activities:** Visiting museums, fishing, boating, swimming, hiking. **Nearby Attractions:** Museum of the Cherokee Strip, Railroad Museum of Oklahoma, Great Salt Plains State Park. **Additional Information:** Greater Enid Chamber of Commerce, (888) 229-2443 or (580) 237-2494.

RESTRICTIONS

Pets: On leash, cleaned up after. **Fires:** In grills. **Alcoholic Beverages:** At sites. **Vehicle Maximum Length:** None.

TO GET THERE

From the junction of Hwy. 81 and Hwy. 60, go north on 81/60 for 2.2 mi. Turn left at the sign into the entrance.

EUFAULA

Bridgeport RV Park

Rte. 6 Box 379, Eufaula 74432. T: (918) 689-5177; bkent@icok.net.

RV ★★★ Tent n/a

Beauty: ★★★ Site Privacy: ★★★★
Spaciousness: ★★★★ Quiet: ★★★
Security: ★★★★★ Cleanliness: ★★★★★
Insect Control: ★★★★ Facilities: ★★★

The setting for this campground is somewhat rural, with woods bordering the north, west, and south. Sites are laid out in four rows. Row A has 60-foot back-ins that back to the highway to the east, and are the least desirable for this fact. The 60-foot pull-throughs in Row C (in the middle of the park) have most of the shade trees—all but 2. The 60-foot pull-throughs in Row D contain arguably the best sites (in the southwest corner), which are next to the woods, and furthest from the highway and the entrance but do not have any shade. The electric eye on the gate and the on-site manager make this campground extremely secure, while the immaculate rest rooms in both the bathhouse and the clubhouse ensure that guests will be comfortable. This campground is geared toward overnighters and clubs—sometimes filling to capacity with the latter. Phone ahead to ensure that there are spaces, as this is a good campground that can make a nice destination or just a one-night stay.

BASICS

Operated By: Bill & Cindy Kent. **Open:** Mar. 1–Oct. 31. **Site Assignment:** Flexible, depending on site availability; verbal reservations OK. **Registration:** In office. (Late arrivals select an available site & pay in the morning.) **Fee:** RV $17 (checks, no credits cards). **Parking:** At site.

FACILITIES

Number of RV Sites: 53. **Number of Tent-Only Sites:** 0. **Hookups:** Water, sewer, electric (30 amps). **Each Site:** Picnic table. **Dump Station:** No (sewer at all sites). **Laundry:** Yes. **Pay Phone:** Yes. **Rest Rooms and Showers:** Yes. **Fuel:** No. **Propane:** No. **Internal Roads:** Gravel. **RV Service:** Call-in. **Market:** 6 mi. to Eufaula. **Restaurant:** 1 mi. south. **General Store:** Yes. **Vending:** No. **Swimming:** No. **Playground:** No. **Other:** Clubhouse (with kitchen), storm shelter, electric eye on gate. **Activities:** Fishing, boating, swimming, golfing. **Nearby Attractions:** Lake Eufaula, 2 golf courses, Whole Hawg Day. **Additional Information:** Eufaula Chamber of Commerce, (918) 689-2791.

RESTRICTIONS

Pets: On leash, cleaned up after. **Fires:** In grills. **Alcoholic Beverages:** At sites. **Vehicle Maximum Length:** None.

TO GET THERE

From the junction of Hwy. 69 and Hwy. 150 (Fountainhead state Park Exit): on the northwest side of the highway overpass, turn left onto the frontage road, then immediately left onto Bridgeport Rd. Turn right at the sign into the entrance.

GORE
MarVal Family Resort

Rte. 1 Box 314M, Gore 74435. T: (918) 489-2295; F: (918) 489-2671; www.marvalresort.com; marvalre @crosstel.net.

RV ★★★★ Tent ★★★★★

Beauty: ★★★★	Site Privacy: ★★
Spaciousness: ★★★	Quiet: ★★★★
Security: ★★★★★	Cleanliness: ★★★★
Insect Control: ★★★★	Facilities: ★★★★

This campground is positively huge, with sites scattered from the river up to the entrance drive. Assuming availability, there is truly a site for any camper's tastes. (Note that aside from H, the lettered sites to the west and south of the pool are seasonal sites, and not for overnight use.) Sites 102–108 are 70-foot back-ins right along the riverbank, where a camper could put a canoe or small boat into the water, while 400–408 are back-ins close to the swimming access area. Across from these sites, 216–219 also offer proximity to the swimming beach. Sites 110–112, in the northeast corner, are 60-foot pull-throughs that are one row away from the water's edge. Fishermen will want to camp in sites 410–415, which are back-ins (as long as 75 feet) that run along the bank of the trout pond. Sites 207–215 are are smaller back-ins (45 feet long), suitable for a pop-up. Some very nice, more developed, back-ins are 510–518, which have a concrete pad and wooden walkway on one side. These sites back to a row of trees, beyond which is a huge open field. A large field in the southeast corner provides more than enough tenting space, although only one site (22) has a large shade tree. (18 has several much smaller trees.) This field has excellent grass, and is surrounded by woods, lending it a nice wild feel. The rest rooms are individual unisex units that are very clean and modern. The showers are also very clean and cozy, if a little compact. This campground guarantees water fun for all ages, and should be a definite destination for families.

BASICS

Operated By: Val & Marc Marcum, Dan & Leia Nosalek, Lynn & Gary Cleek. **Open:** All year. **Site Assignment:** Most sites by reservation; credit card required. No holiday cancellations. **Registration:** In office. (No late arrivals. Gates locked at 10 p.m.) **Fee:** $15–27; varies widely by season & day of week. **Parking:** At site.

FACILITIES

Number of RV Sites: 111. **Number of Tent-Only Sites:** 14. **Hookups:** Water, sewer, electric (30, 50 amps). **Each Site:** Picnic table. **Dump Station:** Yes. **Laundry:** Yes. **Pay Phone:** Yes. **Rest Rooms and Showers:** Yes. **Fuel:** No. **Propane:** No. **Internal Roads:** Gravel. **RV Service:** No. **Market:** 1.25 mi. south. **Restaurant:** 1 mile south. **General Store:** Yes. **Vending:** Yes. **Swimming:** Pool, river. **Playground:** Yes. **Other:** Mini golf, basketball, cabins, snack bar, trout fishing, horseback riding, events with activities director, recreation field. **Activities:** Volleyball, fishing, swimming. **Nearby Attractions:** Cherokee Courthouse. **Additional Information:** Gore Chamber of Commerce, (918) 489-2534.

RESTRICTIONS

Pets: On leash, cleaned up after. **Fires:** In grills. **Alcoholic Beverages:** At sites. **Vehicle Maximum Length:** None. **Other:** No ATVs.

TO GET THERE

From I-40 Exit 287, turn north onto Hwy. 100 and go 5.9 mi. Turn right onto Gore Landing Rd. and go 0.2 mi. Turn left onto Marval Ln. and go straight into the campground.

GROVE
Cedar Oaks RV Resort

1550 83rd St., Grove 74344. T: (800) 880-8884 or (918) 786-4303; F: (918) 786-4303.

RV ★★★★★ Tent n/a

Beauty: ★★★★★	Site Privacy: ★★★★
Spaciousness: ★★★★	Quiet: ★★★★★
Security: ★★★★★	Cleanliness: ★★★★★
Insect Control: ★★★★	Facilities: ★★★★★

This RV park lives up to the standards implied by the word "resort." Sites are highly developed, averaging 30 feet wide, with nice grassy sections next to paved strips. The park is divided into two sections: the main park to the north and a smaller loop to the south. In the main section, sites 1–17 lie along the entrance road, and have nothing to recommend them (besides being in a nice park). Sites 18–31 back to the first 17 sites, and like them are 58-foot back-ins without any outstanding features. Sites 32–45 and 50–63 are 65-foot pull-throughs in the middle of the park that have decent views of the lake when the park is mostly empty. 46–49 and 74–76 are 51-foot back-ins located in a strip along the north edge. 76 is a good alternative to one of the pull-throughs, as it commands a very nice view of the lake. The most exquisitie sites, however, are 64–73. These are 65-foot pull-throughs facing the lake. End site 73 has an enormous grassy section adjacent to it. The southern section of the park contains sites 77–110 in a large loop. These are all 45-foot back-ins on the outside of the loop. (The inside will contain some enormous 100-foot pull-throughs, but they are as-yet unfinished.) Sites 88–96 have the best views, while 80–86 are closest to the bathhouse. All facilities are sparkling clean, and the park has a security guard for peace of mind. Campers in this resort can count on a comfortable and secure stay.

Basics

Operated By: The Coats Family. **Open:** All year. **Site Assignment:** Assigned upon registration (verbal reservations "highly recommended"). **Registration:** In office. (Late arrivals use drop box.) **Fee:** $19.50 (checks, V, MC). **Parking:** At site.

Facilities

Number of RV Sites: 126. **Number of Tent-Only Sites:** 0. **Hookups:** Water, sewer, electric (30, 50 amps). **Each Site:** Picnic table. **Dump Station:** Yes. **Laundry:** Yes. **Pay Phone:** Yes. **Rest Rooms and Showers:** Yes. **Fuel:** No. **Propane:** No. **Internal Roads:** Paved/gravel. **RV Service:** No. **Market:** 1.5 mi. over bridge. **Restaurant:** Less than 0.5 mi. southeast. **General Store:** Yes. **Vending:** No. **Swimming:** Lake. **Playground:** No. **Other:** Dock, boat ramps, private cove, meeting rooms (with kitchen), RV & boat storage, dataport, pavilion. **Activities:** Boating, swimming, fishing, shuffleboard, horseshoes. **Nearby Attractions:** Har-Ber Village. **Additional Information:** Grove Area Chamber of Commerce, (918) 786-9079.

Restrictions

Pets: On leash, cleaned up after. **Fires:** In grills. **Alcoholic Beverages:** At sites. **Vehicle Maximum Length:** None.

To Get There

From the junction of Hwy. 10 North and Hwy. 59 North, turn northwest onto Hwy. 59 and go 3.2 mi. Turn left at the sign into the entrance.

GUTHRIE
Pioneer RV Park

1601 Seward Rd., Guthrie 73044. T: (405) 282-3557; F: (405) 282-5376.

RV ★★★★ | Tent ★★★

Beauty: ★★★★	Site Privacy: ★★★★
Spaciousness: ★★★★	Quiet: ★★★★
Security: ★★★★	Cleanliness: ★★★★
Insect Control: ★★★★	Facilities: ★★★

Laid out in strips, this campground offers grassy pull-throughs throughout the park and back-ins along the eastern edge. These back-ins (1–12) back to a chain-link fence, beyond which lie green agricultural fields. Sites 13–21 are 70-foot pull-throughs on the eastern side of the park, and 24–30 are 75-foot pull-throughs dead in the middle. Being an end site, 21 has a more generous amount of space and a shade tree, which make it one of the nicest sites in the park. To the west lie two rows of 70-foot pull-throughs, of which the southernmost strip (37–48) has slightly nicer sites due to their proximity to the tenting area and the view to the south. (The best views are from 30 and 36.) Site 32 has extremely limited space due to the landscaping and a fountain that encroaches on this space. Tenting is permitted on a strip along the southern edge of the campground. There is nice grass, but no real shade. RVers will be pleased with this campground, and tenters will enjoy a pleasant enough stay at this park.

Basics

Operated By: Bill & Sue True. **Open:** All year. **Site Assignment:** Assigned upon registration. Reservations require credit card; cancellation requires one week's notice. **Registration:** In office. (Late arrivals pay in morning.) **Fee:** RV $17.50 (full), tent $10. (checks, V, MC). **Parking:** At site.

FACILITIES

Number of RV Sites: 63. **Number of Tent-Only Sites:** 4. **Hookups:** Water, sewer, electric (30, 50 amps). **Each Site:** Picnic table. **Dump Station:** No (sewer at all sites). **Laundry:** Yes. **Pay Phone:** Yes. **Rest Rooms and Showers:** Yes. **Fuel:** No. **Propane:** Yes. **Internal Roads:** Gravel. **RV Service:** No. **Market:** 6 mi. north. **Restaurant:** 6 mi. north. **General Store:** Yes. **Vending:** Yes. **Swimming:** No. **Playground:** No. **Other:** Clubhouse. **Activities:** Tours to Oklahoma City, visiting museums. **Nearby Attractions:** Scottish Rite Temple, State Capital Publishing Museum, Oklahoma City. **Additional Information:** Guthrie CVB, (800) 299-1889 or (405) 282-1947.

RESTRICTIONS

Pets: On leash, cleaned up after. **Fires:** In grills. **Alcoholic Beverages:** At sites. **Vehicle Maximum Length:** None.

TO GET THERE

From I-35 Exit 151, go 0.55 mi. Turn right at the sign into the campground.

GUYMON

Southwind RV Park

3941 Southwest Hwy. 54, Rte. 3 Box 52-A, Guymon 73942. T: (877) 861-8103 or (580) 338-7415; swindrv@ptsi.net.

RV ★★★ Tent ★★

Beauty: ★★★	Site Privacy: ★★★★
Spaciousness: ★★★★	Quiet: ★★★
Security: ★★★★	Cleanliness: ★★★
Insect Control: ★★★★	Facilities: ★★★

This campground is arranged in rows of odd and even numbered pull-through sites. The odd numbered sites in the row on the east side are 36 45 feet, while the even numbered sites to the west are longer: 36 × 65 feet. The best sites are odd numbers 3–23, as they are longer, they face an agricultural field, they are located away from the mobile homes, and they have larger trees. The least desirable sites are the even numbered sites 2–18, which are shorter pull-throughs next to the manager's mobile home and the office, which brings registration traffic right past these sites. There are mobile homes at the southwest end, and some in the campground itself (27, 29). The tent area has a thin grass covering over hard dirt. There is only one site under tree coverage—the rest are out in the open and have no shade whatsoever. There is also scattered equipment and a shed in this area, making it less attractive. However, tent sites are well removed from the road, which makes them feel more private. The rest room and showers are modern and clean. The TV lounge has a greenhouse with an absolutely monster-sized agave cactus. RVers will enjoy this campground slightly more than tenters, who may want to check out one of the region's state parks.

BASICS

Operated By: Eddy Ainsworth. **Open:** All year. **Site Assignment:** Assigned upon registration. Verbal reservations OK, unless arriving after 6 pm, which requires a credit card. Same day cancellation before 6 p.m. for refund. **Registration:** In office. (Late arrivals use drop box.) **Fee:** RV $17 (30 amps), $20 (50 amps), tent $9 (V, MC, D). Senior discount of $2. **Parking:** At site.

FACILITIES

Number of RV Sites: 40. **Number of Tent-Only Sites:** 10. **Hookups:** Water, sewer, electric (30, 50 amps). **Each Site:** Tree, a few picnic tables. **Dump Station:** No (sewer at all sites). **Laundry:** Yes. **Pay Phone:** Yes. **Rest Rooms and Showers:** Yes. **Fuel:** No. **Propane:** Cylinder exchange. **Internal Roads:** Dirt/gravel. **RV Service:** No. **Market:** 1.75 mi. northeast. **Restaurant:** 1 mile northeast. **General Store:** No. **Vending:** No. **Swimming:** No. **Playground:** Yes. **Other:** Dataport, city water, TV lounge. **Activities:** Visiting museums, fishing, boating, swimming. **Nearby Attractions:** Large rodeo (May 1), museums, Optima Lake. **Additional Information:** Guymon Chamber of Commerce, (580) 338-3376.

RESTRICTIONS

Pets: On leash, cleaned up after. **Fires:** In grills. **Alcoholic Beverages:** At sites. **Vehicle Maximum Length:** 65 ft. **Other:** No generators, additional charge for more than 2 people.

TO GET THERE

From the junction of Hwy. 3/136/412 and Hwy. 54, turn onto Hwy. 54 West and go 1.3 mi. southwest. (Keep your eyes peeled for the sign on the left-hand side.) Turn left at the sign onto the dirt road entrance.

HINTON

Red Rock Canyon State Park

P.O. Box 502, Hinton 73047. T: (800) 654-8240 or (405) 542-6344; F: (405) 542-6342; www.touroklahoma.com; redrockcanyon@hintonnet.net.

RV ★★★★ Tent ★★★★★

Beauty: ★★★★★ Site Privacy: ★★★★
Spaciousness: ★★★★ Quiet: ★★★★★
Security: ★★★★ Cleanliness: ★★★
Insect Control: ★★★ Facilities: ★★★

Stunning views of red canyon walls and campsites smothered in shade trees: if that sounds unattractive to you, stay away from this campground. But everyone else should definitely make a stop here! This campground has sites divided into Areas 1–4. Area 1 has water and electric sites right up against the canyon walls. There are loads of trees, but some sites have only dirt and no grass. The section of the road leading to 5–7 is in disrepair, and may present a challenge. Sites 11–18 are 40–65-foot grassy back-ins, while 8 could fit a rig of any size. Some sites are not perfectly level. This area is also used for rappelling on the rocks, and therefore it sees a fair amount of day traffic. Area 2 offers group camping with 45-foot back-ins. These sites are more open, with shade trees around the perimeter. Area 3 has full hookups and open 50-foot back-ins in an area separated from the road. All sites have concrete slabs and grass, and some have shade trees. This is the easiest place for RVs to camp, as it involves the least amount of turns or technical driving. Area 4 is for overflow camping, but is used even when the other areas are not all full. These are the furthest sites in, and are less developed. These grassy, shaded sites are well off the road, but also have some degree of slope. Sites at the extreme south end (in the 50s and 60s) are in an open field with little shade. The rest rooms are small but quite clean. This is a beautiful campground that will appeal to the whole family, whether in an RV or tents.

Basics

Operated By: Oklahoma State Park. **Open:** All year. **Site Assignment:** First come, first served; no reservations. **Registration:** Can register in office. Fees collected at sites. **Fee:** RV $17 (full), $14 (water, electric), tent $7. **Parking:** At site.

Facilities

Number of RV Sites: 52. **Number of Tent-Only Sites:** 32. **Hookups:** Water, sewer, electric (30, 50 amps). **Each Site:** Picnic table, grill. **Dump Station:** Yes. **Laundry:** No. **Pay Phone:** Yes. **Rest Rooms and Showers:** Yes. **Fuel:** No. **Propane:** No. **Internal Roads:** Paved, gravel. **RV Service:** No. **Market:** 6 mi. in Hinton. **Restaurant:** 6 mi. in Hinton. **General Store:** No. **Vending:** No. **Swimming:** Pool. **Playground:** Yes. **Other:** None. **Activities:** Swimming, rappelling, rockhounding, volleyball, hiking, horseback riding. **Nearby Attractions:** Ft Cobb State Park, Crowder Lake State Park. **Additional Information:** Hinton Chamber of Commerce, (405) 542-6428.

Restrictions

Pets: On leash, cleaned up after. **Fires:** In grills. **Alcoholic Beverages:** At sites. **Vehicle Maximum Length:** None. **Other:** 14 days max. stay limit, no amplified music.

To Get There

From I-40, take Exit 101 and turn south onto Hwy. 2/281. Go 5.2 mi. then turn left at the sign into the entrance. The entrance road is steep and winding.

KINGFISHER

Sleepee Hollo RV Park

918 North Main, Kingfisher 73750. T: (405) 375-5010.

RV ★★★★ Tent ★★★

Beauty: ★★★★ Site Privacy: ★★★★
Spaciousness: ★★★★ Quiet: ★★★
Security: ★★★★ Cleanliness: ★★★★
Insect Control: ★★★★ Facilities: ★★★

Farms surround this campground to the north, west, and south, giving it a rural feel. Sites are grassy and level pull-throughs, many of which are not numbered. Sites 1–7 are all super-long (105–120-foot) pull-throughs, all but one of which are well-shaded. A row of unnumbered back-in sites to the south range in length from 45 feet (in the southeast corner) to 90 feet (in the southwest corner). One RV site just in front of the office is a shady, all-grass site that is quite attractive. The rest of the sites to the west and north are unnumbered sites on an open grassy field. These are huge back-ins, ranging from 45 feet to 90 feet long. There is a potential to pull-through on some sites, if neighboring sites are vacant. Tenters have a huge open space to the west in which to pitch a tent. The field is grassy, but has no shade trees. This is an attractive campground with lots of trees inside, and farms with cattle surround the perimeter. It makes a nice stop for any kind of camper, although is slightly better for RVs than tents.

Basics

Operated By: Joe Farrell. **Open:** All year. **Site Assignment:** Assigned upon registration; verbal reservations OK. **Registration:** In office. (Late arrivals select an available site & pay in the morning.) **Fee:** RV $19.50 (50 amps), $16.50 (30 amps), tent $8. **Parking:** At site.

Facilities

Number of RV Sites: 29. **Number of Tent-Only Sites:** Undesignated sites. **Hookups:** Water, sewer, electric (30, 50 amps). **Dump Station:** Yes. **Laundry:** Yes. **Pay Phone:** Yes. **Rest Rooms and Showers:** Yes. **Fuel:** No. **Propane:** No. **Internal Roads:** Gravel. **RV Service:** No. **Market:** 2 mi. south. **Restaurant:** 2 mi. south. **General Store:** No. **Vending:** Yes. **Swimming:** No. **Playground:** No. **Other:** Basement for entertainment or storm shelter, pet walk area. **Activities:** Hiking, tours, biking. **Nearby Attractions:** Chisolm Trail Museum & Governor Seay Mansion, Oklahoma City. **Additional Information:** Kingfisher Chamber of Commerce, (405) 375-5176.

Restrictions

Pets: On leash, cleaned up after. **Fires:** In grills. **Alcoholic Beverages:** At sites. **Vehicle Maximum Length:** None.

To Get There

From the junction of Hwy. 33 and Hwy. 81, go 0.8 mi. north on Hwy. 81. Turn left at the sign into the entrance.

LAWTON

Lawton Campground

3701 Southwest 11th St., Lawton 73501. T: (580) 355-1293.

RV ★★★ Tent ★★★

Beauty: ★★★	Site Privacy: ★★★
Spaciousness: ★★★	Quiet: ★★★★
Security: ★★★★	Cleanliness: ★★★★
Insect Control: ★★★	Facilities: ★★★

This is a new campground (less than two years old), and consequently still a little unfinished. While it may be rustic in style, however, fixtures are brand-new and clean. Laid out in three strips, sites are unnumbered and a little difficult to locate. There are four full hookups near the rest rooms (the red barn next to the house) and two sites just east of the barn under a large shade tree. These two are the nicest sites in the park, due to the overhanging tree. Apart from these, the rest of the sites are undelineated spaces in a grassy field. There is little to distinguish one from the other save for the hookups, but this does allow for a rig of any size to occupy pretty much any site. All sites are very level and grassy, and the setting is quiet and rural. Tenting is allowed in the southern portion of the central and eastern strips. The grass ground covering is excellent, and there are trees for protection to the eastern side. This small campground has a very homey feel, and will only get better as it becomes more established.

Basics

Operated By: Pat Reynolds. **Open:** All year. **Site Assignment:** Flexible, depending on availabilitiy; verbal reservations OK. **Registration:** In office. (Late arrivals use drop box in bath house). **Fee:** RV $12 (full), $9 (water, electric), tent $6. **Parking:** At site.

Facilities

Number of RV Sites: 30. **Number of Tent-Only Sites:** 0. **Hookups:** Water, sewer, electric (30 amps). **Dump Station:** No. **Laundry:** No. **Pay Phone:** No. **Rest Rooms and Showers:** Yes. **Fuel:** No. **Propane:** No. **Internal Roads:** Gravel. **RV Service:** No. **Market:** 2.5 mi. north. **Restaurant:** 2 mi. north. **General Store:** No. **Vending:** No. **Swimming:** No. **Playground:** No. **Other:** Easy access off the interstate, golf course next door. **Activities:** Golf, visiting museums. **Nearby Attractions:** Fort Sill Military Reservation, Museum of the Great Plains, Wichita Mountains National Wildlife Refuge. **Additional Information:** Lawton Chamber of Commerce & Industry, (800) 872-4540 or (580) 355-3541.

Restrictions

Pets: On leash, cleaned up after. **Fires:** In grills. **Alcoholic Beverages:** At sites. **Vehicle Maximum Length:** None.

To Get There

From I-44, take Exit 33. Go 0.7 mi. north on

11th St. Turn right into the gravel entrance across from Coobs St. (just south of the golf course). The office is in the house on the left.

MUSKOGEE
Crossroads RV Park

P.O. Box 95-5, Porter 74454. T: (918) 686-9104; F: (918) 683-8685.

RV ★★★ Tent ★★★

Beauty: ★★★ Site Privacy: ★★★
Spaciousness: ★★★★ Quiet: ★★★
Security: ★★★★ Cleanliness: ★★★★
Insect Control: ★★★★ Facilities: ★★★

As this RV park has numerous long-term residents, a sign indicates to all visitors that only sites 1–17 and B1–8 are for overnighters. Sites 1–17 are all large gravel sites in the north part of the park. Sites 1–10 are open-ended pull-throughs that can fit a rig of any size. End site 10 has a grassy space, which the other sites lack. In a row slightly east of the first strip, sites 11–17 are open-ended back-ins that can reasonably accomodate about 50–60 feet before encroaching on the (undefined) gravel drive. Sites B1-8 are in the southeast corner of the park. All of these sites are open-ended pull-throughs that can take RVs of almost any size (with the exception of B8, which is somewhat restricted in size due to its proximity to another site.) All other sites in the park are for long-term guests or mobile homes. This is a good overnight stay for RVers—more so than for tenters—but lacks a certain something to make it as a destination.

Basics

Operated By: Janie Burwell. **Open:** All year. **Site Assignment:** Assigned upon registration; verbal reservations OK. **Registration:** In office. (Late arrivals use drop box.) **Fee:** RV $14 (full), tent $7. **Parking:** At site.

Facilities

Number of RV Sites: 25. **Number of Tent-Only Sites:** 5. **Hookups:** Water, sewer, electric (30, 50 amps). **Each Site:** Picnic table, grill. **Dump Station:** Yes. **Laundry:** Yes. **Pay Phone:** Yes. **Rest Rooms and Showers:** Yes. **Fuel:** No. **Propane:** No. **Internal Roads:** Gravel. **RV Service:** No. **Market:** 7 mi. to Muskogee. **Restaurant:** 6 mi. to Muskogee. **General Store:** Yes. **Vending:** Yes. **Swimming:** No. **Playground:** No. **Other:** Pavilion. **Activities:** Fishing, boating, swimming, hiking. **Nearby Attractions:** Ataloa Lodge Museum, Five Civilized Tribes Museum, Sequoya Bay State Park. **Additional Information:** Muskogee Convention & Tourism, (918) 684-6363.

Restrictions

Pets: On leash, cleaned up after. **Fires:** In grills. **Alcoholic Beverages:** At sites. **Vehicle Maximum Length:** None.

To Get There

From the junction of Hwy. 16/62 and Hwy. 69, go north on Hwy. 69 for 4.8 mi. (2 mi. north of the Arkansas River). At the junction with Hwy. 51B, turn right and go striaght into the campground.

OKLAHOMA CITY
Sands Motel

721 South Rockwell Ave., Oklahoma City 73128. T: (405) 787-7353.

RV ★★★ Tent n/a

Beauty: ★★ Site Privacy: ★★★
Spaciousness: ★★★ Quiet: ★★★
Security: ★★★ Cleanliness: ★★
Insect Control: ★★★★ Facilities: ★★★

Located behind (to the south of) the office, RV sites in this park are operated in conjunction with a motel. There are 6 rows in all, and not all sites are numbered, which makes finding your site potentially difficult. Row 1 contains 60-foot pull-throughs next to the motel. (There is a possibility of sticking out to about 70 feet.) Sites B and C share an electricity pylon that encroaches on their space. Row 3 has probably the nicest sites, which are all nicely shaded. However, the pull-throughs are a little shorter in this row (54 feet long). Row 4 contains 40-foot back-ins that back to a culvert and an unsightly storage shed. The southernmost sites, in Row 6, back to a fence, which adds to their security and privacy, but G also abuts a storage shed. This RV park is an acceptable overnight stay, and the pool makes for pleasant recreation, but it is not a destination.

BASICS

Operated By: Sands Motel. **Open:** All year. **Site Assignment:** Assigned upon registration; no reservations. **Registration:** In office (24 hours). **Fee:** RV $13.90. **Parking:** At site.

FACILITIES

Number of RV Sites: 34. **Number of Tent-Only Sites:** 0. **Hookups:** Water, sewer, electric (30, 50 amps). **Dump Station:** No (sewer at all sites). **Laundry:** Yes. **Pay Phone:** Yes. **Rest Rooms and Showers:** Yes. **Fuel:** No. **Propane:** No. **Internal Roads:** Gravel/dirt. **RV Service:** No. **Market:** 0.5 mi. east. **Restaurant:** 2 mi. east. **General Store:** Yes. **Vending:** No. **Swimming:** Pool. **Playground:** Yes. **Activities:** Golf, tennis, tours, theater, swimming, basketball, automobile racing, horse racing, shopping. **Nearby Attractions:** Crystal Bridge at Myriad Botanical Gardens, National Cowboy Hall of Fame & Western Heritage Center, Oklahoma City Art Museum, Oklahoma City National Memorial. **Additional Information:** Oklahoma City Convention & Tourism Bureau, (800) 225-5652 or (405) 297-8912.

RESTRICTIONS

Pets: On leash, cleaned up after. **Fires:** In grills. **Alcoholic Beverages:** At sites. **Vehicle Maximum Length:** None. **Other:** No busses.

TO GET THERE

From I-40 Exit 143 (Rockwell Ave.), turn south onto Rockwell Ave. On the south side of the highway interchange, take the first right into the motel parking lot.

PONCA CITY

Snyder's RV Park

3171 West North Ave., Ponca City 74601. T: (580) 762-4686.

RV ★★★ | Tent n/a

Beauty: ★★	Site Privacy: ★★★
Spaciousness: ★★★	Quiet: ★★★★
Security: ★★★★	Cleanliness: ★★★
Insect Control: ★★★★	Facilities: ★★★

As there are no rest rooms, this RV park accepts only rigs that are self-contained. RV sites are located behind the store, in two small rows. All sites are level, gravel sites, and all but 10 are well-shaded. Site 7 is next to a shed, making it slightly less desirable. Sites are often occupied by road crews and other long-term guests, so a phone call would be worthwhile before arriving. The store really jumps around lunch time, and this is not the best time to check in, as all staff will be busy. This park is a functional stop that offers convenience services (gas, food, etc.), but won't likely become a repeat destination for most travelers.

BASICS

Operated By: Dave Snyder. **Open:** All year. **Site Assignment:** Flexible, depending on site availability; verbal reservations OK. **Registration:** In store. (Late arrivals select an available site & pay in the morning.) **Fee:** RV $12. **Parking:** At site.

FACILITIES

Number of RV Sites: 10. **Number of Tent-Only Sites:** 0. **Hookups:** Water, sewer, electric (20, 30, 50 amps), cable. **Dump Station:** Yes. **Laundry:** No. **Pay Phone:** Yes. **Rest Rooms and Showers:** No. **Fuel:** Yes. **Propane:** No. **Internal Roads:** Gravel. **RV Service:** No. **Market:** 3 mi. east. **Restaurant:** Limited on-site; 2 mi. east. **General Store:** Yes. **Vending:** No. **Swimming:** No. **Playground:** No. **Other:** ATM, sandwiches. **Activities:** Fishing, boating, swimming, hiking. **Nearby Attractions:** Kaw Lake, Marland Estate Mansion, Ponca City Cultural Center. **Additional Information:** Ponca City Area Chamber of Commerce, (580) 765-4400.

RESTRICTIONS

Pets: On leash, cleaned up after. **Fires:** In grills. **Alcoholic Beverages:** At sites. **Vehicle Maximum Length:** None.

TO GET THERE

From the junction of Hwy. 60 and Hwy. 156, turn south onto Hwy. 156 (toward Marland) and go 0.4 mi. Turn left onto North Ave. and go 0.85 mi. Turn left at the sign into the entrance.

SALLISAW

Lakeside RV Park

P.O. Box 1414, Sallisaw 74955. T: (918) 775-7522; F: (918) 775-0457.

RV ★★★★ | Tent n/a

Beauty: ★★★	Site Privacy: ★★★★★
Spaciousness: ★★★★★	Quiet: ★★★★
Security: ★★★★	Cleanliness: ★★★★★
Insect Control: ★★★★	Facilities: ★★★★

With woods to the north, east, and west, this campground has a definite rural feel, despite the numerous residences in close proximity to it. Sites are arranged in two rows of pull-throughs, with back-ins along the east and west sides. (Sites 21–28 to the west are reserved for long-term guests.) Back-ins 1–6 on the eastern edge of the campground are 60 × 45 feet. Site 6 is closest to the (covered) pool, whereas end sites 1 and 11 are furthest from the entrance and closest to the woods to the north, making these the nicest overnight spots. The eastern strip of pull-throughs boasts some incredibly long sites that range in length from 75 feet (13) to 90 feet (14) to 105 feet (15). End site 20 is slightly shorter, at 65 feet. The rec room is comfortable and tastefully furnished, and the rest rooms (individual unisex units) would look great in anyone's home. One small drawback is that the coin-op shower runs for only four minutes per quarter. All facilities are clean and incredibly comfy, making this a very pleasant stay. (Note that there is an overt Christian theme to the park, with pamphlets, iconography, and other religious paraphernalia scattered throughout.)

Basics

Operated By: Paula & Mike Mouzakis. **Open:** Mar. 15–Nov. 15. **Site Assignment:** Assigned upon registration, but flexible; verbal reservations OK. **Registration:** In office. (Late arrivals use drop box.) **Fee:** RV $18 (50 amps), $16 (30 amps). **Parking:** At site.

Facilities

Number of RV Sites: 28. **Number of Tent-Only Sites:** 0. **Hookups:** Water, sewer, electric (30, 50 amps). **Each Site:** Picnic table. **Dump Station:** No (sewer at all sites). **Laundry:** Yes. **Pay Phone:** No. **Rest Rooms and Showers:** Yes. **Fuel:** No. **Propane:** Yes. **Internal Roads:** Gravel. **RV Service:** No. **Market:** 7 mi. to Sallisaw. **Restaurant:** 2 blocks. **General Store:** Across street. **Vending:** No. **Swimming:** Pool. **Playground:** No. **Other:** Rec room (w/ TV & chairs), pavilion. **Activities:** Board games. **Nearby Attractions:** Fourteen Flags Museum, Sequoyah's Home site. **Additional Information:** Sallisaw Chamber of Commerce, (918) 775-2558.

Restrictions

Pets: On leash, cleaned up after. **Fires:** In grills. **Alcoholic Beverages:** At sites. **Vehicle Maximum Length:** None.

To Get There

From I-40 Exit 308, turn south onto Hwy. 59 and go 7.2 mi. Turn left at the sign into the campground.

SAWYER

Sawyer RV Park

HC 66 Box 1430, Sawyer 74756. T: (580) 326-0830.

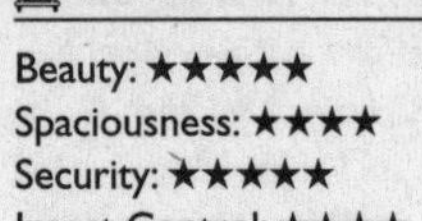

Beauty: ★★★★★ Site Privacy: ★★★★
Spaciousness: ★★★★ Quiet: ★★★★★
Security: ★★★★★ Cleanliness: ★★★★★
Insect Control: ★★★★ Facilities: ★★★★

Surrounded by forest and pasture land, this campground has both a wilderness and an on-the-farm feel. The campground is very pretty (there are flowers and a small white fence that run along the entryway), and is located just one mile from the Hugo Lake Recreation Area. Sites are back-ins arranged on the outside of a loop. Sites 1–8 are 40-foot back-ins, while sites 14–17 can accommodate an RV of any size. Sites 10 and (especially) 11 have the best shade in the park and can likewise accommodate a big rig. Sites 1–4 have grassy patches but little shade. The rest room facility is a small individual rest room and shower in the laundry. All facilities are kept extremely clean. This is definitely one of the nicest parks in the region. Although small, it is a deserving destination for RV campers. Even campers who don't take advantage of the nearby Hugo Lake facilities will enjoy a stay at this park.

Basics

Operated By: Jan Park. **Open:** All year. **Site Assignment:** Flexible, depending on availability; verbal reservations OK. **Registration:** In office (trailer 13). **Fee:** $15 (checks, no credit cards). **Parking:** At site.

Facilities

Number of RV Sites: 19. **Number of Tent-Only Sites:** 0. **Hookups:** Water, sewer, electric (30 amps). **Each Site:** Picnic table. **Dump Station:** No (sewer at all sites). **Laundry:** Yes. **Pay Phone:** No. **Rest Rooms and Showers:** Yes. **Fuel:** No. **Propane:** No. **Internal Roads:** Gravel. **RV Service:** No. **Market:** 12 mi. to Hugo. **Restaurant:** 12 mi. to Hugo. **General Store:** No. **Vending:** No. **Swimming:** No. **Playground:** No. **Other:** 6 overflow sites, wildlife. **Activities:** Swimming, boating, fishing. **Nearby Attractions:** Hugo Lake, Raymond Gary State Park. **Additional Information:** Choctaw County Chamber of Commerce, (580) 326-7511.

RESTRICTIONS

Pets: On leash, cleaned up after. **Fires:** In grills. **Alcoholic Beverages:** At sites ("party elsewhere"). **Vehicle Maximum Length:** None. **Other:** No refunds.

TO GET THERE

From the junction of Hwy. 70 and Hwy. 147, turn north onto Hwy. 147 and go 2.6 mi. Turn at the sign for Virgil Point Park.

SEMINOLE
Round-Up RV Park

Rte. 3 Box 285F, Seminole 74868. T: (405) 382-7957.

RV: ★★★ Tent: n/a

Beauty: ★★★	Site Privacy: ★★★
Spaciousness: ★★★	Quiet: ★★★
Security: ★★★	Cleanliness: ★★★
Insect Control: ★★★★	Facilities: ★★★

Although this park is located in an urban setting, it has some features (such as flowering bushes and a wooden fence) that make it more attractive. In addition, each site has a shade tree, which makes a stay there more comfortable than it would otherwise be (especially in late summer). The restaurant parking lot (as well as the highway) lies to the west of the park, residences border it in the southeast and northeast, and a fishing pond (with a pretty pavilion) sits to the east. The RV sites, all pull-throughs, average 75 × 30 feet in size. End sites 1 and 14 are closest to the pond (1 is right next to the pavilion and its two grills), while end sites 13 and 27 are closest to the parking lot. The best area is in the middle of the south row (sites 19–22, more or less), which faces an open field and is away from both the entrance and the residences. The rest rooms are air conditioned, but rather small and basic. They also seem to suffer from some amount of neglect. Nevertheless, this park and its very nice restaurant make for quite a decent overnight stop.

BASICS

Operated By: Larry Kinslow. **Open:** All year. **Site Assignment:** First come, first served; no reservations. **Registration:** In restaurant. (Late arrivals use drop box.) **Fee:** RV $14.10 (checks, V, MC, AE, D). **Parking:** At site.

FACILITIES

Number of RV Sites: 27. **Number of Tent-Only Sites:** 0. **Hookups:** Water, sewer, electric (50 amps). **Each Site:** Picnic table. **Dump Station:** Yes. **Laundry:** No. **Pay Phone:** Yes. **Rest Rooms and Showers:** Yes. **Fuel:** No. **Propane:** No. **Internal Roads:** Gravel. **RV Service:** No. **Market:** 7 mi. in town. **Restaurant:** On site. **General Store:** No. **Vending:** No. **Swimming:** No. **Playground:** Yes. **Other:** Fishing pond (catch & release), dog walk, covered pavilion with 2 grills. **Activities:** Fishing, festivals. **Nearby Attractions:** Jasmine Moran Children's Museum, festivals. **Additional Information:** Seminole Chamber of Commerce, (405) 382-3640.

RESTRICTIONS

Pets: On leash, cleaned up after. **Fires:** In grills. **Alcoholic Beverages:** At sites. **Vehicle Maximum Length:** None.

TO GET THERE

From I-40 (Exit 200): on the south side of the highway, go 0.2 mi. south on Hwy. 99 to the 2nd commercial complex. Turn left at the sign for the restaurant into the entrance.

SPIRO
Rockin' Horse RV Park

Rte. 1 Box 267, Spiro 74959. T: (918) 962-2524.

RV: ★★★ Tent: ★★★

Beauty: ★★★	Site Privacy: ★★★★
Spaciousness: ★★★	Quiet: ★★★★
Security: ★★★★	Cleanliness: ★★★
Insect Control: ★★★★	Facilities: ★★

This rural campground has grassy RV sites situated along a loop. Not all sites are numbered. Sites 2–7 are gravel pull-throughs without any shade. Sites 10 and 15 are 75-foot pull-throughs, while end site 12 is a 60-foot pull-through. Sites 21 and those to either side of 21 are 60-foot back-ins that back to a grassy field and then to woods. These are the nicest sites due to the grass and the natural surroundings. One site (possibly 16) in the southeast corner is exceptionally spacious. Tenting is possible in the field to the south of the RV sites. Tent sites have thick grass but no shade. The one rest room and one shower are acceptably clean. Please note that the campground has recently been sold to new owners, and any number of changes may be expected.

BASICS

Operated By: Jack & Jeanie. **Open:** All year. **Site Assignment:** Assigned upon registration; verbal reservations OK. **Registration:** In office. (Late arrivals use drop box.) **Fee:** RV $15 (full), tent $8 (checks). **Parking:** At site.

FACILITIES

Number of RV Sites: 22. **Number of Tent-Only Sites:** Undesignated sites. **Hookups:** Water, sewer, electric (30 amps). **Dump Station:** No (sewer at all sites). **Laundry:** Yes. **Pay Phone:** No. **Rest Rooms and Showers:** Yes. **Fuel:** No. **Propane:** No. **Internal Roads:** Gravel. **RV Service:** No. **Market:** Less than 1 mi. east. **Restaurant:** Less than 1 mi. east. **General Store:** No. **Vending:** Yes. **Swimming:** No. **Playground:** No. **Other:** Storm shelter, RV & boat storage. **Activities:** Fishing, boating, swimming, hiking. **Nearby Attractions:** Spiro Mounds Archaeological State Park, Robert S. Kerr Lake. **Additional Information:** Spiro Area Chamber of Commerce, (918) 962-3816.

RESTRICTIONS

Pets: On leash, cleaned up after. **Fires:** In grills. **Alcoholic Beverages:** At sites. **Vehicle Maximum Length:** None.

TO GET THERE

From the junction of Main St. and Hwy. 9/271, turn west onto Hwy. 271 and go 1.2 mi. Turn right at the sign into the entrance.

TALEQUAH

Diamondhead Resort

12081 Hwy. 10, Talequah 74464. T: (800) 722-2411 or (918) 456-4545.

RV ★★★ Tent ★★★★

Beauty: ★★★★	Site Privacy: ★★★
Spaciousness: ★★★★	Quiet: ★★★★★
Security: ★★★★★	Cleanliness: ★★★
Insect Control: ★★★	Facilities: ★★★

All of the RV sites here are situated in a row in the northwest portion of the campground. These grassy, undeveloped sites are unnumbered. Counting from the southwest by the gravel road, sites 1–10 and 12–16 are under large shade trees, which make them more attractive. Sites 11–22 could conceivably be pull-throughs, if the campground is relatively empty, but 1–10 back to trees and cannot be anything other than back-ins. However, since the field in which they sit is so large, these sites can take a rig of any size. There are loads of tenting sites, none of which are numbered. Since the campground is so natural and is surrounded by woods and the river, this is an ideal site for tenting. Restroom facilities are basic, and rather small for such a large campground. The building they are housed in needs a good cleaning, but the facilities themselves are well maintained. Note that campers who stay here are expected to take float trips, making this campground somewhat unusual. However, this seems to be a common restriction among "float" campgrounds in the area (which has many).

BASICS

Operated By: Joyce Eastham. **Open:** Apr. 1–Oct. 1. **Site Assignment:** First come, first served; verbal reservations OK. **Registration:** In office, or with guard (nights & weekends). **Fee:** RV $15 (electric), tent $10, car (V, MC, D). **Parking:** At site.

FACILITIES

Number of RV Sites: 22. **Number of Tent-Only Sites:** Undesignated sites. **Hookups:** Electric (30 amps). **Each Site:** Picnic table, grill. **Dump Station:** Yes. **Laundry:** No. **Pay Phone:** No. **Rest Rooms and Showers:** Yes. **Fuel:** No. **Propane:** No. **Internal Roads:** Gravel. **RV Service:** No. **Market:** 7 mi. to Talequah. **Restaurant:** 3 mi. towards Talequah. **General Store:** Yes. **Vending:** No. **Swimming:** River. **Playground:** No. **Other:** Canoe rentals. **Activities:** Canoe floating, volleyball, basketball. **Nearby Attractions:** Fishing. **Additional Information:** Talequah Area Chamber of Commerce, (800) 456-4860 or (918) 456-3742.

RESTRICTIONS

Pets: On leash, cleaned up after. **Fires:** In grills. **Alcoholic Beverages:** At sites. **Vehicle Maximum Length:** None. **Other:** Only floaters may stay in campground. No glass or styrofoam on or near river.

TO GET THERE

From the junction of Hwy. 51/62/82 and Hwy. 10 in town by Wal-Mart, go northeast on Hwy. 10/51/62/82 for 2.2 mi. Turn right onto Downing St. (3rd light) and go 1.9 mi. Turn left onto Scenic Hwy. 10 and go 5.3 mi. Turn right at the sign into the entrance. (Follow the gravel road to the back of the campground for electrical sites.)

TONKAWA

Woodland Camper Park

16600 West South Ave., Tonkawa 74653. T: (580) 628-2062.

RV ★★★ Tent ★★★

Beauty: ★★★ Site Privacy: ★★★
Spaciousness: ★★★ Quiet: ★★★
Security: ★★★★ Cleanliness: ★★★
Insect Control: ★★★★ Facilities: ★★★

Just off the interstate, this campground is bordered by a gas station to the west and fields to the north and south. Mostly unnumbered, sites range from 75 feet (east row) to 95 feet (west row) long. They are all undeveloped grassy sites, averaging 40 feet wide. The least desirable sites are the end sites to the south, which are closest to the highway (especially the southeast end site, which also has no shade tree). The most desirable site, in the northeast corner, has a large shade tree, abuts a field, and is furthest from the highway. There is an enormous area where tenting is possible. The best tent site is in front of the house, under a large shade tree (unfortunately, closer to the road). The rest rooms and showers are passable, but there was paint flaking from the shower stalls during our visit, and the floor is unpainted cement. This campground is mainly an overnighter, about equally decent for tenters and RVers.

BASICS

Operated By: Gary & Jo Wood. **Open:** All year. **Site Assignment:** Flexible, depending on site availability; verbal reservations OK. **Registration:** In office. (Late arrivals use drop box.) **Fee:** RV $14 (full), tent $8. **Parking:** At site.

FACILITIES

Number of RV Sites: 38. **Number of Tent-Only Sites:** Undesignated sites. **Hookups:** Water, sewer, electric (30 amps). **Dump Station:** Yes. **Laundry:** No. **Pay Phone:** Across street. **Rest Rooms and Showers:** Yes. **Fuel:** No. **Propane:** No. **Internal Roads:** Paved. **RV Service:** No. **Market:** 2 mi. east. **Restaurant:** Across street. **General Store:** Across street. **Vending:** No. **Swimming:** No. **Playground:** No. **Other:** None. **Activities:** Boating, swimming, fishing. **Nearby Attractions:** Ponca City, Great Salt Plains State State Park. **Additional Information:** Tonkawa Chamber of Commerce, (580) 628-2220.

RESTRICTIONS

Pets: On leash, cleaned up after. **Fires:** In grills. **Alcoholic Beverages:** At sites. **Vehicle Maximum Length:** None.

TO GET THERE

From I-35 (Exit 214): on the west side of the highway, go 0.15 mi. west. Turn right at the sign into the entrance.

TULSA

Tulsa Northeast KOA

19605 East Skelly Dr., Catoosa 74015. T: (800) KOA-7657 or (918) 266-4227; www.koa.com/where/OK/36106.htm.

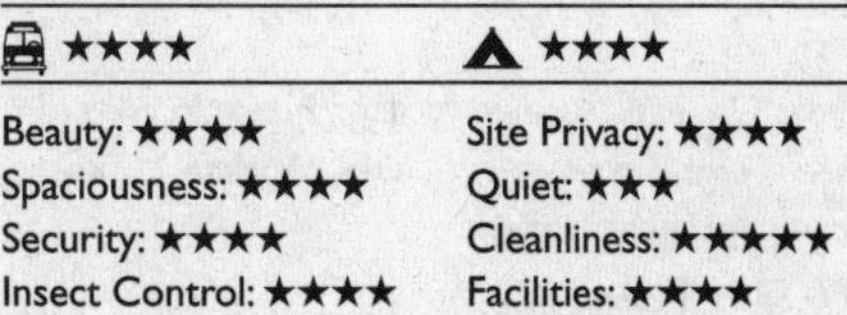

RV ★★★★ Tent ★★★★

Beauty: ★★★★ Site Privacy: ★★★★
Spaciousness: ★★★★ Quiet: ★★★
Security: ★★★★ Cleanliness: ★★★★★
Insect Control: ★★★★ Facilities: ★★★★

This campground offers open grassy sites in the front section and more shaded sites behind the office. All sites are pull-throughs. The front section has 75-foot sites that are roomier than most of the sites in the back (24 feet wide versus 18 feet wide). Northern end sites (116, 130, 143, 153, 163, 177, 191, and 205) are closest to the entrance road and are therefore less desirable. End sites closer to the office (112 and 158 especially) receive more passing traffic from registering campers. Of the southern sites, the two rows (the 40s and 50s) directly behind the office are the widest and most suitable for rigs with slide-outs. Of the remaining sites, 10 and 16 in the eastern side are closest to a storage shed. Sites in the southwestern corner (77, 84, 91, 98, 104, 100) are furthest from the entrance and the office. Tent sites are directly behind the office, in a strip of grassy sites. The rest rooms and showers are absolutely spotless and very comfortable. This campground makes a great home base for exploring Tulsa and its environs.

BASICS

Operated By: Private operator. **Open:** All year. **Site Assignment:** Assigned upon registration Credit card required for reservation; 24-hours cancellation policy. **Registration:** In office. (Late arrivals use drop box.) **Fee:** RV $24 (full), $20 (water, electric), tent $18. **Parking:** At site.

Facilities

Number of RV Sites: 118. **Number of Tent-Only Sites:** 9. **Hookups:** Water, sewer, electric (30, 50 amps). **Each Site:** Picnic table, grill. **Dump Station:** Yes. **Laundry:** Yes. **Pay Phone:** Yes. **Rest Rooms and Showers:** Yes. **Fuel:** No. **Propane:** Yes. **Internal Roads:** Gravel. **RV Service:** No. **Market:** 3 blocks south. **Restaurant:** 0.25 mi. south. **General Store:** Yes. **Vending:** Yes. **Swimming:** Pool. **Playground:** Yes. **Other:** Cabins, pet walk, dataport, rec room, video games. **Activities:** Swimming, volleyball, fishing, boating, swimming, tours, golf, softball/baseball, horse racing. **Nearby Attractions:** Trail of Tears, amusement parks, casinos, lakes, Tulsa Zoo. **Additional Information:** Tulsa CVB, (800) 558-3311 or (918) 585-1201.

Restrictions

Pets: On leash, cleaned up after. **Fires:** In grills. **Alcoholic Beverages:** At sites. **Vehicle Maximum Length:** None.

To Get There

From I-44 (Exit 240A: 193rd Ave.), turn north onto 193rd Ave. and go 0.15 mi. Turn right at the sign into the entrance. Follow the entrance road past the trucking companies. Turn right at the sign into the campground.

WAURIKA

Moneka Park

1645 South 101st Ave., Tulsa 74128. T: (580) 963-2111; www.lasr.net/lasr/oklahoma/waurika/body.html.

RV: ★★★ Tent: ★★★★

Beauty: ★★★★	Site Privacy: ★★★★
Spaciousness: ★★★★	Quiet: ★★★★★
Security: ★★★	Cleanliness: ★★★★
Insect Control: ★★	Facilities: ★★

Sites in this wilderness campground are situated around a loop. Depending on your preference, you can select a site on the outside of the loop (on the right side), nestled into the forest, or on the more open inside of the loop (left side). (Inside sites 12–23 at the south end are also totally forested.) Sites on the west side of the loop (1, 4, 6, and odd 7–17) have short footpaths to the creek. Sites 3 and 36–38 offer the best opportunity to recreate in the grassy field. Less desirable sites are 12 and 13, located at the intersection of two internal roads and therefore sunject to road traffic. Sites 18–20 are apt to receive more passing foot traffic due to the proximity of the hiking trail between 18 and 19. Perhaps the only downside to this beautiful campground is that the rest rooms are small (one non-flush toilet) and only naturally lit, but they are clean. This campground is a quiet and fun destination for RVers and tenters alike, as long as you can stand getting back to basics a little.

Basics

Operated By: Army Corps of Engineers. **Open:** Mar. 1–Oct. 31. **Site Assignment:** First come, first served; no reservations. **Registration:** At pay station. **Fee:** $8. **Parking:** At site.

Facilities

Number of RV Sites: 38. **Number of Tent-Only Sites:** 0. **Hookups:** None. **Each Site:** Picnic table, grill, wooden "prep table" by grill. **Dump Station:** No. **Laundry:** No. **Pay Phone:** No. **Rest Rooms and Showers:** Yes (No showers). **Fuel:** No. **Propane:** No. **Internal Roads:** Paved. **RV Service:** No. **Market:** 8 mi. to Waurika. **Restaurant:** 8 mi. to Waurika. **General Store:** No. **Vending:** No. **Swimming:** Lake. **Playground:** No. **Other:** Hiking trail. **Activities:** Hiking, swimming, boating, fishing. **Nearby Attractions:** Waurika Lake, Beaver Creek Trail. **Additional Information:** Waurika Chamber of Commerce, (580) 228-2081.

Restrictions

Pets: On leash, cleaned up after. **Fires:** In grills. **Alcoholic Beverages:** At sites. **Vehicle Maximum Length:** None.

To Get There

From the junction of Hwy. 70 and Hwy. 5, turn west onto Hwy. 5 and go 5.3 mi. Turn right at the wooden sign for Waurika Lake. Go 0.9 mi. (past the Project Office and Information Center), and veer left when the road starts along the lake. Go 0.8 mi. and turn left into the campground.

WOODWARD

Corky's Get and Go

802 Northwest Hwy. 270, Woodward 73801. T: (405) 254-9161.

RV ★★★ Tent ▲ ★★

Beauty: ★★★	Site Privacy: ★★★
Spaciousness: ★★★	Quiet: ★★
Security: ★★★	Cleanliness: ★★★★
Insect Control: ★★★★	Facilities: ★★

An RV park managed in conjunction with a convenience store, this park has 2 rows of 5 back-in sites. Sites 1–5 are directly behind the store, while 6–10 back to a residential area. All sites are open and level, measure 40 × 25 feet, and have excellent grass. Site 6 has a nice shade tree, making it the most desirable. Sites 8 and 9 share a smaller tree, but are a better pick than the other treeless sites. Sites 1 and 10 (especially 1) are least desirable, as they border a city street. Site 1 also has the RV dump station next to it. While there may be several long-term guests in the numbered sites, campers who only want to stay one night and can afford to forgo hookups can park in the field that abuts the RV park at no cost. Tenting is possible in the field, which has a very nice grass floor. There is no charge for tents, assuming that no hookups are used. If Corky's park is full, there is a motel right next door that offers overnight RV parking spaces, but these are on a tar surface and do not have any shade trees.

BASICS

Operated By: Corky Chestnut. **Open:** All year. **Site Assignment:** First come, first served; verbal reservations OK. **Registration:** In convenience store (5p.m.–midnight). (Late arrivals select an available site & settle in the morning.) **Fee:** $10 (free for no hookups) (V, MC, AE, D). **Parking:** At site, in field for no hookups.

FACILITIES

Number of RV Sites: 10. **Number of Tent-Only Sites:** 0. **Hookups:** Water, sewer, electric (30 amps). **Dump Station:** Yes. **Laundry:** No. **Pay Phone:** Yes. **Rest Rooms and Showers:** Rest rooms in convenience store. **Fuel:** Yes. **Propane:** No. **Internal Roads:** Gravel. **RV Service:** No. **Market:** 1.5 mi. southeast. **Restaurant:** 0.5 mi. southeast. **General Store:** Yes. **Vending:** Yes. **Swimming:** No. **Playground:** No. **Other:** None. **Activities:** Visiting museums. **Nearby Attractions:** Plains Indians & Pioneers Museum, Southern Plains Range Research Station. **Additional Information:** Woodward Chamber of Commerce, (800) 364-5352 or (580) 256-7411.

RESTRICTIONS

Pets: On leash, cleaned up after. **Fires:** In grills. **Alcoholic Beverages:** At sites. **Vehicle Maximum Length:** 45 ft.

TO GET THERE

From the junction of Hwys 3/15/183/270/412, go 0.3 mi. north on Hwy. 270 (Old Fort Supply Rd.). Turn right at the Conoco sign into Corky's Convenience Store.

Texas

Texans are proud of the size of their state. Our team, a bunch of Easterners, grew more impressed as each day passed. When we hadn't reached El Paso by the 25th day of our westbound tour of Texas, we became listless and discouraged. But the discovery of Texas's natural beauty, colorful history, and rich culture is worth the drive.

Texans divide their state into seven geographic and cultural regions. Big Bend Country begins at **El Paso** and is bordered by New Mexico to the north and the Rio Grande River on the south. Big Bend Country is home to two breathtaking national parks: **Guadalupe Mountains** and **Big Bend.**

The Panhandle Plains includes **Amarillo, Lubbock, Wichita Falls,** and **Abilene.** Amarillo is the gateway to the nation's second largest canyon, **Palo Duro.** Lubbock, Wichita Falls, and Abilene experienced massive growth in the 1880s, when railroad expansion fueled the cattle industry.

The Prairies and Lakes region is bordered on the north by Oklahoma, stretches south to the Gulf Coast region, and includes the **Dallas–Fort Worth Metroplex**. Lake recreation, urban tourist attractions, and business draw millions to this area annually.

The eastern Piney Woods region borders Arkansas and Louisiana and stretches from **Texarkana** to north of **Houston.** In the heart of the rolling hills of the Piney Woods, tranquil **Angelina National Forest** surrounds massive **Sam Rayburn Reservoir.**

Texas's Gulf Coast region stretches from industrial **Beaumont** to the important agricultural area near **Brownsville.** In the 1970s the coast was transformed by OPEC's embargo on oil exported to the United States, which caused Texas oil prices to skyrocket and stimulated industrial growth.

The South Texas Plains stretch from **San Antonio** to **McAllen** and are bordered on the southwest by the Rio Grande. Greatly influenced by Mexican culture, this region has been the focus of numerous territory disputes, wars, and skirmishes. In the famous battle of the **Alamo** (1835), Texas Revolutionary forces were defeated by the Mexican army.

The Hill Country is anchored by **Austin** on its eastern border and includes the charming tourist towns of **Fredericksburg** and **Kerrville.** The **Lyndon B. Johnson National Historic Park,** near **Stonewall,** includes the president's boyhood home, grave, and family ranch. Lady Bird Johnson still occupies the ranch and greets tourists when time allows.

When planning your trip, call for the newest Texas State Travel Guide. There are so many tourist attractions in Texas that we have chosen to list only those easily accessed from major cities.

Austin attractions: **Lyndon B. Johnson Library and Museum, Lady Bird Johnson Wildflower Center, State Capitol Complex,** the **University of Texas.** Corpus Christi attractions: **Texas State Aquarium, Padre Island National Seashore, *USS Lexington* Museum on the Bay.** Dallas-Fort Worth attractions: the Dallas Cowboys, **Dallas Zoo, Fair Park, Six Flags Over Texas, Billy Bob's Texas** (world's largest honky-tonk, yahoo!), **Fort Worth Museum of Science and History, Fort Worth Zoo, Texas Motor Speedway.** El Paso attractions: **Juarez** tours, **Fort Bliss, Old Missions.** Houston attractions: **Astrodome, Downtown Houston Theater District, Museum District** (includes 14 museums, galleries, and gardens), **Six Flags AstroWorld/WaterWorld, Space Center Houston.** San Antonio attractions: **the Alamo, Military Bases Complex, Missions of San Antonio, San Antonio Zoo, Sea World of Texas, Six Flags Fiesta Texas.**

ALAMO

Alamo Palms

1341 Business Hwy. 83, Alamo, 78516. T: (956) 787-7571; F: (956) 787-7594; www.gocampingamerica.com/alamopalms, or www.alamopalms.com.

RV ★★★ | Tent n/a

Beauty: ★★★ | Site Privacy: ★★
Spaciousness: ★★ | Quiet: ★★★★
Security: ★★★★ | Cleanliness: ★★★★
Insect Control: ★★★★ | Facilities: ★★★★

"Alamo Palms" is a misnomer. Incredibly, the park's brochure also boasts about its trees. Alas, the campground is almost completely treeless. But Alamo Palms does offer top-notch amenities and recreation, including 20 shuffleboard courts, eight billiard tables, and weekly ballroom dances. Alamo Palms is a community-oriented adult-only park. The campground consists of row after row of nearly identical sites. So choose your site based on location; sites in the 200s, 300s, and 400s are close to the pool and clubhouse. All RV sites are small and nondescript, with paved back-in parking. Suburban Alamo Palms is convenient to shopping and restaurants. Drive to the beach or to Mexico in about an hour. Fenced and gated at night, security is good. Don't visit south Texas in the heat of summer. Make reservations well in advance in the winter.

Basics

Operated By: Hynes Group. **Open:** All year. **Site Assignment:** Reservations for one month or more, $200 nonrefundable deposit, call (800) 780-7571. **Registration:** At office. **Fee:** $20 per night for 2 people, $1 for each additional person. **Parking:** At site.

Facilities

Number of RV Sites: 351. **Number of Tent-Only Sites:** 0. **Hookups:** Water, sewer, electric (30, 50 amps), cable TV, dataport. **Each Site:** No amenities. **Dump Station:** No. **Laundry:** Yes. **Pay Phone:** Yes. **Rest Rooms and Showers:** No showers. **Fuel:** No. **Propane:** Yes. **Internal Roads:** Paved. **RV Service:** 2 mi. **Market:** 1 mi. **Restaurant:** 1 mi. **General Store:** 0.5 mi. **Vending:** Yes. **Swimming:** Pool. **Playground:** No. **Other:** Spa, tennis courts, exercise facilities, pool room, game room, ballroom, car & RV wash area, storage facilities. **Activities:** Shuffleboard, dancing, crafts, table tennis. **Nearby Attractions:** Sabal Palm Audubon Center & Sanctuary, Gladys Porter Zoo, Brownsville Battlefields, CAF/ Confederate Air Force Rio Grande Valley Wing, Historic Brownsville Museum. **Additional Information:** Alamo Chamber of Commerce (956) 787-2117, Rio Grande Valley Chamber of Commerce, (956) 968-3141.

Restrictions

Pets: Not allowed. **Fires:** In your own grill only. **Alcoholic Beverages:** Allowed. **Vehicle Maximum Length:** 40 ft.

To Get There

Travel south on US 281 (south of San Antonio), pass the US 83 East exit, and take the next exit, Business 83 East. This will take you to Alamo. The campground is 5 mi. ahead on the right just after Cesar-Chavez Rd.

ALEDO

Cowtown RV Park

7000 I-20, Aledo, 76008. T: (817) 441-7878; F: (817) 441-6567; www.gocamopingamerica.com/cowtown; cowtown@gocampingamerica.com.

RV ★★★ | Tent n/a

Beauty: ★★★ | Site Privacy: ★★★
Spaciousness: ★★★ | Quiet: ★★★
Security: ★★★ | Cleanliness: ★★★★
Insect Control: ★★★ | Facilities: ★★★

Approximately 20 miles west of downtown Fort Worth, plain-looking Cowtown provides convenient and tidy campsites. "Cowtown" is an old nickname for Fort Worth and not descriptive of this area. A bustling suburb with plenty of restaurants and shops, Aledo is no cow-town. Arranged in two long, straight rows of pull-throughs and two smaller sections containing back-in sites, all sites are narrow and basically unattractive. Each site contains a paved parking pad, a grassy area, and a sapling. The young trees break the visual monotony, but provide no shade or privacy. For couples, we recommend sites in the 90s and 100s—furthest from the interstate, these are likely the quietest. Families should look for a site in the front, near the pool and playground. Close to I-20, with no gates and no security guard, security at Cowtown is poor. For the nicest weather, visit northeastern Texas in spring or fall.

Basics

Operated By: The Beadels. **Open:** All year. **Site Assignment:** For reservations, call (800) 781-

4678; credit card number holds site, no-show charged one night. **Registration:** At office. **Fee:** $25 per night for 2 people, $1 per extra person over age 11. **Parking:** At site.

Facilities

Number of RV Sites: 104. **Number of Tent-Only Sites:** None. **Hookups:** Water, sewer, electric (30, 50 amps). **Each Site:** Some picnic tables, some grills. **Dump Station:** Yes. **Laundry:** Yes. **Pay Phone:** Yes. **Rest Rooms and Showers:** Yes. **Fuel:** No. **Propane:** Yes. **Internal Roads:** Some paved, some gravel. **RV Service:** 7 mi. east in Fort Worth. **Market:** 2 mi. in Willow Park. **Restaurant:** 2 mi. in Willow Park. **General Store:** At park. **Vending:** Yes. **Swimming:** Pool. **Playground:** Yes. **Other:** Rally room, mail service, fax service, car rental. **Activities:** volleyball, horseshoes, planned activities. **Nearby Attractions:** Trinity Meadows Race Track, Texas Opry, Six Flags Over Texas, Fort Worth Cowtown Coliseum, Fort Worth Sundance Square, Fort Worth Zoo, Fort Worth Museum of Science & History. **Additional Information:** Fort Worth CVB (800) 433-5747.

Restrictions

Pets: On leash & not allowed in playground or pool area. **Fires:** In grills only. **Alcoholic Beverages:** Not allowed inside buildings. **Vehicle Maximum Length:** 45 ft. **Other:** Speed limit 7 mph. You may rent a site for the RV price & tent-camp on it.

To Get There

From Fort Worth head west on I-30. Pass the junction of I-30 with I-20 and continue west on I-20 to exit 418 (Ranch House Rd.). Campground is one mile east on South Access Rd.

ARLINGTON

Treetops RV Village

1901 West Arbrook Rd., Arlington, 76015. T: (817) 467-7943; F: (817) 468-7607; www.flash.net/~tweetops/treetop.html; tweetops@flash.net.

RV ★★★ | Tent n/a

Beauty: ★★★★	Site Privacy: ★★★★
Spaciousness: ★★★	Quiet: ★★★
Security: ★★★	Cleanliness: ★★★★
Insect Control: ★★★	Facilities: ★★★

Convenient and attractive, Treetops is located in a thriving suburb about halfway between Dallas and Fort Worth. Spend your days off property; area shopping, dining, and tourist attractions are plentiful, while amenities at the campground are not. Sites include both back-ins and pull-throughs, and they are laid out on a winding road. Site size varies, but most are small and crowded. Even so, sites feel private thanks to 2001 shady oak trees and landscaped shrubbery between many sites. Each site contains a gravel RV parking space and a grassy area. Sites 338–361 are the furthest from busy roads and likely to be the quietest. We also recommend any of the sites along the small creek that runs through the park. There are no gates at this park, making security marginal. This park stays busy, so we recommend year-round advance reservations.

Basics

Operated By: Privately owned. **Open:** All year. **Site Assignment:** Reservations accepted, credit card number holds site, 24-hour cancellation notice required. **Registration:** At office. **Fee:** $28 per night for 2 people, $3 for each additional person over age 5. **Parking:** Gravel.

Facilities

Number of RV Sites: 165 (90 are reserved for monthly guests). **Number of Tent-Only Sites:** 0. **Hookups:** Water, sewer, electric (30, 50 amps), cable TV. **Each Site:** Picnic table, cement patio. **Dump Station:** Yes. **Laundry:** Yes. **Pay Phone:** Yes. **Rest Rooms and Showers:** Yes. **Fuel:** No. **Propane:** Yes. **Internal Roads:** Paved. **RV Service:** 15 mi. west in Fort Worth. **Market:** 0.25 mi. **Restaurant:** 0.25 mi. **General Store:** 0.25 mi. **Vending:** None. **Swimming:** Pool. **Playground:** No. **Other:** Dog walking area, dataport, mailboxes, newspaper vending, pavilion. **Activities:** Swimming. **Nearby Attractions:** Six Flags, Hurricane Harbor, Fort Worth Stockyards, Texas Motor Speedway, Texas Rangers Baseball, Lone Star Park, DFW International Airport, Dallas Mavericks, Mesquite Rodeo, Dallas Cowboys, convention centers, numerous retail shops. **Additional Information:** Fort Worth CVB (800) 433-5747, Dallas CVB (800) 232-5527.

Restrictions

Pets: Small pets only, must be on leash. **Fires:** None, bring your own grill. **Alcoholic Beverages:** Allowed. **Vehicle Maximum Length:** 45 ft. **Other:** No pop-ups or tents allowed.

To Get There

From I-20, take exit 449 (Cooper St.). Go north one block and veer left onto Melear Dr. Turn left onto Arbrook Rd. Entrance is on the right.

ATLANTA

Atlanta State Park

Rte. 1 Box 116, Atlanta 75551.T: (512) 389-8900 or (800) 792-1112; F: (512) 389-8959; www.tpwd.state.tx.us; e-mail.reservations@tpwd.state.tx.us.

RV: ★★★★ Tent: ★★★★★

Beauty: ★★★★	Site Privacy: ★★★★
Spaciousness: ★★★★	Quiet: ★★★★★
Security: ★★★★	Cleanliness: ★★★★
Insect Control: ★★	Facilities: ★★★

This state park offers two of the things that all RVers love in a campsite: full hookups and pull-throughs. (Of the nearly 60 sites in the park, about half are 110-foot pull-throughs, and nearly a third have full hookups.) While this park does not offer any sites right on the water's edge, sites 15–17 in the Kights Bluff area have decent lake views. (16 and 17 are pull-throughs.) Sites 4 and 5 are the most secluded, being 40-foot back-ins at the end of a roundabout. Sites 1 and 8 are closest to the entrance to this area and are therefore less desirable. Sites 16–23 are pull-throughs but are all quite open to the sun. The Wilkins Creek camping area offers forested pull-throughs away from the water's edge. Even-numbered sites 32–36 are particularly well-shaded. Site 65 is the only back-in in the area, and seems out of place: it looks like an outdated hookup that may not be in use. Like Knights Bluff, white Oak Ridge offers views of the lake (especially sites 51–54), but no sites on the water's edge. These sites are slightly smaller back-ins (35 feet) than in Knights Bluff, and are all pretty well-shaded. These sites, unlike the others, have a dirt floor instead of grass. Sites 52 and 53, at the end of a roundabout, are the most secluded. The rest rooms in this park are clean and have flush toilets, and each camping area has hot-water showers. This is a worthwhile destination for a family outing or a loner's getaway. There is something to suit just about anyone who doesn't mind getting out and about.

BASICS

Operated By: Texas Parks & Wildlife. **Open:** All year. **Site Assignment:** First come, first served. (Credit card required to make a reservation. $3 reservation service fee; $5 cancellation fee.). **Registration:** In office. (Late arrivals use drop box at entrance.). **Fee:** RV: $13 (full), $11 (water, electric), plus $2/person entrance fee (V, MC, D accepted in the office or for reservation.). **Parking:** At site.

FACILITIES

Number of RV Sites: 59. **Number of Tent-Only Sites:** Combined. **Hookups:** Water, sewer, electric (20, 30 & 50 amps). **Each Site:** Picnic table, grill, fire pit, lantern post, tent pad, water. **Dump Station:** Yes. **Laundry:** No. **Pay Phone:** Yes. **Rest Rooms and Showers:** Yes. **Fuel:** No. **Propane:** No. **Internal Roads:** Paved. **RV Service:** No. **Market:** 10 mi. to Queen's City. **Restaurant:** 10 mi. to Queen's City. **General Store:** Yes. **Vending:** Yes. **Swimming:** Lake. **Playground:** Yes. **Other:** Ampitheatre, group picnic area, fish cleaning station. **Activities:** Swimming, boating, fishing, hiking, mountain biking. **Nearby Attractions:** Lake Wright Patman, Caddo Lake State Park, Starr Family State Historical Park. **Additional Information:** Park Office: (903) 796-6476.

RESTRICTIONS

Pets: On 6-ft. leash, cleaned up after. **Fires:** In grills. **Alcoholic Beverages:** None. **Vehicle Maximum Length:** None. **Other:** Each visitor must pay $2 entrance fee per day.

TO GET THERE

From the junction of Hwy. 436 and Hwy. 59, go 1.35 mi. north on Hwy. 59 to FM 96. Turn west onto FM 96 and go 7.2 mi. Turn right onto FM 1154 and go 1.6 mi. to Park Rd. 42, which leads to the park entrance.

AUSTIN

Austin Lone Star RV Resort

7009 South IH-35, Austin, 78744.T: (512) 444-6322; F: (512) 444-8719; www.austinlonestar.com; austinlonestar@austinlonestar.com.

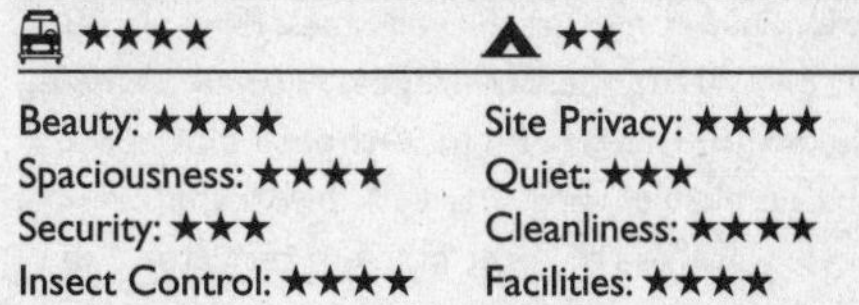

With convenient interstate access and a variety of nearby restaurants and shopping, Austin Lone Star is an excellent choice if you're touring the capital city. Sites at this pretty park are fairly spacious, with gravel parking and grassy plots at each site. Laid out in a series of tidy rows, sites include both back-ins and pull-throughs. Most sites are shaded by ash and other species. The shadiest sites include 105–138, which are bordered by trees to the south. Families should go for sites near the neat playground and other recreation at the front of the park. The rest rooms are outstanding—clean, spacious, and private. Unfortunately, the small, unattractive tent sites are not recommended. Visit Austin in spring or fall for the nicest weather. Luckily, insects are rarely a concern—Austin's famous bat community feeds on mosquitoes. With no gates, security is poor at this urban campground.

Basics

Operated By: The Rowleys. **Open:** All year. **Site Assignment:** Reservations accepted, credit card number holds site, 24-hour cancellation notice required, (800)284-0206. **Registration:** At office. **Fee:** $35 per night, RV or tent. **Parking:** At site.

Facilities

Number of RV Sites: 150 w/full hookups. **Number of Tent-Only Sites:** 4 w/electricity & water only. **Hookups:** Water, sewer, electric (30, 50 amps), phone, & cable TV. **Each Site:** Picnic tables, BBQ pits. **Dump Station:** Yes. **Laundry:** Yes. **Pay Phone:** Yes. **Rest Rooms and Showers:** Yes. **Fuel:** No. **Propane:** Yes. **Internal Roads:** Paved. **RV Service:** 0.5 mi. **Market:** 0.5 mi. **Restaurant:** In park. **General Store:** In park. **Vending:** Yes. **Swimming:** Pool. **Playground:** Yes. **Other:** Hot tub, mini-mart, gift shop, lodge. **Activities:** Tours, organized activities, pool tables, horseshoes, volleyball, basketball. **Nearby Attractions:** Texas state capitol, National Wildflower Center, Zilker Park, Pioneer Farm, Slaughter-Leftwich Winery, Mexican Free-Tailed Bat Colony, Barton Creek Greenbelt Preserve. **Additional Information:** Austin CVB (800) 926-2282.

Restrictions

Pets: On 6-ft. max. leash at all times. **Fires:** In BBQ pits only. **Alcoholic Beverages:** Allowed. **Vehicle Maximum Length:** None. **Other:** 5 mph speed limit, no bicycle riding after dark, high water pressure; suggest use of water pressure regulator, 3 day tent limit.

To Get There

If heading north on I-35, take Exit 228 and it is one block on the right side. If heading south on 35, take exit 227, make a U-turn to the left, go back under the interstate onto the service road heading north. Park is 0.5 mi. ahead on the right.

BASTROP

Bastrop State Park

P.O. Box 518, Bastrop, 78602-0518. T: (512) 321-2101; F: (512) 321-3300; www.tpwd.state.tx.us.

RV ★★★★ Tent ★★★★

Beauty: ★★★★★ Site Privacy: ★★★★
Spaciousness: ★★★★ Quiet: ★★★★
Security: ★★★ Cleanliness: ★★★★
Insect Control: ★★★ Facilities: ★★★★★

Part of a recreation complex including Lake Bastrop, Buescher State Park, and Lake Somerville State Park, the area is home to the "Lost Pines," a stand of isolated loblolly pines. Fauna includes the endangered Houston toad (mating and male trilling peak in Feb. and Mar.). The park's amenities are excellent. Though campsites at Buescher are more private and spacious than campsites here, there are fewer insects at drier Bastrop. The Piney Hill area offers RV sites with full hookups and gravel pull-throughs (we fancied sites 1, 23, 24, and 25). The Copperas Creek area includes multi-use sites with water and electric hookups and gravel back-in parking. Tent campers should "rough it" at serene Creekside campground. All sites are spacious, with lovely tree cover. There is no gate, but Bastrop's rural setting makes it reasonably safe. Visit during the week. Only 32 miles from Austin, the park stays busy weekends Mar. through Nov.

Basics

Operated By: Texas Parks & Wildlife. **Open:** All year. **Site Assignment:** Reservations (512) 389-8900; reservations must be made at least 48 hours in advance; deposit (equivalent to first night's fee) required to hold reservation; cancellations more than two days prior to reservation result in $5 fee, cancellations within two days of reservation result in loss of deposit. **Registration:** Headquarters. **Fee:** $3 per person per day for anyone aged 13 & over, $15 for sites w/water, electric, & sewer, $12 for sites w/water & electric, $9 for sites w/water only, $7 for primitive tent sites (cash, checks, D,V, MC). **Parking:** At most sites.

Facilities

Number of RV Sites: 54 sites w/full hookups. **Number of Tent-Only Sites:** 23 sites w/water at each. **Hookups:** Water, sewer, electric (30, 50 amps). **Each Site:** Picnic table, fire ring, grill. **Dump Station:** Yes. **Laundry:** No. **Pay Phone:** Yes. **Rest**

Rooms and Showers: Yes. **Fuel:** No. **Propane:** No. **Internal Roads:** Paved. **RV Service:** 8 mi., west of Bastrop. **Market:** 1 mi. east in Bastrop. **Restaurant:** 1 mi. east in Bastrop. **General Store:** Wal-Mart, 1 mi. east in Bastrop. **Vending:** Beverages. **Swimming:** Pool. **Playground:** No. **Other:** 18-hole golf course (6152 yards, Bermuda greens, electric & pull carts for rent), picnic area, cabins, lodges, group barracks, group dining hall, outdoor sports area, cabins, gift shop. **Activities:** Golfing, hiking, backpacking, fishing, canoeing, swimming, road cycling, & guided tours. **Nearby Attractions:** Lake Bastrop, Buescher State Park, Lake Somerville State Park & Trailway, Austin (32 mi. west). **Additional Information:** Austin CVB (800) 926-2282, Smithville Chamber of Commerce (512) 237-2313, Bastrop Chamber of Commerce (512) 321-2419.

Restrictions

Pets: On leash only. **Fires:** In fire rings only. **Alcoholic Beverages:** prohibited. **Vehicle Maximum Length:** 50 ft.

To Get There

From Bastrop, drive east on State Hwy. 21 for 1 mi. Park entrance is on the right. The park is also accessible from Buescher State Park and State Hwy. 71.

BIG BEND NATIONAL PARK

Chisos Basin and Cottonwood Campgrounds

P.O. Box 129, Big Bend National Park 79834-0129. T: (915) 477-2251; F: (915) 477-1175; www.nps.gov/bibe; bibeinformation@nps.gov.

RV ★★★★★ Tent ★★★★★

Beauty: ★★★★★	Site Privacy: ★★★
Spaciousness: ★★★★	Quiet: ★★★★★
Security: ★★★★★	Cleanliness: ★★★★★
Insect Control: ★★★★	Facilities: ★★★★

Big Bend is breathtaking. It's worth the long and sometimes desolate drive. The park's southern border is the Rio Grande River, with its dramatic cliffs. There are also vast acres of Chihuahuan desert punctuated by the Chisos Mountains (Emory Peak is the highest in the park at 7,825 feet). Flora and fauna are diverse because of extreme elevation changes and the park's location on the range borders of many Central and North American species. Each campground at Big Bend is different. Though shaded by a few cottonwood trees, the RV campground at Rio Grande Village is the least attractive of the lot. If you can forego hookups, stay elsewhere. Chisos Basin (el. 5,401 feet) offers sites with a little shade and privacy provided by high mountain junipers, small oaks, and pinions. Cottonwood campground offers little privacy, but sites are deliciously shaded by a mature stand of cottonwood trees. Gravel, back-in parking is most common. Security is not a concern. Visit in spring or fall to avoid massive crowds at the camping areas.

Basics

Operated By: National Park Service. **Open:** All year. **Site Assignment:** First come, first served; no reservations accepted (except group camping). **Registration:** Self-registration. **Fee:** $8 for up to 9 people (cash only). **Parking:** At site (recommended no more than one car).

Facilities

Number of RV Sites: 94. **Number of Tent-Only Sites:** None. **Hookups:** None (water available, no generators allowed at Cottonwood). **Each Site:** Picnic table, grill. **Dump Station:** Yes (not at Cottonwood). **Laundry:** No (only at Rio Grande Village). **Pay Phone:** Yes (not at Cottonwood). **Rest Rooms and Showers:** Flush toilets at Chisos Basin, pit toilets at Cottonwood. **Fuel:** Yes (at Panther Junction & Rio Grande Village in the Park). **Propane:** Yes (at Rio Grande Village). **Internal Roads:** Paved. **RV Service:** 4 mi. outside west entrance in Study Butte/Terlingua. **Market:** Park stores, 100 mi. in Alpine. **Restaurant:** On-site at Chisos Basin, 4 mi. outside west entrance in Terlinqua. **General Store:** Hardware 100 mi. in Alpine, Wal-Mart 120 mi. in Fort Stockton. **Vending:** No. **Swimming:** No. **Playground:** No. **Other:** Visitor Center, picnic areas, amphitheaters, boat launches, gift shop. **Activities:** Nature trails, hiking, backpacking, rafting, canoeing, off-roading, scenic drive, birdwatching, historic sites, ranger programs. **Nearby Attractions:** Big Bend Ranch State Park Complex, Chihuahuan Desert Research Institute, Chinati Hot Springs, Davis Mountains Indian Lodge & Balmorhea State Parks, Alpine crafts & antiques, Museum of the Big Bend. **Additional Information:** Alpine Chamber of Commerce (800) 561-3735.

Restrictions

Pets: On leash only. **Fires:** Ground fires not allowed. **Alcoholic Beverages:** Allowed (at sites only). **Vehicle Maximum Length:** None (Chisos Basin not over 24 ft.). **Other:** 14-day stay limit, 28-

days per year, quiet hours enforced (no generators at Cottonwood), no dumping of gray water.

To Get There

From Alpine (junction of US 90 w/State Hwy. 118), take 118 south 80 mi. to the west entrance of the park. To get to the north entrance, take US 90 east 23 mi. and turn south on US 385. Drive approximately 45 mi. south to the north entrance. The Chisos Basin campground is 29 mi. from the west entrance and 38 mi. from the north entrance. The Cottonwood campground is 35 mi. from the west entrance and 64 mi. from the north entrance.

BLANCO

Blanco State Park

P.O. Box 493, Blanco 78606. T: (830) 833-4333 or (800) 792-1112; F: (830) 833-5388; www.tpwd.state.tx.us

RV ★★★ Tent ★★★

Beauty: ★★★	Site Privacy: ★★★
Spaciousness: ★★★	Quiet: ★★★
Security: ★	Cleanliness: ★★★
Insect Control: ★★★	Facilities: ★★★

At 104 acres, Blanco is neither large nor pretty. It feels like a city park, although original facilities were built by the Civilian Conservation Corps in the 1930s. Fishing along the Blanco River is the most popular activity. Catches include rainbow trout, perch, catfish, and bass. The campground consists of two small loops. Site size is adequate. Sites 1–10 have full hookups and are slightly smaller than sites 11–30. Most sites have paved, back-in parking (site 16 is the only pull-through). There are a few shady sites, but most are open to neighbors and the elements. Families should try for sites 27 or 31, near the playground. Otherwise, there is little difference between sites. There is no gate at Blanco, making security marginal. Visit in late spring, summer or fall, avoiding holiday weekends.

Basics

Operated By: Texas Parks & Wildlife. **Open:** All year. **Site Assignment:** Reservations (512) 389-8900, reservations must be made at least 48 hours in advance, deposit required (equivalent to first night's fee) to hold reservation, cancellations more than two days prior to reservation result in $5 fee, cancellations within two days of reservation result in loss of deposit. **Registration:** Headquarters. **Fee:** $3 per person per day for anyone aged 13 & older, plus $12 for sites w/water & electric, $14 for sites w/water, electric, & sewer (cash, checks, D,V, MC). **Parking:** At site.

Facilities

Number of RV Sites: 10. Number of Tent-Only Sites. **Hookups:** Water, sewer, electric (30 & 50 amps). **Each Site:** picnic table, fire ring. **Dump Station:** Yes. **Laundry:** No. **Pay Phone:** Yes. **Rest Rooms and Showers:** Yes. **Fuel:** No. **Propane:** No. **Internal Roads:** Paved. **RV Service:** 20 mi. south in Spring Branch. **Market:** 1 mi. south. **Restaurant:** 200 yards from park. **General Store:** 40 mi. west in Fredericksburg. **Vending:** No. **Swimming:** No. **Playground:** Yes. **Other:** Gift shop, group day-use facilities, screened shelters. **Activities:** Swimming in Blanco River, picnicking, hiking, boating (electric motors only), fishing. **Nearby Attractions:** Nearby attraction include Lyndon B. Johnson State Historical Park & LBJ Ranch, Pedernales Falls & Guadalupe River state parks, Canyon Lake, Cascade Caverns, Natural Bridge Caverns, Aquarena Springs. **Additional Information:** Blanco Chamber of Commerce (830) 833-5101, www.texashillcountryinfo.com.

Restrictions

Pets: Leash Only. **Fires:** In fire rings only. **Alcoholic Beverages:** Not allowed. **Vehicle Maximum Length:** 50 ft. **Other:** Max. 8 people per campsite, Quiet time 10 p.m.–6 a.m., fourteen day stay limit, swim at your own risk, gathering of firewood prohibited.

To Get There

From Austin, drive west on US 290 for 42 mi. Turn left on US 281, and go south for 10 mi. Go through Blanco, then turn right onto Park Rd. 23. The park entrance is within 200 yards. From San Antonio, drive north on US 281. Cross State Rte. 46 and continue until reaching Blanco (about 30 mi.). Cross the Blanco River and then take the first left, onto Park Rd. 23. The park entrance is within 200 yards.

BOERNE

Alamo Fiesta RV Resort

33000 IH-10 West, Boerne, 78006. T: (830) 249-4700; F: (830) 249-4654; www.alamofiestarv.com.

RV ★★★ Tent ★★★

Beauty: ★★★	Site Privacy: ★★★

Spaciousness: ★★★★ Quiet: ★★★★
Security: ★★★ Cleanliness: ★★★
Insect Control: ★★★★ Facilities: ★★★★

Alamo Fiesta is a good camping option if you would like to tour the hill country and San Antonio without switching campgrounds. Bandera, Kerrville, and Fredericksburg are within 40 miles of Boerne. Downtown San Antonio is a little closer and 6 Flags Fiesta Texas is 12 miles away. The campground consists mainly of rows of pull-throughs with back-in sites along the perimeter of the park. Sites are on the large side of average, and most have no shade. There is some well-intentioned (but poorly maintained) landscaping. Each site has a grassy plot, which often bleeds haphazardly into the gravel parking spaces. Near the playground, sites 1–5 and 128–133 are good choices for families. For tranquility, obtain a back-in site in the back of the park (70–94). With no gates, this small town/suburban park has marginal security. Visit Texas Hill Country on weekdays for breezy touring.

Basics

Operated By: Cliff & Linda Dorsey. **Open:** All year. **Site Assignment:** Reservations held w/credit card number, call (800) 321-CAMP, all credit cards, checks & cash accepted; check out at 11 a.m. **Registration:** At office. **Fee:** $22 for 2 people in an RV, $2 for each extra person over age 6, $16.50 for pop-ups & vans, $15.50 for tents. **Parking:** At site.

Facilities

Number of RV Sites: 221. **Number of Tent-Only Sites:** Tent area available. **Hookups:** Water, sewer, electric (20, 30, 50 amps), cable TV, dataport. **Each Site:** Picnic table. **Dump Station:** Yes. **Laundry:** Yes. **Pay Phone:** Yes. **Rest Rooms and Showers:** Yes. **Fuel:** No. **Propane:** Yes. **Internal Roads:** Paved. **RV Service:** 1.5 mi. southeast in Boerne. **Market:** 1 mi. southeast in Boerne. **Restaurant:** 1 mi. southeast in Boerne. **General Store:** 0.5 mi. southeast in Boerne. **Vending:** Yes. **Swimming:** Pool. **Playground:** Yes. **Other:** Basketball courts, banquet rooms, soccer field, tennis court, horseshoe pit, pavilion. **Activities:** Horseshoes, washer pitching. **Nearby Attractions:** King House Museum, The Alamo, Six Flags/ Fiesta Texas, Historic Missions, Sea World, Riverwalk, Cowboy Artists of America Museum. **Additional Information:** San Antonio CVB (800) 447-3372, Boerne Chamber of Commerce (888) 842-8080.

Restrictions

Pets: On leash only. **Fires:** Not allowed. **Alcoholic Beverages:** Allowed. **Vehicle Maximum Length:** 75 ft.

To Get There

From San Antonio, head west on I-10. Take Exit 542 and make an immediate right turn.

BROWNSVILLE

River Bend Resort

Rte. 8 Box 649, Brownsville, 78520. T: (956) 548-0194; F: (956) 548-0191.

RV ★★★★ Tent n/a

Beauty: ★★★★★ Site Privacy: ★★★
Spaciousness: ★★★★ Quiet: ★★★★
Security: ★★★★ Cleanliness: ★★★★★
Insect Control: ★★★★★ Facilities: ★★★★★

Seniors-only River Bend is among the most attractive parks in south Texas. The park's facilities are outstanding considering how few sites it offers. The swimming pool and clubhouse overlook a pretty bend in the Rio Grande River, and the golf course features many holes with nice river views. The campground consists of back-in sites laid out along two main roads. Sites are spacious and incredibly tidy. Landscaping at each site adds to the manicured look of the park, but provides no shade or privacy—there are no trees. All parking is paved. The nicest sites overlook the golf course. Brownsville is convenient to attractions, restaurants, and shopping galore. Gates lock at night, making security at this suburban park fair. Make reservations months in advance for winter visits. Avoid south Texas in the summer.

Basics

Operated By: John Alberg. **Open:** All year. **Site Assignment:** Reservations are required & are taken Mon–Fri. from 9 a.m.-noon; Check-in at 12 p.m.-5 p.m. firm, unless previous night registration arrangements have been made; check out at 10 a.m. **Registration:** At office. **Fee:** $21 per day for 2 people, $2.50 for each additional person, $2 A/C charge per day per unit, $4 charge per day for more than 30-amp usage. **Parking:** At site.

Facilities

Number of RV Sites: 30. **Number of Tent-Only Sites:** 0. **Hookups:** Water, sewer, electric (30, 50 amps), cable TV. **Each Site:** None. **Dump**

Station: No. **Laundry:** Yes. **Pay Phone:** Yes. **Rest Rooms and Showers:** Yes. **Fuel:** No. **Propane:** No, daily service comes to the park, Mon.–Sat. **Internal Roads:** Paved. **RV Service:** 60 mi. northwest in McAllen. **Market:** 5 mi. east in Brownsville. **Restaurant:** 5 mi. east in Brownsville. **General Store:** 4 mi. east in Brownsville. **Vending:** Beverages only. **Swimming:** Pool. **Playground:** No. **Other:** 18-hole golf course, tennis courts, rec hall, dance hall. **Activities:** Horseshoes, shuffleboard, swimmimg, arts & crafts, golf. **Nearby Attractions:** Gladys Porter Zoo, CAF/Confederate Air Force Rio Grande Valley Wing, South Padre Island, Boca Chica Beach. **Additional Information:** Brownsville Chamber of Commerce (956) 542-4341.

Restrictions

Pets: On leash only. **Fires:** In grills only, bring your own. **Alcoholic Beverages:** Not allowed. **Vehicle Maximum Length:** 40 ft.

To Get There

From Hwy. US 77/83, exit at local route 802. Go west 2 mi. to US 281. Turn right on Hwy. 281 and go west 3 mi. Entrance is on the left.

BROWNWOOD

Lake Brownwood State Park

RR 5 Box 160, Lake Brownwood 76801. T: (915) 784-5223 or (800) 792-1112; F: (915) 784-6203; www.tpwd.state.tx.us

RV ★★★★ Tent ★★★★

Beauty: ★★★★	Site Privacy: ★★★
Spaciousness: ★★★★	Quiet: ★★★★
Security: ★★★★	Cleanliness: ★★★★
Insect Control: ★★	Facilities: ★★★★

Fishermen enjoy Lake Brownwood, an 8,000-acre reservoir supporting crappie, perch, catfish, and bass. There are extensive fishing and boating facilities. Landlubbers explore the shoreline, especially when adorned with spring wildflowers. There are four types of sites in three campgrounds. Those seeking peace, quiet, and full hookups should obtain a site at the Council Bluff loop. Tent campers should ask for sites 60–67—with water and electric hookups, these are the only heavily wooded sites. Boaters prefer lake level sites at Willow Point, with water and electric hookups. All sites are relatively spacious, with back-in gravel parking and at least a little shade. The park's extremely rural location makes it fairly safe even though there is no locked gate at night. The Panhandle Plains are cold in the winter and hot in the summer. Visit in spring or fall. Avoid summer weekends, when this state park more closely resembles a theme park.

Basics

Operated By: Texas Parks & Wildlife. **Open:** All year. **Site Assignment:** Reservations (512) 389-8900, reservations must be made at least 48 hours in advance, deposit required (equivalent to first night's fee) to hold reservation, cancellations more than two days prior to reservation result in $5 fee, cancellations within two days of reservation result in loss of deposit. **Registration:** Headquarters. **Fee:** $3 per person per day for anyone aged 13 & older, $8 tent-only camp sites, $11sites w/electric, $12 sites w/electric & sewer, $2 for third vehicle at a campsite (cash, checks, D, V, MC). **Parking:** At site.

Facilities

Number of RV Sites: 8. **Number of Tent-Only Sites:** 12 sites w/water in area, 8 sites w/water, electric. **Hookups:** water, electric (30, 50 amps), sewer. **Each Site:** picnic table, grill. **Dump Station:** Yes. **Laundry:** No. **Pay Phone:** Yes. **Rest Rooms and Showers:** Yes. **Fuel:** No. **Propane:** No. **Internal Roads:** Paved. **RV Service:** Inquire at campground. **Market:** 8 mi. southwest toward Brownwood. **Restaurant:** 8 mi. southwest toward Brownwood. **General Store:** Wal-Mart 20 mi. in Brownwood. **Vending:** Beverages. **Swimming:** No. **Playground:** No. **Other:** Volleyball court, basketball court, softball field, park store, boat launches, floating boat dock w/boat slip & courtesy fuel dock, cabins, screened shelters, group camping, dining, & lodge facilities. **Activities:** picnicking, hiking, boating (motors, water skis & jet skis all allowed), fishing, swimming, bird-watching. **Nearby Attractions:** Howard Payne College, Douglas McArthur Academy of Freedom, Camp Bowie Memorial Park, Coleman City Park, Camp Colorado Museum Replica. **Additional Information:** Brownwood Chamber of Commerce (915) 646-9535.

Restrictions

Pets: Leash Only. **Fires:** In grills & fire rings only. **Alcoholic Beverages:** Prohibited. **Vehicle Maximum Length:** 65 ft. (all sites are back-in). **Other:** Max. 8 people per campsite, Quiet time 10 p.m.–6 a.m., fourteen day stay limit, gathering of firewood prohibited, special pet restrictions, number of vehicles per campsite is restricted (call for details), swim at your own risk.

To Get There

From Brownwood, go northwest on State Hwy. 279 for 16 mi. Turn right on Park Rd. 15 and follow it for 6 mi. to the park entrance.

BURNET
Inks Lake State Park

Rte. 2 Box 31, Burnet 78611. T: (512) 793-2223; F: (512) 793-2065; www.tpwd.state.tx.us.

RV ★★★★ Tent ★★★★

Beauty: ★★★★ Site Privacy: ★★★
Spaciousness: ★★★ Quiet: ★★★
Security: ★★★★ Cleanliness: ★★★★
Insect Control: ★★★★ Facilities: ★★★★

Pink granite hills, cedar and oak woodlands, and a constant level of activity: Inks Lake provide the backdrop for a variety of recreation, including a 9-hole golf course. Inks Lake supports bass, crappie, and catfish, while the land supports turkey quail and many other species. The area is famous for its spring wildflowers. Campgrounds are partially shaded, with mid-sized sites and paved back-in parking. Tent sites include paved tent pads. Tent campers looking for ample space and lake views should ask for 311, 314, 317, 333, or 346. RV campers should ask for 43, 48, 65, 67, 92, 279, or 287. Families should consider a site adjacent to one of the six playgrounds or the swimming beach. Spring and early summer are ideal times to visit, since late summer is very hot and autumn can be rainy. There is no gate at Inks Lake, but its remote location makes it fairly safe.

Basics

Operated By: Texas Parks & Wildlife. **Open:** All year. **Site Assignment:** Reservations (512) 389-8900; reservations must be made at least 48 hours in advance; deposit (equivalent to first night's fee) required to hold reservation; cancellations more than two days prior to reservation result in $5 fee, cancellations within two days of reservation result in loss of deposit. **Registration:** Headquarters. **Fee:** $4 per person per day for anyone aged 13 & over, $15 for sites w/water & electric, $10 for sites w/water only, $8 for primitive tent sites, excess fee required for more than two vehicles per site (cash, checks, V, MC, D). **Parking:** At most sites.

Facilities

Number of RV Sites: 137 w/water & 50-amp hookups. **Number of Tent-Only Sites:** 50 tent only w/water at each site, 10 walk-in, tent only w/water & electric, 9 walk-in primitive. **Hookups:** Water, electric (30, 50 amps). **Each Site:** picnic table, lantern hanger, fire pit/grill combination. **Dump Station:** Yes. **Laundry:** No. **Pay Phone:** Yes. **Rest Rooms and Showers:** Yes. **Fuel:** No. **Propane:** No. **Internal Roads:** Paved. **RV Service:** 21 mi. south in Marble Falls. **Market:** 12 mi. east in Burnet. **Restaurant:** Floating restaurant on Inks Lake, 3 mi. east or west. **General Store:** In park, hardware 12 mi. in Burnet, Wal-Mart 21 Mi. in Marlboro Falls. **Vending:** Yes. **Swimming:** No. **Playground:** Yes. **Other:** 9-hole golf course, picnic area, amphitheater, fishing piers, boat ramp, mini cabins, screened shelters, park store. **Activities:** Hiking, backpacking, golf (cart & club rental available), lake swimming, fishing, waterskiing, scuba diving, guided tours at specific times, boating (canoe, paddle boat, & surfbike rentals available at park store). **Nearby Attractions:** Lyndon B. Johnson Ranch & State Historical Parks, Vanishing Texas river cruise, Lake Buchanon & Buchanon Dam, towns of Burnet, Fredericksburg, & Johnson City, numerous Hill Country lakes & state parks. **Additional Information:** Inks Lake & Lake Buchanon Chamber of Commerce (512) 793-2803, Burnet Chamber of Commerce (512) 756-4297.

Restrictions

Pets: On leash. **Fires:** In fire rings only. **Alcoholic Beverages:** Prohibited. **Vehicle Maximum Length:** 70 ft. **Other:** Follow boat launch protocol; swim at your own risk.

To Get There

From Burnet, drive west on State Hwy. 29 for 9 mi. Turn left on Park Rd. 4 and drive south for 3 mi. to the park headquarters.

CADDO
Possum Kingdom State Park

P.O. Box 70, Caddo 76429. T: (940) 549-1803 or (800) 792-1112; F: (940) 549-0741; www.tpwd.state.tx.us.

RV ★★★ Tent ★★★

Beauty: ★★★ Site Privacy: ★★★
Spaciousness: ★★★ Quiet: ★★★
Security: ★★★★★ Cleanliness: ★★★
Insect Control: ★★ Facilities: ★★★★

The 20,000-acre Lake Possum Kingdom offers exceptionally clear water, attracting snorkelers and scuba divers. The lake supports crappie, perch, and various bass and catfish species. The park offers extensive fishing facilities. Five campgrounds are situated along the lakeshore. Walk-in campsites have no potties and fire-rings only. Happy with water only? Try sites 79–85 and 100, 104, 105, and 113 in the Chaparral Trail area. With full hookups and proximity to the playground and beach, the Spanish Oaks area is good for RV campers with children. Tent campers enjoy the Lakeview area, which offers water and electric hookups. Sites 22–26 have nice views. Most sites are partially shaded, with paved back-in parking. Site size varies immensely—arrive early for your choice of sites. Security is excellent due to extreme remoteness. Low year-round humidity and pleasant swimming make this park bearable (and crowded) in late summer. Visit any time except busy summer weekends.

Basics

Operated By: Texas Parks & Wildlife. **Open:** All year. **Site Assignment:** Reservations (512) 389-8900, reservations must be made at least 48 hours in advance, deposit required (equivalent to first night's fee) to hold reservation, cancellations more than two days prior to reservation result in $5 fee, cancellations within two days of reservation result in loss of deposit. **Registration:** Headquarters. **Fee:** $3 per person per day for anyone aged 13 & older, $6 walk-in primitive tent camping, $10 water-only sites, $10 water & electric, $15 premium water & electric (cash, checks, V, MC, D). **Parking:** At most sites.

Facilities

Number of RV Sites: 60 sites w/water, electric. **Number of Tent-Only Sites:** 55 sites w/water close by. **Hookups:** Water, electric (30 amps). **Each Site:** Picnic table, either fire ring or grill. **Dump Station:** Yes. **Laundry:** No. **Pay Phone:** Yes. **Rest Rooms and Showers:** Yes. **Fuel:** Yes. **Propane:** No. **Internal Roads:** Paved. **RV Service:** 50 mi. east in Mineral Wells. **Market:** Marina store in park. **Restaurant:** 18 mi. North on Possum Kingdom Lake. **General Store:** Marina store in park, 32 mi. to Wal-Mart in Breckinridge or Graham. **Vending:** Beverages only. **Swimming:** No. **Playground:** Yes. **Other:** Concrete boat ramp w/courtesy dock, gas dock, covered slip rental, marina store (hours vary w/season), fishing pier, fish-cleaning facility. **Activities:** Boating (motorized & non-motorized boat rentals available), jet skiing (rentals available), fishing, waterskiing, swimming, hiking, biking. **Nearby Attractions:** Fort Griffin & Fort Richardson state historical parks. **Additional Information:** Possum Kingdom Chamber of Commerce (888) 779-8330.

Restrictions

Pets: Leash Only. **Fires:** In grills & fire rings only. **Alcoholic Beverages:** Not allowed. **Vehicle Maximum Length:** 40 ft. **Other:** Max. 8 people per campsite, Quiet time 10 p.m.–6 a.m., 14 day stay limit, swim at your own risk, follow boat launch protocol, gathering of firewood prohibited.

To Get There

From I-20, take exit 414. Go west on US 180, through the towns of Weatherford and Palo Pinto. Continue to go west on 180 for 25 mi. past Palo Pinto, until you reach a blinking light. Then turn right onto Park Rd. 33. Go north on Park Rd. 33 for 17 mi. Road ends at park entrance.

CALLIHAM, THREE RIVERS

Choke Canyon State Park

P.O. Box 2, Calliham 78007. T: (361) 786-3868; F: (361) 786-3414.

RV ★★★★ Tent ★★★★

Beauty: ★★★	Site Privacy: ★★★★
Spaciousness: ★★★★	Quiet: ★★★★
Security: ★★★★★	Cleanliness: ★★★★
Insect Control: ★	Facilities: ★★★★★

Many Mexican bird species grace Choke Canyon Reservoir, which forms the northern border of their natural range. Birding is augmented with feeders and trails. Of the two park units, Calliham hosts more birds and is more densely wooded. The reservoir supports various bass, catfish, and sunfish species, as well as crappie, bluegill, carp, and gar. The park provides excellent facilities for anglers. The campgrounds aren't gorgeous, but they are tidy and functional. Sites are large, with gravel, back-in parking. Most have partial shade. For water views, head for RV sites 115–131 at Calliham. RV sites 106–108 are the most shady and private. For tents, we prefer sites 200–218, which are situated on a 75-acre lake at Calliham. Security is excellent at Choke Canyon; the park is extremely remote with locked gates at night. For the best weather, visit in spring or fall. Crowds are only a problem on holiday weekends.

Basics

Operated By: Texas Parks & Wildlife. **Open:** All year. **Site Assignment:** Reservations (512) 389-8900, reservations must be made at least 48 hours in advance, deposit required (equivalent to first night's fee) to hold reservation, cancellations more than two days prior to reservation result in $5 fee, cancellations within two days of reservation result in loss of deposit. **Registration:** Headquarters. **Fee:** $3 per person per day for anyone aged 13 & older, $14 for sites w/water & electricity, $9 for sites w/water only (cash, checks, V, MC, D). **Parking:** At most sites.

Facilities

Number of RV Sites: 40 sites w/water & electricity. **Number of Tent-Only Sites:** 19 sites w/water only. **Hookups:** Water, electric (30, 50 amps). **Each Site:** Picnic table, lantern post, fire ring, shade covers at Calliham Unit. **Dump Station:** Yes. **Laundry:** No. **Pay Phone:** Yes. **Rest Rooms and Showers:** Yes. **Fuel:** 0.25 mi. outside park. **Propane:** 0.25 mi. outside park. **Internal Roads:** Paved. **RV Service:** 75 mi. southeast in Corpus Christi. **Market:** 12 mi. east in Three Rivers. **Restaurant:** 3.5 mi. east of park. **General Store:** 12 mi. east in Three Rivers. **Vending:** Beverages only. **Swimming:** Pool (Memorial Day–Labor Day). **Playground:** Yes. **Other:** Calliham Unit: screened shelters, picnic area, group picnic area, group dining hall, group rec hall, amphitheater, sports complex (including gym & stage), swimming pool bathhouse, shuffleboard, tennis, volleyball, & full basketball courts, wildlife viewing blind, bird trail w/feeders, interpretive center, boat ramps. South Shore Unit: Shaded picnic area, group picnic pavilions, concession stand, baseball diamond, volleyball court, boat ramps, canoe launch, fishing platform, fish cleaning area, overlook shelters, The North Shore Area (1700 acres includes primitive group camping, equestrian camping, boat ramps, hunting in season). **Activities:** Picnicking, boating, fishing, hiking, backpacking, birding, lake beach & pool swimming, various team sports, educational & interpretive programs. **Nearby Attractions:** Lake Corpus Christi State Park, Lipantitlan State Historical Park, San Antonio (about 80 mi.), Corpus Christi (about 70 mi.). **Additional Information:** Three Rivers Chamber of Commerce (361) 786-2528, San Antonio CVB (800) 447-3372, Corpus Christi Area Convention & Tourist Bureau (800) 678-6232.

Restrictions

Pets: On leash only. **Fires:** In fire rings only. **Alcoholic Beverages:** Prohibited. **Vehicle Maximum Length:** 50 ft.

To Get There

To reach the South Shore Unit from Three Rivers, drive west on State Hwy. 72 for 3.5 mi. To reach the Callaham Unit from Three Rivers, drive west on State Hwy. 72 for 12 mi.

CANYON

Palo Duro Canyon State Park

RR 2 Box 285, Canyon, 79015. T: (806) 488-2227; F: (806) 488-2556; www.tpwd.state.tx.us.

RV ★★★★ Tent ★★★★

Beauty: ★★★★	Site Privacy: ★★★
Spaciousness: ★★★	Quiet: ★★★
Security: ★★★★★	Cleanliness: ★★★★
Insect Control: ★★★	Facilities: ★★★★

At 800 feet deep, 120 miles long, and 0.5 to 20 miles wide, Palo Duro is the second-largest canyon in the U.S. Exposed rock includes white gypsum, red claystone, and gray, yellow, and lavendar mudstone. The park's mascot is "The Lighthouse", a 300-foot rock spire. Hardwoods throughout the canyon include juniper and mesquite. The canyon rim supports short grass prairie. Campsites vary in privacy and spaciousness, with some 60 feet from neighbors and others stacked together. Low trees and brush provide no shade. Parking is paved. RV campers enjoy pull-throughs at the Hackberry area (30-amp service). Need 50-amp service? Try the Sagebrush area (sites 137 and 139 are pull-throughs). The Mesquite area has gorgeous views of red rock formations. Security is excellent— the park is in a remote area and locks its gate at night. If you're not seeing *Texas,* the musical, visit in spring or fall. Otherwise, visit during the week.

Basics

Operated By: Texas Parks & Wildlife. **Open:** All year. **Site Assignment:** Reservations (512) 389-8900; reservations must be made at least 48 hours in advance; deposit (equivalent to first night's fee) required to hold reservation; cancellations more than two days prior to reservation result in $5 fee, cancellations within two days of reservation result in loss of deposit. **Registration:** Headquarters. **Fee:** $3 per person per day for anyone aged 13 & over, $12 for sites w/water & electric, $9 for primitive tent camping (cash, checks, V, MC, D). **Parking:** At site.

FACILITIES

Number of RV Sites: 83 sites w/water & electricity. **Number of Tent-Only Sites:** 22 w/water nearby. **Hookups:** Water, electric (30, 50 amps). **Each Site:** Picnic table, grill, some have shade shelters. **Dump Station:** Yes. **Laundry:** No. **Pay Phone:** Yes. **Rest Rooms and Showers:** Yes. **Fuel:** Yes. **Propane:** No. **Internal Roads:** Paved. **RV Service:** 30 mi. north in Amarillo. **Market:** In park. **Restaurant:** In park. **General Store:** In park, or Wal-Mart 14 mi. west in Canyon. **Vending:** Yes. **Swimming:** No. **Playground:** Yes. **Other:** Equestrian area, interpretive center, gift shop, park store, picnic area, amphitheatre, historical markers, equestrian camping area, separate trails for hiking, mountain biking, & equestrian use. **Activities:** Guided tours, hiking, horseback riding, mountain biking, bird-watching, & scenic drives, TEXAS musical drama nightly during the summer (no Wed. performances). **Nearby Attractions:** Cowboy Morning at Figure 3 Ranch, Panhandle Plains Museum, Storyland Zoo for Children, Nielson Memorial Museum, Alibates Flint Quarries National Monument, Lake Meredith National Recreation Area, Amarillo. **Additional Information:** Amarillo Convention & Visitor Council (800) 692-1338, TEXAS box office (806) 655-2181.

RESTRICTIONS

Pets: On leash only. **Fires:** In grill only. **Alcoholic Beverages:** Prohibited. **Vehicle Maximum Length:** 60 ft. **Other:** Be aware of flash flood precautions & rough terrain.

TO GET THERE

From I-27, take Exit 106, State Hwy. 217. Go east on 217 for 8 mi.

CEDAR HILL

Cedar Hill State Park

1570 FM 1382, Cedar Hill, 75104. T: (972) 291-6641; F: (972) 291-0209; www.tpwd.state.tx.us.

RV ★★★★★ Tent ★★★★★

Beauty: ★★★★★	Site Privacy: ★★★★
Spaciousness: ★★★★	Quiet: ★★★★★
Security: ★★★★★	Cleanliness: ★★★★
Insect Control: ★★	Facilities: ★★★★★

This is one of the finest suburban parks we've seen. The 7,500-acre Lake Joe Pool supports catfish, crappie, and largemouth and white bass. The on-site Penn Farm Agricultural History Center houses a cast of farm animals, headlined by Vern the fainting goat. The park's endangered tallgrass prairie remnants include a variety of grasses and wildflowers. Four campgrounds contain 355 multi-use sites. Sites have paved, back-in parking. Most are large with shady trees and foliage between sites. For proximity to the beach and marina, RV campers prefer sites on the outside of loop G (Lakeview Camping Area). Families prefer sites on the inside of loop G, which encircles the playground. Tent campers should ask for a lake view (sites 263–265 and 267–270 are lovely). This park is perennially crowded—avoid busy summer weekends. If visiting on a holiday, book 11 months in advance. Excellent security includes vigilant peace officers and locked gates at night.

BASICS

Operated By: Texas Parks & Wildlife. **Open:** All year. **Site Assignment:** Reservations (512) 389-8900; reservations must be made at least 48 hours in advance; deposit (equivalent to first night's fee) required to hold reservation; cancellations more than two days prior to reservation result in $5 fee, cancellations within two days of reservation result in loss of deposit. **Registration:** Headquarters. **Fee:** $5 per person per day for anyone aged 13 & over, $15 for sites w/water & electric, $7 for primitive tent camping (cash, checks, V, MC, D). **Parking:** At site, except for primitive tent sites.

FACILITIES

Number of RV Sites: 325. **Number of Tent-Only Sites:** 30 walk-in primitive sites. **Hookups:** Water, electric (30 amps). **Each Site:** Fire ring/grill combination, lantern post, picnic table, tent pad. **Dump Station:** Yes. **Laundry:** No. **Pay Phone:** Yes. **Rest Rooms and Showers:** Yes. **Fuel:** Inside park at marina store. **Propane:** 1.5 mi. east in Cedar Hill. **Internal Roads:** Paved. **RV Service:** 1.5 mi. east in Cedar Hill. **Market:** 1.5 mi. east in Cedar Hill. **Restaurant:** 1.5 mi. east in Cedar Hill. **General Store:** K-Mart 1.5 mi. east in Cedar Hill. **Vending:** Yes. **Swimming:** No. **Playground:** Yes. **Other:** Penn Farm Agricultural History Center (self guided tours, farm animals, organic garden), marina store (groceries, fast food grill, boat rentals, fishing barge, gasoline), two boat ramps, picnic area, group picnic area, gift shop, extensive compost demonstration site. **Activities:** Hiking, mountain biking, picnicking, boating, waterskiing, jet skiing, fishing, lake swimming, bird-watching. **Nearby Attractions:** Dallas-Fort Worth Metroplex attractions (see Texas introduction). **Additional Informa-**

tion: Joe Pool Marina Store (972) 299-9010, Dallas CVB (800) 232-5527, Fort Worth CVB (800) 433-5747.

RESTRICTIONS

Pets: On leash only. **Fires:** In fire ring only. **Alcoholic Beverages:** Prohibited. **Vehicle Maximum Length:** 50 ft.

TO GET THERE

From I-20 take Exit 457, Hayes Rd. (FM 1382). Drive south for 4 mi. The park entrance is on the right. From Cedar Hill and US 67, exit at FM 1382 and go north for 2.5 mi. The entrance is on the left.

COMSTOCK

Seminole Canyon State Historical Park

P.O. Box 820, Comstock 78837. T: (915) 292-4464 or (800) 792-1112; F: (915) 292-4596; www.tpwd.state.tx.us.

RV ★★★★★ Tent ★★★★★

Beauty: ★★★★★ Site Privacy: ★★★★
Spaciousness: ★★★★ Quiet: ★★★★★
Security: ★★★★★ Cleanliness: ★★★★★
Insect Control: ★★★ Facilities: ★★★★

Deep canyons, big skies, and rocky terrain create a stunning landscape. Awesome vistas at Seminole Canyon belie the region's harshness (annual rainfall is 15 to 18 inches). The brochure states, "almost everything in this environment bites, stings, or scratches." Nonetheless, human habitation dates back thousands of years. Prehistoric petroglyphs endure in rock shelters (viewed by guided tour only). Diverse wildlife includes many bird species unique to Mexican borderlands. The multiuse campground contains few sites—forget about choosing your own. Sites are spacious with enough short scrubby brush between them to provide a little privacy. There is no shade here, so plan accordingly. Most every site has a stunning view. Parking is back-in and paved. Security is excellent at Seminole Canyon due to its extreme remoteness. Plan to visit in the fall, as this park experiences heavy traffic in the spring and intense heat in the summer.

BASICS

Operated By: Texas Parks & Wildlife. **Open:** All year. **Site Assignment:** Reservations (512) 389-8900, reservations must be made at least 48 hours in advance, deposit required (equivalent to first night's fee) to hold reservation, cancellations more than two days prior to reservation result in $5 fee, cancellations within two days of reservation result in loss of deposit. **Registration:** Headquarters. **Fee:** $2 per person per day for anyone aged 13 & older, $11 for sites w/electricity, $8 for sites w/water only (cash, checks, V, MC, D). **Parking:** At site.

FACILITIES

Number of RV Sites: 23. **Number of Tent-Only Sites:** None. **Hookups:** Water, electric (30 amps). **Each Site:** Picnic table, shade shelter, tent pad, fire ring or grill. **Dump Station:** Yes. **Laundry:** No. **Pay Phone:** Yes. **Rest Rooms and Showers:** Yes. **Fuel:** No. **Propane:** No. **Internal Roads:** Paved. **RV Service:** 42 mi. east in Del Rio. **Market:** 9 mi. east in Comstock. **Restaurant:** 9 mi. east in Comstock. **General Store:** 42 mi. east in Del Rio. **Vending:** Snacks at park headquarters 8 a.m. to 5 p.m. **Swimming:** No. **Playground:** No. **Other:** Interpretive center, picnic area, gift shop. **Activities:** Guided Tours of Seminole Canyon, Hiking, mountain biking, historical study, nature interpretation. **Nearby Attractions:** Judge Roy Bean Visitor Center in Langtry, Lake Amistad National Recreation Area (about 35 mi.), Whitehead Memorial Museum & The Old Perry Store in Del Rio (about 42 mi.). **Additional Information:** Del Rio Chamber of Commerce (830) 775-3551, Judge Roy Bean Visitor's Center (830) 291-3340.

RESTRICTIONS

Pets: Leash only. **Fires:** in designated areas only. **Alcoholic Beverages:** Not allowed. **Vehicle Maximum Length:** 45 ft. **Other:** Canyons are closed to the public except for guided tours, Max. 8 people per campsite, Quiet time 10 p.m.–6 a.m., fourteen day stay limit, gathering of firewood prohibited.

TO GET THERE

From Del Rio drive west on US 90 for 40 mi. The park entrance is 9 mi. past the town of Comstock, just east of the Pecos River Bridge.

CONCAN

Garner State Park

HCR 70 Box 599, Concan, 78838. T: (830) 232-6132; F: (830) 232-6139; www.tpwd.state.tx.us.

RV ★★★★ Tent ★★★★★

Beauty: ★★★★★ Site Privacy: ★★★★
Spaciousness: ★★★★ Quiet: ★★★★

Security: ★★★★ Cleanliness: ★★★★
Insect Control: ★★★★ Facilities: ★★★★★

Garner's campgrounds are the most popular in the state. It's no wonder—the campgrounds are in a valley surrounded by beautiful rolling hills adorned with crooked Spanish and lacey oak. Garner offers unique recreation including jukebox dances and inner tubing the rapids of the Frio River. In season, the Friends of Garner State Park present the "Cowboy Sunset Serenade," celebrating American cowboys through poetry and songs. Of five camping areas, three have hookups. We prefer Live Oak area, which is quieter than Oakmont and Shady Meadows. It's also the best for families, with a playground next to the washhouse. Sites are spacious, with paved, back-in parking (pull-throughs available at other camp areas). Most are shady. We recommend even-numbered sites 334–358, which are a stone's throw from the Frio River. Security is very good at this remote park. Campgrounds are crowded spring, summer, and fall—make advance reservations.

Basics

Operated By: Texas Parks & Wildlife. **Open:** All year. **Site Assignment:** Reservations (512) 389-8900, reservations must be made at least 48 hours in advance, deposit required (equivalent to first night's fee) to hold reservation, cancellations more than two days prior to reservation result in $5 fee, cancellations within two days of reservation result in loss of deposit. **Registration:** Headquarters. **Fee:** $2 per person per day for anyone aged 13 & older, $20 for sites w/water & electricity, $10 for sites w/water only (cash, checks, V, MC, D). **Parking:** At site.

Facilities

Number of RV Sites: 146 reservable sites. **Number of Tent-Only Sites:** 205 (water only). **Hookups:** Water, electric (30 amps). **Each Site:** Picnic table, grill, fire ring, tent pad, some w/lantern hooks & shade shelters. **Dump Station:** Yes. **Laundry:** Yes. **Pay Phone:** Yes. **Rest Rooms and Showers:** Yes. **Fuel:** 9 mi. north in Leakey. **Propane:** 9 mi. north in Leakey. **Internal Roads:** Paved. **RV Service:** 100 mi. west in Del Rio. **Market:** In park. **Restaurant:** 9 mi. north in Leakey. **General Store:** 9 mi. north in Leakey. **Vending:** Beverages only. **Swimming:** No. **Playground:** Yes. **Other:** Screened shelters, overflow camping area, picnic shelter w/kitchen, dining hall, picnic sites, group camp area w/screened shelters, surfaced road area for bike riding & day hiking, unpaved hiking trails, gift shop, snack bar, mini-golf course, paddle boats & inner tubes. **Activities:** River swimming, tubing, boating, hiking, walking, bicycling, mini-golf, picnicking, fishing, & juke box dancing nightly in the summer. **Nearby Attractions:** Hill Country, Lost Maples, & Devil's Sinkhole Natural Areas, Kickapoo Cavern State Park, John Nance "Cactus Jack" Garner Museum in Uvalde, historic Mission Nuestra Senora de la C&elaria del Canon, Camp Sabinal, & Fort Inge. **Additional Information:** Frio Canyon Chamber of Commerce (830) 232-5222, Uvalde Chamber of Commerce (830) 278-3361.

Restrictions

Pets: On leash only. **Fires:** In fire rings only. **Alcoholic Beverages:** Prohibited. **Vehicle Maximum Length:** 30 ft. **Other:** Read safety warnings.

To Get There

From San Antonio take US 90 West to Sabinal. At Sabinal turn right onto US 127 and follow it for 30 mi. Turn right onto US 83 and go 8 mi. to FM 1050. Go 0.2 mi. and turn right onto Park Rd. 29.

COOPER

Cooper Lake State Park (Doctor's Creek Unit)

Rte. 3 Box 741, Cooper 75482. T: (512) 389-8900 or (800) 792-1112; F: (512) 389-8959; www.tpwd.state.tx.us; e-mail.reservations@tpwd.state.tx.us.

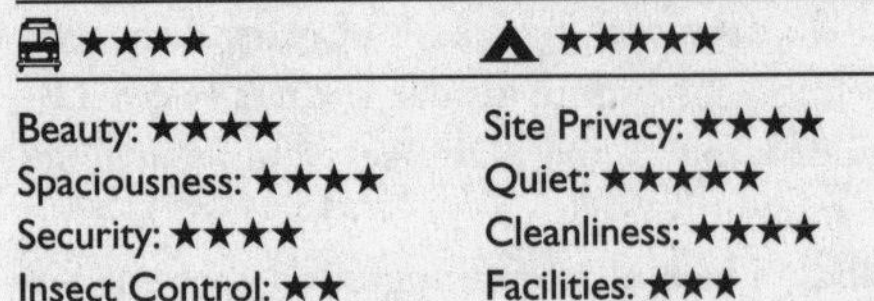

★★★★ ★★★★★

Beauty: ★★★★ Site Privacy: ★★★★
Spaciousness: ★★★★ Quiet: ★★★★★
Security: ★★★★ Cleanliness: ★★★★
Insect Control: ★★ Facilities: ★★★

Sites in this wilderness park are mostly grassy and forested, and they include 55-foot back-ins and 120-foot pull-throughs. Sites 1 and 42 at the entrance are well shaded, but rather close to the internal road. Site 4 is similarly close to the intersection of two internal roads, and it may not suit many campers due to the higher volume of passing traffic (which, admittedly, is still rather limited). Site 8 is reserved for the park host, and the sites on either side seem to be popular with campers either seeking the added security or the added companionship. Sites 12 and 13 are both back-ins on a concrete slab, and are very open to the sun. The best sites, depending on taste, are either 15–17 (although 17 is next to a parking area); 22 and 23, which back to the edge of the lake; or 22 (especially if 23 is unoccupied), which is well shaded, by the water, and somewhat secluded. The rest rooms are quite clean, well-lit, and spacious, with modern facilities. And as for activities in the park, there is plenty to do for anyone in the family. This park is a typical high-quality Texas state park, with water activities, sports, and hiking available. A definite destination for a family holiday.

Basics

Operated By: Texas Parks & Wildlife. **Open:** All year. **Site Assignment:** First come, first served. (Credit card required to make a reservation. $3 reservation service fee; $5 cancellation fee.). **Registration:** In office. (Late arrivals use drop box at entrance.). **Fee:** Water, electric: $12, water: $8, plus $2 entrance fee (V, MC, D accepted in the office or for reservation.). **Parking:** At site.

Facilities

Number of RV Sites: 42. **Number of Tent-Only Sites:** Combined. **Hookups:** Water, electric (30 amps). **Each Site:** Picnic table, grill, fire pit, lantern post. **Dump Station:** Yes. **Laundry:** No. **Pay Phone:** Yes. **Rest Rooms and Showers:** Yes. **Fuel:** No. **Propane:** No. **Internal Roads:** Paved. **RV Service:** No. **Market:** 3 mi. to Cooper. **Restaurant:** 3 mi. to Cooper. **General Store:** Yes. **Vending:** Yes. **Swimming:** Lake. **Playground:** Yes. **Other:** 6 shelters, 1 cottage, ampitheatre. **Activities:** Swimming, boating, fishing, hiking, mountain biking. **Nearby Attractions:** Sam Bell Maxey House State Historical Park, Bonham State Park, Lake Bob S&lin State Park. **Additional Information:** Doctor's Creek Unit Office: (903) 395-3100.

Restrictions

Pets: On 6-ft. leash, cleaned up after. **Fires:** In grills. **Alcoholic Beverages:** None. **Vehicle Maximum Length:** None. **Other:** All visitors must pay $2 entrance fee per day.

To Get There

From Business Hwy. 24 and Hwy. 154 (First and Dallas in the town square), go 1.3 mi. east on Hwy. 154 (Dallas), then turn south onto FM 1529 and go 1.6 mi. Turn right at the sign into the entrance.

CORPUS CHRISTI

Colonia del Rey RV Park

1717 Waldron Rd., Corpus Christi, 78418. T: (361) 937-2435; F: (361) 937-2929; www.gocamping america.com/coloniadelray; cldelrey@intcomm.net.

RV ★★★ Tent n/a

Beauty: ★★★★	Site Privacy: ★★★
Spaciousness: ★★★	Quiet: ★★★
Security: ★★★	Cleanliness: ★★★
Insect Control: ★★	Facilities: ★★★

This suburban park is convenient to cosmopolitan Corpus Christi attractions, Corpus Christi Naval Air Station, and gorgeous beaches at Padre Island National Seashore and Mustang Island. Most of the sites at this nice-looking campground are laid out in tidy rows of pull-throughs. Sites are decent-sized and partially shaded by palm and other tree species. Parking is on grass. The most attractive sites are in section 32. Families should head for sites 16–23, large sites near the pool and playground. The quietest sites are those in section 60. With no gates and no fence around the property, security is poor at Colonia Del Rey. Although the city regularly sprays, insects can be unbearable in this area. Prepare yourself with bug spray, and avoid southern Texas in late summer.

Basics

Operated By: Jan Moya. **Open:** All year. **Site Assignment:** Advance reservations are accepted, credit card number holds site for daily or weekly camping, $50 for monthly camping; 24-hour-7-day notice for cancellation. Sites are usually assigned by the campground. Check-in after 11 a.m. Check out by noon. **Registration:** Office. **Fee:** $23.00 for 2 people. $1.50 extra per person. $2 extra for a concrete lot. **Parking:** At site.

Facilities

Number of RV Sites: 200. **Number of Tent-Only Sites:** 0. **Hookups:** Water, sewer, electric (30, 50 amps), cable TV, phone, & dataport. **Each Site:** Picnic table. **Dump Station:** Yes. **Laundry:** Yes. **Pay Phone:** Yes. **Rest Rooms and Showers:** Yes. **Fuel:** No. **Propane:** Yes. **Internal Roads:** Paved. **RV Service:** Colonia del Rey RV Sales, (361) 937-5703. **Market:** 0.5 mi. north. **Restaurant:** 0.5 mi. north. **General Store:** 0.5 mi. north Wal-Mart. **Vending:** Beverages. **Swimming:** Pool. **Playground:** Yes. **Other:** rec hall. **Activities:** Planned activities, Mexico tours, swimming. **Nearby Attractions:** USS Lexington, Texas State Aquarium, The Colombus Ships, Greyhound Racetrack, Padre Island National Seashore. **Additional Information:** Corpus Christi Area Convention & Tourist Bureau (800) 678-6232, Padre Island National Seashore (361) 949-8068.

Restrictions

Pets: Leash only. **Fires:** No ground fires. **Alcoholic Beverages:** Allowed. **Vehicle Maximum Length:** 50 ft.

To Get There

From I-358, exit at Waldron Rd. Go south 0.5 mi. Entrance is on the left.

DAINGERFIELD

Daingerfield State Park

Rte. 3 Box 286-B, Daingerfield 75638. T: (512) 389-8900 or (800) 792-1112; F: (512) 389-8959; www.tpwd.state.tx.us; e-mail.reservations@ tpwd.state.tx.us.

RV: ★★★★★ Tent: ★★★★★

Beauty: ★★★★★ Site Privacy: ★★★★★
Spaciousness: ★★★★★ Quiet: ★★★★★
Security: ★★★★ Cleanliness: ★★★★
Insect Control: ★★ Facilities: ★★★

This state park has three smallish camping areas (approx 10 units each), which can all take RVs, but one of which (Big Pine) is off-limits for tents. This is just as well, since these are huge (120-foot) pull-throughs that overlook the water (1–5) or back to the water (6–10), and make the trip worthwhile for an RVer. The space is very generous, as is typical in Texas state parks, and any rig that can drive on the highway can fit into these sites. The rest room in the camping area also leaves nothing to be desired: it is big and clean, and has flush toilets and hot showers. The Dogwood camping area provides shaded electrical sites in a loop near the water. Site 17 is particularly close, while 18 and 19 have nice views of the lake. The Mountain View area is also in a loop, and offers secluded 40-foot back-ins away from the water (but with nary a mountain in view!). The best sites for someone wanting to get away from it all are 31, 33, and 34, which are on the furthest edge of a dead-end roundabout. Families, couples, and anyone with a love of the outdoors should find their way to Daingerfield State Park, which offers activities galore in a beautiful wilderness setting.

Basics

Operated By: Texas Parks & Wildlife. **Open:** All year. **Site Assignment:** First come, first served. (Credit card required to make a reservation. $3 reservation service fee; $5 cancellation fee.). **Registration:** In office. (Late arrivals use drop box at entrance.). **Fee:** RV: $14 (full), $12 (water, electric), plus $2 entrance fee (V, MC, D accepted in the office or for reservation.). **Parking:** At site.

Facilities

Number of RV Sites: 52. **Number of Tent-Only Sites:** Combined. **Hookups:** Water, sewer, electric (30 amps). **Each Site:** Picnic table, grill, fire pit, lantern post. **Dump Station:** Yes. **Laundry:** No. **Pay Phone:** Yes. **Rest Rooms and Showers:** Yes. **Fuel:** No. **Propane:** No. **Internal Roads:** Paved. **RV Service:** No. **Market:** 3 mi. to Daingerfield. **Restaurant:** 3 mi. to Daingerfield. **General Store:** Yes. **Vending:** Yes. **Swimming:** Lake. **Playground:** Yes. **Other:** Lodge, ampitheatre, boat ramp, fish cleaning station. **Activities:** Swimming, boating, fishing, hiking, mountain biking. **Nearby Attractions:** Lake Bob S&lin, Starr Mansion Historical State Park, Caddo Lake State Park, Atlanta State Park.

Restrictions

Pets: On 6-ft. leash, cleaned up after. **Fires:** In grills. **Alcoholic Beverages:** None. **Vehicle Maximum Length:** None. **Other:** All visitors must pay $2 entrance fee per day.

To Get There

From the junction of Hwy. 259 and Hwy. 49, go 2.4 mi. east on Hwy. 49. Turn right at the sign onto a paved road (the sign bearing the street name and number—Park Rd. 17—is not visible from Hwy. 49) and follow it to the entrance of the park.

DALLAS/FORT WORTH

Trader's Village RV Park and Campground

2602 Mayfield Rd., Gr& Prairie, 75052. T: (972) 647-8205; F: (972) 647-8585; www.tradersvillage.com; tvgprv@flash.net.

RV: ★★★ Tent: ★

Beauty: ★★★ Site Privacy: ★★
Spaciousness: ★★★ Quiet: ★★★

Security: ★★★ Cleanliness: ★★★
Insect Control: ★★★★ Facilities: ★★★

Trader's Village Flea Market covers 100 acres and accommodates 1,800 dealers. Open Sat. and Sun. all year, the flea market also offers food stands and children's rides and games. Call ahead for special event information. The campground is bland and completely flat. A few trees make the park aesthetically bearable but provide little shade. Most sites offer pull-through parking. Those on the perimeter of the campground offer back-in parking. Parking is paved, and each site has a little patch of grass. Sites in the 40s, 50s, 60s, 70s 80s, and 90s have the most mature trees. However, families should go for sites in the 200s, the closest to the pool and rec hall. We don't recommend this suburban campground unless you're buying or selling at Trader's Village. Security is fair—gates are never locked but the campground is patrolled by armed guards. Make advance reservations at Christmastime.

Basics

Operated By: Traders Village. **Open:** All year. **Site Assignment:** Advance reservations recommended, credit card number holds site, one day cancellation notice, call from 8:30 a.m. to 8 p.m.V, MC, AE, D, personal check & cash accepted. Check-in & check-out at 1 p.m. Sites held until 6 p.m. unless previous arrangements are made. **Registration:** At office. **Fee:** $25 for RV, $16 for tent. **Parking:** At site.

Facilities

Number of RV Sites: 212. **Number of Tent-Only Sites:** Tent area (40 ft. × 120 ft.) w/electricity & water in area. **Hookups:** Water, sewer, electric (50 amps). **Each Site:** Picnic table, BBQ pit. **Dump Station:** Yes. **Laundry:** Yes. **Pay Phone:** Yes. **Rest Rooms and Showers:** Yes. **Fuel:** Yes, no diesel. **Propane:** Yes. **Internal Roads:** Paved. **RV Service:** 10 mi. in Dallas. **Market:** In park. **Restaurant:** 0.25 mi. **General Store:** 0.25 mi. **Vending:** Yes. **Swimming:** Pool. **Playground:** Yes. **Other:** rec hall, mini-mart, hair salon. **Activities:** Shopping on weekends, festivals. **Nearby Attractions:** Six Flags, Hurricane Harbor, Fort Worth Stockyards, Texas Motor Speedway, Texas Rangers Baseball, Lone Star Park, DFW International Airport, Dallas Mavericks, Mesquite Rodeo, Dallas Cowboys, convention centers, numerous retail shops. **Additional Information:** Fort Worth CVB (800) 433-5747, Dallas CVB (800) 232-5527.

Restrictions

Pets: 2 pets per site, on leash only, never unattended. **Fires:** Not allowed. **Alcoholic Beverages:** Allowed. **Vehicle Maximum Length:** 45 ft. **Other:** Speed limit of 10 mph strictly enforced.

To Get There

From I-20, take the Great Southwest Pkwy. exit. Go north on Great Southwest Pkwy. 0.25 mi. to Mayfield Rd. Take a left on Mayfield Rd. Entrance is 300 yards on the right.

DENISON

Eisenhower State Park

50 Park Rd. 20, Denison 75020-4898.T: (512) 389-8900 or (800) 792-1112; F: (512) 389-8959; www.tpwd.state.tx.us; e-mail.reservations@tpwd.state.tx.us.

RV: ★★★★ Tent: ★★★★

Beauty: ★★★★ Site Privacy: ★★★
Spaciousness: ★★★★ Quiet: ★★★★★
Security: ★★★★ Cleanliness: ★★★★
Insect Control: ★★ Facilities: ★★★

This park is divided into five camping areas, along with a screened lean-to area. Armadillo Hill has 45-foot grassy back-ins. The sites are very open but are surrounded by forest. Sites 4 and 5 are very close to the playground, which some campers may not prefer. Sites 16–22 have a partial view of the water, but all sites are some distance from the water's edge. The rest rooms are clean and modern and have flush toilets, but there is no shower. Bois d'Arc Ridge has all 110-foot pull-throughs, making it the best bet for larger rigs, or anyone who doesn't want to spend time parking. These grassy sites are forested, offering good shade, but are also away from the water. The Cedar Hollow Group Trailer area consists of 110-foot pull-throughs on the blacktop, with no shade and no direct access to the water—not the prettiest camping area. Fossil Ridge, however, is much nicer, with grassy, forested sites that overlook the water (especially 152–155). The Elm Point area is similarly close to the water, with 40-foot back-ins but no shade. It would be difficult not to find a campsite to your liking in this state park, but as the office staff agree, don't come in the dead heat of Aug.!

Basics

Operated By: Texas Parks & Wildlife. **Open:** All year. **Site Assignment:** First come, first served.

(Credit card required to make a reservation. $3 reservation service fee; $5 cancellation fee.). **Registration:** In office. (Late arrivals use drop box at entrance.). **Fee:** RV: $15 (full), $13 (water, electric), water: $10, plus $2 entrance fee per person (V, MC, D accepted in the office or for reservation.). **Parking:** At site.

FACILITIES

Number of RV Sites: 214. **Number of Tent-Only Sites:** Combined. **Hookups:** Water, sewer, electric (30 amps). **Each Site:** Fire ring. **Dump Station:** Yes. **Laundry:** No. **Pay Phone:** Yes. **Rest Rooms and Showers:** Yes. **Fuel:** No. **Propane:** No. **Internal Roads:** Paved. **RV Service:** No. **Market:** 8 mi. south (Exit 69). **Restaurant:** 3 mi. across lake. **General Store:** Yes (marina). **Vending:** Yes. **Swimming:** Lake. **Playground:** Yes. **Other:** rec hall, pavillion, fish cleaning station, lighted fishing pier. **Activities:** Swimming, boating, fishing, hiking, mountain biking. **Nearby Attractions:** Eisenhower Birthplace Historical State Park, Bonham State Park, Lake Texoma, Hagerman National Wildlife Refuge. **Additional Information:** Eisenhower State Park Office: (903) 465-1956.

RESTRICTIONS

Pets: On 6-ft. leash, cleaned up after. **Fires:** In grills. **Alcoholic Beverages:** None. **Vehicle Maximum Length:** None. **Other:** All visitors must pay $2 entrance fee per day.

TO GET THERE

From Hwy. 75, take Exit 72 and turn north onto Hwy. 91. Go 1.7 mi. and turn left at the sign for the park (at the beginning of the dam). Follow the road 1.8 mi. to the park entrance.

DONNA

Victoria Palms

602 North Victoria Rd., Donna, 78537. T: (956) 464-7801; F: (956) 782-3232; www.victoriapalms.com; vicpalms@acnet.net.

RV ★★★ | Tent n/a

Beauty: ★★★★	Site Privacy: ★★★
Spaciousness: ★★★★	Quiet: ★★★★
Security: ★★★★	Cleanliness: ★★★★
Insect Control: ★★★★	Facilities: ★★★★

This retirement resort in suburban Donna offers extensive and well-maintained recreational facilities. Scheduled classes and entertainment (in-season) help this large complex retain a community atmosphere. It also offers easy access to shopping and restaurants and extremely tidy sites. The spacious sites are laid out in rows, and most feature back-in parking. All parking is paved. New sites are completely open, with no shade and no privacy. We recommend the older sites, which enjoy a bit of shade and privacy. Each of the older sites contains one lovely mature palm trees and one mature grapefruit tree. Guests are encouraged to pick their own grapefruits. In all other respects, the sites are exactly alike. This gated and fenced property offers good security. Avoid the Lower Rio Grande Valley in the summer, and be sure to make advance reservations in the winter.

BASICS

Operated By: Stephen Hynes. **Open:** All year. **Site Assignment:** Reservations for 1–3 month min., w/$250 deposit, $25 cancellation fee w/notice, call (800) 551-5303. **Registration:** At office. **Fee:** $23–$30. **Parking:** At site.

FACILITIES

Number of RV Sites: 760. **Number of Tent-Only Sites:** 0. **Hookups:** Water, sewer, electric (50 amps), cable TV, dataport. **Each Site:** 1 palm tree, 1 grapefruit tree, concrete parking slots, concrete patio. **Dump Station:** No. **Laundry:** Yes. **Pay Phone:** Yes. **Rest Rooms and Showers:** Yes. **Fuel:** No. **Propane:** Yes. **Internal Roads:** Paved. **RV Service:** 5 mi. south in Donna. **Market:** 5 mi. south in Donna. **Restaurant:** On site, open in the winter only. **General Store:** 10 mi. southwest in Weslaco. **Vending:** Yes. **Swimming:** Pool. **Playground:** No. **Other:** Tennis courts, mail room, card rooms, library, ballroom, beauty & barber shop, recreation center, lounge, sewing room, billiard room, exercise facilities, computer club, poolside bar. **Activities:** Fishing, hunting, arts & crafts, dancing, shuffleboard, horseshoes, golf. **Nearby Attractions:** Sabal Palm Audubon Center & Sanctuary, Gladys Porter Zoo, Brownsville Battlefields, CAF/ Confederate Air Force Rio Grande Valley Wing, Historic Brownsville Museum. **Additional Information:** Donna Chamber of Commerce (956) 464-3272, Rio Grande Valley Chamber of Commerce (956) 968-3141.

RESTRICTIONS

Pets: On leash only. **Fires:** In your own grill only. **Alcoholic Beverages:** Allowed. **Vehicle Maximum Length:** 60 ft.

TO GET THERE

From US 83, exit at Victoria Rd. and go south 0.25 mile, entrance on the left.

EL PASO

Mission RV Park

1420 RV Dr., El Paso 79928. T: (800) 447-3795 or (915) 859-1133; F: (915) 859-5201.

RV ★★★★	Tent ★★★
Beauty: ★★★	Site Privacy: ★★★★
Spaciousness: ★★★	Quiet: ★★★★
Security: ★★★★★	Cleanliness: ★★★★★
Insect Control: ★★★★	Facilities: ★★★★★

This huge RV park is laid out like a V, with the 2 branches off-limits to pets. While most areas border nothing much to look at (there is a mobile home along the "E" strip to the south/southwest and a residential area to the northeast), there is a farily nice view of the mountains from sites E69–97, only slightly spoiled by a commercial area in the foreground. Most of the perimeter of the park is fenced off with barbed wire; in the rest of the areas, a stone or chainlink fence provides security. Pull-throughs are a good 70 feet long and 21 feet wide; back-ins are equally wide and vary up to 45 feet long. While most sites are open to the sun without any tree cover, end sites do get the benefit of trees and other vegetation and are therefore the best sites. Back-ins D49–97 also have a tree and are therefore a good choice for those willing to forego a pull-through. The recreation areas are fenced off and well maintained. Likewise, the laundry facilities are huge, modern, and clean, with plenty of space and even an ironing board. Rest rooms and showers are clean and modern. This campground is a clean, safe, and delightful campground, lacking only in shade trees to be an unbeatable destination.

BASICS

Operated By: Dan Martinez. **Open:** All year. **Site Assignment:** Assigned upon registration (Flexible). **Registration:** In office. (Late arrivals register w/security in guard box at gate.). **Fee:** Full: $24, van: $17, tent: $15. **Parking:** At site.

FACILITIES

Number of RV Sites: 188. **Number of Tent-Only Sites:** 25. **Hookups:** Water, sewer, electric (30 & 50 amps). **Each Site:** Overturned cable spool for a table. **Dump Station:** Yes. **Laundry:** Yes. **Pay Phone:** Yes. **Rest Rooms and Showers:** Yes. **Fuel:** No. **Propane:** Yes (Mon. only). **Internal Roads:** Paved, in perfect condition. **RV Service:** Yes. **Market:** 4 mi. north or south. **Restaurant:** 2 mi. west. **General Store:** Yes. **Vending:** Yes. **Swimming:** Pool (indoor). **Playground:** Yes. **Other:** Jacuzzi, wash/wax RV service, dog walk, RV storage, sell utility trailers. **Activities:** Basketball, tennis, horseshoes, Mexico tours. **Nearby Attractions:** Casinos, Mexico. **Additional Information:** El Paso Chamber of Commerce, (915) 534-0500.

RESTRICTIONS

Pets: On leash, cleaned up after, restricted from 1/2 of park. **Fires:** In grills. **Alcoholic Beverages:** At sites. **Vehicle Maximum Length:** 75 ft. **Other:** No motorcycles (Rule sheet provided inside campground map).

TO GET THERE

From I-10, take Exit 34 east onto the north loop of Americas Ave. and drive 1.8 mi. As soon as possible, get into the far left lane and take the turnaround under the overpass. Drive 1.6 mi. on Joe Battle Blvd (straight through past the Van Buren exit). Turn right onto Rojas and drive 0.2 mi. Turn right onto RV Dr., then go another 0.2 mi. and turn left at the sign into the campground entrance. Pull in as far as possible past the office on the right to allow for others to enter.

GALVESTON

Galveston Island State Park

Rte. 4 Box 156A, Galveston 77554. T: (409) 737-1222, for Information Only (800) 792-1112; F: (409) 737-5496; www.tpwd.state.tx.us.

RV ★★★	Tent ★★
Beauty: ★★★	Site Privacy: ★
Spaciousness: ★★	Quiet: ★★★
Security: ★★★	Cleanliness: ★★★
Insect Control: ★	Facilities: ★★★★

Campsites are cookie-cutter dull and extremely close to one another. The draw is the pristine beach (mere yards from campsites) and its wildlife. Over 300 species of birds have been recorded here. Observation blinds and platforms enrich the bird-watching experience. Anglers appreciate the choice of ocean or freshwater intermittently stocked with bass, catfish, perch, and rainbow trout.Each Lilliputian campsite has paved back-in parking, and absolutely no shade or privacy. There is also a group camping area. Mosquitoes and heat can be brutal here. We recommend insect repellent and a golf-style umbrella for each member of the family. Visit during the week to avoid crowds. Go during late spring, summer, or fall if you plan to sun and swim. We visited in Dec., and the weather was pleasant for beach walks. This suburban park is situated on a major roadway—valuables should be protected, though gates are locked at night.

Basics

Operated By: Texas Parks & Wildlife. **Open:** All year. **Site Assignment:** Reservations (512) 389-8900, reservations must be made at least 48 hours in advance, deposit required (equivalent to first night's fee) to hold reservation, cancellations more than two days prior to reservation result in $5 fee, cancellations within two days of reservation result in loss of deposit. **Registration:** Headquarters. **Fee:** $3 per person per day for anyone aged 13 & over, $20 for premium sites w/50-amp hookups, $15 for premium sites w/30-amp hookups, $15 for standard sites w/50-amp hookups, $12 for standard sites w/30-amp hookups, excess fee required for more than two vehicles per site (cash, checks, D,V, MC). **Parking:** At site.

Facilities

Number of RV Sites: 170. **Number of Tent-Only Sites:** None. **Hookups:** water, electric (30, 50 amps). **Each Site:** Picnic table, grill, fire ring. **Dump Station:** Yes. **Laundry:** No. **Pay Phone:** Yes. **Rest Rooms and Showers:** Yes. **Fuel:** No. **Propane:** No. **Internal Roads:** Paved. **RV Service:** 25 mi. west in La Marque. **Market:** 2 mi. East in Galveston. **Restaurant:** 1 mi. East in Galveston. **General Store:** Wal-Mart 10 mi. East in Galveston. **Vending:** Beverages only. **Swimming:** No. **Playground:** No. **Other:** Bathhouse on the beach, outdoor showers, interpretive center, gift shop, screened shelters, fish cleaning shelter. **Activities:** Picnicking, fishing, bird-watching, hiking, walking, mountain biking, swimming (at your own risk). **Nearby Attractions:** Moody Gardens, numerous historical homes in Galveston, the Railroad Museum, the Str& Historical District, Tall Ship Elissa (an 1877 sailing vessel), the Seaport Museum, Ocean Star Offshore Drilling Rig & Museum, attractions in Houston & San Jacinto. **Additional Information:** Galveston Chamber of Commerce (409) 763-5326.

Restrictions

Pets: Leash Only. **Fires:** In grills & fire rings only. **Alcoholic Beverages:** Prohibited. **Vehicle Maximum Length:** 40 ft. **Other:** Max. 8 people per campsite, Quiet time 10 p.m.–6 a.m., 14 day stay limit, swim at your own risk, no glass on beach, beware of poisonous snakes, jellyfish, & undercurrents.

To Get There

From I-45, drive south on 61st St. to Seawall Blvd. Turn right on Seawall Blvd., and then right on Seawall (FM 3005). Follow FM 3005 for 10 mi. Park entrance is on the left.

HOUSTON

Houston Leisure RV Resort

1601 South Main St., Highlands 77562. T: (281) 426-3576; F: (281) 426-5258; www.gocampingamerica.com/houstonleisure; hlrvresort@houston.rr.com.

RV ★★★ | Tent ★★★

Beauty: ★★★ | Site Privacy: ★★★
Spaciousness: ★★★ | Quiet: ★★★
Security: ★★★ | Cleanliness: ★★★★
Insect Control: ★★ | Facilities: ★★★

Located in suburban Highlands, Houston Leisure is approximately 19 miles east of downtown Houston. There are restaurants and shopping within minutes of the park, and attractions such as Space Center Houston and the Battleship *Texas* are easily accessible. The campground is attractive and consists of nine rows of long narrow pull-throughs and five rows of back-ins. Parking spaces were paved in the past, but they now more closely resemble gravel. Site size is average, and site privacy is poor. Many of the sites have a shady tree or two while a few others are completely open. Security is fair—the office is attended until 11 p.m., but there are no gates. Avoid Houston in the heat of the summer.

Basics

Operated By: LLC. **Open:** All year. **Site Assignment:** Sites assigned; credit card number holds reservation, no-show charged one night. **Registration:** Office in store, night host & self-registration. **Fee:** $25 RV, $18 tent (3 nights max.); prices for 2 people, $2 per additional person (cash, checks, V, MC, D, AE). **Parking:** At site, in parking lot.

Facilities

Number of RV Sites: 205. **Number of Tent-Only Sites:** 5. **Hookups:** Water, sewer, electric (30, 50, 100 amps). **Each Site:** Picnic table, asphalt pad. **Dump Station:** Yes. **Laundry:** Yes. **Pay Phone:** Yes. **Rest Rooms and Showers:** Yes. **Fuel:** No. **Propane:** Yes. **Internal Roads:** Paved.

RV Service: 5 mi. in Channel View. **Market:** 1 mi. north. **Restaurant:** Within 1 mi. **General Store:** Park store, hardware 2 mi. in Highlands, Wal-Mart 10 mi. in Houston. **Vending:** No. **Swimming:** Pool. **Playground:** Yes. **Other:** Pavilion, exercise room. **Activities:** Basketball, tennis, horseshoes, shuffleboard. **Nearby Attractions:** Space Center Houston, Battleship Texas, Moody Gardens aquarium, rainforest & discovery pyramids, San Jacinto Monument & Battleground, Arm& Bayou Nature Center, Traders Village outdoor market, Lone Star Flight Museum in Galveston. **Additional Information:** Greater Houston CVB (800) 4-HOUSTON.

Restrictions

Pets: 6-ft. leash max. **Fires:** Not allowed (bring your own grill). **Alcoholic Beverages:** Allowed. **Vehicle Maximum Length:** 45 ft. (sites vary). **Other:** Quiet hours enforced.

To Get There

From Houston, take I-10 east to Exit 787/ Crosby-Lynchburg Rd. Drive north 0.5 mile on Crosby-Lynchburg Rd. and the Resort is on the right.

HUNTSVILLE

Huntsville State Park

P.O. Box 508, Huntsville 77342. T: (936) 295-5644, for information only call (800) 792-1112; F: (936) 295-9426; www.tpwd.state.tx.us.

RV ★★★★ Tent ★★★★

Beauty: ★★★★	Site Privacy: ★★★
Spaciousness: ★★★	Quiet: ★★★
Security: ★★★★	Cleanliness: ★★★
Insect Control: ★★★	Facilities: ★★★★

Because of its proximity to Houston and its rural feel, Huntsville State Park is one of the most popular state parks in Texas, with campgrounds booking to capacity months in advance. The 210-acre Lake Raven is stocked with crappie, perch, catfish, and bass. The gently sloping terrain is complemented by plenty of open space and three playgrounds. Huntsville is a great place for children to expend their seemingly limitless energy. Loblolly and short-leaf pines, trees typical of the Texas Pineywoods region, provide excellent shade cover. Campsites are spacious, with paved parking and some pull-throughs large enough to handle 56-foot RVs. The most private sites, 174 and 175, are quickly taken year-round. When planning your visit, avoid hot, humid Aug. and rainy Sep. Gates are locked at 10 p.m. making security good.

Basics

Operated By: Texas Parks & Wildlife. **Open:** All year. **Site Assignment:** Reservations (512) 389-8900, reservations must be made at least 48 hours in advance, deposit required (equivalent to first night's fee) to hold reservation, cancellations more than two days prior to reservation result in $5 fee, cancellations within two days of reservation result in loss of deposit. **Registration:** Headquarters. **Fee:** $3 per person per day for anyone aged 13 & older, plus $9 for tent-camping, $12 for RV camping (cash, checks, V, MC, D). **Parking:** At site.

Facilities

Number of RV Sites: 61. **Number of Tent-Only Sites:** 127. **Hookups:** Water, electric (20 amps). **Each Site:** Picnic table, grill, fire ring, lantern post. **Dump Station:** Yes. **Laundry:** No. **Pay Phone:** Yes. **Rest Rooms and Showers:** Yes. **Fuel:** No. **Propane:** No. **Internal Roads:** Paved. **RV Service:** 10 mi. south in New Waverly. **Market:** 5 mi. north in Huntsville. **Restaurant:** 5 mi. north in Huntsville. **General Store:** 5 mi. north in Huntsville. **Vending:** Beverages only, concession stand open May through Sep. **Swimming:** No. **Playground:** Yes. **Other:** S&y beach on lake, interpretive center, gift shop, group picnic shelter (capacity 75 people), group lodge (capacity 150 people). **Activities:** Picnicking, swimming, boating (rental of canoes, paddle boats, & flat-bottomed boats in season), fishing, hiking, biking, horseback riding. **Nearby Attractions:** General Sam Houston's Old Homestead, Sam Houston Memorial Museum, Sam Houston Visitor Center & Statue, The Walls Unit (the first Texas prison), the Prison Museum, Historic Huntsville (one of Texas' oldest towns). **Additional Information:** Horseback riding at Lake Raven Stables (936) 295-1985, Huntsville Chamber of Commerce (936) 295-8113.

Restrictions

Pets: Leash Only. **Fires:** In grills & fire rings only. **Alcoholic Beverages:** Prohibited. **Vehicle Maximum Length:** 56 ft. **Other:** Max. 8 people per campsite, Quiet time 10 p.m.–6 a.m., fourteen day stay limit, gathering of firewood prohibited.

To Get There

From Exit 109 on I-45, drive 6 mi. southwest on Park Rd. 40.

JOHNSON CITY

Pedernales Falls State Park

Rte. 1 Box 450, Johnson City 78636. T: (830) 868-7304, for information only call (800) 792-1112; F: (830) 868-4186; www.tpwd.state.tx.us.

RV ★★★★★ Tent ★★★★★

Beauty: ★★★★★	Site Privacy: ★★★★★
Spaciousness: ★★★★★	Quiet: ★★★★★
Security: ★★★	Cleanliness: ★★★★★
Insect Control: ★★★	Facilities: ★★★★

Striking limestone falls resulted from 300 million years of geological change. Hikers appreciate twenty miles of trails in this park. Ash and cypress trees are found along the river, while the drier woodlands support oak and juniper stands. Hill Country fauna includes the elusive golden-cheeked warbler. Multipurpose campsites with paved back-in parking are situated in one area. Spacious and heavily wooded, with dense foliage between each site, these are some of the most beautiful campsites in the state. The park also maintains a sponsored youth camping area. Atop the river bluffs is a hike-in primitive tent-camping area with nearby water and chemical toilets. Although there are no locked gates, security is good here because of the park's remote location (nine miles from Johnson City). Aug. and Sep. are wet and hot, and winter can be very cold here. Plan to visit in spring, early summer, or fall.

BASICS

Operated By: Texas Parks & Wildlife. **Open:** All year. **Site Assignment:** Reservations (512) 389-8900, reservations must be made at least 48 hours in advance, deposit required (equivalent to first night's fee) to hold reservation, cancellations more than two days prior to reservation result in $5 fee, cancellations within two days of reservation result in loss of deposit. **Registration:** Headquarters. **Fee:** $2 per person per day for anyone aged 13 & older, $16 for sites w/water, electric, $7 for tent-camping in primitive area (cash, checks, V, MC, D). **Parking:** At most sites.

FACILITIES

Number of RV Sites: 66. **Number of Tent-Only Sites:** 0. **Hookups:** Water, electric (20, 30 amps). **Each Site:** Picnic tables, fire ring, flat tent pad. **Dump Station:** Yes. **Laundry:** No. **Pay Phone:** Yes. **Rest Rooms and Showers:** Yes. **Fuel:** No. **Propane:** No. **Internal Roads:** Paved. **RV Service:** 34 mi. north in Marble Falls. **Market:** 10 mi. west in Johnson City. **Restaurant:** 10 mi. west in Johnson City. **General Store:** 34 mi. north in Marble Falls. **Vending:** Beverages. **Swimming:** No. **Playground:** No. **Other:** Horse corral (day use only), covered bird viewing station, amphitheater, sponsored youth group area, gift shop. **Activities:** picnicking, hiking, river swimming, tubing, wading, mountain biking, fishing, bird-watching, horseback riding. **Nearby Attractions:** Lyndon B. Johnson National & State Historic Parks (Johnson City), Admiral Nimitz Museum & Historical Center (Fredericksburg), numerous state parks & natural areas, numerous wineries, Austin attractions. **Additional Information:** Fredericksburg CVB (830) 997-6523, Austin CVB (800) 926-2282,.

RESTRICTIONS

Pets: Leash Only. **Fires:** In grills & fire rings only. **Alcoholic Beverages:** Prohibited. **Vehicle Maximum Length:** 45 ft. **Other:** Max. 8 people per campsite, Quiet time 10 p.m.–6 a.m., fourteen day stay limit, gathering of firewood prohibited, swim at your own risk, no pets or open fires allowed in primitive camping area.

TO GET THERE

From Austin, drive west on US 290 for 32 mi., then turn right on FM 3232. Drive north on FM 3232 for 6 mi. to the park entrance. From Johnson City drive east on FM 2766 for 9 mi. to the park entrance.

KARNACK

Caddo Lake State Park

Rte. 2 Box 15, Karnack 75661. T: (512) 389-8900 or (800) 792-1112; F: (512) 389-8959; www.tpwd.state.tx.us; e-mail.reservations@tpwd.state.tx.us.

RV ★★★★★ Tent ★★★★★

Beauty: ★★★★★	Site Privacy: ★★★★
Spaciousness: ★★★★	Quiet: ★★★★★
Security: ★★★★	Cleanliness: ★★★
Insect Control: ★★	Facilities: ★★★

Visitors to this state park who come in RVs should take note that the entrance road is quite steep in some areas, but visitors delight in the humongous pull-throughs with full hookups once they've negotiated their way in. The road is also a little more complicated because of several one-way streets, making it necessary to drive first to the day-use area (near Big Cypress Bayou), then cutting across to the left to the camping areas. The first camping area you come across is Mill Pond, which is off-limits to RVs. These are 40-foot sites that are very close to the water's edge (61–65 are right on the water), which can make them buggy. The most remote site is 60, at the end of the roundabout. The next camping area is Squirrel Haven, which merges into Armadillo Run. These two areas consist of 40-foot forested and grassy sites. Sites 37–45 are located across from a row of screened shelters. The best sites are 29 and 30, at the end of a roundabout. The last camping area, Woodpecker Hollow, is designed with the big rig in mind. These are 120-foot pull-through sites with full hookups. All sites are forested and grassy, and the best two are next to the camp host (21 and 23) at the end of the roundabout. These are probably the safest, most comfortable sites in the park. Anyone with an interest in nature or living in the wild should come to Caddo Lake State Park for a camping holiday. Boat rentals are available and make for a fun afternoon—especially if you catch sight of one of the lake's native alligators! Like other parks this far south, however, July and Aug. are unbearably hot, and Sep. and Oct. are very busy.

Basics

Operated By: Texas Parks & Wildlife. **Open:** All year. **Site Assignment:** First come, first served. (Credit card required to make a reservation. $3 reservation service fee; $5 cancellation fee.). **Registration:** In office. (Late arrivals use drop box at entrance.). **Fee:** RV: $15 (full), $12 (water, electric), water: $8, plus $2 entrance fee per person (V, MC, D accepted in the office or for reservation.). **Parking:** At site.

Facilities

Number of RV Sites: 28. **Number of Tent-Only Sites:** 20. **Hookups:** Water, sewer, electric (30 amps). **Each Site:** Picnic table, grill, fire pit. **Dump Station:** Yes. **Laundry:** No. **Pay Phone:** Yes. **Rest Rooms and Showers:** Yes. **Fuel:** No. **Propane:** No. **Internal Roads:** Paved. **RV Service:** No. **Market:** 13 mi. to Marshall. **Restaurant:** 13 mi. to Marshall. **General Store:** Yes. **Vending:** Yes. **Swimming:** Lake. **Playground:** Yes. **Other:** Canoe/boat rentals & tours, interpretive center, rec hall, cabins, ampitheatre, fishing pier. **Activities:** Swimming, boating, fishing, hiking, mountain biking, wildlife viewing. **Nearby Attractions:** Starr Family State Historical Park. **Additional Information:** Marshall Chamber of Commerce, (903) 935-7868; Caddo Lake Office, (903) 679-3351.

Restrictions

Pets: On 6-ft. leash, cleaned up after. **Fires:** In grills. **Alcoholic Beverages:** None. **Vehicle Maximum Length:** None. **Other:** All visitors must pay $2 entrance fee per day.

To Get There

From the junction of Hwy. 43/134 and FM 2198, go 0.5 mi. east on FM 2198. Turn left onto Park Rd. 2 and follow it to the park entrance.

KERRVILLE

Guadalupe River RV Resort

2605 Junction Hwy. 27, Kerrville, 78028. T: (830) 367-5676; F: (830) 367-3003; www.guadaluperiver rvresort.com; info@grrvr.com.

RV ★★★ | Tent n/a

Beauty: ★★★★	Site Privacy: ★★★
Spaciousness: ★★★★	Quiet: ★★★★
Security: ★★★	Cleanliness: ★★★★
Insect Control: ★★★★	Facilities: ★★★★

This new resort offers excellent amenities, including separate adult and family swimming pools. Charming Kerrville is known as a cultural hub. With fantastic weather, Kerrville is also known as a gateway to great outdoor recreation. Lost Maples State Natural Area and Kerrville-Schreiner State Park are both nearby. Many sites at Guadalupe River are extremely attractive, while others are unappealing. Stay away from the dull, noisy sites near Hwy. 27. Instead, try to score a riverfront site (1–10 or 50–61) and enjoy the gorgeous view of the gently sloping riverbank. Riverside sites have back-in parking, but most other sites are pull-throughs. All sites are spacious, with a large patch of grass at each site. Many are shady, though few are very private. All parking is paved. Security is passable; there are no gates, but the park is very remote. Visit popular Kerrville during the week.

Basics

Operated By: Gene, Marianne, & Martin Ellis. **Open:** All year. **Site Assignment:** Credit card required to hold reservation, call (800) 582-1916. 48 hour cancellation policy. Check-out at noon. **Registration:** At office. **Fee:** $26 per night for 2 people, $2 per extra person over age 6, $.09 per kilowatt hour for electricity. Cash or personal check are the only accepted forms of payment. **Parking:** On paved area at each site.

FACILITIES

Number of RV Sites: 202. **Number of Tent-Only Sites:** 0. **Hookups:** Water, sewer, electric (30, 50 amps), phone, cable TV. **Each Site:** Picnic tables, BBQ pits. **Dump Station:** Yes. **Laundry:** Yes. **Pay Phone:** Yes. **Rest Rooms and Showers:** Yes. **Fuel:** Once per week, otherwise, 1 mi. away. **Propane:** Once per week, otherwise, 1 mi. away. **Internal Roads:** Paved. **RV Service:** 0.25 mi. **Market:** 0.5 mi. **Restaurant:** 1 mi. **General Store:** At park. **Vending:** Yes. **Swimming:** Pool. **Playground:** Yes. **Other:** Two group facilities, pavilion w/BBQ pit, fireplace & dance floor, health spa, jacuzzi, steam room, sauna, game room, clubhouse, adult-only area. **Activities:** fishing, walking, boating, horseshoes, tetherball, ping pong, shuffleboard, volleyball, basketball, organized activities. **Nearby Attractions:** Hill County Arts Foundation, Point Theater, Stonehenge II, Scott Schreiner Municipal Golf Course, H.E.B. Municipal Tennis Center, Texas Arts & Crafts Fair, Cowboy Artists of America Museum. **Additional Information:** Kerrville CVB (800) 221-7958.

RESTRICTIONS

Pets: On 10-ft. max. leash at all times, even in river. **Fires:** In fire pits only. **Alcoholic Beverages:** Allowed. **Vehicle Maximum Length:** 55 ft. **Other:** No tent camping allowed.

TO GET THERE

From San Antonio, take I-10 west toward El Paso and take exit 505. Drive about 2 mi. south on FM 783. Take a right onto Hwy. 27 heading west, and the campground will be 2.5 mi. on the left.

LUMBERTON

Village Creek State Park

P.O. Box 8565, Lumberton 77657. T: (409) 755-7322; www.tpwd.state.tx.us.

RV ★★★★ Tent ★★★★

Beauty: ★★★★	Site Privacy: ★★★★
Spaciousness: ★★★★	Quiet: ★★★★★
Security: ★★★★★	Cleanliness: ★★★★
Insect Control: ★★★	Facilities: ★★★★

Village Creek is a wooded retreat surrounded by suburbia. The flat-water creek, a favorite amongst anglers and paddle-sports enthusiasts, winds southeasterly and eventually joins the Neches River. Abundant rainfall supports cypress swamps, water tupelo, and river birch. Birders spot egrets and herons. The campground includes long and narrow yet attractive sites. Site size and privacy vary—some are incredibly huge and secluded, others ho-hum. There are no creek-side RV sites due to flooding. However, tent-campers may choose walk-in sites along Village Creek. All sites are nicely wooded and shady. At the RV area, all sites are back-ins with paved parking. Sites 1 and 3 are very secluded. Security is good-the park is gated at night. Although native bats dine on mosquitoes, insects flourish after heavy rains in the warmer months. Call before you visit Village Creek to check on water levels. Make advance reservations at this extremely popular park.

BASICS

Operated By: Texas Parks & Wildlife. **Open:** All year. **Site Assignment:** Reservations (512) 389-8900; reservations must be made at least 48 hours in advance; deposit (equivalent to first night's fee) required to hold reservation; cancellations more than two days prior to reservation result in $5 fee, cancellations within two days of reservation result in loss of deposit. **Registration:** Office, after hours register next morning (gate locks at 10 p.m.). **Fee:** $10 developed, $6 primitive, plus $2 entrance fee per person 13 & older up to 8 people max. (cash, checks, V, MC, D). **Parking:** At site (2 cars), in parking lot about 75 yards from walk-in sites.

FACILITIES

Number of RV Sites: 25. **Number of Tent-Only Sites:** 16 walk-in primitive sites w/tent pad or clearing. **Hookups:** Water, electric (30 amps). **Each Site:** Picnic table, fire ring, lantern pole. **Dump Station:** Yes. **Laundry:** No. **Pay Phone:** Yes. **Rest Rooms and Showers:** Yes. **Fuel:** No. **Propane:** No. **Internal Roads:** Paved (gravel road to walk-in sites). **RV Service:** 2 mi. in Lumberton. **Market:** 1 mi. in Lumberton. **Restaurant:** 2 mi. in Lumberton. **General Store:** Park store, hardware & Wal-Mart 3 mi. in Lumberton. **Vending:** Beverages, ice. **Swimming:** No. **Playground:** Yes. **Other:** Picnic area, pavilion, rec hall, meeting room. **Activities:** swimming, fishing (local canoe rentals & fishing supplies), hiking, mountain biking, bird-watching, year-round nature study programs. **Nearby Attractions:** Sea Rim & Martin Dies Jr. State Parks, Big Thicket National Preserve, Cattail Marsh, Pleasure Island, Sabine Pass Battlefield, Beaumont museums, 80 mi. to Houston. **Additional Information:** Beaumont CVB (409) 880-3749 www.beaumont cvb.com.

Restrictions

Pets: 6-ft. leash max. **Fires:** Allowed, in fire rings (except under fire ban). **Alcoholic Beverages:** Not allowed. **Vehicle Maximum Length:** 55 ft. (sites vary). **Other:** No gathering firewood, dumping gray water.

To Get There

From Beaumont, drive north approximately 9 mi. on US 69/96 and take the Mitchell Rd. exit. Drive almost 0.5 mi. on the access road and turn right (east) onto Mitchell Rd. Immediately turn left (north) onto FM 3513/Village Creek Pkwy. Drive approximately 2 mi. and turn right (east) onto Alma Dr. Cross the railroad tracks, veer to the left and go 0.5 mi. to the park entrance.

MATHIS

Lake Corpus Christi State Park

Box 1167, Mathis 78368. T: (512) 547-2635; www.tpwd.state.tx.us.

RV ★★★★ Tent ★★★★

Beauty: ★★★★	Site Privacy: ★★★★
Spaciousness: ★★★★	Quiet: ★★★★
Security: ★★★★	Cleanliness: ★★★★
Insect Control: ★★★★	Facilities: ★★★

Anglers fish for catfish, bass, sunfish, and crappie in 21,000-acre Lake Corpus Christi. Adjacent Lake Corpus Christi State Park is instrumental in conserving the mesquite grassland ecosystem. Despite the park's gorgeous setting, there are no walking trails. There are four main camping loops: two contain full hookups and pull-through parking while the other two contain no hookups and back-in parking. For RVs, sites 1–23 are larger and more private than sites 24–48. There are no lakefront RV sites. Tent campers (or RVs foregoing hookups) should head for waterfront sites, including 57–66 and 91–99. All sites are spacious, with shade and privacy provided by mesquite trees and other brushy flora. Parking is paved and each site has a large patch of grass. Security is good at this remote park. Gates lock at night, and peace officers live on property. Convenient to Corpus Christi, the park stays busy from Feb. to Aug. Visit in autumn for tranquility.

Basics

Operated By: Texas Parks & Wildlife. **Open:** All year. **Site Assignment:** Inquire at campground. **Registration:** Inquire at campground. **Fee:** $16 for sites w/full hookups, $14 for sites w/water & electric, $8 for primitive tent sites, day use fee of $3 per person aged 13 & over. **Parking:** At site.

Facilities

Number of RV Sites: 60. **Number of Tent-Only Sites:** None. **Hookups:** Water, sewer, electric. **Each Site:** Picnic table (some covered), either BBQ pit or fire ring & grill. **Dump Station:** Yes. **Laundry:** No. **Pay Phone:** Yes. **Rest Rooms and Showers:** Yes. **Fuel:** No. **Propane:** No. **Internal Roads:** Paved. **RV Service:** 30 mi. southeast in Odem. **Market:** 3 mi. east in Mathis. **Restaurant:** 3 mi. east in Mathis. **General Store:** 3 mi. east in Mathis. **Vending:** Beverages only. **Swimming:** No. **Playground:** Yes. **Other:** Screened shelters, gift shop, picnic area, picnic pavilion, boat ramp, fishing pier, fish cleaning facility, scenic overlook. **Activities:** Lake swimming (at your own risk), fishing, boating, nature study. **Nearby Attractions:** Choke Canyon, Goose Island, & Mustang Island State parks; Fulton Mansion & Goliad State Historical parks, Padre Island National Seashore, Aransas Wildlife Refuge, Corpus Christi attractions. **Additional Information:** Corpus Christi Area Convention & Tourist Bureau (800) 678-6232.

Restrictions

Pets: Leash only. **Fires:** Fire rings, BBQ pits only. **Alcoholic Beverages:** Not allowed. **Vehicle Maximum Length:** 35 ft. **Other:** No lifeguards.

To Get There

From I-37, take exit 34 and drive southwest on TX 359 for 4 mi. Turn right onto FM 1068. The park entrance is on the left.

MEDINA

Las Avenues RV Resort

17740 State Hwy. 16 North, Medina, 78055. T: (830) 589-7766; F: (830) 589-2606; unameit@wire web.net.

RV ★★★ Tent n/a

Beauty: ★★★	Site Privacy: ★★★
Spaciousness: ★★★	Quiet: ★★★
Security: ★★	Cleanliness: ★★
Insect Control: ★★★★	Facilities: ★★★★

Las Avenues caters to residents, but overnighters also enjoy the nicely landscaped pool, golf course, and other amenities. Oddly, the campsites are not nearly as tidy as the recreational areas. The campground is laid out in an oblong loop with a creek flowing through the middle. Site size varies greatly, with long, tight pull-throughs and amply sized back-ins. Most sites are nicely shaded by live oak (complete with Spanish moss) and other tree species. Parking is on gravel with a grassy plot at each site. Sites 28–32 are the quietest and enjoy a lovely view of the hills. Security at Las Ave.s is fair. Gates are kept open during the day and the park is visible from Hwy. 16. Though the park has the mellow atmosphere of a retirement community, children are welcome. Visit Texas Hill Country in the spring when wildflowers are blooming.

Basics

Operated By: Private. **Open:** All year. **Site Assignment:** Reservations accepted, no deposit required, site choice is first come, first served upon check-in. V, MC, D, checks & cash are accepted forms of payment. Check-out is at noon. **Registration:** At office. **Fee:** $20 per night for two people, $2 for each additional adult. **Parking:** On site.

Facilities

Number of RV Sites: 64. **Number of Tent-Only Sites:** 0. **Hookups:** Water, sewer, electric (50 amps), phone, cable TV. **Each Site:** Picnic table. **Dump Station:** No. **Laundry:** Yes. **Pay Phone:** Yes. **Rest Rooms and Showers:** Yes. **Fuel:** No. **Propane:** Once per week, otherwise, two mi. away. **Internal Roads:** Gravel. **RV Service:** 20 mi. in Boerne. **Market:** 2 mi. **Restaurant:** 2 mi. **General Store:** 3 mi. **Vending:** Yes. **Swimming:** Pool. **Playground:** No. **Other:** 9 hole par-3 golf course, nature trails, exercise room, jacuzzi, rec hall. **Activities:** Horseshoes, shuffleboard, pool, ping-pong, fishing, card-playing, volleyball. **Nearby Attractions:** Stonehenge II, Texas Arts & Crafts Fair, Texas Cowboy Artists of America Museum, Agricultural Heritage Center Museum, Bat Railroad Tunnel, Cibolo Wilderness Trail. **Additional Information:** Kerrville CVB (800) 221-7958; Bandera Chamber of Commerce, (830) 796-3045; Boerne Chamber of Commerce, (888) 842-8080.

Restrictions

Pets: On leashes—no pit bulls, rottweilers, or German shepherds allowed. **Fires:** In grills only. **Alcoholic Beverages:** Allowed. **Vehicle Maximum Length:** 48 ft. **Other:** Speed limit 5 mph.

To Get There

From San Antonio, take I-410 (loop) Exit 13A and head northwest on State Hwy. 16. Drive approximately 50 mi. to Medina and the campground is on the right. If you are headed south on I-10, exit at Hwy. 16 south at Kerrville, then take exit Hwy. 173 heading south. From there, take FM 2828 west to Hwy. 16 north to Medina. Note that this seems round-about, but there are portions of Hwy. 16 that are unsuitable for RVs.

MERIDIAN

Meridian State Park

Rte. 2 Box 2465, Meridian 76665. T: (254) 435-2536; F: (254) 435-2076; www.tpwd.state.tx.us.

RV: ★★★★ Tent: ★★★★★

Beauty: ★★★★★	Site Privacy: ★★★★
Spaciousness: ★★★★	Quiet: ★★★★★
Security: ★★★★	Cleanliness: ★★★★
Insect Control: ★★★	Facilities: ★★★★

Heavily wooded with ash, juniper, oak, and other species, Meridian offers extremely attractive campgrounds. Sites are large and shady, with paved back-in and pull-through parking. Site privacy varies, with dense greenery between some and others open to neighbors. RVs should head for one of the pull-throughs with full hookups. Tent campers should head for one of the pretty lakefront sites (no hookups). Meridian's rolling woods support myriad wildlife, including golden cheeked warblers in the spring. The 72-acre lake supports bream, crappie, catfish, bass, and rainbow trout (winter only). Security is good at this extremely rural park which locks its gates at night. Visit Meridian in the spring, early summer, or fall for the nicest weather. Avoid this park on summer weekends, when the small campgrounds are likely to be crowded.

Basics

Operated By: Texas Parks & Wildlife. **Open:** All year. **Site Assignment:** Reservations (512) 389-8900; reservations must be made at least 48 hours in advance; deposit (equivalent to first night's fee) required to hold reservation; cancellations more than two days prior to reservation result in $5 fee, cancellations within two days of reservation result in loss of deposit. **Registration:** Park Headquarters, after hours self-registration (gate locks at 10 p.m.). **Fee:** $25 screened shelter, $17 pull-through (water, electric & sewer), $15 back-in (water & electric), $12 tent w/water, $10 tent without water, plus $3 entrance fee per person over 13 years (cash, personal check, V, MC, D). **Parking:** At site (2 cars).

Facilities

Number of RV Sites: 15. **Number of Tent-Only Sites:** 14 (8 w/water nearby, 6 without water or electricity). **Hookups:** Water, sewer, electric (30 amps). **Each Site:** Picnic table, fire ring. **Dump Station:** Yes. **Laundry:** No. **Pay Phone:** Yes. **Rest Rooms and Showers:** Yes. **Fuel:** No. **Propane:** No. **Internal Roads:** Paved. **RV Service:** 45 mi. in Waco. **Market:** Park store, grocery 2 mi. in Meridian. **Restaurant:** 2 mi. in Meridian. **General Store:** Hardware 2 mi. in Meridian, Wal-Mart 45 mi. in Waco. **Vending:** Beverages only. **Swimming:** No. **Playground:** No. **Other:** Screened shelters, picnic area, boat ramp, boat dock, group dining hall, gift shop. **Activities:** Lake swimming, boating (no-wake lake), pedal boat rentals summertime, fishing, bird-watching, hiking, road biking. **Nearby Attractions:** Meridian golf, Bosque County Courthouse, Norse historic Norwegian settlement, Dinosaur Valley, Lake Whitney & Cleburne State Parks, Fossil Rim, Waco historic homes, Homestead Heritage Traditional Crafts Village, Texas Sports Hall of Fame. **Additional Information:** Meridian Chamber of Commerce, (254) 435-2966; Waco CVB, (800) 321-9226.

Restrictions

Pets: 6-ft. max leash (not in shelters or buildings). **Fires:** Allowed, fire ring only. **Alcoholic Beverages:** Not allowed. **Vehicle Maximum Length:** 45 ft. (back-in sites 20 ft.). **Other:** No-wake lake.

To Get There

From Waco, take TX 6 northwest approximately 45 mi. to Meridian and turn left (southwest) on TX 22. Drive 2.5 mi. and turn right on Park Rd. 7, directly into the park.

MEXIA

Fort Parker State Park

Rte. 3 Box 95, Mexia 76667. T: (254) 562-5751; F: (254) 562-9787; www.tpwd.state.tx.us.

RV ★★★★ Tent ★★★★

Beauty: ★★★★★	Site Privacy: ★★★
Spaciousness: ★★★★	Quiet: ★★★★★
Security: ★★★	Cleanliness: ★★★★
Insect Control: ★★★	Facilities: ★★★★

Most campsites here offer stunning views of the sunset over 700-acre Fort Parker Lake. The lake supports crappie, bass, catfish, and trout (in season). Guided boat tours of the lake are available (call for schedule). The RV campground consists of one area alongside the lake. There are back-in and pull-through sites with paved parking. Some sites could cause mild claustrophobia, while others are amply sized. Most are nicely shaded, but none are very private. Arrive early and angle for a lakefront site, the prettiest of which is number 18—a gorgeous pull-through. The primitive tent-camping area is nicely wooded. Visit popular Fort Parker on weekdays between Mar. and June when wildfowers are blooming and crowds are at a minimum. Security is fair at this small-town park; there are no gates.

Basics

Operated By: Texas Park & Wildlife Dept. **Open:** All year. **Site Assignment:** Reservations (512) 389-8900; reservations must be made at least 48 hours in advance; deposit (equivalent to first night's fee) required to hold reservation; cancellations more than two days prior to reservation result in $5 fee, cancellations within two days of reservation result in loss of deposit. **Registration:** Park Headquarters, after hours register next morning. **Fee:** $12 developed, $8 primitive, plus entry fee $2 per adult (cash, checks, V, MC, D). **Parking:** At site, in parking lot.

Facilities

Number of RV Sites: 25. **Number of Tent-Only Sites:** 10 primitive w/picnic table. **Hookups:** Water, electric (30 amps). **Each Site:** Picnic table, fire ring grill combination, lantern pole. **Dump Station:** Yes. **Laundry:** No. **Pay Phone:** Yes. **Rest Rooms and Showers:** Yes. **Fuel:** No. **Propane:** No. **Internal Roads:** Paved. **RV Service:** 40 mi. in Waco. **Market:** 5 mi. in Groesbeck. **Restaurant:** 5 mi. in Groesbeck. **General Store:** 7 mi. in Mexia. **Vending:** Beverages only. **Swimming:** No. **Playground:** Yes. **Other:** Activity center, screened shelters, picnic area & shelter, boat ramp, fish cleaning station. **Activities:** Lake swimming, fishing, canoe & paddle boat rentals, Cynthia Ann boat tours, hiking, biking trails. **Nearby Attractions:** Confederate Reunion Grounds, Old Fort Parker Historic Site, Waco historic homes, Homestead Heritage Traditional Crafts Village, Texas Sports Hall of Fame. **Additional Information:** Waco CVB (800) 321-9226.

RESTRICTIONS

Pets: On leash only. **Fires:** Allowed, fire rings only (except under fire ban). **Alcoholic Beverages:** No. **Vehicle Maximum Length:** None (sites vary). **Other:** Texas State Park regulations apply.

TO GET THERE

From US 84 in Mexia, turn south on TX 14. Drive 7 mi. to the park entrance on the right. The campground is one mile inside the park.

MINERAL WELLS

Lake Mineral Wells State Park and Trailway

100 Park Rd. 71, Mineral Wells 76067. T: (940) 328-1171, for information only call (800) 792-1112; F: (940) 325-8536; www.tpwd.state.tx.us.

RV ★★★★★   Tent ★★★★★

Beauty: ★★★★★   Site Privacy: ★★★★★
Spaciousness: ★★★★★   Quiet: ★★★★★
Security: ★★★   Cleanliness: ★★★★
Insect Control: ★★★   Facilities: ★★★★

The only major rock climbing and rappelling region in north Texas, Mineral Wells offers 85 climbs (difficulty ranges from 5.5 to 5.11d). Nearby, the State Trailway is a 20-mile "rail to trail" conversion open to pedestrians, cyclists, and equestrians. The lake supports bass, catfish, crappie, and perch. Three campgrounds are lakeside: The Post Oak tent-only area contains 11 gorgeous sites under a romantic post oak canopy. The Plateau area offers water and electric sites (ask for 59, 60, and 64–66 for the best lake views). The Live Oak area contains water-only sites (ask for 31–34 for the nicest lake views). Sites are spacious and situated on loops with back-in gravel parking. The entrance is within Mineral Wells city limits, so protect your valuables (gates lock at night). Apr. and May are the wettest months. Winters can be very cold and summers very hot. Visit in Mar., June (on weekdays), Sep., or Oct.

BASICS

Operated By: Texas Parks & Wildlife. **Open:** All year. **Site Assignment:** Reservations (512) 389-8900, reservations must be made at least 48 hours in advance, deposit required (equivalent to first night's fee) to hold reservation, cancellations more than two days prior to reservation result in $5 fee, cancellations within two days of reservation result in loss of deposit. **Registration:** Headquarters. **Fee:** $3 per person per day for anyone aged 13 & older, $6 for primitive walk-in tent camping, $8 for water-only sites, $11 water & electric, $15 premium water & electric (cash, checks, D,V, MC). **Parking:** At most sites.

FACILITIES

Number of RV Sites: 108. **Number of Tent-Only Sites:** 25 hike-in (about 2.5 mi.) primitive. **Hookups:** water, electric (30 amps). **Each Site:** picnic table, fire ring, grill. **Dump Station:** Yes. **Laundry:** No. **Pay Phone:** Yes. **Rest Rooms and Showers:** Yes. **Fuel:** No. **Propane:** No. **Internal Roads:** Paved. **RV Service:** 0.5 mi. west of park. **Market:** 3 mi. west in Mineral Wells. **Restaurant:** 3 mi. west in Mineral Wells. **General Store:** Wal-Mart, 3 mi. west in Mineral Wells. **Vending:** Park concession open daily Mar. through Dec. **Swimming:** No. **Playground:** No. **Other:** Picnic sites, equestrian camp-sites, screened shelters, seasonal park store, boat ramp, fishing piers, screened shelters. **Activities:** Swimming, fishing, boating (row boat, canoe, & paddle boat rental available), rock climbing, rappelling, mountain biking, equestrian camping, horseback riding, hiking. **Nearby Attractions:** Fort Richardson State Historical Park, Lost creek Reservoir State Trailway, Possum Kingdom State Park, Cleburne State Park, Dinosaur Valley State Park, Clark Gardens, The Brazos River, Possum Kingdom Lake. **Additional Information:** Mineral Wells Area Chamber of Commerce, (800) 252-MWTX.

RESTRICTIONS

Pets: Leash Only. **Fires:** In grills & fire rings only. **Alcoholic Beverages:** Prohibited. **Vehicle Maximum Length:** 45 ft. **Other:** Max. 8 people per campsite, Quiet time 10 p.m.–6 a.m., fourteen–day stay limit, gathering of firewood prohibited, climbers & rappelers must check in at headquarters, no skiing, jet skiing, or tubing permitted.

TO GET THERE

From Mineral Wells, drive east on US 180 for 4 mi. From Weatherford, drive west on US 180 for 14 mi.

MISSION

Bentson-Rio Grande Valley State Park

P.O. Box 988, Mission 78573-0988. T: (956) 585-1107, for information only call (800) 792-1112; F: (956) 585-3448; www.tpwd.state.tx.us.

RV ★★★★ Tent ★★★★

Beauty: ★★★★★ Site Privacy: ★★★
Spaciousness: ★★★ Quiet: ★★★★
Security: ★★★ Cleanliness: ★★★★
Insect Control: ★ Facilities: ★★★★

Year-round warmth makes for delightful winter or early spring retreats at this campground. Situated on a resaca—a former Rio Grande River channel (now still-water)—the lush flora and varied fauna of the park are typical of the Mexican subtropics. Fish for bass and catfish in the resaca. The surrounding brushlands form natural habitats for exotic cats such as ocelot and jaguarundi. Exotic birds include paraque, groove-billed ani, black-bellied whistling duck, and scores more. The lovely campsites are large, usually shady and flat. Tent sites offer paved back-in parking and water at each site. Tent campers will find the prettiest sites lining the resaca (110–139). Searching for exotic birds and full hookups? Try sites 3–36. RV sites offer fewer trees and paved pull-through parking. In spite of its quiet feel, this suburban park is about 3 miles from afternoon traffic jams. Watch your valuables even though the gates lock at 10 p.m.

Basics

Operated By: Texas Parks & Wildlife. **Open:** All year. **Site Assignment:** Reservations (512) 389-8900, reservations must be made at least 48 hours in advance, deposit required (equivalent to first night's fee) to hold reservation, cancellations more than two days prior to reservation result in $5 fee, cancellations within two days of reservation result in loss of deposit. **Registration:** Headquarters. **Fee:** $3 per person per day for anyone aged 13 & older, $12 per night for sites w/water, $18 per night for full hookups (cash, checks, V, MC, D). **Parking:** At site.

Facilities

Number of RV Sites: 78 sites w/water, electric, & sewer. **Number of Tent-Only Sites:** 65 sites w/water only. **Hookups:** Water, sewer, electric (20, 30, 50 amps). **Each Site:** Grill, picnic table, fire ring, lantern post. **Dump Station:** Yes. **Laundry:** No. **Pay Phone:** Yes. **Rest Rooms and Showers:** Yes. **Fuel:** No. **Propane:** No. **Internal Roads:** Paved. **RV Service:** 5 mi. north in Mission. **Market:** 3 mi. north in Palmview. **Restaurant:** 3 mi. north in Palmview. **General Store:** K-Mart 5 mi. north toward McAllen. **Vending:** Beverages, ice. **Swimming:** No. **Playground:** Yes. **Other:** Bicycle rental, volleyball court, shuffleboard, fish cleaning table, bird observation blinds, birding information center Dec. through Mar. **Activities:** hiking, picnicking, bird-watching, boating, bicycling, & fishing. **Nearby Attractions:** Falcon State Park, Santa Ana National Wildlife Refuge, Sabal Palm Sanctuary, Mexico attractions. **Additional Information:** Mission Chamber of Commerce, (956) 585-2727; Rio Grande Valley Chamber of Commerce, (956) 968-3141; McAllen Convention & Visitor Bureau (956) 682-2871.

Restrictions

Pets: Leash Only. **Fires:** In grills & fire rings only. **Alcoholic Beverages:** Prohibited. **Vehicle Maximum Length:** 40 ft. **Other:** Max. 8 people per campsite, Quiet time 10 p.m.–6 a.m., 14-day stay limit, gathering of firewood prohibited.

To Get There

From McAllen, go west on I-83. Exit at Bentsen Palm Blvd., turn left, and drive south. After crossing Business 83, Bentsen Palm Blvd. becomes FM 2062. The park entrance is about 3 mi. from I-83.

MISSION
Chimney RV Park

4224 South Conway St., Mission, 78572. T: (956) 585-5061; F: (956) 519-8348; www.gocampingamerica.com/chimneypark.

RV ★★★ Tent n/a

Beauty: ★★★ Site Privacy: ★★★
Spaciousness: ★★★ Quiet: ★★★
Security: ★★★★ Cleanliness: ★★★
Insect Control: ★★★ Facilities: ★★★

Another seniors-only park in south Texas, Chimney Park is sandwiched between a levee and the Rio Grande River. However, the river view is deadened by the concrete sea wall that runs the length of the park. The park's namesake is a 1907 steam-powered water-pump chimney. The park's aged facilities are not as extensive as those at many of the competing resorts. Campsites are generally plain and small—we imagine you'll get to know your neighbors. With little shade or privacy, each site has paved back-in parking, a grassy area, and a concrete patio. Permanent park models occupy all of the riverfront sites. The nicest available sites, including 16–20, 150–154, and 261–268, have trees nearby. Fenced and guarded, security is excellent at suburban Chimney Park. Within a mile, there are restaurants and shops galore. Stay away from South Texas in the summer, and make advance reservations in the winter.

BASICS

Operated By: Private. **Open:** All year. **Site Assignment:** Reservations accepted, payable w/V, MC, D, personal check, or cash. **Registration:** At office. **Fee:** $22 per night for 2 people, $2 per night per extra person. **Parking:** On site.

FACILITIES

Number of RV Sites: 276. **Number of Tent-Only Sites:** None. **Hookups:** Water, sewer, electric, phone, dataport & cable TV. **Each Site:** Fire ring. **Dump Station:** No. **Laundry:** Yes. **Pay Phone:** Yes. **Rest Rooms and Showers:** Yes. **Fuel:** No. **Propane:** Yes. **Internal Roads:** Paved. **RV Service:** 0.5 mi. **Market:** 0.5 mi. **Restaurant:** 0.25 mi. **General Store:** 0.5 mi. **Vending:** Yes. **Swimming:** Pool. **Playground:** No. **Other:** Boat ramp, boat dock, floating dock, fishing dock, jacuzzi, game room. **Activities:** Horseshoes, shuffleboard, fishing, boating, billiards, variety shows, card games, dances, bingo, ice cream socials. **Nearby Attractions:** Azalduas Dam, Banworth Park, Mission Nature Park. **Additional Information:** Mission Chamber of Commerce, (956) 585-2727.

RESTRICTIONS

Pets: On leash. **Fires:** In grills only. **Alcoholic Beverages:** Allowed. **Vehicle Maximum Length:** 38 ft.

TO GET THERE

Traveling south from Corpus Christi or Kingville on US 77, exit onto US 83 west. Travel approxiamately 45 mi. to Mission and exit onto Conway St. The park is 0.25 mi. south on the right.

MONAHANS

Monahans Sandhills State Park

P.O. Box 1738, Monahans, 97956. T: (915) 943-2092; F: (915) 943-2806; www.tpwd.state.tx.us.

RV: ★★★	Tent: ★★★
Beauty: ★★★★	Site Privacy: ★★★
Spaciousness: ★★★	Quiet: ★★★
Security: ★★	Cleanliness: ★★★★
Insect Control: ★★★	Facilities: ★★★

At the end of a vast dune field which continues 200 miles northeast into New Mexico, the park contains "active dunes" that move and change seasonally because they're not anchored by vegetation. Try dusk or dawn wildlife viewing at the ponds. Look for coyote, bobcat, porcupine and others. The unique shinoak tree is mature at under four feet tall. The campgrounds are odd. Sites nestle into the dunes in pairs, with each pair sharing a shade shelter. Each site has its own picnic table. While you are nose-to-nose with your shelter-mate, dunes and ample space provide privacy between pairs of sites. Some sites offer paved pull-through parking. All others have paved back-in parking. You will be assigned a site. There are no gates, and we easily entered the park after dark. Be cautious with your valuables—the entrance is yards from the freeway exit. Visit Monahans any time but late summer.

BASICS

Operated By: Texas Parks & Wildlife. **Open:** All year. **Site Assignment:** Reservations (512) 389-8900; reservations must be made at least 48 hours in advance; deposit (equivalent to first night's fee) required to hold reservation; cancellations more than two days prior to reservation result in $5 fee, cancellations within two days of reservation result in loss of deposit. **Registration:** Headquarters. **Fee:** $2 per person per day for anyone aged 13 & over, $9 for sites w/water & electric, $6 for sites w/water only (cash, checks, V, MC, D). **Parking:** At site.

FACILITIES

Number of RV Sites: 15. **Number of Tent-Only Sites:** 0. **Hookups:** Water, electric (20, 30, 50 amps). **Each Site:** Grill, picnic table. **Dump Station:** Yes. **Laundry:** No. **Pay Phone:** Yes. **Rest Rooms and Showers:** Yes. **Fuel:** 5 mi. west in Monahans. **Propane:** 5 mi. west in Monahans. **Internal Roads:** Paved. **RV Service:** 30 mi. east in Odessa. **Market:** 5 mi. west in Monahans. **Restaurant:** 5 mi. west in Monahans. **General Store:** 5 mi. west in Monahans. **Vending:** Yes. **Swimming:** No. **Playground:** No. **Other:** Interpretive center, equestrian day use area, group dining hall, one working oil well, picnic area, sand toboggan & disc rental. **Activities:** Hiking, picnicking, sand surfing, bird-watching at interpretive center. **Nearby Attractions:** Million Barrel Museum, Balmorhea State Park, Odessa Meteor Crater. **Additional Information:** Odessa Chamber of Commerce, (915) 332-9111; Monahans Chamber of Commerce, (915) 943-2187.

RESTRICTIONS

Pets: On leash only. **Fires:** In grill only. **Alcoholic Beverages:** Prohibited. **Vehicle Maximum Length:** 45 ft. **Other:** No "four-wheelers" or motorcycles allowed.

TO GET THERE

From I-20, take Exit 86 to Park Rd. 41. The park entrance is visible from the interstate.

NEEDVILLE

Brazos Bend State Park

21901 FM 762, Needville, 77461. T: (979) 553-5101; F: (979) 553-5108; www.tpwd.state.tx.us.

★★★★ ★★★★

Beauty: ★★★★	Site Privacy: ★★★
Spaciousness: ★★★★	Quiet: ★★★
Security: ★★★★	Cleanliness: ★★★★
Insect Control: ★	Facilities: ★★★★

A nature-lover's paradise, Brazos Bend contains fascinating ecosystems, including river flood-plains, upland coastal prairies, freshwater marshes, oxbow lakes, the Brazos River, and creeks. Wildlife spotted from the observation tower and viewing platforms includes feral hogs and 270 bird species. The 0.5-mile, paved Creek-feild Lake Nature Trail is handicapped accessible and includes tactile interpretive panels and audio tours. On property, George Observatory offers public star-gazing—call for schedule. Attractive campgrounds consist of two loops of back-in sites with gravel parking. Large campsites are shaded by black willow, sycamore, and cottonwood trees. There is little privacy. Many sites in both sections are situated along "Big Creek". Pretty creekside sites include101, 214, and 215. For privacy, we recommend site 105. Grassy tent pads are found at each site. Security is good at this rural park. Popular with Houston city slickers, Brazos Bend stays busy on all but the most inclement week-ends. Visit on weekdays.

BASICS

Operated By: Texas Parks & Wildlife. **Open:** All year. **Site Assignment:** Reservations (512) 389-8900, reservations must be made at least 48 hours in advance, deposit required (equivalent to first night's fee) to hold reservation, cancellations more than two days prior to reservation result in $5 fee, cancellations within two days of reservation result in loss of deposit. **Registration:** Headquarters. **Fee:** $3 per person per day for anyone aged 13 & older, $12 for overnight camping (cash, checks, V, MC, D). **Parking:** At site.

FACILITIES

Number of RV Sites: 77. **Number of Tent-Only Sites:** 0. **Hookups:** Water, electric (20, 30 amps). **Each Site:** Picnic table, fire ring, grill. **Dump Station:** Yes. **Laundry:** No. **Pay Phone:** Yes. **Rest Rooms and Showers:** Yes. **Fuel:** No. **Propane:** No. **Internal Roads:** Paved. **RV Service:** 30 mi. northeast in Sugarland. **Market:** Convenience store 1 mi. south in community of Woodrow, full market 18 mi. northwest in Needville. **Restaurant:** Deli 1 mi. south in community of Woodrow, full service 18 mi. northwest in Needville. **General Store:** Wal-Mart, 18 mi. south in West Columbia. **Vending:** Beverages only. **Swimming:** No. **Playground:** Yes. **Other:** George Observatory (call for hours), interpretive center, group dining hall, group picnic pavilions, picnic areas, screened shelters, amphitheater, gift shop, fishing piers, fish cleaning area, handicapped accessible nature trail. **Activities:** Picnicking, hiking, bicycling, mountain biking, boating, fishing, interpretive tours & educational programs, stargazing (special parties & programs). **Nearby Attractions:** San Jacinto Battleground Historical Complex including the San Jacinto Monument & Battleship "Texas", Galveston Island State Park, George Ranch, Houston. **Additional Information:** Houston CVB (800) 4-HOUSTON, Fort Bend Convention/Visitor Services (281) 491-0800.

RESTRICTIONS

Pets: On leash only. **Fires:** In fire rings only. **Alcoholic Beverages:** Prohibited. **Vehicle Maximum Length:** 45 ft. **Other:** Special alligator precautions: do not feed or molest the alligators, no swimming or wading, keep pets & children away from alligators, stay at least 30 ft. away from alligators.

TO GET THERE

From Houston, follow TX 288 to Rosharon. At Rosharon, turn left on FM 1462 and travel west for roughly 9 mi. Park entrance on right.

PADRE ISLAND

Padre Island National Seashore, Malaquite Beach Campground

P.O. Box 181300, Corpus Christi, 78480. T: (361) 949-8068; F: (361) 949-9951; www.nps.gov/pais/pphtml/camping.html.

Beauty: ★★★★
Site Privacy: ★★
Spaciousness: ★★★
Quiet: ★★★
Security: ★★★★
Cleanliness: ★★★★
Insect Control: ★
Facilities: ★★★★

At seventy miles long, Padre Island National Seashore is one of the largest pieces of undeveloped shoreline in the U.S. The island is rich in folklore concerning buried pirate's treasure. It's also rich in natural beauty and wildlife, including graceful waterfowl such as herons. Much of the island is accessible only by foot or four-wheel drive. Attractive Malaquite Campground is 100 feet from the beach, nestled into graceful dunes. There is no vegetation other than dune grasses. Sites have parallel paved parking and are completely open to each other. All sites are small, and there is no shade. If your RV doesn't have an awning, bring large umbrellas. Sites are all the same, so choose your site based on location. Mosquitoes thrive at Padre Island, so come prepared. Security is good—although there are no gates, the campground is extremely remote. Rarely crowded, Malaquite is an excellent destination in late spring, early summer, and autumn.

Basics

Operated By: National Park Service. **Open:** All year. **Site Assignment:** No reservations are accepted. **Registration:** Visitor Center. **Fee:** $8 per night, in addition to day use fees of $10 per car or $5 per cyclist or pedestrian. **Parking:** At site.

Facilities

Number of RV Sites: 46 plus non-designated sites on the beach. **Number of Tent-Only Sites:** Non-designated oceanfront sites. **Hookups:** None. **Each Site:** Picnic table. **Dump Station:** Yes. **Laundry:** No. **Pay Phone:** Yes. **Rest Rooms and Showers:** Yes. **Fuel:** No. **Propane:** No. **Internal Roads:** Paved except for beach driving. **RV Service:** 18 mi. north in Corpus Christi. **Market:** In park. **Restaurant:** 10 mi. north in Corpus Christi. **General Store:** In park, 25 mi. in Corpus Christi. **Vending:** Yes. **Swimming:** No. **Playground:** No. **Other:** Visitor center, scenic drive, observation deck, bathhouses. **Activities:** Wind surfing, trash walks, picnicking, four-wheel-driving, hiking, birdwatching, beachcombing, swimming, surfing, boating, volunteering, waterskiing, fishing, guided tours, & activities. **Nearby Attractions:** Texas State Aquarium, USS Lexington, Ships of Christopher Colombus. **Additional Information:** Corpus Christi Area Convention & Tourist Bureau (800) 678-6232.

Restrictions

Pets: On leash only. **Fires:** Contained fires only. **Alcoholic Beverages:** Allowed. **Vehicle Maximum Length:** None.

To Get There

From Corpus Christi, take US 358 to Rte. 22. Drive approximately 20 mi. and follow the signs to camping areas.

PORT ARANSAS

Mustang Island State Park

P.O. Box 326, Port Aransas 78373. T: (361) 749-5246; F: (361) 749-6455; www.tpwd.state.tx.us.

RV ★★★ Tent ★★★★★

Beauty: ★★★
Site Privacy: ★
Spaciousness: ★★
Quiet: ★★★
Security: ★★★
Cleanliness: ★★★★
Insect Control: ★★★
Facilities: ★★

Tent campers are in luck at Mustang Island—gorgeous beachfront tent sites include a picnic table and shade shelter at each site (call ahead regarding beach conditions). RV sites are disappointing. The RV campground is a sea of unnecessary pavement. Sites are small, extremely close together, and offer no shade or privacy. All sites are back-in, and there is no vegetation in the campground. It doesn't matter which site you choose. The beach and birding are the draws here. The park provides nice, not extensive, beach facilities and no special birding facilities. Though the park feels rural, restaurants are 10 minutes away. The mosquitoes can be oppressive here, so come prepared with insect repellant. Mustang Island is busiest in the spring and summer. For tranquility, visit in the fall. Security is good; the front gates are locked at night, and the campground is a long walk from Hwy. 361.

Basics

Operated By: Texas Parks & Wildlife. **Open:** All year. **Site Assignment:** Reservations (512) 389-8900; reservations must be made at least 48 hours in advance; deposit (equivalent to first night's fee) required to hold reservation; cancellations more than two days prior to reservation result in $5 fee, cancellations within two days of reservation result in loss of deposit. **Registration:** Park headquarters, after hours register next morning. **Fee:** $15 developed, $7 primitve, plus $3 entrance fee per person over 13 years (cash, checks, V, MC, D). **Parking:** At site (2 cars), on beach for primitive camping.

Facilities

Number of RV Sites: 48. **Number of Tent-Only Sites:** 300 (beach). **Hookups:** Water, electric (50 amps). **Each Site:** Covered shelter, BBQ pit. **Dump Station:** Yes. **Laundry:** no. **Pay Phone:** Yes. **Rest Rooms and Showers:** Yes. **Fuel:** No. **Propane:** No. **Internal Roads:** Paved. **RV Service:** 15 mi. in Corpus Christi. **Market:** 10 mi. in Corpus Christi. **Restaurant:** 5 mi. in Corpus Christi. **General Store:** 10 mi. in Corpus Christi. **Vending:** Yes. **Swimming:** No. **Playground:** No. **Activities:** Fishing, swimming, surfing, beach combing, bird-watching. **Nearby Attractions:** USS Lexington, Texas State Aquarium, The Colombus Ships, Greyhound Racetrack, Padre Island National Seashore, University of Texas Marine Science Center, Port Aransas Birding Center. **Additional Information:** Port Aransas Chamber of Commerce, (361) 749-5919; Corpus Christi Area Convention & Tourist Bureau, (800) 678-6232.

Restrictions

Pets: On leash only. **Fires:** Allowed on the beach only (or grill). **Alcoholic Beverages:** No. **Vehicle Maximum Length:** 40 ft. **Other:** No lifeguards, water sports at your own risk.

To Get There

From Corpus Christi, take TX 358 southeast until it becomes Park Rd. 22. Cross the causeway and drive 1 mi. to the traffic light. Turn left on TX 361 and drive 5 mi. to the park.

PORT ARANSAS

Pioneer RV Resort

120 Gulfwind Dr., Port Aransas, 78373. T: (361) 749-6248; F: (361) 749-6250; www.gocampingamerica.com/pioneerrv; info@pioneerrvresorts.com.

RV: ★★★ Tent: n/a

Beauty: ★★★★	Site Privacy: ★★★
Spaciousness: ★★★	Quiet: ★★★★
Security: ★★★	Cleanliness: ★★★★
Insect Control: ★★★★	Facilities: ★★★★

Port Aransas on Mustang Island is known for its excellent birding, with boardwalks and raised observation towers at both the Port Aransas Birding Center and the Port Aransas Wetlands Park. Excellent deep-sea fishing and lovely beaches appeal to families and retirees. Pioneer's campground is attractive and tidy, with both back-in and pull-through spaces. The L-shaped campground hugs a pretty pond that attracts many birds. Sites are situated in long rows and feature paved parking. There are no trees, but each site has a grassy area. Most sites are of average size. We recommend the premium sites (the 300s), which are larger, quieter, and closer to the beach. Security is fair at Pioneer—there are no gates, but the park's serene location gives no cause for concern. Insects are not as problematic here as at nearby Mustang Island State Park. For solitude, visit Port Aransas in the fall.

Basics

Operated By: Don Temple. **Open:** All year. **Site Assignment:** For reservations, call (888) 480-3246; credit card number holds reservation, monthly reservations require one month deposit. You may request a certain area, but not a certain site. Payment may be made by V, MC, D, personal check, or cash. **Registration:** At office. **Fee:** $21 per night for 2 people in a back-in, $23 for a pull-through, $2 for each additional adult. **Parking:** On site.

Facilities

Number of RV Sites: 330. **Number of Tent-Only Sites:** 0. **Hookups:** Water, sewer, electric (30, 50 amps), phone, cable TV. **Each Site:** Concrete patio, picnic table. **Dump Station:** Yes. **Laundry:** Yes. **Pay Phone:** Yes. **Rest Rooms and Showers:** Yes. **Fuel:** No. **Propane:** Yes. **Internal Roads:** Concrete. **RV Service:** 30 mi. in Corpus Christi. **Market:** 3.5 mi. north in Port Aransas. **Restaurant:** 3.5 mi. north in Port Aransas. **General Store:** 25 mi. in Aransas Pass. **Vending:** Beverages, c&y, ice, beer. **Swimming:** Pool. **Playground:** Yes. **Other:** Spa, rec hall, fish cleaning facility, trolley service. **Activities:** Birding areas, arts & crafts, deep sea fishing trips, aerobics, dancing, golf, ladies lunches, cribbage, washers, dominoes, bridge, bunko, pool, horseshoes, shuffleboard, quilting. **Nearby Attractions:** Texas State Aquarium, The USS Lexington, Corpus Christi Greyhound Racetrack, University of Texas Marine Science Center, Port Aransas Birding Center. **Additional Information:** Port Aransas Chamber of Commerce, (361) 749-5919; Corpus Christi Area Convention & Tourist Bureau (800) 678-6232.

Restrictions

Pets: On leash only; must be approved if over 50 lbs., absolutely no pit bulls, dobermans, rottweilers, chows, or wolf hybrids allowed. **Fires:** In grills only. **Alcoholic Beverages:** Allowed. **Vehicle Maximum Length:** 60 ft.

To Get There

From Corpus Christi, take TX 358 which becomes Park Rd. 22. After you cross the JFK Causeway, take a left at the next traffic light (Hwy. 361) and the park will be 15 mi. on the right.

PORT ISABEL

Long Island Village

P.O. Box 695, Port Isabel 78578. T: (956) 943-6449 or (800) 292-7261; F: (956) 943-3113.

RV ★★★★ Tent n/a

Beauty: ★★★★	Site Privacy: ★★★
Spaciousness: ★★★★	Quiet: ★★★★
Security: ★★★★★	Cleanliness: ★★★★★
Insect Control: ★★★★	Facilities: ★★★★★

Ultra-tidy Long Island Village welcomes families and retirees and maintains extensive facilities, including an 18-hole golf course. Located on Long Island, south of Port Isabel, the park is convenient to South Padre Island and restaurants and shopping. Though sites are small and crowded, the campground is laid out in a series of rows dissected by picturesque canals. Waterfront sites often have private docks. The sites are extremely clean with paved, back-in parking. There are few trees. Landscaping enhances the park's beauty, though it provides no shade or privacy. Since Long Island is so large, families should look for a site near the pool. Couples should ask for a quiet site in the back. Security is excellent; the complex is gated and surrounded by water. Popular with families in the spring and summer and popular with snow birds in the winter, it's best to visit Long Island in the fall.

Basics

Operated By: Outdoor Owners Assoc. of Long Island Texas. **Open:** All year. **Site Assignment:** Lots assigned; credit card number holds lot, 48-hour cancellation notice required or fee is charged; check-in 3 p.m., check-out 11 a.m. **Registration:** Office, register w/security at night. **Fee:** $30 for 3 people, $2 per additional person, 8 people max. (cash, personal Check, V, MC, AE, D). **Parking:** At site only.

Facilities

Number of RV Sites: 200. **Number of Tent-Only Sites:** None. **Hookups:** Water, sewer, electric (50 amps), cable. **Each Site:** Concrete pad. **Dump Station:** No. **Laundry:** Yes. **Pay Phone:** Yes. **Rest Rooms and Showers:** Yes. **Fuel:** No. **Propane:** Service. **Internal Roads:** Paved. **RV Service:** 0.5 mi. in Port Isabel. **Market:** 0.5 mi. in Port Isabel. **Restaurant:** On-site (seasonal), also within one block of resort. **General Store:** Within 2 blocks. **Vending:** Yes. **Swimming:** Pool (indoor & outdoor). **Playground:** No. **Other:** Rec hall, exercise room, sauna, library, ballroom, billiard room. **Activities:** 18-hole par 3 golf course, mini-golf, tennis, shuffleboard, volleyball, basketball, horseshoes, arts & crafts. **Nearby Attractions:** Padre Island National Seashore, Port Isabel Lighthouse & Boca Chica State Parks, dolphin watching, charter fishing, Rio Grande, South Padre Island. **Additional Information:** Port Isabel Chamber of Commerce, (800) 527-6102; South Padre Island CVB, (800) SO-PADRE.

Restrictions

Pets: On leash only. **Fires:** Not allowed (bring your own grill). **Alcoholic Beverages:** Allowed. **Vehicle Maximum Length:** 60 ft. **Other:** No pop-ups, vans or tents, no fish-cleaning on picnic tables.

To Get There

From US 77/83, take TX 100 east approximately 25 mi. Just before the causeway, turn right on Garcia St. and follow it 0.5 mi. to the Resort at the end.

QUANAH

Copper Breaks State Park

RR 2 Box 480, Quanah 79252-9420. T: (940) 839-4331; F: Fax:; www.tpwd.state.tx.us.

RV ★★★★ Tent ★★★★

Beauty: ★★★★	Site Privacy: ★★★★
Spaciousness: ★★★★	Quiet: ★★★★
Security: ★★★★	Cleanliness: ★★★★
Insect Control: ★★★	Facilities: ★★★★

Taking its name from the copper deposits found in the area, this park boasts striking rock formations with alternating layers of gypsum, red clays, and shales. Recreation revolves around the 60-acre lake, which is stocked with rainbow trout in the winter. Lake Copper Breaks also hosts many migratory waterfowl, including great blue heron. Part of the Texas state longhorn herd lives at Copper Breaks. Comanche campground (water/electric) is not as pretty as Kiowa (no hookups). Both offer spacious, paved, back-in sites. Kiowa includes sites shaded by tall trees and secluded by foliage between many sites. Families might appreciate Kiowa's proximity to the swimming beach. Comanche's sites are cookie-cutter boring and have no shade and little privacy. Security is good at this rural park. North Texas experiences cold winters and hot summers; visit in spring, early summer, or fall.

BASICS

Operated By: Texas Parks & Wildlife. **Open:** All year. **Site Assignment:** Inquire at campground. **Registration:** Headquarters. **Fee:** $11 for sites w/water & electricity, $8 for sites without water & electricity, $6 for primitive tent camping. **Parking:** At site.

FACILITIES

Number of RV Sites: 25. **Number of Tent-Only Sites:** 24. **Hookups:** Water, electric. **Each Site:** Fire ring, grill, picnic table. **Dump Station:** Yes. **Laundry:** No. **Pay Phone:** Yes. **Rest Rooms and Showers:** Yes. **Fuel:** No. **Propane:** No. **Internal Roads:** Yes. **RV Service:** 63 mi. northeast in Altus, OK. **Market:** 13 mi. north in Quanah. **Restaurant:** 8 mi. south in Crowell. **General Store:** 13 mi. north in Quanah. **Vending:** Yes. **Swimming:** No. **Playground:** Yes. **Other:** Visitor's center, meeting room, picnic area, picnic pavilion, swimming beach, boat ramp, boat dock, fishing pier, amphitheater, scenic overlook, group camp, equestrian camping,. **Activities:** Hiking, backpacking, equestrian trails, swimming, boating, fishing, paddle boat rental (in-season), horseshoes, basketball, volleyball. **Nearby Attractions:** Hardeman County Historical Museum, Medicine Mound (on private property), Firehall Museum in Crowell, Lake Pauline, Greenbelt Reservoir. **Additional Information:** Inquire at campground.

RESTRICTIONS

Pets: Leash only. **Fires:** Fire rings only. **Alcoholic Beverages:** Not allowed. **Vehicle Maximum Length:** 50 ft.

TO GET THERE

From Quanah, drive south on State Hwy. 6 for 25 mi. Park Rd. 62 entrance is on the right.

QUITAQUE

Caprock Canyons State Park and Trailway

P.O. Box 204, Quitaque 79255. T: (806) 455-1492; F: (806) 455-1254; www.tpwd.state.tx.us.

RV ★★★★★ Tent ★★★★★

Beauty: ★★★★★	Site Privacy: ★★★★
Spaciousness: ★★★★★	Quiet: ★★★★★
Security: ★★★★	Cleanliness: ★★★★★
Insect Control: ★★★	Facilities: ★★★★

This gorgeous state park is adjacent to 64-mile Caprock Canyon Trailway, a multi-use "rail to trail" conversion completed in 1993. Catering to expert hikers and mountain bikers, 25 miles of extremely rugged trails are found inside the park. Wildlife includes African aoudad sheep, a herd of pronghorn antelope, and the largest herd of buffalo in the state park system. Pretty Honea Flat campground features sites with paved back-in RV parking. Site size varies. Cottonwood trees and foliage provide shade and privacy at some sites, while others are more open. Families should go for sites 15 and 17 (near the playground and potties). Those seeking privacy should try to score site 23. The tent-only campgrounds are also very attractive. Visit Caprock on weekdays in spring, summer, or fall. Call ahead to avoid special event weekends. Security is good-there are no gates, but the park is extremely remote.

BASICS

Operated By: Texas Parks & Wildlife. **Open:** All year. **Site Assignment:** Reservations (512) 389-8900; reservations must be made at least 48 hours in advance; deposit (equivalent to first night's fee) required to hold reservation; cancellations more than two days prior to reservation result in $5 fee, cancellations within two days of reservation result in loss of deposit. **Registration:** Park headquarters, after hours self-registration. **Fee:** $12 RV, $7-$10 tent, plus $2 entrance fee per additional person up to 8 max (cash, checks, V, MC, D). **Parking:** At site (2 cars, $2 per additional vehicle).

FACILITIES

Number of RV Sites: 35. **Number of Tent-Only Sites:** 39. **Hookups:** Water, some electric (30 amps). **Each Site:** Picnic table, fire ring, lantern pole. **Dump Station:** Yes. **Laundry:** No. **Pay Phone:** Yes. **Rest Rooms and Showers:** Yes. **Fuel:** No. **Propane:** No. **Internal Roads:** Paved. **RV Service:** Inquire at campground. **Market:** 3 mi. in Quitaque. **Restaurant:** 3 mi. in Quitaque. **General Store:** 3 mi. in Quitaque. **Vending:** Beverages only. **Swimming:** No. **Playground:** Yes. **Other:** Interpretive exhibits, gravel equestrian loop, amphitheater, backpacking trails, picnic pavilion, fishing pier boat ramp. **Activities:** hiking, horseback riding, seasonal horse rentals, mountain biking, boating, fishing, lake swimming, scenic drive, guided tours. **Nearby Attractions:** Turkey, Panhandle-Plains Historical Museum & West Texas State University in Canyon, Palo Duro Canyon & Copper Breaks State Parks, Lake Mackenzie, Ranching Heritage Center, 2 hours from Amarillo & Lubbock. **Additional Information:** Turkey City Hall (806) 423-1033, Amarillo Convention & visitors Bureau (800) 692-1338, Lubbock CVB (800) 692-4035.

Restrictions

Pets: On leash only. **Fires:** Allowed, fire rings only. **Alcoholic Beverages:** Not allowed. **Vehicle Maximum Length:** None.

To Get There

From I-27, take Exit 74 and head east on TX 86 approximately 45 mi. to Quitaque. Turn north on FM 1065 and drive 3 mi. to the park.

RUSK

Rusk Campground, Rusk/Palestine State Park and Texas State Railroad Historical Park

P.O. Box 39, Rusk 75785. T: (903) 683-5126; F: (903) 683-2212; www.tpwd.state.tx.us.

RV ★★★★ Tent ★★★★

Beauty: ★★★★	Site Privacy: ★★★★
Spaciousness: ★★★★	Quiet: ★★★
Security: ★★★★	Cleanliness: ★★★★
Insect Control: ★★★★	Facilities: ★★★★

Rusk and Palestine recreation areas are connected by the 25-mile Texas State Railroad. The park maintains four steam engines and four antique diesel engines and offers four-hour, 50-mile round trip excursions between Rusk and Palestine (depart at either terminus). Children especially enjoy visiting the engineer and touring the steam engine cab. After the trains, explore the lake and woods. We prefer the RV campground at Rusk, which is nicer than Palestine, with tall pine trees providing shade at most sites. Pull-through sites offer full hookups and paved parking. Sites are comfortably spaced, but not huge. Sites 7–12, situated away from Hwy. 84, are the quietest. Families enjoy sites 17 and 19, which are adjacent to the playground. Site 14, the only back-in, is the most secluded. Assiduously avoid Rusk/Palestine on summer weekends. Opt for weekday and off-season visits. Security is good at this rural recreation area. Gates lock at 10 p.m.

Basics

Operated By: Texas Parks & Wildlife Dept. **Open:** All year. **Site Assignment:** Reservations (512) 389-8900; reservations must be made at least 48 hours in advance; deposit (equivalent to first night's fee) required to hold reservation; cancellations more than two days prior to reservation result in $5 fee, cancellations within two days of reservation result in loss of deposit. **Registration:** Park Office, after hours register next morning. **Fee:** $10 plus entry fee $2 per adult (cash, checks, V, MC, D). **Parking:** At site (2 cars), in parking lot.

Facilities

Number of RV Sites: 34. **Number of Tent-Only Sites:** 16 water & electric. **Hookups:** Water, sewer, electric (30, 50 amps). **Each Site:** Picnic table, grill, fire ring (amenities at tent & multipurpose sites). **Dump Station:** Yes. **Laundry:** No. **Pay Phone:** Yes. **Rest Rooms and Showers:** Yes. **Fuel:** No. **Propane:** No. **Internal Roads:** Paved. **RV Service:** 30 mi. in Nacogdoches. **Market:** 4 mi. in Rusk. **Restaurant:** 5 mi. in Rusk. **General Store:** 5 mi. in Rusk. **Vending:** Beverages only. **Swimming:** No. **Playground:** Yes. **Other:** Picnic areas & pavilions, gift shop & food at train depots, group dining hall, fishing jetty, tennis courts. **Activities:** Steam engine tours (weekends Mar.-Nov.), lake swimming, fishing, pedal boat & canoe rentals, nature trails, biking, volleyball, horseshoes. **Nearby Attractions:** Mission Tejas & Caddoan Mounds State Historical Parks, Tyler & Fairfield State Parks, Museum of East Texas, NASA Scientific Balloon Base. **Additional Information:** Palestine CVB (800) 659-3484.

Restrictions

Pets: On leash only. **Fires:** Allowed, fire rings (except under fire ban). **Alcoholic Beverages:**

Not allowed. **Vehicle Maximum Length:** 40 ft. (sites vary). **Other:** Checkout 2 p.m., daytime visitors must exit park by 10 p.m.

To Get There

From US 84, about 1 mile west of downtown Rusk, turn south onto Park Rd. 76 and drive 0.25 mile to the park.

SABINE PASS

Sea Rim State Park

P.O. Box 1066, Sabine Pass, 77655. T: (409) 971-2559; F: (409) 971-2917; www.tpwd.state.tx.us.

RV ★★★ Tent ★★★★

Beauty: ★★★	Site Privacy: ★
Spaciousness: ★★	Quiet: ★★★
Security: ★★★	Cleanliness: ★★
Insect Control: ★	Facilities: ★★★

Spend little time in the uninspired campgrounds. Rather, enjoy the often deserted beach or explore the Sea Rim marshlands via canoe, kayak, or boardwalk. This biologically important area includes marsh grasses that inhabit a tidal zone, and it's a winter home for numerous bird species. RV sites are small and crowded. The entire campground is paved, with no trees or shrubs. Bring your own shade and live without privacy. All sites are unattractive, so pick one near the beach. Tent campers fare better—sites are more spacious and attractive, but offer little privacy. For sheer beauty, the best option for tent campers is primitive camping on the beach. Sep. is the wettest month at Sea Rim. Visit in late spring or early summer before the heat becomes unbearable. Security is good at this very rural park. We cannot overstate the terror caused by Sea Rim mosquitoes. Prepare to battle these beasts.

Basics

Operated By: Texas Parks & Wildlife. **Open:** All year. **Site Assignment:** Reservations (512) 389-8900; reservations must be made at least 48 hours in advance; deposit (equivalent to first night's fee) required to hold reservation; cancellations more than two days prior to reservation result in $5 fee, cancellations within two days of reservation result in loss of deposit. **Registration:** Headquarters. **Fee:** $2 per person per day for anyone aged 13 & over, $11 for RV sites, $8 for tent-only sites, $6 for primitive tent camping on the beach (cash, checks, D,V, MC). **Parking:** At site.

Facilities

Number of RV Sites: 20. **Number of Tent-Only Sites:** 10. **Hookups:** Water, electric (30 amps). **Each Site:** Picnic table, grill, tent-only sites also have lantern hook & tent pad. **Dump Station:** Yes. **Laundry:** No. **Pay Phone:** Yes. **Rest Rooms and Showers:** Yes. **Fuel:** No. **Propane:** No. **Internal Roads:** Paved. **RV Service:** 25 mi. northeast in Port Arthur. **Market:** 10 mi. east in Sabine Pass. **Restaurant:** 10 mi. east in Sabine Pass. **General Store:** Wal-Mart 20 mi. northeast in Port Arthur. **Vending:** Yes. **Swimming:** No. **Playground:** No. **Other:** S&y swimming beach, picnic area, gift shop, visitor's center, observation deck, observation blinds for bird-watching, air boat tours (by reservation only). **Activities:** Hiking, walking, bicycling, bird-watching, beach combing, boating (canoe & kayak rentals available), beach swimming, fishing, seasonal waterfowl hunting. **Nearby Attractions:** Sabine Pass Battleground State Historical Park, festivals & historic homes in Port Arthur & surrounding towns. **Additional Information:** Port Arthur convention & Visitors Bureau (800) 235-7822.

Restrictions

Pets: On leash only. **Fires:** Ground fires allowed on beach or in fire rings. **Alcoholic Beverages:** Prohibited. **Vehicle Maximum Length:** 40 ft. **Other:** Swim at your own risk, don't approach, annoy, or feed the alligators.

To Get There

From I-10, take Exit 829 at Winnie and drive 28 mi. east on TX 73. Turn south on TX 82 and drive 10 mi. to the traffic light in Sabine Pass at State Hwy. 87. Turn right and drive 10 mi. into the park.

SAN ANGELO

San Angelo State Park

3900-2 Mercedes, San Angelo 76901. T: (915) 949-4757 or (800) 792-1112; F: (915) 947-2963; www.tpwd.state.tx.us; sasp@wcc.net.

RV ★★★ Tent ★★★

Beauty: ★★★	Site Privacy: ★★★
Spaciousness: ★★★★	Quiet: ★★★★
Security: ★★★	Cleanliness: ★★★★
Insect Control: ★★★	Facilities: ★★★

Three campgrounds are situated along the North Concho River, and four are adjacent to O.C. Fisher Lake. Sites are spacious, if lackluster. RV campers looking for elbow room should ask for pull-through sites 1–11 (Red Arroyo area). Tent campers looking for lake views should head for sites 13–16 (Red Arroyo area). Many sites have partial lake views since there are few trees. Gravel parking is the norm. Ecologically diverse, this park is home to roughly 350 species of birds. The Concho River is named after indigenous freshwater mussels that produce iridescent pink or purple "Concho pearls." Also of interest are dinosaur tracks and Native American petroglyphs (access via reserved group tours). Suburban (fewer than three miles from San Angelo), but with locked gates at night, security is decent. The weather at this park can be extreme, so try to visit in spring, early summer, or fall.

Basics

Operated By: Texas Parks & Wildlife. **Open:** All year. **Site Assignment:** Reservations (512) 389-8900, reservations must be made at least 48 hours in advance, deposit required (equivalent to first night's fee) to hold reservation, cancellations more than two days prior to reservation result in $5 fee, cancellations within two days of reservation result in loss of deposit. **Registration:** Headquarters. **Fee:** $2 per person per day for anyone aged 13 & older, $10 for sites w/water, electric, $6 for primitive sites (cash, checks, V, MC, D). **Parking:** At site.

Facilities

Number of RV Sites: 80. **Number of Tent-Only Sites:** 100 primitive sites. **Hookups:** Water, electric. **Each Site:** Picnic table, fire ring, grill. **Dump Station:** Yes. **Laundry:** No. **Pay Phone:** Yes. **Rest Rooms and Showers:** Yes. **Fuel:** No. **Propane:** No. **Internal Roads:** Paved. **RV Service:** 3 mi. southeast in San Angelo. **Market:** Super Wal-Mart 3 mi. southeast in San Angelo. **Restaurant:** 3 mi. southeast in San Angelo. **General Store:** Super Wal-Mart, 3 mi. southeast in San Angelo. **Vending:** Beverages. **Swimming:** No. **Playground:** Yes. **Other:** High & low level boat ramps, courtesy docks, fishing platform, log shelters, group camping & picnic areas, equestrian camping, gift shop. **Activities:** Picnicking, hiking, mountain biking, horseback riding, swimming, fishing, boating, birding, group tours upon request. **Nearby Attractions:** Fort Concho, Concho Ave. shopping district, Concho River Walk, Miss Hattie's Museum. **Additional Information:** San Angelo Convention & Visitor's Bureau (800) 375-1206.

Restrictions

Pets: Must be kept on leash at all times. **Fires:** In fire rings & grills only. **Alcoholic Beverages:** Prohibited. **Vehicle Maximum Length:** 60 ft. **Other:** Max. 8 people per campsite, Quiet time 10 p.m.–6 a.m., fourteen day stay limit, gathering of firewood prohibited.

To Get There

To reach the south shore park entrance from San Angelo, take US 67 south for about 2 mi. and then turn right on FM 2288. To reach the north shore park entrance from San Angelo, go north on US 87 for about 2 mi., and then turn left on FM 2288.

SAN ANTONIO

Admiralty RV Resort

1485 North Ellison Dr., San Antonio, 78251. T: (210) 647-7878; F: (210) 521-4443; www.admiraltyresort.com; arvrllc@aol.com.

RV: ★★★ | Tent: n/a

Beauty: ★★★★	Site Privacy: ★★★
Spaciousness: ★★★	Quiet: ★★★
Security: ★★★	Cleanliness: ★★★★★
Insect Control: ★★★★★	Facilities: ★★★★

This gleefully tidy park is convenient to SeaWorld, restaraunts, and shopping. Six Flags Fiesta Texas, the Alamo, and the River Walk are within 30 miles. Spending the day at the park? Facilities are well maintained. The nicely landscaped campground is laid in rows of pull-throughs, with back-ins along the perimeter of the park. Sites are small, with little privacy. Some sites enjoy shady trees, but many are open. RV parking is paved, though some internal roads are gravel. Families should head for sites 1–10, 101–110, or 201–210, the closest to the playground. Couples looking for a little solitude should go for sites in the 600s. Security is fair at this suburban campground-there are no gates, but a guard patrols the property at night. The brochures claim that San Antonio has mild weather all year, but it sometimes gets chilly in the winter; visit in spring or fall.

Basics

Operated By: Corporate. **Open:** All year. **Site Assignment:** Reservations accepted all year, (800)

999-7872; credit card number holds site, no-show charged one night; deposit & refund policies vary for weekly & monthly stays. Check out at 11 a.m. **Registration:** At office. **Fee:** $34 per night for two people, $3.50 for 3rd, 4th, & 5th person, $5 for 6th, 7th, & 8th person. **Parking:** At site.

FACILITIES

Number of RV Sites: 240 w/full hookups. **Number of Tent-Only Sites:** 0. **Hookups:** Water, sewer, electric (30, 50 amps), dataport, & cable TV. **Each Site:** Picnic table, concrete pads, brick patio, some grills. **Dump Station:** Yes. **Laundry:** Yes. **Pay Phone:** Yes. **Rest Rooms and Showers:** Yes. **Fuel:** No. **Propane:** No. **Internal Roads:** Paved. **RV Service:** 2 mi. west. **Market:** 2 mi. east in San Antonio. **Restaurant:** 7 mi. east in San Antonio. **General Store:** 7 mi. north in San Antonio. **Vending:** Yes. **Swimming:** Pool. **Playground:** Yes. **Other:** Game room, exercise room, adult jacuzzi, clubhouse. **Activities:** Basketball, water aerobics, volleyball, year-round schedule of activities, including bingo, crafts, dances, ice cream socials, etc. **Nearby Attractions:** The Alamo, Botanical Gardens, San Antonio Zoo & Aquarium, Sea World, Mexican-American Cultural Center, Riverwalk, McNay Art Museum, Market Square, IMAX Theater, Institute of Texan Cultures. **Additional Information:** San Antonio CVB (800) 447-3372.

RESTRICTIONS

Pets: On 6-ft. max. leash at all times. **Fires:** Only in BBQ grills. **Alcoholic Beverages:** Allowed. **Vehicle Maximum Length:** 60 ft.

TO GET THERE

From I-410 (loop), take Exit 9A and drive northwest 2 mi. on State Hwy. 151. Turn left on Potranco Rd. and drive 2 mi. to North Ellison Rd. Turn right and the resort is one mile on the left.

SAN BENITO

Fun 'n' Sun

1400 Zillock Rd., San Benito, 78586. T: (956) 399-5125; F: (956) 399-7725; www.gocampingamerica.com/funnsun/; funnsun@acnet.net.

RV: ★★★	Tent: n/a
Beauty: ★★★	Site Privacy: ★★★
Spaciousness: ★★★	Quiet: ★★★
Security: ★★★★	Cleanliness: ★★★★
Insect Control: ★	Facilities: ★★★★

Open to seniors only, Fun 'n' Sun offers activities galore and keeps its extensive facilities in good shape. South Padre Island, Brownsville, and Mexico are easy to reach, as well as a plethora of restaurants and shopping. Though Fun 'n' Sun only accepts reservations for one month or longer, there are eight overnight sites near the front gate. Sites are small and have little privacy. Some are shaded by trees. All have paved, back-in parking. Each site has a little grassy area. Ask for sites 5–8, which are away from Zillock Rd. and quieter. Security is good. The gate is attended 24-hours. Don't visit south Texas in the summer, and be prepared for major crowds in the winter.

BASICS

Operated By: Lee & Jan Campbell. **Open:** All year. **Site Assignment:** Reservations for one month or more, $200 nonrefundable deposit, call (800) 399-5127; V, MC, checks, & cash accepted. **Registration:** At office, Mon–Fri., 8 a.m.–5 p.m.; at security building after hours. **Fee:** $24. **Parking:** At site.

FACILITIES

Number of RV Sites: 1408. **Number of Tent-Only Sites:** 0. **Hookups:** Water, sewer, electric (30, 50 amps), cable TV. **Each Site:** No amenities. **Dump Station:** No. **Laundry:** Yes. **Pay Phone:** Yes. **Rest Rooms and Showers:** Yes. **Fuel:** No. **Propane:** Yes. **Internal Roads:** Paved. **RV Service:** 15 mi. **Market:** 1 mi. **Restaurant:** 2 mi. **General Store:** 3 mi. **Vending:** Yes. **Swimming:** Pool. **Playground:** No. **Other:** Barber & beauty shops, post office, chapel, woodworking shop, music room, meeting rooms, rec hall, dance hall, sewing room, library, lapidary shop, tennis courts, hot tub, silver smithing shop. **Activities:** Dancing, pool, shuffleboard, horseshoes, bocci ball, birding. **Nearby Attractions:** South Padre Island Beaches, Gladys Porter Zoo, Mexico. **Additional Information:** San Benito Chamber of Commerce, (956) 399-5321.

RESTRICTIONS

Pets: On leash only. **Fires:** In grills only. **Alcoholic Beverages:** Allowed. **Vehicle Maximum Length:** 40 ft. **Other:** All rates are based on occupancy of 2 people per unit. One person must be at least 55 years old & the other person at least 40 years old.

TO GET THERE

From US 77/83, take the Paso Real/Hwy. 509 exit. Stay on the frontage road 0.25 mi. past Paso Real and turn right on Zillock Rd. The campground is 0.25 mi.

SAN MARCOS

United RV Resort

1610 IH 35 North, San Marcos, 78666. T: (512) 353-5959; F: (512) 353-8271; www.gocampingamerica.com/unitedrv/index.html; united-rv@sanmarcos.net.

RV ★★★ Tent ★★★

Beauty: ★★★★ Site Privacy: ★★★
Spaciousness: ★★★ Quiet: ★★★
Security: ★★★ Cleanliness: ★★★
Insect Control: ★★★ Facilities: ★★★

Though clean and pretty, United lacks the recreational facilities found at many of the better parks. Just off of I-35, we recommend United as a convenient stopover or if you plan on spending most of your time outside the park. Restaurants and shopping are nearby. Most of the sites are laid out in rows of pull-throughs. However, we recommend sites in the 40s, 50s, and 60s—shady back-ins along the southern perimeter of the park. Families should consider sites 1–20, which are closer to the pool and playground. Comfortably spaced, most sites enjoy some shade and a little privacy. Parking is on gravel and each site has a long grassy area. When we visited, the suburban park was experiencing a loitering problem, raising questions about security. Visit San Marcos in the summertime if you want to take the kids to nearby Schlitterbahn Water Park.

BASICS

Operated By: Ed & Josephine Morrill. **Open:** All year. **Site Assignment:** Reservations accepted (800) 344-9906, credit card number holds site, 24-hour cancellation notice required. Check-in & check-out are at noon. **Registration:** At office. **Fee:** $21.60 per night for 2 people (RV & tent sites w/electricity), $20.70 for tent sites w/water only, $3 per extra person over age 3. **Parking:** 2 places per site, gravel.

FACILITIES

Number of RV Sites: 100. **Number of Tent-Only Sites:** 5 w/electricity & water, 9 w/water only. **Hookups:** Water, sewer, electric (30, 50 amps), cable (91 sites w/full hookups). **Each Site:** Picnic table, some grills. **Dump Station:** Yes. **Laundry:** Yes. **Pay Phone:** Yes. **Rest Rooms and Showers:** Yes. **Fuel:** No. **Propane:** Yes. **Internal Roads:** Paved. **RV Service:** 14 mi. north in Buda. **Market:** 2 mi. north in San Marcos. **Restaurant:** 0.5 mi. north in San Marcos. **General Store:** At park. **Vending:** Yes. **Swimming:** Pool. **Playground:** Yes. **Other:** Lounge, fax, copier services, cc telephone, clubhouse, pet park, video services. **Activities:** Horseshoes, shuffleboard, Ping-Pong. **Nearby Attractions:** Aquarena Center, Camping World, Wonder World, Schlitterbahn Water Park. **Additional Information:** San Marcos CVB (888) 200-5620.

RESTRICTIONS

Pets: On leash at all times. **Fires:** In grills only. **Alcoholic Beverages:** Allowed. **Vehicle Maximum Length:** 70 ft. **Other:** Due to high water pressure, water pressure regulators are recommended.

TO GET THERE

From San Antonio, head north on I-35 toward Austin. Take Exit 206 and stay to the right. Park will be on the right just off the service road.

SMITHVILLE

Buescher State Park

P.O. Box 75, Smithville, 78957-0075. T: (512) 237-2241; F: (512) 237-2580; www.tpwd.state.tx.us.

RV ★★★★★ Tent ★★★★★

Beauty: ★★★★★ Site Privacy: ★★★★★
Spaciousness: ★★★★★ Quiet: ★★★★★
Security: ★★★★ Cleanliness: ★★★★
Insect Control: ★ Facilities: ★★★★★

Part of a complex of state parks, Buescher connects to Bastrop State Park with a 13-mile paved, winding, hilly road that's appreciated by experienced cyclists. Unlike Bastrop, Buescher's facilities surround a small lake (approximately 25 acres) supporting catfish, bass, crappie, perch, and seasonal rainbow trout. The "Lost Pines" of Texas are prominent on the road from Bastrop. Post and live oak steal the show at Buescher. We prefer sites at Buescher over Bastrop because of their gorgeous foliage between sites. But mosquitoes are far worse here—stay at drier Bastrop if it's been raining. Three campgrounds dot the small lake. RV campers find paved, back-in sites at Cozy Circle. With shady oak trees and paved back-in parking, we prefer the multi-use sites at Oak Haven. All sites are spacious. Rural location and locked nighttime gates make security excellent. Plan to visit on weekdays to avoid the mob.

Basics

Operated By: Texas Parks & Wildlife. **Open:** All year. **Site Assignment:** Reservations (512) 389-8900; reservations must be made at least 48 hours in advance; deposit (equivalent to first night's fee) required to hold reservation; cancellations more than two days prior to reservation result in $5 fee, cancellations within two days of reservation result in loss of deposit. **Registration:** Headquarters. **Fee:** $3 per person per day for anyone aged 13 & over, $10 for sites w/water & electric, $7 for sites w/water only (cash, checks, V, MC, D). **Parking:** At most sites.

Facilities

Number of RV Sites: 40. **Number of Tent-Only Sites:** 25 sites w/water only. **Hookups:** Water, electric (30 amps). **Each Site:** Picnic table, grill, fire ring. **Dump Station:** Yes. **Laundry:** No. **Pay Phone:** Yes. **Rest Rooms and Showers:** Yes. **Fuel:** No. **Propane:** No. **Internal Roads:** Paved. **RV Service:** 45 mi. west in Austin. **Market:** 1 mi. southwest in Smithville. **Restaurant:** 1 mi. southwest in Smithville. **General Store:** 1 mi. southwest in Smithville. **Vending:** Beverages only. **Swimming:** No. **Playground:** Yes. **Other:** Picnic area, group picnic pavilion, rec hall, gift shop, screened shelters. **Activities:** Hiking, boating, fishing, lake swimming, road biking. **Nearby Attractions:** Lake Bastrop, Bastrop State Park, Lake Somerville State Park & Trailway, towns of Smithville & Bastrop, Texas state capitol Austin. **Additional Information:** Austin CVB (800) 926-2282, Smithville Chamber of Commerce, (512) 237-2313; Bastrop Chamber of Commerce, (512) 321-2419.

Restrictions

Pets: On leash only. **Fires:** In fire ring only. **Alcoholic Beverages:** Prohibited. **Vehicle Maximum Length:** 50 ft.

To Get There

From Smithville, go northwest on TX 71 for 2 mi. Turn right on FM 153 and go north for 0.5 mi. to Park Rd. 1.

SNYDER

Wagon Wheel Dude Ranch

5996 CR 2128, Snyder, 79549. T: (915) 573-2348; F: (915) 573-5277; www.wagonwheel.com; wagonwr @snydertex.com.

 ★★★★  ★★★★

Beauty: ★★★★ Site Privacy: ★★★
Spaciousness: ★★★★ Quiet: ★★★★
Security: ★★★ Cleanliness: ★★★★
Insect Control: ★★★★ Facilities: ★★★★★

Wagon Wheel is an excellent destination for families with energetic children. In addition to planned recreation, kids love to run around and explore the ranch. If your group is big enough (10 or more people), you can schedule a chuck wagon meal. The campground includes old and new sections, though sites at both are basically the same. Both offer pull-throughs with gravel parking and a patchy grass and dirt area. Sites are large, some a long as 90 feet. With few trees and scrubby foliage, there is little shade or privacy at the campground. Families should pick a site close to the bathrooms. Tent campers should head for the more picturesque area near the pond (no hookups). Extremely remote, security is not a problem at Wagon Wheel. The panhandle plains sometimes experience extreme weather and should be avoided during winter and late summer.

Basics

Operated By: Billy Ray & Pam Browning. **Open:** All year. **Site Assignment:** Reservations recommended, credit card deposit, one week cancellation notice required, check-in at 3 p.m., check-out at noon. **Registration:** At office. **Fee:** $19.50 for 50-amp site, $16.50 for 30-amp site, $10 for tent. **Parking:** At site.

Facilities

Number of RV Sites: 25. **Number of Tent-Only Sites:** Tenting allowed near pond or near electricity hookups. **Hookups:** Water, sewer, electric (30, 50 amps). **Each Site:** Picnic table. **Dump Station:** Yes. **Laundry:** Yes. **Pay Phone:** Yes. **Rest Rooms and Showers:** Yes. **Fuel:** No. **Propane:** No. **Internal Roads:** Gravel. **RV Service:** 8 mi. east in Snyder. **Market:** 8 mi. east in Snyder. **Restaurant:** On site. **General Store:** 8 mi. east in Snyder. **Vending:** Beverages. **Swimming:** Pool. **Playground:** Yes. **Other:** Horseback riding lessons, trail rides, paddleboats, pleasure trails, game room, party barn. **Activities:** Washer pitching, horseshoes, softball, horseback riding, fishing, basketball, hiking, skeet shooting, quail & dove hunting. **Nearby Attractions:** Buffalo Gap Historic Village, Scurry County Museum, Abilene Zoo, Grace Museum, Dyess Air Force Base. **Additional Information:** Snyder Chamber of Commerce, (915) 573-3558; City of Snyder (915) 573-4957.

Restrictions

Pets: On leash only. **Fires:** In fire ring only. **Alcoholic Beverages:** Allowed. **Vehicle Maximum Length:** 50 ft.

To Get There

From Lubbock, take the Post Exit (US 84) off of Loop 289. Continue southeast toward Snyder. 37 mi. past the town of Post, turn left on CR 2128. Go 3 mi. to ranch; entrance on the left.

SOMERVILLE

Lake Somerville State Park and Trailway

Rte. 1 Box 499, Somerville, 77879-9713. T: (979) 535-7763; F: (979) 535-7718; www.tpwd.state.tx.us.

RV ★★★★★ Tent ★★★★★

Beauty: ★★★★★
Site Privacy: ★★★★★
Spaciousness: ★★★★★
Quiet: ★★★★★
Security: ★★★★
Cleanliness: ★★★★★
Insect Control: ★
Facilities: ★★★

Comprising over 8,700 acres, gorgeous Lake Somerville consists of three units: Nails Creek, Birch Creek, and the Somerville Wildlife Management Area (a public hunting area). Nails Creek and Birch Creek are connected by a 13-mile multi-use trail known for its spring wildflowers. Both Nails Creek and Birch Creek have lovely campgrounds with spacious sites. Exceptional privacy is provided by dense trees, including post oak, hickory, blackjack oak, and others. Each site has paved back-in parking and a large grassy area. Birch Creek is popular with college students. Families and couples prefer quieter Nails Creek. At Nails Creek, there are gorgeous lakefront sites in the Cedar Creek Loop. At Birch Creek, the prettiest views are at the Cedar Elm camping area (no hookups). Security is fair—there are no gates, but both campgrounds are extremely remote. Mosquitoes proliferate when it's rainy, so come prepared. For optimal weather, visit in spring or fall.

Basics

Operated By: Texas Parks & Wildlife. **Open:** All year. **Site Assignment:** Reservations (512) 389-8900; reservations must be made at least 48 hours in advance; deposit (equivalent to first night's fee) required to hold reservation; cancellations more than two days prior to reservation result in $5 fee, cancellations within two days of reservation result in loss of deposit. **Registration:** Headquarters. **Fee:** $2 per person per day for everyone aged 13 & older, $12 for equestrian sites, $9 for sites w/water & electricity, $8 for sites w/water only. **Parking:** At site.

Facilities

Number of RV Sites: 40 sites w/water & electricity. **Number of Tent-Only Sites:** 10. **Hookups:** Water, electric (30, 50 amps). **Each Site:** Picnic table, fire ring, lantern post, tent pad. **Dump Station:** Yes. **Laundry:** No. **Pay Phone:** Yes. **Rest Rooms and Showers:** Yes. **Fuel:** No. **Propane:** No. **Internal Roads:** Paved. **RV Service:** 20 mi. west in Giddings. **Market:** 12 mi. south in Burton. **Restaurant:** 3 mi. west of park. **General Store:** 12 mi. south in Burton. **Vending:** Beverages only. **Swimming:** No. **Playground:** No. **Other:** Birch Creek Unit: equestrian camping, group picnic pavilions, group camping, group dining hall, fish cleaning shelter, boat ramps, boat dock, volleyball courts, gift shop. Nails Creek Unit: group picnic area, equestrian camping, fish cleaning shelter, boat ramp, volleyball courts, gift shop. **Activities:** Picnicking, boating, fishing, swimming, hiking, backpacking, bicycling, mountain biking, horseback riding, volleyball, group tours available. **Nearby Attractions:** Bluebell Creamery, Presidential Corridor between Austin & College Station, Bastrop & Buescher State Parks, Stephen F. Austin & Washington-on-the-Brazos State Historical Parks, Austin (about 85 mi.), College Station (about 60 mi.). **Additional Information:** Austin Convention & Visitor's Bureau (800) 926-2282, Bryan-College Station Convention & Visitor's Bureau (800) 777-8292.

Restrictions

Pets: On leash only. **Fires:** In fire rings only. **Alcoholic Beverages:** Prohibited. **Vehicle Maximum Length:** 50 ft.

To Get There

To access Birch Creek Unit from Somerville, drive north on State Hwy. 36 for 4 mi. to the town of Lyons. Then drive west on State Hwy. 60 for 8 mi. and turn left onto Park Rd. 57. To get to Nails Creek Unit from Giddings, head east on TX 290 for 6 mi. Turn left on FM 180 and follow it for 15 mi.

SPRING BRANCH
Guadalupe River State Park

3350 Park Rd. 31, Spring Branch 78070. T: (830) 438-2656 or (800) 792-1112; F: (830) 438-2229; www.tpwd.state.tx.us.

RV ★★★★★ Tent ★★★★★

Beauty: ★★★★★	Site Privacy: ★★★★
Spaciousness: ★★★★★	Quiet: ★★★★★
Security: ★★★★★	Cleanliness: ★★★★
Insect Control: ★	Facilities: ★★★

Three campgrounds nestle into a bend in the Guadalupe River. For tent campers only, Cedar Sage Camping area has water at each site and paved back-in parking spaces. Sites 33–37 are the roomiest, and families with children should ask for sites 24 or 26, which flank the playground. Turkey Sink camping area contains spacious sites with paved back-in parking for RVs. The Guadalupe is lined with bald cypress and limestone bluffs. A variety of hardwoods provide shade and privacy for campers. Birdwatchers look for golden-cheeked warblers who nest in the park's virgin ashe juniper woodlands. Adjacent Honey Creek State Natural Area is home to live-oak grassland, a vanishing Central Texas ecosystem (access by guided tour only). Security is excellent here, with gates that lock at 10 p.m. Only 30 miles from San Antonio, this park is an excellent, quick getaway for city folk. Plan a visit during mild spring or autumn.

BASICS

Operated By: Texas Parks & Wildlife. **Open:** All year. **Site Assignment:** Reservations (512) 389-8900, reservations must be made at least 48 hours in advance, deposit required (equivalent to first night's fee) to hold reservation, cancellations more than two days prior to reservation result in $5 fee, cancellations within two days of reservation result in loss of deposit. **Registration:** Headquarters. **Fee:** $3 per person per day for anyone aged 13 & older, $15 for sites w/water & electric, $12 for water-only or walk-in primitive camping, $4 excess vehicle charge (cash, checks, D,V, MC). **Parking:** At most sites.

FACILITIES

Number of RV Sites: 48. **Number of Tent-Only Sites:** 20 primitive walk-in sites. **Hookups:** Water, electric. **Each Site:** Picnic table, fire ring, 16-ft. × 16-ft. tent pad. **Dump Station:** Yes. **Laundry:** No. **Pay Phone:** Yes. **Rest Rooms and Showers:** Yes. **Fuel:** No. **Propane:** No. **Internal Roads:** Paved. **RV Service:** 13 mi. west in Boerne. **Market:** 7 mi. east in Bulverde. **Restaurant:** 7 mi. east in Bulverde. **General Store:** 3 mi. west in Bergheim. **Vending:** Beverages. **Swimming:** No. **Playground:** Yes. **Other:** Interpretive Center, gift shop, amphitheater. **Activities:** Canoeing, tubing, fishing, swimming, picnicking, hiking. **Nearby Attractions:** Honey Creek State Natural Area, Blanco State Park, San Antonio, Boerne, New Braunfels, & San Marcos attractions. **Additional Information:** San Antonio CVB (210) 270-8700, Boerne Convention & Visitor's Bureau (800) 842-8080, New Braunfels Convention & Visitor's Bureau (800) 572-2626, San Marcos Convention & Visitor's Bureau (888) 200-5620.

RESTRICTIONS

Pets: Leash Only. **Fires:** In fire rings only. **Alcoholic Beverages:** Prohibited. **Vehicle Maximum Length:** 58 ft. **Other:** Max. 8 people per campsite, Quiet time 10 p.m.–6 a.m., fourteen day stay limit, gathering of firewood prohibited.

TO GET THERE

From I-10 (Boerne), drive east on TX 46 for 13 mi., and then turn left on Park Rd. 31. From San Antonio, drive North on US 281, and then turn left on TX 46. Drive west on TX 46 for 8 mi., and then turn right on Park Rd. 31. The park entrance is at the north end of Park Rd. 31.

SULPHER SPRINGS
Cooper Lake State Park (South Sulpher Unit)

Rte. 3 Box 741, Sulpher Springs 75482. T: (512) 389-8900 or (800) 792-1112; F: (512) 389-8959; www.tpwd.state.tx.us; e-mail.reservations@tpwd.state.tx.us.

RV ★★★★ Tent ★★★★★

Beauty: ★★★★	Site Privacy: ★★★★
Spaciousness: ★★★★	Quiet: ★★★★★
Security: ★★★★	Cleanliness: ★★★
Insect Control: ★★★	Facilities: ★★★

This state park is divided up into four camping areas, several day-use areas, and a screened shelter and cabin area on the water's edge. RV campers will be mostly concerned with the Bright Star and Deer Haven camping areas, unless they wish to bring a horse to the Buggy Whip equestrian area. All sites are grassy and forested, although often the trees that encircle the sites do not shade them. The Bright Star area is laid out in a loop, with sites on the inside being more open to the sun. (A shaded picnic table at these sites helps reduce exposure.) Site 2 is well-shaded, but close to a dumpster. Also very well-shaded are 12–15 (which back to the lake) and 19. Of these, 14 and 15 are 110-foot pull-throughs. Nominally part of the Deer Haven area, sites 47–58 and 78–87 are located along the internal road, and are for this reason less desirable than those closer to the water and off the beaten path. Even-numbered sites 62–66, which back to the water, are the best sites in this area for their superior shade. The Oak Grove area provides walk-in tenting sites on a dirt (not grass) floor. The best sites are 92 and 94–101, which are right on the water; the least desirable is 88, right by the entrance to Oak Grove. For those campers with horses, Buggy Whip offers back-in sites as spokes around a looped road. Each site has a trailhead that leads to horse trails. More than nearly any other campground, this park offers a huge selection of activities, and everyone should enjoy their stay enough to return year after year.

Basics

Operated By: Texas Parks & Wildlife. **Open:** All year. **Site Assignment:** First come, first served. (Credit card required to make a reservation. $3 reservation service fee; $5 cancellation fee.). **Registration:** In office. (Late arrivals use drop box at entrance.). **Fee:** Water, electric: $12, water: $8, plus $3 entrance fee per person (V, MC, D accepted in the office or for reservation.). **Parking:** At site, additional parking for walk-ins.

Facilities

Number of RV Sites: 102. **Number of Tent-Only Sites:** 15. **Hookups:** Water, electric (30 amps). **Each Site:** Picnic table, grill, fire pit, lantern post. **Dump Station:** Yes. **Laundry:** No. **Pay Phone:** Yes. **Rest Rooms and Showers:** Yes. **Fuel:** No. **Propane:** No. **Internal Roads:** Paved. **RV Service:** No. **Market:** 12 mi. to Sulpher Springs. **Restaurant:** 12 mi. to Sulpher Springs. **General Store:** No. **Vending:** Yes. **Swimming:** Lake. **Playground:** Yes. **Other:** Boat ramp, fish cleaning station, pavillion, cabins, shelters, firewood. **Activities:** Swimming, boating, fishing, hiking, mountain biking. **Nearby Attractions:** Sam Bell Maxey Historical State Park, Bonham State Park, Lake Bob S&lin State Park. **Additional Information:** South Sulpher Unit Office: (903) 945-5256.

Restrictions

Pets: On 6-ft. leash, cleaned up after. **Fires:** In grills. **Alcoholic Beverages:** None. **Vehicle Maximum Length:** None. **Other:** All visitors must pay $3 entrance fee per day.

To Get There

From the junction of Hwy. 19/154 and Hwy. 71, go 4.25 mi. west on Hwy. 71. Turn north onto FM 3505 and go 1.5 mi. to the entrance.

VALLEY VIEW

Ray Roberts State Park (Johnson Branch Unit)

100 PW 4153, Valley View 76272. T: (512) 389-8900 or (800) 792-1112; F: (512) 389-8959; www.tpwd.state.tx.us; e-mail.reservations@tpwd.state.tx.us.

RV ★★★★ | Tent ★★★★

Beauty: ★★★★	Site Privacy: ★★★★
Spaciousness: ★★★★	Quiet: ★★★★★
Security: ★★★★	Cleanliness: ★★★★★
Insect Control: ★★★	Facilities: ★★★

This park is divided into four camping areas. The Dogwood Canyon area is the first campground inside the entrance. It is furthest from the water, and also the most primitive, suitabale for tents but not RVs. (Sites are walk-ins.) The rest rooms have non-flush toilets. Oak Point is likewise a walk-in area suitable for tenting. Sites are open and grassy with great views of the lake. There is a small flush toilet but no showers. The Juniper Cove area is the very antithesis of Dogwood Canyon—some of its sites are right up by the water's edge (7–14), and the rest rooms are very clean and modern, with flush toilets and hot showers. These sites are 40-foot back-ins separated from the water by a row of wild bushes (except for 11–13, which are right on the water). Much less "natural" (and bordering on the ugly) are sites 1–6, 25, and 36–39, which are very open sites located on the blacktop. (Sites 5, 6, 36, 37 are pull-throughs.) While these may appeal to certain campers, they definitely miss the point of coming to such a beautiful lake. In the Walnut area, most sites are open to the sun, but sites 57 and 73 have exceptional shade. Sites

45, 49–52, and 55 have views of the water, while 41–44 and 87–89 are open blacktop sites like those described above. The rest rooms are clean and modern, like those in Juniper Cove. This campground is a delightful destination for anyone who enjoys water activities or just going "wild" for a while.

Basics

Operated By: Texas Parks & Wildlife. **Open:** All year. **Site Assignment:** First come, first served. (Credit card required to make a reservation. $3 reservation service fee; $5 cancellation fee.). **Registration:** In office. (Late arrivals use drop box at entrance.). **Fee:** Water, electric: $12, water (walk-in): $9, primitive (walk-in): $6, all add $3 entrance fee (V, MC, D accepted in the office or for reservation.). **Parking:** At site.

Facilities

Number of RV Sites: 104. **Number of Tent-Only Sites:** 83. **Hookups:** Water, electric (30 amps). **Each Site:** Picnic table, grill, fire pit, lantern post. **Dump Station:** Yes. **Laundry:** No. **Pay Phone:** Yes. **Rest Rooms and Showers:** Yes. **Fuel:** No. **Propane:** No. **Internal Roads:** Paved. **RV Service:** No. **Market:** 7 mi. to Valley View. **Restaurant:** 7 mi. to Valley View. **General Store:** Yes. **Vending:** Yes. **Playground:** Yes. **Other:** Pavillion, fish cleaning station, boat ramp. **Activities:** Swimming, boating, fishing, hiking, mountain biking. **Nearby Attractions:** Eisenhower State Park, Tioga, Frank Buck Zoo, Morton Museum. **Additional Information:** Johnson Branch Unit Office: (940) 637-2294.

Restrictions

Pets: On 6-ft. leash, cleaned up after. **Fires:** In grills. **Alcoholic Beverages:** None. **Vehicle Maximum Length:** None. **Other:** All visitors must pay $3 entrance fee per day.

To Get There

From I-35, take Exit 483 and go 6.5 mi. east on FM 3002. Turn right at the sign into the entrance.

VANDERPOOL

Lost Maples State Natural Area

HCR 1 Box 156, V&erpool 78885. T: (830) 966-3413; www.tpwd.state.tx.us.

 ★★★★  ★★★★

Beauty: ★★★★★ | Site Privacy: ★★★
Spaciousness: ★★★★ | Quiet: ★★★★
Security: ★★★★★ | Cleanliness: ★★★★★
Insect Control: ★★ | Facilities: ★★★

Famed for its isolated stand of Uvalde bigtooth maples, this natural area is popular with autumn "leaf peepers." However, the trees include other showy species such as sumac, and complement the area's striking granite outcroppings year-round. Built in a valley, the small campground offers exceptionally lovely views. The campsites are contained in one area and offer paved, back-in parking. Sites are decent-sized, with a little shade at most. Those without many trees benefit from the shaded picnic table found at each site. Few sites are very private. The most secluded are 17 and 18—we recommend these for tent campers and small RVs. Security at Lost Maples is fine. The park is so remote that gates are unnecessary. If you must visit in the fall, plan your trip for a weekday and make advance reservations. Ticks can proliferate here, so examine your hair and clothes regularly.

Basics

Operated By: Texas Parks & Wildlife. **Open:** All year. **Site Assignment:** Inquire at campground. **Registration:** Headquarters. **Fee:** $14 for sites w/water & electric, $5 per person day use fee. **Parking:** At site except primitive.

Facilities

Number of RV Sites: 30. **Number of Tent-Only Sites:** None. **Hookups:** Water, electric. **Each Site:** Shaded picnic table. **Dump Station:** Yes. **Laundry:** No. **Pay Phone:** Yes. **Rest Rooms and Showers:** Yes. **Fuel:** No. **Propane:** No. **Internal Roads:** Paved. **RV Service:** 48 mi. northeast in Kerrville. **Market:** 4 mi. south in V&erpool. **Restaurant:** 15 mi. south in Utopia. **General Store:** 15 mi. south in Utopia. **Vending:** No. **Swimming:** No. **Playground:** No. **Other:** Picnic sites, scenic drive, gift shop. **Activities:** Hiking, nature trail. **Nearby Attractions:** Garner & Kerrville-Schreiner State Parks, Hill Country State Natural Area, Frontier Times Museum, rodeos in B&era. **Additional Information:** B&era CVB (800) 364-3833.

Restrictions

Pets: Leash only. **Fires:** Fire rings only. **Alcoholic Beverages:** Not allowed. **Vehicle Maximum Length:** 50 ft. **Other:** Campfires not allowed in primitive sites.

To Get There

From Vanderpool, drive 5 mi. north on Ranch Rd. 187. The park is on the left.

WHITNEY
Lake Whitney State Park

P.O. Box 1175, Whitney, 76692. T: (254) 694-3793; F: (254) 694-6934; www.tpwd.state.tx.us.

RV ★★★ | Tent ★★★

Beauty: ★★
Spaciousness: ★★★
Security: ★★★
Insect Control: ★★★★
Site Privacy: ★★★
Quiet: ★★★
Cleanliness: ★★★
Facilities: ★★★

If you don't mind the crowds, visit in the spring, when over 40 species of wildflowers bloom. The rest of the year, this is one of the least attractive state parks in Texas. The park is in a rural area, but the town of Whitney is visible from the campgrounds. Even so, the park stays busy Mar. through Oct. due to its unique offerings, including an airstrip. There are three types of campsites in a number of separate areas. No sites with full hookups have water views. We recommend the water/electric areas, which contain a number of waterfront sites. Sites are spacious and parking is paved. There are both back-in and pull-through sites. Waterfront pull-throughs 124–130 are the nicest. With very few trees in the campgrounds, snag a site with a shade shelter. Tent campers have no trouble finding a waterfront site. Security is good, with locked gates at night.

Basics

Operated By: Texas Parks & Wildlife. **Open:** All year. **Site Assignment:** Reservations (512) 389-8900, reservations must be made at least 48 hours in advance, deposit required (equivalent to first night's fee) to hold reservation, cancellations more than two days prior to reservation result in $5 fee, cancellations within two days of reservation result in loss of deposit. **Registration:** Headquarters. **Fee:** $2 per person per day for anyone aged 13 & older, $20 for sites w/full hookups & shade shelters, $13 for sites w/full hookups, $12 for sites w/water & electricity, $8 for sites w/water only (cash, checks, D, V, MC). **Parking:** At site.

Facilities

Number of RV Sites: 24 w/full hookups, 42 w/electricity & water only. **Number of Tent-Only Sites:** 71. **Hookups:** Water, sewer, electric (30 amps). **Each Site:** Fire ring, stand-up grill, some picnic tables & shade shelters. **Dump Station:** Yes. **Laundry:** No. **Pay Phone:** Yes. **Rest Rooms and Showers:** Yes. **Fuel:** No. **Propane:** No. **Internal Roads:** Paved. **RV Service:** 30 mi. north in Cleburne. **Market:** 4 mi. east in Whitney. **Restaurant:** 4 mi. east in Whitney. **General Store:** 4 mi. east in Whitney. **Vending:** Beverages, ice, & wood. **Swimming:** No. **Playground:** Yes. **Other:** Airstrip, 21 screened shelters. **Activities:** Hiking, picnicking, boating, fishing, swimming, scuba diving, waterskiing, nature study, birding, & limited mountain biking. **Nearby Attractions:** Cleburne, Meridian, Dinosaur Valley, & Mother Neff State Parks, The Confederate Museum, Texas Ranger Hall of Fame, Fossil Rim Exotic Wildlife Ranch. **Additional Information:** Lake Whitney Chamber of Commerce, (254) 694-2540.

Restrictions

Pets: Must be on leash at all times, must have proof of current shots, not allowed in swimming area. **Fires:** Allowed in fire rings only. **Alcoholic Beverages:** Not allowed. **Vehicle Maximum Length:** 100 ft.

To Get There

From I-35, take the Hillsboro exit. In Hillsboro take TX 22 west approximately 15 mi. to Whitney. At the first traffic light, turn right on TX 933 and drive 0.5 mile to FM 1244. Turn left and the park is in 3 mi.

ZAVALLA
Angelina National Forest, Boykin Springs and Sandy Creek Recreation Areas

Rte. 2 Box 242, Zavalla 75980. T: (936) 897-1068; F: (936) 897-3406; www.southernregion.fs.fed.us/texas.

RV ★★★★★ | Tent ★★★★★

Beauty: ★★★★★
Spaciousness: ★★★★★
Security: ★★★★
Insect Control: ★★★
Site Privacy: ★★★★★
Quiet: ★★★★★
Cleanliness: ★★★★
Facilities: ★★★★

About 150,000 acres of national forest flank the Sam Reyburn Reservoir, with incredibly inexpensive camping areas. Boykin Springs, near man-made Boykin Lake, is the largest. Sandy Creek, a smaller camping area, contains sites with water views. The untidy campground host sites were disappointing. Sites at both campgrounds are beautiful and fairly similar, though Boykin's are often more private. The woods are lovely and provide shade at both campgrounds. Most sites are back-ins with gravel parking. Site size varies at both. At Sandy Creek, try to score site 10 (private and heavily wooded, with a lake view). At Boykin, head for sites 12, 14, and 15, bordering picturesque Boykin Creek. Security is good at Angelina National Forest owing to campground remoteness. Boykin Springs stays busy on spring and summer weekends—visit in autumn or during the week. Sandy Creek is less popular and may be visited on all but the busiest holiday weekends.

Basics

Operated By: USDA Forest Service. **Open:** All year. **Site Assignment:** First come, first served; no reservations. **Registration:** Pay station, self-registration. **Fee:** $6 for 8 people (cash, checks). **Parking:** At site (2 vehicles).

Facilities

Number of RV Sites: 48. **Number of Tent-Only Sites:** 4 (Boykin Springs). **Hookups:** None (water available). **Each Site:** Picnic table, fire ring &/or grill, tent pad. **Dump Station:** yes (at Caney Creek). **Laundry:** No. **Pay Phone:** No. **Rest Rooms and Showers:** Yes (cold only at S&y Creek). **Fuel:** No. **Propane:** No. **Internal Roads:** Paved. **RV Service:** 20 mi. in Jasper. **Market:** 20 mi. in Jasper. **Restaurant:** 20 mi. in Jasper. **General Store:** 20 mi. in Jasper. **Vending:** No. **Swimming:** No. **Playground:** No. **Other:** Sheltered picnic areas, boat launches. **Activities:** Fishing, hunting, swimming beaches (no lifeguard), horse trails, hiking, backpacking, mountain biking, canoeing, kayaking, bird-watching. **Nearby Attractions:** Jasper "Bass Fishing Capitol of the World," Museum of East Texas, Texas Forestry Museum, Millards Crossing historic Nacogdoches, antiques & flea markets, Sabine National Forest, Martin Dies Junior State Park. **Additional Information:** Lufkin/Angelina County chamber of Commerce, (936) 634-6644.

Restrictions

Pets: On leash only, must be kept quiet, not allowed on beaches. **Fires:** Allowed, fire rings, grills only. **Alcoholic Beverages:** Allowed, at sites. **Vehicle Maximum Length:** 24 ft. (sites vary). **Other:** No generators 10 p.m.–7 a.m.

To Get There

From Zavalla, drive east on State Hwy. 63. To get to Boykin Springs, drive 11 mi. and turn right (south) on Forest Service Rd. 313. Drive 2.5 mi. To get to Sandy Creek, drive 17.5 mi. and turn left (north) on Forest Service Rd. 333. Drive 3 mi.

Supplemental Directory of Campgrounds

ARKANSAS

Alma

Alma RV Park, 405 Heather Ln., 72921. T: (501) 632-0909. RV/tent: 50. $5–$22. Hookups: electric (30, 50 amps), water, sewer.

Ft. Smith/Alma KOA, 3539 North Hwy. 71, 72921. T: (800) 562-2703 or (501) 632-2704. www.koa.com/where/AR/04110. RV/tent: 78. $20–$24. Hookups: electric (30, 50 amps), water, sewer.

Indian Creek Campground, 13324 Indian Creek Rd., 72732. T: (501) 656-3145. www.ReserveUSA.com/nrrs/ar/ind2. RV/tent: 20. $13–$15. Hookups: electric (30 amps).

Arkadelphia

Alpine Ridge Campground, 729 Channel Rd., 71923. T: (870) 246-5501. www.ReserveUSA.com/nrrs/ar/alpr. RV/tent: 49. $10–$14. Hookups: electric (20, 30 amps).

Arlie Moore Campground, 729 Channel Rd., 71923. T: (870) 246-5501. www.ReserveUSA.com/nrrs/ar/arli. RV/tent: 71. $10–$14. Hookups: electric (20, 30 amps).

Caddo Drive Campground, 729 Channel Rd., 71923. T: (870) 246-5501. www.ReserveUSA.com/nrrs/ar/cadv. RV/tent: 72. $10. Hookups: electric (20, 30 amps).

Edgewood Campground, 729 Channel Rd., 71923. T: (870) 246-5501. www.ReserveUSA.com/nrrs/ar/edge. RV/tent: 51. $10–$14. Hookups: electric (20, 30 amps).

Iron Mountain Campground, 729 Channel Rd., 71923. T: (870) 246-5501. www.ReserveUSA.com/nrrs/ar/irom. RV/tent: 69. $10–$14. Hookups: electric (20, 30 amps).

Shouse Ford Campground, 729 Channel Rd., 71923. T: (870) 246-5501. www.ReserveUSA.com/nrrs/ar/shou. RV/tent: 100. $10–$14. Hookups: electric (20, 30, 50 amps).

Ashdown

Beards Bluff Campground, 1528 Hwy. 32 East, 71822. T: (870) 388-9556. www.ReserveUSA.com/nrrs/ar/beab. RV/tent: 30. $9–$14. Hookups: electric (20, 30 amps).

Cottonshed, 1528 Hwy. 32 East, 71822. T: (870) 287-7118. www.ReserveUSA.com/nrrs/ar/cotn. RV/tent: 46. $13–$15. Hookups: electric (20, 30 amps), water.

Millwood State Park, 1564 Hwy. 32 East, 71822. T: (870) 898-2800. www.ArkansasStateParks.com. RV/tent: 117. $9–$17. Hookups: electric (30 amps), water.

Benton

JB's RV Park & Campground, 8601 J.B. Baxely Rd., 72015. T: (501) 778-6050. RV/tent: 44. $14–$16. Hookups: electric (30, 50 amps), water, sewer.

Bismarck

DeGray State Park, 2027 State Park Entrance Rd., 71929. T: (501) 865-2801. www.ArkansasStateParks.com. RV/tent: 113. $14–$16. Hookups: electric (30 amps), water.

Bluff City

White Oak Lake State Park, Rte. 2 Box 28, 71722. T: (870) 685-2748 or (870) 685-2132. www.ArkansasStateParks.com. RV/tent: 45. $6–$14. Hookups: electric (30 amps), water.

Blytheville

Knights of the Road RV Park, 3801 South Division, 72315. T: (501) 763-7161. RV/tent: 12. $18. Hookups: electric (20, 30, 50 amps), water, sewer.

Brinkley

Super 8 RV Park, P.O. Box 828, 72021. T: (501) 734-4680. RV/tent: 34. $13–$17. Hookups: electric (30 amps), water, sewer.

ARKANSAS (continued)

Cotter

White River Campground & Cottages, P.O. Box 99, 72626. T: (870) 453-2299. F: (870) 453-3232. RV/tent: 86. $17. Hookups: electric (30, 50 amps), water, sewer.

Dardanelle

Mount Nebo State Park, No. 1 State Park Dr., 72834. T: (501) 229-3655. www.ArkansasStateParks.com. RV/tent: 35. $6–$12. Hookups: electric (30 amps), water.

DeQueen

Bellah Mine Campground, 706 DeQueen Lake Rd., 71832. T: (870) 584-4161. www.ReserveUSA.com/nrrs/ar/bell. RV/tent: 20. $10–$14. Hookups: electric (20, 30 amps), water.

Cossatot Reefs Campground, 706 DeQueen Lake Rd., 71832. T: (870) 584-4161. www.ReserveUSA.com/nrrs/ar/coss. RV/tent: 26. $9–$15. Hookups: electric (20, 30 amps), water.

Big Coon Creek Campground, 706 DeQueen Lake Rd., 71832. T: (870) 584-4161. www.ReserveUSA.com/nrrs/ar/bigc. RV/tent: 31. $13–$15. Hookups: electric (20, 30 amps), water.

Dierks

Blue Ridge Campground, 952 Lake Rd. P.O. Box 8, 71833. T: (870) 286-2346. www.ReserveUSA.com/nrrs/ar/blur. RV/tent: 17. $9–$13. Hookups: electric (20, 30 amps), water.

Eureka Springs

Green Tree Lodge & RV Park, Rte. 6 Box 130, 72632. T: (501) 253-8807. RV/tent: 24. $17–$19. Hookups: electric (20, 30, 50 amps), water, sewer.

Hidden Cove, 700 C.R. 1089, 72632. T: (501) 253-2939. F: (501) 253-0591. www.eurekaweb.com/hiddencove. RV/tent: 80. Hookups: electric (20, 30, 50 amps), water, sewer.

Kettle Campground, Hwy. 62 East, Rte. 4 Box 615, 72632. T: (800) 899-CAMP or (501) 253-9100. www.eureka-net.com/kettle. RV/tent: 80. $12–$19. Hookups: electric (20, 30, 50 amps), water, sewer.

Starkey Campground, 3994 Mundell Rd., 72631. T: (501) 253-5866. www.ReserveUSA.com/nrrs/ar/star. RV/tent: 23. $11. Hookups: electric (20, 30 amps).

Wanderlust RV Park, Rte. 1 Box 946, 72632. T: (800) 253-7385. RV/tent: 90. $19. Hookups: electric (20, 30, 50 amps), water, sewer.

Fairfield Bay

Golden Pond RV Park, Box 1520, 72088. T: (501) 723-8212. F: (501) 723-8414. www.golden-pond.com. RV/tent: 35. $19. Hookups: electric (30, 50 amps), water, sewer.

Flippin

Cedar Hollow RV Park, 76 MC 8119, 72634. T: (877) 747-3633 or (870) 453-8643. www.billyhill.com/cedarhollowrv. RV/tent: 26. $17. Hookups: electric (20, 30, 50 amps), water, sewer.

Garfield

Lost Bridge South Campground, 12001 Buckhorn Cir., 72732. T: (501) 359-3312. www.ReserveUSA.com/nrrs/ar/loss. RV/tent: 36. $13. Hookups: electric (20, 30 amps).

Gilbert

Buffalo Camping and Canoeing, P.O. Box 45, 72636. T: (870) 439-2888 or (870) 439-2386. www.gilbertstore.com/lodging.htm. RV/tent: 86. $5–$15. Hookups: electric (30 amps), water.

Greenbrier

Woolly Hollow State Park, 82 Woolly Hollow Rd., 72058. T: (501) 679-2098. www.ArkansasStateParks.com. RV/tent: 32. $9–$14. Hookups: electric (30 amps), water.

Hampton

Silver Eagle RV Campground, P.O. Box 1165, 71744. T: (870) 798-3798. www.silvereaglerv.com. RV/tent: 35. $18. Hookups: electric (20, 30, 50 amps), water, sewer.

Harrisburg

Lake Poinsett State Park, 5752 State Park Ln., 72432. T: (870) 578-2064. www.ArkansasStateParks.com. RV/tent: 30. $12–$16. Hookups: electric (30 amps), water.

Harrison

Harrison Village Campground, Rte. 4 Box 15, 72601. T: (501) 743-3388. RV/tent: 79. $18. Hookups: electric (20, 30, 50 amps), water, sewer.

Shady Oaks Campground and RV Park, 960 Hwy. 206 East, 72601. T: (870) 743-2343. www.camptheoaks.com. RV/tent: 50. $12–$22. Hookups: electric (20, 30, 50 amps), water, sewer.

Heber Springs

Devils Fork Campground, 700 Heber Springs Rd. North, 72543. T: (501) 362-2416. www.ReserveUSA.com/nrrs/ar/devf. RV/tent: 56. $12–$17. Hookups: electric (20, 30 amps).

ARKANSAS (continued)

Heber Springs (continued)

Hill Creek Campground, 700 Heber Springs Rd. North, 72543. T: (501) 362-2416. www.ReserveUSA.com/nrrs/ar/hill. RV/tent: 41. $12–$15. Hookups: electric (30, 50 amps), water, sewer.

John F Kennedy Campground, 700 Heber Springs Rd. North, 72543. T: (501) 362-2416. www.ReserveUSA.com/nrrs/ar/john. RV/tent: 74. $15–$18. Hookups: electric (20, 30 amps), water.

Hot Springs

Camp Lake Hamilton, 6191 Central Ave., 71901. T: (501) 525-8204. RV/tent: 80. $12. Hookups: electric (30, 50 amps), water, sewer.

Hot Springs KOA, 838 McClendon Rd., 71901. T: (800) 562-5903 or (501) 624-5912. www.koa.com/where/AR/04106. RV/tent: 86. $24–$26. Hookups: electric (20, 30, 50 amps), water, sewer.

Lake Catherine State Park, 1200 Catherine Park Rd., 71913. T: (501) 844-4176. www.ArkansasStateParks.com. RV/tent: 70. $14–$16. Hookups: electric (30 amps), water.

Lakeside Trailer Park & Cottages, Inc., 451 Lakeland Dr., 71901. T: (501) 525-8878. RV/tent: 20. $13. Hookups: electric (30 amps), water, sewer.

Mill Pond Mobile Home & RV Village, 1 Peakness Dr., 71901. T: (501) 525-3959. RV/tent: 21. $10. Hookups: electric (30, 50 amps), water, sewer.

Pit Stop RV Park & Restaurant, 3040 Albert Pike, 71901. T: (501) 767-6830. RV/tent: 15. $18. Hookups: electric (30, 50 amps), water.

River View Paradise RV Park & Condos, 200 River Oaks Dr., 71901. T: (501) 767-9821. RV/tent: 65. $20. Hookups: electric (30 amps), water, sewer.

Timbercrest RV & Mobile Home Park, 3921 Central Ave., 71901. T: (501) 525-8361. RV/tent: 53. $15. Hookups: electric (50 amps), water, sewer.

Wagon Wheel RV Park, 205 Treasure Isle Rd. No. 99, 71913. T: (501) 767-6852. RV/tent: 62. $15–$18. Hookups: electric (30 amps), water, sewer.

Huntsville

Withrow Springs State Park, Rte. 3 Box 29, 72750. T: (501) 559-2593. www.ArkansasStateParks.com. RV/tent: 26. $6–$14. Hookups: electric (30 amps), water.

Jonesboro

Lake Frierson State Park, 7904 Hwy. 141, 72401. T: (870) 932-2615. www.ArkansasStateParks.com. RV/tent: 12. $12. Hookups: electric (30 amps), water.

Perkins RV Park, 1821 Parker Rd., 72404. T: (870) 935-4152. RV/tent: 44. $8–$19. Hookups: electric (30, 50 amps), water, sewer.

Kirby

Daisy State Park, 103 East Park, 71950. T: (870) 398-4487. www.ArkansasStateParks.com. RV/tent: 117. $6–$16. Hookups: electric (30 amps), water.

Lake Village

Lake Chicot State Park, 2542 Hwy. 257, 71653. T: (870) 265-5480. www.ArkansasStateParks.com. RV/tent: 127. $6–$17. Hookups: electric (30 amps), water, sewer.

Lakeview

Bull Shoals State Park, 129 Bull Shoals Park, 72756. T: (870) 431-5521. www.ArkansasStateParks.com. RV/tent: 105. $6–$16. Hookups: electric (30 amps), water, sewer.

Riverside Mobile/RV Park, 449 River Rd., 72642. T: (870) 431-5419. F: (870) 431-5419. www.riversidervpark.com. RV/tent: 21. $10–$15. Hookups: electric (20, 30, 50 amps), water, sewer.

Lamar

Dad's Dream RV Park, Rte. 2 Box 19, 72846. T: (501) 865-2322. RV/tent: 40. $12. Hookups: electric (30, 50 amps), water, sewer.

Lowell

Green Country RV Park, 110 Pleasant Grove Rd., 72745. T: (501) 659-8850. RV/tent: 71. $16–$18. Hookups: electric (30, 50 amps), water, sewer.

Hickory Creek Park, 12618 Hickory Creek Rd., 72745. T: (501) 750-2943. www.ReserveUSA.com/nrrs/ar/hic2. RV/tent: 61. $13–$15. Hookups: electric (20, 30 amps).

Magnolia

Coachman's Inn & RV Park, 420 East Main St., 71753. T: (870) 234-6122. RV/tent: 10. $15. Hookups: electric (30, 50 amps), water, sewer.

Mena

Queen Wilhelmina State Park, 3877 Hwy. 88 West, 71953. T: (501) 394-2863. www.ArkansasStateParks.com. RV/tent: 41. $6–$14. Hookups: electric (30 amps), water.

Morrilton

Cherokee Campground, 1 Quincy Rd., 72110. T: (501) 329-2986. www.ReserveUSA.com/nrrs/ar/che3. RV/tent: 33. $16. Hookups: electric (20, 30 amps), water.

ARKANSAS (continued)

Morrilton (continued)

Lewisburg Bay RV Park, 1020 South Bridge St., 72110. T: (501) 354-5601. RV/tent: 20. $11. Hookups: electric (30 amps), water, sewer.

Mount Ida

Marilyn's RV Park, 3551 Hwy. 270 West, 71957. T: (870) 867-0168. F: (870) 867-0168. RV/tent: 12. $15. Hookups: electric (15 amps), water.

Mountain Home

Bidwell Point Campground, P.O. Box 2070, 72654. T: (870) 467-5375. www.ReserveUSA.com/nrrs/ar/bidw. RV/tent: 48. $14. Hookups: electric (20, 30 amps).

Buck Creek Campground, P.O. Box 2070, 72654. T: (870) 785-4313. www.ReserveUSA.com/nrrs/ar/buck. RV/tent: 42. $9–$16. Hookups: electric (20, 30 amps).

Cranfield Park Campground, P.O. Box 2070, 72654. T: (870) 492-4191. www.ReserveUSA.com/nrrs/ar/cran. RV/tent: 69. $13–$16. Hookups: electric (20, 30 amps).

Gamaliel Campground, P.O. Box 2070, 72654. T: (870) 425-2700. www.ReserveUSA.com/nrrs/ar/gama. RV/tent: 64. $13–$16. Hookups: electric (20, 30 amps).

Jordan Park Campground, P.O. Box 2070, 72654. T: (870) 499-7223. www.ReserveUSA.com/nrrs/ar/jord. RV/tent: 33. $11–$14. Hookups: electric (20, 30 amps).

Panther Bay Campground, P.O. Box 2070, 72654. T: (870) 425-2700. www.ReserveUSA.com/nrrs/ar/pant. RV/tent: 22. $11. Hookups: electric (20, 30 amps).

Robinson Point Campground, P.O. Box 2070, 72654. T: (870) 492-6853. www.ReserveUSA.com/nrrs/ar/robp. RV/tent: 102. $13–$16. Hookups: electric (20, 30 amps).

White Buffalo Resort and Campground, 418 White Buffalo Tr., 72653. T: (870) 425-8555. RV/tent: 52. $18–$23. Hookups: electric (20, 30, 50 amps), water, sewer.

Mountain Pine

Lake Ouachita State Park, 5451 Mountain Pine Rd., 71956. T: (501) 767-9366. www.ArkansasStateParks.com. RV/tent: 118. $6–$17. Hookups: electric (30 amps), water, sewer.

Mountain View

Blue Sky RV Park, HC 72 Box 136, 72113. T: (870) 269-8132. www.blueskyrvpark.com. RV/tent: 87. $17. Hookups: electric (20, 30 amps), water, sewer.

Ozark RV Park, HC 71 Box 540, 72560. T: (501) 269-2542. RV/tent: 56. $14. Hookups: electric (20, 30 amps), water, sewer.

Mountainburg

Lake Fort State Park, P.O. Box 4, 72946. T: (501) 369-2469. www.ArkansasStateParks.com. RV/tent: 12. $14. Hookups: electric (30 amps), water.

Murfreesboro

Cowhide Cove Campground, Rte. 1, 71958. T: (870) 285-2151. www.ReserveUSA.com/nrrs/ar/cown. RV/tent: 50. $8–$14. Hookups: electric (20, 30 amps).

Crater of Diamonds State Park, 209 State Park Rd., 71958. T: (870) 285-3113. www.ArkansasStateParks.com. RV/tent: 60. $14.00. Hookups: electric (30 amps), water.

Self Creek Campground, Rte. 1, 71958. T: (870) 285-2151. www.ReserveUSA.com/nrrs/ar/self. RV/tent: 72. $12–$14. Hookups: electric (20, 30 amps).

Omaha

Ozark Vue RV Park, Rte. 1 Box 126D, 72662. T: (501) 426-5166. RV/tent: 31. $14. Hookups: electric (20, 30, 50 amps), water, sewer.

Cricket Creek Campground, 20110 Boat Dock Rd., 72662. T: (870) 426-3331. www.ReserveUSA.com/nrrs/ar/cric. RV/tent: 35. $11–$14. Hookups: electric (20, 30 amps).

Ozark

Aux Arc Campground, 6042 Lock and Dam Rd., 72949. T: (501) 667-2129. www.ReserveUSA.com/nrrs/ar/auxa. RV/tent: 63. $14–$19. Hookups: electric (20, 30, 50 amps), water, sewer.

Perryville

Coffee Creek Landing & Resort, P.O. Box 31, 72126. T: (501) 889-2745. F: (501) 889-5485. www.coffeecreekresort.com. RV/tent: 63. $15. Hookups: electric (20, 30, 50 amps), water, sewer.

Plainview

Quarry Cove Campground, Nimrod Lake Quarry Cove Park, 3 Hwy. 7 South, 72857. T: (501) 272-4233. www.ReserveUSA.com/nrrs/ar/quar. RV/tent: 31. $14. Hookups: electric (20, 30 amps), water.

ARKANSAS (continued)

Plainview (continued)

Sunlight Bay Campground, Sunlight Bay 3 Hwy. 7 South, 72857. T: (501) 272-4234. www.ReserveUSA.com/nrrs/ar/sunl. RV/tent: 28. $14. Hookups: electric (20, 30 amps), water.

Powhatan

Lake Charles State Park, 3705 Hwy. 25, 72458. T: (870) 878-6595. www.ArkansasStateParks.com. RV/tent: 61. $14–$16. Hookups: electric (30 amps), water.

Rogers

Lost Bridge North Campground, 2260 North 2nd, 72756. T: (501) 359-3312. www.ReserveUSA.com/nrrs/ar/lost. RV/tent: 48. $13–$15. Hookups: electric (20, 30 amps).

Royal

Brady Mountain Campground, 1201 Blakely Dam Rd., 71968. T: (501) 767-2108. www.ReserveUSA.com/nrrs/ar/bran. RV/tent: 74. $12–$14. Hookups: electric (20, 30 amps).

Denby Point Campground, 1201 Blakely Dam Rd., 71968. T: (501)767-2108. www.ReserveUSA.com/nrrs/ar/denb. RV/tent: 67. $8–$14. Hookups: electric (20, 30 amps).

Russellville

Lake Dardanelle State Park, 2428 Marina Rd., 72802. T: (501) 967-5516. www.ArkansasStateParks.com. RV/tent: 83. $14–$17. Hookups: electric (30 amps), water, sewer.

Piney Bay Campground, 1598 Lock And Dam Rd., 72802. T: (501) 885-3029. www.ReserveUSA.com/nrrs/ar/pinb. RV/tent: 91. $13–$16. Hookups: electric (20, 30 amps), water.

Siloam Springs

Greentree RV Park, 1800 West Hwy. 412, 72761. T: (501) 524-8898. RV/tent: 37. $17–$19. Hookups: electric (30, 50 amps), water, sewer.

South Plainview

Carter Cove Campground, 3 Hwy. 7, 72857. T: (501) 272-4983. www.ReserveUSA.com/nrrs/ar/cart. RV/tent: 34. $14. Hookups: electric (20, 30 amps), water.

County Line, 3 Hwy. 7, 72857. T: (501) 272-4945. www.ReserveUSA.com/nrrs/ar/coul. RV/tent: 20. $14. Hookups: electric (20, 30 amps), water.

Springdale

Springdale Whisler RV Park, 1101 South Old Missouri Rd., 72764. T: (501) 751-9081. F: (501) 756-9388. RV/tent: 64. $15. Hookups: electric (30, 50 amps), water, sewer.

Star City

Cane Creek State Park, P.O. Box 96, 71667. T: (870) 628-4714. www.ArkansasStateParks.com. RV/tent: 30. $14–$16. Hookups: electric (30 amps), water.

Van Buren

Park Ridge RV Campground, 1616 Rena Rd., 72956. T: (501) 410-GORV (4678). F: (501) 474-2282. RV/tent: 28. $16–$24. Hookups: electric (30, 50 amps), water, sewer.

West Fork

Devil's Den State Park, 11333 West Hwy. 74, 72774. T: (501) 761-3325. www.ArkansasStateParks.com. RV/tent: 148. $6–$16. Hookups: electric (30 amps), water.

West Memphis

Tom Sawyer's Mississippi River RV Park, 1286 South 8th, 72301. T: (870) 735-9770. RV/tent: 90. $20–$22. Hookups: electric (30, 50 amps), water, sewer.

COLORADO

Alamosa

Alamosa Economy Campground, 12532 Hwy. 160 East, 81101. T: (719) 589-5574. RV/tent: 30. $10–$15. Hookups: electric (20, 30, 50 amps), water.

Almont

Three Rivers Resort & Outfitting, Rafting, Fishing, Kayaking, P.O. Box 339, 81210. T: (888) 761-3474 or (970) 641-1303. RV/tent: 62. $20. Hookups: electric (20, 30 amps), water, sewer.

Antonito

Camp Twin Rivers Cabins & RV Park, 34044 Hwy. 17, 81120. T: (888) 689-6787 or (719) 376-5710. F: (719) 376-5954. RV/tent: 46. $13–$18. Hookups: electric (20, 30, 50 amps), water, sewer.

Narrow Gauge RR Inn & RV Park, 5200 CO 285, P.O. Box 636, 81120. T: (800) 323-9469 or (719) 376-5441. F: (719) 376-5443. RV/tent: 10. $12. Hookups: electric (20, 30 amps), water, sewer.

Ponderosa Campground & Cabins, 18234 West Hwy. 17, 81120. T: (719) 376-5857. RV/tent: 34. $16–$22. Hookups: electric (20, 30 amps), water.

Arboles

Arboles Campground, Navajo State Park, 1526 CR 982, Box 1697, 81121. T: (970) 883-2208. http://parks.state.co.us/navajo. RV/tent: 52. $18. Hookups: electric (30 amps).

Mancos State Park, 1526 CR 982, Box 1697, 81121. T: (970) 883-2208. http://parks.state.co.us/mancos. RV/tent: 25. $18. Hookups: none.

Piñon Park Campground, RV Resort & Lodging, P.O. Box 1729, 81121. T: (888) 926-1749 or (970) 883-3636. RV/tent: 55. $12–$20. Hookups: electric (20, 30, 50 amps), water, sewer.

Aurora

Cherry Creek State Park (Cherry Creek Campground), 4201 South Parker Rd., 80014. T: (303) 699-3860. http://parks.state.co.us/cherry_creek. RV/tent: 102. $18. Hookups: electric (30 amps).

Denver Meadows RV Park, 2075 Potomac St., 80011. T: (800) 364-9487 or (303) 364-9483. F: (303) 366-7289. RV/tent: 278. $25. Hookups: electric (20, 30, 50 amps), water, sewer.

Bayfield

Riverside RV Park, 41743 Hwy. 160, P.O. Box 919, 81122. T: (888) 884-2475 or (970) 884-2475. F: (970) 884-6163. RV/tent: 97. $12–$19. Hookups: electric (20, 30 amps), water, sewer.

Vallecito Resort, 13030 CR 501, 81122. T: (970)884-9458 (Apr–Sept) or (480) 671-9848 (Oct–Apr). RV/tent: 213. $15–$33. Hookups: electric (20, 30, 50 amps), water, sewer.

Bellevue

Archer's Poudre River Resort, 33021 Poudre Canyon Hwy., 80512. T: (888) 822-0588 or (970) 881-2139. RV/tent: 9. $17–$25. Hookups: electric (20, 30, 50 amps), water, sewer.

Home Moraine Trailer Park, 37797 Poudre Canyon Hwy., 80512. T: (970) 881-2356. RV/tent: 32. $15. Hookups: electric (20, 30, 50 amps), water, sewer.

Mountain Park, Hwy. 14, 80512. T: (970) 881-2157. www.ReserveUSA.com/nrrs/co/mout. RV/tent: 55. $18. Hookups: electric (20, 30 amps).

Rustic Resort, Restaurant, Lounge, & Store, 31443 Poudre Canyon Hwy., 80512. T: (970) 881-2179. RV/tent: 18. $14–$16. Hookups: electric (20, 30 amps), water, sewer.

Sportsman's Lodge & Store, 44174 Poudre Canyon Hwy., 80512. T: (800) 270-2272 or (970) 881-2272. RV/tent: 14. $25. Hookups: electric (20, 30 amps), water, sewer.

Blanca

Blanca RV Park, 521 Main St., 81123. T: (719) 379-3201. RV/tent: 36. $15. Hookups: electric (20, 30, 50 amps), water, sewer.

Brighton

Barr Lake Campground, 17180 East 136th Ave., 80601. T: (800) 654-7988 or (303) 659-6180. RV/tent: 108. $19–$28. Hookups: electric (20, 30, 50 amps), water, sewer.

Buena Vista

Buena Vista KOA, 27700 CR 303, 81211. T: (800) 562-2672 or (719) 395-8318. F: (719) 395-2192. www.koa.com. RV/tent: 87. $18–$27. Hookups: electric (50 amps), water, sewer.

Crazy Horse Camping Resort, 33975 Hwy. 24 North, 81211. T: (800) 888-7320. www.crazyhorseresort.com. RV/tent: 85. $19–$28. Hookups: electric (20, 30 amps), water, sewer.

Mt. Princeton RV Park, 30380 CR 383, 81211. T: (719) 395-6206. RV/tent: 86. $20. Hookups: electric (30, 50 amps), water, sewer.

Snowy Peaks RV & Mobile Park, 30430 North Hwy. 24, 81211. T: (719) 395-8481. www.snowypeaksrvpark.com. RV/tent: 65. $18–$20. Hookups: electric (20, 30, 50 amps), water, sewer.

COLORADO (continued)

Canon City

Buffalo Bill's Royal Gorge Campground, 30 CR 3-A, 81212. T: (800) 787-0880 or (719) 269-3211. F: (719) 269-3211. www.camproyalgorge.com. RV/tent: 46. $20–$22. Hookups: electric (20, 30, 50 amps), water, sewer.

Conejos River Campground, 26714 Hwy. 17, 81120. T: (719) 376-5943. RV/tent: 56. $18. Hookups: electric (30, 50 amps), water, sewer.

Fort Gorge Campground & RV Park, 45044 Hwy. 50, 81212. T: (719) 275-5111. F: (719) 276-3069. RV/tent: 90. $15–$22. Hookups: electric (20, 30, 50 amps), water, sewer.

Indian Springs Ranch, P.O. Box 405, 81215. T: (719) 372-3907. www.coloradodirectory.com/indianspringsranch. RV/tent: 80. $15–$20. Hookups: electric (20, 30, 50 amps), water, sewer.

Royal Gorge/Canon City KOA, P.O. Box 528, 81215. T: (800) 562-5689. F: (719) 275-6116. www.koa.com. RV/tent: 153. $20–$27. Hookups: electric (20, 30, 50 amps), water, sewer.

Royal View Camp Resort, 43590 Hwy. 50 West, 81212. T: (866) 290-2461 or (719) 275-1900. F: (719) 275-0498. www.royalviewcampground.com. RV/tent: 53. $15–$35. Hookups: electric (20, 30, 50 amps), water, sewer.

Yogi Bear's Jellystone Park, 43595 Hwy. 50, 81212. T: (719) 275-2128. RV/tent: 81. $22–$31. Hookups: electric (20, 30 amps), water, sewer.

Cascade

Lone Duck Campground & Fishing Pond, P.O. Box 25, 80809. T: (800) 776-5925 or (719) 684-9907. RV/tent: 99. $19–$25. Hookups: electric (20, 30, 50 amps), water, sewer.

Cedaredge

Alexander Lake Lodge, P.O. Box 900, 81413. T: (970) 856-2539. F: (970) 856-2540. RV/tent: 17. $20. Hookups: electric (20, 30, 50 amps), water, sewer.

Mesa View RV Park, 195 Southwest 15th Cir., 81413. T: (970) 856-7689. F: (970) 856-7693. RV/tent: 10. $15. Hookups: electric (20, 30 amps), water, sewer.

Shady Creek, 205 North Grand Mesa Dr. (Hwy. 65), 81413. T: (970) 856-7522. F: (970) 856-7563. RV/tent: 16. $20. Hookups: electric (30, 50 amps), water, sewer.

Central City

Central City/Blackhawk KOA, 661 Hwy. 46, 80403. T: (800) 562-1620 or (303) 582-9979. F: (303) 582-3475. www.koa.com. RV/tent: 37. $16–$24. Hookups: electric (15, 20, 50 amps), water, sewer.

Cimarron

Black Canyon RV Park & Campground, P.O. Box 128, 81220. T: (970) 249-1147. RV/tent: 31. $15–$22. Hookups: electric (20, 30, 50 amps), water, sewer.

Clark

Pearl Lake State Park Lower Loop, P.O. Box 750, 80428. T: (970) 879-3922. http://parks.state.co.us/pearl. RV/tent: 15. $14. Hookups: none.

Pearl Lake State Park Upper Loop, P.O. Box 750, 80428. T: (970) 879-3922. http://parks.state.co.us/pearl. RV/tent: 21. $14. Hookups: none.

Coaldale

Hidden Valley Campground & Trail Rides, P.O. Box 220, 81222. T: (719) 942-4171. RV/tent: 63. $14–$19. Hookups: electric (20, 30, 50 amps), water, sewer.

Collbran

Wallace Guides & Outfitters, P.O. Box 380, 81624. T: (970) 487-3235. F: (970) 487-0118. RV/tent: 4. $10. Hookups: electric (20, 30 amps), water.

Colorado Springs

Conifer Ridge Campground, Mueller State Park, P.O. Box 39, 80814. T: (719) 687-2366. http://parks.state.co.us/mueller. RV/tent: 28. $18. Hookups: electric (30 amps).

Cross Creek Campground, Eleven Mile State Park, 4229 CR 92, 80827. T: (719) 748-3401. http://parks.state.co.us/eleven_mile. RV/tent: 13. $14. Hookups: none.

Fountain Creek RV Park, 3023 1/2 West Colorado Ave., 80904. T: (719) 633-2192. RV/tent: 114. $24–$28. Hookups: electric (20, 30, 50 amps), water, sewer.

Goldfield Campground, 411 South 26th, 80904. T: (719) 471-0495. RV/tent: 50. $20–$23. Hookups: electric (20, 30, 50 amps), water, sewer.

Grouse Mountain Campground, Mueller State Park, P.O. Box 39, 80814. T: (719) 687-2366. http://parks.state.co.us/mueller. RV/tent: 32. $18. Hookups: electric (30 amps).

Howbert Point Campground, Eleven Mile State Park, 4229 CR 92, 80827. T: (719) 748-3401. http://parks.state.co.us/eleven_mile. RV/tent: 10. $14. Hookups: none.

Lazy Boy Campground, Eleven Mile State Park, 4229 CR 92, 80827. T: (719) 748-3401. http://parks.state.co.us/eleven_mile. RV/tent: 14. $14. Hookups: none.

COLORADO (continued)

Colorado Springs (continued)

Mountaindale Campground & Cabins, 2000 Barrett Rd., 80926. T: (719) 576-0619. F: (719) 576-0619. RV/tent: 93. $15–$22. Hookups: electric (20, 30, 50 amps), water, sewer.

North Shore Campground, Eleven Mile State Park, 4229 CR 92, 80827. T: (719) 748-3401. http://parks.state.co.us/eleven_mile. RV/tent: 89. $14. Hookups: none.

Northwoods Village RV Park, 3100 Wood Ave., 80907. T: (719) 633-7564. RV/tent: 143. $20. Hookups: electric (50 amps), water, sewer.

Peak View Campground, Mueller State Park, P.O. Box 39, 80814. T: (719) 687-2366. http://parks.state.co.us/mueller. RV/tent: 5. $18. Hookups: electric (30 amps).

Peak View Inn & RV Park, 4950 North Nevada Ave., 80918. T: (800) 551-CAMP or (719) 598-1434. RV/tent: 120. $20–$25. Hookups: electric (20, 30 amps), water, sewer.

Revenuers Ridge Campground, Mueller State Park, P.O. Box 39, 80814. T: (719) 687-2366. http://parks.state.co.us/mueller. RV/tent: 34. $18. Hookups: electric (30 amps).

Rocking Chair Campground, Eleven Mile State Park, 4229 CR 92, 80827. T: (719) 748-3401. http://parks.state.co.us/eleven_mile. RV/tent: 13. $14. Hookups: none.

Rocky Ridge Campground, Eleven Mile State Park, 4229 CR 92, 80827. T: (719) 748-3401. http://parks.state.co.us/eleven_mile. RV/tent: 140. $14. Hookups: electric (30 amps).

Witcher Cove Campground, Eleven Mile State Park, 4229 CR 92, 80827. T: (719) 748-3401. http://parks.state.co.us/eleven_mile. RV/tent: 26. $14. Hookups: none.

Wrangler RV Ranch & Motel, 6225 East Platte Ave. (Hwy. 24), 80915. T: (719) 591-1402. RV/tent: 110. $26–$28. Hookups: electric (20, 30, 50 amps), water, sewer.

Cortez

La Mesa Campground, 2430 East Main St., 81321. T: (970) 565-3610. RV/tent: 45. $19. Hookups: electric (20, 30 amps), water, sewer.

Lazy G Campground, P.O. Box 1048, 81321. T: (800) 628-2183 or (970) 565-8577. F: (970) 565-0123. RV/tent: 79. $14–$20. Hookups: electric (20, 30, 50 amps), water, sewer.

Sundance RV Park, 815 East Main, 81321. T: (800) 880-9413 or (970) 565-0997. RV/tent: 68. $24. Hookups: electric (20, 30, 50 amps), water, sewer.

Creede

Antlers Rio Grande Resort, 26222 Hwy. 149, 81130. T: (719) 658-2423. F: (719) 658-0804. RV/tent: 24. $23. Hookups: electric (30, 50 amps), water, sewer.

Broken Arrow Ranch, HC 70, 32728 Hwy. 149, 81130. T: (719) 658-2484. RV/tent: 10. $15. Hookups: electric (20, 30, 50 amps), water, sewer.

Cripple Creek

Cripple Creek Gold Campground & Horse Company, P.O. Box 601, 80813. T: (719) 689-2342 or (719) 689-0131. RV/tent: 25. $12–$14. Hookups: electric (20, 30 amps).

Cripple Creek Hospitality House & Travel Park, P.O. Box 957, 80813. T: (800) 500-2513 or (719) 689-2513. RV/tent: 88. $16–$19. Hookups: electric (20, 30, 50 amps), water, sewer.

Cripple Creek KOA, P.O. Box 699, 80813. T: (800) 562-9125 or (719) 689-3376. www.koa.com. RV/tent: 82. $20–$25. Hookups: electric (20, 30, 50 amps), water, sewer.

Prospectors RV Park, P.O. Box 1237, 80813. T: (719) 689-2006. RV/tent: 27. $5–$20. Hookups: electric (20, 30 amps), water, sewer.

Del Norte

Woods & River Campground, P.O. Box 64, 81132. T: (877) 354-6922 or (719) 657-4530 or (719) 657-4530. RV/tent: 46. $12–$19. Hookups: electric (20, 30 amps), water, sewer.

Delta

Four Seasons River Inn & RV Park, 676 Hwy. 50 North, 81416. T: (888) 340-4689 or (970) 874-9659. RV/tent: 30. $18–$21. Hookups: electric (30, 50 amps), water, sewer.

Over-The-Hill RV Ranch, 1675 Hwy. 92, 81416. T: (970) 874-0200. RV/tent: 51. $18–$21. Hookups: electric (20, 30, 50 amps), water, sewer.

Riverwood Inn and RV Park, 677 Hwy. 50 North, 81416. T: (888) 213-2124 or (970) 874-5787. F: (970) 874-4872. www.riverwoodn.com/rvpark.htm. RV/tent: 39. $11–$22. Hookups: electric (30, 50 amps), water, sewer.

Divide

Alpine Lakes Resort, 4145 Omer Rd., P.O. Box 669, 80814. T: (719) 687-7337. RV/tent: 85. $18–$24. Hookups: electric (20, 30, 50 amps), water.

COLORADO (continued)

Dolores

Dolores River RV Park & Cabins, 18680 Hwy. 145, 81323. T: (800) 200-2399 or (970) 882-7761. F: (970) 882-4829. RV/tent: 91. $14–$25. Hookups: electric (20, 30, 50 amps), water, sewer.

Groundhog Lake Fishing Camp & Outfitters, P.O. Box 27, 81323. T: (970) 882-4379. RV/tent: 10. $7–$13. Hookups: electric (20, 30 amps).

Outpost Motel, Cabins, & RV Park, 1800 Central Ave., 81323. T: (800) 382-4892 or (970) 882-7271. RV/tent: 16. $25. Hookups: electric (20, 30 amps), water, sewer.

Priest Gulch Campground & RV Park, 27646 Hwy. 145, 81323. T: (970) 562-3810. www.priestgulch.com. RV/tent: 93. $18–$23. Hookups: electric (20, 30, 50 amps), water, sewer.

Stoner Creek Cafe, Store, Cabins, & RV Park, 25113 Hwy. 145, 81323. T: (970) 882-2204. F: (970) 882-2204. RV/tent: 35. $13–$20. Hookups: electric (20, 30, 50 amps), water, sewer.

Durango

Alpen Rose RV Park, 27847 Hwy. 550 North, 81301. T: (877) 259-5791 or (970) 247-5540. RV/tent: 100. $29. Hookups: electric (30, 50 amps), water, sewer.

Bueno Tiempo Ranch, 27846 Hwy. 550, 81301. T: (877) 247-9796 or (970) 247-9796. RV/tent: 118. $12–$25. Hookups: electric (20, 30 amps), water.

Cottonwood Camper Park, 21636 US 160, P.O. Box 1456, 81302. T: (970) 247-1977. RV/tent: 75. $17–$22. Hookups: electric (20, 30, 50 amps), water, sewer.

Durango North KOA, 13391 CR 250, 81301. T: (800) 562-2792 or (970) 247-4499. F: (970) 259-9545. www.koa.com. RV/tent: 131. $19–$29. Hookups: electric (20, 30 amps), water, sewer.

Five Branches Camper Park & Cabins, 4677 CR 501-A, 81122. T: (800) 582-9580 or (970) 884-2582. F: (970) 884-9765. RV/tent: 108. $13–$17. Hookups: electric (20, 30 amps), water, sewer.

Golden Terrace South, 17801 West Colfax, 80401. T: (303) 279-6279. RV/tent: 167. $25. Hookups: electric (30, 50 amps), water, sewer.

Hermosa Meadows Camper Park & Camper Cabins, 31420 Hwy. 550, 81301. T: (800) 748-2853 or (970) 247-3055. RV/tent: 150. $21–$30. Hookups: electric (20, 30, 50 amps), water, sewer.

Lightner Creek Campground, 1567 CR 207, 81301. T: (970) 247-5406. RV/tent: 97. $22–$27. Hookups: electric (20, 30 amps), water, sewer.

United Campground of Durango, 1322 Animas View Dr., 81301. T: (970) 247-3853. RV/tent: 193. $19–$31. Hookups: electric (20, 30, 50 amps), water, sewer.

Empire

Conestoga Wagon Stop RV Campground & Cabin Lodging, 7364 US 40, P.O. Box 334, 80438. T: (888) 428-9604 or (303) 569-3066. F: (303) 569-0251. RV/tent: 20. $13–$19. Hookups: electric (20, 30, 50 amps), water, sewer.

Mountain Meadow Campground, P.O. Box 2, 80438. T: (877) 931-2500 or (303) 569-2424. F: (303) 569-2424. RV/tent: 45. $16–$26. Hookups: electric (20, 30 amps), water, sewer.

Englewood

Flying Saucer RV Park, 2500 West Hampden, 80110. T: (303) 789-1707. RV/tent: 150. $24. Hookups: electric (20, 30, 50 amps), water, sewer.

Estes Park

Blue Arrow, 1665 Hwy. 66, 80517. T: (800) 582-5342 or (970) 586-5342. www.estes-park.com. RV/tent: 175. $20–$31. Hookups: electric (30, 50 amps), water, sewer.

Estes Park Campground, P.O. Box 3517, 80517. T: (888) 815-2029 or (970) 586-4188. www.estes-park.com/epcampground. RV/tent: 68. $21–$24. Hookups: electric (20, 30 amps), water.

Manor RV Park & Motel, 815 Riverside Dr., 80517. T: (800) 344-3256 or (970) 586-3251. RV/tent: 110. $28–$31. Hookups: electric (20, 30 amps), water, sewer.

Mary's Lake Campground & RV Park, P.O. Box 2514, 80517. T: (800) 445-6279 or (970) 586-4411. RV/tent: 150. $20–$26. Hookups: electric (20, 30, 50 amps), water, sewer.

National Park Resort Campground & Cabins, 3501 Fall River Rd., 80517. T: (970) 586-4563. RV/tent: 96. $25–$27. Hookups: electric (20, 30 amps), water, sewer.

Paradise RV Park & Motel, 815 East Riverside Dr., 80517. T: (800) 344-3256 or (970) 586-3251. www.campestespark.com. RV/tent: 110. $27. Hookups: electric (30 amps), water, sewer.

Spruce Lake RV Park, 1050 Mary's Lake Rd., 80517. T: (970) 586-2889. www.estes-park.com/sprucelake. RV/tent: 110. $22–$32. Hookups: electric (30 amps), water, sewer.

Yogi Bear's Jellystone Park of Estes, 5495 US 36, 80517. T: (800) 722-2928. www.jellystoneofestes.com. RV/tent: 99. $25–$35. Hookups: electric (20, 30, 50 amps), water, sewer.

COLORADO (continued)

Falcon

Falcon Meadow Campground, 11150 Hwy. 24, 80831. T: (719) 495-2694. www.campcolorado.com. RV/tent: 30. $12–$17. Hookups: electric (20, 30 amps), water, sewer.

Fort Collins

Blue Spruce Mobile Home & RV Park, 2730 North Shields, 80524. T: (970) 221-3723. RV/tent: 14. $15. Hookups: electric (20, 30, 50 amps), water, sewer.

Heron Lake RV Park, P.O. Box 1100, 80522. T: (877) 254-4063. RV/tent: 190. $26–$28. Hookups: electric (20, 30, 50 amps), water, sewer.

Fort Garland

Ute Creek Campground, P.O. Box 188, 81133. T: (719) 379-3238. F: (719) 379-3238. RV/tent: 32. $10–$15. Hookups: electric (20, 30 amps), water, sewer.

Ft. Collins KOA, Box 600, 6670 North Hwy. 287, 80535. T: (800) 562-2648. F: (970) 493-9758. www.koa.com. RV/tent: 59. $19–$25. Hookups: electric (20, 30, 50 amps), water, sewer.

Glenwood Springs

Rock Gardens Campground, Rafting, & Jeep Tours, 1308 CR 129, 81601. T: (800) 958-6737 or (970) 945-6737. F: (970) 945-2413. RV/tent: 77. $21–$25. Hookups: electric (20, 30, 50 amps), water, sewer.

Golden

Dakota Ridge RV Park, 17700 West Colfax Ave., 80401. T: (800) 398-1625 or (303) 279-1625. RV/tent: 141. $32. Hookups: electric (20, 30, 50 amps), water, sewer.

Reverends Ridge Campground, Golden Gate Canyon, 3873 Hwy. 46, 80403. T: (303) 582-3707. http://parks.state.co.us/golden_gate. RV/tent: 62. $18. Hookups: electric (30 amps).

Granby

Arapaho Bay, c/o USFS P.O. Box 10, 80446. T: (970) 887-4100. www.ReserveUSA.com/nrrs/co/arap. RV/tent: 84. $12. Hookups: none.

Grand Junction

Aspen Grove Campground, Vega State Park Box 186, 81624. T: (970) 487-3407. http://parks.state.co.us/vega. RV/tent: 29. $14. Hookups: none.

Big J RV Park, 2819 Hwy. 50, 81503. T: (877) 240-2527. F: (970) 263-0566. RV/tent: 90. $21. Hookups: electric (20, 30, 50 amps), water, sewer.

Bookcliff Campground, Highline Lake State Park, 1800 11.8 Rd., 81524. T: (970) 858-7208. http://parks.state.co.us/highline. RV/tent: 28. $14. Hookups: none.

Early Settlers Campground, Vega State Park Box 186, 81624. T: (970) 487-3407. http://parks.state.co.us/vega. RV/tent: 34. $18. Hookups: electric (30 amps).

Island Acres Campground, Colorado River State Park, P.O. Box 700, 81520. T: (970) 434-3388. http://parks.state.co.us/Colorado_River. RV/tent: 74. $18. Hookups: electric (30 amps).

Junction West RV Park, 793-22 Rd., 81505. T: (970) 245-8531. RV/tent: 66. $21. Hookups: electric (20, 30, 50 amps), water, sewer.

Mobile City RV Home Park, 2322 Hwys. 6 and 50, 81505. T: (970) 242-9291. RV/tent: 90. $22. Hookups: electric (30 amps), water, sewer.

Oak Point Campground, Vega State Park Box 186, 81624. T: (970) 487-3407. http://parks.state.co.us/vega. RV/tent: 38. $14. Hookups: none.

Grand Lake

Winding River Resort Village & Snowmobiling, P.O. Box 629, 80447. T: (800) 282-5121 or (970) 627-3215 or (303) 623-1121. F: (970) 627-5003. RV/tent: 186. $20–$25. Hookups: electric (20, 30 amps), water, sewer.

Green Mountain Falls

Rocky Top Motel and Campground, P.O. Box 215, 80819. T: (719) 684-9044. RV/tent: 78. $11–$18. Hookups: electric (20, 30 amps), water, sewer.

Gunnison

Gunnison Lakeside Resort, 28357 Hwy. 50 West, 81230. T: (877) 641-0488 or (970) 641-0477. RV/tent: 43. $12–$25. Hookups: electric (20, 30, 50 amps), water, sewer.

Mesa Campground, 36128 West Hwy. 50, 81230. T: (970) 641-3186. www.coloradodirectory.com/mesacamp. RV/tent: 150. $17–$26. Hookups: electric (30, 50 amps), water, sewer.

Rockey River Resort, 4359 CR 10, 81230. T: (970) 641-0174. RV/tent: 26. $20. Hookups: electric (20, 30 amps), water, sewer.

Shady Island Resort, Cabins, & RV Park, 2776 Hwy. 135 North, 81230. T: (970) 641-0416. RV/tent: 40. $20. Hookups: electric (20, 30 amps), water, sewer.

Tall Texan Campground, 194 CR 11, 81230. T: (970) 641 2927. F: (970) 641 2927. RV/tent: 118. Hookups: electric (20, 30, 50 amps), water, sewer.

COLORADO (continued)

Hayden

Juniper Springs Campground, Yampa River State Park, P.O. Box 759, 81639. T: (970) 276-2061. http://parks.state.co.us/Yampa. RV/tent: 6. $14. Hookups: none.

Maybell Bridge Campground, Yampa River State Park, P.O. Box 759, 81639. T: (970) 276-2061. http://parks.state.co.us/Yampa. RV/tent: 5. $14. Hookups: none.

The Elks Campground, Yampa River State Park, P.O. Box 759, 81639. T: (970) 276-2061. http://parks.state.co.us/Yampa. RV/tent: 15. $14. Hookups: none.

Yampa River State Park Headquarters, P.O. Box 759, 81639. T: (970) 276-2061. http://parks.state.co.us/Yampa. RV/tent: 35. $18. Hookups: electric (30 amps).

Hooper

UFO Watchtower & Campground, P.O. Box 583, 81136. T: (719) 378-2271. www.ufowatchtower.com. RV/tent: 24. $10. Hookups: electric (20, 30 amps), water, sewer.

Hotchkiss

Clear Fork Campground, CrawfoRd. State Park, P.O. Box 147, 81415. T: (970) 921-5721. http://parks.state.co.us/crawford. RV/tent: 16. Hookups: none.

Iron Creek Campground, CrawfoRd. State Park, P.O. Box 147, 81415. T: (970) 921-5721. http://parks.state.co.us/crawford. RV/tent: 16. $18. Hookups: electric (30 amps).

Howard

Pleasant Valley RV Park of Howard, 0018 CR 47, 81233. T: (719) 942-3484. RV/tent: 61. $12–$21. Hookups: electric (20, 30, 50 amps), water, sewer.

Idaho Springs

Cottonwood RV Park, 1485 Hwy. 103, 80452. T: (303) 567-2617. RV/tent: 20. $18–$25. Hookups: electric (20, 30, 50 amps), water, sewer.

Indian Springs Resort & Campground, P.O. Box 1990, 80452. T: (303) 989-6666. RV/tent: 32. $18. Hookups: electric (20, 30 amps), water.

Kremmling

Red Mountain RV Park, P.O. Box 1267, 80459. T: (970) 724-9593. RV/tent: 65. $12–$19. Hookups: electric (20, 30, 50 amps), water, sewer.

La Jara

Aspen Glade, Conejos Peak Rd., 15571 CR T-5, 81140. www.ReserveUSA.com/nrrs/co/asgl. RV/tent: 34. $14. Hookups: none.

La Veta

Elk Valley RV Park & Fly Shop, 5535 Hwy. 12, 81055. T: (866) 733-5533. RV/tent: 12. $22. Hookups: electric (20, 30, 50 amps), water, sewer.

Rustic Shack Cabins & RV Park, 404 South Oak, P.O. Box 397, 81055. T: (877) 460-6221 or (719) 742-6221. RV/tent: 14. $15–$20. Hookups: electric (20, 30 amps), water, sewer.

Lake City

Castle Lakes Campground Resort & Cabins, CR 30, P.O. Box 909, 81235. T: (800) 862-6166 or (970) 944-2622. RV/tent: 51. $17–$22. Hookups: electric (20, 30, 50 amps), water, sewer.

Highlander RV Campground, Jeep Rentals, & Gifts, P.O. Box 880, 81235. T: (888) 580-4636 or (970) 944-2878. RV/tent: 28. $20–$25. Hookups: electric (20, 30, 50 amps), water, sewer.

Woodlake Park Campground & Cabins, P.O. Box 400, 81235. T: (800) 201-2694 or (970) 944-2283 (June–Sept) or (817) 536-4079 (Oct–May). RV/tent: 25. $19. Hookups: electric (20, 30 amps), water, sewer.

Lake George

Lake George Cabins & RV Park, 8966 CR 90, 80827. T: (719) 748-3822. F: (719) 748-3822. RV/tent: 13. $15–$20. Hookups: electric (20, 30 amps), water, sewer.

Lamar

Lamar Country Acre's, 29151 US 28, 81052. T: (719) 336-1031. RV/tent: 8. $16–$18. Hookups: electric (20, 30, 50 amps), water, sewer.

Leadville

Baby Doe, Tourquoise Lake, 80461. www.ReserveUSA.com/nrrs/co/baby. RV/tent: 50. $15. Hookups: none.

Sugar Loafin' RV Park and Campground, 303 Hwy. 300, 80461. F: (719) 486-0919. www. sugarloafin@leadville.com. RV/tent: 98. $22–$26. Hookups: electric (20, 30, 50 amps), water, sewer.

Littleton

Chatfield State Park, 11500 North Roxborough Park Rd., 80125. T: (303) 791-7275. www.parks.state.co.us/Chatfield/camping.asp#Individual. RV/tent: 153. $18. Hookups: electric (30 amps).

COLORADO (continued)

Longmont

Westwood Inn Motel & Campground, 1550 North Main, 80501. T: (303) 776-2185. RV/tent: 20. $20. Hookups: electric (20, 30, 50 amps), water, sewer.

Loveland

Boyd Lake State Park, 3720 North CR 11-C, 80538. T: (970) 669-1739. www.parks.state.co.us/Boyd/camping.asp. RV/tent: 148. $18. Hookups: electric (30 amps).

Fireside RV Park & Cabins, 6850 West Hwy. 34, 80537. T: (970) 667-2903. RV/tent: 36. $18–$22. Hookups: electric (20, 30, 50 amps), water, sewer.

Loveland RV Village, 4421 East Hwy. 34, 80537. T: (970) 667-1204. RV/tent: 190. $20–$24. Hookups: electric (30, 50 amps), water, sewer.

Riverview RV Park & Campground, 7806 West Hwy. 34, 80537. T: (800) 447-9910 or (970) 667-9910. F: (970) 613-2023. RV/tent: 160. $20–$27. Hookups: electric (20, 30, 50 amps), water, sewer.

Lyons

Stone Mountain Lodge & Cabins, 18055 North St. Vrain Dr., 80540. T: (800) 282-5612 or (303) 823-6091. www.stonemountainlodge.com. RV/tent: 16. $15–$20. Hookups: electric (20, 30 amps).

Mancos

Echo Basin Guest Ranch Resort & RV Park, 43747 Rd. M, 81328. T: (800) 426-1890 or (970) 533-7000. RV/tent: 100. $17–$25. Hookups: electric (20, 30, 50 amps), water, sewer.

Morefield Campground in Mesa Verde, P.O. Box 277, 81328. T: (800) 449-2288. F: (970) 533-7831. www.visitmesaverde.com. RV/tent: 440. $16–$23. Hookups: electric (20, 30 amps), water, sewer.

A & A Mesa Verde RV Park, 34979 Hwy. 160, 81328. T: (800) 972-6620. F: (970) 565-7141. RV/tent: 70. $20–$25. Hookups: electric (30, 50 amps), water, sewer.

Marble

Meri Daes RV Park, 220 West Park, 81623. T: June–Sept (970) 963-1831 or Oct–May (303) 756-0566. RV/tent: 15. $18. Hookups: electric (20, 30 amps), water.

Meeker

Buford Hunting & Fishing Lodge, Store, Chuckwagon, & Horse Boarding, 20474 CR 8, 81641. T: (970) 878-4745. RV/tent: 8. $20. Hookups: electric (20, 30 amps), water.

North Fork Campground and Group Site, CR 8, 81641. T: (970) 878-4039. www.ReserveUSA.com/nrrs/co/nor2. RV/tent: 40. $12. Hookups: none.

Ute Lodge, Horses, Fishing, and Pack Trips, 393 CR 75, 81641. T: (888) 414-2022 or (970) 878-4669. RV/tent: 12. $15–$25. Hookups: electric (20, 30, 50 amps), water, sewer.

Mesa

Sundance RV Camp & Cabins, 11674 Hwy. 65, 81643. T: (970) 268-5651. RV/tent: 37. $15–$25. Hookups: electric (20, 30, 50 amps), water, sewer.

Montrose

Cedar Creek RV Park & Mini Golf, 126 Rose Ln., 81401. T: (877) 426-3884 or (970) 249-3884. F: (970) 856-6386. RV/tent: 55. $19–$22. Hookups: electric (20, 30, 50 amps), water, sewer.

Hangin Tree RV Park, Campground, Convenience Store, & Gas, 17250 Hwy. 550 South, 81401. T: (888) 657-4131. F: (970) 249-1865. RV/tent: 31. $16–$22. Hookups: electric (20, 30, 50 amps), water, sewer.

King's River Bend RV Park, 65100 Old Chipeta Tr., 81401. T: (970) 249-8235. RV/tent: 70. $15–$19. Hookups: electric (20, 30, 50 amps), water, sewer.

Monument

Lake of the Rockies Retreat, Camping, & Cabin Resort, 99 Mitchell Ave., 80132. T: (800) 429-4228 or (719) 481-4227. F: (719) 481-0039. RV/tent: 235. $18–$30. Hookups: electric (20, 30, 50 amps), water, sewer.

Mosca

Great Sand Dunes Oasis, 5400 Hwy. 150 North, 81146. T: (719) 378-2222. F: (719) 378-2901. RV/tent: 90. $12–$19. Hookups: electric (20, 30, 50 amps), water, sewer.

Nathrop

Brown's Family Campground, Box 39, 11430 CR 197, 81236. T: (800) 643-9727 or (719) 395-8301. F: (719) 395-8337. RV/tent: 75. $16–$25. Hookups: electric (20, 30 amps), water, sewer.

New Castle

New Castle/Glenwood Springs KOA, 0581 CR 241, 81647. T: (800) 562-3240 or (970) 984-2240. F: (970) 984-0349. www.koa.com. RV/tent: 57. $16–$24. Hookups: electric (20, 30, 50 amps), water, sewer.

Ohio City

Rowe's RV Park, Gun Shop, & 1886 Gen'l Store, P.O. Box 61, 81237. T: (970) 641-4272. RV/tent: 8. $13. Hookups: electric (20, 30, 50 amps), water, sewer.

COLORADO (continued)

Orchard

Dunes Campground, Jackson Lake State Park, 26363 CR 3, 80649. T: (970) 645-2551. http://parks.state.co.us/jackson. RV/tent: 18. $14. Hookups: none.

Foxhills Campground, Jackson Lake State Park, 26363 CR 3, 80649. T: (970) 645-2551. http://parks.state.co.us/jackson. RV/tent: 89. $14. Hookups: none.

Lakeside Campground, Jackson Lake State Park, 26363 CR 3, 80649. T: (970) 645-2551. http://parks.state.co.us/jackson. RV/tent: 58. $14. Hookups: none.

Northview Campground, Jackson Lake State Park, 26363 CR 3, 80649. T: (970) 645-2551. http://parks.state.co.us/jackson. RV/tent: 10. $18. Hookups: electric (30 amps).

Pelican Campground, Jackson Lake State Park, 26363 CR 3, 80649. T: (970) 645-2551. http://parks.state.co.us/jackson. RV/tent: 33. $14. Hookups: none.

Sandpiper Campground, Jackson Lake State Park, 26363 CR 3, 80649. T: (970) 645-2551. http://parks.state.co.us/jackson. RV/tent: 28. $18. Hookups: electric (30 amps).

Ouray

Ouray KOA, P.O. Box J, 81427. T: (800) 562-8026 or (970) 325-4736. F: (970) 325-0461. www.koa.com. RV/tent: 123. $19–$26. Hookups: electric (20, 30 amps), water, sewer.

Pagosa Springs

160 West Adult RV Park, P.O. Box 28, 81147. T: (970) 264-5873. F: (970) 264-7225. RV/tent: 28. $22. Hookups: electric (20, 30, 50 amps), water, sewer.

Acres Green RV Park, 10 Leisure Ct., 81147. T: (888) 724-6727 or (970) 264-9264. F: (970) 264-9265. RV/tent: 20. $18. Hookups: electric (30, 50 amps), water, sewer.

Blanco River RV Park, 97 Leisure Ct., 81147. T: (800) 280-9429 or (970) 264-5547. RV/tent: 64. $14–$20. Hookups: electric (20, 30, 50 amps), water, sewer.

Elk Meadows Campground, P.O. Box 238, 81147. T: (970) 264-5482. RV/tent: 35. $15–$18. Hookups: electric (20, 30, 50 amps), water, sewer.

Happy Camper RV Park & Cabin, 9260 West Hwy. 160, 81147. T: (970) 731-5822. F: (970) 731-5620. RV/tent: 90. $12–$18. Hookups: electric (20, 30 amps), water, sewer.

Hide-A-Way RV Park & Campground, P.O. Box 1931, 81147. T: (970) 731-5112. RV/tent: 40. $10–$15. Hookups: electric (20, 30, 50 amps), water, sewer.

Pagosa Riverside Campground & Camper Cabins, P.O. Box 268, 81147. T: (888) 785-3234 or (970) 264-5874. F: (970) 264-5874. RV/tent: 87. $16–$26. Hookups: electric (20, 30 amps), water, sewer.

Sportsman's Supply, Campground, & Cabins, 2095 Taylor Ln., 81147. T: (970) 731-2300. RV/tent: 40. $16–$25. Hookups: electric (20, 30 amps), water, sewer.

The Spa @ Pagosa Springs, Destination Spa & RV Resort, 317 Hot Springs Blvd., P.O. Box 37, 81147. T: (800) 832-5523 or (970) 264-5910. RV/tent: 8. $23. Hookups: electric (20, 30, 50 amps), water, sewer.

Paonia

Redwood Arms Motel & RV Park, 1478 Hwy. 133, P.O. Box 1390, 81428. T: (970) 527-4148. F: (970) 527-4181. RV/tent: 20. $20. Hookups: electric (20, 30, 50 amps), water, sewer.

Parlin

7-11 Ranch, 5291 CR 76, 81239. T: (970) 641-0666. RV/tent: 11. $10. Hookups: electric (20, 30 amps), water, sewer.

Penrose

Floyd's RV Park, 1438 Hwy. 50, 81240. T: (719) 372-3385. F: (719) 372-3385. RV/tent: 47. $12–$20. Hookups: electric (20, 30 amps), water, sewer.

Piru

Green Ridge, P.O. Box 249, 93040. T: (970) 887-4100. www.ReserveUSA.com/nrrs/co/grer. RV/tent: 78. $5. Hookups: none.

Pueblo

Arkansas Point Campground, Lake Pueblo State Park, 640 Pueblo Reservoir Rd., 81005. T: (719) 561-9320. http://parks.state.co.us/pueblo. RV/tent: 95. $18. Hookups: electric (30 amps).

Fort's RV Park, 3015 Lake Ave., 81004. T: (719) 564-2327. RV/tent: 55. $21–$25. Hookups: electric (20, 30, 50 amps), water, sewer.

Fowler RV Park, P.O. Box 306, 81039. T: (719) 263-4287. RV/tent: 41. $10–$20. Hookups: electric (20, 30 amps), water, sewer.

Haggard's RV Campground, 7910 West Hwy. 50, 81007. T: (719) 547-2101. RV/tent: 180. $20–$23. Hookups: electric (20, 30 amps), water, sewer.

Juniper Breaks Campground, Lake Pueblo State Park, 640 Pueblo Reservoir Rd., 81005. T: (719) 561-9320. http://parks.state.co.us/pueblo. RV/tent: 84. $14. Hookups: none.

COLORADO (continued)

Pueblo (continued)

Kettle Creek Campground, Lake Pueblo State Park, 640 Pueblo Reservoir Rd., 81005. T: (719) 561-9320. http://parks.state.co.us/pueblo. RV/tent: 27. $14. Hookups: none.

Prairie Ridge Campground, Lake Pueblo State Park, 640 Pueblo Reservoir Rd., 81005. T: (719) 561-9320. http://parks.state.co.us/pueblo. RV/tent: 82. $18. Hookups: electric (30 amps).

Pueblo South/Colorado City KOA, 9040 I-25 South, 81004. T: (800) 562-8646 or (719) 676-3376. www.koa.com. RV/tent: 109. $18–$32. Hookups: electric (30, 50 amps), water, sewer.

Pueblo West Campground, Cabins, & Arena, 480 East McCulloch Blvd., 81007. T: (877) 547-7070 or (719) 547-9887. RV/tent: 63. $17–$20. Hookups: electric (20, 30, 50 amps), water, sewer.

Yucca Flats Campground, Lake Pueblo State Park, 640 Pueblo Reservoir Rd., 81005. T: (719) 561-9320. http://parks.state.co.us/pueblo. RV/tent: 86. $18. Hookups: electric (30 amps).

Red Feather Lakes

Alpine Lodge, P.O. Box 180, 80545. T: (970) 881-2933. RV/tent: 10. $5–$15. Hookups: electric (20, 30 amps), water, sewer.

Rifle

Elk Run Campground, Sylvan Lake State Park, 0050 CR 219, 81650. T: (970) 625-1607. http://parks.state.co.us/sylvan. RV/tent: 33. $14. Hookups: none.

Fishermans Paradise Campground, Sylvan Lake State Park, 0050 CR 219, 81650. T: (970) 625-1607. http://parks.state.co.us/sylvan. RV/tent: 11. $14. Hookups: none.

Rye

Lodge at San Isabel, RV Park & General Store, 59 CR 371, 81069. T: (719) 489-2280 (lodge) or (719) 489-2601 (store). RV/tent: 15. $15. Hookups: electric (20, 30 amps), water, sewer.

Salida

Five Points Campground, Arkansas Headwaters Recreation Area, 307 West Sackett, 81201. T: (719) 539-7289. www.parks.state.co.us/arkansas/camping.asp. RV/tent: 16. $14. Hookups: none.

Heart of the Rockies Campground, 16105 Hwy. 50, 81201. T: (800) 496-2245 or (719) 539-4051. RV/tent: 65. $14–$20. Hookups: electric (20, 30 amps), water, sewer.

Helca Junction Campground, Arkansas Headwaters Recreation Area, 307 West Sackett, 81201. T: (719) 539-7289. www.parks.state.co.us/arkansas/camping.asp. RV/tent: 11. $14. Hookups: none.

Monarch Spur RV Park and Campground, 18989 West Hwy. 50, 81201. T: (888) 814-3001. www.monarchspurrvpark.com. RV/tent: 49. $17–$25. Hookups: electric (50 amps), water, sewer.

Railroad Bridge Campground, Arkansas Headwaters Recreation Area, 307 West Sackett, 81201. T: (719) 539-7289. www.parks.state.co.us/arkansas/camping.asp. RV/tent: 7. $14. Hookups: none.

Rincon Campground, Arkansas Headwaters Recreation Area, 307 West Sackett, 81201. T: (719) 539-7289. www.parks.state.co.us/arkansas/camping.asp. RV/tent: 4. $14. Hookups: none.

Ruby Mountain Campground, Arkansas Headwaters Recreation Area, 307 West Sackett, 81201. T: (719) 539-7289. www.parks.state.co.us/arkansas/camping.asp. RV/tent: 12. $14. Hookups: none.

Silt

Viking RV Park & Campground, 32958 River Frontage Rd., 81652. T: (970) 876-2443. F: (970) 963-2139. RV/tent: 77. $15–$25. Hookups: electric (20, 30, 50 amps), water, sewer.

Silverton

Molas Lake Camping, Camper Cabins, Stables, Snowmobile Tours, P.O. Box 776, 81433. T: (800) 846-2177 or (970) 387-5848. RV/tent: 78. $14. Hookups: electric (20, 30 amps), water, sewer.

Red Mountain Motel, Cabins, RV Park, Jeep & Snowmobile Rental, P.O. Box 346, 81433. T: (888) 970-5512 or (970) 387-5512. RV/tent: 20. $15–$22. Hookups: electric (20, 30, 50 amps), water, sewer.

Silverton Lakes Campground, P.O. Box 126, 81433. T: (888) 551-CAMP or (970) 387-5721. RV/tent: 75. $14–$17. Hookups: electric (20, 30, 50 amps), water, sewer.

Somerset

Crystal Meadows Resort, 30682 CR 12, 81434. T: (970) 929-5656. F: (970) 929-5957. RV/tent: 45. $27–$30. Hookups: electric (20, 30, 50 amps), water, sewer.

South Fork

AspenRidge Cabins & RV Park, 0710 West Hwy. 149, 81154. T: (719) 873-5921. F: (719) 813-1148. RV/tent: 40. $17. Hookups: electric (20, 30, 50 amps), water, sewer.

Blue Creek Lodge, Cabins, RV Park, & Campground, 11682 Hwy. 149, 81154. T: (800) 326-6408 or (719) 658-2479. F: (719) 658-2915. RV/tent: 33. $20. Hookups: electric (20, 30, 50 amps), water, sewer.

COLORADO (continued)

South Fork (continued)

Budget Host—Ute Bluff Lodge, Cabins, Motel, & RV Park, 27680 West Hwy. 160, 81154. T: (800) 473-0595. RV/tent: 42. $17–$19. Hookups: electric (20, 30, 50 amps), water, sewer.

Chinook Lodge, Cabins, Smokehouse, RV Park, & Trail Rides, Box 1214, 81154. T: (888) 890-9110 or (719) 873-9993. F: (719) 873-1706. RV/tent: 26. $12–$18. Hookups: electric (20, 30, 50 amps), water, sewer.

Cottonwood Cove Lodge, Cabins, Restaurant, Jeeps, & Rafts, 13046 Hwy. 149, 81154. T: (719) 658-2242. F: (719) 658-0802. RV/tent: 25. $20. Hookups: electric (20, 30 amps), water, sewer.

Goodnight's Lonesome Dove Cabins & RVs, P.O. Box 157, 81154. T: (800) 551-3683 or (719) 873-1072. F: (719) 873-1170. RV/tent: 42. $15–$18. Hookups: electric (20, 30 amps), water, sewer.

Moon Valley Ranch Resort Campground & Guided Fishing & Hunting, P.O. Box 265, 81154. T: (719) 873-5216. RV/tent: 61. $15. Hookups: electric (20, 30 amps), water, sewer.

Rainbow Lodge, Cabins, & RV Park, P.O. Box 224, 81154. T: (888) 873-5174 or (719) 873-5571. F: (719) 873-5125. RV/tent: 24. $20. Hookups: electric (20, 30 amps), water, sewer.

Riverbend Resort Cabins & RV Park, P.O. Box 1270, 81154. T: (800) 621-6512 or (719) 873-5344. F: (719) 873-5770. RV/tent: 57. $18–$22. Hookups: electric (20, 30 amps), water, sewer.

Steamboat Springs

Hahns Peak Lake, FR 486. T: (970) 870-2161. www.ReserveUSA.com/nrrs/co/hahn. RV/tent: 26. $10. Hookups: none.

Harding Spur Campground, Stagecoach State Park, 25500 R CR 14 (P.O. Box 98), 80467. T: (970) 736-2436. http://parks.state.co.us/stagecoach. RV/tent: 18. $14. Hookups: none.

Junction City Campground, Stagecoach State Park, 25500 R CR 14 (P.O. Box 98), 80467. T: (970) 736-2436. http://parks.state.co.us/stagecoach. RV/tent: 27. $18. Hookups: electric (30 amps).

Pinnacle Campground, Stagecoach State Park, 25500 R CR 14 (P.O. Box 98), 80467. T: (970) 736-2436. http://parks.state.co.us/stagecoach. RV/tent: 38. $18. Hookups: electric (30 amps).

Sterling

Chimney Grove Campground, North Sterling State Park, 24005 CR 330, 80751. T: (970) 522-3657. http://parks.state.co.us/north_sterling. RV/tent: 44. $14. Hookups: none.

Elks Campground, North Sterling State Park, 24005 CR 330, 80751. T: (970) 522-3657. http://parks.state.co.us/north_sterling. RV/tent: 50. $18. Hookups: electric (30 amps).

Inlet Grove Campground, North Sterling State Park, 24005 CR 330, 80751. T: (970) 522-3657. http://parks.state.co.us/north_sterling. RV/tent: 47. $18. Hookups: electric (30 amps).

Strasburg

Denver East/Strasburg KOA, P.O. Box 597, 80136. T: (800) 562-6538 or (303) 622-9274. F: (303) 622-9274. www.koa.com. RV/tent: 75. $18–$27. Hookups: electric (20, 30, 50 amps), water, sewer.

Stratton

Marshall Ash Village RV Park, 818 Colorado Ave., 80836. T: (800) 577-5795 or (719) 348-5141. RV/tent: 33. $19–$25. Hookups: electric (30, 50 amps), water, sewer.

Texas Creek

Whispering Pines Resort, 24871 Hwy. 50 West, 81223. T: (888) 275-3827 or (719) 275-3827. RV/tent: 118. $9–$18. Hookups: electric (20, 30 amps), water, sewer.

Trinidad

Budget Host—Derrick RV Park & Motel, 10301 Santa Fe Trail Dr., 81082. T: (719) 846-3307. F: (719) 846-3309. RV/tent: 20. $17–$25. Hookups: electric (20, 30, 50 amps), water, sewer.

Carpios Ridge Campground, Trinidad Lake State Park, 32610 Hwy. 12, 81082. T: (719) 846-6951. http://parks.state.co.us/trinidad. RV/tent: 62. $18. Hookups: electric (30 amps).

Walden

Bockman Campground, State Forest State Park, 2746 CR 41, 80480. T: (970) 723-8366. http://parks.state.co.us/state_forest. RV/tent: 52. $14. Hookups: none.

Lake John Resort, 2521 CR 7A, P.O. Box 902, 80480. T: (970) 723-3226. F: (970) 723-3236. RV/tent: 30. $15. Hookups: electric (20, 30, 50 amps), water, sewer.

North Michigan Reservoir Campground, State Forest State Park, 2746 CR 41, 80480. T: (970) 723-8366. http://parks.state.co.us/state_forest. RV/tent: 38. $14. Hookups: none.

Powderhorn Cabins, Star Rte. 102, 35336 Jackson CR 21, 80480. T: (970) 723-4359. F: (970) 723-3712. RV/tent: 6. $18. Hookups: electric (20, 30 amps), water.

COLORADO (continued)

Walden (continued)

Ranger Lakes Campground, State Forest State Park, 2746 CR 41, 80480. T: (970) 723-8366. http://parks.state.co.us/state_forest. RV/tent: 32. $14. Hookups: none.

Walsenburg

Budget Host Motel & Campground, P.O. Box 190. T: (800) 283-4678 or (719) 738-3800. RV/tent: 18. $11–$15. Hookups: electric (20, 30 amps), water, sewer.

Mosca Campground, San Luis State Park, County Ln. 6 North (P.O. Box 175), 81146. T: (719) 378-2020. http://parks.state.co.us/san_luis. RV/tent: 33. $18. Hookups: electric (30 amps).

Pinon Campground, Lathrop State Park, 70 CR 502, 81089. T: (719) 738-2376. http://parks.state.co.us/lathrop. RV/tent: 79. $18. Hookups: electric (30 amps).

Westcliffe

Cross D Bar Trout Ranch & Campground, 2299 CR 328, 81252. T: (800) 453-4379 or (719) 783-2007. F: (303) 733-8859. RV/tent: 36. $11–$18. Hookups: electric (20, 30, 50 amps), water, sewer.

Weston

Stonewall Inn & RV Park, 6673 Hwy. 12, 81091. T: (719) 868-2294 or (719) 269-7071 (Nov 15–May 1). F: (719) 868-2294. RV/tent: 16. $18. Hookups: electric (20, 30, 50 amps), water, sewer.

Winter Park

Sitzmark Chalets/Cabins, RV Park, & Campground, P.O. Box 65, 78253 US 40, 80482. T: (970) 726-5453. RV/tent: 30. $20–$30. Hookups: electric (20, 30 amps), water, sewer.

Snow Mountain Ranch, YMCA of the Rockies, P.O. Box 169, 80482. T: (970) 887-2152 ext 4110 (families) or (800) 777-YMCA (group rates). RV/tent: 54. $19–$23. Hookups: electric (20, 30 amps), water, sewer.

Woodland Park

Diamond RV Park, 900 North Hwy. 67, 80863. T: (719) 687-9684. www.diamondcampground.com. RV/tent: 150. $16–$22. Hookups: electric (20, 30, 50 amps), water, sewer.

Town & Country Resort, P.O. Box 368, 80866. T: (800) 600-0399 or (719) 687-9518. F: (719) 687-9518. RV/tent: 22. $22–$25. Hookups: electric (20, 30, 50 amps), water, sewer.

KANSAS

Arkansas City

Lou Ann's Campground, 9423 292nd Rd., 67005. T: (620) 442-4458. RV/tent: 20. $15. Hookups: electric (30 amps), water, sewer.

Assaria

Shepherd's Gate RV & Recreational Park, 1288 East Lapsley Rd., 67416. T: (785) 667-5795 or (785) 822-8463. F: (785) 667-5796. RV/tent: 35. $10–$15. Hookups: electric (30 amps), water, sewer.

Bird City

Right Motel & RV Park, Hwy. 36, 67731. T: (785) 734-2344. RV/tent: 19. $15–$20. Hookups: electric (30, 50 amps), water, sewer.

Bonner Springs

Cottonwood Camping RV Park & Campground, 115 South 130th St., 66012. T: (913) 422-8038. www.cottonwoodcamping.com. RV/tent: 100. $18–$22. Hookups: electric (20, 30, 50 amps), water, sewer.

Burlington

Damsite Campground, 1565 Embankment Rd. Southwest, 66839. T: (316) 364-8613. www.ReserveUSA.com/nrrs/ks/dams/index.html. RV/tent: 26. $10–$15. Hookups: electric (30 amps), water.

Riverside East Campground, 1565 Embankment Rd. Southwest, 66839. T: (316) 364-8613. www.ReserveUSA.com/nrrs/ks/riea. RV/tent: 53. $10–$15. Hookups: electric (30 amps), water.

Riverside West Campground, 1565 Embankment Rd. Southwest, 66839. T: (316) 364-8613. RV/tent: 43. $10–$15. Hookups: electric (30 amps).

Cherryvale

Big Hill Lake (Overlook Campground), P.O. Box 426, 67335-0426. T: (316) 336-2741. www.ReserveUSA.com/nrrs/ks/chpa. RV/tent: 30. $12. Hookups: electric (20 amps).

KANSAS (continued)

Coffeyville

Walter Johnson Park Campground, P.O. Box 307, 508 Park, 67337. T: (800) 626-3357. www.coffeyville.com. RV/tent: 72. $4. Hookups: electric (20, 30, 50 amps), water.

Columbus

T&S RV Park, 1308 East Hwy. 160, 66725. T: (620) 674-3304. F: (620) 674-3342. RV/tent: 23. $15. Hookups: electric (30, 40, 50 amps), water, sewer.

Council Grove

Canning Creek, 945 Lake Rd., 66846. T: (620) 767-5195. www.ReserveUSA.com/nrrs/ks/cank. RV/tent: 42. $10–$16. Hookups: electric (20, 30 amps), water.

Richey Cove, 945 Lake Rd., 66846. T: (620) 767-5195. www.ReserveUSA.com/nrrs/ks/ricv. RV/tent: 49. $10–$15. Hookups: electric (20, 30 amps), water.

Santa Fe Trail Campground, 945 Lake Rd., 66846. T: (620) 767-5195. www.ReserveUSA.com/nrrs/ks/sant. RV/tent: 39. $9–$16. Hookups: electric (20, 30, 50 amps), water, sewer.

Dodge City

Gunsmoke Trav-L Park, 11070 108 Rd., 67801. T: (800) 789-8247 or (316) 227-8247. RV/tent: 110. $18–$20. Hookups: electric (50 amps), water, sewer.

El Dorado

Bluestem Point Campground, Rte. 3, 67042. T: (316) 321-7180. RV/tent: 286. $15–$16. Hookups: electric (20, 30 amps), water, sewer.

Walnut River Campground, Rte. 3, 67042. T: (316) 321-7180. RV/tent: 177. $15–$16. Hookups: electric (20, 30 amps), water, sewer.

Ellis

Cedar Bluff State Park, Rte. 2 Box 76A, 67637. T: (785) 726-3212. RV/tent: 121. $10–$16. Hookups: electric (20, 30, 50 amps), water, sewer.

Ellis Lakeside Campground, Rte. 2 Box 76A, 67637. T: (785) 726-3212. RV/tent: 28. $7–$10. Hookups: electric (20 amps).

Fall River

Damsite, P.O. Box 37, 67047. T: (620) 658-4445. www.ReserveUSA.com/nrrs/ks/damr. RV/tent: 33. $10–$18. Hookups: electric (20, 30, 50 amps), water, sewer.

Whitehall Bay, P.O. Box 37, 67047. T: (620) 658-4445. www.ReserveUSA.com/nrrs/ks/whha. RV/tent: 29. $10–$18. Hookups: electric (20, 30, 50 amps), water, sewer.

Fredonia

Cottonwood Court, P.O. Box 5, 1002 North 8th St., 66736. T: (620) 378-3468. RV/tent: 13. $10. Hookups: electric (20, 30, 50 amps), water, sewer.

Garden City

Garden City KOA, 4100 East Hwy. 50, 67846. T: (800) KOA-3361 or (316) 276-8741. www.koa.com. RV/tent: 96. $15–$22. Hookups: electric (50 amps), water, sewer.

Goodland

Mid-America Camp Inn, 2802 Commerce Rd., 67735. T: (785) 899-5431. RV/tent: 109. $13–$19. Hookups: electric (20, 30, 50 amps), water, sewer.

Halstead

Spring Lake Campground, Rte. 2, 67056. T: (316) 835-3272. RV/tent: 131. $15. Hookups: electric (30, 50 amps), water, sewer.

Hays

El Charro RV Park, 2020 East 8th St., 67601. T: (785) 625-3423. RV/tent: 5. $16. Hookups: electric (30, 50 amps), water, sewer.

Sunflower Creek Campground & RV Park, 501 Vine St., 67601. T: (785) 623-4769. RV/tent: 24. $15–$20. Hookups: electric (30, 50 amps), water, sewer.

Hesston

Cottonwood Grove Campground, 1001 East Lincoln Blvd., 67062. T: (620) 327-4173. RV/tent: 32. $5–$15. Hookups: electric (30 amps), water, sewer.

Horton

Horse Thief Campground, 200 Horse Thief Rd., 67464. T: (785) 546-2565. F: (785) 546-2343. RV/tent: 40. $7–$15. Hookups: electric (30 amps).

Junction City

Curtis Creek Park, 4020 West Hwy. K-57, 66441. T: (785) 238-4636. www.ReserveUSA.com/nrrs/ks/curc. RV/tent: 78. $10–$16. Hookups: electric (20, 30 amps), water.

Dam Site, 2105 North Pawnee Rd., 66839. T: (316) 364-8613. RV/tent: 32. $10–$15. Hookups: electric (20, 30 amps), water.

Rolling Hills Park West, 4020 West Hwy. K-57, 66441. T: (785) 238-5714. www.ReserveUSA.com/nrrs/ks/rolh. RV/tent: 62. $10–$16. Hookups: electric (30 amps).

Thunderbird Marina, West Rolling Hills Rd., 66441. T: (785) 238-5864. RV/tent: 80. $14. Hookups: electric (15, 20, 30, 50 amps), water.

KANSAS (continued)

La Crosse

Double D RV Park, P.O. Box 699, 67548. T: (785) 222-2457. RV/tent: 14. $13–$17. Hookups: electric (20, 30 amps), water, sewer.

Lawrence

Cedar Ridge, 872 North 1402 Rd., 66049. T: (785) 843-7665. www.ReserveUSA.com/nrrs/ks/cdri. RV/tent: 100. $16. Hookups: electric (20, 30 amps), water.

Hickory Campground, 872 North 1402 Rd., 66049. T: (785) 843-7665. www.ReserveUSA.com/nrrs/ks/hick. RV/tent: 196. $10–$14. Hookups: electric (30 amps).

Walnut, 872 North 1402 Rd., 66049. T: (785) 843-7665. www.ReserveUSA.com/nrrs/ks/waln. RV/tent: 100. $8–$14. Hookups: electric (30 amps).

Leavenworth

Leavenworth RV Park, 24836 Tonganoxie Rd., 66048. T: (913) 351-0505. RV/tent: 5. $22. Hookups: electric (30 amps), water.

Lebo

Sundance Campground, 31051 Melvern Lake Pkwy., 66510-9179. T: (785) 549-3318. RV/tent: 30. $10. Hookups: none.

Lindsborg

Coronado Motel/RV Park, 305 Harrison, 67456. T: (800) 747-2793 or (785) 227-3943. RV/tent: 18. $17. Hookups: electric (20, 30, 50 amps), water, sewer.

Louisburg

Middle Creek RV Park, 33565 South Metcalf, 66053. T: (866) 888-6779 or (913) 376-3304. F: (913) 376-3304. www.rutlateroutpost.com. RV/tent: 24. $20–$22. Hookups: electric (30, 50 amps), water, sewer.

Lucas

Lucas RV Park & Laundry, 119 North Wolf, 67648. T: (785) 525-6396. RV/tent: 5. $17. Hookups: electric (20, 50 amps), water, sewer.

Lyndon

Crossroads RV Park & Campground Inc., P.O. Box 721, 66451. T: (785) 221-5482. RV/tent: 65. $15–$23. Hookups: electric (20, 30, 50 amps), water, sewer.

Marion

Cottonwood Point, 2105 North Pawnee, 66861. T: (620) 382-2101. www.ReserveUSA.com/nrrs/ks/cotp. RV/tent: 94. $14–$16. Hookups: electric (20, 30, 50 amps).

Hillsboro Cove, 2105 North Pawnee, 66861. T: (620) 382-2101. www.ReserveUSA.com/nrrs/ks/hilc. RV/tent: 52. $14. Hookups: electric (20, 30 amps).

Marquette

Riverside, 105 Riverside Dr., 67464. T: (785) 546-2294. www.ReserveUSA.com/nrrs/ks/rive. RV/tent: 40. $10–$14. Hookups: electric (20, 30 amps).

Venango Park, 105 Riverside Dr., 67464. T: (785) 546-2294. RV/tent: 236. $10–$16. Hookups: electric (20, 30 amps).

Mayetta

Prairie Schooner RV Park & Campground, 15680 Pacific St., 66509. T: (785) 966-2952. RV/tent: 39. $18. Hookups: electric (20, 30, 50 amps), water, sewer.

McPherson

Mustang Mobile Park, 1909 Millers Ln., 67460. T: (316) 241-0237. RV/tent: 28. $12. Hookups: electric (20, 50 amps), water, sewer.

Melvern

Arrow Rock Campground, 31051 Melvern Lake Pkwy., 66510-9179. T: (785) 549-3318. RV/tent: 45. $10–$14. Hookups: electric (30 amps).

Coeur d'Alene Campground, 31051 Melvern Lake Pkwy., 66510-9179. T: (785) 549-3318. www.ReserveUSA.com/nrrs/ks/coeu. RV/tent: 60. $10–$14. Hookups: electric (30 amps).

Eisenhower Campground, 31051 Melvern Lake Pkwy., 66510-9179. T: (785) 528-4102. RV/tent: 190. $9–$16. Hookups: electric (30, 50 amps), water, sewer.

Outlet Campground, 31051 Melvern Lake Pkwy., 66510-9179. T: (785) 549-3318. www.ReserveUSA.com/nrrs/ks/oult. RV/tent: 150. $15–$18. Hookups: electric (20, 30 amps), water, sewer.

Turkey Point Campground, 31051 Melvern Lake Pkwy., 66510-9179. T: (785) 549-3318. www.ReserveUSA.com/nrrs/ks/turp. RV/tent: 50. $10–$16. Hookups: electric (20, 30, 50 amps), water.

Merriam

Walnut Grove RV Park, 10218 Johnson Dr., 66203. T: (913) 262-3023. F: (913) 432-5269. www.walnutgrovery.com. RV/tent: 55. $20–$22. Hookups: electric (30, 50 amps), water, sewer.

KANSAS (continued)

Milford

Flagstop Resort & RV Park, P.O. Box 329, 66514. T: (800) 293-1465. www.members.xoom.com/flagstop. RV/tent: 190. $16. Hookups: electric (50 amps), water, sewer.

Langley Point, 4020 West Hwy. K57, 66441. T: (785) 238-5714. RV/tent: 57. $7–$16. Hookups: electric (20, 30, 50 amps), water, sewer.

Timber Creek Park, 4020 West Hwy. K57, 66441. T: (785) 238-5714. RV/tent: $7–$16. Hookups: electric (20, 30, 50 amps), water, sewer.

Morrill

Mulberry Creek Family Retreat, 551 270th St., 66515. T: (888) 459-1595 or (785) 459-2279. RV/tent: 70. $15. Hookups: electric (30, 50 amps), water, sewer.

Mound Valley

Big Hill Lake, P.O. Box 426, 67335. T: (316) 336-2741. www.ReserveUSA.com/nrrs/ks/mova. RV/tent: 72. $12–$17. Hookups: electric (20, 30, 50 amps), water, sewer.

Nickerson

Hendrick's Capybara Lake, 7910 North Roy L. Smith Rd., 67561. T: (888) 489-8039. www.hedricks.com/lake. RV/tent: 16. $15. Hookups: electric (20, 30, 50 amps), water, sewer.

Oakley

Kansas Kountry Inn, 3538 Hwy. 40, 67748. T: (800) 211-6917 or (785) 672-3131. F: (785) 672-3134. RV/tent: 16. $10. Hookups: electric (20, 30, 50 amps), water, sewer.

Paola

Hillsdale State Park, 26001 West 255th St., 66071. T: (913) 783-4507. www.kdwparks.state.ks.us. RV/tent: 80. $10–$17. Hookups: electric (20, 30, 50 amps), water.

Paxico

Mill Creek Campground, Rte. 1 Box 54, 66526. T: (785) 636-5321. RV/tent: 46. $18. Hookups: electric (20, 30, 50 amps), water, sewer.

Perry

Locust Campground, 10419 Perry Park Dr., 66073. T: (785) 597-5144. www.ReserveUSA.com/nrrs/ks/slou. RV/tent: 14. $15. Hookups: electric (20, 30 amps), water.

Longview, 10419 Perry Park Dr., 66073. T: (785) 597-5144. www.ReserveUSA.com/nrrs/ks/lonv. RV/tent: 52. $10–$14. Hookups: electric (20, 30 amps).

Old Town, 10419 Perry Park Dr., 66073. T: (785) 597-5144. www.ReserveUSA.com/nrrs/ks/oldt. RV/tent: 77. $10–$14. Hookups: electric (20, 30 amps).

Rock Creek Peninsula Campground, 10419 Perry Park Dr., 66073. T: (785) 597-5144. www.ReserveUSA.com/nrrs/ks/rocr. RV/tent: 77. $10–$14. Hookups: electric (20, 30 amps), water.

Slough Creek Campground, 10419 Perry Park Dr., 66073. T: (785) 597-5144. www.ReserveUSA.com/nrrs/ks/slou. RV/tent: 273. $10–$15. Hookups: electric (20, 30 amps), water.

Perry

Southpoint Campground, 10419 Perry Park Dr., 66073. T: (785) 597-5144. www.ReserveUSA.com/nrrs/ks/slou. RV/tent: 24. $15. Hookups: electric (20, 30 amps), water.

Worthington Campground, 10419 Perry Park Dr., 66073. T: (785) 597-5144. www.ReserveUSA.com/nrrs/ks/slou. RV/tent: 62. $15. Hookups: electric (20, 30 amps).

Quinter

Sunflower Campground, 1130 Castle Rock Rd., 67752-9400. T: (913) 754-3451. RV/tent: 40. $13–$17. Hookups: electric (30 amps), water, sewer.

Rexford

Shepherd's Staff RV Park, 315 Main St., 67753. T: (888) 687-2565 or (785) 687-2565. RV/tent: 12. $18. Hookups: electric (20, 30, 50 amps), water, sewer.

Richmond

V&P RV Park, 532 East South St., 66080. T: (785) 835-6369. RV/tent: 25. $15. Hookups: electric (30, 50 amps), water, sewer.

Russel

Dumler Estates RV Park, P.O. Box 180, 67665. T: (785) 483-2603. RV/tent: 35. $15. Hookups: electric (20, 30, 50 amps), water, sewer.

Salina

Salina KOA, 1109 West Diamond Dr., 67401. T: (800) 562-3126 or (785) 827-3182. www.koa.com. RV/tent: 82. $16–$21. Hookups: electric (20, 30, 50 amps), water, sewer.

Sundowner West Park, P.O. Box 2388, 67402. T: (785) 823-8335. RV/tent: 91. $20. Hookups: electric (30, 50 amps), water, sewer.

KANSAS (continued)

Scott City

Pine Tree RV Park, 402 North Main St., 67871. T: (620) 872-3076. RV/tent: 25. $17. Hookups: electric (20, 30, 50 amps), water, sewer.

Smith Center

Sunset Park Campground, West Hwy. 36, 705 White Rock, 66967. T: (785) 282-6037. RV/tent: 16. $14. Hookups: electric (20, 30 amps), water, sewer.

South Haven

Oasis RV Park, Hwy. 166 East of I-35, 67140. T: (620) 892-5115. RV/tent: 25. $14. Hookups: electric (20, 30, 50 amps), water, sewer.

St. Francis

Homesteader Motel & RV Park, 414 West Hwy. 36, 67756. T: (800) 750-2169 or (785) 332-2168. RV/tent: 9. $15. Hookups: electric (30, 50 amps), water, sewer.

St. John

Pine Haven Retreat, Rte. 2 Box 140A, 67576. T: (88) 549-CAMP or (620) 549-3444. F: (620) 549-3571. RV/tent: 50. $10–$16. Hookups: electric (20, 30, 50 amps), water, sewer.

Sylvan Grove

Lucas Park, 4860 Outlet Blvd., 67481. T: (785) 658-2551. www.ReserveUSA.com/nrrs/ks/luca. RV/tent: 116. $10–$16. Hookups: electric (20, 30 amps), water.

Minooka Park, 4860 Outlet Blvd., 67481. T: (785) 658-2551. www.ReserveUSA.com/nrrs/ks/mino. RV/tent: 235. $10–$16. Hookups: electric (20, 30 amps), water.

Topeka

Capital City RV Park, 1949 Southwest 49th St., 66609. T: (785) 862-KAMP. RV/tent: 51. $14–$19. Hookups: electric (20, 30, 50 amps), water, sewer.

Lake Shawnee Camping Area, 3435 Southeast Edge Rd., 66609. T: (913) 267-1859. RV/tent: 154. $10. Hookups: electric (30 amps), water.

Toronto

Holiday Hill Campground, 144 Hwy. 105, 66777. T: (316) 637-2213. RV/tent: 30. $7–$10. Hookups: electric (30 amps).

Toronto Point Campground, 144 Hwy. 105, 66777. T: (316) 637-2213. RV/tent: 200. $7–$10. Hookups: electric (20, 30 amps), water.

Vassar

Carbolyn Park, 5260 Pomona Dam Rd., 66543. T: (785) 453-2201. www.ReserveUSA.com/nrrs/ks/carb. RV/tent: 32. $10–$16. Hookups: electric (20, 30 amps), water.

Michigan Valley, 5260 Pomona Dam Rd., 66543. T: (785) 453-2201. www.ReserveUSA.com/nrrs/ks/mich. RV/tent: 158. $10–$16. Hookups: electric (20, 30 amps), water.

Pomona Lake Outlet Campground, 5260 Pomona Dam Rd., 66543. T: (785) 453-2201. www.ReserveUSA.com/nrrs/ks/out2. RV/tent: 36. $14. Hookups: electric (20, 30 amps), water.

Wolf Creek, 5260 Pomona Dam Rd., 66543. T: (785) 453-2201. www.ReserveUSA.com/nrrs/ks/wocr. RV/tent: 87. $10–$14. Hookups: electric (20, 30 amps).

Washington

Rose Garden RV Camp, 127 East Ninth St., 66968. T: (785) 325-2411. RV/tent: 9. $15. Hookups: electric (20, 30, 50 amps), water, sewer.

Wellington

Wheatlands of Wellington RV Park, Rte. 1 Box 227, 67152. T: (877) 914-6114 or (316) 326-6114. RV/tent: 72. $24. Hookups: electric (30, 50 amps), water, sewer.

Wichita

All Seasons RV Park, 15520 Maple Ave., 67052. T: (316) 722-1154. RV/tent: 76. $19–$22. Hookups: electric (20, 30, 50 amps), water, sewer.

Blasi Campgrounds, 11209 West Hwy. 54, 67209. T: (316) 722-2681. RV/tent: 110. $19–$23. Hookups: electric (20, 30, 50 amps), water, sewer.

K & R Tratel RV Park, 3200 Southeast Blvd., 67216. T: (316) 684-1531. RV/tent: 66. $16. Hookups: electric (30, 50 amps), water, sewer.

Waco Wego Campground, 9747 South Broadway, 67120. T: (316) 522-1400. RV/tent: 9. $16. Hookups: electric (20, 30, 50 amps), water, sewer.

Wilson

Hell Creek Campground, Rte. 1 Box 181, 67841. T: (785) 658-2465. RV/tent: 400. $7–$10. Hookups: electric (20, 30 amps), water.

Otoe Campground, Rte. 1 Box 181, 67841. T: (785) 658-2465. RV/tent: 235. $7–$10. Hookups: electric (20, 30 amps), water.

MISSOURI

Anderson

Indian Creek RV Park & Campground, Hwy. 71, 64831. T: (417) 845-6400. RV/tent: 120. $12. Hookups: electric (20, 30, 50 amps), water, sewer.

Arrow Rock

Arrow Rock State Historic Site State Park, P.O. Box 1, 65320. T: (660) 837-3330. RV/tent: 45. $12–$15. Hookups: electric (20, 30 amps), water.

Blue Eye

Old Hwy. 86, HCR 2 Box 136, 65615. T: (417) 779-5376. www.ReserveUSA.com/nrrs/mo/ol86. RV/tent: 71. $12–$16. Hookups: electric (20, 30 amps).

Bonne Terre

St. Francois State Park, 8920 US 67 North, 63628. T: (573) 358-2173. RV/tent: 110. $12–$15. Hookups: electric (20, 30 amps), water.

Branson

Acorn Acres, 159 Acorn Acres Ln., 65737. T: (417) 338-2500. RV/tent: 77. $17–$23. Hookups: electric (30, 50 amps), water, sewer.

America's Best Campground, 499 Buena Vista Rd., 65616. T: (417) 339-2296 or (800) 671-4399. F: (417) 336-6581. www.abc-branson.com. RV/tent: 166. $18–$30. Hookups: electric (30, 50 amps), water, sewer.

Andrew's Landing Resort & RV Park, 5329 Hwy. 165, 65616. T: (800) 678-9780 or (417) 334-5071. www.andrewslanding.com. RV/tent: 25. $16. Hookups: electric (20, 30, 50 amps), water, sewer.

Bar M Resort & Campground, HCR 4 Box 2990; Hwy. DD-24, 65737. T: (417) 338-2593. www.Barmresort.com. RV/tent: 12. $17–$20. Hookups: electric (30 amps), water, sewer.

Branson City Campground, 300 Boxcar Willie Dr., 65616. T: (417) 334-2915. RV/tent: 350. $18. Hookups: electric (30, 50 amps), water, sewer.

Branson KOA, 1025 Headwaters Rd., 65616. T: (800) 562-4177 or (417) 334-7450. F: (417) 334-7457. www.koa.com. RV/tent: 169. $19–$28. Hookups: electric (30, 50 amps), water, sewer.

Branson Shenanigans RV Park, 3675 Keeter St., 65616. T: (800) 338-7275 or (417) 334-1920. www.bransonrvpark.com. RV/tent: 30. $20–$25. Hookups: electric (30, 50 amps), water, sewer.

Branson Stagecoach RV Park, 5751 Hwy. 165, 65616. T: (800) 446-7110 or (417) 335-8185. RV/tent: 47. $22–$25. Hookups: electric (30, 50 amps), water, sewer.

Branson View Campground, 2362 Hwy. 265, 65616. T: (800) 992-9055 or (417) 338-8716. F: (417) 338-2016. www.bransonview.com. RV/tent: 42. $19–$25. Hookups: electric (30, 50 amps), water, sewer.

Compton Ridge Campground, 5040 Hwy. 265, 65616. T: (800) 233-8648 or (417) 338-2911. www.comptonridge.com. RV/tent: 227. $19–$27. Hookups: electric (20, 30, 50 amps), water, sewer.

Cooper Creek Resort & Campground, 471 Cooper Creek Rd., 65616. T: (800) 261-8398 or (417) 334 5250. RV/tent: 91. $20–$27. Hookups: electric (20, 30, 50 amps), water, sewer.

Gerth Campground & Camper Park, 139 Irish Ln., 65616. T: (417) 334-5849. RV/tent: 200. $18. Hookups: electric (30, 50 amps), water, sewer.

Indian Point, 3125 Indian Point Rd., 65616. T: (417) 338-2121. www.ReserveUSA.com/nrrs/mo/indp. RV/tent: 78. $16. Hookups: electric (20, 30 amps).

Lakeview Campground, 2820 Indian Point Rd., 65616. T: (800) 396-2232. www.lakeviewcampground.com. RV/tent: 45. $13–$18. Hookups: electric (30, 50 amps), water, sewer.

Musicland Kampground, 116 North Gretna Rd., 65616. T: (888) 248-9080. www.musiclandkampground.com. RV/tent: 112. $26–$32. Hookups: electric (50 amps), water, sewer.

Ozark Country Campground, 679 Quebec Dr., 65616. T: (800) 968-1300 or (417) 334-4681. www.natins.com/campground/country. RV/tent: 67. $13–$25. Hookups: electric (20, 30, 50 amps), water, sewer.

Stormy Point Camp & Resort, 1318 Stormy Point Rd., 65616. T: (417) 338-2255. www.stormypoint.com. RV/tent: 60. $17–$25. Hookups: electric (20, 30, 50 amps), water, sewer.

Tall Pines Campground, 5558 Hwy. 265, 65616. T: (800) 425-2300. RV/tent: 83. $15–$24. Hookups: electric (30, 50 amps), water, sewer.

Trail's End Resort & RV Park, 71 Dogwood Park Tr., 65616. T: (800) 888-1891 or (417) 338-2633. RV/tent: 12. $12–$16. Hookups: electric (30, 50 amps), water, sewer.

Table Rock State Park, 5272 Hwy. 165, 65616. T: (417) 334-4704. RV/tent: 143. $12–$15. Hookups: electric (20, 30, 50 amps), water, sewer.

Camdenton

Bull Run Bluff RV Park & Campground, 54–82 Lake Rd., HCR 80 Box 775. T: (573) 346-7815. www.funlake.com/accommodations/bullrunbluff. RV/tent: 72. $17–$22. Hookups: electric (30, 50 amps), water, sewer.

MISSOURI (continued)

Cameron

Wallace State Park, 10621 Northeast Hwy. 121, 64429. T: (816) 632-3745. RV/tent: 87. $12–$15. Hookups: electric (20, 30 amps), water.

Cape Fair

Cape Fair, 1092 Shadrack Rd., 65624. T: (417) 538-9999. www.ReserveUSA.com/nrrs/mo/cape. RV/tent: 82. $12–$17. Hookups: electric (20, 30 amps), water.

Carthage

Big Red Barn RV Park, 5089 CL 138, 64836. T: (888) 244-2276 or (417) 358-2432. www.bigbarnrvpark.com. RV/tent: 63. $14–$17. Hookups: electric (30, 50 amps), water, sewer.

Cassville

Big M, HCR 81 Box 9251, 65625. T: (417) 271-3190. www.ReserveUSA.com/nrrs/mo/bigm. RV/tent: 92. $11–$17. Hookups: electric (20, 30 amps).

Roaring River State Park, Rte. 4 Box 4100, 65625. T: (417) 847-2539. RV/tent: 185. $12–$15. Hookups: electric (20, 30 amps), water.

Columbia

Finger Lakes State Park, 1505 East Peabody Rd., 65202. T: (573) 443-5315. RV/tent: 36. $12–$15. Hookups: electric (20, 30 amps), water.

Craig

Big Lake State Park, 204 Lake Shore Dr., 64437. T: (660) 442-3770. RV/tent: 75. $12–$15. Hookups: electric (20, 30 amps).

Cuba

Blue Moon RV & Horse Park, 355 Hwy. F, 65453. T: (877) 440-CAMP or (573) 885-3752. F: (573) 885-3752. www.fidnet.com/~blmoonrv. RV/tent: 55. $10–$19. Hookups: electric (30, 50 amps), water, sewer.

Dadeville

Stockton State Park, Rte. 1 Box 1715, 65635. T: (417) 276-4259. RV/tent: 75. $12–$15. Hookups: electric (20, 30 amps), water.

Danville

Graham Cave State Park, 217 Hwy. TT, 63361. T: (573) 564-3476. RV/tent: 52. $12–$15. Hookups: electric (20, 30 amps), water.

DeSoto

Washington State Park, Rte. 2 Box 450, 63020. T: (636) 586-2995. RV/tent: 51. $12–$15. Hookups: electric (20, 30 amps), water.

Eagle Rock

Eagle Rock, HC 1 Box 1037, 65641. T: (417) 271-3215. www.ReserveUSA.com/nrrs/mo/eagr. RV/tent: 63. $12–$18. Hookups: electric (20, 30 amps), water, sewer.

Paradise Cove Camping Resort, HCR 1 Box 1067, 65641. T: (417) 271-4888. RV/tent: 21. $10–$15. Hookups: electric (20, 30 amps), water, sewer.

Forsyth

Forsyth KOA, 11020 MO 76, 65653. T: (800) 562-7560 or (417) 546-5364. www.koa.com. RV/tent: 67. $22–$25. Hookups: electric (20, 30, 50 amps), water, sewer.

Genevieve

Hawn State Park, 12096 Park Dr., 63670. T: (573) 883-3603. RV/tent: 50. $12–$15. Hookups: electric (20, 30 amps), water.

Golden

Viney Creek, Rte. 1 Box 1023, 65658. T: (417) 271-3860. www.ReserveUSA.com/nrrs/mo/vinc. RV/tent: 46. $11–$16. Hookups: electric (20, 30 amps), water.

Hermitage

Damsite, Rte. 2 Box 2160, 65668. T: (417) 745-2244. www.ReserveUSA.com/nrrs/mo/da10. RV/tent: 130. $10–$18. Hookups: electric (20, 30 amps), water.

Lightfoot Landing, Rte. 2 Box 2160, 65668. T: (417) 282-6890. www.ReserveUSA.com/nrrs/mo/ligl. RV/tent: 35. $10–$12. Hookups: electric (20, 30 amps).

Nemo Landing, Rte. 2 Box 2160, 65668. T: (417) 993-5529. www.ReserveUSA.com/nrrs/mo/nemo. RV/tent: 121. $10–$18. Hookups: electric (20, 30 amps), water, sewer.

Outlet Park, Rte. 2 Box 2160, 65668. T: (417) 745-2290. www.ReserveUSA.com/nrrs/mo/oua2. RV/tent: 28. $8–$10. Hookups: electric (20, 30 amps).

Wheatland Park, Rte. 2 Box 2160, 65668. T: (417) 282-5267. www.ReserveUSA.com/nrrs/mo/whea. RV/tent: 86. $10–$18. Hookups: electric (20, 30 amps), water.

Jamesport

Countryside RV Park, 106 East Second, 64648. T: (660) 684 6392. RV/tent: 16. $13. Hookups: electric (20, 30 amps), water, sewer.

MISSOURI (continued)

Jonesburg

Jonesburg/Warrenton KOA, P.O. Box H, 63351. T: (800) 562-5634 or (636) 488-5630. www.koa.com/where/MO/25105. RV/tent: 52. $17–$24. Hookups: electric (20, 30, 50 amps), water, sewer.

Joplin

Joplin KOA, 4359 Hwy. 43, 64804. T: (800) 562-5675 or (417) 623-2246. www.koa.com. RV/tent: 74. $18–$26. Hookups: electric (20, 30, 50 amps), water, sewer.

Kaiser

Lake of the Ozarks State Park, P.O. Box 170, 65047. T: (573) 348-2694. RV/tent: 182. $12–$15. Hookups: electric (20, 30 amps), water.

Kimberling City

Kimberling City KOA, HCR 5 Box 465, 65686. T: (800) 562-5685 or (417) 739-4627. www.koa.com/where/MO/25107. RV/tent: 94. $18–$25. Hookups: electric (30, 50 amps), water, sewer.

Knob Noster

Knob Noster State Park, 801 Southeast Hwy. 10, 65336. T: (660) 563-2463. RV/tent: 77. $12–$15. Hookups: electric (20, 30 amps), water.

Laclede

Pershing State Park, 29277 Hwy. 130, 64651. T: (660) 963-2299. RV/tent: 39. $12–$15. Hookups: electric (20, 30 amps), water.

LaGrange

Wakonda State Park, Rte. 1 Box 242, 63448. T: (573) 655-2280. RV/tent: 79. $12–$15. Hookups: electric (20, 30 amps), water.

Lake Ozark

Cross Creek RV Park, P.O. Box 936, 65049. T: (888) 250-3885. RV/tent: 76. $10–$15. Hookups: electric (30, 50 amps), water, sewer.

Majestic Oaks Park, P.O. Box 525, 65049. T: (573) 365-1890. F: (573) 365-9609. www.majesticoakspark.com. RV/tent: 85. $16–$22. Hookups: electric (30, 50 amps), water, sewer.

Lampe

Baxter Campground, HCR 1 171-A, 65681. T: (417) 779-5370. www.ReserveUSA.com/nrrs/mo/baxt. RV/tent: 54. $11–$15. Hookups: electric (20, 30 amps).

Mill Creek, HCR Box 1059, 65681. T: (417) 779-5378. www.ReserveUSA.com/nrrs/mo/mil2. RV/tent: 68. $12–$16. Hookups: electric (20, 30 amps).

Lawson

Watkins Woolen Mill State Park, 26600 Park Rd. North, 64602. T: (816) 296-3357. RV/tent: 98. $12–$15. Hookups: electric (20, 30 amps), water.

Leasburg

Ozark Outdoors, 200 Ozark Outdoor Ln., 65535. T: (800) 888-0023 or (573) 245-6839. www.ozark-outdoors.net. RV/tent: 260. $7–$16. Hookups: electric (20, 30, 50 amps), water, sewer.

Onondaga Cave State Park, 7556 Hwy. H, 65535. T: (573) 245-6576. RV/tent: 71. $12–$15. Hookups: electric (20, 30 amps), water.

Lebanon

Bennett Spring State Park, 26250 Hwy. 64A, 65536. T: (417) 532-4338. RV/tent: 140. $12–$15. Hookups: electric (20, 30 amps), water, sewer.

Mansfield

Mansfield House B&B/RV Park, 2991 Hwy. A, 65704. T: (417) 924-2222. F: (417) 924-8619. RV/tent: 52. $18–$20. Hookups: electric (20, 30, 50 amps), water, sewer.

Miami

Van Meter State Park, 65344. T: (660) 886-7537. RV/tent: 21. $12–$15. Hookups: electric (20, 30 amps), water.

Monroe City

Frank Russell, 20642 Hwy. J, 63456. T: (573) 735-4097. www.ReserveUSA.com/nrrs/mo/frar. RV/tent: 60. $12. Hookups: electric (20, 30 amps).

Indian Creek, 20642 Hwy. J, 63456. T: (573) 735-4097. www.ReserveUSA.com/nrrs/mo/ind4. RV/tent: 190. $14. Hookups: electric (20, 30 amps).

Ray Behrens, 20642 Hwy. J, 63456. T: (573) 735-4097. www.ReserveUSA.com/nrrs/mo/rabe. RV/tent: 168. $14. Hookups: electric (20, 30 amps).

Mountain Home

Beaver Creek, P.O. Box 2070, 72654. T: (870) 546-3708. www.ReserveUSA.com/nrrs/mo/bec3. RV/tent: 37. $13–$16. Hookups: electric (20, 30 amps).

Pontiac Park, P.O. Box 2070, 72654. T: (870) 425-2700. www.ReserveUSA.com/nrrs/mo/pont. RV/tent: 38. $9–$16. Hookups: electric (20, 30 amps).

River Run, P.O. Box 2070, 72654. T: (870) 546-3646. www.ReserveUSA.com/nrrs/mo/rivn. RV/tent: 32. $8–$16. Hookups: electric (20, 30 amps).

MISSOURI (continued)

Mountain View

Weaver's RV Park, 5400 CR 3200 No. 19, 65548. T: (417) 469-3351. RV/tent: 15. $12. Hookups: electric (20, 30 amps), water, sewer.

Newburg

Arlington RV Campground, 13003 Arlington Outer Rd., 65550. T: (573) 762-2714. www.arlingtonrv campground.com. RV/tent: 60. $4–$14. Hookups: electric (30 amps), water, sewer.

Park Hills

St. Joe State Park, 2800 Pimville Rd., 63601. T: (573) 431-1069. RV/tent: 80. $12–$15. Hookups: electric (20, 30 amps), water.

Patterson

Sam A. Baker State Park, RFD 1 Box 114, 63956. T: (573) 856-4411. RV/tent: 192. $12–$15. Hookups: electric (20, 30 amps).

Piedmont

Bluff View (Clearwater Lake), Rte. 3 Box 3559-D, 63957. T: (573) 223-7777. www.ReserveUSA.com/nrrs/mo/blu2. RV/tent: 69. $10–$15. Hookups: electric (20, 30, 50 amps), water.

Highway K, Rte. 3 Box 3559-D, 63957. T: (573) 223-7777. www.ReserveUSA.com/nrrs/mo/higw. RV/tent: 61. $10–$13. Hookups: electric (20, 30 amps).

River Road L. Bank, Rte. 3 Box 3559-D, 63957. T: (573) 223-7777. www.ReserveUSA.com/nrrs/mo/rilb. RV/tent: 120. $10–$14. Hookups: electric (20, 30 amps).

Webb Creek, Rte. 3 Box 3559-D, 63957. T: (573) 223-7777. www.ReserveUSA.com/nrrs/mo/webb. RV/tent: 39. $10–$13. Hookups: electric (20, 30 amps), water.

Pittsburg

Pomme de Terre State Park, HC 77 Box 890, 65724. T: (417) 852-4291. RV/tent: 257. $12–$15. Hookups: electric (20, 30 amps), water.

Poplar Bluff

Camelot RV Campground, 1217 Rte. 6, 63901. T: (573) 785-1016. RV/tent: 70. $15–$19. Hookups: electric (30, 50 amps), water, sewer.

Reeds Spring

Aunts Creek, Rte. 5 Box 585, 65737. T: (417) 739-2792. www.ReserveUSA.com/nrrs/mo/aunt. RV/tent: 56. $12–$16. Hookups: electric (20, 30 amps).

Ridgedale

Long Creek, 1036 Long Creek Rd., 65639. T: (417) 334-8427. www.ReserveUSA.com/nrrs/mo/lonc. RV/tent: 47. $12–$17. Hookups: electric (20, 30, 50 amps), water.

Robertsville

Robertsville State Park, P.O. Box 186, 63072. T: (636) 257-3788. RV/tent: 27. $12–$15. Hookups: electric (20, 30 amps), water.

Rock Port

Rock Port KOA, 1409 Hwy. 136 West, 64482. T: (800) 562-5415 or (660) 744-5485. www.koa.com/where/MO/25148. RV/tent: 56. $16–$24. Hookups: electric (20, 30, 50 amps), water, sewer.

Rushville

Lewis and Clark State Park, 801 Lake Crest Blvd., 64484. T: (816) 579-5564. RV/tent: 70. $12–$15. Hookups: electric (20, 30 amps), water.

Salem

Jason Place Campground, HCR 81 Box 90, 65560. T: (800) 333-5628 or (573) 858-3224. F: (573) 858-3341. RV/tent: 175. $11–$24. Hookups: electric (20, 30 amps), water.

Montauk State Park, Rte. 5 Box 279, 65560-9025. T: (573) 548-2201. RV/tent: 154. $12–$15. Hookups: electric (20, 30 amps), water.

Sarcoxie

WAC RV Park, 2041 Cimarron Rd., 64862. T: (417) 548-2258. RV/tent: 144. $14. Hookups: electric (20, 30, 50 amps), water, sewer.

Sedalia

Chaplin's RVs, 22415 Main St., 65301. T: (660) 826-8549. RV/tent: 15. $12. Hookups: electric (30, 50 amps), water, sewer.

Shell Knob

Campbell Point, 792 Campbell Point Rd., 65747. T: (417) 858-3903. www.ReserveUSA.com/nrrs/mo/camb. RV/tent: 765. $12–$18. Hookups: electric (20, 30 amps).

Viola, Rte. 5 Box 5210, 65747. T: (417) 858-3904. www.ReserveUSA.com/nrrs/mo/viol. RV/tent: 57. $11–$16. Hookups: electric (20, 30 amps), water.

Sikeston

Town & Country Camping & RV Park, Hwy. 62 East, P.O. Box 1223, 63801. T: (800) 771-1339 or (573) 472-1339. F: (573) 472-2240. RV/tent: 60. $15. Hookups: electric (30, 50 amps), water, sewer.

MISSOURI (continued)

Springfield

Springfield KOA, 5775 West Farm Rd., 65802. T: (800) 562-1228 or (417) 831-3645. F: (417) 863-0295. www.koa.com. RV/tent: 99. $18–$26. Hookups: electric (20, 30, 50 amps), water, sewer.

St. Louis

KOA St. Louis West at Six Flags, Box 128, 63025. T: (800) 562-6249 or (636) 257-3018. F: (636) 257-6575. www.koa.com. RV/tent: 159. $19–$24. Hookups: electric (20, 30, 50 amps), water, sewer.

KOA St. Louis South, 8000 Metropolitan Blvd., 63012. T: (800) 562-3049 or (636) 479-4449. www.koa.com. RV/tent: 113. $15–$23. Hookups: electric (20, 30, 50 amps), water, sewer.

St. Charles

Sundermeier RV Park & Conference Center, 111 Transit St., 63301. T: (800) 929-0832 or (314) 940-0111. RV/tent: 106. $34–$37. Hookups: electric (30, 50 amps), water, sewer.

Stanton

Stanton/Meramec KOA, Box 177, 63079. T: (800) 562-4498 or (573) 927-5215. F: (573) 927-5215. www.koa.com. RV/tent: 51. $16–$21. Hookups: electric (20, 30, 50 amps), water, sewer.

Stockton

Cedar Ridge, 16435 East Stockton Lake Dr., 65785. T: (417) 995-2045. www.ReserveUSA.com/nrrs/mo/cemo. RV/tent: 54. $10–$16. Hookups: electric (20, 30 amps), water.

Crabtree Cove, 16435 East Stockton Lake Dr., 65785. T: (417) 276-6799. www.ReserveUSA.com/nrrs/mo/crat. RV/tent: 58. $10–$16. Hookups: electric (20, 30 amps), water.

Hawker Point, 16435 East Stockton Lake Dr., 65785. T: (417) 276-7266. www.ReserveUSA.com/nrrs/mo/hawk. RV/tent: 62. $10–$16. Hookups: electric (20, 30 amps).

Ruark Bluff East, 16435 East Stockton Lake Dr., 65785. T: (417) 637-5303. www.ReserveUSA.com/nrrs/mo/ruar. RV/tent: 91. $10–$16. Hookups: electric (20, 30 amps).

Ruark Bluff West, 16435 East Stockton Lake Dr., 65785. T: (417) 637-5279. www.ReserveUSA.com/nrrs/mo/ruaw. RV/tent: 66. $10–$16. Hookups: electric (20, 30 amps).

Stoutsville

Mark Twain State Park, 20057 State Park Office Rd., 65283. T: (573) 565-3440. RV/tent: 101. $12–$15. Hookups: electric (20, 30 amps), water.

Sullivan

Meramec State Park, 2800 South Hwy. 185, 63080. T: (573) 468-6072. RV/tent: 190. $12–$15. Hookups: electric (20, 30, 50 amps), water, sewer.

Trenton

Crowder State Park, 76 Hwy. 128, 64683. T: (660) 359-6473. RV/tent: 42. $7–$12. Hookups: electric (30 amps).

Troy

Cuivre River State Park, 678 SR 147, 63379. T: (636) 528-7247. RV/tent: 80. $12–$15. Hookups: electric (20, 30, 50 amps), water, sewer.

Wappapello

Peoples Creek Campground, HC 2 Box 2349, 63966. T: (573) 222-8234. www.ReserveUSA.com/nrrs/mo/pecr/pecr2. RV/tent: 37. $14. Hookups: electric (20, 30 amps).

Peoples Creek Upper Campground, HC 2 Box 2349, 63966. T: (573) 222-8234. www.ReserveUSA.com/nrrs/mo/pecr/pecr1. RV/tent: 20. $14. Hookups: electric (20, 30 amps).

Redman Creek East, HC 2 Box 2349, 63966. T: (573) 222-8233. www.ReserveUSA.com/nrrs/mo/red2/red21. RV/tent: 68. $14. Hookups: electric (20, 30 amps).

Redman Creek West, HC 2 Box 2349, 63966. T: (573) 222-8233. www.ReserveUSA.com/nrrs/mo/red2/red22. RV/tent: 38. $14. Hookups: electric (20, 30 amps).

Warsaw

Berry Bend, Rte. 2 Box 29A, 65355. T: (660) 438-7317. www.ReserveUSA.com/nrrs/mo/berr. RV/tent: 113. $10–$16. Hookups: electric (20, 30 amps).

Bucksaw, Rte. 2 Box 29A, 65355. T: (660) 438-7317. www.ReserveUSA.com/nrrs/mo/bucs. RV/tent: 136. $10–$16. Hookups: electric (20, 30 amps).

Long Shoal, Rte. 2 Box 29A, 65355. T: (660) 438-7317. www.ReserveUSA.com/nrrs/mo/losh. RV/tent: 123. $10–$16. Hookups: electric (20, 30, 50 amps), water.

Osage Bluff, Rte. 2 Box 29A, 65355. T: (660) 438-7317. www.ReserveUSA.com/nrrs/mo/osag. RV/tent: 68. $10–$16. Hookups: electric (20, 30 amps).

Talley Bend, Rte. 2 Box 29A, 65355. T: (417) 438-7317. www.ReserveUSA.com/nrrs/mo/tale. RV/tent: 76. $10–$16. Hookups: electric (20, 30 amps).

MISSOURI

Thibaut Point, Rte. 2 Box 29A, 65355. T: (660) 438-7317. www.ReserveUSA.com/nrrs/mo/thib. RV/tent: 51. $10–$16. Hookups: electric (20, 30 amps).

Harry S Truman State Park, HCR 66 Box 14, 65355. T: (660) 438-7711. RV/tent: 201. $12–$15. Hookups: electric (20, 30 amps), water.

Weston

Weston Bend State Park, P.O. Box 115, 16600 Hwy. 45 North, 64098. T: (816) 640-5443. RV/tent: 36. $12–$15. Hookups: electric (20, 30 amps), water.

Wildwood

Dr. Edmund A Babler Memorial State Park, 800 Guy Park Dr., 63005. T: (636) 458-3813. RV/tent: 77. $12–$15. Hookups: electric (20, 30 amps).

NEW MEXICO

Alamogordo

Cimmarron Campground, Carson National Forest Community Affairs Office, 208 Cruz Alta Rd., 87571. T: (505) 758-6200. www.fs.fed.us/r3/carson/html_main/list_camping2.html. RV/tent: 36. $10. Hookups: none.

Evergreen Park, 2200 North Florida Ave. No. 50, 88310. T: (505) 437-3721. RV/tent: 45. $16. Hookups: electric (20, 30, 50 amps), water, sewer.

Oliver Lee Memorial State Park, 409 Dog Canyon, 88310. T: (505) 437-8284. www.emnrd.state.nm.us/nmparks/pages/parks/oliver/oliver.htm. RV/tent: 44. $8–$18. Hookups: electric (20, 30 amps).

White Sands Community, 607 South White Sands Blvd., 88310. T: (505) 437-8388. RV/tent: 290. $17–$20. Hookups: electric (30 amps), water, sewer.

Albuquerque

Albuquerque North/Bernalillo KOA, P.O. Box 758, 87004. T: (800) 562-3616 or (505) 867-5227. www.koa.com. RV/tent: 89. $21–$31. Hookups: electric (20, 30, 50 amps), water, sewer.

American RV Park of Albuquerque, 13500 Coronado Fwy. Southwest, 87121. T: (800) 282-8885 or (501) 831-3545. F: (501) 836-6095. www.americanrvpark.com. RV/tent: 202. $26–$30. Hookups: electric (20, 30, 50 amps), water, sewer.

Balloon View RV Park, 500 Tyler Rd. Northeast, 87121. T: (800) 932-9523 or (505) 345-3716. F: (505) 345-3718. RV/tent: 87. $23–$26. Hookups: electric (30, 50 amps), water, sewer.

Best Western American Motor Inn & RV Park, 12999 Central Ave. Northeast, 87123. T: (505) 298-7426. F: (505) 298-0212. RV/tent: 13. $24–$28. Hookups: electric (30, 50 amps), water, sewer, cable.

Enchanted Trails Camping Resort, 14305 Central NW, 87121. T: (800) 326-6317 or (505) 831-6314. F: (505) 831-1000. www.enchantedtrails.com. RV/tent: 135. $20–$22. Hookups: electric (30 amps), water, sewer.

Palisades RV Park, 9201 Central NW, 87121. T: (888) 922-9595 or (505) 831-5000. RV/tent: 112. $22–$24. Hookups: electric (30, 50 amps), water, sewer.

Alto

Elk Run Cabins & RV Park, P.O. Box 406, 88312. T: (800) 687-0620 or (505) 336-4240. www.ruidoso.net/elkrun. RV/tent: 20. $20–$25. Hookups: electric (30, 50 amps), water, sewer.

Angel Fire

Monte Verde RV Park, P.O. Box 520, 87710. T: (505) 377-3404. www.aardvarkrv.com/monteverderv. RV/tent: 28. $18. Hookups: electric (30 amps), water, sewer.

Anthony

El Paso West RV Park, 1415 Anthony Dr., 88021. T: (505) 882-7172. RV/tent: 100. $20. Hookups: electric (30, 50 amps), water, sewer.

Arrey

Arrey RV Park, MM 19, Hwy. 87, 87930. T: (866) 267-1049 or (505) 267-1049. www.zianet.com/mmoyle. RV/tent: 10. $8.50. Hookups: electric (20, 30, 50 amps), water, sewer.

Aztec

Ruins Road RV Park, 312 Ruins Rd., 87410. T: (505) 334-3160. F: (505) 334-3160. RV/tent: 45. $15. Hookups: electric (30, 50 amps), water, sewer.

NEW MEXICO (continued)

Bloomfield

Bloomfield KOA, 1900 East Blanco Blvd., 87413. T: (800) 562-8513 or (505) 632-8339. www.koa.com/where/NM/31156. RV/tent: 84. $16–$23. Hookups: electric (20, 30, 50 amps), water, sewer.

Caballo

Caballo Lake State Park, P.O. Box 32, 87931. T: (505) 743-3942. www.emnrd.state.nm.us/nmparks/pages/parks/caballo/caballo.htm. RV/tent: 200. $8–$18. Hookups: electric (20, 30 amps).

Percha Dam State Park, P.O. Box 32, 87931. T: (505) 743-3942. www.emnrd.state.nm.us/nmparks/pages/parks/percha/percha.htm. RV/tent: 29. $8–$18. Hookups: electric (20, 30 amps).

Canjilon

Canjilon Lakes Campground, Carson National Forest Community Affairs Office, 208 Cruz Alta Rd., 87571. T: (505) 758-6200. www.fs.fed.us/r3/carson/html_main/list_camping2.html. RV/tent: 40. $10. Hookups: none.

Echo Ampitheater Campground, Carson National Forest Community Affairs Office, 208 Cruz Alta Rd., 87571. T: (505) 758-6200. www.fs.fed.us/r3/carson/html_main/list_camping2.html. RV/tent: 10. $10. Hookups: none.

Capitan

Mountain High RV Park, HC 71 Box 1220, 88316. T: (505) 336-4236. RV/tent: 39. $20. Hookups: electric (30 amps), water, sewer.

Carlsbad

Brantley Lake State Park, P.O. Box 2288, 88221. T: (505) 457-2384. www.emnrd.state.nm.us/nmparks/pages/parks/brantley/Brantley.htm. RV/tent: 11. $8–$18. Hookups: electric (20, 30 amps).

Cavern Estates Mobile Home & RV Park, 3022 National Parks Hwy., 88220. T: (505) 887-3274. RV/tent: 50. $15–$17. Hookups: electric (30, 50 amps), water, sewer.

Edeal's Pecos River RV Park & Minimart, 320 East Greene St., 88220. T: (505) 885-5201. RV/tent: 16. $19. Hookups: electric (20, 30, 50 amps), water, sewer.

Windmill RV Park, 3624 National Parks Hwy., 88220. T: (888) 349-7275 or (505) 887-1387. RV/tent: 61. $18–$22. Hookups: electric (30, 50 amps), water, sewer.

Carrizozo

Valley of Fires Recreation Area, P.O. Box 63, 88301. T: (505) 648-2241. F: (505) 648-2241. RV/tent: 25. $10. Hookups: electric (30 amps).

Cedar Crest

Turquoise Trail Campground & RV Park, P.O. Box 582, 22 Calvary Rd., 87008. T: (505) 281-2005. RV/tent: 87. $19. Hookups: electric (20, 30, 50 amps), water, sewer.

Chama

El Vado Lake State Park, P.O. Box 367, 87575. T: (505) 588-7247. www.emnrd.state.nm.us/nmparks/pages/parks/elvado/elvado.htm. RV/tent: 64. $8–$18. Hookups: electric (20, 30 amps).

Little Creel Resort, P.O. Box 781, 87520. T: (505) 756-2382. RV/tent: 67. $15–$35. Hookups: electric (20, 30, 50 amps), water, sewer.

Rio Chama RV Park, 182 North Hwy. 17, 87520. T: (505) 756-2303. RV/tent: 90. $16–$20. Hookups: electric (30, 50 amps), water, sewer.

Twin Rivers RV Park & Campground, P.O. Box 26, 87520. T: (505) 756-2218. RV/tent: 85. $15. Hookups: electric (15, 20, 30, 50 amps), water, sewer.

Church Rock

Red Rock State Park, Box 10, 57311. T: (505) 722-3839. RV/tent: 135. $14. Hookups: electric (30, 50 amps), water.

Cimarron

Cimarron Inn & RV Park, 204 Hwy. 64, 87714. T: (505) 376-2268. F: (505) 376-4504. RV/tent: 12. $17. Hookups: electric (20, 30 amps), water, sewer.

Cloudcroft

Apache Campground, Lincoln Forest, 1101 New York Ave., 88310-6992. T: (505) 682-2551. F: (505) 434-7218. RV/tent: 26. $10. Hookups: none.

Deerhead Campground, Lincoln Forest, 1101 New York Ave., 88310-6992. T: (505) 682-2551. F: (505) 434-7218. RV/tent: 35. $10. Hookups: none.

Pines Campground, Lincoln Forest, 1101 New York Ave., 88310-6992. T: (505) 682-2551. F: (505) 434-7218. RV/tent: 48. $10. Hookups: none.

Silver Campground, Lincoln Forest, 1101 New York Ave., 88310-6992. T: (505) 682-2551. F: (505) 434-7218. RV/tent: 32. $10. Hookups: none.

Sleepy Grass Campground, Lincoln Forest, 1101 New York Ave., 88310-6992. T: (505) 682-2551. F: (505) 434-7218. RV/tent: 45. $10. Hookups: none.

NEW MEXICO

Clovis

West Park Inn RV Park, 1500 West 7th St., 88101. T: (505) 763-7218. RV/tent: 18. $18. Hookups: electric (20, 30 amps), water, sewer, cable.

Conchas Dam

Conchas Lake State Park, P.O. Box 976, 88416. T: (505) 868-2270. www.emnrd.state.nm.us/nm parks/pages/parks/conchas/conchas.htm. RV/tent: 215. $8–$18. Hookups: electric (20, 30 amps).

Deming

81 Palms RV Resort, 2800 West Pine St., 88030. T: (505) 546-7434. RV/tent: 106. $16–$18. Hookups: electric (20, 30, 50 amps), water, sewer.

A Deming Roadrunner RV Park, 2849 East Motel Dr., 88030. T: (800) 226-9937. F: (505) 546-6960. www.zianet.com/roadrunnerrv. RV/tent: 109. $10–$16. Hookups: electric (20, 30, 50 amps), water, sewer.

A Little Vineyard RV Park & Resort, 2901 Motel Dr. East, 88030. T: (800) 413-0312. www.zianet.com/cjbailey. RV/tent: 153. $12. Hookups: electric (20, 30, 50 amps), water, sewer.

Dream Catcher Escapees RV Park, 4400 East Motel Dr., 88030. T: (505) 544-4004. www.escapees.com. RV/tent: 132. $10. Hookups: electric (20, 30, 50 amps), water, sewer.

Hitchin' Post RV Park, 611 West Pine St., 88030. T: (505) 546-9145. RV/tent: 40. $11–$14. Hookups: electric (30 amps), water, sewer.

Rockhound State Park, P.O. Box 1064, 88030. T: (505) 546-6182. www.emnrd.state.nm.us/nm parks/pages/parks/rockh/rockh.htm. RV/tent: 36. $8–$18. Hookups: electric (20, 30 amps).

Starlight Village Resort, P.O. Drawer 1139, 88031. T: (505) 546-0867. F: (505) 546-6029. RV/tent: 64. $17. Hookups: electric (30, 50 amps), water, sewer.

Vista Floridas RV Park, 545 O'Kelley Rd. Southeast, 88030. T: (505) 544-8366. RV/tent: 21. $15. Hookups: electric (20, 30, 50 amps), water, sewer.

Eagle Nest

Eagle Gem RV Park, HCR 71 Box 3, 87718. T: (505) 377-2214 or (505) 377-0522. RV/tent: 60. $17. Hookups: electric (20, 30, 50 amps), water, sewer.

Golden Eagle RV Park, Box 458, 87718. T: (800) 388-6188 or (505) 377-6188. RV/tent: 53. $20. Hookups: electric (30, 50 amps), water, sewer.

Lost Eagle RV Park, 155 East Therma Dr., 87718. T: (800) 581-2374 or (505) 377-2374. RV/tent: 41. $15–$17. Hookups: electric (30, 50 amps), water, sewer.

Elephant Butte

Cozy Cove, Box 427, 87935. T: (505) 740-0745. RV/tent: 29. $13. Hookups: electric (20, 30, 50 amps), water, sewer.

Elephant Butte Lake State Park, P.O. Box 13, 87935. T: (505) 744-5421. www.emnrd.state.nm.us/nm parks/pages/parks/butte/butte.htm. RV/tent: 223. $8–$18. Hookups: electric (20, 30 amps).

Enchanted Views RV Park, P.O. Box 250, 87935. T: (505) 744-5876. RV/tent: 37. $14–$16. Hookups: electric (30, 50 amps), water, sewer.

Espanola

Ohkay RV Park, North Riverside Dr., 87532. T: (505) 753-5067. RV/tent: 84. $21. Hookups: electric (30, 50 amps), water, sewer.

Farmington

Dad & Ann's RV Park, 202 East Pinon, 87401. T: (888) 326-3237. F: (505) 326-1870. RV/tent: 10. $15. Hookups: electric (30 amps), water, sewer.

Downs Hair Salon & RV Park, 5701 Hwy. 64, 87401. T: (505) 325-7094. RV/tent: 42. $17. Hookups: electric (30, 50 amps), water, sewer.

Mom & Pop RV Park, 901 Illinois Ave., 87401. T: (800) 748-2807. RV/tent: 33. $14. Hookups: electric (30 amps), water, sewer.

Paramount RV Park, North Rd. 6220, 87401. T: (505) 598-9824. F: (505) 598-6515. RV/tent: 16. $15. Hookups: electric (20, 30, 50 amps), water, sewer.

Faywood

City of Rocks State Park, P.O. Box 50, 88034. T: (505) 536-2800. www.emnrd.state.nm.us/nm parks/pages/parks/cityrock/cityrock.htm. RV/tent: 57. $8–$18. Hookups: electric (20, 30 amps).

Fort Sumner

Sumner Lake State Park, HC 64 Box 125, 88119. T: (505) 355-2541. www.emnrd.state.nm.us/nm parks/pages/parks/sumner/sumner.htm. RV/tent: 106. $8–$18. Hookups: electric (20, 30 amps).

Gila Hot Springs

Gila Hot Springs RV Park & Vacation Center, HC 68 Box 80, 88061. T: (505) 536-9551. RV/tent: 16. $17. Hookups: electric (30, 50 amps), water, sewer.

Grants

Bar S RV Park, I-40, Exit 79, 87020. T: (505) 876-6002. RV/tent: 51. $12. Hookups: electric (20, 30, 50 amps), water, sewer.

Blue Spruce RV Park, I-40, Exit 81, 87020. T: (505) 287-2560. RV/tent: 23. $11. Hookups: electric (20, 30, 50 amps), water, sewer.

NEW MEXICO (continued)

Grants (continued)

Cibola Sands RV Park, P.O. Box 179, 87020. T: (505) 287-4376. www.cibolarv.com. RV/tent: 46. $16–$20. Hookups: electric (20, 30, 50 amps), water, sewer.

Valencia Village Mobile & RV Park, 1400 East Roosevelt Ave., 87020. T: (505) 287-2744. RV/tent: 60. $15. Hookups: electric (30, 50 amps), water, sewer.

Guadalupita

Coyote Creek State Park, P.O. Box 477, 87722. T: (505) 387-2328. www.emnrd.state.nm.us/nm parks/pages/parks/coyote/coyote.htm. RV/tent: 50. $8–$18. Hookups: electric (20, 30 amps).

Morphy Lake State Park, P.O. Box 477, 87722. T: (505) 387-2328. RV/tent: 60. $8–$18. Hookups: none.

Hobbs

Burnell's RV Park, 100 South Marlind Blvd., 88240. T: (505) 393-3226. F: (505) 393-3226. RV/tent: 27. $16. Hookups: electric (30, 50 amps), water, sewer.

Conner RV Sales & Park, 100 South Marland Blvd., 88240-6349. T: (505) 393-3226. RV/tent: 5. $16. Hookups: electric (30, 50 amps), water, sewer.

Jims RV Park, 615 North Marland Blvd., 88240-5404. T: (505) 397-2551. RV/tent: 21. $13. Hooksups: electric (20, 30, 50 amps), water, sewer.

Jemez Springs

Fenton Lake State Park, 455 Fenton Lake Rd., 87025. T: (505) 829-3630. www.emnrd.state.nm.us/nmparks/pages/parks/fenton/fenton.htm. RV/tent: 40. $8–$18. Hookups: electric (20, 30 amps).

Lakewood

7 Rivers Cove RV Resort at Brantley Lake, P.O. Box 103, 88254. T: (877) 457-2002 or (505) 457-2000. RV/tent: 30. $20–$22. Hookups: electric (30, 50 amps), water, sewer.

Las Cruces

Coachlight Motel & RV Park, 301 South Motel Blvd., 88005. T: (505) 526-3301. RV/tent: 47. $20. Hookups: electric (30, 50 amps), water, sewer.

Dalmonts RV Trailer Corral, 2224 South Valley, 88005. T: (505) 523-2992. RV/tent: 26. $16. Hookups: electric (15, 20, 30 amps), water, sewer.

RV Doc's Park & Service Center, 1475 Ave. de Mesilla, 88005. T: (888) 2RV-DOCS or (505) 526-8401. RV/tent: 66. $20–$23. Hookups: electric (30, 50 amps), water, sewer.

Siesta RV Park, 1551 Ave. de Mesilla, 88005. T: (800) 414-6816 or (505) 523-6816. F: (505) 523-0599. RV/tent: 54. $21–$23. Hookups: electric (30 amps), water, sewer.

Sunny Acres Mobile Village, 595 North Valley Dr., 88005. T: (877) 800-1716 or (505) 534-1716. F: (505) 524-3099. RV/tent: 24. $20. Hookups: electric (30, 50 amps), water, sewer.

Las Vegas

Las Vegas KOA, HC 31 Box 16, 87701. T: (800) 562-3423 or (505) 454-0180. www.koa.com. RV/tent: 60. $19–$27. Hookups: electric (20, 30 amps), water, sewer.

Storrie Lake State Park, HC33 Box 109 No. 2, 87701. T: (505) 425-7278. www.emnrd.state.nm.us/nmparks/pages/parks/storrie/storrie.htm. RV/tent: 112. $8–$18. Hookups: electric (20, 30 amps).

Vegas RV Park, 504 Harris Rd., 87701. T: (505) 425-5640. RV/tent: 33. $18. Hookups: electric (30 amps), water, sewer.

Westward Ho RV Park, 857 AirpoRte. Rd., 87701. T: (505) 425-6978. www.members.tripod.com/~dukesrv. RV/tent: 20. $20. Hookups: electric (30, 50 amps), water, sewer.

Los Alamos

Bandelier National Monument, HCR 1 Box 1, Suite 50, 87544. T: (505) 672-3861. F: (505) 672-9607. RV/tent: 93. $20. Hookups: none.

Los Ojos

Heron Lake State Park, P.O. Box 159, 87511. T: (505) 588-7470. www.emnrd.state.nm.us/nmparks/pages/parks/heron/heron.htm. RV/tent: 400. $8–$18. Hookups: electric (20, 30 amps).

Mesilla

Hacienda RV Resort, P.O. Box 1479, 88046. T: (888) 686-9090 or (505) 528-5800. www.haciendarv.com. RV/tent: 113. $25–$27. Hookups: electric (30, 50 amps), water, sewer.

Moriarty

Zia RV Park & Campground, HC 81 Box 165, 87035. T: (505) 832-9796. RV/tent: 58. $15–$17. Hookups: electric (30, 50 amps), water, sewer.

Navajo Dam

Navajo Lake State Park, 1448 NM 511 No. 1, 87419. T: (505) 632-2278. www.emnrd.state.nm.us/nm parks/pages/parks/navajo/navajo.htm. RV/tent: 451. $8–$18. Hookups: electric (20, 30 amps).

NEW MEXICO (continued)

Nogal

Alto Hombre Gordito, P.O. Box 1445, 88341. T: (877) 466-2734 or (505) 336 7877. www.hombre-gordito.com. RV/tent: 20. $35. Hookups: electric (20, 30, 50 amps), water, sewer.

North Pecos

Santa Barbara Campground, Carson National Forest Community Affairs Office, 208 Cruz Alta Rd., 87571. T: (505) 758-6200. www.fs.fed.us/r3/carson/html_main/list_camping2.html. RV/tent: 22. $10. Hookups: none.

Pena Blanca

Cochiti Area, 82 Dam Crest Rd., 87041. T: (505) 465-0307. www.ReserveUSA.com/nrrs/nm/coca. RV/tent: 60. $5–$11. Hookups: electric (20, 30 amps).

Tetilla Peak, 82 Dam Crest Rd., 87041. T: (505) 465-0307. www.ReserveUSA.com/nrrs/nm/tpea. RV/tent: 52. $7–$11. Hookups: electric (20, 30 amps).

Portales

Oasis State Park, 1882 Oasis Rd., 88130. T: (505) 356-5331. www.emnrd.state.nm.us/nmparks/pages/parks/oasis/oasis.htm. RV/tent: 23. $8–$18. Hookups: electric (20, 30 amps).

Wagon Wheel RV Park, Northeast Hwy. 70, 88130. T: (505) 356-3700. RV/tent: 21. $16. Hookups: electric (20, 30, 50 amps), water, sewer.

Radium Springs

Leasburg Dam State Park, P.O. Box 6, 88054. T: (505) 524-4068. www.emnrd.state.nm.us/nmparks/pages/parks/leasburg/leasburg.htm. RV/tent: 54. $8–$18. Hookups: electric (20, 30 amps).

Ranchos de Taos

Taos RV Park, P.O. Box 729 TL, 87557. T: (800) 323-6009 or (505) 758-1667. F: (505) 758-1989. RV/tent: 24. $21–$23. Hookups: electric (20, 30 amps), water, sewer.

Raton

Kickback RV Park, 1025 Frontage Rd., 87740. T: (505) 445-1200. RV/tent: 45. $20–$22. Hookups: electric (30, 50 amps), water, sewer.

Raton KOA, 1330 South 2nd St., 87740. T: (800) 562-9033 or (505) 445-3488. www.koa.com. RV/tent: 54. $15–$25. Hookups: electric (20, 30, 50 amps), water, sewer.

Sugarite Canyon State Park, HCR 63 Box 386, 87740. T: (505) 445-5607. www.emnrd.state.nm.us/nmparks/pages/parks/sugarite/sugarite.htm. RV/tent: 40. $8–$18. Hookups: electric (20, 30 amps).

Red River

River Ranch, Box 69, 87558. T: (505) 754-2293. www.redrivernm.com/riverranch. RV/tent: 31. $23–$27. Hookups: electric (30, 50 amps), water, sewer.

Red River Canyon

Columbine Campground, Carson National Forest Community Affairs Office, 208 Cruz Alta Rd., 87571. T: (505) 758-6200. www.fs.fed.us/r3/carson/html_main/list_camping2.html. RV/tent: 27. $10. Hookups: none.

Elephant Rock Campground, Carson National Forest Community Affairs Office, 208 Cruz Alta Rd., 87571. T: (505) 758-6200. www.fs.fed.us/r3/carson/html_main/list_camping2.html. RV/tent: 22. $10. Hookups: none.

Fawn Lakes Campground, Carson National Forest Community Affairs Office, 208 Cruz Alta Rd., 87571. T: (505) 758-6200. www.fs.fed.us/r3/carson/html_main/list_camping2.html. RV/tent: 21. $10. Hookups: none.

Junebug Campground, Carson National Forest Community Affairs Office, 208 Cruz Alta Rd., 87571. T: (505) 758-6200. www.fs.fed.us/r3/carson/html_main/list_camping2.html. RV/tent: 22. $10. Hookups: none.

Rio Grande Gorge

BLM Orilla Verde, Carson National Forest Community Affairs Office, 208 Cruz Alta Rd., 87571. T: (505) 758-6200. www.fs.fed.us/r3/carson/html_main/list_camping2.html. RV/tent: 23. $10. Hookups: none.

BLM Wild Rivers Campground, Carson National Forest Community Affairs Office, 208 Cruz Alta Rd., 87571. T: (505) 758-6200. www.fs.fed.us/r3/carson/html_main/list_camping2.html. RV/tent: 35. $10. Hookups: none.

Rio Pueblo

Comales Campground, Carson National Forest Community Affairs Office, 208 Cruz Alta Rd., 87571. T: (505) 758-6200. www.fs.fed.us/r3/carson/html_main/list_camping2.html. RV/tent: 13. $10. Hookups: none.

Duran Canyon Campground, Carson National Forest Community Affairs Office, 208 Cruz Alta Rd., 87571. T: (505) 758-6200. www.fs.fed.us/r3/carson/html_main/list_camping2.html. RV/tent: 12. $10. Hookups: none.

NEW MEXICO (continued)

Rio Pueblo (continued)

La Junta Campground, Carson National Forest Community Affairs Office, 208 Cruz Alta Rd., 87571. T: (505) 758-6200. www.fs.fed.us/r3/carson/html_main/list_camping2.html. RV/tent: 8. $10. Hookups: none.

Rio Rancho

Stagecoach Stop RV Resort, 3650 Hwy. 528, 87124. T: (888) 272-PARK. F: (505) 867-1890. RV/tent: 85. $21–$25. Hookups: electric (30, 50 amps), water, sewer.

Rociada

Pendaries RV Park, P.O. Box 697, 87742. T: (800) 820-8304 or (505) 454-8304. F: (505) 425-6989. www.pendariesrvpark.com. RV/tent: 30. $25. Hookups: electric (20, 30, 50 amps), water, sewer.

Rodeo

Mountain Valley Lodge, 88056. T: (505) 557-2267. www.rodeonewmexico.com/rvparks. RV/tent: 13. $6–$12. Hookups: electric (30, 50 amps), water, sewer.

Roswell

Bottomless Lakes State Park, HC 12 Box 1200, 88201. T: (505) 624-6058. www.emnrd.state.nm.us/nmparks. RV/tent: 76. $8–$18. Hookups: electric (20, 30 amps).

Town & Country RV Park, 331 West Brasher Rd., 88203. T: (800) 499-4364 or (505) 624-1833. www.roswell-usa.com/tandcrv. RV/tent: 131. $18–$20. Hookups: electric (30, 50 amps), water, sewer.

Ruidoso

Blue Spruce RV Park, 302 Mechem, 88345. T: (505) 257-7993. RV/tent: 23. $17. Hookups: electric (30 amps), water, sewer.

Bonito Hollow RV Park, P.O. Box 349, 88312. T: (505) 336-4325. RV/tent: 71. $18–$23. Hookups: electric (20, 30, 50 amps), water, sewer.

Pine Ridge RV Campground, 124 Glade Dr., 88345. T: (505) 378-4164. RV/tent: 73. $16–$21. Hookups: electric (20, 30, 50 amps), water, sewer.

Twin Spruce RV Park, 621 Hwy. 70 West, 88245. T: (505) 257-4310. RV/tent: 102. $25–$26. Hookups: electric (20, 30, 50 amps), water, sewer.

Ruidoso Downs

Circle B RV Park, Box 1800, 88346. T: (505) 378-4990. RV/tent: 202. $18. Hookups: electric (20, 30, 50 amps), water, sewer.

Seeping Springs Trout Lakes & Campground, P.O. Box 997, 88346. T: (505) 378-4216. RV/tent: 65. $20. Hookups: electric (30 amps), water, sewer.

Santa Fe

Hyde Memorial State Park, 740 Hyde Park Rd., 87501. T: (505) 983-7175. www.emnrd.state.nm.us/nmparks/pages/parks/hyde/hyde.htm. RV/tent: 50. $8–$18. Hookups: electric (20, 30 amps).

Los Campos de Santa Fe RV Park, 3574 Cerrillos Rd., 87505. T: (800) 852-8160 or (505) 473-1949. F: (505) 471-9220. RV/tent: 95. $25. Hookups: electric (30, 50 amps), water, sewer.

Rancheros de Santa Fe Campground, 736 Old Las Vegas Hwy., 87505. T: (800) 426-9259 or (505) 466-3482. www.rancheros.com. RV/tent: 121. $26. Hookups: electric (15, 20, 30, 50 amps), water, sewer.

Santa Fe KOA, 934 Old Las Vegas Hwy., 87505. T: (800) 562-1514 or (505) 466-1419. www.koa.com/where/NM/31159. RV/tent: 51. $20–$30. Hookups: electric (30, 50 amps), water, sewer.

Trailer Ranch RV Park, 3471 Cerrillos Rd., 87505. T: (505) 471-9970. www.traillerranch.com. RV/tent: 42. $25–$28. Hookups: electric (30, 50 amps), water, sewer.

Santa Rosa

Santa Rosa KOA, Box 423, 88435. T: (800) 562-0836 or (505) 472-3126. F: (505) 472-3883. www.koa.com/where/NM/31143. RV/tent: 100. $18–$25. Hookups: electric (20, 30, 50 amps), water, sewer.

Santa Rosa Lake State Park, P.O. Box 384, 88433. T: (505) 472-3110. www.emnrd.state.nm.us/nmparks/pages/parks/santa/Santa.htm. RV/tent: 90. $8–$18. Hookups: electric (20, 30 amps).

Seneca

Clayton Lake State Park, Rte. Box 20, 88437. T: (505) 374-8808. www.emnrd.state.nm.us/nmparks/pages/parks/clayton/clayton.htm. RV/tent: 33. $8–$18. Hookups: electric (20, 30 amps).

Silver City

Cedar Ridge RV Park & Campground, 2789 South Hwy. 90, 88061. T: (505) 388-4013. RV/tent: 15. $12. Hookups: electric (20, 30 amps), water, sewer.

Silver City KOA, 11824 Hwy. 180 East, 88061. T: (800) 562-7623 or (505) 388-3351. F: (505) 388-0461. www.koa.com. RV/tent: 77. $18–$27. Hookups: electric (20, 30, 50 amps), water, sewer.

NEW MEXICO

Socorro

Casey's Socorro RV Park, P.O. Box 641, 87801. T: (800) 687-2696 or (505) 835-2234. F: (505) 835-2234. RV/tent: 103. $13. Hookups: electric (30 amps), water, sewer, cable.

Western Motel & RV Park, 404 1st St., 87825. T: (505) 854-2417. F: (505) 854-3217. RV/tent: 12. $15. Hookups: electric (20, 30, 50 amps), water, sewer.

Taos

Enchanted Moon RV Park, 7 Valle Escondido Rd., 87571. T: (505) 758-3338. RV/tent: 69. $20. Hookups: electric (20, 30, 50 amps), water, sewer.

Taos Valley RV Park & Campground, Box 7204 NDCBU, 120 Este Es Rd., 87571. T: (800) 999-7571 or (505) 758-4469. www.camptaos.com/rv. RV/tent: 92. $22–$27. Hookups: electric (20, 30, 50 amps), water, sewer.

Taos Canyon

Capulin Campground, Carson National Forest Community Affairs Office, 208 Cruz Alta Rd., 87571. T: (505) 758-6200. www.fs.fed.us/r3/carson/html_main/list_camping2.html. RV/tent: 11. $10. Hookups: none.

La Sombra Campground, Carson National Forest Community Affairs Office, 208 Cruz Alta Rd., 87571. T: (505) 758-6200. www.fs.fed.us/r3/carson/html_main/list_camping2.html. RV/tent: 13. $10. Hookups: none.

Las Petacas Campground, Carson National Forest Community Affairs Office, 208 Cruz Alta Rd., 87571. T: (505) 758-6200. www.fs.fed.us/r3/carson/html_main/list_camping2.html. RV/tent: 9. $10. Hookups: none.

Tijeras

Hidden Valley Resort, 844B East Hwy. 66, 87059. T: (800) 326-2024 or (505) 281-3363. RV/tent: 99. $18–$23. Hookups: electric (30, 50 amps), water, sewer.

Mountain View Campground & RV Park, 768 Hwy. 66 East, 87059. T: (888) 284-2343 or (505) 281-2343. RV/tent: 24. $15–$18. Hookups: electric (30 amps), water, sewer.

Truth or Consequences

Cielo Vista RV Park, 501 South Broadway, 97901. T: (888) 414-8478 or (505) 894-3738. RV/tent: 72. $21. Hookups: electric (30, 50 amps), water, sewer.

RJ RV Park, 2103 South Broadway, 87901. T: (505) 894-9777. RV/tent: 47. $21. Hookups: electric (30, 50 amps), water, sewer.

Tucumcari

Tucumcari KOA, 6299 Quay Rd., 88401. T: (800) 562-1871 or (505) 461-1841. www.koa.com. RV/tent: 111. $15–$25. Hookups: electric (20, 30, 50 amps), water, sewer.

Tularosa

Mountain Meadow RV Park, 240 Mountain Meadow, 88352. T: (505) 585-4979. RV/tent: 32. $13. Hookups: electric (30 amps), water, sewer.

Vado

Vado RV Park, 16201 Las Aleuras, 88072. T: (505) 233-2573. RV/tent: 71. $16. Hookups: electric (30 amps), water, sewer.

Valle Vidal

Cimmarron Campground, Carson National Forest Community Affairs Office, 208 Cruz Alta Rd., 87571. T: (505) 758-6200. www.fs.fed.us/r3/carson/html_main/list_camping2.html. RV/tent: 36. $10. Hookups: none.

McCrystal Campground, Carson National Forest Community Affairs Office, 208 Cruz Alta Rd., 87571. T: (505) 758-6200. www.fs.fed.us/r3/carson/html_main/list_camping2.html. RV/tent: 60. $10. Hookups: none.

Villanueva

Villanueva State Park, P.O. Box 40, 87583. T: (505) 421-2957. www.emnrd.state.nm.us/nmparks/pages/parks/villanue/villanue.htm. RV/tent: 60. $8–$18. Hookups: electric (20, 30 amps).

Williamsburg

Shady Corner RV Park, Broadway & Rio Grande, 87942. T: (505) 894-7698. RV/tent: 6. $12. Hookups: electric (30, 50 amps), water, sewer.

OKLAHOMA

Afton

Grand Country Mobile & RV Park, Rte. 3 Box 163, 74331. T: (918) 257-5164. RV/tent: 16. $12. Hookups: electric (20, 30, 50 amps), water, sewer.

Canton

Big Bend, P.O. Box 69, 73724. T: (580) 886-3576. www.ReserveUSA.com/nrrs/ok/biok. RV/tent: 115. $11–$16. Hookups: electric (20, 30 amps), water.

Canadian, P.O. Box 69, 73724. T: (580) 886-2989. www.ReserveUSA.com/nrrs/ok/caok. RV/tent: 77. $11–$15. Hookups: electric (20, 30 amps).

Sandy Cove, P.O. Box 69, 73724. T: (580) 274-3576. www.ReserveUSA.com/nrrs/ok/saco. RV/tent: 37. $14. Hookups: electric (20, 30 amps).

Checotah

Terra Starr Park, Rte. 2 Box 2130, 74426. T: (918) 689-2164 or (918) 689-7094. RV/tent: 300. $13. Hookups: electric (20, 30 amps), water, sewer.

Checotah/Henryetta

Checotah/Henryetta KOA, Box 750, 74426. T: (800) 562-7510 or (918) 473-6511. www.koa.com. RV/tent: 83. $18–$20. Hookups: electric (20, 30, 50 amps), water, sewer.

Claremore

Claremore Expo Center, 400 Veterans Pkwy., 74017. T: (918) 342-5357. RV/tent: 44. $15. Hookups: electric (20, 30, 50 amps), water, sewer.

Clayton

Potato Hills Central, HC 60 Box 175, 74536. T: (918) 569-4131. www.ReserveUSA.com/nrrs/ok/pota. RV/tent: 94. $15. Hookups: electric (20, 30 amps), water.

Copan

Post Oak Park, Rte. 1 Box 260, 74022. T: (918) 532-4334. www.ReserveUSA.com/nrrs/ok/post. RV/tent: 20. $14–$18. Hookups: electric (20, 30 amps), water.

Washington Cove, Rte. 1 Box 260, 74022. T: (918) 532-4129. www.ReserveUSA.com/nrrs/ok/wash. RV/tent: 101. $14–$16. Hookups: electric (20, 30, 50 amps), water.

Davis

Turner Falls Park, I-35 Exit 47 or 51. T: (580) 369-2917 or (580) 369-2988. www.turnerfallspark.com. RV/tent: 344. $8–$10. Hookups: electric (30 amps), water.

El Reno

Cherokee KOA, Box 6, 73036. T: (800) 562-5736 or (405) 884-2595. www.koa.com. RV/tent: 79. $15–$21. Hookups: electric (20, 30, 50 amps), water, sewer.

Hensley's RV Park, Country Club Rd., 73036. T: (405) 262-6490. RV/tent: 26. $21. Hookups: electric (30, 50 amps), water, sewer.

Elk City

Elk City/Clinton KOA, P.O. Box 137, 73626. T: (800) 562-4149 or (580) 592-4409. F: (580) 592-4530. www.koa.com. RV/tent: 90. $17–$28. Hookups: electric (20, 30, 50 amps), water, sewer.

Elk Creek RV Park, 20th & South Main, 73644. T: (888) 4RV-OKLA or (580) 225-3160. RV/tent: 74. $17–$19. Hookups: electric (30, 50 amps), water, sewer.

Fort Gibson

Blue Bill Point, Rte. 1 Box 3900, 74434. T: (918) 682-4314. www.ReserveUSA.com/nrrs/ok/blpo. RV/tent: 43. $11–$16. Hookups: electric (20, 30 amps), water.

Dam Site (Fort Gibson Lake), Rte. 1 Box 3900, 74434. T: (918) 682-4314. www.ReserveUSA.com/nrrs/ok/dami. RV/tent: 47. $15. Hookups: electric (20, 30 amps).

Flat Rock Creek, Rte. 1 Box 3900, 74434. T: (918) 682-4314. www.ReserveUSA.com/nrrs/ok/flat. RV/tent: 36. $15–$16. Hookups: electric (20, 30 amps), water.

Rocky Point, Rte. 1 Box 3900, 74434. T: (918) 682-4314. www.ReserveUSA.com/nrrs/ok/rocy. RV/tent: 63. $16. Hookups: electric (20, 30 amps), water.

Taylor Ferry, Rte. 1 Box 3900, 74434. T: (918) 682-4314. www.ReserveUSA.com/nrrs/ok/tafe. RV/tent: 102. $11–$16. Hookups: electric (20, 30, 50 amps), water.

Wildwood, Rte. 1 Box 3900, 74434. T: (918) 682-4314. www.ReserveUSA.com/nrrs/ok/wilw. RV/tent: 30. $16. Hookups: electric (20, 30, 50 amps), water.

Fort Supply

Supply Park, P.O. Box 248, 73841. T: (580) 766-2001. www.ReserveUSA.com/nrrs/ok/supp. RV/tent: 110. $10–$15. Hookups: electric (20, 30 amps), water.

OKLAHOMA (continued)

Gore

Afton Landing, Rte. 2 Box 21, 74435. T: (918) 489-5541. www.ReserveUSA.com/nrrs/ok/afto. RV/tent: 20. $10–$15. Hookups: electric (20, 30 amps), water.

Applegate Cove, Rte. 2 Box 21, 74435. T: (918) 489-5541. www.ReserveUSA.com/nrrs/ok/appg. RV/tent: 27. $15. Hookups: electric (20, 30 amps), water.

Bluff Landing, Rte. 2 Box 21, 74435. T: (918) 489-5541. www.ReserveUSA.com/nrrs/ok/blla. RV/tent: 21. $15. Hookups: electric (20, 30 amps).

Brewers Bend, Rte. 2 Box 21, 74435. T: (918) 489-5541. www.ReserveUSA.com/nrrs/ok/brew. RV/tent: 42. $10–$15. Hookups: electric (20, 30 amps).

Chicken Creek, Rte. 1 Box 259, 74435. T: (918) 487-5252. www.ReserveUSA.com/nrrs/ok/chok. RV/tent: 102. $13–$18. Hookups: electric (20, 30, 50 amps), water.

Cookson Bend, Rte. 1 Box 259, 74435. T: (918) 487-5252. www.ReserveUSA.com/nrrs/ok/cobe. RV/tent: 121. $10–$18. Hookups: electric (20, 30, 50 amps).

Cowlington Point, Rte. 2 Box 21, 74435. T: (918) 489-5541. www.ReserveUSA.com/nrrs/ok/cowl. RV/tent: 38. $8–$13. Hookups: electric (20, 30 amps), water.

Elk Creek Landing, Rte. 1 Box 259, 74435. T: (918) 487-5252. www.ReserveUSA.com/nrrs/ok/elcl. RV/tent: 42. $10–$15. Hookups: electric (20, 30 amps).

Pettit Bay, Rte. 1 Box 259, 74435. T: (918) 487-5252. www.ReserveUSA.com/nrrs/ok/pett. RV/tent: 55. $10–$18. Hookups: electric (20, 30, 50 amps), water, sewer.

Short Mountain Cove, Rte. 2 Box 21, 74435. T: (918) 489-5541. www.ReserveUSA.com/nrrs/ok/shmc. RV/tent: 32. $8–$12. Hookups: electric (20, 30 amps).

Snake Creek, Rte. 1 Box 259, 74435. T: (918) 487-5252. www.ReserveUSA.com/nrrs/ok/sank. RV/tent: 82. $10–$18. Hookups: electric (20, 30, 50 amps), water, sewer.

Spaniard Creek, Rte. 2 Box 21, 74435. T: (918) 489-5541. www.ReserveUSA.com/nrrs/ok/span. RV/tent: 35. $15. Hookups: electric (20, 30 amps), water.

Strayhorn Landing, Rte. 1 Box 259, 74435. T: (918) 487-5252. www.ReserveUSA.com/nrrs/ok/strl. RV/tent: 38. $15–$18. Hookups: electric (20, 30 amps), water, sewer.

Grove

Lee's Grand Lake Resort, 24800 South 630 Rd., 74344. T: (918) 786-4289. RV/tent: 25. $18–$20. Hookups: electric (30, 50 amps), water, sewer.

Kansas

Spencer Ridge Resort, Rte. 1 Box 222, 74347. T: (800) 964-6670 or (918) 597-2269. RV/tent: 32. $14. Hookups: electric (20, 30, 50 amps), water, sewer.

Kellyville

Heyburn Park, Rte. 2 Box 140, 74039. T: (918) 247-6601. www.ReserveUSA.com/nrrs/ok/heyb. RV/tent: 47. $14–$16. Hookups: electric (20, 30 amps), water.

Sheppard Point, 27349 Heyburn Lake Rd., 74039. T: (918) 247-4551. www.ReserveUSA.com/nrrs/ok/shep. RV/tent: 37. $16. Hookups: electric (20, 30 amps), water.

Kingston

Buncombe Creek, 351 Corps Rd., 75020. T: (903) 465-4990. www.ReserveUSA.com/nrrs/ok/bunc. RV/tent: 51. $10–$15. Hookups: electric (20, 30 amps), water.

Burns Run East, 351 Corps Rd., 75020. T: (903) 465-4990. www.ReserveUSA.com/nrrs/ok/burr. RV/tent: 54. $11–$20. Hookups: electric (20, 30 amps), water.

Burns Run West, 351 Corps Rd., 75020. T: (903) 465-4990. www.ReserveUSA.com/nrrs/ok/burw. RV/tent: 127. $11–$20. Hookups: electric (20, 30 amps), water.

Caney Creek, 351 Corps Rd., 75020. T: (903) 465-4990. www.ReserveUSA.com/nrrs/ok/caek. RV/tent: 52. $10–$18. Hookups: electric (20, 30 amps), water.

Johnson Creek, 351 Corps Rd., 75020. T: (903) 465-4990. www.ReserveUSA.com/nrrs/ok/jocr. RV/tent: 40. $18. Hookups: electric (20, 30 amps), water.

Lakeside, 351 Corps Rd., 75020. T: (903) 465-4990. www.ReserveUSA.com/nrrs/ok/lasd. RV/tent: 127. $11–$20. Hookups: electric (20, 30 amps), water.

Platter Flats, 351 Corps Rd., 75020. T: (903) 465-4990. www.ReserveUSA.com/nrrs/ok/plat. RV/tent: 57. $10–$15. Hookups: electric (20, 30, 50 amps), water.

McAlester

Super 8 Motel & RV Park, US 69 Business South, 2400 South Main, 74502. T: (918) 426-5400. RV/tent: 40. $12. Hookups: electric (20, 30 amps), water, sewer.

OKLAHOMA (continued)

Miami

Miami Mobile Home & RV Park, 2001 East Steve Owens, 74354. T: (800) 515-2287 or (918) 542-2287. RV/tent: 48. $14. Hookups: electric (30, 50 amps), water, sewer.

Muskogee

Meadowbrook RV Park, 1305 South 32nd St., 74401. T: (918) 681-4574. RV/tent: 39. $15. Hookups: electric (30, 50 amps), water, sewer.

Oklahoma City

A-OK RV Park, 721 South Rockwell, 73128. T: (405) 787-7356. RV/tent: 34. $14. Hookups: electric (30, 50 amps), water, sewer.

Briscoe's RV Park, 6002 I-35 South, 73149. T: (800) 622-6073. RV/tent: 60. $18. Hookups: electric (20, 30, 50 amps), water, sewer.

Council Road RV Park, 8108 Southwest 8th St., 73128. T: (405) 789-2103. RV/tent: 102. $16. Hookups: electric (20, 30, 50 amps), water, sewer.

Eastland Hills RV Park, 3100 South Douglas Blvd., 73150. T: (405) 736-1013. RV/tent: 53. $12–$15. Hookups: electric (20, 30, 50 amps), water, sewer.

Okie RV Park & Camp Ground, 9824 Southeast 29th St., 73129. T: (405) 732-3093. RV/tent: 35. $8. Hookups: electric (30, 50 amps), water, sewer.

Oklahoma City East KOA, 6200 South Choctaw Rd., 73020. T: (800) 562-5076 or (405) 391-5000. F: (405) 391-5004. www.koa.com. RV/tent: 85. $15–$29. Hookups: electric (20, 30, 50 amps), water, sewer.

Roadrunner RV Park, 4800 South I-35, 73129. T: (405) 677-2373. RV/tent: 80. $19–$21. Hookups: electric (30, 50 amps), water, sewer.

Rockwell RV Park, 720 South Rockwell, 73128. T: (888) 684-3251 or (405) 787-5992. www.campusa.com/ok/rockwell. RV/tent: 126. $20–$24. Hookups: electric (30, 50 amps), water, sewer.

Oologah

Blue Creek, P.O. Box 700, 74053. T: (918) 341-4244. www.ReserveUSA.com/nrrs/ok/blcr. RV/tent: 61. $12–$16. Hookups: electric (20, 30 amps).

Hawthorn Bluff, P.O. Box 700, 74053. T: (918) 443-2319. www.ReserveUSA.com/nrrs/ok/hawt. RV/tent: 93. $14–$18. Hookups: electric (20, 30 amps).

Spencer Creek, P.O. Box 700, 74053. T: (918) 341-3690. www.ReserveUSA.com/nrrs/ok/spen. RV/tent: 84. $12–$16. Hookups: electric (20, 30 amps).

Ouachita

Cedar Lake (Oklahoma), Choctaw Ranger District, HC 63 Box 5184, 74939. T: (918) 653-2991. www.ReserveUSA.com/nrrs/ok/ced3. RV/tent: 24. $10–$20. Hookups: electric (20, 30, 50 amps), water, sewer.

Ponca City

Bear Creek Cove, 9400 Lake Rd., 74604. T: (580) 762-5611. www.ReserveUSA.com/nrrs/ok/brcc. RV/tent: 22. $15. Hookups: electric (20, 30 amps), water.

Coon Creek, 9400 Lake Rd., 74604. T: (580) 762-5611. www.ReserveUSA.com/nrrs/ok/cooe. RV/tent: 304. $16–$18. Hookups: electric (20, 30 amps), water.

Osage Cove, 9400 Lake Rd., 74604. T: (580) 762-5611. www.ReserveUSA.com/nrrs/ok/osac. RV/tent: 94. $16. Hookups: electric (20, 30 amps).

Sarge Creek, 9400 Lake Rd., 74604. T: (580) 762-5611. www.ReserveUSA.com/nrrs/ok/sarg. RV/tent: 301. $16. Hookups: electric (20, 30 amps), water.

Washunga Bay, 9400 Lake Rd., 74604. T: (580) 762-5611. www.ReserveUSA.com/nrrs/ok/waba. RV/tent: 62. $11–$15. Hookups: electric (20, 30, 50 amps), water.

Sallisaw

Sallisaw KOA, P.O. Box 88, 74955. T: (800) 562-2797 or (918) 775-2792. www.koa.com. RV/tent: 82. $15–$21. Hookups: electric (20, 30, 50 amps), water, sewer.

Sand Springs

New Mannford Ramp, 23115 West Wekiwa Rd., 74063. T: (918) 865-2621. www.ReserveUSA.com/nrrs/ok/newm. RV/tent: 39. $10–$17. Hookups: electric (20, 30 amps), water.

Salt Creek North, 23115 West Wekiwa Rd., 74063. T: (918) 865-2621. www.ReserveUSA.com/nrrs/ok/salc. RV/tent: 126. $11–$16. Hookups: electric (20, 30 amps), water.

Washington Irving S Campground, 23115 West Wekiwa Rd., 74063. T: (918) 865-2621. www.ReserveUSA.com/nrrs/ok/wasi. RV/tent: 41. $11–$16. Hookups: electric (20, 30 amps).

Sawyer

Kiamichi Park, P.O. Box 99, 74756. T: (580) 326-3345. www.ReserveUSA.com/nrrs/ok/kiam. RV/tent: 91. $9–$15. Hookups: electric (20, 30 amps), water.

OKLAHOMA (continued)

Sawyer (continued)

Virgil Point, P.O. Box 99, 74756. T: (580) 326-3345. www.ReserveUSA.com/nrrs/ok/virp. RV/tent: 51. $15. Hookups: electric (20, 30 amps).

Skiatook

Birch Cove, HC 67 Box 135, 74070. T: (918) 396-3170. www.ReserveUSA.com/nrrs/ok/birc. RV/tent: 84. $16. Hookups: electric (20, 30 amps).

Tall Chief Cove, HC 67 Box 135, 74070. T: (918) 288-6820. www.ReserveUSA.com/nrrs/ok/tall. RV/tent: 57. $18. Hookups: electric (20, 30 amps), water.

Twin Points, HC 67 Box 135, 74070. T: (918) 396-3170. www.ReserveUSA.com/nrrs/ok/twpo. RV/tent: 54. $14. Hookups: electric (20, 30 amps).

Stigler

Belle Starr, Rte. 4 Box 5500, 74462. T: (918) 799-5843. www.ReserveUSA.com/nrrs/ok/bels. RV/tent: 68. $16–$18. Hookups: electric (20, 30, 50 amps), water.

Brooken Cove, Rte. 4 Box 5500, 74462. T: (918) 799-5843. www.ReserveUSA.com/nrrs/ok/brco. RV/tent: 71. $16. Hookups: electric (20, 30 amps), water.

Dam Site South (Eufaula Lake), Rte. 4 Box 5500, 74462. T: (918) 799-5843. www.ReserveUSA.com/nrrs/ok/dam9. RV/tent: 57. $11–$16. Hookups: electric (20, 30 amps), water.

Gentry Creek, Rte. 4 Box 5500, 74462. T: (918) 799-5843. www.ReserveUSA.com/nrrs/ok/gent. RV/tent: 40. $10–$14. Hookups: electric (20, 30 amps), water.

Highway 9 Landing, Rte. 4 Box 5500, 74462. T: (918) 799-5843. www.ReserveUSA.com/nrrs/ok/hinl. RV/tent: 73. $10–$16. Hookups: electric (20, 30 amps), water.

Porum Landing, Rte. 4 Box 5500, 74462. T: (918) 799-5843. www.ReserveUSA.com/nrrs/ok/poru. RV/tent: 53. $10–$16. Hookups: electric (20, 30 amps), water.

Tahlequah

Arrowhead Camp, 7704 Hwy. 10, 74464. T: (800) 749-1140 or (918) 456-1140. RV/tent: 281. $12–$17. Hookups: electric (15, 20, 30 amps), water, sewer.

Diamondhead Resort, 10281 Hwy. 10, 74464. T: (800) 722-2411 or (918) 456-4545. RV/tent: 118. $12–$15. Hookups: electric (30 amps).

Eagle Bluff Resort, 9800 Hwy. 10, 74464. T: (800) 366-3031. RV/tent: 155. $13–$17. Hookups: electric (30, 50 amps), water, sewer.

Hanging Rock Camp, 7453 Hwy. 10, 74464. T: (800) 375-3088 or (918) 456-3088. F: (918) 456-3670. RV/tent: 506. $3–$15. Hookups: electric (30 amps), water, sewer.

Peyton's Place, 10298 Hwy. 10, 74464. T: (800) 359-0866 or (918) 456-3847. F: (918) 456-4950. RV/tent: 85. $3–$15. Hookups: electric (20, 30, 40 amps), water, sewer.

Riverside Camp, 5116 Hwy. 10, 74464. T: (800) 749-CAMP. RV/tent: 48. $10–$15. Hookups: electric (30 amps).

Sparrowhawk Camp, 21985 North Ben George Rd., 74464. T: (800) 722-9635 or (918) 456-8371. www.sparrowhawkcamp.com. RV/tent: 100. $10–$16. Hookups: electric (30 amps).

Tahlequah Floats, One Plaza South, Ste. 243, 74464. T: (800) 375-6949 or (918) 456-6949. RV/tent: 158. $3/person. Hookups: electric (30 amps).

War Eagle Resort, 13020 Hwy. 10, 74464. T: (800) 722-3834 or (918) 456-6272. www.shop oklahoma.com/wareagle.htm. RV/tent: 532. $10–$16. Hookups: electric (30 amps), water.

Tulsa

Estes Park, 1710 South 79th East Ave., 74112. T: (918) 627-3150. RV/tent: 21. $18. Hookups: electric (30, 50 amps), water, sewer.

Mingo RV Park, 801 North Mingo Rd., 74116. T: (800) 932-8824 or (918) 832-8824. RV/tent: 100. $22. Hookups: electric (30, 50 amps), water, sewer.

Valliant

Little River Park, Rte. 1 Box 400, 74764. T: (580) 876-3720. www.ReserveUSA.com/nrrs/ok/lirp. RV/tent: 89. $10–$15. Hookups: electric (20, 30 amps), water.

Lost Rapids, Rte. 1 Box 400, 74764. T: (580) 876-3720. www.ReserveUSA.com/nrrs/ok/losr. RV/tent: 30. $8–$13. Hookups: electric (20, 30 amps), water.

Pine Creek Cove, Rte. 1 Box 400, 74764. T: (580) 933-4215. www.ReserveUSA.com/nrrs/ok/picr. RV/tent: 40. $10–$15. Hookups: electric (20, 30 amps), water.

Turkey Creek, Rte. 1 Box 400, 74764. T: (580) 876-3720. www.ReserveUSA.com/nrrs/ok/turk. RV/tent: 34. $8–$12. Hookups: electric (20, 30 amps).

OKLAHOMA (continued)

Watonga

Roman Nose, Rte. 1, 73772. T: (800) 892-8690 or (580) 623-4215. RV/tent: 175. $7–$21. Hookups: electric (20, 30, 50 amps), water, sewer.

Waurika

Chisholm Trail Ridge, P.O. Box 29, 73573. T: (580) 439-8040. www.ReserveUSA.com/nrrs/ok/chis. RV/tent: 95. $14–$16. Hookups: electric (20, 30 amps), water.

Kiowa Park I, P.O. Box 29, 73573. T: (580) 963-9031. www.ReserveUSA.com/nrrs/ok/kiow. RV/tent: 180. $14–$16. Hookups: electric (20, 30 amps), water.

Woodward

Cottonwood RV Park, Rte. 1 Box 195, 73801. T: (580) 256-1068. RV/tent: 22. $12. Hookups: electric (30, 50 amps), water, sewer.

TEXAS

Abilene

Abilene RV Park, 6195 East Int. Hwy. 20, 79601. T: (915) 672-0657. RV/tent: 60. $18. Hookups: electric (20, 30, 50 amps), phone (modem).

Abilene State Park, 150 Park Rd. 32, Tuscola, 79562. T: (915) 572-3204. RV/tent: 107. $6–12. Hookups: electric, water.

KOA-Abilene, 4851 West Stamford St., 79603. T: (915) 672-3681. RV/tent: 81. $24. Hookups: electric (20, 30, 50 amps), water, cable TV, central phone (modem), phone (modem).

Alamo

Alamo Rec-Veh Park, 1320 West Frontage Rd., 78516. T: (956) 787-8221. RV/tent: 440. $17. Hookups: electric (20, 30 amps), phone (modem).

Casa Del Valle, 1048 North Alamo Rd., 78516. T: (956) 783-5008. RV/tent: 175. $20. Hookups: electric (30, 50 amps).

Morningside Mobile & RV Park, 105 North Cesar Chavez, San Juan, 78589. T: (956) 787-5784. RV/tent: 504. $18. Hookups: electric (30, 50 amps).

Alpine

Lost Alskan RV Resort, 2401 North Hwy. 118, 79830. T: (800) 837-3604. RV/tent: 93. $18. Hookups: electric (30, 50 amps), cable TV, central phone (modem), phone (modem).

KOA-Amarillo, 1100 Folsom Rd., 79108. T: (800) 335-1792. RV/tent: 142. $19–24. Hookups: electric (20, 30, 50 amps), water.

Overnite RV Park, 900 South Lakeside Dr., 79118. T: (806) 373-1431. elens@juno.com. RV/tent: 77. $23. Hookups: electric (20, 30, 50 amps), water, cable TV, central phone (modem), modem.

Amarillo

The Village East RV Park, 1414 Sunrise Dr., 79104. T: (806) 373-4962. RV/tent: 90. $22. Hookups: electric (20, 30, 50 amps), cable TV, central phone (modem).

Westview RV Park, P.O. Box 2891, 79105. T: (806) 352-8567. RV/tent: 54. $13. Hookups: electric (30, 50 amps).

Aransas Pass

Icw RV Park, 427 East Ransom Rd., 78336. T: (361) 758-1044. RV/tent: 134. $16–21. Hookups: electric (20, 30, 50 amps).

Portobelo Village RV & Mobile Home Park, 2009 West Wheeler (Hwy. 35 West), 78336. T: (361) 758-3378. RV/tent: 125. $16–18. Hookups: electric (100 amps).

Argyle

Paradise RV Park, 1217 FM 407W, 76226. T: (940) 648-3573. RV/tent: 91. $15. Hookups: electric (20, 30, 50 amps).

Arroyo City

Seaway RV Village, 35375 FM 2925 Rio Hondo, 78583-3474. T: (956) 748-2276. cjtenna@att-global.net. RV/tent: 75. $18. Hookups: electric (20, 30, 50 amps), central phone (modem), phone (modem).

Austin

McKinney Falls State Park, 5808 McKinney Falls Pkwy, 78744. T: (512) 243-1643. RV/tent: 84. $12. Hookups: electric, water.

Oak Forest RV Park, 8207 Canoga Ave., 78724. T: (512) 926-8984. RV/tent: 88. $20. Hookups: electric (30, 50 amps), cable TV, phone (modem).

Pecan Grove RV Park, 1518 BaRte.on Springs Rd., 78704. T: (512) 472-1067. RV/tent: 93. $20. Hookups: electric (30 amps), cable TV, central phone (modem), phone (modem).

TEXAS (continued)

Bacliff

Bayside RV Park, 5437 East FM 646, 77518. T: (281) 339-2131. RV/tent: 87. $25–30. Hookups: electric (30, 50 amps), central phone (modem).

Bandera

Pomarosa RV Park, P.O. Box 1118, 78003. T: (830) 796-4339. RV/tent: 50. $18. Hookups: electric (30,50 amps), phone (modem).

Skyline Ranch RV Park, Drawer 1990, 78003. T: (830) 796-4958. skyline@indian-creek.net. RV/tent: 85. $15. Hookups: electric (20, 30, 50 amps), cable TV, central phone (modem), phone (modem).

Yogi Bear's Jellystone Camp-Resort-Bandera, P.O. Box 1687, 78003. T: (830) 796-3751. RV/tent: 210. $17–19. Hookups: electric (20, 30, amps), water.

Baytown

Willow Creek RV Park, 2305 Hwy. 146 North, 77520. T: (281) 422-5423. RV/tent: 62. $15. Hookups: electric (30, 50 amps).

Beaumont

East Lucas RV Park, 2590 East Lucas Dr., 77703-1126. T: (409) 899-9209. d.sorensen@worldnet.att.net. RV/tent: 65. $20. Hookups: electric (20, 30, 50 amps), cable TV, central phone (modem), phone (modem).

Belton

KOA-Belton/Temple/Killeen, P.O. Box 118, 76513. T: (254) 939-1961. RV/tent: 99. $21–22. Hookups: electric (20, 30, 50 amps), water, cable TV, central phone (modem),phone (modem).

Benbrook

Holiday Park, 76126-0619. T: (817) 292-2400. RV/tent: 105. $10–20. Hookups: electric, water.

Big Spring

Texas RV Park Of Big Spring, 4100 South US Highway 87, 79720. T: (915) 267-7900. rbworthy@msn.com. RV/tent: 106. $21. Hookups: electric (20, 30, 50 amps), cable TV, central phone (modem), phone (modem).

Brackettville

Fort Clark Springs, P.O. Box 345, 78832. T: (800) 937-1590. fcsa@ms1.hilconet.com. RV/tent: 84. $17. Hookups: electric (20, 30, 50 amps), cable TV, phone (modem).

Breckenridge

Bridgeview RV Park, 5300 Hwy. 180 W, 76424. T: (254) 559-8582. RV/tent: 43. $15–16. Hookups: electric (30, 50 amps), water.

Brenham

Artesian Park RV Campground, 8601 Hwy. 290 W, 77833. T: (979) 836-0680. RV/tent: 59. $12–14. Hookups: electric (20, 30, 50 amps), water, central phone (modem), phone (modem).

Brookeland

Mill Creek Park, Route 3 P.O. Box 486, Jasper, 75951-9598. T: (409) 384-5716. RV/tent: 110. $11–15. Hookups: electric.

Brookshire

KOA-Houston West Campground, 35303 Cooper Rd., 77423. T: (281) 375-5678. RV/tent: 84. $20–23. Hookups: electric (20, 30, 50 amps), water, central phone (modem), phone (modem).

Brownsville

4 Seasons Mobile Home Park & RV Resort, 6900 Coffee Port Rd., 78521. T: (956) 831-4918. coffeeport@aol.com. RV/tent: 125. $20. Hookups: electric (30 amps), cable TV, phone (modem).

Breeze Lake Campground, 1710 North Vermillion, 78521. T: (877) 296-3329. breezelake@worldnet.att.net. RV/tent: 189. $18–20. Hookups: electric (20, 30, 50 amps), cable TV, central phone (modem), phone (modem).

Crooked Tree Campland, 605 FM 802, 78520. T: (956) 546-9617. RV/tent: 200. $24–28. Hookups: electric (20, 30, 50 amps), central phone (modem), phone (modem).

Paul's RV Park, 1129 North Minnesota Ave., 78521. T: (956) 831-4852. paulrvpark@aol.com. RV/tent: 135. $15–27. Hookups: electric (20, 30, 50 amps), cable TV, central phone (modem), phone (modem).

Rio RV Park, 8801 East Boca Chica, 78521. T: (956) 831-4653. riorvpark@aol.com. RV/tent: 112. $15–27. Hookups: electric (20, 30, 50 amps), cable TV, central phone (modem), phone (modem).

Bryan

Primrose Lane RV & Mh Park, 2929 Stevens Dr., 77803. T: (888)782-2671. RV/tent: 117. $20. Hookups: electric (20, 30, 50 amps).

Buchanan Dam

Shady Oaks RV Park, P.O. Box 725, 78609. T: (512) 793-2718. RV/tent: 64. $17. Hookups: electric (20, 30, 50 amps), cable TV, phone (modem).

Bulverde

Texas 281 RV Park, P.O. BOX 420, 78163. T: (830) 980-2282. RV/tent: 159. $20. Hookups: electric (30, 50 amps), water.

TEXAS

Burleson

Mockingbird Hill Mobile Home & RV Park, 1990 South Burleson Blvd No. 20, 76028. T: (877) 736-7699. RV/tent: 59. $18. Hookups: electric (20, 30, 50 amps), phone (modem).

Caddo Mills

Dallas Northeast Campground, 4268 FM 36 South, 75135-6782. T: (800) 309-0714. RV/tent: 85. $19. Hookups: electric (20, 30, 50 amps), central phone (modem), phone (modem).

Canton

Canton Campground, 30488 State Hwy. 64 Wills Point, 75169. T: (903) 865-1511. cmpcnton@gte.net. RV/tent: 74. $15–18. Hookups: electric (20, 30, 50 amps), water, central phone (modem).

Canyon Lake

Maricopa Ranch Resort, P.O. Box 1659, 78130. T: (830) 964-3731. RV/tent: 142. $15–25. Hookups: electric (30, 50 amps).

Cleburne

Cleburne State Park, 5800 Park Rd. 21, 76031. T: (817) 645-4215. RV/tent: 58. $11–17. Hookups: electric, water.

Clint

Cotton Valley RV Park, P.O. Box 1189, 79836. T: (915) 851-2137. RV/tent: 75. $18. Hookups: electric (20, 30, 50 amps), water.

College Station

University RV Park, 19191 Hwy. 6 South, 77845. T: (409) 690-6056. RV/tent: 42. $18. Hookups: electric (20, 30 amps), water.

Colorado City

Lake Colorado City State Park, 4582 FM 2836, 79512. T: (915) 728-3931. RV/tent: 132. $8–11. Hookups: electric, water.

Columbus

Columbus RV Park & Campground, 2800 Hwy. 71S, 78934. T: (800) 657-6108. RV/tent: 50. $20. Hookups: electric (30, 50 amps).

Comanche

Copperas Creek Park, Route 1, P.O. Box 71 A, 76442-9210. T: (817) 893-7545. RV/tent: 60. $14–32. Hookups: electric (30 amps), water.

Comfort

RV Park Usa, 108 Blue Ridge, 78013. T: (830) 995-2900. RV/tent: 52. $16.50. Hookups: electric (20, 30, 50 amps).

Conroe

Convience RV Park & Repair Center At The Fish Ponds, 17091 State Hwy. 75 North Willis, 77378. T: (936) 344-2027. RV/tent: 52. $18. Hookups: electric (20, 30, 50 amps), phone (modem).

Park on The Lake, 12351 FM 830 Willis, 77378. T: (409) 890-2375. rvpark@flex.net. RV/tent: 85. $15. Hookups: electric (30, 50 amps), central phone (modem), phone (modem).

Corpus Christi

Greyhound RV Park, 5402 LeopaRd. St, 78408. T: (361) 289-2076. RV/tent: 90. $18. Hookups: electric (20, 30, 50 amps), central phone (modem), phone (modem).

Hatch RV Park, 3101 Up River Rd., 78408. T: (800) 332-4509. bettyemcl@msn.com. RV/tent: 130. $25–27. Hookups: electric (20, 30, 50 amps), central phone (modem), phone (modem), cable TV.

Marina Village Park, 78418. T: (361) 937-2560. RV/tent: 135. $17. Hookups: electric (20, 30, 50 amps), central phone (modem).

Puerto Del Sol RV Park, 5100 Timon Blvd, 78402. T: (361) 882-5373. ptdelsol@intcomm.net. RV/tent: 59. $19–21. Hookups: electric (20, 30, 50 amps), water, entral phone (modem), phone (modem).

Corsicana

American RV Park, 4345 West Highway 31, 75110. T: (888) 872-0233. american.rv.@airmail.net. RV/tent: 95. $22.50. Hookups: electric (20, 30, 50 amps), central phone (modem), phone (modem).

Dallas

Dallas Hi Ho RV Park, 200 West Bear Creek Rd. Glenn Heights, 75154-8112. T: (877) 619-3900. RV/tent: 127. $20. Hookups: electric (20, 30, 50 amps), water, central phone (modem), phone (modem).

Sandy Lake RV Park, 1915 Sandy Lake Rd. Carrollton, 75006. T: (972) 242-6808. sandylrv@nation wide.net. RV/tent: 260. $20–22. Hookups: electric (20, 30, 50 amps), central phone (modem), phone (modem).

Dawson

Wolf Creek Park, 1175 FM 667, 76679-9707. T: (817) 578-1431. RV/tent: 74. $10–15. Hookups: electric (20, 30 amps), water.

TEXAS (continued)

Del Rio

American Campground, HCR 3 Box 44, 78840. T: (830) 775-6484. amercamp@delrio.com. RV/tent: 123. $17.95. Hookups: electric (20, 30, 50 amps), water, cable TV, central phone (modem), phone (modem).

Holiday Trav-L-Park, HCR 3 Box 40, 78840. T: (830) 775-7275. RV/tent: 176. $18. Hookups: electric (30, 50 amps), water.

Denton

Dallas Destiny RV Park, 7100 I-35 E, 76205. T: (888) 238-1532. dstnydall@aol.com. RV/tent: 193. $31–34. Hookups: electric (20, 30, 50 amps).

Diana

Brushy Creek Park, 2669 FM 726, Jefferson, 75657. T: (903) 777-3491. RV/tent: 111. $10–20. Hookups: electric, water.

Dickinson

Green Caye RV Park, 2415 Caroline St, 77539. T: (281) 337-0289. RV/tent: 74. $18. Hookups: electric (30, 50 amps), central phone (modem).

Donna

Bit-O-Heaven RV & Mobile Home Park, Rte. 4 Box 4750, 78537. T: (956) 464-5191. RV/tent: 700. $18. Hookups: electric (20, 30, 50 amps).

Palm Shadows RV Park, Rte. 4 Box 4452, 78537. T: (956) 464-3324. RV/tent: 469. $25. Hookups: electric (30, 50 amps), phone (modems).

Dumas

Yerby's Mobile Home & RV Park, Box 774, 79029. T: (806) 935-4940. RV/tent: 52. $12–14. Hookups: electric (30, 50 amps), phone (modems).

Edinburg

Orange Groove RV Park, 4901 East State Highway 107, 78539. T: (956) 383-7931. RV/tent: 524. $22. Hookups: electric (20, 30 amps).

Edna

Lake Texana State Park, P.O. Box 760, 77957-0760. T: (361) 782-5718. RV/tent: 141. $9–12. Hookups: electric, water.

El Paso

El Paso Roadrunner RV Park, 1212 Lafayette Dr., 79907. T: (915) 598-4469. elpasorv@aol.com. RV/tent: 136. $20. Hookups: electric (20, 30 amps), water, central phone (modem), phone (modem).

Ennis

Waxahachie Creek Park, 4000 Observation Dr., 75119-9563. T: (214) 875-5711. RV/tent: 58. $12–16. Hookups: electric (20, 30 amps), water.

Eustace

Purtis Creek State Park, 14225 FM 316, 75124. T: (903) 425-2332. RV/tent: 71. $6–12. Hookups: electric, water.

Fentress

Leisure Camp And RV Park, P.O. Box 277, 78622. T: (512) 488-2563. leisure@thrifty.net. RV/tent: 108. $17–19. Hookups: electric (20, 30, 50 amps), water, central phone (modem), phone (modem).

Fort Davis

Davis Mountains State Park, P.O. Box 1458, 79734. T: (915) 426-3337. RV/tent: 88. $15. Hookups: electric, water.

Fort Stockton

Comanche Land RV Park, 700 North Gillis, 79735. T: (915) 336-6403. RV/tent: 58. $10. Hookups: electric (30 amps).

KOA-Fort Stockton, P.O. Box 627, 79735. T: (915) 395-2494. jokar@netwest.com. RV/tent: 79. $15.50–19.50. Hookups: electric (20, 30, 50 amps), water, central phone (modem), phone (modem).

Fort Worth

Sunset RV Park, 4921 White Settlement Rd., No. 46, 76114. T: (800) 738-0567. sunsetrvpark@earthlink.net. RV/tent: 69. $16. Hookups: electric (20, 30, 50 amps), cable TV, central phone (modem), phone (modem).

Fredericksburg

Fredericksburg-KOA, 5681 East US Highway 290, 78624. T: (830) 997-4796. RV/tent: 109. $25–29. Hookups: electric (20, 30, 50 amps), water, cable TV, central phone (modem), phone (modem).

Oakwood RV Resort, 78 FM 2093, 78624-7154. T: (830) 997-9817. oakwood@ktc.com. RV/tent: 134. $19.50–23. Hookups: electric (20, 30, 50 amps), cable TV, central phone (modem), phone (modem).

Fulton

Goose Island State Park, HC 4 Box 105 Rockport, 78382. T: (361) 729-2858. RV/tent: 127. $8–15. Hookups: electric, water.

TEXAS (continued)

Galveston

Bayou Shores RV Resort, 6310 HeaRd.s Ln., 77551. T: (888) 744-2837. RV/tent: 84. $18–22. Hookups: electric (20, 30, 50 amps), cable TV, central phone (modem), phone (modem).

Glen Rose

Oakdale Park, P.O. Box 548, 76043. T: (254) 897-2321. RV/tent: 300. $16. Hookups: electric (20, 30 amps), water.

Tres Rios RV River Resort, 2322 CR 312, 76043. T: (254) 897-4253. RV/tent: 537. $18–20. Hookups: electric (30, 50 amps), water, central phone (modem).

Goliad

Coleto Creek Reservoir And Park, P.O. Box 68 Fannin, 77960. T: (361) 575-6366. RV/tent: 58. $14–22. Hookups: electric, water (15, 30, 50 amps).

Grapeland

Salmon Lake Park, P.O. Box 483, 75844. T: (936) 687-2594. RV/tent: 525. $16. Hookups: electric (20, 30 amps), water.

Grapevine

Silver Lake Park, 1501 North Dooley, 76051. T: (817) 329-8993. RV/tent: 59. $15. Hookups: electric (30 amps), water.

Harlingen

Encore RV Park Harlington, 1900 Grace Ave., 78550. T: (956) 428-4137. nhctxss@msn.com. RV/tent: 1066. $20. Hookups: electric (30, 50, 100 amps), central phone (modem), phone (modem).

Paradise Park Harlingen, 1201 North Expressway 77, 78552. T: (956) 425-6881. nhctxpp@msn.com. RV/tent: 309. $22. Hookups: electric (30,50 amps), central phone (modem), phone (modem).

Sunburst RV Park, 4525 Graham Rd., 78552. T: (956) 423-1170. nhctxlw@swbell.net. RV/tent: 300. $20. Hookups: electric (30, 50 amps), central phone (modem), phone (modem).

Tropic Winds Mobile Home & RV Park, 1501 North Loop 499, 78552. T: (956) 423-4020. tropicwsrv@aol.com. RV/tent: 477. $22. Hookups: electric (20, 30, 50 amps), cable TV, central phone (modem), phone (modem).

Hempstead

Yogi Bear's Jellystone Park, Rte. 3 Box 83A, 77445. T: (409) 826-4111. RV/tent: 151. $17. Hookups: electric (20, 30, 50 amps), water.

Houston

All Star RV Resort, 10515 Southwest Fwy., 77074. T: (713) 981-6814. allstar@allstar-rv.com. RV/tent: 120. $34–39. Hookups: electric (20, 30, 50 amps), cable TV, central phone (modem), phone (modem).

KOA-Houston Central, 1620 Peachleaf, 77039. T: (281) 442-3700. RV/tent: 75. $18–24. Hookups: electric (20, 30, 50 amps), water, central phone (modem), phone (modem).

South Main RV Park, 10100 South Main, 77025. T: (713) 667-0120. smrvpark@flash.net. RV/tent: 108. $27.95. Hookups: electric (20, 30, 50 amps), water, central phone (modem).

Traders Village, 7979 Eldridge Rd., 77041. T: (281) 890-8846. tvhops@flash.net. RV/tent: 307. $17.95–20. Hookups: electric (20, 30, 50 amps), water, central phone (modem).

Jasper

Martin Dies Jr. State Park, Rte. 4 Box 274, 75951. T: (409) 384-5231. RV/tent: 85. $12. Hookups: electric, water.

Jefferson

Buckhorn Creek, Farm 726, 75657. T: (903) 665-8261. RV/tent: 100. $12–20. Hookups: electric, water.

Johnson Creek Camping Area, 2669 FM, 75657-9780. T: (903) 755-2435. RV/tent: 85. $12–20. Hookups: electric, water.

Johnson City

Roadrunner RV Park, P.O. Box 161, 78636. T: (830) 868-7449. rvpark1@yahoo.com. RV/tent: 52. $16–18. Hookups: electric (20, 30, 50 amps), central phone (modem).

Junction

KOA-Junction, 2145 North Main St., 76849. T: (800) 562-7506. RV/tent: 61. $19.95–21.45. Hookups: electric (20, 30, 50 amps), water.

South Llano River State Park, HC 15 Box 224, 76849. T: (915) 446-3994. RV/tent: 70. $6–12. Hookups: electric, water.

Kerrville

Buckhorn Lake Resort, 4071 Goat Creek Rd., 78028. T: (800) 568-6458. buckhorn@ktc.com. RV/tent: 225. $27. Hookups: electric (20, 30, 50 amps), cable TV, central phone (modem), phone (modem).

TEXAS (continued)

Kerrville (continued)

By the River RV Campground, P.O. Box 2126, 78029. T: (830) 367-5566. RV/tent: 75. $20. Hookups: electric (30 amps), cable TV, central phone (modem).

Take-It-Easy Resort, 703 Junction Hwy., 78028. T: (800) 828-6984. tie@ktc.com. RV/tent: 81. $20. Hookups: electric (20, 30, 50 amps), cable TV, central phone (modem), phone (modem).

Kingsville

Oasis RV & Mobile Home Park, P.O. Box 1689, 78363. T: (361) 592-0764. nomad1@intcomm.net. RV/tent: 147. $15. Hookups: electric (20, 30, 50 amps), phone (modem).

La Feria

Kenwood RV & Mobile Home Plaza Llc, 1221 North Main No. 100, 78559. T: (956) 797-1851. RV/tent: 293. $20. Hookups: electric (20, 30, 50 amps), cable TV, phone (modem).

La Feria RV Park, 450 East Frontage Rd., 78559. T: (956) 797-1043. RV/tent: 153. $20. Hookups: electric (20, 30, 50 amps).

Vip Park, 600 East Frontage Rd., 78559. T: (956) 797-1401. RV/tent: 155. $20. Hookups: electric (20, 30, 50 amps).

La Marque

Little Thicket Travel Park, 408 Volney, 77568. T: (409) 935-5375. RV/tent: 59. $16.50. Hookups: electric (20, 30, 50 amps).

Lajitas

Lajitas On The Rio Grande RV Park, HC 70 Box 435, 79852. T: (915) 424-3471. RV/tent: 78. $18. Hookups: electric (20, 30, 50 amps), cable TV, phone (modem).

Laredo

Lake Casa Blanca International State Park, P.O. Box 1844, 78044. T: (956) 725-3826. RV/tent: 300. $12. Hookups: electric (30 amps), water.

Lavon

Lavonia, 3375 Skyview Dr., 75098-7575. T: (972) 442-3141. RV/tent: 53. $8–16. Hookups: electric, water.

League City

Space Center RV Resort, 301 Gulf Freeway, 77573. T: (888) 846-3478. scrvp@flash.net. RV/tent: 125. $20–32. Hookups: electric (20, 30, 50, 100 amps), cable TV, phone and modem.

Los Fresnos

Palmdale RV Resort, P.O. Box 308, 78566. T: (956) 399-8694. info@PalmdaleRVResort.com. RV/tent: 200. $21. Hookups: electric (30, 50 amps), central phone (modem), phone (modem).

Lubbock

KOA-Lubbock, 5502 County Rd. 6300, 79416. T: (806) 762-8653. RV/tent: 87. $18.95–25.95. Hookups: electric (20, 30, 50 amps), water.

Loop 289 RV Park, 3436 West Loop 289, 79407. T: (806) 792-4348. RV/tent: 85. $19. Hookups: electric (20, 30, 50 amps).

Luling

Riverbend RV Park, P.O. Box 1062, 78648. T: (830) 875-9548. RV/tent: 80. $12–18. Hookups: electric (30, 50 amps), water.

Manvel

Almost Heaven Resort, 4202 Del Bello Rd., 77578. T: (800) 895-CAMP. almostheaven@orbitworld.net. RV/tent: 138. $21.50. Hookups: electric (20, 30, 50 amps), water, central phone (modem).

Marathon

Stillwell Ranch Campground, HC 65 Box 430, Alpine, 79830. T: (915) 376-2244. RV/tent: 66. $13–14. Hookups: electric (30 amps), water.

Marshall

Country Pines RV Park, 5935 US Hwy. 59 North, 75670. T: (800) 848-7087. RV/tent: 100. $13–17. Hookups: electric (20, 30, 50 amps), water, central phone (modem).

Mathis

KOA-Lake Corpus Christi, P.O. Box 1167, 78368. T: (361) 547-5201. RV/tent: 108. $22. Hookups: electric (20, 30, 50 amps), water.

Wilderness Lakes RV Resort, P.O. Box 519, 78368. T: (361) 547-9995. RV/tent: 123. $18. Hookups: electric (20, 30, 50 amps).

McAllen

Citrus Valley RV Park, 2901 State Hwy. 107, 78504. T: (956) 383-8189. RV/tent: 233. $22. Hookups: electric (20, 30 amps).

McAllen Mobile Park, 4900 North McColl Rd., 78504. T: (956) 682-3304. mmpdavid@aol.com. RV/tent: 318. $19. Hookups: electric (20, 30, 50 amps), phone (modem).

TEXAS (continued)

McKinney

Lighthouse RV Resort, Box 350, 1020 US Hwy. 75 North, 75454. T: (800) 844-2196. rvresorttx@aol.com. RV/tent: 114. $24.50–26.50. Hookups: electric (20, 30, 50 amps), water, phone (modem).

Mercedes

Encore RV Park-Mercedes, 8000 Paradise South, 78570. T: (956) 565-2044. nhctxps@msn.com. RV/tent: 490. $10–21. Hookups: electric (30, 50 amps), phone (modem).

Llano Grande Lake Park, 489 Yolanda, 78570. T: (956) 565-2638. RV/tent: 870. $20. Hookups: electric (30, 50 amps).

Midland

Midessa Oil Patch RV Park, 4220 South CR 1290, Odessa, 79765. T: (915) 5632368. RV/tent: 135. $24. Hookups: electric (20, 30, 50 amps), central phone (modem), phone (modem).

Mission

Bentsen Grove Trailer Park, 810 North Bentsen Palm Dr., 78572. T: (956) 585-7011. bentsengrv@aol.com. RV/tent: 850. $20. Hookups: electric (30, 50 amps), cable TV, central phone (modem), phone (modem).

Circle T RV Park, 1820 Clay Tolle St., 78572. T: (956) 585-5381. RV/tent: 268. $15. Hookups: electric (20, 30, 50 amps), phone (modem).

Eldorado Acres RV Park, 2404 North Goodwin Rd. (FM 492), 78572. T: (956) 581-6718. RV/tent: 122. $16. Hookups: electric (30 amps).

Seven Oaks Resort & Country Club, 1300 Circle Dr., 78572. T: (956) 581-0068. RV/tent: 232. $20. Hookups: electric (30 amps).

Montgomery

Havens Landing RV Resort, 19785 Hwy. 105 W, 77316. T: (936) 582-6307. lea.bivins@gte.net. RV/tent: 170. $25. Hookups: electric (20, 30, 50 amps).

Mount Pleasant

Lake Bob Sandlin State Recreation Area, Rte. 5 Box 224, 75686. T: (903) 572-5531. RV/tent: 75. $12–14. Hookups: electric, water.

New Braunfels

Hill Country RV Resort, 131 South Ruekle Rd., 78130. T: (830) 625-1919. RV/tent: 300. $18. Hookups: electric (20, 30, 50 amps).

New Caney

Lone Star Lakes RV Park, 20842 US Highway 59, 77357. T: (800) 290-9301. RV/tent: 78. $17. Hookups: electric (20, 30, 50 amps), water, cable TV, phone (modem).

Orange

Oak Leaf Park Campground, 6900 Oak Leaf Dr., 77632. T: (409) 886-4082. RV/tent: 115. $19. Hookups: electric (20, 30, 50 amps), water, phone (modem).

Ozona

Circle Bar RV Park, P.O. Box 1498, 76943. T: (915) 392-2611. RV/tent: 128. $20. Hookups: electric (20, 30, 50 amps).

Palacios

Serendipity RV Park & Marina, 1001 Main St, 77465. T: (800) 556-0534. RV/tent: 162. $16.50–18.50. Hookups: electric (30, 50 amps).

Paris

Sanders Cove Park, P.O. Box 129, Powderly. T: (903) 732-3020. RV/tent: 89. $10–15. Hookups: electric, water.

Pecos

Trapark RV Park, 3100 Moore St, 79772. T: (915) 447-2137. RV/tent: 61. $15. Hookups: electric (20, 30, 50 amps), water, cable TV, central phone (modem).

Perrin

Mitchell RV Park, P.O. Box 68, 76486. T: (940) 798-4615. dheinz@wf.net. RV/tent: 245. $16. Hookups: electric (20, 30 amps), water, central phone (modem), phone (modem).

Pineland

San Augustine Park, Route 3, P.O. Box 486, Jasper, 75951-9598. T: (409) 384-5716. RV/tent: 100. $12–17. Hookups: electric, water.

Port Aransas

Island RV Resort, Box 1377, 78373. T: (361) 749-5600. RV/tent: 199. $20. Hookups: electric (20, 30, 50 amps), cable TV, phone (modem).

Surfside RV Resort, P.O. Box 179, 78373. T: (888) 565-5929. RV/tent: 45. $20–22. Hookups: electric (50 amps), cable TV, phone (modem).

TEXAS (continued)

Port Isabel

Port Isabel Park Center, P.O. Box 295, 78578. T: (956) 943-7340. Pipkcenter@aol.com. RV/tent: 225. $13–14. Hookups: electric (30, 50 amps), cable TV, central phone (modem), phone (modem).

Portland

Sea Breeze RV Park, 1026 Seabreeze Ln., 78374. T: (361) 643-0744. seabreezrv@aol.com. RV/tent: 142. $20. Hookups: electric (30, 50 amps), water, cable TV, central phone (modem), phone (modem).

Proctor

Sowell Creek Park, Route 1, P.O. Box 71 A, Comancle, 76442-9210. T: (817) 879-2322. RV/tent: 60. $14–50. Hookups: electric (30 amps), water.

Rio Hondo

River Ranch RV Resort, 20054 Reynolds, 78583-3106. T: (956) 748-2286. RV/tent: 125. $20. Hookups: electric (30, 50 amps).

Rockport

Lagoons RV Resort, 600 Enterprise Blvd., 78382. T: (361) 729-7834. lagoonsrv@the-i.net. RV/tent: 298. $21.50–23. Hookups: electric (30, 50 amps), cable TV, central phone (modem), phone (modem).

Woody Acres Mobile Home & RV Resort, Box 236 Fulton, 78358. T: (800) 526-9264. woodyacres@interconnect.net. RV/tent: 225. $17.50–24. Hookups: electric (20, 30, 50 amps), cable TV, central phone (modem), phone (modem).

San Angelo

Spring Creek Marina & RV Park, 45 Fishermans Rd., 76904. T: (800) 500-7801. sprcreek@wcc.net. RV/tent: 83. $18.50–22. Hookups: electric (20, 30, 50 amps), water, cable TV, central phone (modem), phone (modem).

San Antonio

Blazing Star Luxury RV Resort, 1120 West Loop 1604 North, 78251. T: (877) 387-5777. bfurci@express-news.net. RV/tent: 260. $27–35. Hookups: electric (30, 50 amps), cable TV, central phone (modem), phone (modem).

Traveler's World RV Resort, 2617 Roosevelt Ave., 78214. T: (210) 532-8310. tvrwrld@aol.com. RV/tent: 170. $24.50–27. Hookups: electric (30, 50 amps), central phone (modem), phone (modem).

Sanger

Ray Roberts Lake State Park, 100 PW 4137 Pilot Point, 76258-8944. T: (940) 686-2148. RV/tent: 151. $10–14. Hookups: electric (20, 30 amps), water.

Schertz

Stone Creek RV Park, 18905 IH-35 North, 78154. T: (830) 609-7759. stonecrk@onr.com. RV/tent: 256. $19.50–21.50. Hookups: electric (30, 50 amps), central phone (modem), phone (modem).

Seguin

River Shade RV Park, 3995 State Hwy. 123 Bypass, 78155. T: (800) 364-7275. rivershade@prodigy.net. RV/tent: 78. $20–22. Hookups: electric (30, 50 amps), cable TV, central phone (modem), phone (modem).

South Padre Island

Destination South Padre Island, One Padre Blvd., 78597. T: (800) 867-2373. RV/tent: 190. $28–38. Hookups: electric (20, 30, 50 amps).

Spring

Spring Oaks RV & Mobile Home Community, 22014 Spring Oaks Dr., 77389. T: (281) 350-2606. RV/tent: 67. $18. Hookups: electric (30, 50 amps), central phone (modem), phone (modem).

Sugar Land

Usa RV Park, 20825 Southwest Fwy., 77479. T: (281) 343-0626. RV/tent: 114. $14.50. Hookups: electric (30, 50 amps).

Surfside Beach

San Luis Pass County Park, 14001 CR 257 Freeport, 77541. T: (800) 372-7578. RV/tent: 89. $17–20. Hookups: electric (20, 30, 50 amps).

Terlingua

Big Bend Motor Inn & RV Campground, Box 336, 79852. T: (915) 371-2218. RV/tent: 166. $16. Hookups: electric (20, 30, 50 amps), water, cable TV, central phone (modem), phone (modem).

Texarkana

Clear Springs Recreational Area, P.O. Box 1817, 75504-1817. T: (903) 838-8636. RV/tent: 101. $12. Hookups: electric (20, 30 amps), water.

The Colony

Hidden Cove Park, Rte. 2 Box 353H, Frisco, 75034. T: (972) 294-1155. RV/tent: 50. $16–28. Hookups: electric (20, 30 amps), water.

TEXAS (continued)

Tyler

Tyler State Park, 789 Park Rd. 16, 75706-9141. T: (903) 597-5338. RV/tent: 149. $8–12. Hookups: electric (20, 30 amps), water.

Whispering Pines Campground & Resort, 5583 FM 16 East, 75706. T: (800) 559-3817. wpines@gower.net. RV/tent: 140. $17–20. Hookups: electric (20, 30, 50 amps), water, central phone (modem), phone (modem).

Uvalde

Park Chalk Bluff, HCR 33 Box 566, 78801. T: (830) 278-5515. fgwallac@peppersnet.com. RV/tent: 87. $10–18. Hookups: electric (30, 50 amps), water.

Van Horn

KOA-Van Horn, P.O. Box 265, 79855. T: (915) 283-2728. RV/tent: 70. $18.50. Hookups: electric (20, 30, 50 amps), water.

Vernon

Rocking A RV Park, 3725 Harrison, 76384. T: (940) 552-2821. rockinga@chipshot.net. RV/tent: 83. $18–20. Hookups: electric (20, 30, 50 amps), water, central phone (modem), phone (modem).

Victoria

Dad's RV Park, 203 Hopkins, 77901. T: (361) 573-1231. dadrv@txer.lnet. RV/tent: 50. $14–17. Hookups: electric (20, 30, 50 amps), water, cable TV, central phone (modem), phone (modem).

Waco

Speegleville I Park, P.O. Box 8221, 76714. T: (817) 756-5359. RV/tent: 99. $13–16. Hookups: electric (30 amps), water.

Waco North-KOA, P.O. Box 157 West, 76691. T: (254) 826-3869. RV/tent: 76. $20–21. Hookups: electric (20, 30, 50 amps), water, central phone (modem), phone (modem).

Wallisville

Turtle Bayou RV Park, P.O. Box 185, 77597. T: (409) 389-2468. RV/tent: 63. $24. Hookups: electric (30, 50 amps), water.

Weslaco

County Sunshine Loelasco, 1601 South Airport, 78596. T: (956) 969-1557. nhctxcs@msn.com. RV/tent: 245. $20. Hookups: electric (30, 50 amps), phone (modem).

Magic Valley Park, 2300 East State Hwy. 83, 78596. T: (956) 968-8242. RV/tent: 387. $17. Hookups: electric (20, 30 amps), phone (modem).

Snow to Sun RV & Mobile Home Community, 1701 North International Blvd., 78596. T: (956) 968-0322. RV/tent: 316. $25. Hookups: electric (50 amps), phone (modem), central phone (modem).

Whitney

Lake Whitney RV Resort, P.O. Box 1309, 76692-1309. T: (800) 999-9259. RV/tent: 75. $18. Hookups: electric (20, 30, 50 amps).

Wichita Falls

Wichita Falls RV Park, 2944 Seymour Hwy., 76301. T: (800) 252-1532. RV/tent: 135. $20–22.50. Hookups: electric (20, 30, 50 amps), cable TV.

Wylie

East Fork Park, P.0. Box 742585, 75374. T: (972) 442-3141. RV/tent: 63. $8–16. Hookups: electric, water.

Zapata

4 Seasons RV Park, P.O. Box 1007, 78076. T: (956) 765-4241. RV/tent: 175. $15. Hookups: electric (20, 30, 50 amps), water, cable TV, phone (modem)

Index

Arkansas

***Arkansas** (continued)*

Colorado

***Colorado** (continued)*

***Colorado** (continued)*

***Colorado** (continued)*

***Colorado** (continued)*

Kansas

***Kansas** (continued)*

***New Mexico** (continued)*

***New Mexico** (continued)*

***New Mexico** (continued)*

Oklahoma

***Oklahoma** (continued)*

Texas

***Texas** (continued)*

***Texas** (continued)*